1993

HISTORY OF PERSIA UNDER QĀJĀR RULE

HISTORY OF PERSIA UNDER QĀJĀR RULE

Translated from the Persian
of ḤASAN-E FASĀ'I'S
Fārsnāma-ye Nāṣeri

1972 by HERIBERT BUSSE

Columbia University Press, New York & London

ISBN: *0-231-03197-1*
Library of Congress Catalog Card Number: 74-183229
Printed in the United States of America

UNESCO COLLECTION OF REPRESENTATIVE WORKS
The volumes in the Persian Heritage Series
are jointly sponsored by
UNESCO
and Pahlavi Foundation's Royal Institute of
Translation and Publication.

PERSIAN HERITAGE SERIES

Editor: Ehsan Yar-Shater (Columbia University)

Advisory Council

I. Gershevitch (Cambridge University)
G. Lazard (University of Paris)
G. Morgenstierne (University of Oslo)
B. Spuler (University of Hamburg)
G. Tucci (University of Rome)
T. C. Young (Princeton University)

Past members

†A. J. Arberry (Cambridge University)
†W. B. Henning (University of California)
†H. Massé (University of Paris)

Other volumes published in the Persian Heritage Series:

In English

Ferdausi, *Epic of the Kings*, translated by R. Levy
Attar, *Muslim Saints and Mystics*, translated by A. J. Arberry
Rumi, *Mystical Poems I*, translated by A. J. Arberry
Tansar, *Letter of Tansar*, translated by M. Boyce
Rashid al-Din, *The Successors of Genghis Khan*, translated by A. J. Boyle
Tusi, *Nasirean Ethics*, translated by G. M. Wickens
Varavini, *Tales of Marzuban*, translated by R. Levy
Gorgani, *Vis o Ramin*, translated by G. Morrison

In French

Nezami, *Chosroès et Chirine*, translated by H. Massé
Aruzi, *Les Quatre Discours*, translated by I. de Gastine

In Italian

Nezami, *Le Sette Principesse*, translated by A. Bausani

Under press

Anon, *History of Sistan*, translated by M. Gold
Anon, *Samak-e Ayyar I*, translated by F. Razavi
Avicenna, *Metaphysics* (from the *Danesh-nameh* translated by P. Morewedge.
Gardizi, *History*, translated by A. Pontecorvo.

The Persian Heritage Series is published under the joint auspices of UNESCO and the Royal Institute of Publication and Translation of Iran, affiliated with the Pahlavi Foundation. The Series owes its foundation to an initiative of H. M. the Shahanshah of Iran, and enjoys his continuing encouragement and support. The Series aims at making the best of Persian classics available in the major Western languages. The translations in this Series are intended not only to satisfy the needs of the students of Persian history and culture but also to respond to the demands of the intelligent reader who seeks to broaden his intellectual and artistic horizons through an acquaintance with the major world literatures.

FOREWORD

The Qājār dynasty of Persia came to power in the 1780s, some forty years after the Safavids lost their grip over the country. The Qājārs continued on into our own century, until 1921, when they were swept aside by the forces of a nationalist, reformist movement. During the greater part of their rule, the country continued the political, social, and religious traditions of Safavid Persia. Isolated from most of the Muslim world and the West, however, Persia found itself at the turn of the century at a low ebb of its political and cultural power. For about two centuries the country had ceased to experience that mysterious impulse which stimulates nations into eras of dynamic self-determination and innovative approaches. Entrenched in its obsolete ways and incapable of fully recognizing the forces of change which were sweeping over the Middle East, the Qājār dynasty did not prove in the end a match for the more progressive elements which brought about the revolution of 1906 for constitutional government.

Associated with a period of declining fortunes in Persian history, and having suffered an inglorious downfall, the Qājār dynasty has largely failed to arouse the enthusiasm of historians, either native or foreign. And this despite the fact that fairly extensive accounts of the Qājār period exist in both Persian sources and European travel books and narratives.

It is only recently that the history of a period whose beginning is steeped in medieval, traditional Persia and whose last phase is animated by cultural confrontation with the West, national strife, and reformist endeavors, has begun to attract due attention. It is now being increasingly realized that a study of the period not only has its own intrinsic value, but is also essential for an understanding of both the contemporary development of the country and its past experiences.

An objective and coherent history of the Qājārs, however, suffers from an imbalance of the sources in Western languages. Whereas European narratives and comments abound, native accounts available in Western languages are scarce. Sir J. Brydge's *The Dynasty of the Qajars*, a translation of a Persian pragmatic history of ᶜAbd or-Razzaq Maftun Dombali (London, 1833), which is about the only work of its kind available in English, treats of no more than two decades of the Qājār rule. The European works, valuable as they are, particularly for their descriptions of social customs, present Persian events from a non-Persian viewpoint, often tainted by political or religious prejudices. It is to be noted that the Qājār period coincides with the height of European expansion, and therefore it is hardly surprising if the views and attitudes of many a European writer are colored by the prevalent imperialism of the time. The Persian appraisal of events is largely lacking.

The present work provides for the first time a fairly detailed native account of the Qājār dynasty from its beginning down to the year 1882. It is a translation of the first part of Hasan Fas'i's *Fārsnāma*, which although purporting to be a history, geography, and geographical history of the province of Fars, in fact contains one of the fuller accounts of Persian history as a whole under Qājār rule. Its author, a careful and patient scholar who had access to major Persian sources and government archives, as well as eye-witness accounts, was particularly well equipped to treat the Qājār history. His preoccupation with Fars has the added advantage of permitting him to describe the provincial administration of Persia in a typical case with details not to be found elsewhere.

Professor Busse's painstaking and able translation has in more than one way enhanced the usefulness of the work by including equivalent Christian dates, chapter headings and subheadings, various tables, and bibliographies.

Ehsan Yarshater

PREFACE

This translation of Ḥasan-e Fasā'i's History of the Qājārs from the first part of the *Fārsnāma-ye Nāṣeri* is intended to make accessible an important source on the history of Persia in the nineteenth century. As far as I know, no such work has been undertaken since Sir Harford Jones Brydges's translation of the *Ma'āther-e Solṭāniya* by ᶜAbd or-Razzāq ibn Najaf Qoli, which was published under the title *The Dynasty of the Kajars, Translated from the Original Persian Manuscript presented to Sir H. J. Brydges* (London, 1833). Incidentally, the title is even more misleading than the date of publication suggests, since only the time down to the year 1226:1811 is treated, consequently not even two decades of the Qājār rule. There is no lack of summary treatises on the history of the Qājārs written by European historians and scholars; however, most of these books treat only part of the Qājār history, such as Sir John Malcolm's *History of Persia*, in two volumes, which ends with the year 1814. An excellent history of nineteenth-century Persia by R. Watson follows the events down to the year 1858. Sir P. M. Sykes's *History of Persia* is brought down to the year 1921, the date of publication of the two volumes; however, in intensity it remains far behind Watson's book. Finally, E. G. Browne has included a short and capricious chapter on the Qājār rule in the fourth volume of his famous *Literary History of Persia*, first published in 1920. In all these books Persian sources are not widely used. Sir John Malcolm restricts his mention of Persian sources to hinting about "a Persian Manuscript." Watson makes use of the *Roużat oṣ-Ṣafā-ye Nāṣeri* by Reżā Qoli Khān Hedāyat and two Persian eyewitness reports of the siege of Herāt; his other sources are books written exclusively by Europeans. It is undoubtedly true that European sources are essential for the study of nineteenth-century Persia; but it is also evident that the modern student of

Qājār rule must accord the Persian sources at least the same importance as other source material. Only then will the student be entitled to pass judgment on the value and authenticity of non-European statements.

The *Fārsnāma-ye Nāṣeri* consists of two volumes: The first volume contains, on 346 pages, a treatise on the history of Persia and especially Fārs from the beginning of Islam to the year 1300:1882/83. The second volume, which is about the same size, is a descriptive geography of that province and includes a substantial amount of historical information. Both volumes are not altogether new to Orientalists. In 1913, D. Démorgny wrote a treatise on the tribes of Fārs which is based on the second part of the *Fārsnāma-ye Nāṣeri*.[1] E. G. Browne's history of the Moẓaffarids in the third volume of his *Literary History of Persia*, which was published in 1920, is taken from Ḥasan-e Fasā'i's first part. Finally, V. Minorsky uses extensively the *Fārsnāma-ye Nāṣeri*—which he calls "excellent"—in his commentary on the *Ḥudūd al-ᶜĀlam* and refers to it again and again in his various articles on the history and geography of Persia in the first edition of the *Encyclopaedia of Islam*.[2]

Compared to the other Persian chronicles of the nineteenth century, the *Fārsnāma-ye Nāṣeri* has the advantage that it covers nearly a century of Qājār rule. However, the first volume, the history, has to be made accessible before one turns one's attention to the geographical part, which is in a way a history from the geographical point of view. This might suffice to justify my choice. Because Ḥasan-e Fasā'i writes in a plain and clear language, refraining from the bombastic style of the previous centuries, the text needs abridgment in a few passages only. In the main, poems and chronograms have been omitted; poems add nothing to historical information, while the chronograms

1. D. Démorgny, "Les tribus du Fars," in: *Revue du Monde Musulman*, 22 (1913).

2. See the articles Lur, Luristān, Shūlistān Nādir, and the like.

in most cases cannot be translated without depriving them of the point. For the convenience of the reader the text has been divided into four main chapters, according to the rulers treated in the chronicle, and subheadings have been introduced for better understanding of the arrangement of the material. It should be noted that the printed edition has neither chapters nor paragraphs. Notes have been added in those cases where an immediate understanding of the text requires some further information. A full confrontation with other sources, Persian or European, lies outside the scope of a translation. Where the author refers to the second volume of his book, the passages in question have been included in the text or in the notes, most of them in full wording. A list of the shahs, grand viziers, governors, and viziers of Fārs, as far as information on them is to be found in the text, and genealogical tables as well, have been added as an appendix.

Finally, I should like to thank Professor Ehsan Yar-Shater for having included this translation in the Persian Heritage Series. It is to be hoped that this book will stimulate further studies in the much neglected history of nineteenth-century Persia. I also owe much to the patient collaboration of Dr. Abd al-Karim Golshani and Mr. Ivars Alksnis, University of Hamburg. Their help was valuable to me in problems of translation and style. My special thanks go to Miss Phyllis Holbrook and Miss Paula Schonwald, Columbia University Press, without whose help in questions of transliteration and arrangement of the material the book would certainly not have appeared in the present shape. It goes without saying that the responsibility for any shortcomings rests with me alone.

Bochum, 1972 H.B.

Ḥasan-e Fasā'i, the author of the *Fārsnāma-ye Nāṣeri*, came from a family which can be traced back to the fifteenth century. The family was called Dashtaki, after the Dashtak quarter of Shiraz. The Dashtak quarter existed down to the time of the Zand and was incorporated into other quarters in the course of the reshaping of the administration of Shiraz by Karim Khān Vakil.[1] The first ancestor that we have specific information on was Gheyāth od-Din Manṣur (d. about 870:1465/66), who founded a college in Shiraz called Madrasa-ye Manṣuriya; several villages were made a Pious Foundation in favor of this college. Ḥasan-e Fasā'i was administrator of these foundations until the end of his life. At the end of the sixteenth century, a branch of the family settled down at Mecca and acquired great wealth in the form of landed property in the Holy City and its surroundings. A descendant of Gheyāth od-Din Manṣur, Mirzā Neẓām od-Din Aḥmad, went to Hyderabad/Decan and was appointed vizier to the ruler of Golconda, the Quṭb Shāhi ᶜAbdollāh ibn Moḥammad (r. 1612–72). Ṣadr od-Din ᶜAli Khān, the vizier's son, was born in Medina in 1052:1642, lived for some time in India and then went to Shiraz after having performed his *ḥajj*—the pilgrimage to Mecca and Medina and the Holy Places in Mesopotamia. At Shiraz, he became a professor at the Manṣuriya College. Brockelmann lists eight books written by him, among them a Divan, books on philology, and commentaries on poetry.[2] Ṣadr od-Din ᶜAli Khān made his possessions in Mecca a

1. A detailed history of the family is given in *FNN*, II, 29 f., 80 f., and 231 f.

2. See Brockelmann, *Geschichte der arabischen Litteratur, Supplementband*, II, 627 f. Ḥasan-e Fasā'i, *FNN*, II, 86, enumerates the titles of 17 books written by ᶜAli Khān.

Pious Foundation, the administration of which was inherited by his descendants. Ḥasan-e Fasā'i was administrator of the foundation, which yielded a yearly income of 300 toman. Ṣadr od-Din ᶜAli Khān died in about 1117:1705 at Shiraz. His son, Majd od-Din Moḥammad, born in 1105:1693 at Hyderabad, settled down in the village of Rouniz-e bālā, northwest of Fasā. According to the Pious Foundations in favor of the Manṣuriya College mentioned above, the family seems to have acquired estates there as far back as the fifteenth century. This branch of the family from that time on was called Mirzāyān-e Fasā'i. Some of Majd od-Din's sons lived at Fasā, some at Shiraz. Ḥasan, the father of the author, grew up at Shiraz, later returned to Fasā, and lived there on his inherited property. He died in 1327:1821/22 and was buried at Rouniz-e bālā in his father's mausoleum Boqᶜa-ye Mirzā. With this generation the family entered into Persian politics. Ḥasan's elder brother, Moḥammad Ḥosein, known as Mirzā Jāni-ye Fasā'i, was appointed governor of Fasā by Karim Khān Vakil,[3] and was for a short time, during Jaᶜfar Khān-e Zand's reign, governor of Esfahan.[4] When the Zands were overthrown by the Qājārs, Mirzā Jāni did not suffer any harm, but was forced to give two of his sons as hostages.[5] Later, however, he was to enjoy full favor with the Qājārs. He was "one of the most renowned nobles of Fārs" and became councilor to Crown Prince Fatḥ ᶜAli Mirzā, when the latter was governor of Fārs.[6] During Ḥosein ᶜAli Khān's revolt, he was imprisoned and died from poison.[7] His sons and grandsons made splendid careers in the service of the Qājārs. His son Mirzā Hādi became governor of the central part of the province of Fārs.[8] One of Hādi Mirzā's sons, Moḥammad Ḥosein, was appointed Vakil of Fārs,[9] and another son, Abu'l-Ḥasan Khān, received the title "Farzand Maqām."[10] However, this branch of the family also produced

3. See *FNN*, II, 231. 4. See below, p. 23 seq. 5. See below, p. 56.
6. See below, p. 64. 7. See below, p. 82 seq. 8. See below, p. 86 seq.
9. See below, p. 244. 10. See below, p. 196.

renowned theologians; one, the Mojtahed Haji Mirzā Ebrāhim, wrote several treatises on theology.

The author of the *Fārsnāma-ye Nāṣeri*, son of Ḥasan and nephew of Mirzā Jāni-ye Fasā'i, dedicated his life to scholarship. According to his autobiography,[11] he was born in 1237:1821/22 at Fasā, the same year in which his father died.[12] He began the study of theology at Shiraz, continued it at Esfahan, and then again at Shiraz. He then turned to mathematics and medicine. After a short stay in Tehran in 1279:1862/63 and a visit to Mashhad and Yazd, he settled down at Shiraz and took to teaching and practicing medicine. In Shaᶜbān 1283:December 1866, he went to Behbehān and studied calligraphy and Koran interpretation under the guidance of Mollā ᶜAli Aṣghar. Having visited the Holy Places in Mesopotamia in Ramażān 1287:December 1870, he returned to Shirāz. Two years later, after the death of one of his relatives, he was unlawfully deprived of part of his possessions, the Pious Foundation, which lay near Shiraz, Fasā, and in the district of Rāmjerd, north of Shiraz. He engaged in endless endeavors to recover his property, as late as the year 1314:1896/97, not long before his death. A detailed study of this interesting lawsuit is beyond the scope of my introduction; several documents concerning it are included by the author in the second part of his book. In fact, in his introduction, he devotes several passages to the lawsuit.

A detailed background of the writing of the *Fārsnāma-ye Nāṣeri* is given in the introduction to the first volume. On the basis of his exact knowledge of the province of Fārs, Ḥasan-e Fasā'i had drawn maps of the different parts of the province. By order of Masᶜud Mirzā Ẓell os-Solṭān, then governor of Fārs, he combined the maps to make a general map of the province in 1289:1872/73. Three years later, when Moᶜtamad od-Doula

11. See *FNN*, II, 87 f.

12. The author gives the year of his birth in a poem, inserted in *FNN*, II, 87.

Farhād Mirzā had become governor of Fārs, Ḥasan-e Fasā'i drew a new, larger map, which was 2 cubits (about 190 cm.) long and 1 cubit (about 95 cm.) wide. It showed "the names of all the villages and islands, of the large springs, rivers and the famous mountains of the province of Fārs." Although this map had been drawn by the order of Farhād Mirzā, the author presented it to the shah and wrote in its margin a petition concerning the law-suit for his lost property. The shah granted the petition and Farhād Mirzā, as the author tells us, did all that was in his power to back the claims. The connections to Farhād Mirzā proved to be very useful. Probably through his mediation, Ḥasan-e Fasā'i was appointed physician in ordinary to Eḥteshām od-Doula, Farhād Mirzā's son and governor of Behbehān. In 1294:1877, our author accompanied Eḥteshām od-Doula on his campaign from Behbehān to the coast of the Persian Gulf as far as Bandar Kangān. Two years later, he visited the island of Khārk in the governor's company.[13] It was probably also during Farhād Mirzā's governorship (1876–81) that Ḥasan-e Fasā'i married a daughter of a Shirazi merchant.[14] In 1296:1877 he was ordered by Farhād Mirzā to write a geography of Fārs on the basis of the map mentioned above. Complying with this order, Ḥasan-e Fasā'i decided to write a book, the *Fārsnāma-ye Nāṣeri*, in two parts: the first part was to contain the history of the kings, governors, and nobles of Fārs, from the beginning of Islam down to his own time; the second part was to be a geography of Fārs. As we learn from the several dates inserted in the text, the work was not finished until 1305:1887/88.[15] The introduction to the first volume was evidently not written until 1311, for Ḥasan-e Fasā'i mentions there that he intended to follow the events down to that year. Actually, it comes to an end with the year 1300:

13. See below, p. 400 seq.

14. The other wife of Ḥasan-e Fasā'i was a daughter of the calligrapher and poet Mirzā Seiyed ᶜAli, with the penname Nayāz, see *FNN*, II, 90.

15. See *FNN*, I, 4.

1882/83. We learn from the copyist's note that the author had reached the age of seventy and was blind by the end of the first volume. According to this note, also, the fair copy for the lithographed edition was finished in Dhu'l-Qaᶜda 1312: April–May 1895. The printing of the two volumes was not finished before Ṣafar 1314: July 1896, the date of the *fermān* reproduced at the end of the second volume. Although we have no information about the author's death, he was still alive when his book was published. The two volumes are generally bound together in one, as is also the reprint undertaken by the Ketābkhāna-ye Sanā'i in about 1965. The map of Fārs was published separately.[16] A map on a smaller scale is to be found on pages 16–17 of the second volume of the lithographed edition.

As for planning and conception, the *Fārsnāma-ye Nāṣeri* stands at the end of a long tradition. Local history and geography, intermixed with biography, had been quite familiar in Moslem culture since classical times; the *Fārsnāma-ye Nāṣeri* is not an isolated type of literature for the nineteenth century. Especially concerning Fārs, Ḥasan-e Fasā'i had a precursor in the person of Mirzā Moḥammad Jaᶜfar Khān-e Khormuji, who in his *Āthār-e Jaᶜfari* had combined topography and history in one.[17] The book had been published in 1276: 1860 and was known to Ḥasan-e Fasā'i, although he does not quote it *expressis verbis*. One might speculate that because Moḥammad Jaᶜfar Khān, in another work, the *Ḥaqā'eq ol-akhbār-e Nāṣeri*,[18] had put forth harsh accusations against the Qājārs, Ḥasan-e Fasā'i might have deemed it advisable to mention his name but not quote from Moḥammad Jaᶜfar Khān's books.

Farhād Mirzā, our author's patron, was a reformist, as his

16. See Minorsky, *Ḥudūd al-ᶜĀlam*, p. 376.

17. See Storey, p. 343.

18. The book was first published in 1284: 1867/68, and then withdrawn from circulation by order of the Persian government. A new edition has been published by Ḥosein Khadiv-Jam, Tehran 1345: 1967.

famous father, ᶜAbbās Mirzā, had been. He took a great interest in mathematics and geography and translated into Persian an Arabic treatise on mathematics and W. Pinnock's *Comprehensive System of Geography*, adding a chapter on Fārs based on observations during his campaigns and travels through the province.[19] Farhād Mirzā also compiled a small English-Persian Dictionary and thereby contributed to the knowledge of English in Persia. He was a zealous partisan of the introduction of European science into Persia and of the reform of Persian prose writing. His collection and edition of the famous Abu'l-Qāsem Qā'em Maqām's letters, published in Tabriz in 1282:1865/66, bears witness to his endeavors in this field. Ḥasan-e Fasā'i proved a willing student of his patron in the geographical part of his book by making use of Farhād Mirzā's achievements in modern geography. Despite his docility he showed a strong inclination to tradition, for his book contains all the traditional elements of classical geography, as well as much biographical material which does not form part of geography in the strict sense of the word. It is, however, due to precisely this character of his writing that the book is a nearly inexhaustible source for information on Fārs in the nineteenth century. Ḥasan-e Fasā'i was a historiographer, too, and thus he dedicated the first part of his book to history. The style of both parts is plain and simple. Farhād Mirzā's influence is attested by two passages from Sir John Malcolm's *History of Persia* quoted in full by our author.[20] This is, however, nothing more than a decoration, for he is more traditional in the field of history than in that of geography. One might say that he is a true representative of the Medieval Persia that E. G. Browne still found in his travels in the 1880s.

19. See below, p. 393, year 1294:1877/78.

20. The book was translated into Persian by order of the English government of India, at the express wishes of the Persian governor of Kerman, Vakil ol-Molk I (d. 1866), see *Eastern Persia. An Account of the Journeys of the Persian Boundary Commission 1870–71–72*, ed. Sir Frederic John Goldsmid (2 vols., London, Macmillan and Co., 1876), I, 184.

Not following the inspiration which Malcolm's book could have given him, Ḥasan-e Fasā'i wrote his history in the annalistic manner. This form of historiography was abandoned soon after, leaving the *Fārsnāma-ye Nāṣeri* one of if not the last Annals written in Persia. According to Storey, Moḥammad Ḥasan Khān E^{c}temād od-Doula (also called Ṣani^{c} od-Doula) must have finished his chronicle on Nāṣer od-Din Shāh's reign after Ḥasan-e Fasā'i's history.[21]

Writing on the history of Persia, Ḥasan-e Fasā'i had a wealth of source material at his disposal. The nineteenth century is particularly rich in literary works in the field of history. The number of chronicles, including the *Fārsnāma*, written in the last century comes to no fewer than nineteen, the *Fārsnāma* being the eighteenth in chronological order. Of his seventeen predecessors, Ḥasan-e Fasā'i quotes only five *expressis verbis*: 1) Mirzā Moḥammad Kalāntar-e Fārs: *Ruznāma* (Diary), ending with the year 1199:1784; 2) Fatḥ ^{c}Ali Khān-e Kāshāni "Ṣabā:" *Shāhanshāh-nāma*, an epic description of Fatḥ ^{c}Ali Shāh's campaigns, finished in 1225:1810 (Storey, No. 425); 3) Fażlollāh-e Khāveri-ye Shirāzi: *Tārikh-e Dhu'l-Qarnein*, which is brought down to the year 1263:1847 (Storey, No. 429.1); 4) Reżā Qoli Khān "Hedāyat:" *Roużat oṣ-Ṣafā-ye Nāṣeri*, a continuation of Mirkhvānd's chronicle, brought down to about 1863 (Storey, No. 440); 5) Moḥammad Taqi-ye Kāshāni "Sepehr:" *Tārikh-e Qājāriya*, the ninth volume of the *Nāsekh ot-tavārikh*. Sepehr died in 1297:1879/80 (Storey, No. 441). Apart from that, there are a few quotations from other books, such as Nāṣer od-Din Shāh's book on his pilgrimage to the Holy Places in Mesopotamia. In several instances Ḥasan-e Fasā'i speaks summarily of "the Qājār chronicles." Owing to his close connections in government, he had access to archives. He makes use of documents and quotes the following pieces in full (or slightly abridged): 1) agreement entered into by Persia and the Imam of Masqaṭ, 1272:1856

21. See Storey, No. 444.2.

(below, p. 312 seq.); 2) letter of obligation signed by the sons of the Imam of Masqaṭ, 1272:1856 (below, p. 316 seq.); 3) a promulgation published during the English occupation of Bushehr in 1273:1856 (below, p. 325 seq.); 4) letter of Grand Vizier Sepahsālār of the year 1288:1871 (below, p. 375 seq.); 5) *Fermān* issued by Nāṣer od-Din Shāh before his journey to Europe, 1290:1873 (below, p. 378); 6) personal letter addressed to Farhād Mirzā by Nāṣer od-Din Shāh, in connection with No. 5 (below, p. 378 seq.). Finally, the chronicle is based on eyewitness reports; the author refers repeatedly to what has been told to him by "old people of Shiraz."

The *Fārsnāma-ye Nāṣeri* is not merely a local history of Fārs. In accordance with the traditional Persian ideas on the nature of kingship, the author puts the history of the province of Fārs into the framework of the history of the Qājār dynasty. Typical is a sentence like this: "By the good fortune of the shah, the zeal of Moᶜtamad od-Doula Farhād Mirzā, and the endeavors of Qavām ol-Molk, the fortress of Tebr was captured."[22] It should be noted that neither the shah nor Farhād Mirzā took part in the siege of Tebr. However, as in the Persia of ancient times, the prosperity of the empire depends on the fortune of the shah, whose existence alone is a guarantee for success. It is only from the year 1247:1831/32 onward that in the chronicle events in Fārs are treated more extensively than the imperial policy is. The date is significant; after the treaty of Torkmānchāy of February 1828 the power of the Qājārs was considerably weakened. The history of the empire was then not much more than reports of humiliations by the European powers, particularly Russia and England. Whereas, the year 1247:1831/32 is marked by the outbreak of internal strife in the province of Fārs which was to shake the province for several decades. Order was established only when Farhād Mirzā was appointed governor of Fārs in 1873. A complete report of the disorder in Fārs pro-

22. See below, p. 391.

vided Ḥasan-e Fasā'i with the opportunity to describe vividly Farhād Mirzā's government. The European attitudes on Farhād Mirzā have for a long time been based on E. G. Browne's statements in his *A Year amongst the Persians.* In his *Literary History of Persia*, IV, 157, Browne somewhat revises his harsh judgment and writes: "To this security [i.e., of traveling in Persia in about 1887–88] I hardly did justice in the narrative of my travels. . . . And if this remarkable security, which compared favourably with that of many European countries, had originally been brought about by frightful exemplary punishments of robbers and ill-doers, these were no longer in evidence . . . though the ghastly pillars of mortar with protruding human bones outside the gate of Shiraz still bore witness of the stern rule of the Shah's uncle Farhād Mirzā Moᶜtamed od-Doula, whom I met only in the capacity of a courtly and learned bibliophile." Authors writing later than Browne are less restrained; one may, however, question whether their opinions on Farhād Mirzā's policy are based on new sources. Storey writes (p. 204 of his *Persian Literature*): "His administration was oppressive and unpopular and during the four years of his second term of office [ending about 1880, according to E. G. Browne], he is said to have caused no less than 700 hands to be cut off for various offences." Rypka, *Iranische Literaturgeschichte* (p. 334), says exactly the same: "Wegen seiner rücksichtslosen Strenge berüchtigt, schaffte er als zweimaliger Gouverneur von Fārs für lange Zeit Ordnung." From Ḥasan-e Fasā'i we cannot, of course, expect a critical judgment on Farhād Mirzā either. His report of Farhād Mirzā's government could be taken word for word from a traditional "Mirror for Princes."[23] The truth lies, as it often does, somewhere in between. Ḥasan-e Fasā'i's chronicle is, in any case, a valuable testimonial of the beliefs and feelings of a nineteenth-century Persian and as such deserves our full interest.

23. For this type of literature, see H. Busse, "Fürstenspiegel und Fürstenethik im Islam," in *Bustan*, 1/1968, pp. 12–19.

CONTENTS

CHAPTER I : ĀQĀ MOḤAMMAD SHĀH — I

Offspring and Early Life — I

The Origin of the Qājār Tribe; The Ancestors of Āqā Moḥammad Khān; His Early Life.

The Conquest of Northern Persia — 5

The Conquest of Māzandarān; Division in Shiraz After Karim Khān Vakil's Death; Abu'l-Fatḥ Khān Zand Succeeds to the Throne; Ṣādeq Khān-e Zand appears on the Scene; ^{c}Ali Morād Khān-e Zand, Another Pretender, Captures Esfahan and Tehran; The Drunkard Abu'l-Fatḥ Khān-e Zand Deposed by Ṣādeq Khān; ^{c}Ali Morād Khān's Activities in Northern Persia; The Qājārs Weakened by Internal Strife; The Conquest of Semnān, Dāmghān, Shahrud, and Besṭām; The Conquest of Gilān, Khamsa, Qazvin, and Zenjān; Marriages of Fatḥ ^{c}Ali Khān; First Siege of Tehran; Zand Attack on Māzandarān Fails; A Change on the Zand Throne; Āqā Moḥammad Khān Conquers Tehran; Ja^{c}far Khān occupies Esfahan; Zand Campaign to Jandaq; Esfahan Reoccupied by Āqā Moḥammad Khān; Ja^{c}far Khān Undertakes a Campaign to Kuh-e Giluya and Behbehān; Zand attack on Yazd Fails; Another Pretender to the Crown Appears on the Scene; Ja^{c}far Khān-e Zand Subdues Lārestān; Yazd Occupied by the Qājār Army; Esfahan Lost to Ja^{c}far Khān-e Zand for a Short While; Loṭf ^{c}Ali Khān, Brother of Ja^{c}far Khān-e Zand, Sent on Campaign to the Persian Gulf; Murder of Ja^{c}far Khān; Seiyed Morād Khān Ascends the Zand Throne; Loṭf ^{c}Ali Khān Defeats Seiyed Morād Khān and Assumes Rulership.

The Overthrow of the Zand Rule — 33

Āqā Moḥammad Khān Undertakes His First Campaign to Shiraz; Five sons born to Fatḥ ^{c}Ali Khān; Preparations for the Conquest of Southern Persia; Loṭf ^{c}Ali Khān-e Zand Undertakes Campaign to Kerman; Pretensions of Ja^{c}far Qoli Khān to the Qājār Throne; Qājār Campaign to Ādherbāyjān; Haji Ebrāhim Khān's Defection from the Zand; Loṭf ^{c}Ali Khān Retreats to the Persian Gulf Coast; Haji Ebrāhim Khān Appointed Qājār Governor of Fārs; The Qājār Troops Suffer a Defeat at Kāzerun; The Tribal Soldiers of the Zand Expelled from Shiraz; Loṭf ^{c}Ali Khān Occupies Zarqān; Loṭf ^{c}Ali Khān Fails to Recapture Shiraz; Āqā Moḥammad Khān Suffers a Stroke, Sends Army to Shiraz; Battle Outside the Gates of Shiraz; Āqā Moḥammad Khān Goes in Person to Shiraz; The

Qājār Ruler Again in Fārs; Loṭf ᶜAli Khān Conquers Kerman; Āqā Moḥammad Khān Undertakes Campaign to Kerman; Loṭf ᶜAli Khān's Flight and Death; Fatḥ ᶜAli Khān Appointed Governor of Fārs.

Attempt to revive the Safavid Empire 65

Qājār Campaign to Armenia and Georgia; Coronation of Āqā Moḥammad Shāh; Campaign to Khorasan; Russian Intervention in Georgia; The Murder of Āqā Moḥammad Shāh.

CHAPTER 2 : FATH ᶜALI SHĀH 77

The Consolidation of Power 77

The Crown Prince Goes from Shiraz to Tehran; Campaign to Subdue Rebels in Ādherbāyjān; Ḥosein Qoli Khān, Brother of Fatḥ ᶜAli Shāh, Appointed Governor of Fārs; Punishment of Āqā Moḥammad Shāh's Murderers; Burial of Āqā Moḥammad Shāh at Najaf; Coronation of Fatḥ ᶜAli Shāh; The Royal Court at Solṭāniya; Rebellion of Ḥosein Qoli Khān; Appointments and Promotions; Two Palaces Built; ᶜAbbās Mirzā Appointed Crown Prince.

The Conquest of Khorasan 89

First Campaign to Khorasan; Miscellaneous Events; Ḥosein ᶜAli Mirzā, Son of Fatḥ ᶜAli Shāh, Appointed Governor of Fārs, Receives Title "Farmān-Farmā"; Another Campaign to Khorasan; Conclusion of a Treaty with England; Deposal of Grand Vizier Haji Ebrāhim Khān Eᶜtemād od-Doula; New Rebellion of Ḥosein Qoli Khān; Vahhābi Sack of Kerbelā; Third Campaign to Khorasan; Crown Prince ᶜAbbās Mirzā Married to Qājār Princess; Punishment of a Turkoman Tribe; Mashhad Captured; Murder of the Persian Ambassador to India.

Toward the Peace Treaty of Golestān 107

The Russians Invade Armenia and Ādherbāyjān; A Strange Story of Zizianov's Murder; Deposal of Charāgh ᶜAli Khān, Vizier of Fārs; Reforms in the Central Government; Napoleon Offers a Treaty of Friendship; Soleimān Pasha Taken Prisoner by the Persians; War with Russia Continued; Arrival of Gardane, Conclusion of a Treaty with France; Miscellaneous Events; Diplomatic Activities in Tehran; Treaty of Friendship Concluded with England; Holy War Declared on Russia; Appointment of a Persian Ambassador to London; New Campaign to Armenia and Georgia; Appointments in the Central Government and in Fārs; Russian Peace Offer; Sir John Malcolm at Solṭāniya; Persian Troops Assist the Imam of

Masqaṭ against Vahhābis; The Shah travels to Esfahan; Arrival of an Ottoman Embassy in Tehran; The Shah at Solṭāniya; Sir Gore Ouseley Appointed Ambassador to Persia; Arghun Khān's Tomb Discovered; Haji Ebrāhim Khān's Son Restored to Office in Shiraz; The Shah at Solṭāniya; The Peace Treaty of Golestān.

A Period of Negotiations Foreign and Consolidation Home 144

Appointments and Promotions; Envoys from the Arabian Peninsula in Tehran; The Shah Pays Debts of a Courtier; Appointment of a New Vizier in Shiraz; Foreign Relations; Arrest of the Governor of Astārabād; A Case of Blood Revenge; Suppression of a Local Revolt; The Shah Travels to Different Parts of the Country; The Persian Ambassador's Negotiations in St. Petersburg; Another Change in the Vizierate of Shiraz; A Russian Ambassador Sent to Persia; The Governor of Fārs Undertakes Campaign to the Persian Gulf; Movements of the Royal Court; Persian Ambassadors Sent to Several European Countries; The Shah Undertakes Campaign to Khorasan; The Shah Visits the Shrine at Mashhad; The Vizier of Shiraz Murdered; Diplomatic Relations with Austria; Movements of the Royal Court; Death of the Prime Minister; Marriage of Crown Prince Moḥammad Mirzā; Appointment of a "Chief of the Tribes" of Fārs; The Shah Receives Gifts from the Russian Emperor; Measures Taken Against a Sufi Order; Tribal Quarrels in Fārs Settled; Diplomatic Relations with England and Egypt; The Shah Travels to Khorasan; The Royal Court at Solṭāniya; Persia Ravaged by Plague; A Revolt Planned by the Governor of Khorasan; Death of the Prime Minister; Treaty Concluded with Turkey; Earthquakes in Southern Persia; The Shah Travels to Esfahan and Establishes Order There; Appointments and Promotions; Thirtieth Anniversary of the Shah's Accession to the Throne; Miscellaneous Events.

Last Attempt to Recover Armenia and Ādherbāyjān 174

Holy War Declared on Russia; Vain Efforts of the Russian Ambassador to Stop Hostilities; The Persian Army Lays Siege on Shushā; Persian Defeat Near Ganja; Return of the Royal Court to Tehran By Way of Tabriz; A New Persian Campaign Opened; Tabriz Occupied by Russian Troops; Peace Negotiations at Khārqān; Conclusion of a peace treaty at Torkmānchāy.

Concentration on Internal Policy 185

A New Prime Minister Appointed; The Shah Travels to Qom and Solṭānābād; The Russian Ambassador Griboyedov Murdered in Tehran; A Son of the Crown Prince Sent to Saint Petersburg; Appointments to High Positions in the Government; Rise and Downfall of the Nuri Family in Shiraz; The Shah Travels to Fārs to Settle the Affairs of That Province;

An Attempt at the Shah's Life; the Court Returns to Tehran; Arrival of an Ambassador from Sind; The Shah Travels to Kermānshāh and Esfahan to Settle Affairs There; Birth of Nāṣer od-Din Mirzā; Crown Prince ᶜAbbās Mirzā Sent to Khorasan; Alleviation of Taxes Granted to the Governor of Fārs.

Troubles in Fārs 201

Sheikh ᶜAbd or-Rasul Khān Expelled from Bushehr; The Governor of Fārs Goes to Bushehr and Establishes Order There; Rivalries in Shiraz; Behbehān Occupied by Mirzā Manṣur Khān; Appointment of New Governors to Several Districts of Fārs; The Qashqā'i and Other Tribes Move from Fārs to Kerman; Naṣir Khān Reappointed Governor of Lārestān; The Governor of Fārs Undertakes Campaign to Kerman; Murder of Sheikh ᶜAbd or-Rasul Khān at Dālaki; The Deputy Governor of Fārs Marches to Bushehr; The Governor of Fārs Reconciles the Qashqā'i Tribe and Settles Affairs in Kerman; Unsuccessful Attempt of Sheikh ᶜAbd or-Rasul Khān's son to Conquer Bushehr; Holāgu Mirzā's Appointment to the Governorship of Kerman Confirmed by the Shah; An Unusually Cold Winter; Measures Taken Against Moshir ol-Molk, the Former Vizier of Fārs; Military Reforms in Fārs; Death of Crown Prince ᶜAbbās Mirzā; The Governor of Fārs Subdues the Qashqā'i Khāns; Moshir ol-Molk Reappointed Vizier of Fārs; Arrival of an English Military Mission.

Last Measures 227

Moḥammad Mirzā Appointed Crown Prince; The Shah Travels to Esfahan to Settle Affairs in Southern Persia; Death of Fatḥ ᶜAli Shāh.

CHAPTER 3 : MOḤAMMAD SHĀH 231

The Struggle for succession 231

The Prime Minister Incites Ḥosein ᶜAli Mirzā Farmān-Farmā, the Governor of Fārs, to Assume Rulership; Moḥammad Shāh Ascends the Throne in Tabriz and Tehran; The Governor of Fārs Claims the Throne; Firuz Mirzā Appointed Governor of Fārs; the Rebels Suffer Defeat Near Izadkhvāst; Indecision and Uproar in Shiraz; Shiraz Occupied By the Royal Army; the Governor Arrested; The Governor of Fārs Is Brought to Tehran and Dies There; Haji Mirzā Āqāsi Appointed Prime Minister; Nāṣer od-Din Mirzā Appointed Crown Prince; Reorganization of the Province of Fārs; Vali Khān, Chief of the Mamassani Lors, Subdued.

Attempt to Establish Persian Supremacy over Afghanistan 250

Attempt to Conquer Herāt Fails; Moᶜtamad od-Doula Summoned From Shiraz to Tehran; The Shah Settles the Affairs of Turkoman Tribes in

Khorasan; Firuz Mirzā Sent to Kerman; Faridun Mirzā Farmān-Farmā Appointed Governor of Fārs; The Shah Undertakes Campaign to Afghanistan; Herāt Beleaguered By the Persian army; Siege of Herāt Raised After English intervention In the Persian Gulf.

Policy in Southern Persia 261

Miscellaneous Events in the Province of Fārs; Disturbance and Civil War in Shiraz; Nāṣer od-Din Mirzā Appointed Prince Governor, Farhād Mirzā Deputy Governor of Fārs; Farhād Mirzā Subdues the Chiefs of the Mamassani Lors; Farhād Mirzā Settles Affairs In the Coastal Area of the Persian Gulf; Several Districts Separated from the Province of Fārs; New Governor of Kuh-e Giluya and Behbehān Appointed by Farhād Mirzā; Farhād Mirzā's Successful Administration of Fārs; Farhād Mirzā Summoned to Tehran; Mirzā Nabi Khān's Unsuccessful Government of Fārs; Ḥosein Khān Appointed Governor of Fārs; Irrigation Work Undertaken in the Shiraz Area; A Change in the Vizierate of Fārs; Quarrels Among the Qashqā'i Khāns; Ḥosein Khān Goes to Tehran to Close the Accounts of Fārs; Foundation of the Bābi Faith; Ḥosein Khān Returns to Fārs and Settles Affairs in the Qashqā'i Region; Ḥosein Khān Finishes Irrigation Work In the Shiraz Area; Death of Moḥāmmad Shāh.

CHAPTER 4 : NĀṢER OD-DIN SHĀH 282

Internal Difficulties 282

Nāṣer od-Din Shāh Ascends the Throne; The People of Shiraz Rise in Rebellion Against Ḥosein Khān Neẓām od-Doula; Bahrām Mirzā Moᶜezz od-Doula Appointed Governor of Fārs; Sheikh Naṣr Khān Appointed Governor of Bushehr and Defends Himself Successfully Against a Pretender; Firuz Mirzā Noṣrat od-Doula Appointed Governor of Fārs; Bābi Disturbances at Fasā and Niriz; Appointments in Shiraz; Sheikh Naṣr Khān of Bushehr Summoned to Shiraz and Sent to Tehran; Quarrels About the Governorship of Kuh-e Giluya and Behbehān; Police Stations Established In the Persian Cities and Towns; The Shah Travels to Esfahan; The Governor of Fārs Settles Affairs in Behbehān and Mamassani; A New Prime Minister Appointed; Firuz Mirzā Settles Affairs In the Southern Districts of Fārs; Bābis' Attempt At the Shah's Life; Firuz Mirzā Settles Affairs At Bushehr and Surroundings; Earthquake in Shiraz; Ṭahmāsp Mirzā Mo'eiyed od-Doula Appointed Governor of Fārs.

Quarrel with the Imam of Masqaṭ About the Possession of Bandar ᶜAbbās 303

Persian Attempt to Occupy Bandar ᶜAbbās Fails; Bandar ᶜAbbās Conquered By Persian Troops; Ṭahmāsp Mirzā Returns To Shiraz; Bandar ᶜAbbās Lost and Reconquered; Ṭahmāsp Mirzā Appoints His Son Governor of Kuh-e Giluya and Behbehān; French Ambassador Arrives at Bushehr; The Imam of Masqaṭ Confirmed In the Possession of Bandar ᶜAbbās; Appointments in the Province of Fārs; Quarrel Between Lor and Bakhteyāri Tribes Settled.

New Attempt to Establish Persian Supremacy Over Afghanistan and English Intervention In the Persian Gulf 319

Bushehr Occupied By English Troops Upon Persian Campaign to Afghanistan; The Governor of Fārs Prepares Campaign to Bushehr; Persian Attack On the English Camp Near Borāzjān; The Persian Troops Rally At Nanizak; Persian Advance To the Vicinity of Bushehr; Peace Treaty Concluded In Paris; Appointments and Promotions.

Fārs In a State of Unrest 335

Miscellaneous Events; Fārs Haunted By Plague; Governor of Lārestān Subdued; Miscellaneous Events; Reorganization of the Central Government; Solṭān Morād Mirzā Ḥosām os-Salṭana Appointed Governor of Fārs; Appointments and Promotions; New Governors Appointed to Several Districts of Fārs; The Bahārlu and Inālu Tribes Subdued; The Shah Travels to Kurdistan and Solṭāniya; The Governor of Fārs Settles Affairs at Bushehr; Street Riots in Shiraz; Mahdi Qoli Mirzā Subdues Local Ruler of Bastak; A Change in the Governorship of Bandar ᶜAbbās; The governor of Fārs sent to Khorasan; Ṭahmāsp Mirzā Mo'eiyed od-Doula Again Appointed Governor of Fārs; Ṭahmāsp Mirzā Constructs Bridge Across the Parvāb River; Proceedings at the Royal Court; Moẓaffar od-Din Mirzā Appointed Crown Prince; Solṭān Masᶜud Mirzā Yamin od-Doula Ẓell os-Solṭān Appointed Governor of Fārs; A Change in the Vizierate of Fārs; Solṭān Oveis Mirzā Eḥteshām od-Doula's Successful Administration of Kuh-e Giluya and Behbehān; Proceedings at the Royal Court; Death of Qavām ol-Molk; His Sons Promoted to High Offices; Solṭān Oveis Mirzā Establishes Order in Kuh-e Giluya; Uproar in Shiraz, Upon Which the Vizier Is Deposed; Solṭān Morād Ḥosām os-Salṭana Again Governor of Fārs, Executes Head of the Rebels; Solṭan Oveis Mirzā Constructs Water Conduit at Behbehān; The Shah Travels to Māzandarān; Famine in Shiraz; The Shah Travels to Mashhad.

Final Settlement of the Bandar ᶜAbbās Question 358

Solṭān Morād Mirzā Ḥosam os-Salṭana Occupies Bandar ᶜAbbās; The Bahārlu and Inālu Tribes Complain about Qavām ol-Molk's Oppression; Offer to the Imam of Masqaṭ Concerning the Possession of Bandar ᶜAbbās;

The Shah Orders New Distribution of the Government Schedules; New Governor Appointed to Dārāb and the Bahārlu and Inālu Tribes; Qavām ol-Molk's Machinations in Tehran with Regard to the Governorship of Dārāb and Fasā; Appointment of New Governors to Bandar ᶜAbbās, Lārestān, and Bushehr; Bandar ᶜAbbās Restituted to the Imam of Masqaṭ; Final Settlement of the Possession of Bandar ᶜAbbās; Solṭān Masᶜud Mirzā Ẓell os-Solṭān Again Appointed Governor of Fārs; Shiraz and Fārs Infested With Plague; Miscellaneous Events.

Coexistence with Ottoman Turkey Adopted 368

The Shah's Pilgrimage to the Holy Places in Mesopotamia; A Son Born to Solṭān Masᶜud Mirzā; The Author's Pilgrimage to Mecca and Medina; Appointments and Promotions; Moḥammad Qāsem Khān Vāli Appointed Governor of Fārs.

A Step Toward Reforms and Modernization 374

Prime Minister Haji Mirzā Ḥosein Khān Announces Reforms in the Civil Service; Famine in Several Parts of Fārs; Solṭān Masᶜud Mirzā Ẓell os-Solṭān Appointed Governor of Fārs a Third Time; Change in the Governorship of Bandar ᶜAbbās; The Shah Travels to the Shores of the Caspian Sea; The Shah's First Visit to Europe; Mirzā Fatḥ ᶜAli Khān-e Shirazi Appointed Prime Minister; Solṭān Morād Mirzā Ḥosām os-Salṭana's Third Term of Office as Governor of Fārs; The "Chest of Justice": A New Experiment of Internal Reforms; Yaḥyā Khān Moᶜtamad ol-Molk Appointed Governor of Fārs, Gives Moshir ol-Molk Plenipotentiary Power; Administrative difficulties in Several Districts of Fārs; The Shāh Travels to the Shore of the Caspian Sea; Increase of Crime and Highway Robbery in Fārs; Proceedings at the Royal Court.

Fārs Ruled by Efficient and Enlightened Governor 386

Moᶜtamad od-Doula Farhād Mirzā Appointed Governor of Fārs; Moᶜtamad od-Doula Appoints New Governors to Several Districts of Fārs; Reforms of Taxation and Civil Service in Fārs; The Fortress of Tebr, Stronghold of Highway Robbers Conquered; Eḥteshām od-Doula, Governor of Kuh-e Giluya and Behbehān, Subdues Rebels in the Coastal Area of the Persian Gulf; The Shah's Second Visit to Europe; Repair of Irrigation Canals in the Shiraz Area; Eḥteshām od-Doula Undertakes Another Campaign to the Coastal Area; Proceedings at the Royal Court; An Eclipse of the Sun; Qavām ol-Molk Repairs Irrigation Canals Near Shiraz; Eḥteshām od-Doula Sent to the Coastal Area a Third Time; Miscellaneous Events; The Author Accompanies Eḥteshām od-Doula on the Fourth Campaign to the Coastal Area and Visits the Island of Khārk; Sheikh

Madhkur Khān-e Kangāni Subdued; The Shah Travels to Māzandarān; The Province of Fārs in Perfect Order; Mo^ctamad od-Doula returns to Tehran; Examples of His Wise Government of the Province of Fārs; Mo^ctamad od-Doula's Activities in the Field of Scholarship and Writing; Administrative Reorganization of Southern Persia; Solṭān Ḥosein Mirzā Jalāl od-Doula Appointed Governor of Fārs; Panj ^cAli Beg of the Inālu Tribe Subdued; Administrative Activities of Governor and Vizier of Fārs; Cavalry Detachment from Fārs Stationed in Tehran; Miscellaneous Events; Death of Moshir ol-Molk and Qavām ol-Molk.

Appendices 421

Bibliography 433

Index 441

HISTORY OF PERSIA UNDER QĀJĀR RULE

CHAPTER I

Āqā Moḥammad Shāh

OFFSPRING AND EARLY LIFE

THE ORIGIN OF THE QĀJĀR TRIBE. [227] The most venerable Qājārs are descendants of Qājār Nuyān, son of the Mongol Sertāq Nuyān, who was tutor (atābeg) of the Persian king Arghun Khān.[1] When the descendants of Qājār Nuyān increased in number, they and all the different branches of the tribes were called "Qājār" after their ancestor. In the year 736,[2] the Qājārs migrated to Syria and made that region their abode. When Timur Gurkān undertook his campaign to Egypt and Syria,[3] he ordered the Qājārs to migrate from Syria to Turkistan. When they arrived in Ādherbayjān, they stopped at Ganja[4] and Erevan; one group of them which settled down at the upper course of the river was called "Yukhāribāsh." Turkish "Yuqāri" has become "Yukhāri," meaning "upper part"; "bāsh" means "head." The other group, which settled down at the lower course of the river was called "Ashshāqbāsh," which means

1. "Nuyān" (Mongolian "noyon, noyan") was the title of military commanders in the Mongol army, see B. Spuler, *Die Mongolen in Iran* (3d ed. Berlin, Akademie-Verlag, 1968), p. 401. Arghun Khān (r. 1284–91) was the fourth Ilkhanid ruler of Persia. According to other sources, Sertāq was tutor of Ghāzān Khān (r. 1295–1304), the son of Arghun Khān, and was murdered in 1295 because he was a follower of Gaikhātu Khān (r. 1291–95), see EI[1] II, s.v. Ḳādjār (Cl. Huart).

2. 736:1335/36, that is, at the end of the Ilkhanid Abu Saᶜid's rule (1316–35).

3. That is, A.D. 1400/01. In contemporary Islamic sources, Gurkān is explained as "son in law," because Timur tried to legitimate his rule by marrying a Mongol princess.

4. The town was renamed Elisavetpol after the Russian occupation, and Kirovabad in 1935, see EI[2] I, s.v. Gandja.

"below the head."[5] This was the first subdivision of the Qājārs. After that, each of both groups was subdivided into several branches, which were called differently: the one after its home, its ancestor, or its leader, the other one after the animals it reared: the sheep, in Turkish "qoyun," and the camel, in Turkish "deveh," to which was added the ending "lu," which means "owner, possessor." In this way the Ashshāqbāsh are called "Qoyunlu," [228] "ᶜEzz od-Dinlu," "Zeyādlu," and "Dāshlu";[6] the Yukhāribāsh "Devehlu," "Qeyākhlu," and "Khezānadārlu."[7]

THE ANCESTORS OF ĀQĀ MOḤAMMAD KHĀN; HIS EARLY LIFE. In the time of the Safavid ruler Shāh Soleimān,[8] Shāh Qoli Khān-e Qājār Qoyunlu proceeded from Ganja, the abode of his forefathers, to Astarābād and married a daughter of one of the nobles of that town. He had two sons: Fatḥ ᶜAli Khān, who was to become the ancestor of the Qājār dynasty, and Fażl ᶜAli Khān, the ancestor of the Qājār Qoyunlu khāns. Fatḥ ᶜAli Khān inherited his father's leadership. His murder has been described under the events of the year 1139.[9] His successor as leader and chief, nay as ruler and king, was his eldest son Moḥammad

5. Reżā Qoli Khān Hedāyat, *Roużat oṣ-ṣafā-ye Nāṣeri*, IX, 4–6, gives three versions of the origin of the Qājārs. The version given here by Ḥasan-e Fasā'i corresponds on the whole with Hedāyat's version no. 1. According to other sources, the Qājārs were located at Ganja and Erevan in the time of the Safavids only; the subdivision into Yukhāribāsh and Ashshāqbāsh is referred to the Safavids, too, and said to have taken place in the region of Astarābād/Gorgan, not at Ganja and Erevan, see EI[1] II, s.v. Ḳādjār.

6. "ᶜEzz od-Din" ("strength of religion") and "Zeyād" are personal names of Islamic origin; "Dāsh" ("stone") occurs often as part of Turkish names, as for instance in "Bektāsh."

7. "Khezānadār" is not a personal name, but means "treasurer."

8. He reigned 1666–94.

9. Fatḥ ᶜAli Khān, together with Ṭahmāsp Qoli Khān (the later Nāder Shāh), was in the service of the Safavid Shah Ṭahmāsp II. On a campaign to Mashhad, he was murdered by Ṭahmāsp Qoli Khān under the pretext of pretensions to Shah Ṭahmāsp's throne, see *FNN*, I, 164 s.

Ḥasan Khān, as has been told under the events of the year 1172.[10] Then rulership and kingship were bestowed upon Moḥammad Ḥasan Khān's eldest son Āqā Moḥammad Khān. The circumstances of his early life before he claimed the rule were as follows: He was born on Sunday, 7th Moḥarram of the year 1155[11] at Astarābād, in the house of Seiyed Mofid-e Astarābādi,[12] because at that time Nāder Shāh[13] ruled over the whole of Persia, Khvārezm, Turkistan, India, and Dāghestān.[14] His father, Moḥammad Ḥasan Khān, out of fear of Nāder Shāh, was hiding in the Turkoman desert, and Āqā Moḥammad Khān's mother—daughter of Eskandar Khān-e Qājār Qoyunlu, sister of Moḥammad Khān, and paternal aunt of Amir-e Kabir Soleimān Khān—had taken refuge in the house of Seiyed Mofid, who was granting refuge and help to high and low. Seiyed Mofid concealed the birth, pretended the child was his own, gave him the name "Āqā Moḥammad," and brought him up with his own children. When ᶜAli Qoli Khān-e Afshār, known as "ᶜĀdel Shāh," son of Nāder Shāh's brother, assumed the rule,[15] a group of opponents betrayed Āqā Moḥammad Khān to that ruler. ᶜĀdel Shāh sent for Āqā Moḥammad Khān and had him brought to Khorasan. When he arrived there, ᶜĀdel Shāh's intention was to put him to death. Upon the intercession of a benevolent friend, ᶜĀdel Shāh spared the life of the Qājār prince, but ordered him to be

10. In 1172:1758/59, Moḥammad Ḥasan Khān suffered a defeat in Māzandarān and was killed when he tried to escape, see *FNN*, I, 212.

11. March 14, 1742.

12. Astarābād/Gorgān was named "dār ol-mo'menin" ("home of the believers"), probably because of the many seiyeds living there, see EI² I, s.v. Astarābādh (R. N. Frye).

13. Nāder Shāh reigned 1736–47.

14. Dāghestān, "Land of the mountains," is the region on the western shore of the Caspian Sea, now an Autonomous Republic of the R.S.F.S.R., see EI² II, s.v. Dāghistān (W. Barthold–A. Bennigsen). Nāder Shāh's rule over Dāghestān was firmly established only for a short while.

15. ᶜĀdel Shāh reigned 1747–48 in Khorasan; he was Nāder Shāh's nephew.

deprived of his manhood. When ᶜĀdel Shāh died, Āqā Moḥammad Khān won his freedom, went to his father, and remained with him. When Moḥammad Ḥasan Khān was murdered,[16] his sons were removed from Astarābād at the instigation of Moḥammad Ḥosein Khān-e Qājār Devehlu, the beglerbegi of Astarābād, and by order of Karim Khān Vakil.[17] Except for Mortażā Qoli Khān and Moṣṭafā Qoli Khān, the sons of the beglerbegi's sister, who were allowed to stay, Reżā Qoli Khān, Jaᶜfar Qoli Khān and ᶜAli Qoli Khān were brought to Qazvin, while Āqā Moḥammad Khān, the eldest of them, together with his brother Ḥosein Qoli Khān, was sent to Shiraz. They stayed as hostages at Karim Khān Vakil's court. Karim Khān Vakil, known for his kindness,[18] treated them with both paternal affection and respect. He allowed them to sit in his assembly and took council in the affairs of the government with Āqā Moḥammad Khān, whom he used to call "Pirān of the government."[19] Ḥosein Qoli Khān was appointed governor of Dāmghān. In the year 1185,[20] Fatḥ ᶜAli Shāh, the eldest son of Ḥosein Qoli Khān, was born of the daughter of Moḥammad Khān-e ᶜEzz od-Dinlu. Because he was given the name of his ancestor Fatḥ ᶜAli Khān, he was nicknamed

16. See above, note 10.

17. Karim Khān Vakil-e Zand (r. 1750–79), a descendant of the Lak branch of the Kurdish tribes, was the most successful of the petty rulers among whom Persia was divided after Nāder Shāh's death. From Shiraz he ruled over most parts of southern and central Persia. To 1794, as recounted here, he and his successors were the most dangerous opponents of the Qājārs.

18. "Muḥammad's reign of almost thirty years was one of clemency and moderation, and the country flourished under his enlightened rule," see Bosworth, *The Islamic Dynasties*, p. 177.

19. Pirān was one of the generals of Afrāseyāb, a legendary king of the Turanians, praised in Firdousi's Shāh-nāma, see Justi, *Iranisches Namenbuch*, p. 252. It is remarkable that Karim Khān Vakil, himself of Iranian offspring, respected the feelings of his Qājār guest of Turkish origin so much that he nicknamed him after a hero of the Turanians, who were considered as the ancestors of the Turks.

20. 1185:1771/72. The date is uncertain, see below, p. 229.

"Bābā Khān."[21] In the year 1188,[22] three men of the Turkoman tribe Yomut murdered Ḥosein Qoli Khān near Fandarask.[23]

THE CONQUEST OF NORTHERN PERSIA

THE CONQUEST OF MĀZANDARĀN.[24] The day of Karim Khān Vakil's death,[25] Āqā Moḥammad Khān, who had spent about fifteen years as a hostage at the Vakil's court, was falconing and hunting at Mahārlu, 8 parasangs from Shiraz.[26] His paternal aunt, a lady of the Vakili harem, informed him of what had happened. He did not return to Shiraz, but proceeded with fourteen followers (molāzemin) to Esfahan, where he arrived three days later. In the evening of 20th Ṣafar,[27] he arrived at the shrine of ᶜAbd ol-ᶜAzim,[28] performed the rites of pilgrimage and implored divine help for his important undertaking. The day before, in the district of Varāmin,[29] he met Mirzā Moḥammad Khān, Reżā Khān and other Qājār Devehlu khāns, who long since had been bitter enemies of the Qājār Qoyunlu and lived on

21. "Bābā" means "father, daddy," or "uncle."

22. 1188:1774/75.

23. Fandarask belongs now to the modern bakhsh of Rāmyān, which lies about 42 miles east-northeast of Astarābād/Gorgān, see *Farhang*, II, 205, s.v. Fandarask.

24. This paragraph starts on p. 220 of the original text; the story of the origin of the Qājārs and the ancestors of Āqā Moḥammad Khān is told by the author in connection with Āqā Moḥammad Khān's accession to the throne in Tehran, p. 227 of the text (p. 23 of my translation).

25. March 3, 1779, see *FNN*, I, 218. Other sources have March 13, see EI[1] II, s.v. Ḳādjārs (Cl. Huart).

26. Mahārlu lies about 25 miles southeast of Shiraz, near the Daryācha-ye Bākhtegān (also called Daryācha-ye Mahārlu), the biggest salt lake of southern Persia, see *FNN*, II, 194.

27. March 10, 1779.

28. At that time the shrine was outside the gates of Tehran. The reason for the visit was that the skull of Āqā Moḥammad Khān's father was buried within the precincts (ḥaram) of the shrine, see *FNN*, I, 212.

29. A small town about 30 miles southeast of Tehran.

terms of blood revenge with them. Āqā Moḥammad Khān showed regret over the enmity and hostility between both parties, and they changed their attitude and accepted him joyfully. Thereupon Āqā Moḥammad Khān proceeded confidently to Māzandarān.[30] Now, although he had made friends of his enemies outside, his brothers Mortażā Qoli Khān and Reżā Qoli Khān did not accept his kingship, assumed a hostile attitude towards him, and took blatant measures of defense. Āqā Moḥammad Khān's hopes that he might not be compelled to fight his first battle against his own brothers, were not fulfilled. On 15th Rabi^c I of that year,[31] he defeated his enemies and brought Māzandarān under his sway.

DIVISION IN SHIRAZ AFTER KARIM KHĀN VAKIL'S DEATH; ABU'L-FATḤ KHĀN SUCCEEDS TO THE THRONE. One should know that Moḥammad Karim Khān Vakil had four sons: first, Moḥammad Raḥim Khān, who died in the year 1190, eighteen years old.[32] The second son was Abu'l-Fatḥ Khān; the third and fourth were Moḥammad ^{c}Ali Khān and Ebrāhim Khān. Abu'l-Fatḥ Khān entered into an agreement with Naẓar ^{c}Ali Khān and the sons of Sheikh ^{c}Ali Khān and twelve other Zand khāns and made them his supporters. Moḥammad ^{c}Ali Khān made friends with Zaki Khān, the son of the late Karim Khān Vakil's paternal uncle,[33] went to Zaki Khān's house, assembled the tribal soldiers and the government servants near

30. It was after the downfall of the Safavids only, in the first half of the eighteenth century, that the Qājārs had extended their rule from Astarābād to the southern shore of the Caspian Sea. For the governors of Astarābād and Māzandarān in Safavid times, see K. Röhrborn, *Provinzen und Zentralgewalt Persiens im 16. und 17. Jahrhundert*, pp. 36, 121.

31. April 2, 1779.

32. 1190:1776/77.

33. According to Zambaur, *Manuel*, p. 264, Zaki Khān was Karim Khān Vakil's brother, not his cousin as stated here. There are other mistakes in Zambaur's genealogical table of the Zand rulers, see below, p. 7, note 37.

the Enderun-e kuchek,[34] which lies in the vicinity of Zaki Khān's house, and they rioted. The tribes and servants put themselves under the command of Moḥammad ᶜAli Khān and Zaki Khān and surrounded Abu'l-Fatḥ Khān and the Zand nobles in the citadel. Because there were no provisions in the citadel, the beleaguered lived for three days on the roasted meat of three gazelles which were kept in the garden of the citadel. Then, the mother of the late Moḥammad Raḥim Khān mediated an agreement, which was accepted by Zaki Khān. When Naẓar ᶜAli Khān together with the other Zand khāns who were trapped in the citadel presented themselves at Moḥammad Rahim Khān's house, near the garden of the citadel, to conclude the peace treaty with Moḥammad ᶜAli Khān and Zaki Khān, the latter violated the truce and sent a group of soldiers who put them all to death and sent Naẓar ᶜAli Khān's skull to Zaki Khān. Then Abu'l-Fatḥ Khān and Moḥammad ᶜAli Khān were both together proclaimed king.[35]

ṢĀDEQ KHĀN-E ZAND APPEARS ON THE SCENE. When Ṣādeq Khān at Basra[36] was informed of Karim Khān Vakil's death, he took the troops who were staying with him and returned to Shiraz. He halted outside the city and sent his brother Jaᶜfar Khān, the son of Zaki Khān's sister,[37] to the city to win the favor (of the new rulers). Finding no sympathy, Jaᶜfar Khān returned to the camp. Then Zaki Khān sent to the people of the camp the following message: "If you do not obey me, I shall do

34. The "small courtyard," built by Karim Khān Vakil, later on known as "House of Abu'l-Fatḥ Khān," see below, p. 239.

35. They were, however, mere puppets of Zaki Khān, as the context indicates, see also below, p. 9.

36. He had been sent to Basra by Karim Khān Vakil in 1192:1778 to subdue the Bani Montafeq Arabs. Karim Khān Vakil's attempt to occupy Basra was, on the whole, a failure and caused heavy losses both to ᶜErāq and Persia, as stated by Ḥasan-e Fasā'i, see *FNN*, I, 218.

37. According to Zambaur, *Manuel*, p. 264, Jaᶜfar Khān was Ṣādeq Khān's son, which is, however, not correct.

away with all your relations in the city." The people of the camp deserted Ṣādeq Khān group by group and entered the city. Ṣādeq Khān, who had been friendly to the people of Kerman, hurried with Moḥammad Ḥasan Khān-e Sistāni[38] to Kerman. Zaki Khān sent a group of soldiers after him, but they suffered a defeat when they encountered Ṣādeq Khān and returned to Shiraz without success.

ᶜALI MORĀD KHĀN-E ZAND, ANOTHER PRETENDER, CAPTURES ESFAHAN AND TEHRAN. Because ᶜAli Morād Khān, the son of Zaki Khān's sister and stepson of Ṣādeq Khān, was in dread of his uncle and had joined Abu'l-Fatḥ Khān in order to be sent to some other place, under the pretext of disorder in Esfahan and ᶜErāq,[39] Abu'l-Fatḥ Khān appointed him commander of a large army and sent him to that region. Having established [221] order there, ᶜAli Morād Khān proceeded to Tehran. Some time later he left Tehran, planning a revolt against Zaki Khān. Arriving at Qom he realized that the whole army was in mortal fear of Zaki Khān's obstinacy and cruelty, so he treated the officers amicably and gradually disclosed his plans. At the Holy Shrine at Qom[40] he entered into an agreement with the nobles of his army to refuse obedience to Zaki Khān. Then he marched to Esfahan and beat the drum of revolt with great noise. When Zaki Khān in Shiraz received intelligence of that, he immediately went outside the city and sent the townspeople a herald with the following message: "Everybody who is called a man, except the merchants and craftsmen, will be punished unless he joins the camp." All the emirs and nobles, most of them wearing shagreen-leather slippers, set out on their way and

38. He was the local ruler of Bam, southeast of Kerman, see below, p. 37, note 179.

39. That is, "Persian" ᶜErāq, the region between Qom and Esfahan.

40. The sepulcher of Fāṭema, the sister of ᶜAli ibn Musā ar-Rižā, the Eighth Emām of the Shia, who is buried at Mashhad (d. 203:818).

joined the camp at Bājgāh, 1 parasang north of Shiraz.[41] When Zaki Khān arrived at Izadkhvāst,[42] 9 stations north of Shiraz, he was informed that ᶜAli Morād Khān had followed on the heels of the officials who were bringing the public treasure of Esfahan to Shiraz, and brought it back to Esfahan. He blamed the people of Izadkhvāst, saying: "Why did you not prevent ᶜAli Morād Khān from doing that, and why did you not fight him?" Then he ordered the inhabitants to be killed and sacked. At night, ᶜAli Khān-e Māfi[43] and several other people proceeded to Zaki Khān's resting place, fired their pistols at him, and sent him on his last journey.

THE DRUNKARD ABU'L-FATḤ KHAN-E ZAND DEPOSED BY ṢĀDEQ KHĀN. The late Lord Mayor Mirzā Moḥammad[44] writes in his diary:

The usurpation of Zaki Khān lasted a hundred days. After Zaki Khān's murder, which occurred on 23d Jomādi I of that year,[45] we took Abu'l-Fatḥ Khān and Moḥammad ᶜAli Khān and conducted them to Shiraz. On the day of their arrival, about 100,000 people came out of the city to welcome Abu'l-Fatḥ Khān and to congratulate him on his kingship. The day before, his name had been mentioned on the pulpits and put on the coins. We distributed about 50,000 toman among the army and

41. "Custom-house," a small village 6 miles northeast of Shiraz, on the highway to Esfahan.

42. About 85 miles south of Esfahan (now named Samirom).

43. The Māfi were (apart from the Zand, to which the ruling family belonged, and other tribes) a subdivision of the Kurds, see EI[1] III, s.v. Lak (V. Minorsky).

44. Mirzā Moḥammad was lord mayor of Shiraz during the time of the Zand rule; in the last years of his life he was in the service of Āqā Moḥammad Khān, and he died in Tehran in 1200:1786, see *FNN*, I, 227, and below, p. 23, note 106. His diary ("Ruznāma") was published by ᶜAbbās Eqbāl, Tehran 1325. The following quotation is to be found on pp. 72 s. of that edition. Ḥasan-e Fasā'i has shortened the text considerably; on the other hand, ᶜAbbās Eqbāl had no access to the manuscript used by Ḥasan-e Fasā'i, so the divergencies between Ḥasan-e Fasā'i's text and Eqbāl's edited text may be the result of different versions of the Ruznāma.

45. June 8, 1779.

other people. But what was it good for? Being a young man—"The sugar of youth is sweeter than the sugar of wine"—the king spent the first night of his rule drinking wine in the company of beautiful women, spent the day in idleness, and did not attend to the affairs of the government, the army, and the defense of the state. His friends asked me to advise him: "Your late father took to drinking wine after ten years of fortunate kingship only, whereas you, having not yet spent ten hours of your kingship, indulge in doings which spoil the affairs of this and the future life, not leaving them for one single hour!" Thereupon he accepted my advice outwardly; inwardly, however, he did not care for it, and drank more than before. Several days later I advised him a second time to respect his father's last will and testament and to think over his bad behavior. He promised most solemnly to give up drinking from that day onward. He abstained from drinking for three or four days, then he started again. The third time I was in a state of desperation, because the order of his government was approaching dissolution, and I told him what had to be said. In accordance with the rules of human behavior his appetite for the forbidden increased, so that his blood remained not even one hour without the hotness of wine, and he spent not a moment outside the company of beautiful women. Then Ṣādeq Khān arrived from Kerman, paid his respects to him, and gave him good advice. Abu'l-Fatḥ Khān, however, did not accept his advice, and Ṣādeq Khān perceived the king's true nature. Ṣādeq Khān then befriended most of the nobles of the army. Furthermore, a group of people who disapproved of Abu'l-Fatḥ Khān's behavior, aroused Ṣādeq Khān, saying: "Would it be disgraceful if you assumed independent rulership yourself?" For several days while Ṣādeq Khān deceived the king by promising to arrange a marriage for him, he made preparations with the officers to assume the rulership. When I, my brother Mirzā Jāni,[46] and 5 or 6 other people who were safeguarding the late Karim Khān Vakil's rights, went to Ṣādeq Khān to advise him, he returned to his original attitude and acknowledged Abu'l-Fatḥ Khān's kingship. Again the group of troublemakers incited him to depose Abu'l-Fatḥ Khān and to confine him to his house. In spite of all that, Abu'l-Fatḥ Khān did not desist from drinking and doing forbidden things. So, when he was intoxicated,

46. This brother of Mirzā Moḥammad is not mentioned in Eqbāl's text.

Ṣādeq Khān arrested him and put him in prison, according to the saying: "When Khosrou becomes haughty, an unexpected gust of wind throws the crown off his head." Several days later Ṣādeq Khān had Abu'l-Fatḥ Khān blinded. Because he had violated the last will and testament of Karim Khān Vakil, Ṣādeq Khān got his retribution within a short while, according to the saying: "There is recompense for the violence of character." Abu'l-Fatḥ Khān's government had lasted seventy days. Then Ṣādeq Khān's name was mentioned on the pulpits and put on the coins."

ᶜALI MORĀD KHĀN'S ACTIVITIES IN NORTHERN PERSIA. After Zaki Khān's murder, ᶜAli Morād Khan publicly assumed Abu'l-Fatḥ Khān's succession. He appointed Āqā Bāqer-e Khorāsgāni[47] governor of Esfahan and bestowed the title "Khān" upon him. When he received a report that Dhu'l-Feqār Khān-e Afshār of Khamsa[48] had occupied Qazvin, he departed with a great army from Esfahan to destroy him. Upon his arrival in that region, the army of Afshārs and Khamsa people suffered a defeat, and Dhu'l-Feqār Khān took to flight. He was taken prisoner at Khalkhāl,[49] sent to ᶜAli Morād Khān, and put to death upon his arrival. Then ᶜAli Morād Khān departed for Tehran.

When Āqā Moḥammad Khān had established his rule over the whole of Māzandarān, ᶜAli Morād Khān appointed Maḥmūd Khān, the son of Āzād Khān-e Afghān, commander in chief of the Zand and Afghān army and sent him to Māzandarān. Āqā Moḥammad Khān sent his brother Jaᶜfar Qoli Khān against him. The Qājār army gained a decisive victory, and Maḥmūd Khān arrived in Tehran as a fugitive.[50]

47. Khorāsgān is a small village east of Esfahan.

48. The "Five districts," the hilly region west of Qazvin, the center of which was Zenjān, about 90 miles northwest of Qazvin.

49. The region of Herouābād, about 50 miles south-southeast of Ardebil, see *Farhang*, IV, 450, s.v. Garrus.

50. After that, ᶜAli Morād Khān captured Esfahan and sent an army against Ṣādeq Khān in Shiraz; this passage of the text has been omitted in the translation, because it is not so much related to the history of the Qājārs.

THE QĀJĀRS WEAKENED BY INTERNAL STRIFE. [222] At the end of the year 1194[51] Āqā Moḥammad Khān, having conquered Māzandarān and seeing no obstacle to his rule, dispatched the detachments of his army, each for the conquest of a particular province. He himself, together with his nephews Fatḥ ᶜAli Khān ("Bābā Khān") and Ḥosein Qoli Khān and the mother of both princes, sat confidently on the throne of rulership at Bārforush.[52] However, Reżā Qoli Khān, his brother, found himself without kingship and waited for some good opportunity. When he heard that Āqā Moḥammad Khān had dispersed his army, he marched to Bārforush with a group of Lārijāni musketeers[53] and rose in revolt. They encircled Āqā Moḥammad Khān's house and opened fire. Āqā Moḥammad Khān retreated to a chimney[54] and offered resistance for several hours. Seeing no escape, he surrendered to his unhospitable brother. However, Mirzā Faridun, known as Haji Khān-e Jān, Āqāsi Khān, and other followers of Reżā Qoli Khān, who secretly sympathized with Āqā Moḥammad Khān, promised him protection. They brought him from Bārforush to the village of Band-e Pay[55] and treated him with utmost respect. Āqā Moḥammad Khān settled down there, hoping for divine help. When Mortażā Qoli Khān, another of Āqā Moḥammad Khān's brothers, who had occupied Astarābād, heard what had happened, he grew angry at Reżā Qoli Khān's

51. That is, Autumn 1780.

52. Renamed Bābol in 1927, about 18 miles east-northeast of Āmol. The Safavid Shah ᶜAbbās I (r. 1588–1629) used to visit the town and laid out a garden called "Bāgh-e Shāh" or "Bāgh-e Eram," see EI² I, s.v. Bārforush (L. Lockhart).

53. Lārijān is the mountainous region south of Āmol, around the Demavend, the highest elevation of the Elburz range, see *Farhang*, III, 266, s.v. Lārijān.

54. "Bādgir" in Persian: "Airy house" or "a funnel perforated in every part for the admission of air" (see Steingass, *Persian-English Dictionary*, s.v.). The device is used in the hot regions of Persia to bring the cool breeze down to a subterranean room.

55. "Qarya-ye Band-e Pay," probably the center of the district south of Bābol, see Keihān, *Jughrāfiyā-ye mofaṣṣal-e Irān*, II, 293.

depravity, and departed on 5th Moḥarram of the year 1195[56] for the liberation of his brother, together with a group of Qājār and Turkoman cavalry. Reżā Qoli Khān dispatched a detachment of his supporters against Mortażā Qoli Khān; he himself departed from Bārforush behind them. When the vanguard of his army reached the town of Sāri,[57] it was defeated by Mortażā Qoli Khān's soldiers and took to flight. Reżā Qoli Khān repented what he had done and went to the village of Band-e Pay to offer excuses to Āqā Moḥammad Khān and to find support. However, because his fortune had changed and because he did not get what he wanted, he fled from Māzandarān, proceeded to Esfahan, and entered the service of ᶜAli Morād Khān. Seeing that he could not stay there, he went to Shiraz and entered the service of Ṣādeq Khān. Some time later he went to Khorasan and died there. When Reżā Qoli Khān left the village of Band-e Pay, his brothers Mirzā Faridun "Haji Khān" and Āqāsi Khān[58] entered the service of Āqā Moḥammad Khān, went from Band-e Pay to Bārforush, and put him on the throne. Their army of about 3,000 or 4,000 men they put at his disposal. From Sāri, Mortażā Qoli Khān sent his brothers to Bārforush to congratulate Āqā Moḥammad Khān on his accession to the throne. A group of evildoers, however, incited Mortażā Qoli Khān to claim the rule for himself. So he waged war with Āqā Moḥammad Khān, but was defeated in each battle he fought. Finally, Āqā Moḥammad Khān in his benevolence gave him the province of Astarābād and the districts of Do Danga and Chahār Danga in the region of Hezār Jarib as a fief (tiyul).[59]

56. January 1, 1781.

57. About 25 miles east of Bārforush/Bābol.

58. A few lines above they are called "followers," not brothers of Reżā Qoli Khān.

59. Chahār Dānga and Do Dānga are now a district (bakhsh) south and southeast of Sāri, the center of Chahār Dānga is Keyāsar, about 36 miles southeast of Sāri. This means that Mortażā Qoli Khān was given, apart from Astarābād, the eastern part of Māzandarān.

THE CONQUEST OF SEMNĀN, DĀMGHĀN, SHAHRUD, AND BESṬĀM. [233] When ᶜAli Morād Khān received information that Āqā Moḥammad Khān had taken possession of the whole of Māzandarān and Astarābād, he appointed Amir Guna Khān-e Afshār-e Ṭāromi[60] commander in chief of the army and sent him to conquer Māzandarān. When Amir Guna Khān arrived in that region, the people of Lārijān preferred to put themselves under his command and escorted him to Lārijān. From Bārforush, Āqā Moḥammad Khān marched with his army of Qājār warriors and people from Māzandarān[61] against Amir Guna Khān. A battle was fought near Sabza Meidān,[62] in which Amir Guna Khān was defeated; thence he fled to Tehran. After that victory Āqā Moḥammad Khān added the districts of Semnān, Dāmghān, Shahrud, and Besṭām[63] to his possessions.

THE CONQUEST OF GILĀN, KHAMSA, QAZVIN, AND ZENJĀN.[64] [224] In the year 1196[65] Āqā Moḥammad Khān departed from Māzandarān and proceeded to Astarābād, his home and the seat of the government and realm of his ancestors. Having renewed the treaty with his brothers and nephews and the Qājār emirs, he returned to Māzandarān. The same year he marched with a great army to conquer Rasht and Gilān. Because Hedāyatollāh Khān, the governor of Gilān, knew that he was

60. Ṭārom is the region on the Safid Rud, which flows into the Caspian Sea near Rasht, see EI[1] IV, s.v. Ṭārum (V. Minorsky).

61. This means that Āqā Moḥammad Khān's army was composed of tribal forces (Qājārs) and of indigenous musketeers (tofangchis) from Māzandarān.

62. The place is not mentioned in my sources. In any case, the victory gained near Sabza Meidān ("Green Square") allowed Āqā Moḥammad Khān to extend his rule to the southern slope of the Elburz range.

63. The region east of Tehran and south of the mountain range which separates Gorgān (Astarābād) from the Dasht-e Kavir.

64. In the meantime, ᶜAli Morād Khān had conquered Shiraz, after a siege which lasted nearly a year, and had done away with Ṣādeq Khān; this passage of the text has not been translated.

65. Began December 17, 1781.

unable to resist Āqā Moḥammad Khān, he abandoned his possessions and treasures, took his family, boarded a ship, and sailed to Shirvān.[66] And Āqā Moḥammad Khān entered Rasht, took over the government, laid hand on the innumerable riches in cash and kind of the governor of Rasht, and provided the officers of his army with gold and brocade.

Then Āqā Moḥammad Khān sent his army under the command of his brother Jaᶜfar Qoli Khān to conquer Khamsa[67] and to do away with Ramażān Khān-e Zand—also called Reżā Khān-e Zand in several chronicles—who in the service of ᶜAli Morād Khān was staying with an army of Lors at Sāvoj Bolāgh in the region of Raiy.[68] When both armies met, Ramażān Khān was defeated, and Jaᶜfar Qoli Khān sent the skulls of the dead and the prisoners to Āqā Moḥammad Khān. Then Jaᶜfar Qoli Khān marched off to conquer Qazvin and to do away with Moulā Verdi Khān-e Dhu'l-Qadr,[69] the governor of that region. After several skirmishes he occupied the town and took Moulā Verdi Khān prisoner. The royal court then marched from Gilān to the district of Solṭāniya,[70] and the town of Zenjān was added to Āqā Moḥammad Khān's possessions. When the autumn was over and the winter near, the royal court left Solṭāniya and settled down in Māzandarān.

66. The mountainous region northwest of Baku.

67. For its conquest by the Zand, see above, p. 11.

68. Perhaps the same as Sāvuch Bolāgh ("cold fountain") near Karaj, about 25 miles northwest of Tehran, see *Farhang*, Vol. I, Introduction (synoptical tables of the districts).

69. The Dhu'l-Qadr had formed, together with the Qājārs, Afshārs, and other tribes, the Qizilbash order, the main supporters of Safavid rule.

70. About 30 miles southeast of Zenjān, later on one of the most favored summer resorts of the Qājār rulers down to the middle of the nineteenth century. The town of Solṭāniya, a Mongol foundation, was the capital of Ilkhanid Persia. It was perhaps not by chance that the Qājārs, who considered themselves as of Mongolian offspring, favored that region. Later on, Arghun Khān's tomb was discovered near Solṭāniya, and ᶜAbbās Mirzā put on a Mongolian mail shirt when he marched against the Russians, see below, pp. 108, 139.

MARRIAGES OF FATḤ ͨALI KHĀN. That year the daughter of Jaͨfar Khān, son of Qāder Khān-e ͨArab-e ͨĀmeri-ye Besṭāmi,[71] a famous emir, was given in marriage to Fatḥ ͨAli Khān, Āqā Moḥammad Khān's nephew, who was eleven years old, and a royal wedding feast was celebrated. Also that year, the daughter of Fatḥ ͨAli Khān-e Qājār Devehlu was married to Fatḥ ͨAli Khān. She was put on a gilded litter and escorted from the town of Dāmghān to Māzandarān, and the wedding feast lasted two weeks.

FIRST SIEGE OF TEHRAN. The New Year fell on 5th Rabiͨ II of the year 1197.[72] Āqā Moḥammad Khān departed from Māzandarān to conquer Reiy and to do away with Ghafur Khān-e Tehrāni, the governor of that region. He laid siege to Tehran. However, as the siege grew lengthy, the air of the town became bad, and the plague spread from the town to the Qājār camp. Āqā Moḥammad Khān therefore ordered to raise the siege and marched to ͨAli Bolāgh, that is, "ͨAli's spring," near Dāmghān.[73] Then he returned to Māzandarān and spent the winter there.

ZAND ATTACK ON MĀZANDARĀN FAILS. When ͨAli Morād Khān ruled over the whole of Persia except Māzandarān, Khorasan, and Ādherbāyjān[74] and no enemy was left, he

71. Probably the ruling family of the Arabs living in the district of Besṭām which had been added to the Qājār dominions shortly before.
72. March 10, 1783 (should be March 21).
73. One of the summer houses of the Persian kings, about 9 miles northwest of Dāmghān, "so called because it is said to be one of the miracles which Ali performed, at the prayers of the inhabitants of this dry country, who were starving from the effects of a great drought. He spoke, and the water flowed," see James Morier, *Travels*, p. 369, and the map facing page 349. There is a "Bāgh-e Shāh" on the 1:500,000 map, about 7 miles northwest of Dāmghān, in the highland near Kalāta.
74. Ādherbāyjān was in the possession of Kurdish emirs of the Shaqāqi branch, see below, p. 40, while Shāhrokh (r. 1748–95), a grandson of Nāder Shāh, controlled the eastern part of Khorasan from his capital Mashhad.

conceived the idea of conquering Astarābād and Māzandarān. He spent the New Year of 1198[75] at Esfahan, assembled a huge army, the cavalry of which consisted of more than 12,000 men, appointed his fifteen-year-old son Sheikh Veis Khān commander in chief, and sent him to Māzandarān. He himself followed his son with troops from Esfahan, marched to Tehran and stayed there. When Sheikh Veis Khān arrived in Māzandarān [225] most of the nobles deserted Āqā Moḥammad Khān and joined the Zand prince. Seeing that everybody was against him, Āqā Moḥammad Khān, in order to save his family and possessions, left Māzandarān, settled down at Astarābād, and strengthened the defenses of the town. Sheikh Veis Khān established his rule over the whole of Māzandarān, Firuzkuh, Lārijān, and Rostamdār, that is, Nur va-Kujur.[76] Āqā Moḥammad Khān's brother Mortażā Qoli Khān, who had no affection at all toward his brother and claimed the rule over Māzandarān, proceeded to Sheikh Veis Khān and humbled himself. When ᶜAli Morād Khān in Tehran heard that, he sent Moḥammad Ẓāher Khān-e Zand, the son of Zaki Khān's sister and ᶜAli Morād Khān's maternal aunt,[77] with a group of Bakhteyāri and other people, about 8,000 men, for the conquest of Astarābād. Moḥammad Ẓāher Khān entered Māzandarān and passed the "Ditch of Golbād,"[78] which

75. March 21, 1784.

76. The districts listed here cover the eastern part of Māzandarān, including Firuzkuh on the southern slope of the Elburz range; for Nur va-Kujur see below, p. 92.

77. According to Zambaur, *Manuel*, p. 264, ᶜAli Morād Khān's mother was married in second marriage to Ṣādeq Khān, the brother of Karim Khān Vakil.

78. Ḥasan-e Fasā'i describes the ditch a few lines below: "To establish order in Māzandarān, the Safavid Shah ᶜAbbās I (1588–1629) ordered a group of Turkomans from Āsib to dig a deep ditch from the hills near Ashraf (near the modern town of Behshehr, about 35 miles east of Sāri and 43 miles west of Astarābād/Gorgān) to the coast of the Caspian Sea, over a distance of 4 parasangs (about 15 miles), which could not be passed by horsemen. In the ditch and on its edge large and thick trees from Māzandarān were planted, which formed a thicket. Therefore, the crossing of the

he left imprudently unguarded. Having arrived in the vicinity of Astarābād, he put up an earthwork and took shelter in it. Āqā Moḥammad Khān attended to the guard of the ramparts and towers constantly, and every day a group of valiant Qājār warriors left the town, gave battle, and returned. When the siege grew lengthy and Āqā Moḥammad Khān learned that the "Ditch of Golbad," which had to be passed by the caravans from Māzandarān that supplied Moḥammad Ẓāher Khān's camp with provisions, was not guarded, he ordered Ḥamza Solṭān, one of his faithful and upright followers, to occupy the ditch with musketeers from Astarābād and to prevent people from crossing it. Accordingly, Ḥamza Solṭān-e Anzāni-ye Astarābādi[79] occupied the ditch with musketeers from Anzān in the province of Māzandarān and cut the Zand camp off from supplies. When the communications between Māzandarān and the camp were interrupted, the Zand camp was visited with famine and starvation, the soldiers became hungry and very weak, and fortune smiled upon Āqā Moḥammad Khān. A few days later, when the horses for want of fodder were not able to speed and the soldiers for want of victuals not able to speak, Āqā Moḥammad Khān attacked the Zand soldiers with his army, broke through at the first attempt, and nobody escaped his grip. They all fled in different directions. The commander in chief, Moḥammad Ẓāher Khān, made his escape to the desert of Gorgān,[80] but was taken prisoner by the Turkomans and brought before Āqā Moḥammad Khān in a state of humiliation and disdain. When the order was given to put him to death, he was cut into pieces

---

ditch is very difficult, if not impossible. Traveling from Māzandarān to Astarābād is confined to that road. Because that ditch is situated near the village of Golbād, it is called "Jerr-e Golbād."

79. Anzān is a village near Bandar Gaz, about 27 miles west of Astarābād.

80. That is, the plain on the eastern shore of the Caspian Sea, north of Astarābad/Gorgān.

by the Qājār and Turkoman swords. All those who fled in the direction of the Ditch of Golbād were taken prisoner by Ḥamza Solṭān (who in several chronicles is called Ḥamza Khān-e Noukandi). In that victorious battle more than 10,000 people were killed.

On 1st Moḥarram of the year 1199[81] Āqā Moḥammad Khān returned with his army from Astarābād to Māzandarān. He first hurried to the region of Ashraf ol-Belād[82] where Mehr ᶜAli Khān, chief of the guard (nasaqchi bāshi) of ᶜAli Morād Khān, and Hāji Reżā Khān-e Farāhāni were staying with 7,000 men. They were defeated and joined Sheikh Veis Khān, because they were not able to defend Sāri. Sheikh Veis Khān, who during his stay in Māzandarān had done nothing but oppress and sack the townspeople and therefore did not trust them, left his belongings and fled in disgrace, on 10th Moḥarram,[83] to Tehran. Two or three nobles of Veis Khān's followers were executed by order of ᶜAli Morād Khān because they abandoned Māzandarān without battle and had gone to Tehran.

To prepare a new campaign ᶜAli Morād Khān gathered together several thousand soldiers and sent them to Māzandarān under the command of Rostam Khān, the son of his paternal uncle, who was a famous warrior of the Zand. Āqā Moḥammad Khān sent his brother Jaᶜfar Qoli Khān with a detachment of his army against him. When both armies met, the Zand army suffered a defeat and took flight. Because they feared ᶜAli Morād Khān's punishment they hurried to Esfahan, where they had their houses and families. Bāqer Khān-e Khorāsgāni, the beglerbegi of Esfahan, closed the doors, and they had to spend the whole winter in the region of Esfahan, suffering heavily from snow and ice.

81. November 14, 1784.
82. Near the modern town of Behshehr, about 28 miles east-northeast of Sāri, see also below, p. 354, note 240.
83. November 23, 1874.

A CHANGE ON THE ZAND THRONE; ĀQĀ MOḤAMMAD KHĀN CONQUERS TEHRAN. Then ᶜAli Morād Khān summoned his half-brother Jaᶜfar Khān, who was staying in Kurdistan, and sent him to Tehran to establish order in Ādherbāyjān and Khamsa. When Jaᶜfar Khān arrived in that region, he became self-willed and unruly and marched by way of Qalamrav-e ᶜAli Shakar[84] to Esfahan. When ᶜAli Morād Khān was informed, the first thing he did was to give leave to the army commanded by Jaᶜfar Khan and to order them to go home. Upon the arrival of that order the army of Jaᶜfar Khān dispersed. Jaᶜfar Khān proceeded repentfully to Hamadān and thence to Kazzāz,[85] because at Hamadān he was not able to secure his goal. At Kazzāz he was joined by a group of soldiers who in the campaign to Māzandarān had quarreled with Rostam Khān and fled. The late lord mayor of Shiraz Moḥammad, who at that time was serving at ᶜAli Morād Khān's court, writes (in his diary):[86]

ᶜAli Morād Khān, who until the time he fell ill was not used to wine, became a drunkard because of the bad conditions of the state and the depravities which were spreading [226], and his health was weakened. His mother, who was Jaᶜfar Khān's mother, too, informed the latter that ᶜAli Morād Khān was in a bad state of health; that there was no hope of recovery. Then Jaᶜfar Khān left Zenjān and raised the banner of revolt. When ᶜAli Morād Khān was informed of that, he entrusted Tehran to his son Sheikh Veis Khān and traveled in spite of his serious illnes and cold and snow to Esfahan. On 1st Rabiᶜ II of that year[87] he died at Murcha-ye Khurt.[88]

When ᶜAli Morād Khān had left Esfahan for Tehran, he had appointed Bāqer Khān-e Khorāsgāni governor of Esfahan. Having received news

84. That is, the province of Hamadān, see Röhrborn, *Provinzen und Zentralgewalt Persiens*, p. 8.

85. The region southwest of Solṭānābād/Arāk, see *Farhang-e Irān Zamin*, Vol. XIV (1966–67), map facing p. 264.

86. Continuation of the diary (Ruznāma) mentioned above, p. 9, Eqbāl's edition pp. 83 s.

87. February 11, 1785.

88. About 30 miles north-northeast of Esfahan.

of the ruler's death, Bāqer Khān fancied he could assume the rule. He took the royal insignia of ʿAli Morād Khān and summoned 4,000 or 5,000 musketeers from Chahār Maḥall,[89] Samirom,[90] Kordon,[91] and Qomesha.[92] Then he summoned the nobles of the Lakziya army,[93] which was staying at Esfahan, revealed his secret plans to them and won them over by promises and rewards. He proceeded from his house to the Ṭālār-e Ṭavila[94] and ascended the throne with royal splendor. His name was mentioned on the pulpits and put on the coins. With the different classes of people he conversed in the manner of kings. On the pulpits and on the coins he was styled "Shāh Bāqer." When Shāh Bāqer heard the sound of Jaʿfar Khān's cannons from the station of Chāl-e Seyāh,[95] he became worried and gave the nobles of the army a huge sum of money out of ʿAli Morād Khān's treasury, to make them march against Jaʿfar Khān's army for the consolidation of his rule. They left the city through one gate and returned through another before one hour had elapsed. In the afternoon of Thursday 7th Rabiʿ II,[96] four and a half days after Shāh Bāqer's accession to the throne, 5,000 to 6,000 tribal warriors entered, sword in hand, the Ṭālār-e Ṭavila. Shāh Bāqer received three or four blows and escaped to another building and fled through the Behesht Ā'in Palace.[97] The tribal warriors reported this

89. "Four districts," the region west of Esfahan.

90. About 90 miles south of Esfahan.

91. About 55 miles east-southeast of Esfahan.

92. Now called Shahreżā, about 50 miles south of Esfahan. In Eqbāl's edition, p. 84, the region of Yazd (aṭrāf-e Yazd) is added to the places mentioned here.

93. "Sepāh-e Lakziya"; "Lakziya" is derived from Lakz, the name of a people (Lezgians) of southern Dāghestān, see EI^2 II, s.v. Dāghistān, column 86a (W. Barthold–A. Bennigsen).

94. "Long hall," part of the famous ʿAli Qapu palace, which in Safavid times was used as royal reception hall, see Loṭfollāh Honarfar, *Ganjina-ye āthār-e tārikhi-ye Eṣfahān*, Esfahan, Ketābforushi-ye Thaqafi, 1344, p. 752 (quoted from Mirzā Ḥosein Khān, *Joghrāfeyā-ye Eṣfahān*, pp. 22 s.).

95. "Black well," perhaps the same as Chāh-e Seyāh, about 20 miles northwest of Esfahan (chāh is another word for chāl, "well").

96. February 17.

97. Honarfar, *Ganjina*, p. 622, describes the Kākh-e hasht behest ("Pavilion of seven paradises"), built by Shah Soleimān (r. 1666–94), which might be the "Behesht Ā'in" mentioned here.

God-given victory to Jaᶜfar Khān and invited him to the city. The next day Jaᶜfar Khān entered Esfahan with all pomp and assumed rulership. Two days later Shāh Bāqer was arrested at Dudasht,[98] brought before Jaᶜfar Khān, and put in prison. Jaᶜfar Khān used to repeat in the public reception every day: "Heaven be praised that I have conquered the inherited empire with the sword and acquired the rule of my fathers and forefathers."[99]

When Āqā Moḥammad Khān received news of ᶜAli Morād Khān's death, he departed from Māzandarān without hesitation. When he arrived outside Tehran, the inhabitants shut the gates and sent him the following message: "Jaᶜfar Khān has ascended the throne at Esfahan. We are obedient servants of the king. We obey everybody who ascends the throne." Āqā Moḥammad Khān agreed to the proposal and departed for Esfahan. When Jaᶜfar Khān heard of that, he considered it, compared with his own bravery and experience, a fairy tale without real substance. He made superficial preparations and set a detachment under the command of Najaf Khān, his maternal uncle, to Qom. When Najaf Khān arrived opposite the Qājār camp, he fled without giving battle. Then Jaᶜfar Khān sent 7,000 cavalry and infantry under the command of Aḥmad Khān, the son of Āzād Khān-e Afghān, in support of Najaf Khān. The army of Āqā Moḥammad Khān advanced cautiously and slowly from Qom to Kāshān. Imagining that the Qājār army was fleeing and would fall easy prey to him, Aḥmad Khān departed with great haste. When he met the Qājār army near Naṣrābād in the vicinity of Kāshān,[100] he fled after brief skirmishing, and the Zand army was defeated. Having received intelligence of the defeat, Jaᶜfar Khān was so afraid that he did not even take supper; he abandoned the royal insignia, even Karim Khān Vakil's jewel studded qalyān,[101] his mother and sisters and 23 servants of the royal harem, and fled to Shiraz before

98. Dudasht is perhaps the same as Tudashk (see map 1:500,000), a small town about 55 miles east of Esfahan, on the highway to Yazd, see also Farhang X 52 (Tudashg).

99. The statement claims a twofold legitimation of rulership: by conquest and inheritance, that is, both kinds of legitimation on which rule is based according to the Islamic concept of state.

100. About 12 miles northwest of Kāshān.

101. A pipe for smoking through water (nargile).

sunrise. [227] The following day Āqā Moḥammad Khān and the Qājār army entered Esfahan.

Two months later Āqā Moḥammad Khān departed for the conquest of ᶜErāq[102] and the submission of Aḥmad Khān-e Afghān and the Bakhteyāri tribe. Having subdued the rebels, he returned to Esfahan. Then the governorship of Esfahan was entrusted to Bāqer Khān-e Khorāsgāni who for some time had been imprisoned by Jaᶜfar Khān.

On 27th Shavvāl of that year[103] Āqā Moḥammad Khān departed for the conquest of Tehran and sent Majnun Khān-e Pazuki[104] in advance. Having arrived at Tehran, Majnun Khān occupied the town and informed Āqā Moḥammad Khān of the conquest. Then the royal court marched by way of Hamadān to Tehran. On Sunday, 11th Jomādi I of the year 1200,[105] when the sun entered the sign of Aries, Āqā Moḥammad Khān ascended the throne of the empire of the world.[106]

JAᶜFAR KHĀN OCCUPIES ESFAHAN. [228] When news of Āqā Moḥammad Khān's accession to the throne reached Shiraz, Jaᶜfar Khān assembled an army of 22,000 cavalry and infantry and marched from Shiraz to Esfahan. Bāqer Khān-e Khorāsgāni, the beglerbegi of Esfahan, left the city and took shelter in the citadel of Ṭabaruk.[107] On 21st Moḥarram of the year 1201[108] Jaᶜfar Khān stormed the citadel and put Bāqer Khān to death; his family was sent to Shiraz. The governorship of Esfahan was

102. That is, "Persian Eraq" (ᶜErāq-e ᶜajami), the region northwest of Esfahan, as far as Hamadān and Qom. A long passage on Mirzā Moḥammad's personal experiences has been omitted in the translation.

103. September 2, 1785.

104. In Safavid times the Pazuki were living at Semnān and Demavand, the region east and north of Tehran, see Röhrborn, *Provinzen und Zentralgewalt Persiens*, p. 136. Pazukis of Kurdish origin are mentioned in EI[1] II, s.v. Kurden (V. Minorsky).

105. March 12, 1786.

106. Here ends Mirzā Moḥammad's diary; Ḥasan-e Fasā'i inserts at the end of the quotation a short note on the date of Mirzā Moḥammad's death: end of the year 1200: October 1786.

107. This famous citadel of Esfahan was pulled down not long ago, see Honarfar, *Ganjina*, p. 39 (with photograph of the citadel).

108. November 13, 1786.

entrusted to Mirzā Jāni-ye Shirāzi, known as Fasā'i. This Mirzā Jāni is the uncle of the author of this book; Mirzā Jāni is the grandson of Seiyed ᶜAli Khān-e ᶜAllāma-ye Shirāzi, known as Madanī.[109]

Then Jaᶜfar Khān left Mir Veis Khān-e Zand, the brother of Seiyed Morād Khān, with a detachment of the army at Esfahan for the defense of the city and sent Haji ᶜAli Qoli Khān-e Kāzeruni with several detachments to Kāshān and Qom. Jaᶜfar Khān himself departed for Hamadān. When he arrived there, Esmāᶜil Khān, the governor of Hamadān, fled. Then Moḥammad Hosein Khān-e Garrusi,[110] ᶜAli Khān-e Khamsa'i, and a group of Qaraguzlu gathered together and marched to the vicinity of Hamadān. Jaᶜfar Khān marched against them, suffered a defeat 1 parasang from Hamadān and returned to Esfahan.

ZAND CAMPAIGN TO JANDAQ; ESFAHAN REOCCUPIED BY ĀQĀ MOḤAMMAD KHĀN. When Moḥammad Ḥasan Khān-e ᶜArab-e ᶜĀmeri, the governor of Jandaq,[111] rose in rebellion, Jaᶜfar Khān sent Haji ᶜAli Qoli Khān-e Kāzeruni to punish him. When ᶜAli Qoli Khān arrived at Jandaq, Moḥammad Ḥasan Khān suffered a defeat and entrenched himself on the citadel of Jandaq. Haji ᶜAli Qoli Khān promised him by solemn oath safety of his life and goods and escorted him to Esfahan. However, Jaᶜfar Khān violated the oath and put Moḥammad Ḥasan Khān in prison. [229] By this act, Jaᶜfar Khān caused Haji ᶜAli

109. See Introduction, p. xi.

110. There are in Ādherbāyjān three places named Garrus: 1) near Marand, 2) near Marāgha, and 3) in the district of Khalkhāl, which adjoins Khamsa (see above, p. 11, note 48). The last mentioned may be the home of Moḥammad Ḥosein Khān, because he appears together with a khān of Khamsa.

111. About 180 miles northeast of Esfahan, on the southern fringe of the Dasht-e Kavir. ᶜĀmeri Arabs of Besṭām (north of the Dasht-e Kavir) are mentioned above, p. 16. According to Sven Hedin, *Zu Land nach Indien*, I, 318, Jandaq was an important stopping place and trading center for the caravan traffic from northern to southern Persia.

Qoli Khān to plan a revolt, because the people of the southern region of Fārs consider the violation of an oath a great crime. Haji ᶜAli Qoli Khān, the khāns of Lirāvi,[112] and the nobles of Fārs, who had been obedient servants of Jaᶜfar Khān, were very angry about his depravity and decided to leave him and to return home.

Āqā Moḥammad Khān, however, departed from Tehran to Esfahan. When Jaᶜfar Khān got news of that, he fled without hesitation to Shiraz. Āqā Moḥammad Khān occupied Esfahan without difficulties, stationed his brother Jaᶜfar Qoli Khān with 6,000 men in that city, and proceeded to the pasture of Sangbārān.[113] Then news arrived of the revolt of ᶜAli Khān-e Khamsa'i. Āqā Moḥammad Khān, therefore, had no choice but to march to Khamsa. When he arrived there, ᶜAli Khān repented his doing, came out to meet Āqā Moḥammad Khān and to offer all excuses, and was generously received. The royal court stayed several days at Zenjān and returned then to Tehran with pomp.

JAᶜFAR KHĀN UNDERTAKES A CAMPAIGN TO KUH-E GILUYA AND BEHBEHĀN. Having arrived at Shiraz, Jaᶜfar Khān sent ᶜAbd or-Razzāq Khān-e Kāshi to Kāzerun to subdue Haji ᶜAli Qoli Khān. He was granted security by solemn oath and brought to Shiraz. A few days later, he was imprisoned in the citadel in an inexcusable manner. When the summer was over, Jaᶜfar Khān departed for Kuh-e Giluya.[114] Having arrived at Kāzerun, he stayed there for three months, appointed his brother Moḥammad Khān commander of the army and sent him to punish the Mamassani tribe.[115] Having established perfect order in that region, Moḥammad Khān returned to Kāzerun and marched to

112. Lirāvi is the region of Bandar Deilam (northwest of Bushehr), forming a district (nāḥeya) of Kuh-e Giluya, see *FNN*, II, 279.

113. Sangbārān lies about 90 miles west-northwest of Esfahan, and 30 miles south of Golpāygān.

114. The mountainous region northwest of Kāzerun.

115. A branch of the Lors of Kuh-e Giluya, in the district of Fahleyān, about 40 miles north of Kāzerun.

Behbehān in the company of Ja^{c}far Khān. Because Sheikh Ghażabān of the Bani Ka^{c}b tribe,[116] the governor of Falāḥi and Moḥammara,[117] was disobedient, Ja^{c}far Khān sent his brother Moḥammad Khān, the commander of the army (sardār), and ^{c}Abdollāh Khān to sack the Bani Ka^{c}b. When they arrived there, they obtained rich booty, punished the Jā'iki Bakhteyāri[118] on their way back, and returned to Behbehān. Ja^{c}far Khān spent the whole winter at Behbehān.

ZAND ATTACK ON YAZD FAILS; ANOTHER PRETENDER TO THE CROWN APPEARS ON THE SCENE. The New Year of 1201 fell on 1st Jomādi II.[119] Five days after the feast, Ja^{c}far Khān departed from Behbehān to Shiraz. A few days later he grew suspicious of Seiyed Morād Khān and imprisoned him together with his own brother and a group of Zand khāns in the citadel, where they were put into the company of Haji ^{c}Ali Qoli Khān. When Taqi Khān, the governor of Yazd, refused obedience, Ja^{c}far Khān departed from Shiraz to Yazd in order to punish him. Having arrived at Abarquh,[120] he sent his brother, the commander in chief of the army of Fārs, in advance. Taqi Khān asked Amir Moḥammad Khān-e ^{c}Arab-e Zangu'i, the governor of Ṭabas in Khorasan,[121] for support, prepared the

116. The Bani Ka^{c}b were an Arab tribe who in 1170:1756/57 left the region of Baghdad and settled in the coastal area of Khuzestān. The ancient name of the area was Douraq, which was changed into Falāḥi after the immigration of the Bani Ka^{c}b, who took to agriculture (falāḥa), see *FNN*, II, 238. Further references in the EI, II^{2}, s.v. Dawraḳ (L. Lockhart).

117. For Falāḥi, see preceding note. Moḥammara is the modern town of Khorramshehr, on the Persian bank of the Shaṭṭ al-^{c}Arab.

118. The western boundary of the Bakhteyāri region was Masjed-e Soleimān in northern Khuzestān. Accordingly, Moḥammad Khān and Abdollāh Khān marched from the coastal area to the north, before they returned to Behbehan.

119. March 21, 1787.

120. About 120 miles northeast of Shiraz, 85 miles from Yazd.

121. Ṭabas, an oasis on the fringes of the Dasht-e Kavir and the Dasht-e Lut, lies about 190 miles northwest of Yazd. When Sven Hedin visited

towers and the rampart of Yazd for defense, and entrenched himself behind the fortifications. Then Moḥammad Ḥasan Khān laid siege to Yazd. Having left ᶜAbd or-Raḥim Khān, the brother of the lord mayor of Shiraz, Haji Ebrāhim,[122] with a detachment at Abarquh for the transmission of news from Esfahan, Jaᶜfar Khān hastened to Yazd and joined Moḥammad Ḥasan Khān's camp. Then they attacked the city several times, but things did not work out. One day Jaᶜfar Khān ordered the army to attack the city on all sides. When they executed this plan, news arrived that Amir Moḥammad Khān of Ṭabas had appeared with 1,000 horsemen. In his unpleasant manner, Jaᶜfar Khān stopped the attack. When Moḥammad Khān, son of Naṣir Khān-e Lāri,[123] who with 500 musketeers was fighting in the sight of Jaᶜfar Khān, saw the latter's behavior, he retreated from the battle. Jaᶜfar Khān used Moḥammad Khān's retreat as a pretext to abandon the artillery, the baggage, the tents, and the royal pavilion and to flee to Shiraz. The army of Fārs dispersed in all directions. The same day Amir Moḥammad Khān of Ṭabas entered Yazd and laid hand upon the entire artillery and baggage of Jaᶜfar Khān. His pride grew so as to claim kingship. Aiming at the conquest of the whole world, he gathered together 3,000 to 4,000 cavalry and infantry from Nā'in, Kuhpāya, and Ardestān,[124] took the Zand artillery and the royal baggage and hurried toward Esfahan. He put up the royal pavilion in the

---

Ṭabas in 1906, the governor, ᶜEmād ol-Molk, told him that his ancestors possessed Ṭabas for 200 years and that his grandfather Ḥasan Khān built the new town of Ṭabas about 120 years ago, see Sven Hedin, *Zu Land nach Indien*, II, 51 seq.

122. The story of this famous man who eventually was appointed grand vizier of Persia is told below, p. 36 seq.

123. His family ruled over Lārestān since the Afghan invasion. Naṣir Khān was appointed beglerbegi of Lārestān by Nāder Shāh and was practically an independent ruler of that province, see *FNN*, II, 283 seq.

124. That is, from the whole region east of Esfahan.

district of Dudasht.[125] And Jaᶜfar Qoli Khān, Āqā Moḥammad Khān's brother, departed from Esfahan against Amir Moḥammad Khān. After two or three attacks the army of the Khān of Ṭabas was defeated and put to flight. The artillery and the royal baggage fell into Jaᶜfar Qoli Khān's hands.

JAᶜFAR KHĀN-E ZAND SUBDUES LĀRESTĀN. Jaᶜfar Khān arrived in Shiraz in the month of Moḥarram of the year 1202.[126] Declaring Moḥammad Khān's behavior the cause of his own flight, he bestowed the title "Jahānbāni"[127] upon his son Loṭf ᶜAli Khān and sent him with a detachment of Zand scouts (qalāvusān) to Lārestān to punish Moḥammad Khān. When ᶜAbdollāh Khān and Moḥammad Khān, the sons of Naṣir Khān-e Lāri, heard of Loṭf ᶜAli Khān's departure, they entrusted the citadel of Lār, which lies upon a high hill and overlooks the town, to Moḥammad ᶜAli Khān, their uncle, and hastened to the districts of Lārestān to gather together the musketeers. Loṭf ᶜAli Khān laid siege to the citadel and sent a group behind Moḥammad Khān and ᶜAbdollāh Khān. Both suffered a defeat when the Zand army came up with them, and took to flight. When Moḥammad ᶜAli Khān received news of this occurrence, he delivered the citadel, which had been besieged for nearly four months. Then Loṭf ᶜAli Khān conducted the family of Naṣir Khān-e Lāri to Shiraz. So that year the whole province of Fārs came under Jaᶜfar Khān's sway.

YAZD OCCUPIED BY THE QĀJĀR ARMY. In the spring of that year[128] Āqā Mohammad Khān proceeded from Tehran to Esfahan and sent his brother's son Fatḥ ᶜAli Khān with several

125. The town east of Esfahan, where Shāh Bāqer was captured, see above, p. 22, note 98.
126. Began on October 13, 1787.
127. "Builder of the world"; the same title was bestowed upon Fatḥ ᶜAli Khān when he was appointed governor of Fārs, Kerman, and Yazd, see below, p. 64.
128. That is, spring of the year 1788.

detachments of the army for the conquest of Yazd. Āqā Moḥammad Khān himself went to the pasture of Gandomān[129] and Kushk-e Zard in Fārs[130] in order to sack [230] the Qashqā'i tribes. When the tribes became aware of that plan, they retreated to the highland of Rour va-Ravāt[131] and settled down there. Then the royal court traveled from Kushk-e Zard to Mashhad-e Omm on-Nabi, known as Mashhad-e Morghāb,[132] hoping that Jaᶜfar Khān stretching his head out of the fortifications of Shiraz and seeing the royal power would renounce rulership. However, Jaᶜfar Khān considered this news farfetched and rested behind the heaven-high fortifications of Shiraz. Āqā Moḥammad Khān, however, was discussed among the inhabitants of Fārs near and far and returned to Esfahan. Several days before, Fatḥ ᶜAli Khān who had been sent for the conquest of Yazd, having defeated Taqi Khān and obtained hostages, had returned to Esfahan. Then ᶜAli Qoli Khān, the brother of Āqā Moḥammad Khān, was ordered to stay at Esfahan with 3,000 men, and the royal court made its way back from Esfahan to Tehran.

ESFAHAN LOST TO JAᶜFAR KHĀN-E ZAND FOR A SHORT WHILE. In the month of Moḥarram of the year 1203[133] Jaᶜfar Khān saw a good chance for the conquest of Esfahan and marched off. Having been informed of that intention, ᶜAli Qoli

129. Gandomān lies about 68 miles southeast of Esfahan, near the sources of the Karūn River, the main river of Khuzestān.

130. Kushk-e Zard lies on the upper course of the Polvār Rud, about 27 miles southwest of Ābāda, and about 100 miles southeast of Gandomān, see *FNN*, II, 220.

131. This is most probably the mountainous region between Gandomān and Kushk-e Zard, which is nearly uninhabited.

132. Mashhad-e Omm on-Nabi, about 65 miles northeast of Shiraz, is the ancient Pasargadae; the name means "burial place of the prophet's mother." According to Ḥasan-e Fasā'i, the prophet in question was the legendary Persian hero Jamshid, whom the Persians believed to be a prophet. After the Arabic conquest, Jamshid was identified with King Salomo, see *FNN*, II, 301.

133. Began on October 2, 1788.

Khān at Esfahan sent Naṣrollāh Khān-e Qaraguzlu with 1,000 horsemen to Qomesha. When Jaᶜfar Khān arrived at Esfarjān,[134] he sent his brother Moḥammad Khān with a detachment to Qomesha. Having reached Qomesha, Moḥammad Khān stormed the citadel, took the whole force of 1,000 men prisoner, except 3 or 4 of them, and disarmed them. Naṣrollāh Khān and the other officers were put in fetters, the other prisoners dismissed. Because ᶜAli Qoli Khān received no order from Āqā Moḥammad Khān to engage in fighting, he left Esfahan and hurried to Kāshān. Two days later Jaᶜfar Khān entered Esfahan and put up his camp in the Bāgh-e Saᶜādatābād,[135] When Āqā Moḥammad Khān was informed of the occurrence, he departed from Tehran without hesitation, whereupon Jaᶜfar Khān, having heard of the former's departure, packed his baggage with haste and fled to Shiraz. Two or three days later Āqā Moḥammad Khān arrived at Esfahan. Having established order there, he returned to Tehran.

LOṬF ᶜALI KHĀN, BROTHER OF JAᶜFAR KHĀN-E ZAND, SENT ON CAMPAIGN TO THE PERSIAN GULF. In the month of Rabiᶜ I of that year[136] Jaᶜfar Khān sent his brother Loṭf ᶜAli Khān by way of Firuzābād to punish Bāqer Khān, the governor of Galladār,[137] and the sheikhs of Āl-e Ḥaram,[138] who were the chiefs (kalāntar) of the towns of Bandar ᶜAsluya,[139] Bandar Nāband,[140] and

134. About 25 miles south of Qomisha/Shahreżā, west of the modern highway Shiraz–Esfahan.

135. A large garden laid out by Shāh ᶜAbbās II (r. 1642–66) south of the Zāyanda Rud River, see Honarfar, *Ganjina*, p. 575.

136. Began on November 30, 1788.

137. Near the coast of the Persian Gulf, about 140 miles southeast of Bushehr.

138. A tribe of Arabs whose chief was governor of that region, see *FNN*, II, 292.

139. About 12 miles south of Galladār, on the coast.

140. The Āl-e Ḥaram first settled down at Bandar Nāband, a seaport with an important pearlfishery; then they moved to Bandar ᶜAslūya, not far away from Bandar Nāband, which was abandoned, see *FNN*, II, 291.

Kushk-e Kenār.[141] The people of Galladār fled and joined the Āl-e Ḥaram sheikhs at Bandar ᶜAsluya, and Loṭf ᶜAli Khān entered the deserted town of Galladār.

MURDER OF JAᶜFAR KHĀN; SEIYED MORĀD KHĀN ASCENDS THE ZAND THRONE. All the people whom Jaᶜfar Khan kept for some time in prison in the citadel of Shiraz were engaged in planning their escape; they one day by deception won the friendship of a small boy who had contact with them and waited for some good opportunity. When Jaᶜfar Khān fell seriously ill —it was said that a female slave had administered poison to him— and had to stay in bed for two or three days, the boy brought the prisoners a file. By means of that file they broke their fetters at midnight and rushed before sunrise upon Jaᶜfar Khān's chamberlain; this occurred on 25th Rabiᶜ II of that year.[142] Hearing the uproar, Jaᶜfar Khān despite his weakness jumped out of his bed, punched the faces of Shāh Morād Khān and Jahāngir Khān, the brothers of Seiyed Morād Khān, and knocked them out. Then Ebrāhim Khān, the son of Esmāᶜil Khān-e Zand, an inexperienced youth, entered the room, a broomstick in hand, behind Jaᶜfar Khān's back, raised the broomstick, and smashed it upon Jaᶜfar Khān in such a way that his uncovered skull was split, and that great man fell to the ground. And Seiyed Morād Khān, Veis Morād Khān, and Yāri Khān, the brothers of Seiyed Morād Khān, and Haji ᶜAli Qoli Khān-e Kāzeruni rushed upon Jaᶜfar Khān and finished him off with clubs, broomsticks, stones, and bricks. Then they cut off his head and threw it down from the doorway of the citadel at sunrise, whereupon the guards of the citadel dispersed. Out of sheer necessity the emirs and nobles of Fārs made Seiyed Morād Khān king, and his name was mentioned on the pulpits and put on the coins.

141. Probably the same as Kushk ("kiosk"), about 40 miles northwest of Galladār, see *FNN*, II, 245.

142. January 23, 1789.

LOṬF ᶜALI KHĀN DEFEATS SEIYED MORĀD KHĀN AND ASSUMES RULERSHIP. The officers of Loṭf ᶜAli Khān's army, who had houses and families in Shiraz, received a written statement containing promises and threats. When they were informed of what had happened, they convened a council at once and gathered together around Loṭf ᶜAli Khān's tent. The latter rushed with two of his followers to the stable, jumped on an unsaddled horse, and hastened toward Bushehr. His army dispersed in all directions. At the same time that Loṭf ᶜAli Khān arrived at Bushehr, Nāṣer Khān, the governor of Bushehr, died.[143] Forty days after New Year, which fell on 22d Jomādi II of that year,[144] Sheikh Naṣr Khān, the son of Sheikh Nāṣer Khān, and Amir ᶜAli Khān-e Ḥayyāṭ-e Dā'udi of Dashtestān[145] joined Loṭf ᶜAli Khān with a large number of soldiers. And Seiyed Morād Khān sent an army under the command of his brother Shāh Morād Khān against Loṭf ᶜAli Khān. When Loṭf ᶜAli Khān arrived at Borāzjān, 10 parasangs from Bushehr,[146] Shāh Morād Khān reached the village of Dālaki.[147] Then ᶜAli Himmat Khān-e Kolyā'i, Fażl ᶜAli Khān, and Naqd ᶜAli Khān, the sons of Naẓar ᶜAli Khān-e Zand,[148] and the officers, upon information from Mirzā Moḥammad Ḥosein-e Farāhāni, the vizier of Fārs, and Haji Ebrāhim, the lord mayor of Shiraz, arrested Shāh Morād Khān, put him in fetters, and brought him to Borāzjān, 4

143. Apart from Bushehr he ruled over Bahrein and was appointed "commander of Nāder Shāh's ships in the Persian Golf." In about 1738 (according to Ḥasan-e Fasā'i), he moved from Rishehr to Bushehr; Ḥasan-e Fasā'i calls him the "builder" (bāni) of Bushehr, see *FNN*, II, 204. The town was, however, an ancient foundation, see EI² I, s.v. Bushahr (L. Lockhart)

144. March 21, 1789.

145. Ḥayyāt-e Dā'ud is the region northwest of Bushehr, the center of which is Bandar Rig.

146. Borāzjān lies about 35 miles northeast of Bushehr, and is now the most important settlement between Kāzerun and the coast.

147. About 13 miles north-northeast of Borāzjān.

148. Naẓar ᶜAli Khān had been murdered in the troubles following Karim Khān Vakil's death, see above, p. 7.

parasangs from Dālaki. After arriving there they put Shāh Morād Khān to death, and the whole army, Zand warriors and soldiers from Fārs,[149] joined Loṭf ᶜAli Khān, and marched to Shiraz to overthrow Seiyed Morād Khān. In the evening of 10th Shaᶜbān of that year[150] Vizier Mirzā Moḥammad Ḥosein and Lord Mayor Haji Ebrāhim, Mirzā Jāni-ye Fasā'i, and the nobles of the Zand and of Fārs, out of affection for Loṭf ᶜAli Khān, rose in rebellion, laid siege to the citadel, and informed Loṭf ᶜAli Khān at Kāzerun[151] of their action. On 12th Shaᶜbān[152] Loṭf ᶜAli Khān entered Shiraz with the splendor of Rostam[153] and the pomp of Nader[154] and displayed benevolence towards the nobles. [231] Two days later he stormed the citadel and put Seiyed Morād Khān and his followers to death. By the intercession of the nobles of Fārs the life of Hāji ᶜAli Qoli Khān-e Kāzeruni was spared. Then Loṭf ᶜAli Khān ascended the throne. At that time he was twenty-three years old.

THE OVERTHROW OF THE ZAND RULE

ĀQĀ MOḤAMMAD KHĀN UNDERTAKES HIS FIRST CAMPAIGN TO SHIRAZ. When Āqā Moḥammad Khān received news of Jaᶜfar Khan's murder and Seiyed Morād Khān's usurpation, he departed from Tehran for the conquest of Fārs. Having arrived in Fārs, on the plain of Khosrav-e Shirin,[155] he was informed of what had happened to Seiyed Morād Khān and Loṭf ᶜAli Khān. He departed without hesitation and put up his camp

149. The army was composed of Zand warriors and native musketeers (tofangchi) from Fārs, see also above, p. 14, note 61.

150. May 6, 1789.

151. Loṭf ᶜAli Khān had marched in the meantime about 40 miles, the distance between Borāzjān and Kāzerun.

152. May 8, 1789. 153. A legendary hero of Persian epics.

154. To be understood as an allusion Noudar, the son of Manuchehr, praised in Firdousi's Shāhnāma.

155. About 100 miles north-northwest of Shiraz, on the southern slope of the Kuh-e Seyāh.

on the plain of Hezār in the district of Beiżā, 5 parasangs from Shiraz,[156] on 12th Shavvāl of that year.[157] Leaving the portage there under the command of his brother Jaᶜfar Qoli Khān, he took several thousand cavalry and infantry and marched the next day to the plain of Dinkān and Anjira, 2 parasangs north of Shiraz.[158] Loṭf ᶜAli Khān marched against him with 20,000 soldiers to the village of Dinkān, 0.5 parasangs from Āqā Moḥammad Khān's camp. When the brave warriors on both sides engaged in fighting, three or four cowardly soldiers of the lower ranks of the Qājār army went to Loṭf ᶜAli Khān and addressed him in the following manner: "Brave hero, conqueror of the battle line, man-eating lion! There is Jaᶜfar Qoli Khān's camp; the right wing of the army is staying with him. Its defeat will be your victory!" And Loṭf ᶜAli Khān, who had the heart of a wolf, the vigor of a lion, and the speed of a greyhound, and was always waiting for the chance of such a battle, hastened with 2,000 dagger-skilled horsemen to attack Jaᶜfar Qoli Khān, the heart of the Qājār army. Having reached the right wing, he pressed on Jaᶜfar Qoli Khān, the support of bravery. Then Āqā Moḥammad Khān sent a group from the center under the command of Moḥammad Qoli Khān-e Qājār in support of his brother. When they arrived there, the weakness of the right wing was transformed to a strength, and Loṭf ᶜAli Khān's army was debilitated. Moḥammad Khān, paternal uncle of Loṭf ᶜAli Khān, out of fear of the Qājār sword, fled with his followers to Shulestān,[159] the home of the Mamassani, the tribe from which his

156. Beiżā and surroundings is an area of rich cultivation, about 25 miles north of Shiraz. Tell-e Beiżā is the successor to the once famous town of Beiżā. The village of Hezār lies about 8 miles southeast of Tell-e Beiżā, see *FNN*, II, 185.

157. June 25, 1789.

158. The plain is a patch of cultivation about 8 miles northwest of Shiraz, on the river which supplies Shiraz with water.

159. Shulestān is the region of Noubandagān, which lies about 30 miles northwest of Kāzerun, see *FNN*, II, 302.

mother came. His flight caused the defeat of the whole army of the Zand and of Fārs. Loṭf ᶜAli Khān escaped to the coast of salvation by diving into the Qājār army like a leviathan. He marched through the garden area of Masjed-e Bardi, 0.75 parasangs from Shiraz,[160] and put up his camp in expectation of the runaways of his army. Considering survival the aim of that campaign, he marched to Shiraz and entrenched himself behind the fortifications. Āqā Moḥammad Khān set up his camp on the plain of Koshan and Qebla[161] and beleaguered Shiraz until 18th Dhu'l-Ḥejja of that year.[162] Realizing that he had no chance to conquer the city, he postponed its capture to another time and returned to Tehran.

FIVE SONS BORN TO FATḤ ᶜALI KHĀN. In that auspicious year God gave Fatḥ Ali Khān "Bābā Khān," the son of Āqā Moḥammad Khān's brother, five sons:

1. Moḥammad ᶜAli Mirzā, born in Rabiᶜ II[163] from Gorjiya[164]

2. Moḥammad Qoli Mirzā, born in Ramażān[165] from the daughter of Moḥammad Khān-e Qājār, maternal uncle of Āqā Moḥammad Khān

3. Moḥammad Vali Mirzā, born on 1st Shavvāl[166] from Esfahāniya[167]

160. Masjed-e Bardi lies 3 miles northwest of Shiraz. This means that Loṭf ᶜAli Khān retreated in the direction of Shiraz.

161. Kushān and Qebla are villages in the garden area west of Shiraz, 2 to 3 miles from the city.

162. September 7, 1789. According to this statement, the siege lasted about ten weeks.

163. Began on December 30, 1788.

164. "The Georgian"; women from Georgia were appreciated by the Persians for their beauty. They were brought to Persia as slave girls, in most of the cases as booty of raids undertaken in that Christian country.

165. Began on May 26, 1789.

166. June 25, 1789.

167. She was given the title Tāj od-Doula ("Crown of the Dynasty"), see below, p. 171.

4. ᶜAbbās Mirzā, born on 4th Dhu'l-Ḥejja[168] from the daughter of Fatḥ ᶜAli Khān-e Qājār Devehlu[169]

5. Ḥosein ᶜAli Mirzā, born on the Festival of Sacrifices (10th Dhu'l-Ḥejja)[170] from the daughter of Jaᶜfar Khān, the son of Qāder Khān-e ᶜArab-e ᶜĀmeri-ye Vali Besṭāmi.[171]

Each of them became a fruit-producing arbor in the garden of Persia.[172]

PREPARATIONS FOR THE CONQUEST OF SOUTHERN PERSIA. The New Year fell on 2d Rajab 1204.[173] Āqā Moḥammad Khān celebrated the New Year's feast, and on the 3d Ramażān of the same year[174] he left Tehran for the conquest of the province of Fārs. Having put up his camp on the pasture of Gandomān,[175] he sent his brother ᶜAli Qoli Khān and his cousin Moḥammad Qoli Khān to the region of Kuh-e Giluya. As the inhabitants of that region and Mirzā Solṭān Moḥammad Khān, the governor of Behbehān, were angry with the Zands because of their depravity, they submitted and paid peshkash, expecting to be restored to their offices.[176]

LOṬF ᶜALI KHĀN-E ZAND UNDERTAKES CAMPAIGN TO KERMAN. In Shiraz Loṭf ᶜAli Khān prepared for battle, gathered

168. August 26, 1789.

169. The marriage is mentioned above, p. 16.

170. September 1, 1789.

171. The marriage is mentioned above, p. 16.

172. The statement is an allusion to Fatḥ ᶜAli Shāh's numerous offspring, see below, p. 230.

173. March 18, 1790 (should be March 21).

174. May 17, 1790.

175. Āqā Moḥammad Khān had visited the place in 1202:1786 in order to sack the Qashqā'i khāns, see above, p. 29.

176. Kuh-e Giluya had come into the possession of the Ṭabāṭaba'i family before the Zand took over at Shiraz. In 1170:1757, Karim Khān Vakil-e Zand occupied Behbehān and sent the governor, Mirzā ᶜAli Reżā-ye Behbehāni, in fetter to Shiraz. The governor's son, Mirzā Solṭān Moḥammad Khān, reconquered Behbehān in 1200:1785/86, see *FNN*, II, 267 seq.

several thousand cavalry and infantry, and left Shiraz [232] to march against the Qājārs. He stayed some days outside the gate of the city of Shiraz, expecting news of the Qājār army. Then he received intelligence that Āqā Moḥammad Khān had left the pasture of Gandomān for Zenjān and Qazvin, in order to settle affairs in the region of Khamsa.[177] When Loṭf ᶜAli Khān realized that he had nothing to fear from this side, he committed the governorship of the city of Shiraz to his brother Khosrou Khān, who was still a boy, and appointed Lord Mayor (kalāntar) Haji Ebrāhim his brother's vizier. The fortifications of Shiraz and the tower and rampart guards he entrusted to Barkhudār Khān-e Zand, and the guard of the harem and the palace (ark-e shāhi) to Chamberlain (eshik āqāsi) Moḥammad ᶜAli Khān-e Zand. In the month Ṣafar of the year 1205[178] he marched off to Kerman by way of the town of Niriz.[179] When he reached Sirjān,[180] the people of the province of Kerman submitted to his authority, whereas the inhabitants of the city of Kerman took shelter behind the fortifications. On his arrival, therefore, Loṭf ᶜAli Khān laid siege to the city. After one day the inhabitants of the city sent out the qāżi and sheikh ol-eslām to the camp of Loṭf ᶜAli Khān, in order to intercede for them. They offered 20,000 toman in cash and valuable objects of Kerman as a peshkash, imploring him to raise the siege and postpone the occupation of the city of Kerman to a later time. Loṭf ᶜAli Khān, however, was full of pride and said that he would not raise the siege before Seiyed

177. Khamsa was conquered in 1196:1782, see above, p. 14.

178. September/October, 1790.

179. After the death of Karim Khān Vakil 1193:1779, Kerman had become the prey of the Afghan rulers of Sistān and Baluchistan. Loṭf ᶜAli Khān's campaign to Kerman was the result of an invitation to conquer the province, offered by the local ruler of Bam, Moḥammad Ḥasan (or Ḥosein) Khān-e Sistāni, whose rule was threatened by Seiyed Abu'l-Ḥasan Khān, mentioned below; see Vaziri, *Tārikh-e Kerman*, pp. 341 seq.

180. The western district of the province of Kerman; the town of Sirjān was renamed Saᶜidābād at the beginning of the nineteenth century. Sirjan/Saᶜidābād lies about 70 miles southwest of Kerman.

Abu'l-Hasan Khān-e Kuhaki, the governor of Kerman,[181] and all the nobles and aldermen (kadkhodā) had come out of the city to the encampment. When the qāżi and the sheikh ol-eslām returned unsuccessful to the city, Abu'l-Hasan Khān took greater care in the defense of the fortress than he had done before. When the winter came and roads and paths were blocked by snow and rain, the camp was cut off from provisions. For some time the people in the camp were satisfied with eating the meat of horses and donkeys, and patiently endured snow and rain. When things, however, became unbearable, the soldiers folded their tents and moved off. Loṭf ᶜAli Khān could not but do the same, and in the month of Jomādi I of that year[182] he returned to Shiraz.

When the news of the failure of Loṭf ᶜAli Khān's campaign came to the ears of Āqā Moḥammad Khān, he was reassured with regard to Loṭf ᶜAli Khān and determined on the conquest of Ādherbāyjān, and an order was issued summoning the nobles of the country and the commanders of the army.

PRETENSIONS OF JAᶜFAR QOLI KHĀN TO THE QĀJĀR THRONE. Jaᶜfar Qoli Khān, commander in chief of the army, for years had displayed great eagerness in the service of his high-ranking brother, fighting and rushing into danger, even braving victoriously the jaw of the shark and the claw of the lion. He considered himself heir to the throne of the empire and his brother's successor, always awaiting a sign from his brother and happy news concerning this heritage. As time went on, however,

181. Seiyed Abu'l-Ḥasan Khān (d. 1206:1791/92) was the ancestor of the famous Āqā Khān. Later on, the family gained the favor of the Qājārs. The grandson of Seiyed Abu'l-Ḥasan Khān was married to a daughter of Fatḥ ᶜAli Shāh and received the honorary title "Āqā Khān." In 1838 he revolted in Kerman, but was defeated, and fled to India and established himself in Bombay, since then the permanent residence of the head of the Ismaili sect, see Vaziri, *Tārikh-e Kerman*, pp. 332, 438, and EI² II, s.v. Āghā Khān (H. A. R. Gibb).

182. January/February, 1791.

no sign was apparent. In the last years he even conjectured that the ruler considered nobody but Fatḥ ᶜAli Khān deserving of crown and throne. When he was sure of the latter's being appointed heir to the throne in the near future, his zeal in fulfilling the duties of his office diminished. Being informed of the attack on Ādherbāyjān, he showed no concern and thereby incurred the wrath of the ruler. Moḥammad Zamān Khān-e Qājār and Moḥammad Khān-e Qājār ᶜEzz od-Dinlu, his maternal cousins, came to his house, and giving him guarantees brought him into the presence of the ruler. Asserting their innocence, they accused him of coveting the throne and of having a secret agreement with the khāns of Khorasan against his brother, moreover that he was only waiting for the right opportunity to open hostilities. The accusation of the cousins deeply impressed the ruler; and according to the proverb "Kingship is barren," he ordered special officers of his court to kill his brother, though his heart was afflicted with grief for him. One evening when Jaᶜfar Qoli Khān was returning from a royal assembly to his house, some servants of the king, on a corner of the street, threw a rope round the neck of this disobedient commander and extinguished the star of his life. He was born in the year 1165, and he died in 1205.[183] Wise men have said: "When you have an opinion contrary to that of the Solṭān, you must make a sacrifice of your blood."

QĀJĀR CAMPAIGN TO ĀDHERBĀYJĀN. In the spring of that year,[184] Fatḥ ᶜAli Khān, the Qājār crown prince, was appointed commander (sardār) of ᶜErāq and ordered to protect Esfahan and the borders to the province of Fārs. Āqā Moḥammad Khān set out for the campaign to Ādherbāyjān and encamped in the region of Ṭārom.[185] Soleimān Khān-e Qājār was sent to

183. 1165:1751/52; 1205:1790/91.
184. Spring, 1791.
185. For Ṭārom, see above, p. 14, note 60.

Ṭālesh.[186] Having arrived there, he sacked the settlements, and according to his orders the womenfolk among the inhabitants were sent to Qazvīn. Then the court proceeded from Ṭārom to Sarāb[187] for the chastisement of Ṣādeq Khān-e Shaqāqi. Having burnt Sarāb, which was made a "Sarāb" [mirage], Āqā Moḥammad Khān took up his quarters in Ardebil and did the required homage at the shrine of Shāh Ṣafi.[188] Thence he proceeded to Qarācha Dāgh[189] and entrusted the governor of Khoy and Tabriz to Ḥosein Qoli Dombali.

HAJI EBRĀHIM KHĀN'S DEFECTION FROM THE ZAND. The Qājār crown prince set up his camp on the pasture of Gandomān and waited there for news from Fārs. During the absence of Loṭf ᶜAli Khān, when he was on his campaign to Kerman, a quarrel about rank arose among Haji Ebrāhim, lord mayor of Shiraz, and Barkhurdār Khān-e Zand, commander of the citadel of Shiraz, and Moḥammad ᶜAli Khān-e Zand, guardian of the palace. Haji Ebrāhim's independent handling of affairs had given rise to enmity, and they plotted his destruction. In the presence of Loṭf ᶜAli Khān they accused him of treason and obstinacy. Although Loṭf Ali ᶜKhān did not heed their accusations, it was obvious from his behavior toward Haji Ebrāhim that his confidence and respect for him had changed. Prior to this something had happened which lessened Haji Ebrāhim Khān's confidence in Loṭf ᶜAli Khān. The point in question was this:

186. The coastal area east of Ardebil.

187. There are several places in Ādherbāyjān called Sarāb. This Sarāb is probably the town which lies 48 miles southwest of Ardebil. The Shaqāq (Shakkāk) were Kurds who occupied the region from east of Lake Urmia to Lake Van (on Ottoman territory), see EI[1] IV, 311, s.v. Shakāk (V. Minorsky).

188. That is, Sheikh Ṣafi od-Din (d. 735:1334), the founder of the mystical order of the Ṣafaviya and ancestor of the Safavid rulers. From the fourteenth century onward, mystics and saints were styled "Shāh."

189. The region north of Tabriz, on the southern bank of the Araxes River.

Some people who were suspected of being involved in the murder [233] of Ja^cfar Khān had been acquitted by the intercession of Haji Ebrāhim. One of them was a man named Mirzā Mahdi, who in the days of Jaᶜfar Khān had held the office of secretary of the Army (lashgar-nevis). One day it had become known that he had embezzled a sum of money belonging to the Divan. By the command of Jaᶜfar Khān one of his ears was cut off and he was disgraced. He was removed from his office and lived in seclusion. On the day when the head of Jaᶜfar Khān, as has been reported,[190] was thrown down from the wall of the palace and the people of the bazaar played with and dishonored this venerable skull, the rumor spread among the inhabitants of the city that Mirzā Mahdi had wrought vengeance for his amputated ear on the ear of Jaᶜfar Khān. Mirzā Mahdi, however, from the beginning to the end, had no responsibility whatsoever in this affair. Since Haji Ebrāhim considered him innocent, he interceded for him with Loṭf ᶜAli Khān, and the latter said: "Even if this accusation should be true, I would turn my eye from his fault for the sake of Haji Ebrāhim." After some months had elapsed, he presented robes of honor to the emirs of the court, and Mirzā Mahdi too, was given a robe of honor like the others. When Loṭf ᶜAli Khān's mother heard of this, she lamented: "He gives presents to the murderers of his father. Not only has he bestowed robes of honor upon them, now he treats in the same manner this son of a dog who has done such abominable things to the skull of Jaᶜfar Khān!" Loṭf ᶜAli Khān was enraged at these utterances of his mother and summoned Mirzā Mahdi, who having come into his presence was asked: "If somebody accords bad treatment to his benefactor, what does he deserve?" Mirzā Mahdi could only answer: "He must be burnt alive." Loṭf ᶜAli Khān retorted: "This traitor is you" and ordered him to be burned at the stake.

The result of this was that the confidence of Haji Ebrāhim in

190. See above, p. 31.

Loṭf ᶜAli Khān and that of Loṭf ᶜAli Khān in Haji Ebrāhim came to an end; this lack of confidence between king and vizier became obvious to everybody. Loṭf ᶜAli Khān, however, was aware of the fact that the death of Haji Ebrāhim meant his own death, too, as he knew that the people of Shiraz had great respect for Haji Ebrāhim and that the governors of the districts and the emirs of the tribes had a strong affection for him and that most of the infantry of Loṭf ᶜAli Khān were under the command of Haji Ebrāhim's brothers. As it was clear from the conduct of Loṭf ᶜAli Khān that he was waiting for the right opportunity and that Haji Ebrāhim had nothing to hope for but death, the latter decided to overthrow the Zand dynasty. When Loṭf ᶜAli Khān, at the beginning of Dhu'l-Ḥejja of that year,[191] made up his mind to conquer Esfahan, he conferred, as he had done before his campaign to Kerman, the governorship on Khosrou Khān and appointed Haji Ebrāhim the latter's vizier. The citadel and ramparts of the city and the command over the defense troops of Shiraz were entrusted to Barkhurdār Khān-e Zand, the guarding of the palace and the harem to Moḥammad Khān-e Zand. This he did in the persuasion that Haji Ebrāhim would be unable to offer effective resistance. At the moment of the army's departure he ordered Mirzā Moḥammad, the eldest son of Haji Ebrāhim, who had no office yet, to accompany him. After this order Haji Ebrāhim, if there was a doubt remaining, was assured that he could expect nothing good from Loṭf ᶜAli Khān. Thereupon he resolved to deliver the city of Shiraz to the Qājār ruler.

Sir John Malcolm, the English historian, says: "Haji Ebrāhim always declared that a desire to save his country from the continual petty wars with which it was afflicted was one of the principal motives. None except some plundering soldiers cared whether a Zand or a Qājār was upon the throne; but all desired that Persia should be great and powerful, and enjoy internal tranquillity. Haji Ebrāhim had, perhaps, persuaded

191. Began on August 1, 1791.

himself, that by this act of treason he was only anticipating an event which must occur and saving his country from the misery of a protracted war between two rival families; but there can be no doubt his real motive was that of self-preservation." 192

When Loṭf ʿAli Khān had advanced several marches on his way to the pasture of Gandomān, Haji Ebrāhim, under pretext of an administrative council, invited Barkhurdār Khān-e Zand and Chief Chamberlain (eshik āqāsi bāshi) Moḥammad ʿAli Khān-e Zand to his house. Aided by a corps which he had recruited from among the citizens of Shiraz and put under the command of his younger brother, Moḥammad Ḥosein Khān, he arrested the Zand emirs and imprisoned them, without any bloodshed. On 26th Dhu'l-Ḥejja of that year193 he passed information of what had happened to his other brothers, ʿAbd or-Raḥim Khān and Moḥammed ʿAli Khān, who were commanders of two Fārsi detachments in Loṭf ʿAli Khān's camp at Samirom-e ʿolyā, 2 parasangs from Qumesha in the district of Esfahan. The army of the Qājār crown prince was staying at Qomesha. ʿAbd or-Raḥim Khān informed his friends of the incident. The officers who were allied to him ordered the Fārsi musketeers and those of the tribes to discharge their muskets by sunset in the direction of Loṭf ʿAli Khān's tent and to raise a clamor. This they agreed upon as a sign for the meeting of the friends. When according to the plan the whole camp raised an uproar and the detachments one after the other began to move, Loṭf ʿAli Khān was astonished and confounded by the clamor and the crowd and sent men to collect information. The messengers reported on their return: "The proper action is for you to jump on an unbridled horse and save your life. The whole army has risen against you!" When nobody obeyed the orders he issued, Loṭf ʿAli Khān was convinced of the revolt and moved off in the company of Ṭahmāsp Khān-e Fili and 70 soldiers of the

192. Sir John Malcolm, *History of Persia*, II, 183.
193. August 26, 1791.

latter's detachment. Supposing Shiraz and the palace still to be in the possession of Barkhurdār Khān and Moḥammad ᶜAli Khān, he hurried to Shiraz. In the region of Abarj and Dashtak[194] he received news of what had happened in Shiraz. As about 300 horsemen joined him on the way, he did not lose courage. He marched outside the citadel of Shiraz and sent a messenger to Haji Ebrāhim, asking him for the reason of the incident. Haji Ibrāhim answered: "Tell Loṭf ᶜAli Khān: 'I was informed of your intention and saw no other device for my salvation than to remove you from the throne.' Tell him further: 'Give up hope in Shiraz. Proceed [234] to another country, if you want to escape with your life!'" Loṭf ᶜAli Khān laughed at this talk and said: "This traitor is only a citizen and his followers are merchants and dealers. They cannot compete with the victorious army, which is trained in handling musket and sword only!" Meanwhile about 2,000 soldiers of the scattered camp of Samirom had rallied round him, and on the 2d Moḥarram of the year 1206[195] he laid siege to Shiraz.

Haji Ebrāhim sent a message to the army to the effect that everybody who had a family and relatives in Shiraz must leave Loṭf ᶜAli Khān and go to his house without delay. If they did not obey his order, their families would suffer death and their goods would be confiscated. When Loṭf ᶜAli Khān's army came to know this, all those who had a family and possessions in Shiraz deserted their colors within two to three hours and went to Shiraz.

LOṬF ᶜALI KHĀN RETREATS TO THE PERSIAN GULF COAST. Loṭf ᶜAli Khān moved off to Dashtestān[196] and Bandar Būshehr,

194. Two districts at the foot of the Emāmzāda Kuh (48 miles north of Shiraz); according to *FNN*, II, 170, the center of Abarj was the qaṣba of Dashtak, which "lies on top of a high mountain."

195. September 1, 1791.

196. The coastal area stretching from Bandar Deilam as far as Bandar Bushehr, see *FNN*, II, 203–10.

together with his uncle Moḥammad Khān and the governor of Khesht,[197] Zāl Khān, and 4 or 5 other people. Haji Ebrāhim sent a detachment in their pursuit, while Loṭf ᶜAli Khān with his 4 or 5 men fought in the manner of attack and retreat. After twenty-four hours they came to the foot of the mountain which lies between Kāzerun and Kamārej,[198] and Reżā Qoli Khān, brother of Haji Qoli Khān-e Kāzeruni, came close to them with 1,000 musketeers, and they began to fight. Loṭf ᶜAli Khān displayed utmost bravery and killed several of his opponents. When his horse, which had been running two days and one night, died, he continued to fight on foot and retreated to the mountain mentioned above. In the meantime, the musketeers of Khesht arrived to his support, and he was rescued and entered Khesht safely. Thence he went to Bushehr. Since Sheikh Naṣr Khān, the governor of Bushehr, contrary to a previous agreement, did not give him the permission to enter Bushehr, he went to Bandar Reg[199] to take refuge with Mir ᶜAli Khān-e Ḥayyāṭ-e Dā'udi, the governor (żābeṭ), and he was honorably received.

Sheikh Naṣr Khān, who was a bitter enemy of Mir ᶜAli Khān, suspecting that the refugee [Loṭf ᶜAli Khān] had betaken himself to the latter, gathered together about 3,000 men from Dashtestān and asked Haji Ebrāhim for help. Haji Ebrāhim sent reinforcements of 3,000 horsemen and infantry under the command of Reżā Qoli Khān-e Shāhsevan from Shiraz to Dashtestān. When he arrived at Borāzjān,[200] about 3 parasangs from Bushehr, Naṣr Khān joined him. When Loṭf ᶜAli Khān received news of this, there were no more than 5 or 6 soldiers with him. Then Solṭān ᶜAli Khān-e Zand Hezāra'i, who had made his escape from Shiraz with 70 horsemen, arrived and

197. About 18 miles west-southwest of Kāzerun.

198. Kamārej lies about 11 miles west of Kāzerun, south of the road from Kāzerun to Borāzjān.

199. At the Persian Gulf, about 31 miles northwest of Bushehr.

200. Today, the largest town between Kāzerun and Bushehr, about 31 miles northeast of Bushehr.

joined Loṭf ᶜAli Khān. Amir ᶜAli Khān-e Ḥayyāṭ-e Dā'udi, having collected a host, arrived too, and Loṭf ᶜAli Khān having at his disposal an army which counted less than 1,000 men, with great boldness attacked the army of Shāhsevan and that from the region of Dashtestān, near the village of Tangestān,[201] and routed them completely. Sheikh Naṣr Khān fled to Bushehr and Reżā Qoli Khān-e Shāhsevan to Kāzerun. And 250 ᶜAbd ol-Maleki horsemen, who had been under the command of Reżā Qoli Khān, joined Loṭf ᶜAli Khān.

ḤAJI EBRĀHIM KHĀN APPOINTED QĀJĀR GOVERNOR OF FĀRS. When Haji Ebrāhim heard of the defeat of Reżā Qoli Khān, he sent a respectful petition to Āqā Moḥammad Khān, together with Haji ᶜAli Qoli Khān-e Kāzeruni, asking for help. He presented 3,000 mares, property of the Zand and on pasture in Fārs, as a gift. Haji ᶜAli Qoli Khān was received in audience in the region of Khamsa, the royal court being on its way back from Ādherbāyjān. He submitted the petition of Haji Ebrāhim and the people of Fārs, and royal grace was bestowed and a royal fermān with the appointment of Haji Ebrāhim to the governorship of Fārs and the bestowal of the title "Khān" was issued. Hereafter he was called "Haji Ebrāhim Khān, Beglerbegi of the province of Fārs." And the title "Solṭān" was bestowed upon Mirzā Reżā Qoli Navā'i, Chancellor of the Empire (monshi ol-mamālek). And Seiyed ᶜAli Khān-e Qazvini was sent to Shiraz to confiscate the possessions of the Zand and to escort the family and relations of Loṭf ᶜAli Khān (to Tehran). The crown prince was ordered to station Moṣṭafā Khān-e Qājār Devehlu with 4,000 horsemen at Ābāda, a town between Shiraz and Esfahan, so that he was at the disposal of Haji Ebrāhim.

THE QĀJĀR TROOPS SUFFER A DEFEAT AT KĀZERUN. Haji Ebrāhim, in order to destroy Loṭf ᶜAli Khān, assembled 7,000 horsemen and infantry, put them under the command of Reżā

201. Tangestān is the region east of Bushehr, see *Farhang*, II, 55.

Qoli Khān-e Shāhsevan, Loṭf ᶜAli Khān-e Firuzābādi,[202] Ra'is Qāsem Khān-e Kuh-e Marra'i,[203] and Reżā Qoli Khān, brother of Haji ᶜAli Qoli Khān-e Kāzeruni, and sent them to Dashtestān against Loṭf ᶜAli Khān. At the same time as the army of Fārs arrived at Kāzerun, Loṭf ᶜAli Khān arrived, too. The army of Fārs was routed and retreated to the citadel of Kāzerun. After three or four days Loṭf ᶜAli Khān captured the citadel and had Reżā Qoli Khān-e Kāzeruni and his son ᶜAli Naqi Khān deprived of their sight. About 2,000 men were taken prisoner. Then he marched from Kāzerun to the plain of Juyom, 5 parasangs north of Shiraz, where he stayed for ten days. Thence he marched to Masjed-e Bardi, which lies 1 parasang from Shiraz. There he put up his camp.

THE TRIBAL SOLDIERS OF THE ZAND EXPELLED FROM SHIRAZ. Haji Ebrāhim took measures for the defense of the city of Shiraz. Five sixths of the army which he had recruited among the tribes demanded that if a Zand was to be dethroned another Zand was to be put in his place. As it was the intention of Haji Ebrāhim to depose the Zand and to confer the government upon the Qājārs, it was very unlikely that the tribes would assent to his proposal, and so he reflected upon appropriate measures to be taken; eventually he issued the order that the whole army recruited from among the tribes should assemble the following day in the Masjed-e Vakīl.[204] Everybody would receive his pay in the course of a review to take place on the plain of Jaᶜfarābād[205] [235] He further ordered a group of citizens of Shiraz to establish themselves in the Bāzār-i Vakil and to act according to the orders to be given. On the following day

202. Firuzābād lies about 50 miles south of Shiraz.

203. Kuh-e Marra forms part of the hilly region north of Kāzerun, see *FNN*, II, 247.

204. Masjed-e Jāmeᶜ-e Vakil, built by Karim Khān Vakil in about 1180:1766/67, at the western side of the Bazār-e Vakil, see *FNN*, II, 160.

205. Jaᶜfarābād is a small village 4 miles southeast of Shiraz, see *Farhang*, VII, 191.

he proceeded to the Masjed-e Vakil, and the tribal army advanced group by group and received their purse of money. As they proceeded from the sword-cutlers Bāzār to the Bāzār-e Vakil, the citizens laid hand on them group by group, took away their clothes and turned them out of the city through the Esfahan gate. By this means the whole tribal army, naked and disarmed, was removed from the city. Nobody knew what happened to the others. Then their families were expelled from the city. They were instructed to settle in the villages of the districts of Fārs.

LOṬF ᶜALI KHĀN OCCUPIES ZARQĀN. The disarmed tribal warriors joined Loṭf ᶜAli Khān, who assigned as abode to their families the fortress of Zarqān.[206] He himself proceeded from Masjed-e Bardi to Zarqān, which lies 5 parasangs north of Shiraz. As the inhabitants of Zarqān offered resistance, he took the fortress by force. Then he brought the families of the nobles of the tribes to that place and completed its fortification. And Haji Ebrāhim dispatched 500 musketeers under the command of Bāqer Khān-e Galladāri and Hādi Khān-e Borujerdi to Zarqān. When they arrived there and realized that the fortress was in the possession of Loṭf ᶜAli Khān's adherents, they hid in the valley of the Kuh-e Zarqān[207] and sent a message to Shiraz. When Loṭf ᶜAli Khān came to know their position, he sent a detachment against them. Hādi Khān was killed whereas Bāqer Khān and all the musketeers were taken prisoner and brought into his presence. Bāqer Khān was taken into custody, the other prisoners were disarmed and sent home.

LOṬF ᶜALI KHĀN FAILS TO RECAPTURE SHIRAZ. Having completed the fortification of Zarqān, Loṭf ᶜAli Khān appointed a detachment to its defense and returned to Masjed-e Bardi.

206. About 16 miles northeast of Shiraz.

207. Probably the mountain south of Zarqān; the town itself lies in the valley of the Kur Rud, which passes 5 miles to the northeast.

Then he sent a message to Haji Ebrāhim: "We have the desire to stop fighting. We promise solemnly and take an oath upon the Holy Koran that we are ready to forget what has happened. As to you, take into account the benefits of the Zand dynasty you have enjoyed for so many years! Open the gates, so that we might live better than before or else send my family, who are children of your benefactor, from Shiraz to me so that I might take them and proceed to India or Turkey!" Haji Ebrāhim accepted none of those proposals and dispatched Rabiᶜ Khān-e Marvdashti[208] to Moṣṭafā Khān-e Qājār Devehlu, who with 4,000 horsemen, by order of the crown prince, was staying at Ābāda, 6 marches north of Shiraz.[209] Moṣṭafā Khān marched on byroads to Shiraz and took up his quarters in the Bāgh-e Jahān-namā-ye Vakili, which lies an arrow-shot north of Shiraz and is surrounded by a wall of limestone. This happened in great secret. Then the keeper of the Esfahan gate sent a message to Loṭf ᶜAli Khān: "When you arrive tonight, I shall open the gate to you." Loṭf ᶜAli Khān arrived at the gate with 300 horsemen. He realized that Haji Ebrāhim had invented this agreement in order to make him the target of the musketeers when he arrived at the gate. The same night he returned to Masjed-e Bardi, thence he proceeded by way of Kushk-e Bibi Chāh[210] and the plain of Bājgāh[211] in the direction of Zarqān. Moṣṭafā Khān outflanked the Zand horsemen by marching through the pass of Allāh Akbar[212] and the plain of the icehouse (yakh chāl) and defeated them on the plain of Bājgāh, 2 parasangs from Shiraz; the Zand army was scattered. Loṭf ᶜAli Khān received news of this just when he was

208. Marvdasht is the region around Persepolis, northeast of Shiraz.

209. See above, p. 46.

210. Situated 9 miles northwest of Shiraz, see *Farhang*, VII, 193.

211. The village of Bājgāh lies 6 miles northeast of Shiraz, on the road to Zarqān, see also above, p. 9, note 41. This means that Loṭf ᶜAli Khān first marched in a northern direction and then turned off to the east.

212. The famous pass east of Shiraz, on which a gateway has been erected.

offering his morning prayer. He assembled the defeated soldiers, advanced with 2 or 3 groups of valiant warriors against Moṣṭafā Khān and defeated him. Following on his heels as far as outside the city gate of Shiraz, they took 2,000 men prisoner. Loṭf ᶜAli Khān brought them to Zarqān, put their officers in prison, disarmed the private soldiers, and sent them home to (Persian) ᶜErāq.

ĀQĀ MOḤAMMAD KHĀN SUFFERS A STROKE, SENDS ARMY TO SHIRAZ. On 17th Rabiᶜ II of that year,[213] Āqā Moḥammad Khān while he was sitting on his throne and talking to some courtiers, suffered a stroke all of a sudden and stopped talking. Soleimān Khān-e Qājār, who was standing near him, inquired into the illness and dismissed the courtiers, employing a subtle trick. With the help of several eunuchs he brought the king into the harem, and Mirzā Masiḥ and Mirzā Aḥmad, physicians from Esfahan, were summoned. After one night had passed they treated him by tearing out the hair from his head and by other medical ministrations. When news of this occurrence and of the restoration of the ruler's health arrived at Shiraz, Haji Ebrāhim handed to Mirzā Reżā Qoli Navā'i and Seiyed ᶜAli Khān-e Qazvini some precious objects out of the property of the Zand, namely a box studded with pearls, a dagger studded with jewels, and jewels for the decoration of horsemen and infantry. They traveled to Tehran on byroads; and news of Moṣṭafā Khān's defeat and the misfortune of Haji Ebrāhim were submitted to the king. Then he ordered Jān Moḥammad Khān and Reżā Qoli Khān-e Qājār Devehlu with 7,000 horsemen to march via Herāt-e Morust and Arsenjān[214] to Fārs.

BATTLE OUTSIDE THE GATES OF SHIRAZ. As Loṭf ᶜAli Khān was informed by his tax collectors, who were dispersed over all the districts in order to collect the taxes, of the arrival of the new Qājār army, the Zand leaders deemed it advisable to

213. December 14, 1791.

214. They marched east of the road which was blocked because of Loṭf ᶜAli Khān's staying at Zarqān.

march against the Qājārs. Loṭf ᶜAli Khān, however, although proud of his bravery, put forth: "We must keep back. When this army has entered Shiraz and has joined Moṣṭafā Khān and the auxiliary forces of Fārs, we shall entice them outside the city and finish the whole thing at one blow." Thereupon Jān Moḥammed Khān and Reżā Qoli Khān entered Shiraz undisturbed in the month of Jomādi I of that year.[215] Three or four days later the whole army, the main body and newly arrived forces, Qājārs and detachments recruited from the districts of Fārs, under the command of ᶜAbd or-Raḥim Khān and Moḥammad ᶜAli Khān, brothers of Haji Ebrāhim Khān, and the Qājār commanders marched out of the city and lined up for battle on the plain of Qebla and Koshan.[216] Loṭf ᶜAli Khān drew up his army of about 20,000 horsemen and infantry opposite them [236] and charged from two sides. His warriors fought with great bravery. When he sent a detachment of his horsemen to the vicinity of the Kuh-e Derāk,[217] 1 parasang to the west of Shiraz, the Qājār commanders, supposing them to flee, attacked them while they were moving, put them to flight and charged the center of the Zand army. Loṭf ᶜAli Khān resisted with great vigor and fought in such a manner as to force the Qājār army to retreat, and he pushed them back as far as the city gate of Shiraz. Reżā Qoli Khān-e Qājār Devehlu was taken prisoner, and a great number of Qājār soldiers were either taken prisoner or killed. Since in the last three to four years the locust plague was spread in Fārs and the farmers were reduced to misery by the coming and going of the Zand and Qājār armies and the camp of the Zand outside the city of Shiraz suffered from famine and scarcity of provisions, Loṭf ᶜAli Khān marched from Masjed-e Bardi to the fortress of Zarqān.

215. December, 1791/January, 1792.

216. West of Shiraz, see also above, p. 35, note 161.

217. "A high mountain 2 parasangs west of Shiraz. In summertime the snow is brought thence to Shiraz," see *FNN*, II, 337.

At the same time a group of Māfi and Nānkoli,[218] who had always been faithful followers of Haji Ebrāhim, seceded and plotted his murder. Haji Ebrāhim came to know of this and assigned the district of Beiżā as their abode. When they left the city, they joined the army of Loṭf ᶜAli Khān.

ĀQĀ MOḤAMMAD KHĀN GOES IN PERSON TO SHIRAZ. When the distress of the province of Fārs came to the ears of the Qājār ruler, he departed in the spring of the same year from Tehran for Fārs. On the 14th Shavvāl of that year[219] he arrived at Shahrak in the district of Abarj,[220] several parasangs north of Shiraz. Loṭf ᶜAli Khān removed his whole family and his relatives from the fortress of Zarqān and brought them to the fortress of Rashmāyjān in the district of Marvdasht.[221] With 3,000 horsemen he marched against the Qājār army in order to make a night attack. At sunset of that day a group in the vicinity of the Qājār army saw the Zand troops and reported this to the king. He ordered Ebrāhim Khān-e Ashrafi-ye Māzandarāni with 300 musketeers from Dāmghān to take up a hidden position in the valley which is between Marvdasht and the district of Abarj. At midnight Loṭf ᶜAli Khān arrived at this valley. The Dāmghāni musketeers tried to block the road by discharging their muskets. Loṭf ᶜAli Khān ordered an attack and advanced against the enemy himself. Ebrāhim Khān-e Māzanderāni was killed;

218. The Māfi and Nānkoli (Nānaki ?) are tribal branches of the Lak, that is, the southern Kurds of Persia. Karim Khān Vakil was an offspring of the Zande-ye käla (?), another group of the Lak, see EI[1] III, s.v. Lak (V. Minorsky), and above, p. 4, note 17.

219. June 5, 1792.

220. A village in the valley of the Kur River, in the district of Abarj (see above, p. 44, note 194), 17.5 miles east of Ardekān, see *Farhang*, VII, 144.

221. The region round Eṣṭakhr and Persepolis; according to *FNN*, II, 301, Rashmāyjān lies more than 1 parasang south of Fatḥābād, that is, 2 parasangs north of Zarqān.

several of the musketeers, too, were killed, several wounded and taken prisoner. Loṭf ᶜAli Khān marched through the valley safely. He gave two detachments of horsemen to his paternal uncles ᶜAbdollāh Khān and Moḥammad Khān-e Zand and ordered them to attack the Qājār camp from two sides. He himself marched to the bazaar of the camp (ordubāzār) and there created noise and clamor. And Āqā Moḥammad Khān decided to keep vigil the entire night. The emirs and viziers remained with him, and the musketeers, muskets in hand and matches ready, were standing behind the breastwork around the royal pavilion awaiting the enemy. Then 30 to 40 horsemen of the Zand rode through the bazaar of the camp and invaded the breastwork around the royal pavilion, raising a clamor like that of the Day of Judgment. Mirzā Fatḥollāh-e Ardelāni left the camp of the Qājārs, went to Loṭf ᶜAli Khān and reported: "The king has fled, the musketeers in the entrenchment around the royal pavilion are only shooting for their own protection. It is advisable to stop fighting. As soon as the new day dawns and the flight of the king is known, the camp will be yours without resistance." When Loṭf ᶜAli Khān considered this generous advice he stopped fighting, went to rest in a corner of the camp, and forbade any charge. Nobody should enter the entrenchment around the royal pavilion. The soldiers obeyed, dispersed in the camp, and, having taken everything they could find, carried their booty to Marvdasht, leaving not much more than 1,000 horsemen with Loṭf ᶜAli Khān. At daybreak the king ordered the muezzin to call to prayer. And Loṭf ᶜAli Khān rose to offer his prayers. The king, too, offered his prayers, then he ordered the call to horse. This showed both sides that Āqā Moḥammad Khān and a group of guards (qaravolān) in the entrenchment around the royal pavilion had a strong position and were going to fight. When they realized the small number and disorder of the enemy, they remained where they were, as the situation was hopeful. When Loṭf ᶜAli Khān woke up from the sleep of negligence and realized that Mirzā Fatḥollāh-e Ardelāni was a spy sent by Āqā Moḥammad Khān and that he had been deceived, he made his escape in the direction of the valley in great haste.

Sir John Malcolm states in his *History*: "This daring attempt of Loṭf ᶜAli Khān to recover his power ought not to be deemed an act of desperate temerity, in which success was impossible. That prince well knew from experience that in an army composed like the one which he attacked, confusion, if once introduced, was likely to become irremediable. He also knew that in the actual state of Persia the minds of a number of chiefs of tribes fluctuated between him and Āqā Moḥammad Khān. These leaders, it was obvious, from recent occurrences, always acted upon the impulse of the moment: and as the party they took was blindly adopted by their followers, he had a right to expect that brilliant success would turn the tide in his favour and that he should be able to overcome his enemies with the very means they had collected for his destruction. The plan of the attack was able: he proceeded with every caution, and completely surprised the advance corps of his enemy. The advantage he took of his first success showed at once his skill and his determined courage. Victory was snatched from him by one of those accidents which have so often decided the fate of battles and of empires. If Loṭf ᶜAli Khān deserved success, Āqā Moḥammad Khān had also merited the crown which the result of this day fixed upon his brow. He had evinced, amid a scene of consternation and confusion, all that calm resolution and self-possession which marked his extraordinary character. His mind loved to dwell upon the events of this period: and we are told he used often to observe, that in the modern History of Persia three achievements alone were worthy of being transmitted to posterity. [237] First, the policy and firmness of Haji Ebrāhim, who, aided by a few shopkeepers, took and maintained for months the city of Shiraz against all the warlike tribes of that province. Second, the daring heroism of Loṭf ᶜAli Khān, who, with four or five hundred men, ventured to attack an army of thirty thousand; and, lastly, that fortitude which he himself had displayed, by remaining at his quarters when all around him fled; and that calmness in danger which made him direct the common crier to announce morning prayers in the usual manner, that both his own army and that of his enemy might learn he was at his post, and undisturbed by all that had passed."[222]

From Abarj, Loṭf ᶜAli Khān went to Marvdasht. After a two days' stay he proceeded by way of Niriz and Kerman to Ṭabas in Khorāsān. And on 1st Dhu'l-Ḥejja of that year,[223] the shah entered Shiraz and took up his quarters in the Bāgh-e Vakili. He held a general audience in the pavilion which lies above the sepulcher of Karim Khān Vakil. At the end of the audience Mirzā Moḥammad Khān-e Lārijāni was charged with the exhumation of the corpse of the deceased monarch. His corpse was removed from the sepulcher, transferred to Tehran, and buried in the middle of the threshold (keryās) of the Karim Khāni Convent. Several years later, Fatḥ ᶜAli Shāh Qājār gave orders to unearth these mortal remains and to transfer them to Najaf. And Āqā Moḥammad Khān confirmed Haji Ebrāhim Khān in the governorship of Fārs as before, and he ordered the harem of Loṭf ᶜAli Khān and the families of the nobles of the Zand to be conducted to Tehran. By his order, two columns, each consisting of one piece, and pieces of marble from the window gratings (ezāra) and gate wings with wood carving of fine quality were removed from the buildings in the Vakili palace and conveyed to Tehran. Āqā Moḥammad Khān left Shiraz for Tehran on 11th Moḥarram of the year 1207.[224]

THE QĀJĀR RULER AGAIN IN FĀRS. The New Year fell on Saturday, the 7th Shaᶜbān of that year.[225] Āqā Moḥammad Khān left Tehran and put up his camp on the pasture of Āsopās[226] in

222. Malcolm, *History of Persia,* II, 191–93.
223. July 21, 1792.
224. August 29, 1792. The transfer of pieces of the Vakili palace to Tehran is to be understood as an attempt to win the divine grace (farr), which in Persian tradition, is vested not only in persons but also in things, especially the palace doors.
225. March 20, 1793 (should be March 21).
226. Located 41 miles south-southeast of Ābāda, in the valley of the Kur River.

the province of Fārs. He summoned Haji Ebrāhim and the nobles of Fārs, and royal favors were bestowed upon them. Jān Moḥammad Khān-e Qājār was ordered to pull down the citadel of Shiraz, which had been built by Karim Khān Vakil of mortar, stones, and bricks over a period of many years. I have been told by several old people of Shiraz that when pickaxes and hatchets had no effect on the walls of the fortress, a group of stone cutters, in order to destroy that mountain-like fortification, had to employ tools and means which serve for cutting stones out of a quarry. Then he ordered all the nobles of Fārs to surrender women and boys as hostages. Haji Ebrāhim surrendered his son Asadollāh Khān, a boy of nine years, and the boy's mother, daughter of one of the nobles of Dashtestān, and they were conveyed to Qazvin. Mirzā Jāni-ye Fasā'i was ordered to surrender two hostages. The reason was that Loṭf ᶜAli Khān had more complaints about him than about any other people of Fārs. Mirzā Esmāᶜil and Mirzā Ebrāhim, two of his sons, were sent as hostages. Mirzā Esmāᶜil died on his arrival in Esfahan, and the shah sent an order for a substitute. So Mirzā Jāni sent his younger brother Mirzā Ḥasan, father of the author of this book. He stayed for some time in Tehran.

When the shah had settled the affairs of Fārs, the nobles of that province were allowed to leave Āsopās, and on 14th Moḥarram of the year 1208[227] the royal court departed for Tehran.

LOṬF ᶜALI KHĀN CONQUERS KERMAN. And Loṭf ᶜAli Khān at Ṭabas, having heard of the destruction of the citadel of Shiraz, set out for Shiraz with 300 horsemen, whom Amir Ḥasan Khān, governor of Ṭabas, had put at his disposal. When he arrived at Yazd, the road was blocked by ᶜAli Naqi Khān, son of Taqi Khān, the governor of Yazd, together with a vast host. By his first charge, Loṭf ᶜAli Khān rolled up the army of Yazd, which numbered ten times more than his own troops, like a paper

227. August 23, 1793.

scroll and drove them back to the citadel of the town. Thence he proceeded to Abarquh and captured the citadel. When the shah heard of Loṭf ᶜAli Khān's return, he sent Moḥammad Ḥosein Khān-e Qājār Qoyonlu, his maternal cousin and chamberlain, known by the name of Dudāgh, to Fārs. When Moḥammad Ḥosein Khān "Dudāgh" arrived at Abarquh, he learned that Loṭf ᶜAli Khān had entrusted the citadel of Abarquh to his uncle Naṣrollāh Khān, and that Loṭf ᶜAli Khān himself had marched through Bavānāt[228] and Eṣṭahbānāt[229] and had captured the citadel of Dārāb, the abode of Jaᶜfar Khān-e Dārābi. When Moḥammad Ḥosein Khān's siege of the citadel of Abarquh had gone on for some time, an order arrived from the shah: "It is not worthwhile carrying on the siege of the citadel of Abarquh and letting Loṭf ᶜAli Khān escape. Leave Abarquh and continue your campaign!" Moḥammad Ḥosein Khān, accordingly, departed from Abarquh and proceeded to Shiraz. When he received news that Loṭf ᶜAli Khān had left Dārāb and entered Niriz, he departed with haste from Shiraz, marched through Sarvestān over the pass of Tang-e Karam near Fasā[230] and encamped at the foot of the Kuh-i Kharmān.[231] And Loṭf ᶜAli Khān proceeded from Niriz by way of Khir[232] to Rouniz-e bālā,[233] 1 parasang from the camp of Moḥammad Ḥosein Khān. He established himself in the deserted "fortress of the Mirzā" (Qalᶜa-ye Mirzā). The next day he marched against the Qājār troops. His well-trained horsemen charged from two sides and continued by fighting hand-to-hand. At nightfall both parties

228. The region at the northern foot of the Kuh-e Khahin; the small town of Bavānāt lies about 30 miles southeast of Deh Bid.

229. The region on the southern shore of the Daryācha-ye Bākhtegān, west of Niriz.

230. Tang-e Karam is a village about 12 miles north of Fasā, on the road from Fasā to Eṣṭahbānāt, see *FNN*, II, 237.

231. It was 3 parasangs north of Fasā (3,200 m. high), see *FNN*, II, 337.

232. A district (nāḥeya) belonging to Eṣṭahbānāt, on the southern shore of the Daryācha-ye Bākhtegān, see *FNN*, II, 178.

233. About 19 miles north-northeast of Fasā.

returned to their camps and rested. For eleven days they fought from morning to night, without one side defeating the other. One night Loṭf ᶜAli Khān marched to the camp of his opponents to make a night attack. [238] However, as one of his followers had deserted and entering the service of Moḥammad Ḥosein Khān had revealed Loṭf ᶜAli Khān's secret, the Qājār camp was prepared for battle. When Loṭf ᶜAli Khān arrived at the camp, he found them on their guard and returned to his own camp. On the following morning Moḥammad Ḥosein Khān decided to fight and drew up his lines. Loṭf ᶜAli Khān, standing opposite him, charged first, and both parties battled and fought with the utmost vigor. Eventually, Loṭf ᶜAli Khān's soldiers, losing their enthusiasm, turned to flight. Loṭf ᶜAli Khān gave up his designs on Fārs and proceeded to Ṭabas. Upon his arrival, on the advice of Amir Ḥasan Khān-e Ṭabasi, he marched in the direction of Kandahār to ask support from Timur Shāh Afghān.[234] When he arrived at Qā'en,[235] he was informed of the death of Timur Shāh. While in a state of indecision and depression, he received letters from Moḥammad Khān, son of Aᶜẓam Khān-e Afghān, and Jahāngir Khān, son of Moḥammad Ḥosein Khān-e Sistāni, offering obedience on behalf of Bam and Narmashir, two districts lying to the east of Kerman. Loṭf ᶜAli Khān joined them with 300 horsemen. Upon his arrival at Narmashir, Moḥammad Khān-e Afghān was ready to submit and offered him 500 Afghāni horsemen and, upon his arrival at Bam, Jahāngir Khān, too, hoping for royal reward, entered into an alliance with him and put 500 Sistāni horsemen at his disposal. Then they marched off, their goal being the conquest of Kerman. On his arrival he consigned one half of his army to his uncle ᶜAbdollāh Khān-e Zand, a man of great bravery and highly esteemed by his followers. He ordered him to attack the city from one side. While the defenders of the citadel were engaged in battle with

234. Timur Shāh Dorrāni, reigned 1187–1207:1773–93.
235. A distance of 125 miles east of Ṭabas.

ᶜAbdollāh Khān, Loṭf ᶜAlī Khān himself with the other half of his army approached the other side of the city, put up ladders, descended from the wall without being noticed by the townsfolk, and rushed upon the defenders of the citadel. After a short fight, Moḥammad Ḥosein Khān-e Qaraguzlu and ᶜAbd or-Raḥim Khān, son of Taqi Khān-e Yazdi, fled to Yazd. Many of their followers were killed. The treasury fell to Loṭf ᶜAli Khān. On the following day he assumed the title "Pādeshāh," and his name was mentioned on the pulpits and put on the coins. All this occurred at the beginning of the month of Shaᶜbān of that year.[236]

ĀQĀ MOḤAMMAD KHĀN UNDERTAKES CAMPAIGN TO KERMAN. When the shah heard of this, he made up his mind to conquer Kerman and to deal with Loṭf ᶜAli Khān with the whole army. On 3d Shavvāl[237] he left Tehran. Haji Ebrāhim Khān and the nobles of Fārs, who had been summoned before, but because of heavy snow and rain and the swollen Qom River had been halted at Esfahan, joined the army of the shah during its march from Houż-e Solṭān[238] to the station Pol-e Dallāk near Qom.[239] On 22d Shavvāl[240] the royal army encamped on the pasture of Kushk-e Zard[241] in the province of Fārs. After three days it departed by way of Bavānāt to Kerman. The vanguard

236. Began on March 4, 1794.

237. May 4, 1794.

238. Situated 31 miles northeast of Qom, about 11 miles east of the modern road Qom–Tehran (now ruined).

239. About 12 miles northeast of Qom, near the junction of the Qom River and the Qara Chay River. Inundations in that region happened more than once; a breach of the dam of the Qara Chay River in the year 1883 is mentioned by Sven Hedin, *Zu Land nach Indien*, II, 181. It seems that the road west of the ancient connection between Qom and Tehran first came into use at that time.

240. May 23, 1794.

241. Located 5 parasangs northwest of Āsopās, in the valley of the Kur River, see *FNN*, II, 220 (marked on the map 1:500,000 as a ruin), and above, p. 29, note 130.

was commanded by Ḥasan ᶜAli Khān-e Qājār. When he arrived outside the city of Kerman, he was defeated by Loṭf ᶜAli Khān, who had come out of the city, and retreated to the main body. Then the shah drew near and laid siege to the city. Loṭf ᶜAli Khān, being of good cheer, displayed circumspection and perseverance in the art of defensive warfare.

And this happened: One day a gold coin, struck in the name of Loṭf ᶜAli Khān, came to the sight of the shah. His anger being aroused, he sent a fermān to Tehran to the following effect: "Fatḥollāh Khān, son of Loṭf ᶜAli Khān, the boy, who was brought from Shiraz to Tehran with his father's harem, is to be castrated!"

After four months of besieging Kerman, Loṭf ᶜAli Khān's troops were exhausted and tired from fighting, and their harmony changed to discord. One afternoon, the musketeers of the districts of Māhun and Rubdāl[242] both of which belong to Kerman, who were in charge of the defense works of one side of the city, surrendered the citadel to the Qājār army, and 3,000 infantry men entered the city. When Loṭf ᶜAli Khān heard of this, he fought bravely, killed many, and, at nightfall, drove the rest out of the city. Several days later, Najaf Qoli Khān-e Khorāsāni, an inhabitant of Kerman and one of the supporters of Loṭf ᶜAli Khān, who, with 500 musketeers, was in charge of the defense of the citadel which borders on the desert, entered into a compact with the Qājār emirs, and on Friday, the 29th Rabiᶜ I of the year 1209,[243] he surrendered the citadel; 12,000 Qājār horsemen, entering through the citadel, invaded the city of Kerman. Loṭf ᶜAli Khān with several of his followers was exposed to great danger. When he saw that there was nothing to

242. Māhān, the burial place of the famous mystic and saint Shāh Neᶜmatollāh Kermāni, lies 22 miles southeast of Kerman, on the road to Bam. Rudbāl (see Schwarz, *Iran im Mittelalter*, III, 255) or Rudbār is the region on the lower course of the Halil Rud River, southwest of Bam, see Le Strange, *Lands*, p. 315, and *Farhang*, VIII, 211.

243. October 24, 1794.

gain, he retreated, together with Jahāngir Khān-e Sistāni and his cousins and uncles, to the Solṭāniya gate and after three hours' fighting took possession of it. Waiting until nightfall, he fixed one of the planks of the bridge, dashed out of the gateway, and safely escaped. When on the next day the shah heard of Loṭf ᶜAli Khān's flight, he grew so angry that he ordered the slaughter of the inhabitants of Kerman. About 8,000 women and children were distributed as slaves among the army; all the men were either killed or deprived of their sight.[244]

Mirzā Moḥammad ᶜAli Khān, brother of Fatḥ ᶜAli Khān Malek osh-shoᶜarā with the pen name Ṣabā,[245] was scribe (monshi) in the service of Loṭf ᶜAli Khān. Once, by the order of Loṭf ᶜAli Khān, he had written a letter to the shah, in which abusive language was used. When he had been brought into the presence of the shah, he was asked: "How could you dare address a royal personage like me in such a manner?" [239] He answered: "I was in his service, whereas you were far away." The shah, losing his temper, ordered his hand to be cut off.

LOṬF ᶜALI KHĀN'S FLIGHT AND DEATH. Lotf ᶜAli Khān, in the space of twenty-four hours, dashed from Kerman to the citadel of Bam, nearly 40 parasangs away. His followers, especially, Jahāngir Khān-e Sistāni, had dispersed in all directions. When Jahāngir Khān's brothers asked about him, Loṭf ᶜAli Khān said that he would probably arrive shortly. After two days had elapsed without a trace of him, they presumed him to have been taken prisoner by the Qājār army. Moḥammad ᶜAli Khān, therefore, decided to arrest Loṭf ᶜAli Khān and send him to the shah; by rendering this service he hoped to

244. This famous sack of Kerman was the last catastrophe which befell the city. A few years later, the town was rebuilt on a smaller scale outside the ruins of the ancient city.

245. Ṣabā (d. 1238:1822/23) made his career under the Qājārs and became poet-laureate (malek osh-shoᶜarā) to Fatḥ ᶜAli Shāh, see Browne, IV, 309–10.

obtain the liberation of his brother. When the followers of Loṭf ᶜAli Khan came to know of Moḥammad ᶜAli Khān's plot, they reported this to their master. Out of pride or even fatalism, he paid no attention to their warnings. His followers being scattered in all directions, a body of Sistānis surrounded his camp and asked him to surrender. According to the poet's saying "High heaven cannot bind my hand" he rushed upon this body of men, sword in hand, and dispersed them. When he tried to mount his horse, Gharrān, which was swifter than wind and lightning, one of them stopped the horse.[246] All alone Loṭf ᶜAli Khān charged this group with the boldness of a lion and killed one of them. As they wounded him in the head and in his right hand by two strokes with the sword applied from behind, he stopped fighting. Then they seized him, bound him in chains and ropes, and sent a messenger to the Qājār camp. The next day, Jahāngir Khān-e Sistāni arrived at Bam; his brothers repented their useless action. Upon the arrival of Moḥammad Vali Khān-e Qājār Qoyunlu, Loṭf ᶜAli Khān was brought before the shah. Enraged to the utmost degree he ordered the Turkoman slaves to do what had been done by the people of Lot. Then he had him deprived of his sight and sent to Tehran. Upon his arrival he was killed according to the order. He was buried in the shrine of Emāmzāda Zeid.

The royal name was taken away from the Zand family. Their kingdom had lasted from about the year 1170[247] to the year 1208.[248] Six of them were sovereigns: Vakil od-Doula Karim Khān, Abu'l-Fatḥ Khān, Ṣādeq Khān, ᶜAli Morād Khān, Jaᶜfar Khān, and Loṭf ᶜAli Khān.

In the city of Kerman there is a famous story that a Zoroastrian astrologer had predicted the exact day of the capture of Kerman and the arrest of Loṭf ᶜAli Khān. Some days previous to

246. The author says in rhymed prose: asb-rā pey va-doulat-e Zandeya-ra tey namud ("he stopped the horse and thereby caused the downfall of the Zand dynasty").

247. 1756/57. 248. 1793/94.

the capture, Loṭf ᶜAli Khān heard of this prediction. He ordered the astrologer to be imprisoned in his house, giving him water and bread for the number of days he had foretold: If his prediction turned out to be true, he would be liberated by the Qājār army; if not, he would remain imprisoned until his death. By chance it happened exactly as he had predicted.

During the time in which Loṭf ᶜAli Khān was a prisoner of Moḥammad ᶜAli Khān-e Sistāni, he removed from his bracelet three famous jewels and forwarded them to the shah. The first of these jewels is called "Ocean of Light" (daryā-ye nur), the weight of which amounts to 8½ miskal; the second is called "Crown of the Moon" (tāj-e māh), the weight of which is estimated at 6 miskal; the third is known by the name "Akbar Shāhi," the weight of which is 4 miskal.[249] After Nāder Shah, these three jewels had come into the possession of ᶜAlam Khān-e ᶜArab.[250] By mediation of the emirs of Khorasan they were presented as a gift to Moḥammad Ḥasan Khān-e Qājār Nā'eb os-Salṭana.[251] From him they came to Karim Khān Vakil and from then on they were in the possession of the Zand dynasty up to the time when, by law of inheritance they came into the ownership of the Qājār dynasty. Heaven be praised that now they are preserved in the treasury of the Qājārs, together with some pieces which have been added since.

FATḤ ᶜALI KHĀN APPOINTED GOVERNOR OF FĀRS. After the battle of Kerman, the plundering of the city, the capture of

249. Since 1 miskal = 4.6 grams, see Hinz, *Masse und Gewichte*, p. 6, then 1 Ṣirāfi = 24 Nokhud = 1 miskal. Accordingly, the "Ocean of Light" weighed 39.1 grams, the "Crown of the Moon" 27.6 grams, and the "Akbar Shāhi" 18.4 grams.

250. Mentioned among the khāns of Khvārezm who were taken prisoner by Nāder Shāh in 1745, see Moḥammad Kāẓem *ᶜĀlam-ārā-ye Nāderi*, III, fol. 80 b (the manuscript reads "ᶜAlamd Khān," see the Index to Vol. III).

251. He was the father of Āqā Mohammad Shāh, see above, p. 2 seq.

its inhabitants, and the destruction of the citadel, the royal army marched into the province of Fārs. Marching by way of Sirjān and Niriz, they entered Shiraz at the beginning of Jomādi I of that year.[252] Previous to the siege of Kerman, Crown Prince Fatḥ ᶜAli Khān Nā'eb os-Salṭana had proceeded to Bam, Narmāshir, and Jiroft in order to conquer the southern parts of Kerman. Having subdued this region, he settled its affairs. When he received news of the capture of Kerman and the arrest of Loṭf ᶜAli Khān, he departed from Rudbār, one of the southern districts of Kerman, and marched through Rudān, Aḥmadi,[253] Sabᶜa,[254] and Lārestān. ᶜAbdollāh Khān, son of Naṣir Khān-e Lāri, governor (beglerbegi) of this district, paid homage to Crown Prince Fatḥ ᶜAli Khān and received honors. Together with the shah, the crown prince, proceeding from Lārestān, entered Shiraz.

In the month of Jomādi II of that year[255] the governorship of the provinces of Fārs, Kerman, and Yazd was conferred upon Crown Prince Fatḥ ᶜAli Shāh; he was given the title "Jahānbāni"[256] and was ordered to put up his residence in Fārs. Mirzā Naṣrollāh ᶜAliābādi Māzandarāni was appointed minister of finance of Fārs; Mirzā Jāni-ye Fasā'i, one of the most distinguished nobles of Fārs, was made counselor of the crown prince; and Haji Ebrāhim Khān, beglerbegi of the province of Fārs, was appointed grand vizier. After the pattern of the Safavids, the shah conferred upon Haji Ebrāhim the honorific title "Eᶜtemād od-Doula." He was ordered to reside at the royal court. Also,

252. Began on November 24, 1794.

253. According to *FNN*, II, 216, the two districts of Rudān and Aḥmadi had been united. The town of Rudān lies about 62 miles east-northeast of Bandar ᶜAbbās, Aḥmadi about the same distance from Bandar ᶜAbbās to the north-northeast.

254. The "Seven Districts"; they had been united under the Zand. The central place then had become Forg, about 75 miles northeast of Lār.

255. Began on December 24, 1794.

256. The same title had been bestowed upon Loṭf ᶜAli Khān-e Zand, see above, p. 28.

the shah bestowed favors of different kinds upon all the Seiyeds, learned men, distinguished persons, and renowned sheikhs of the whole province of Fārs, and assigned everybody according to his rank emoluments (waẓifa) and pay (mostamarri).

ATTEMPT TO REVIVE THE SAFAVID EMPIRE

QĀJĀR CAMPAIGN TO ARMENIA AND GEORGIA. [240] Having settled the affairs of Fārs, the shah left Shiraz for Tehran. Seeing that most of the provinces of Persia had come in his possession, he aimed at the conquest of Shirvān, Karabagh, and Georgia and decreed that all the emirs of the army, together with their troops, should assemble at the beginning of spring of that year in Tehran. According to the royal command the whole army, which numbered more than 60,000 horsemen and infantry, assembled at the court. Nobody except E^{c}temād od-Doula knew the aim of the campaign. Fifty-three days after the New Year's feast[257] he divided the army into three parts. The right wing was sent to Moghān, Shirvān, and Dāghestān, the detachments of the left wing to Erevan. He himself with the center marched to the fortress of Shushā,[258] a well-known fortress in Karabagh. The district of Karabagh lies on the banks of the Araxes River. Ebrāhim Khalil Khān-e Javānshir, ruler of the province of Karabagh, refusing obedience to the shah, had gathered a vast host from Tiflis, Darband, Dāghestān, Baku, and Shirvān, claiming independent rule. With several thousand horsemen he moved off in order to block the road to the shah. Being defeated in battle, he retreated to Shushā. Amir Soleimān Khān-e Qājār Qoyunlu and Moṣṭafā Khān-e Qājār Devehlu followed on his heels as far as the citadel of Shushā and built a bastion opposite the fortress. When the royal army arrived, the

257. May 12, 1795.

258. This famous fortified place lies about 38 miles north of the Araxes River; it had been founded after Nāder Shāh's death by the father of Ebrāhim Khalil Khān-e Javānshir, the local ruler of Karabagh, see Sarkisyanz, *Geschichte der orientalischen Völker Rußlands*, p. 154.

shah at once ordered the attack. Ebrāhim Khalil Khān, coming out of Shushā with several detachments and charging daringly in a hand-to-hand fight, suffered a defeat. On the following day the nobles of Baku surrendered and were given pardon. All the time of the siege of Shushā, which lasted from the 20th Dhu'l-Ḥejja of that year[259] to the 23d Moḥarram of the year 1210,[260] Ebrāhim Khalil Khān-e Jarānshir charged with his brave horsemen every day, was defeated, and returned to Shushā. When his vigor was exhausted, he sent a group of Javānshir tribesmen into the presence of the shah, offering to pay taxes (bāj va-kharāj) and to give hostages. The shah passed over his fault and accepted his offer.

The court then left the citadel of Shushā and encamped in the region of Ganja. The shah ordered a letter to be addressed to Erakli Khān, governor (vāli) of Tiflis and Georgia,[261] to the following effect:

> Shah Esmāᶜil Ṣafavi ruled over the province of Georgia. When in the days of the deceased king[262] we were engaged in conquering the provinces of Persia, we did not proceed to this region. As most of the provinces of Persia have come into our possession now, you must, according to ancient law, consider Georgia part of the empire and appear before our majesty. You have to confirm your obedience; then you may remain in the possession of your governorship. If you do not do this, you will be treated as the others.

Erakli Khān in his answer pointed out that he acknowledged no other rule but that of the Russian empress.[263] When the shah heard of this, he left behind a detachment for the protection of this region and proceeded in person to Tiflis, the capital of

259. July 8, 1795. 260. August 9, 1795.

261. Irakli II of Kartli and Kakhetia had recognized Russian suzerainty in 1783. He is called "vāli" in our source, because he was considered as a vassal of Persia, which the rulers of Georgia had been in Safarid times.

262. That is, Moḥammad Ḥasan Khān (d. in 1758/59), father of Āqā Moḥammad Khān.

263 That is, Catherine II (r. 1762–96).

Georgia. Several days previous to this, the left wing had been ordered to join the center of the army. In the region of Ganja, the right wing joined them, too. Although the number of the army was diminished by the detachments which had been left behind at Shushā and Erevan, its number still came to about 40,000 men. The emir of Tiflis prepared for battle 4 parasangs outside the city. By order of the shah, some detachments marched against the Georgian army, which, on being defeated, fled to the citadel of Tiflis. Upon his entering the city, Erakli Khān took his family and rode with haste to the province of Kartil and Kakhetia. The royal army entered the city and killed a group of soldiers who had been taken prisoner in battle. Several priests were bound in ropes and thrown into the river. As the winter commenced, the conquest of Kartil and Kakhetia was delayed until another time.

After nine days' stay in the city of Tiflis, the royal army marched off to Ganja. About 15,000 boys, girls, and young women were taken away from Tiflis. Javād Khān-e Qājār, governor of Ganja, and Moḥammad Khān-e Qājār Zeyādlu Erevani were received in audience and confirmed in their office. Taking into consideration the fact that the whole region had been conquered, the shah ordered winter quarters to be put up on the plain of Moghān near the confluence of the river Kura, one of the finest rivers of Georgia, and the river Araxes. During this time most of the rebels of Shirvān, Armenia and Georgia subdued. When the winter had passed, the shah marched from Moghān to Tehran and took up his residence in this city. And the governorship of Qom was conferred upon a boy of thirteen, Asadollāh Khān, son of Haji Ebrāhim Khān-e Shirāzi Eᶜtemād od-Doula.

CORONATION OF ĀQĀ MOḤAMMAD SHĀH. Notwithstanding the fact that the shah had been ruling already for some time, he had not officially put the crown on his head. He used to say: "As long as the whole population of Persia does not obey my rule, it is not becoming that I call myself king." This time, however, when he returned from the conquest of Karabagh, Shirvān, and Georgia, the nobles of the empire, seiyeds, courtiers, emirs of the army, and the nobles of Persia presented themselves at the court and submitted the following proposal: "When you refused the title of 'Shah,' it was your intention to remove the enemies and rebels from the provinces of Persia. Thank heavens all the rebels have submitted, although the province of Khorasan still remains unconquered. If you would only proceed to the threshold of the shrine of Emām Reżā, [241], that the water of the Oxus might be incorporated in the Empire!" To this he answered: "If, according to your desire, I put the crown on my head, this will cause you, in the beginning, toil and hardship, as I take no pleasure in bearing the title of king as long as I am not one of the greatest kings of Persia. This petition will not be granted but by toil and fatigue." Thereupon Haji Ebrāhim Khān E^c^temād od-Doula, the grand vizier, and the Qājār emirs and nobles of religion and state determined upon crowning him. In future nobody would withhold his money and his person from a royal decree. Then the crown of the Kayanids was put on his head and the bracelet studded with the "Ocean of Light" and the "Crown of the Moon" attached to his arm; the strings of pearls, each pearl of which was as big as a sparrow's egg and as white as camphor, hung down his back to the left and right; and the sword, which was imbued with the blessing of the shrine of Shāh Ṣafi at Ardebil, was girded round his waist. Since the time of the Safavids it was a custom to suspend the royal sword at the sepulcher of Shāh Ṣafi for one night, whilst a group of sufis, during this night, offered continual praises and intercessory prayers on behalf of the king. On the following day a banquet was given, the shah girded this sword round his waist, and distributed alms among the poor.[264]

264. The coronation took place in the spring of the year 1210:1796. A statement concerning the date by Ḥasan-e Fasā'i, in which the space provided for the insertion of the date is left blank, has been omitted in the translation.

CAMPAIGN TO KHORASAN. That same year, with an army bigger than the one the year before, the shah set out for the conquest of Khorasan. On 7th Dhu'l-Qaᶜda of that year[265] he arrived at Mashhad, having chastised on his way, at Astarābād, a group of Turkomans who had made those parts of the province the field of their plundering. The emirs whom he met on his march submitted, as they saw no opportunity of escaping the yoke of obedience. Special favors were allotted to Esḥāq Khān, governor of Torbat-e Ḥeidari.[266] When the royal army arrived in the vicinity of Mashhad, Nāder Mirzā, ruler of Khorasan, son of blind Shāhrokh Shāh, son of Reżā Qoli Mirzā, son of Nāder Shāh, fled to Afghanistan, deserting his blind father.[267] It was submitted that Mirzā Mahdi, mojtahed of Mashhad, in the company of blind Shāhrokh Shāh and Shāhrokh's son Qahhār Qoli Mirzā, was willing to welcome the victorious army. The shah ordered his nephew Ḥosein Qoli Khān to receive Shāhrokh Shāh, showing him every respect. If Mirzā Mahdi was riding in front of Shāhrokh Shāh, he should, for the prophet's pleasure, dismount and shake his hand. But if Shāhrokh Shāh came first, he should salute him on horseback upon his arrival.

When the shah was sitting in audience, he summoned Mirzā Mahdi, Shāhrokh Shāh, and Qahhār Qoli Mirzā. Shāhrokh Shāh was given permission to sit at the foot of the throne, on a chair which had been put there for royal visitors; and Mirzā Mahdi was allowed to sit down.

Then he ordered Soleimān Khān with 8,000 men to enter the city, in the company of Mirzā Mahdi, and to reassure the inhabitants. On the following day, with pious intention and in pure faith, he dismounted, and walking a distance on foot entered the city through the Kheyābānān gate; displaying signs of weakness, poverty, humility, and submissiveness, and shedding

265. May 14, 1796.
266. About 65 miles south of Mashhad.
267. Shāhrokh had been deposed and blinded in Moḥarram 1163 : December 1749; shortly after that he had returned to the throne and was finally deposed in connection with the events described by Ḥasan-e Fasā'i.

tears, he walked to the shrine and kissed the blessed soil. For a space of twenty-three days he was engaged on this sanctified soil in serving God, acting obediently, and offering prayers. During the time of his pilgrimage he served like a servant of the blessed shrine of the venerable Emām.

At that time, by order of the shah, the sepulcher of Nāder Shāh, which was adjacent to the Ḥaram,[268] was destroyed. His corpse was buried on the threshold of the Karim Khāni Convent (in Tehran), by the side of the mortal remains of Karim Khān Vakil. Several years later, by order of Fatḥ ᶜAli Shāh, the bodies of both monarchs were transferred to Najaf.

In the chronicles it is stated that in the acquisition of rank and money Āqā Moḥammad Shāh exceeded the bounds, especially in the acquisition of jewels, as has been reported under the events of the year 1209, relating to Loṭf ᶜAli Khān and the three famous jewels which Nāder Shāh had brought from India.[269] Now, during his stay in Khorasan, he took away several jewels from the emirs of Khorasan. The keeping of jewels of this kind by whomsoever he considered a great crime, declaring their possession the prerogative of the reigning monarch. As he knew that some of the jewels of Nāder Shāh were in the possession of Shāhrokh Shāh he demanded them of him. When Shāhrokh Shāh confirmed by oath that he had none, the shah ordered him to be tortured. Having suffered great torments, he produced some jewels, which were fetched from a garden wall or from the bottom of a well. They went so far as to put a ring of paste on his head and poured melted butter on it. Then he produced a large hyacinth which had been a sparkling jewel of the crown of Aurangzeb, king of India.[270] When the shah heard of that hyacinth he ordered his men to stop tormenting Shāhrokh, saying that he had attained his aim. Then he sent Shāhrokh Shāh

268. That is, the enclosure of the sanctuary.
269. See above, p. 63.
270. Moghul emperor of India, r. 1658–1707.

with his whole family from Khorasan to Māzandarān, assigning them a domicile in that region. When they arrived at Dāmghān, Shāhrokh Shāh died; he was sixty-three years old. The shah took women and sons as hostages from all the emirs of Khorasan and sent them to Tehran.

RUSSIAN INTERVENTION IN GEORGIA. When the shah was about to invade [242] the regions of Balkh and Bokhara, letters arrived from the emirs of Ādherbāyjān to the following effect: "The Empress of Russia, Catherine II, wife of Peter III, is said to have become very angry and to have sworn vengeance when she heard of the slaughter and capture of the Georgians and the plundering of their country, as the Georgians considered themselves to be living under the protection of the Russian empire for a long time. The Russian empress is said to have ordered 40,000 foot soldiers and 22,000 horsemen and 100 cannons under the command of Qizil Ayāgh to invade Persia, marching from the region of Darband. (Qizil Ayāgh is a Turkish word meaning *gold leg*. Because his leg had been smashed by a cannon ball, they had made him a leg of pure gold, and thenceforward he was called by this name.[271]) The people of Baku, Sāleyān, and Ṭālesh,[272] out of fear of Qizil Ayāgh, have submitted. A detachment from Shirvān and Ganja has been defeated." When Āqā Moḥammad Shāh heard of this, he was extremely annoyed. Having left behind Moḥammad Vali Khān-e Qājār with 10,000 horsemen to settle the affairs of Khorasan and having appointed Fatḥ ᶜAli Khān-e Kotvāl as protector of Mashhad, entrusting to him the renovation of the shrine of Emām Reżā and the tax collection (*nimethāl-e divānkhāh-e*), Āqā Moḥammad Shāh

271. The general in question was Valerian Zubov, brother of Platon Zubov, the favorite of Catherine II. He captured Darband in 1796, later in the summer Baku, Shamākhi, and Ganja and was recalled after Catherine's death in November, 1796, see Lang, *The Last Years of the Georgian Monarchy*, pp. 221–23.

272. Sāleyān is the region on the estuary of the Araxes River, south of Baku, Ṭālesh the region adjoining to the south.

hurried to Tehran. Royal decrees were issued and dispatched to the provinces to the effect that the commanders of the army in the spring of that year should assemble in Tehran, fully equipped, for the invasion of Ādherbāyjān and the attack upon the Russian army. Fatḥ ᶜAli Khān Nā'eb os-Salṭana Jahānbāni, governor of the province of Fārs, was summoned, too, together with the nobles of the province. After much admonition and advice, the shah summoned the emirs of the army and the nobles of the country and appointed Fatḥ ᶜAli Khān anew his crown prince and deputy,[273] recommending him to be kind and gentle toward the whole population of the empire and exhorting the army and the people to accord him obedience and devotion.

THE MURDER OF ĀQĀ MOḤAMMAD SHĀH. The New Year fell on the 23d Ramażān of the year 1211.[274] A most remarkable story about the horoscope is told: The astrologer Mirzā Ḥasan, being asked by the shah what the ascendant of that year indicated, answered: "Prosperity for the country and peace for its inhabitants." The shah, looking at the crown prince, said: "Bābā Khān,[275] the astrologer Mirzā Ḥasan announces the death of your uncle, for as long as he lives, nobody will enjoy welfare and peace!" And it happened as had been predicted.

In the month of Dhu'l-Ḥejja of that year[276] the shah departed for Ādherbāyjān, Karabagh, Shirvān, and Georgia. After five-days' stay on the pasture of Solṭāniya news arrived of the death of Catherine II[277] and the withdrawal of Qizil Ayāgh. As during the last campaign the question of the governorship of Karabagh and Shushā had not been settled and Ebrāhim Khalil Khān, governor of that region, had not submitted, the shah considered

273. It is very likely that the bestowal of the title "Jahānbāni" was Fatḥ ᶜAli Khān's first appointment as crown prince, see above, p. 64.

274. March 21, 1797.

275. For this name of Fatḥ ᶜAli Khān, see above, p. 4 seq.

276. Began on May 28, 1797.

277. She died on November 17, 1796. News of her death arrived in Persia six months later!

it expedient to conquer the city of Shushā first and then settle the affairs of the province of Georgia. Therefore he marched by way of Meyāna and Ardebil to Ādinabāzār[278] and put up his camp there. An envoy arrived from the nobles of Shushā submitting the following petition: "As we are convinced that Ebrāhim Khalil Khān was planning evil against the Persian empire, we had the intention of rebelling and putting him in prison. Now he has taken his family and fled from Shushā to Dāghestān. Therefore we beseech you to come to us and to occupy the city of Shushā." Accordingly the shah left the main body of the army and Ḥosein Qoli Khān, brother of the crown prince, and the princes ᶜAbbās Mirzā, Ḥosein ᶜAli Mirzā, and Moḥammad Qoli Mirzā, sons of the crown prince, at Ādinabāzār, putting them under the command of Haji Ebrāhim Khān Eᶜtemād od-Doula and Amir-e Kabir Soleimān Khān-e Qājār. Taking with himself 5,000 horsemen and 3,000 footmen, he departed for Shushā. When he came to the river Araxes and found it swollen high with water, he ordered the horsemen to ride through the river, whereas the footmen were ordered to cross the river by means of several leaky boats and inflated sheepskins; many of them drowned. Then the army entered Shushā. Three days later a quarrel arose between a Georgian servant named Ṣādeq and the valet Khodādād-e Esfahani. They raised their voices to such a pitch that the shah became angry and ordered both to be executed. Ṣādeq Khān-e Shaqāqi, a prominent emir, interceded on their behalf, but was not listened to. The shah, however, ordered their execution to be postponed until Saturday, as this happened to be the evening of Friday, and allowed them to go back to their duties in the royal pavilion, unfettered and unchained. From experience, however, they knew that he would

278. A "River of Adinabazār" is mentioned in the peace treaty of Torkmānchāy, see Hurewitz, I, 97. According to the context, the "small river of Odinabazar" seems to be identical with the upper course of the Bolgar Chay, the source of which lies about 50 miles north of Ardebil.

keep to what he had ordered, and, having no hope, they turned to boldness. When the shah was sleeping, they were joined by the valet ᶜAbbās-e Māzandarāni, who was in the plot with them, and the three invaded the royal pavilion and with dagger and knife murdered the shah.[279]

The murderers took away the box of jewels, the bracelet studded with diamonds, the sword studded with jewels, and the jewels called "Ocean of Light" and "Crown of the Moon" and sent them to Ṣādeq Khan-e Shaqāqi. All these precious objects in his possession, he put the murderers of the shah under his protection, and the same night, taking along his followers, he left Shushā and marched to Tabriz.

This dreadful act took place in the night of 21st Dhu'l-Ḥejja of that year.[280] The chronogram [243] was found in these words: "tārikh-e in shahādat" ("the date of this martyrdom").[281] This monarch reached the age of fifty-six. All his life he had honored the injunctions of the Sharia. As long as he lived he performed his prayers at the time prescribed, and each midnight, though he had passed the day in toil and exertion, he rose to offer a prayer. He did not postpone the chastisement of evildoers and the punishment of criminals. He chastised the governors of the provinces and the nobles of the army when they transgressed the fundaments of the law. As he had seen the fruit of the disunity of the Afshār and Zand, he endeavored to destroy the Qājār tribes, and, on the other hand, to win them over; he discarded some, such as his brothers, and bestowed favors upon others, the crown prince and Amir-e Kabir Soleimān Khān.[282] He did not like exaggeration and flattery and forbade

279. The author adds that Āqā Moḥammad Shāh was born in 1155: 1742/43.

280. June 17, 1797.

281. The assassination is called a "martyrdom" (shahādat), because the shah was waging the Holy War. According to Moslem belief everybody who is killed in the Holy War is a martyr. In this case one should also take into consideration the fact that one of the murderers was a Georgian, a nonbeliever.

282. He was a nephew of Āqā Moḥammad Shāh's mother, see above, p. 3.

the use of honorific titles in the decrees. He approved of writing succinctly. When a poor man or an indigent soldier wanted to submit a petition, he could do it without mediator. Without explicit decree of the shah, no emir of the army and no vizier had any authority. He used to wear simple dress without ornaments. When traveling or hunting he would sit on the floor with the emirs of the army and eat what was at hand.

At daybreak news of the murder of the shah spread among the army. As they had no means of transporting the corpse, they left it behind and dispersed. Moḥammad Ḥosein Khān-e Qājār, the chamberlain, known by the name of Dudāgh, and Mirzā Reżā Qoli Navā'i, chancellor of the empire (monshi ol-mamālek), gathered as much equipment as they could and marched off to Tehran. The people of Shushā plundered the camp and took from the royal household (boyutāt) and the luggage of the emirs and soldiers what they found. The ulema of Shushā, taking care to bury the shah according to the laws of the Sharia, performed the burial rites and committed him to earth provisionally at a fitting place.

When news of the occurrence reached the main body of the army at Ādinabāzār, the emirs abandoned the heavy baggage and went their way. The princes ᶜAbbās Mirzā, Ḥosein ᶜAli Mirzā, Moḥammad Qoli Mirzā, and Ḥosein Qoli Khān, brother of the crown prince, went to Tehran by way of Rasht. Haji Ebrāhim Khān Eᶜtemād od-Doula, with the horsemen from Fārs and the musketeers from Māzandarān, marched to Tehran by way of Ardebil and Zenjān.

ᶜAli Qoli Khān, brother of the murdered shah, was very eager to become king. With great haste he established himself in the fortress of ᶜAli Shāh, 6 parasangs from Tehran.[283] The royal princes and Haji Ebrāhim Khān by chance met at Qazvin. On the advice of Haji Ebrāhim they waited some days, so that

283. Probably the same as ᶜAli Shāh ᶜEvaż, on the Karaj River, about 19 miles west of Tehran, see *Farhang*, I, 143.

the scattered army might assemble. In full order they drew up in the plain of Dulāb in the vicinity of Tehran.[284] Mirzā Moḥammad Khān-e Qājār Devehlu, who by order of the murdered shah was in charge of the defense of the city of Tehran, shut the gates to all emirs, and awaited, in the citadel of Tehran the arrival of Crown Prince Fatḥ ᶜAli Khān.

284. East of Tehran, from which one of the eastern gates of the city has its name.

CHAPTER 2

Fatḥ ᶜAli Shāh

THE CONSOLIDATION OF POWER

THE CROWN PRINCE GOES FROM SHIRAZ TO TEHRAN. When the unfortunate murder of the shah had taken place, the courier Bābā Yusuf, who on foot was quicker than lightning and swifter than the wind, departed from the citadel of Shushā, the distance of which from Shiraz is about 250 parasangs,[1] and arrived at Shiraz on 2d Moḥarram of the year 1212.[2] He informed the crown prince of what had happened. When Fatḥ ᶜAli Khān heard the sad story, he recited the verse of the Koran: "We belong to God and to Him we return."[3] Having summoned the nobles he informed them of the deed. He dispatched orders and decrees to the provinces of the empire and the governors that they should assemble at a fixed date in the capital Tehran and not venture to rise in revolt or attempt to seize power. Then he spent three days and three nights in mourning. After this he entrusted authority over Fārs to Moḥammad ᶜAli Mirzā, his eldest son, who was a boy of nine years and staying at his father's court. The vizierate remained, as before, with Mirzā Naṣrollāh-e ᶜAliābādi Māzandarāni. The experienced emirs, like Mirzā Jāni-ye Fasā'i and Āqā Moḥammad Zamān, lord mayor of Shiraz, in the service of the crown prince, were ordered to accompany him (to Tehran). At the end of the month of Moḥarram of that year the crown prince departed from Shiraz. Passing by the sepulcher of Ḥāfeẓ, he asked for the poet's Divan. Having opened the book for an omen his glance fell upon those two verses at the head of the right-hand leaf: "When during prayer I remembered your beauty, I became so excited that the

1. About 780 miles as the crow flies.
2. June, 27, 1797. 3. Koran II, 156.

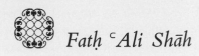

Meḥrāb started shouting: Oh bride of victory, do not complain about fate. Adorn the nuptial chamber of beauty, for, behold, the bridegroom is coming." Then he asked the spirit of the poet for good auspices and departed for Tehran. At the station of Kanāra Gerd, 6 parasangs from Tehran,[4] Ḥosein Qoli Khān and Haji Ebrāhim E^c^temād od-Doula and the other emirs joined him. They put forward that ^c^Ali Qoli Khān, brother of the deceased Āqā Moḥammad Shāh, had not attended to the latter's last will and testament and put no trust in the regulation of the succession; that rising in rebellion, he considered himself owner of crown and throne by the law of inheritance. Thereupon the crown prince sent Ḥosein Qoli Khān together with several other persons to his uncle, bidding him to proceed to Tehran so that they might settle the dispute about the throne. On 20th Ṣafar of that year[5] he established himself in Tehran. Several days later ^c^Ali Qoli Khān entered the city with pretension to the throne. After encountering the shah, he was deprived of his sight and sent to Māzandarān, to abide in the town of Bārforush.

CAMPAIGN TO SUBDUE REBELS IN ĀDHERBĀYJĀN. As has been reported after the frightful murder of the shah, the royal jewels were handed over to Ṣādeq Khān-e Shaqāqi. He was under the impression that possession of the jewels conferred the crown upon him. Gathering part of the scattered troops of Shushā, he rose in rebellion and subdued most of the province of Ādherbāyjān. In previous years his family had been sent as hostages to Qazvin, so he left Ādherbāyjān to conquer [244] Qazvin and liberate his family. The inhabitants of Qazvin, offering resistance, shut the gates and defended themselves bravely. Submitting petition after petition to the shah they asked for assistance. Accordingly, Ḥosein Khān-e Qājār Qazvini,

4. About 21 miles southwest of Shahr Reiy, 1 mile east of the modern road to Qom, see *Farhang*, I, 184.

5. August 15, 1797.

commander of the pages (qollar aqasi), out of loyalty to the people of Qazvin, marched off, and Moḥammad Vali Khān-e Qājār, who by order of the deceased shah had been put in charge of the protection of Khorasan,[6] arrived with 6,000 horsemen. The shah then decided to proceed to Qazvin himself. From the surroundings of Qazvin, Ṣādeq Khān marched against the royal army. They met at the station of Khāk-e ᶜAli in the region of Qazvin,[7] and both sides prepared for battle. While attacking each other, they raised a clamor as if it were the Day of the Last Judgment. Eventually the army of the shah carried the day. Nearly 20,000 men of Ṣādeq Khān's army were either killed or taken prisoner, the rest escaped. From the battlefield the royal army entered the town.

ḤOSEIN QOLI KHĀN, BROTHER OF FATḤ ᶜALI SHAH, APPOINTED GOVERNOR OF FĀRS. As Ḥosein Qoli Khān had displayed extraordinary courage in this battle, favors were bestowed upon him and he was appointed governor of the province of Fārs. Moḥammad ᶜAli Mirzā, then governor of Fārs, was summoned to the court, whereas Mirzā Naṣrollāh-e ᶜAliābādi remained in his office as vizier of Fārs. Jān Moḥammad Khān was dispatched to settle affairs in the region of Lārestān. At the end of Rabiᶜ I of that year[8] Ḥosein Qoli Khān entered Shiraz.

PUNISHMENT OF ĀQĀ MOḤAMMAD SHĀH'S MURDERERS. It was at this time that the Georgian Ṣādeq and Khodādād-e Esfahani, who both had committed the crime of murdering the shah, were brought into the presence of the shah and sentence was passed. One of them was cut to pieces with the sword by Ḥosein Qoli Khān, the other one fell victim to the executioner,

6. See above, p. 71.

7. About 23 miles north of Ābik, which lies 34 miles east of Qazvin, see *Farhang*, I, 77.

8. About September 20, 1797.

who cut off his extremities piece by piece. ᶜAbbās-e Māzandarāni, the third of the murderers, was caught near Kermānshāh and brought to Tehran. He was put to the stake.

BURIAL OF ĀQĀ MOḤAMMAD SHĀH AT NAJAF. From Qazvin the shah departed for Ādherbāyjān to settle affairs there. Upon his arrival at Zenjān he was informed that a plague had broken out in Ādherbāyjān. Therefore he stayed for some time at Zenjān appointing emirs to the governorship of each district of Ādherbāyjān. As for Ṣādeq Khān-e Shaqāqi, a royal order was issued to the effect that if he would deliver the jewels which the Georgian Ṣādeq and Khodādād-e Esfahani had handed over to him at Shushā, he would be pardoned. The fermān was dispatched with Ebrāhim Khān-e Qājār. Upon his arrival, Ṣādeq Khān embraced the opportunity to hand over all the jewels to Ebrāhim Khān. He was pardoned and appointed governor of Sarāb and Garmrud in the province of Ādherbāyjān.[9] Ḥosein Qoli Khān-e Qājār ᶜEzz od-Dinlu was sent to Shushā to transfer the corpse of the murdered shah, and Ebrāhim Khalil Khān-e Javānshir was ordered by a royal fermān to put the corpse of the shah on a litter and arrange the transfer with the honors due a king. In the month of Jomādi II of that year[10] the shah took up his residence in Tehran. Ḥosein Qoli Khān transferred the corpse of the murdered shah to the shrine of ᶜAbd ol-ᶜAzim (near Tehran). Having passed one week in mourning, the shah ordered Moḥammed ᶜAli Khān-e Qājār with 2,000 horsemen and 10,000 miskal minted gold to transfer the corpse to Najaf, accompanied by the theologian Moṣṭafā Qomesha'i and the chief astrologer, Mirzā Musā. When they were near Baghdad, Soleimān Pasha, governor of Baghdad, came out of the city to meet them and to do homage to the deceased. Then the corpse was brought to Najaf and committed to earth.

9. Garm Rud is the region round Meyāna, see Le Strange, *Lands*, p. 170; Sarāb lies about 37 miles north of Meyāna.

10. Began on November 21, 1797.

CORONATION OF FATḤ ᶜALI SHĀH. On the New Year's feast, which coincided with the ᶜId ol-Fiṭr,[11] the shah put the crown (kolāh-e kayāni) on his head and ascended the throne. He promised the people justice and benevolence and remitted to the landowners of the provinces of the empire tax-arrears in the amount of about 500,000 toman, which corresponds to 1 crore. Fatḥ ᶜAli Khān from Kāshān, with the pen name Ṣabā, composed the following chronogram on the date of the shah's ascending the throne: "Az takht Āqā Moḥammad Khān shod va-neshest Bābā Khān" ("Āqā Moḥammad Khān left the throne and Bābā Khān ascended the throne"). Bābā Khān had been the name of the ruler before his appointment as crown prince. Farhād Mirzā, son of Crown Prince ᶜAbbās Mirzā, son of Fatḥ ᶜAli Shāh, also found the word *Bābā* for the date of the enthronement: if one writes the numerical values of those four characters in the sequence used in geometry, one comes to the figure 1212.

The governorship of Kuh-i Giluya was conferred upon Moḥammad Ḥosein Khān, brother of Haji Ebrāhim Khān.

THE ROYAL COURT AT SOLṬĀNIYA; REBELLION OF ḤOSEIN QOLI KHĀN. On 18th Dhū'l-Ḥejja of that year,[12] the court left Tehran in order to chastise the rebels of Ādherbāyjān and encamped for several days on the pasture of Solṭāniya. Since the rebels of Ādherbāyjān were unable to offer resistance, Ṣādeq Khān hurriedly employed the mediation of Amir-e Kabir Soleimān Khān. The shah, accordingly, pardoned him and bestowed favors upon him; and Jaᶜfar Qoli Khān-e Dombali [another chief of the rebels], having no success, moved off to Turkey. Thereupon the court left Solṭāniya; after marching through Marāgha and Salduz they encamped, on 6th Moḥarram of the year 1213,[13] outside the town of Urmiya; on the 17th of that month they moved to Khoy. After several days of enjoyment and pleasure news arrived of the revolt of Ḥosein Qoli Khān, governor of the province of Fārs.

11. March 21, 1798. 12. June 3, 1798. 13. June 20, 1798.

The late Mirzā Fażlollāh-e Khāveri-ye Shirāzi, in his *Tārikh-e Dhu'l-Qarnein*, writes:

Although the shah and Ḥosein Qoli Khān outwardly were offsprings of the same parents, inwardly they differed as much as east differs from west, owing to the dissimilarity of their characters. The one was guided by pure and lucid reason, the other by sheer ignorance. The one was intoxicated with the drink of tyranny, the other maintained law and justice. The one was a jewel of divine mercy, the other a mark of God's eternal wrath. The one had in his possession the signet ring of fortune, the other that of misfortune. Though they had the same parents, their characters were totally different, just as a mixture of honey [245] and colocynth is composed of completely different substances.

The detailed story of Ḥosein Qoli Khān's revolt runs as follows: The royal decree with his appointment to the governorship of Fārs having been issued, he left Qazvin, and arrived at Shiraz at the end of Rabiᶜ I of the year 1212.[14] For the period of several months he treated the emirs and nobles with courtesy, but then he began to display unfriendliness toward the governors of the districts (bolukāt). By bringing a charge against each of them, he gained much money, and having become enormously wealthy, he turned rebellious. Some people from among the rabble led him astray, and he deviated from the path of obedience. Realizing that Mirzā Naṣrollāh-e ᶜAliābādi-ye Māzandarāni, the minister of finance, and Mirzā Jāni-ye Fasā'i, uncle of the author of this book and one of the industrious courtiers, and in charge, moreover, of most of the administrative affairs of Fārs, and Āqā Moḥammad Zamān, the lord mayor and brother of Prime Minister Haji Ebrāhim, and several other people were disturbing his plans, he put them all in fetters and imprisoned them. Mirzā Naṣrollāh, Āqā Moḥammad Zamān, Mirzā Esmāᶜil Shirazi-e Kotvāl, Aḥmad Khān, and Āqā Moḥsen, all of them adherents of the prime minister, were deprived of their sight. The houses of Mirzā Jāni and Āqā Moḥammad and their

14. About September 20, 1797.

families were put under custody. Mirzā Jāni, being forced to eat poisoned food, died. When his corpse was brought from the Vakili palace to the shrine of Shāh Charāgh, some of his family and relatives came out of his house, which lies halfway between the two, and joined the funeral procession. Having entered the shrine they established themselves inside. Ḥosein Qoli Khān ordered a group of people to cut off provisions from this family of seiyeds. One day and one night passed; the imam of the Friday prayers of the province of Fārs, the most reverend Sheikh Moḥammad Mofid, came to their aid, brought them to his house, and ministered to their needs.

Ḥosein Qoli Khān sent a group to arrest Jān Moḥammad Khān, who by order of the shah had been sent to Lārestān to settle affairs in this district. Hearing of his forthcoming arrest he fled to (Persian) ᶜErāq. Then Ḥosein Qoli Khān appointed administrative officers (ᶜāmel) to each district and exercised his despotic rule without mercy. Upon Āqā Maᶜṣum-e Kheżri he bestowed the title "Khān," appointed him to the governorship of Fasā and entrusted upon him the destruction of the possessions of Mirzā Jāni. After his arrival at Fasā he obstructed all the irrigation canals (qanavāt) of the district of Fasā and pulled down the fortresses. The inhabitants were fined and banished, and Āqā Maᶜṣūm lived in the ruins of the destroyed villages like an owl.

When Ḥosein Qoli Khān saw that everything went according to his wishes, he entrusted the city of Shiraz to Rostam Khān-e Bayyāt, one of his confidants, and put up the standard of rebellion against his brother. At the end of Moḥarram of that year[15] he marched from Shiraz to Esfahan. When the shah heard of this, he entrusted the governorship of Ādherbāyjān to Soleimān Khān-e Qājār Qoyonlu and proceeded to ᶜErāq in order to discipline his insane brother. At Esfahan Ḥosein Qoli Khān was engaged in collecting taxes from the merchants and dealers of that region and storing supplies for his revolt. Thence he marched

15. About July 10, 1798.

to Farāhān,[16] and several thousand soldiers from (Persian) ᶜErāq and Esfahan joined him. In his camp at Darjazzin near Hamadān[17] the shah heard of Ḥosein Qoli Khān's arrival at Farāhān and gave orders to march off without delay. Encamping at Sāruq,[18] which belongs to Farāhān, he stayed there for three days and arranged his troops. Then the queen mother arrived, and it came to be known, upon news of the revolt of Ḥosein Qoli Khān, that she had tried to persuade him by sending appropriate letters and messengers to desist from his unlawful rebellion; that, when this had no effect, she got into a camel litter and traveled to her son and met him in the camp of Chāl-e Seyāh;[19] that she had given him good advice, which, however, turned out to be of no use; and that she had had no other choice than to proceed to the camp of the shah. Then she tried to mediate between her two sons: that the temerity of Ḥosein Qoli Khān should not be understood as open revolt; rather the revenues of Fārs were not sufficient to meet the expenses. If the shah considered this affair with brotherly love, he should incorporate the province of Kerman into that of Fārs; having done this, his brother would have no more reason to complain. Out of respect for his mother the shah agreed. When Ḥosein Qoli Khān heard of this proposal, he demanded the governorship of Esfahan, too. Eventually, he accepted the proposal of the queen mother, but then raised new demands. Realizing that the injudicious appetite of his brother could not be restricted except by the sword, the shah entrusted the camp of Sāruq to the prime minister, Haji Ebrāhim, and marched with several thousand experienced soldiers to give

16. Farāhān, now belonging to the shahrestān of Arāk (the former Solṭānābād), lies north of Arāk, see *Farhang*, II. 198.

17. About 55 miles northeast of Hamadān, 3.5 miles east of the road Razan-Hamadān, see *Farhang*, V, 174 (on the 1:500,000 map: Daryazin).

18. A small village about 23 miles northwest of Arāk/Solṭānābād.

19. The 1:500,000 map shows the village of Shāh-e Seyāh about 22 miles northwest of Esfahan; however, the text reads clearly Chāl-e Seyāh (unknown to the *Farhang*), see also above, p. 21, note 35.

battle at Farāhān. Two parasangs from the camp of Ḥosein Qoli Khān he made a halt, and on 28th Ṣafar of that year[20] he drew up his army on the plain of Kamara.[21] As a last resort he sent the chief astrologer, Mirzā Musā Gilāni, to Ḥosein Qoli Khān with a letter containing messages of promise and threat meant to arouse fear and hope. When the chief astrologer arrived, Ḥosein Qoli Khān advanced some steps to meet him. Having heard the courteous message, he quoted [246] those two verses by Ḥāfeẓ: "I thank God that all I have solicited Him for I have luckily received for attaining my end." Then he stepped out of the battle order to negotiate. Upon his arrival in the middle of the square he dismounted. Shedding tears he advanced toward the shah. The shah stretched out his hands in brotherly love and embraced him, both weeping about the misfortune of the time. Then the shah took Ḥosein Qoli Khān by his hand and escorted him from the field of fight to the field of delight, quoting the verse of the Holy Koran: "There is no reproof against you this day."[22] Both armies returned to their camp, and the next day both armies, from ᶜErāq and Fārs, broke up and joined the royal army.

The author of this book was told by some old people from Shiraz that Ḥosein Qoli Khān's reason for submitting to the shah had been his fear of the emirs of his army. Haji Ebrāhim Khān Eᶜtemād od-Doula had contrived a plan and attained his aim by sending a man as a messenger to the emirs of Ḥosein Qoli Khān's army, bearing several letters sealed with the signet ring, to the following effect: "I have submitted your request to the shah, reminding him of your former services. He attested to your faithful loyalty, but does not consider it befitting to attack the camp. The best you can do is that as soon as the army is arranged

20. August 11, 1798.

21. A district about 25 miles southeast of Arāk/Solṭānābād, see the map in *Farhang-e Irān Zamin* 14 (1966–67), facing p. 364.

22. Koran XII, 92.

for battle, you push on faster than the others; prostrating yourself at the hooves of the shah's horse, you will be pardoned." Then the letters were wrapped in linen, coated with wax, and sewn in the soles of the messenger's shoes. He was instructed that after his arrival at Ḥosein Qoli Khān's camp he should behave like a thief or spy, mingling with the crowd in the enclosure of the leader's pavilion and sleeping in the corners of the different tents. The man arrived at the camp and behaved as he had been ordered. One of the servants of Ḥosein Qoli Khān, perceiving his intention, arrested him. After some torture the letters came to light and, without being opened, were brought to Hosein Qoli Khān. Having read them he realized that he was alone and that there was no remedy but to act as he eventually did.

APPOINTMENTS AND PROMOTIONS; TWO PALACES ARE BUILT. The governorship of the province of Fārs was conferred upon Moḥammad ᶜAli Khān-e Qājār Qoyonlu, known by the name of Khālu;[23] and Mirzā Moḥammad Khān, eldest son of Haji Ebrāhim Khān, was appointed tax collector of this province. The settling of the affairs of Kuh-i Giluya was entrusted to Nouruz Khān-e Qājār ᶜEzz od-Dinlu. On 11th Rabiᶜ I of that year[24] the shah departed for Tehran. Ḥosein Qoli Khān was appointed governor of Semnān.

It was in that year that Mirzā Hādi, whose illustrious father, Mirzā Jāni-ye Fasā'i, had been poisoned by Ḥosein Qoli Khān, according to a royal decree presented himself at the court in Tehran. Upon his arrival his wounds were healed by royal favors and he was confirmed in the functions of his father, the governorship of the districts of Fārs, as: Huma-ye Shiraz, Kuh-e Marra, Seyākh, Kavār, Khvāja, Firuzābād, Ṣimekān, Khafr, Juyom and Bidshehr, Dārāb, Niriz, and Eṣṭahbānāt.[25] The pen-

23. *Khālu* means "maternal uncle." 24. August 23, 1798.

25. Huma-ye Shiraz is the district around the city of Shiraz. The capital of Kuh-e Marra is Shikoft, 32 miles southwest of Shiraz, see *FNN*, II, 280. Dārenjān-e Khvāja (*FNN*), the center of Seyākh, lies 34 miles southwest

sions (vaẓāyef) and emoluments of his family were confirmed and increased. The district of Kamin[26] remained fief (tiyul) in his and his brother's possession as before, and he was given splendid robes of honor. As the shah during his stay in the province of Fārs had been on confidential terms with Mirzā Hādi and had honored him by addressing him "companion" (rafiq), he continued to address him in this manner now that the whole of Persia was under his sway. After four-months' stay at the court in Tehran Mirzā Hādi returned to Shiraz.

The same year about 100,000 toman from the treasury were sent to Qom for the renovation of the shrine and the buildings of the sanctuary of Emāmzāda Fāṭema.

And that year, by royal orders, two palaces were built, both of them known by the name "Takht-e Qājār," one of them half a parasang north of Tehran,[27] the other a quarter of a parasang

---

of Shiraz, *FNN*, II, 224. Kavār, the center of the district (boluk) likewise called Kavār, lies 37 miles south-southeast of Shiraz, *FNN*, II, 262. The center of Khvāja is Zanjirān, 16 miles north of Firuzābād, on the western slope of the Kuh-e Safid, *FNN*, II, 198. Firuzābād lies 60 miles south of Shiraz, in the vicinity of the Kuh-e Meimand. Ṣimekān is the valley of the Ṣimekān River, a western tributary of the Mānd Rud, west of Jahrom, between the Kuh-e Sim in the northeast and the Kuh-e Meimand in the southwest, *FNN*, II, 225. Juyom and Bidshehr are two districts southeast of Jahrom, *FNN*, 66, 181. Eṣṭahbānāt lies west of Niriz. Khafr is a district which lies to the north of the district of Ṣimekān, its center, Khafr, lies about 65 miles southeast of Shiraz, *FNN*, II, 196 seq., and *Farhang*, VII, 89. Accordingly, Mirzā Hādi was governor of 15 of the 64 districts (bolukāt) of Fārs (including the district of Kamin, mentioned below); moreover, the 15 districts formed the central part of the province.

26. The region on the banks of the Polvār River, northwest of Persepolis, see *FNN*, II, 260. The special position of this district with regard to Mirzā Hādi is underlined by the fact that it was isolated from the other districts, which formed a nearly continuous stretch of land from Dārāb in the east to Shikoft in the west.

27. A description of this palace which is "entièrement bati de briques et très-inférieur aux constructions des siècles précédents" is given by Dubeux, *La Perse*, p. 14. See also Curzon, *Persia and the Persian Question*, I, 340 seq.

north of Shiraz.[28] Both are situated on top of a hill, and both contain many agreeable lodgings. In the enclosures gardens were laid out, which within a short time were flourishing with different kinds of trees. The produce of the garden of Takht-e Qājār at Shiraz is 1,250 mann of wheat at the weight of 720 miskal-e Ṣirāfi.[29] According to the technical terminology of the people of Shiraz this corresponds to 100 peimān of soil. As has been reported, Amir Atābeg-e Qarācha, vizier of the Saljuqids and governor of Fārs and Khuzestān, about the year of the hegira 520,[30] had some houses built on the top of this hill. He had the water conducted from far away and brought to the top of this hill, and accordingly it was called "Takht-e Qarācha."[31] It remained under cultivation for years and is still called by this name even now, though no trace of the cultivation is left.

ᶜABBĀS MIRZĀ APPOINTED CROWN PRINCE. The New Year fell on 13th Shavvāl of that year.[32] Having completed the celebration of the feast, the shah, according to the last will and

28. It was the site of an older construction before the Saᶜāda gate of Shiraz, in the direction of Yazd, see Le Strange, *Lands*, p. 251.

29. On the basis of 1 miskal-e Ṣirāfi = 4.6 grams (see Hinz, *Masse und Gewichte*, p. 6), 1 mann would be the equivalent of 3.312 kilograms. According to Hinz, l. c., p. 19, the mann-e Tabrizi weighed 3.175 kilograms in the year 1802, whereas the mann-e Shirazi was 3.328 kilograms as early as the tenth century, l. c., p. 17. Supposing 1 mann to be 3.312 kilograms, the yield of the garden amounted to 4,140 kilograms per peimān.

30. 520:1126/27.

31. See *FNN*, I, 28, under the year 526:1131/32: "The Atābeg Qarācha built the Madrasa-ye Qarācha at Shiraz, which is mentioned in the chronicles; of this madrasa no trace is left. Furthermore, he built the palace (ᶜemārat) of Takht-e Qarācha 1 mile north of Shiraz, which now is known as the Takht-e Qājār after being renovated in the year 1208:1793/94 by order of Āqā Moḥammad Shāh. Another of the atābeg's projects is the irrigation-canal at Kāzerun called Qanāt-e Qarācha." Āqā Moḥammad Shāh visited Shiraz in 1209:1794/95, see above, p. 55, where, however, nothing is mentioned of the renovation of the palace.

32. March 20, 1799 (should be March 21).

testament of the murdered Āqā Moḥammad Shāh, appointed ᶜAbbās Mirzā crown prince and deputy (nā'eb os-salṭana), as he was the highest ranking of his brothers on account of his mother.[33] He was given the robe of honor, due the crown prince, which consists of coat, sword, girdle, and dagger studded with jewels. All the princes, emirs, and nobles of the empire offered their congratulations and felicitations. Then Amir-e Kabir Soleimān Khān-e Qājār and Seiyed Mirzā ᶜAli, known by the name Mirzā ᶜIsā-ye Farāhāni, who had been brought up at Shiraz in the service of his maternal uncle Mirzā Ḥosein-e Farāhāni, with the pen name Vafā, vizier of the deceased Karim Khān-e Zand, were appointed adjutants of the crown prince, and the governorship and the vizierate of the province of Ādherbāyjān were conferred upon them.

THE CONQUEST OF KHORASAN

FIRST CAMPAIGN TO KHORASAN. [247] As has been reported, in 1210 Nāder Mirzā Nāderi had hastened to Herāt when Āqā Moḥammad Shāh was marching to Khorasan.[34] After the death of the shah, when Moḥammad Vali Khān-e Qājār, commander in chief (sepahsālār) of Khorasan, had departed from Mashhad for Tehran, Nāder Mirzā went from Herāt to Mashhad without being disturbed by anybody. The inhabitants of Mashhad accepted his authority. Having completed the organization of the Persian empire with the exception of Khorasan, Fatḥ ᶜAli Shah mobilized his army and departed from Tehran on 15th Dhu'l-Ḥejja[35] of that year. Haji Ebrāhim Khān Eᶜtemād od-Doula and Mirzā Shafiᶜ-e Māzandarāni were ordered to his company. When he encamped in the district of Nishāpur, Jaᶜfar Khān-e Bayyāt, governor of Nishāpur, joined the camp and ᶜAli Qoli Khān, the latter's son, and the nobles of Nishāpur appeared at the court. When the shah ordered the surrender of the fortifications of

33. His mother was a Qājār princess, see above, p. 36.
34. See above, p. 69. 35. May 20, 1799.

Nishāpur to his troops and appointed an officer of the camp commander (kotvāl) of the town, ^{c}Ali Qoli Khān disapproved of his father's decision and sent the soldiers appointed by the shah back to the camp. The shah became angry and gave orders to attack and destroy Nishāpur. While Ja^{c}far Khān-e Bayyāt tried to excuse the disobedience of his son and the shah's anger was calming down, Haji Ebrāhim Khān and Mirzā Shafi^{c}-e Māzandarāni proceeded to Nishāpur to give the inhabitants words of encouragement. When they approached the citadel, Ḥosein Qoli Beg, paternal cousin of Ja^{c}far Khān-e Bayyāt, came out of the citadel and put himself at the disposal of the vizier. The rest of the garrison, however, continued their preparations for revolt, thus rousing the anger of the shah. The order for attack being issued, Ja^{c}far Khān-e Bayyāt again tried to persuade his son ^{c}Ali Qoli Khān, giving as hostage his other son, a handsome boy who was staying in the camp of the shah. He was to be killed if his father did not return. Ja^{c}far Khān, however, having entered the town, joined the defenders and redeemed his promise by the firing of muskets and guns. In accordance with the agreement his son, who had reached the age of fourteen only, was put to death. His corpse was surrendered to his father. Then the order was issued to lay waste the gardens and villages of the surroundings of Nishapur and to devastate those districts. For forty days the unfortunate inhabitants of Nishāpur were exposed to the anger of the shah. Lamenting the scarcity of provisions they elected as their mediator the imam of the Friday prayers Haji Ruḥ ol-Amin. Proceeding to the royal camp he should ask for pardon on behalf of Ja^{c}far Khān and the inhabitants of the town. Accordingly, the shah pardoned all the inhabitants, and Chief Mollā ^{c}Ali Aṣghar, having entered the town together with the imam of the Friday prayers, presented the foolish Ja^{c}far Khān to the shah, sword and Koran in hand. He was confirmed in the governorship of Nishāpur as before. For ten years he mourned his young son amid tears.

After the royal army marched off from Nishāpur, the shah gave orders to encamp outside Mashhad, Nāder Mirzā sitting behind the fortifications and the rampart of the town. For religious considerations the shah did not order an attack on the sanctuary, and no harm was done to anybody except that the coming and going of caravans and the transport of provisions were interrupted. By this mean the defenders were caused such distress that a group of Reżavi seiyeds, ulema and sheikhs came out of the town to ask for pardon on behalf of themselves and of Nāder Mirzā as the latter's representatives and made the Koran their mediator. The shah ordered the newcomers to rest, accepted Nāder Mirzā's request, and allowed them to return. Nāder Mirzā was pardoned and given the robe of honor befitting such an occasion. On the 15th Rabi^c I of the year 1214,[36] the royal court departed from outside Mashhad and entered Tehran on 15th Rabi^c II of that year.

MISCELLANEOUS EVENTS. In the middle of Jomādi I of that year[37] the daughter of Amir Guna Khān-e Kord Za^{c}farānlu, governor of Khabushān in Khorasan,[38] was married to Ḥosein ^{c}Ali Mirzā. The wedding feast lasted several days and nights. These were the first nuptials to be celebrated in the time of this glorious dynasty.

At the same time Mirzā Mahdi ^{c}Ali Khān-e Khorasani, by order of the British governor general of India, arrived at the court in Tehran, having been escorted with all honors from Bushehr through Shiraz and Esfahan.

HOSEIN ^{c}ALI MIRZĀ, SON OF FATḤ ^{c}ALI SHAH, APPOINTED GOVERNOR OF FĀRS, RECEIVES TITLE "FARMĀN-FARMĀ." It was in that year, too, that Ḥosein ^{c}Ali Mirzā was appointed

36. August 17, 1799. 37. October 15, 1799.

38. Khabushān is now called Quchān (about 95 miles northwest of Mashhad), see Le Strange, *Lands*, p. 393.

governor of the province of Fārs, receiving the title "Farmān-Farmā"; and Charāgh ᶜAli Khān-e Nawā'i, chief keeper of the arsenal (qur yasāvol bāshi), who had made his career under this dynasty, was appointed vizier of Farmān-Farmā. About 800 musketeers enlisted from the 18 districts (maḥalla) of Nur[39] were sent together with Farmān-Farmā [248] to Shiraz, their commander being Naṣrollāh Khān, brother of Mirzā Asadollāh Khān, the secretary of the army (lashgar nevis). Two years later all their families and relatives from the districts of Nur came to Shiraz. They established themselves in the Murdestān quarter,[40] which had been deserted since the time of the Zand, and built houses, everybody according to his fortune.

ANOTHER CAMPAIGN TO KHORASAN. The New Year fell on the night of Friday, 24th Shavvāl.[41] The spring of that year saw the arrival of Amir Ṭorra Bāz Khān-e Afghān in the name of Vafādār Khān, prime minister of Zamān Shāh, king of Afghanistan,[42] for a meeting with Haji Ebrāhim Khān Eᶜtemād od-Doula. He submitted the following message of the vizier of Afghanistan: "The kingdom of Khorasan, because of its close neighborship, suitably is to remain in the possession of Zamān Shāh, king of Afghanistan, whereas the other provinces of Persia shall belong to the Persian Shah. In the same manner as the king of Afghanistan does not interfere with the other provinces of Persia, no attack shall be launched against Khorasan by the other side. The king of Afghanistan shall be considered the younger

39. The district (Nur va-Kujur) lies in Māzandarān, on the Caspian Sea, east of the town of Āmol. Now it is subdivided into 15 dehestan, see *Farhang*, II, 308, and above, p. 17, note 76.

40. Old name of a quarter which officially was no more in existence after Karim Khān Vakil had reshaped the administrative division of Shiraz, see *FNN*, II, 22.

41. March 17, 1800 (should be March 21).

42. Zamān Shāh (r. 1793–1800) was third of the Dorrāni kings of Afghanistan, who had established a protectorate over Khorasan, see Bosworth, *The Islamic Dynasties*, pp. 214 seq., and the Bibliography given there.

brother of the shah, whilst the possession of Khorasan shall be ceded to the king of Afghanistan." After deliberating the prime minister answered as follows: "The intention of the shah's proceeding to Khorasan is the occupation of all the countries which belong to Persia: Nishāpur, Sabzavār, Kāhel, and Kandahār.[43] Now we are preparing the conquest of Afghanistan." Hearing this harsh answer Ṭorra Bāz Khān repented of having undertaken this mission and returned to Afghanistan.

On 9th Dhu'l-Ḥejja of that year[44] the royal army left Tehran and marched off to Khorasan. On 5th Moḥarram of the year 1215[45] they encamped on the plain of Mazinān.[46] Having dispatched a detachment for the conquest of Sabzavār,[47] the shah stayed at Mazinān to perform the rites of mourning for Emām Ḥosein. Then he departed for Sabzavār and had the royal pavilion put up outside the town. From his shelter behind the rampart of the town, Allāh Yār Khān presented a humble petition asking the shah if he might be allowed to postpone his appearance before the throne to another time. Jaᶜfar Khān-e Bayyāt, governor of Nishāpur and residing in the citadel of Nishāpur, behaved in the same manner. When the siege of both towns was protracted, Ṭorra Bāz Khān arrived again in the name of the king of Afghanistan and submitted the following proposal: "The inhabitants of Sabzavār and Nishāpur, being prisoners in the grip of Allāh Yār Khān and Jaᶜfar Khān, submitted a petition to the court of the king of Afghanistan, upon which the following mediation has been proposed: A delay of several days shall be granted to both of the foolish governors, and the Persian court shall return to Tehran. Upon my own responsibility I undertake to tame their ferocity and to convey

43. That is, Khorasan proper, which had formed part of the Safavid empire.

44. May 4, 1800. 45. May 29, 1800.

46. About 155 miles west of Mashhad, south of the highway Tehran–Mashhad.

47. About 40 miles east of Mazinan.

them to the Afghan court in due course. If, however, they violate this agreement, they shall be punished." In consideration of the old families the shah accepted the mediation of the king of Afghanistan and sent back Ṭorra Bāz Khān with a favorable answer. On 27th Ṣafar of that year[48] the royal court departed from outside the town of Sabzavār for Tehran and arrived there on 14th Rabiᶜ II.[49]

CONCLUSION OF A TREATY WITH ENGLAND. In the same year, Ambassador Sir John Malcolm, one of the confidants of the British government and a distinguished nobleman, was sent in the name of the English king on a mission to the Persian court with letters of friendship and valuable gifts.[50] When news of his arrival at Bandar Būshehr arrived, the deputy of the chief chamberlain of the divan, Fatḥ ᶜAli Khān-e Nuri, was by royal decree appointed his mehmāndār. He proceeded to Fārs and escorted the ambassador with highest respect from Bandar Bushehr by way of Shiraz, Esfahan, Qom, and Kāshān to Tehran. Taking quarters in the palace of Haji Ebrāhim Khān Eᶜtemād od-Doula as a guest of this incomparable vizier he was able to forget the inconveniences and troubles of his voyage. Two or three days later he was received in audience. By competent remarks and amicable speeches he gained the profound respect of the shah. The next day he distributed presents and gifts from Europe and India, and in the name of the British agents presented a treaty sealed by the governor general of India, which was ratified by the signatures of the scribes and the seal of

48. July 20, 1800. 49. September 4, 1800.

50. Sir John Malcolm (1769–1833) began his career in the service of the East India Company. The author of our chronicle quotes passages from Malcolm's History of Persia, see also the Bibliography at the end of this book.

The month of Ramażān of 1215 (date mentioned at the end of this paragraph) ended on February 15, 1801. According to Hurewitz, the treaty was concluded on January 28, 1801. The text is reproduced by Hurewitz, I, 68–70.

the grand vizier, Haji Ebrāhim, and handed over to the ambassador. The treaty included the following five articles: "1) God willing, the friendship between the two great governments will be everlasting. 2) Whenever the Afghans attack India, the shah shall send an army against them, and the English agents shall pay the Persian officials compensation for the expenditure of the campaign. 3) Whenever one of the rulers of Afghanistan concludes a treaty of peace with one of the two governments, the other government shall take part in the treaty. 4) Whenever the Afghans enter upon a war with France or Persia, the English government shall come to the assistance of Persia. 5) The Persian government does not allow the French to establish themselves on Persian soil, by land or by water, nor even to set foot on it." Having accomplished his mission, the ambassador was presented with a sword and a dagger studded with jewels, and Haji Khalil Khān-e Kor Oghlu Qazvini, alderman of the merchants (malek ot-tojjār), was appointed envoy to India in the name of the Persian government. Carrying befitting gifts and presents from the Persian government, he departed from Tehran at the end of Ramażān of that year in the company of the ambassador, Sir John Malcolm.

DEPOSAL OF GRAND VIZIER HAJI EBRĀHIM KHĀN E^cTEMĀD OD-DOULA. The New Year [249] fell on 6th Dhu'l-Qa^cda of 1215.[51] In that year, Grand Vizier Haji Ebrāhim was removed from his office; his fortune coming to an end and his star descending. Nearly every historian, according to the views of his time, has described this event in detail. Nearest to the truth come the statements put forward by the late Mirzā Fażlollah-e Khāveri-ye Shirazi in his *Tārikh-e Dhu'l-Qarnein*:

As I was in the charge of checking each transaction which had been ordered verbally by the shah and of writing down his orders without omission or addition, I asked him when I was engaged in writing down

51. March 21, 1801.

this story what had happened. He told me to write that neither he who had punished had made a mistake nor he who was punished had acted unloyally, that both of them were without fault. Putting my trust in God I took pen and paper and committed to writing this well-arranged exposition: "By decision of nature the quality of jealousy has been added to the soul and body of the beings of this world, and the mark of this reprehensible attribute has been put on their forehead. A lucid example of this is the treatment which Cain accorded to his brother Abel. If, then, fate elects one who by his essence is a sinner to sit on the throne of honor, then those who by their essence are equal to him, their hearts being peirced by the sting of jealousy, draw the sword of opposition against him everywhere, and true friends become treacherous enemies. Officials and secretaries especially are exposed to this danger, as they are a shelter for mankind and a refuge for high-ranking men and common people. Soldiers and subjects harbor desires in their minds and ambition in their hearts. If, however, he complies with the desire of one, the other will feel grief at this, and the number of friends diminishes, while the number of enemies increases. In addition to this: whereas courtiers and emirs may well be allowed to plan the ruin of one of their opponents and to convene gatherings for his betrayal, a king violates the rules of sovereignty and kingship by scheming and intriguing, and his action will be judged as unkingly behavior."

After these introductory remarks Khāveri writes with regard to the grand vizier, Haji Ebrāhim, as follows:

The aforementioned Haji was one of the highborn people of Shiraz. The genealogy of his family is well known: Their illustrious ancestor married a lady of the family of the renowned Haji Qavām od-Din-e Shirazi. His descendants were connected to Haji Qavām od-Din generation after generation, as Ḥāfeẓ says in one of his poems: "The green ocean of the horizon and the moonship are abundantly replete with the beneficence of our Haji Qavām."

The author of this book says: Trustworthy people at Shiraz are convinced that Haji Ebrāhim was an offspring from the male line of the renowned Haji Qavām od-Din. In any case, he is a member of this family. Haji Maḥmud, the grandfather of Haji

Ebrāhim Khān, has gained great wealth by trading. Toward the end of the time of the Safavids he erected a mosque and a college (madrasa) in the Balā Keft quarter at Shiraz and made some of his possessions a Pious Foundation on their behalf. Mosque and college were called "Hāshemiya." His son Haji Hāshem, at the time of the civil war of Afghān Ashrāf,[52] was appointed chief kadkhodā of the Ḥeidari Khāna quarters of Shiraz, a function corresponding to about half the office of a lord mayor.[53] By order of Nāder Shāh one of his eyes was blinded in 1160.[54] Haji Ṭāleb and Haji Ebrāhim, sons of Haji Hāshem, in the time of the Zand, were confirmed in the office of their father. As has been reported, ᶜAli Morād Khān-e Zand, in the year 1196,[55] sent Lord Mayor Mirzā Moḥammad, Mirzā Jāni-ye Fasā'i, and Haji Ebrāhim Khān and other nobles of Fārs as hostages to Esfahan. After the death of ᶜAli Morād Khān and the accession to the throne of Jaᶜfar Khān-e Zand, Mirzā Moḥammad Khān decided to enter the service of Āqā Moḥammad Shāh and went to Tehran. Haji Ebrāhim Khān, however, entered into an agreement with Jaᶜfar Khān and returned to Shiraz. After the death of Lord Mayor Mirzā Moḥammad in Tehran, Jaᶜfar Khān-e Zand conferred the office of lord mayor of Shiraz upon Haji Ebrāhim Khān. Also, as has been reported, under the events of the respective year, Haji Ebrāhim destroyed the fundament of the rule of the Zand in Fārs and attached himself to the Qājār rulers.[56] For four years he was an independent vizier of the deceased Āqā Moḥammad Shāh, and for another four years of Fatḥ ᶜAli Shāh. He had permission to sit in the royal council, was plenipotentiary in the affairs of the empire, and was confidant of the ruler. His eldest brother, ᶜAbd or-Raḥim Khān, had been

52. From 1723 onward.

53. Ḥeidari Khāna comprised five out of ten quarters of Shiraz, see below, p. 264, note 114.

54. 1160:1747/48.

55. See *FNN*, I, 223 seq., under the year 1196:1782.

56. See above, p. 40 seq.

appointed to the governorship of Esfahan and ᶜEraq. His younger brother Moḥammad Ḥosein Khān was governor of Kuh-e Giluya and Behbehān. Āqā Moḥammad Zamān, another of his brothers, had been appointed lord mayor of Shiraz. Mirzā Moḥammad Khān, the eldest son of Haji Ebrāhim Khān, had been appointed beglerbegi of Fārs, and as such he had in hand the administration of the divan affairs of that province, while Charāgh ᶜAli Khān, vizier of Fārs in name, was restricted to keeping the accounts (ṣurat-e ḥesābi). Another son of Haji Ebrāhim, Asadollāh Khān, though still a boy at the beginning of his career, had been appointed governor of Borujerd, Lorestān-e Fili,[57] Shoshtar, and Dezful. In fact, the governorship of the whole of Persia was held by the brothers and sons of Haji Ebrāhim Khān.

When the degrees of honor of Haji Ebrāhim's family exceeded those of the Barmakids, several people paled with envy. Every day courtiers and other people submitted false accusations and mendacious indictments to the shah with regard to Haji Ebrāhim. The shah tried to ignore them, until one day they submitted letters the seals of which had a striking similarity to Haji Ebrāhim's seal. The letters were addressed to Ḥosein Qoli Khān, brother of the shah, and several Persian emirs, who were urged to enter into a conspiracy and to renounce their allegiance to the shah. In addition to this some officers, namely Imāni Khān-e Farāhāni and Haji Rabiᶜ Khān-e Kazzāzi, in strict confidence, told the shah lies, accusing Haji Ebrāhim Khān of planning to overthrow the empire. Although nobody knew whether these letters and testimonies were true or not, the shah changed his attitude toward Haji Ebrāhim and ordered him and his family to be punished. This procedure has much similarity to the sentences of the Sharia courts of justice: If a witness in a lawsuit gives false evidence [250], on the basis of which a sentence is passed, and

57. The western part of Lorestān, also called Posht-e Kuh, see below, p. 342, note 180.

later the untruthfulness of the witness is established before the same or another judge, the sentence nevertheless remains valid, and the witness is merely fined. As all the brothers and sons and followers of the grand vizier were independent governors of provinces, the courtiers had to consider that if the grand vizier was arrested and put into fetters, his followers in the provinces would perhaps rise in revolt. Therefore they took measures that on a given day the grand vizier and his followers in the province were to be arrested and made prisoners of the shah. Accordingly, trustworthy men were sent into the provinces. On 1st Dhu'l-Ḥejja of that year,[58] the grand vizier was arrested in the royal chancery and subjected to a harsh trial concerning his actions. The letters with his seal were presented to him one after the other. Though he vigorously protested his innocence, asserting that the letters and the seals were not his and that jealous and envious people had falsified them, his assertions were of no use. They tore out his eyes and cut out his tongue—which in this situation he had used to insult his opponents rather than ask for mercy! Then they assigned to him and his wife and children Qazvin as a domicile, later on Ṭāleqān,[59] and here he was killed. On 1st Dhū'l-Ḥejja his brothers, sons, and relatives, too, everybody at his respective place, were either killed or deprived of their sight. In this way ᶜAbd or-Raḥim Khān, Moḥammad Ḥosein Khān, and Mirzā Moḥammad Khān were killed and Asadollāh Khān and Ḥasan Khān, sons of ᶜAbd or-Raḥim Khān, were deprived of their sight. Mirzā ᶜAli Reżā, son of the grand vizier, was castrated. All the possessions of the Hāshemiya family were confiscated. They were called "confiscated estates" (amlāk-e żabti) to distinguish them from the state property (khāleṣajāt-e divāni).

Then the vizierate was conferred upon Mirzā Shafiᶜ-e Māzandarāni as independent holder of this office. The lord mayorship

58. April 15, 1801.
59. The region northwest of Qazvin, see Le Strange, *Lands*, p. 225.

of Shiraz was entrusted to Mirzā Ebrāhim-e Shirazi, son of the chief alderman (kadkhodā bāshi) of the five Neᶜmati Khāna quarters of Shiraz, Mirzā Moḥammad ᶜAli. The independent governorship of Behbehān and Kuh-e Giluya was entrusted to Mirzā Solṭān Moḥammad Khān, as before.

NEW REBELLION OF ḤOSEIN QOLI KHĀN. In Ṣafar 1216[60] Ḥosein Qoli Khān, brother of the shah, governor of the town of Kāshān and holder of that fief, again committed self-deceit. A man from Lorestān named Moḥammad Qāsem Pirān Vand who pretended to know alchemy, appeared before Ḥosein Qoli Khān offering his suspicious services. Ḥosein Qoli Khān, immature and young, was of the opinion that he could count the arrival of this man a gain for his plan to become ruler. In the middle of Rabiᶜ I of that year[61] he hastened to Esfahan and alleged that Haji Moḥammad Ḥosein Khān had been removed from the governorship of Esfahan. The latter having fled upon news of his alleged removal, Ḥosein Qoli Khān took possession of Esfahan and its resources. He had coins struck in his name and appointed Moḥammad Qāsem his vizier. When the shah heard of this occurrence he departed for Esfahan. Hearing of the shah's departure, Ḥosein Qoli Khān proceeded to the region of Silākhur[62] and Borujerd. Several days later the shah followed him with haste to the region of Golpāygān.[63] Being disappointed everywhere and by everybody, Ḥosein Qoli Khān went to Qom (seeking refuge at the shrine of Fāṭema). A short time later the shah, too, arrived at Qom. Ḥosein Qoli Khān buckled on his sword and asked for pardon, prostrating himself submissively before the shah. Because of the intercession of the queen mother he was pardoned, and the shah gave him the district of Qom as a

60. Began on June 13, 1801. 61. July 26, 1801.

62. The region on the upper course of the Āb-e Dez (southeast of Borujerd), see Schwarz, *Iran*, V, 578.

63. The town of Golpāygān lies about 85 miles northwest of Esfahan.

fief (soyurghāl). In Jomādi I of that year[64] the shah returned to the Qājār palace in Tehran. However, several months later, when the inhabitants of Qom complained of the bad behavior of Ḥosein Qoli Khān, he was removed from the governorship of Qom; he chose as his abode the village of Dezāshub near Tehran.[65] In the following year, after the death of the queen mother, he was blinded in both eyes; a year later he died.

VAHHĀBI SACK OF KERBELĀ. The New Year fell on 16th Dhu'l-Qaᶜda of that year.[66] That year there took place the unfortunate attack by Saᶜud, son of ᶜAbd ol-ᶜAziz Najdi, upon Kerbelā. Although the detailed narrative of this event is outside the scope of this book, I have written down what I found in the chronicles and what I deemed to be true. It is a strange and remarkable event, and one which was mourned over by more than a few people of Persia. In fact there were very few Persian towns or villages wherein the inhabitants did not deplore the death of a group of their fellow villagers who were killed in that slaughter.

One should know that an Arab bedouin named ᶜAbd ol-Vahhāb came from Najd to Basra to take up his studies with the theologians of that town. Thence he proceeded to Esfahan, where he settled down, devoting his time to a thorough study of morphology, syntax, theory of style, rhethoric, theology (kalām), and religious law. Then he started acting as a mojtahed, inventing in his ejtehād novelties in the religious doctrines, fundamental and derived: God sent messages to the prophets; revelation came to an end with the Prophet Moḥammad, who received the Koran. God taught him His religion in a perfect way. After Moḥammad the Four Caliphs were mojtaheds altogether. Jaᶜfar Ṣādeq and the Four Imāms of the Sunna were

64. Began on September 9, 1801.
65. A small village ½ mile east of Tajrish, 9 miles north of Tehran, see *Farhang*, I, 88.
66. March 21, 1802.

mojtaheds of their age; by their ejtehād they explained what had been left out before them. It is incumbent on the mojtahed to solve problems and questions by syllogisms the premises of which are taken from the Book of God.

ᶜAbd ol-Vahhāb considered many actions of the Moslems to be innovations and aberrations, such as the high cupolas and spacious shrines over the sepulchers of prophets, caliphs, and saints and the golden ornaments applied to them, the suspension of precious objects at the sepulchers notwithstanding the poverty of the Moslems, and walking around the sepulchers and shrines except the walking around the Kaᶜba; all these actions he declared pure idolatry, admitting no difference between those who performed such actions and those who worship idols. He said further that the idolaters [251] cut stones and gold and silver, making of these materials figures of different shapes and that they believed that the souls of those figures are mediators with God—but their God, not the Creator of all things! Every Moslem who walks around a place of pilgrimage and any sepulcher in order to make the soul of its occupant his mediator with God, will be an idolater himself.

With these teachings in mind ᶜAbd ol-Vahhāb departed from Esfahan and returned to the desert of Najd. Meeting ᶜAbd ol-ᶜAziz, one of the nobles of that region,[67] he convinced him of his doctrines. He also wrote treatises on the subject, and making use of the power of ᶜAbd ol-ᶜAziz, he spread the teachings of his treatises among the brutish multitude of Najd and called the followers of his sect after his name "Vahhābiya." ᶜAbd ol-ᶜAziz continuously assembled his adherents to spread this sect and fought with the Arab sheikhs. Having gained power, he built in the region of Najd a fortress which he called Derᶜiyya.[68] He then

67. The first supporter of the Vahhābiya was not ᶜAbd ol-ᶜAziz (r. 1765–1803), but the father of ᶜAbd ol-ᶜAziz, Moḥammad ibn Saᶜud (r. 1746–65), the ancestor and founder of the now ruling family of Saudi Arabia.

68. About 12 miles northwest of Riyadh, the present capital of Saudi Arabia. ᶜAbd ol-Vahhāb came to Derᶜiyya in 1157:1744, see EI² II, s.v.

proceeded to slaughter and plunder his neighbors so that his power increased. Sa^{c}ud, his eldest son, added to the influence of his father by fighting the Arabs in other regions. Then father and son, with a well-arranged army, marched upon Mecca and Medina. They occupied Medina and plundered the treasures of the Mosque and the Holy Sepulcher and all the quarters of the city. From the wood of the Holy Sepulcher, they made firewood for cooking their coffee and burned all the books they could get hold of, except the Koran. The Mosque of the Sepulcher they used as a stable for their beasts. Some days later they moved off. Then Sa^{c}ud made another unsuccessful attempt to conquer Najaf.

And in the year 1216 Sa^{c}ud, son of ^{c}Abd ol-^{c}Aziz, with several thousand Arabs, marched upon Kerbelā. He arrived on 18th Dhu'l-Ḥejja,[69] the "Feast of the Pond of Khomm,"[70] and occupied the town. They killed 5,000 people within six hours after daybreak. Plundering everything they found, they took the women's jewels and clothes away and used force with all of them. They destroyed the blessed sepulcher and took away the candelabra of silver and gold and the precious jewels, brought from many countries, which for years had been suspended in the sanctuary. After six hours they left the town and marched off to Der^{c}iyya, their camels laden with the booty.

THIRD CAMPAIGN TO KHORASAN. At the end of that year the shah decided upon the third campaign to Khorasan. A royal decree was dispatched into the provinces, and after short time the army assembled in Tehran. On 17th Moḥarram of the year 1217[71] the royal army departed for Khorasan. On 8th Rabi^c I of

---

al-Dir^{c}iyya (G. Rentz). The name is derived from Der^c, which means "armor, coat of mail." The full name of the town, typical for this warlike movement, should be *al-Madīna ad-Der^{c}iyya*. "Armored City."

69. April 21, 1802.

70. The feast is celebrated by the Shiis in memory of ^{c}Ali's appointment as successor of the Prophet, which took place at that pond (near Mecca).

71. May 20, 1802.

that year[72] they put up their camp outside Mashhad and laid siege to the city. Within a short time, a famine broke out in the beleaguered town. When the siege had lasted a month, the inhabitants held a gathering in the house of Mojtahed Mirzā Mahdi and sent the latter to the royal camp for mediation. Having entered the royal pavilion, he submitted the following proposal: "The inhabitants of Mashhad do not submit voluntarily to the rule of Nāder Mirzā. If, however, the royal army will occupy the town by force, many thousands of Moslems, indigenous and pilgrims, will perish. This is certainly not the intention of the just shah. If the shah, returning to Tehran, postpones the occupation of the town to another time and appoints a competent emir to stay in this region, all the nobles of the town promise to deliver the town to that emir, once they have had an opportunity of depriving Nāder Mirzā of his power." All the emirs of Khorasan confirmed the truth of this statement. Out of reverence for the holy shrine and mercy for the community of the Prophet, the shah agreed with the proposal of Mirzā Mahdi and sent him back to the town. Having appointed Moḥammad Vali Mirzā governor of Khorasan and Ḥosein Khān-e Qājār Qazvini commander in chief (sardār) the shah returned with the army from outside Mashhad to Tehran, and arrived there in the beginning of Jomādi I of that year.[73]

CROWN PRINCE ᶜABBĀS MIRZĀ MARRIED TO A QĀJĀR PRINCESS. In that year, according to the last will and testament of Āqā Moḥammad Shāh,[74] the daughter of Amir Mirzā Moḥammad Khān-e Qājār Devehlu was married to the crown prince, ᶜAbbās Mirzā Nā'eb os-Salṭana. And royal decrees were issued to the effect that Ḥosein ᶜAli Mirzā Farmān-Farmā of Fārs and the other princes and nobles of the provinces of Persia should assemble at the court. They arrived in due course. The late

72. July 9, 1802. 73. September, 180

74. It is rather doubtful whether this testament existed in writing; there are several allusions to it in the text, especially below, p. 160.

Mirzā Fażlollāh-e Khāveri-ye Shirazi writes in his *Tārikh-e Dhu'l-Qarnein*:

The perfect love of the shah on the crown prince is testified by this occurrence: In order to bring the enjoyments of the wedding feast to perfection, the shah gave the permission to drink wine, although he himself ordinarily refrained from intoxicating liquors. Pronouncing a religious opinion (fetvā) based upon reason (ᶜaql), he opened the door of delight to all. Thereby the pious hypocrites were detected, in accordance with the saying "What is concealed comes to light." This permission, however, was limited to the wedding feast of the crown prince, and that was all.

PUNISHMENT OF A TURKOMAN TRIBE; MASHHAD CAPTURED. The New Year fell on 27th Dhu'l-Qaᶜda of that year.[75] In the month of Ṣafar of the year 1218,[76] the royal army marched off to punish a Turkoman tribe. On 7th Jomādi II of that year[77] the shah returned to Tehran, having attained his aim.

That year, too, Moḥammad Vali Mirzā and Ḥosein Khān-e Qājār Qazvini completed the fourth month of the siege of Mashhad. The inhabitants grew weary of the length of the siege, the famine, and the sternness of Nāder Mirzā, and surrendered the town. Supposing that they had surrendered the town by permission of Mojtahed Mirzā Mahdi, Nāder Mirzā with two men rushed to the mojtahed's house and killed him and fled. The following day Nāder Mirzā was taken prisoner and brought to the town. Then he was [252] taken to Tehran, with his whole family. At the end of Dhu'l-Qaᶜda of that year[78] he was arrested in the presence of the shah. After a trial he and some of his brothers were executed; the rest were deprived of their sight.

MURDER OF THE PERSIAN AMBASSADOR TO INDIA. As has been reported, Haji Khalil Khān Malek ot-Tojjār had been sent, in the year 1215, as Persian ambassador to India, together

75. March 21, 1803.
76. Began on June 3, 1803.
77. October 5, 1803.
78. End of March 1803.

with the British ambassador, Sir John Malcolm.[79] After his arrival in Bombay the agents of the governor general of India conferred upon him perfect respect and honor and put him up in a splendid palace. In his honor a guard consisting of 200 Indian soldiers and four British officers was posted at the gate of the palace. One day at sunset two or three of the ambassador's servants shot at the birds which were sitting on the roof and trees, killing some. As the Indians hold the life of animals sacred, they tried to stop the shooting. Upon this a quarrel arose, the rest of the servants came out of the palace and there was fighting between the soldiers and the servants. Haji Khalil Khān, coming out of the palace to settle the dispute, was struck by a ball and killed. The governor of Bombay had all the soldiers and the officers imprisoned and reported the affair to the governor general of India. The governor general submitted an *aide-mémoire* and an explanation of the occurrence and sent to the Persian court the consul (balliyuz) of Basra with several English gentlemen, clad in black, the color of mourning. The shah answered forgivingly and ordered the Indian soldiers and British officers imprisoned in Bombay to be released. And Moḥammad Nabi Khān-e Shirazi, a wealthy and distinguished man, well educated, and brother-in-law of Haji Khalil Khān, was appointed ambassador to India and proceeded to Bombay in the company of the consul of Basra and several other officers. At his arrival he was welcomed by 200,000 people and put up in a splendid lodging. Every day they took care of him in the most indulgent manner, and he stayed in Bombay for five months in most comfortable accommodations. Then he traveled to Calcutta and spent one year there, honored and prosperous. And Moḥammad Esmāʿil Khān, the son of Haji Khalil Khān, was paid an indemnity of 50,000 toman, and in addition to this he received a monthly allowance. For many years he lived in a prosperous condition in Paris and London, always clad in the Persian style. All his life

79. See above, p. 95.

he wore the high headgear of black lambskin, the long-sleeved coat, the cloak, the short padded coat, the wide trousers, and shoes of shagreen leather with high heels. He died in Paris about the year 1280.[80]

TOWARD THE PEACE TREATY OF GOLESTĀN

THE RUSSIANS INVADE ARMENIA AND ĀDHERBĀYJĀN. In the year 1218 the Russian emperor decided to invade Ādherbāyjān, Armenia, and Karabagh. Therefore he sent Zizianov, a famous Russian minister whom the Armenians in jest called "Ishpokhdur,"[81] with several detachments of horse and foot soldiers and artillery to Tiflis. Gorgin Khān, the governor of Tiflis,[82] being pleased at his arrival, surrendered the city of Tiflis by his free will to the Russian troops. Having settled the affairs of Tiflis, Ishpokhdur marched on Ganja. On 1st Shavvāl of that year[83] he occupied Ganja by force, ordering a universal slaughter. Javād Khān-e Qājār Zeyādlu, governor of Ganja, was killed in battle. Then by order of Ishpokhdur the surviving Moslems were ejected from the town and all the quarters handed over to the soldiers and the Armenians. The town of Erevan, which since the beginning of the Qājār rule had been governed by Moḥammad Khān-e Qājār Qoyunlu, submitted to Ishpokhdur without battle. When the shah received intelligence on this, he first dispatched Crown Prince ᶜAbbās Mirzā against Ishpokhdur, with several detachments of horse and foot soldiers. The

80. 1863/64.

81. Zizianov was a Georgian of noble birth who had been brought up in Russia. As commander in chief of the Russian troops in Caucasia he undertook from 1802–5 cruel campaigns to subdue the rebellious population south of the Caucasus. *Ishpokhdur* means "Inspector" (pronounced "Ishpekhtor"); it is perhaps influenced by the popular etymology invented by the Turkish-speaking Adherbayjanis, meaning "his work is dirt," see Browne, IV, 375*n*1.

82. In Persia, King Giorgi XII was called Gurgin Khān; however, Giorgi XII had died in 1800, see Lang, *The Last Years*, p. 243.

83. January 14, 1804.

crown prince decorated his chest with a mail shirt, which had been handed down from Jochi Khān, son of Chingis Khān to the royal treasury. The vizierate of the city of Tehran was conferred upon Mirzā ᶜIsā, vizier to the crown prince. The grand vizier, Mirzā Shafiᶜ-e Māzandarāni, was appointed counselor to the crown prince and administrator of his affairs. On 28th Dhu'l-Ḥejja of that year[84] the crown prince departed from Tehran. The royal court marched off to Ādherbāyjān in the middle of Moḥarram of the year 1219,[85] proceeding to the pasture of Solṭāniya. All this time the shah was awaiting news from the crown prince. Then a courier arrived and news was spread that the crown prince had had many encounters with Ishpokhdur, several of which he had carried and several of which he had lost. Dispatching a Khorasani detachment in advance, Fatḥ ᶜAli Shāh marched off from the pasture of Solṭāniya. When he arrived in forced marches at the river Araxes, he crossed the ocean-like river, trusting in God, with the whole army, making use of rafts and boats, and put up his quarters in the camp of the crown prince, 3 parasangs from Erevan. As Ishpokhdur had laid siege to the town and was encamping in the Friday mosque of Erevan which is outside the town, the crown prince advanced on the following day to a corner of that mosque and attacked the Russians. The following day, Moḥammad Khān-e Qājār Qoyunlu, governor of Erevan, sent a message (to the Persian camp): "As the guardians of the town of Erevan are Armenians, [253] I fear lest for the sake of their religion and faith, collaborating with the Russians, they surrender the town." Without delay the shah dispatched a detachment of horsemen for the defense of the town, and this detachment, excelling in bravery, entered the town. The following day he ordered another detachment to cut off the camp of Ishpokhdur from its provisions. They blocked the roads, taking away the contributions in kind which

84. April 9, 1804. 85. April 26, 1804.

were brought from all directions. Thereby they aggravated Ishpokhdur's situation considerably. Having no other remedy at hand, he took his army to reconquer the provisions. At this spot, however, the shah had placed ᶜAli Qoli Khān-e Shāhsevan on one side and Pir Qoli Khān on the other. Taking the camp in the middle, 4,000 Russians were either taken prisoner or killed. The Persians returned and erected, by order of the shah, in a corner of the camp pyramids of the skulls of the slain Russian soldiers. The prisoners were taken to Khorasan, ᶜErāq, and Fārs. Fifty men, their officer being a man known by the name Aras Khān, were sent under the custody of a trustworthy man to Shiraz. There they remained for some time. Aras Khān had the good fortune to embrace the Moslem faith.

Upon this defeat, Ishpokhdur, one midnight at the beginning of Jomādi I,[86] desisted from the siege of Erevan and marched off with his troops to Tiflis. When at daybreak the shah received word of this, he immediately dispatched Moḥammad Ḥosein Khān-e Qājār Qoyunlu (called "Dudāgh" on account of his thick lips) in pursuit of Ishpokhdur. He pursued him and his men as far as the surroundings of Tiflis, killing all whom he found on his way. As the cold season was approaching, the shah entrusted all the districts of Karabagh and Ādherbāyjān to experienced emirs and departed for Tehran, arriving there on 17th Rajab of that year.[87]

In that year royal decrees were issued to the effect that a hundred pieces of artillery should be cast of copper and brass, with all the accessories, in the provinces of Ādherbāyjān and Fārs, and to be delivered after completion. In accordance with the order, the crown prince, ᶜAbbās Mirzā, had the guns assigned to Ādherbāyjān fabricated under the supervision of Mirzā ᶜIsā, known by the name Mirzā Bozorg, vizier at Tabriz. Ḥosein ᶜAli Mirzā, governor of Fārs, had the guns assigned to his province,

86. Began on August 8, 1804. 87. September 22, 1804.

with all the accessories, manufactured under the supervision of Charāgh ᶜAli Khān-e Navā'i, vizier of Fārs, and sent them off.

The New Year fell on 19th Dhū'l-Ḥejja of that year.[88] After the feast the shah ordered the horsemen of the army to see to their arms and their riding equipment, made of silver and gold, and the footmen, too, to embellish their equipment with silver and gold, so that in addition to their regular pay (moqarrari-ye divāni) they might have at their disposal a sum for their livelihood at the time of the campaign. After the army had gathered, the shah departed from Tehran for Ādherbāyjān on 24th Ṣafar of the year 1220[89] and put up his camp on the pasture of Solṭāniya. On 16th Rabiᶜ I of that year[90] the court marched off, and on 13th Rabiᶜ II[91] news arrived of the crown prince's defeat of the Russian troops and the flight of their leader. At the same time news arrived from Rasht that Russian troops, coming from the sea, had occupied Bandar Enzeli and that they had been defeated and put to flight by Mirzā Musā, the chief astrologer (monajjem bāshi) and governor of Gilān, who had pushed them back to the sea. Suspecting that the Russian troops would return to Gilān and taking into account the importance of this affair and the close distance, the shah crossed the river Araxes and put up his camp at Aṣlānduz.[92] After several days news arrived from the crown prince that he had had several encounters with Ishpokhdur and the Russian corps and that he had gained a continuous chain of victories. Because of the disturbances the shah conferred the governorship of Ādherbāyjān and Karabagh, from Qaplān Kuh[93] as far as Darband, upon the crown prince, ᶜAbbās Mirzā, Nā'eb os-Salṭana and he himself returned to Tehran at the

88. March 21, 1805. 89. May 24, 1805. 90. June 14, 1805. 91. July 11, 1805.

92. On the right bank of the Araxes River, near the mouth of the Qara Su, see Morier, *Persia*, map of Ādherbāyjān facing p. 232.

93. The mountain range west of Meyāna, see Sven Hedin, *Zu Land nach Indien*, I, 133.

end of Jomādi I of that year.[94] Every day news arrived from Ādherbāyjān, Karabagh and Armenia to the effect that Ishpokhdur, the Russian leader, had passed by this or that place, that he fought against this or that Persian commander and that he had been sometimes defeated and at other times victorious; and then, on 6th Dhu'l-Ḥejja,[95] his head and hand were brought from Ādherbāyjān before the shah.

This is what happened in detail: When the Russian troops arrived in the vicinity of Baku, Ishpokhdur resorted to a ruse. In order to deceive Ḥosein Qoli Khān, the governor of Baku, and to win him over by promises and gifts, he sent an eloquent messenger to the khān, asking for an interview. Accepting his proposal, Ḥosein Qoli Khān worked out a scheme, too, and fixed a place for the interview which was situated halfway between the camp of Ishpokhdur and the town of Baku. The next day, Ḥosein Qoli Khān proceeded to that place, together with his nephew, Ebrāhim Khān, and two other men from Baku. Ishpokhdur, too, with three men, was present. During the discussion, Ebrāhim Khān fired his musket [254] at Ishpokhdur's back, so that the ball came out of his chest. Then they cut off his head and hand and sent them to Tehran.

A STRANGE STORY OF ZIZIANOV'S MURDER. A strange story is reported in all the chronicles about the rule of the Qājārs: one day several courtiers were discussing the calamity caused by the Russian troops in Ādherbāyjān and the depravity of Ishpokhdur, in the presence of Mirzā Moḥammad-e Akhbāri-ye Nishāpuri, a renowned theologian who was fully versed in the sciences dealing with obscure and strange things. By allusions they suggested that perhaps he could protect the Moslems from the depravity of Ishpokhdur; that he should engage in the Holy War. Mirzā Moḥammad agreed, adding that he bet his own

94. About August 20, 1805. 95. February 25, 1806.

head that he would bring the head of Ishpokhdur before the shah, within forty days. Some of the participants of the discussion took a note of the fixed term; the shah having been informed, the said term was registered in the books. In the first volume of the *Tārikh-e Qājāriya*, which forms part of the *Nāsekh ot-Tavārikh*, the author states:

"Haji Mirzā Moḥammad retreated to the hermitage of the shrine of Shāhzāda ᶜAbd ol-ᶜAẓim, drew a picture of a man resembling Ishpokhdur on the wall of the cell, and sitting down in front of that picture recited his usual prayers. One night, ᶜAbd ol-Ḥosein Khān, son of the grand vizier, Haji Moḥammad Ḥosein Khān-e Eṣfahāni, renowned among Arabs and Persians for his accomplishments and knowledge and whose veracity and integrity were lucid as the sun in full daylight, reported to the writer of these lines as follows: "In those days, when Haji Mirzā Moḥammad was engaged in this difficult affair, I went to the hermitage in the shrine of ᶜAbd ol-ᶜAẓim and watched him; he had tied a rope round himself and fixed both ends of it at the two sides of the picture which he had drawn on the wall of the cell. He stared at the face of the man in that picture in such a way that both his eyes were suffused with blood, and he uttered words without interruption. He had become absorbed in his imagination to such a degree that he perceived neither my coming nor my going." The above he did until the day of the appointed term drew near. Then he took a knife and dug it into the chest of the picture. Having done this he left the hermitage and said: "Ishpokhdur has been killed at this moment." The officials of the court counted each day, until the morning of the fortieth day, and the shah sent Haji Mirzā Moḥammad a message, that the space of time had elapsed. The latter answered: "The head of Ishpokhdur will arrive today." The people were watching the road until the afternoon prayer. Then the shah sent a message again, saying that the space of time had elapsed and nothing was known of Ishpokhdur's head. He answered: "It is not my fault, if the horse of the bearer of the head is lame, so that he will arrive some hours after the fixed term." And one hour had not yet passed, when the courier arrived carrying head and hand of Ishpokhdur. Then it was known that his horse had started limping 6 parasangs from Tehran and in consequence was only able to gallop with difficulty. After this event the courtiers demanded Mirzā Moḥammad to treat the Russian emperor in the same way. He answered: "Kings one cannot harm as easily as that. I shall be killed in revenge for Ishpokhdur, who was a great and valiant general." His prediction was confirmed. When the courtiers accepted his excuse, he left Tehran and went to Baghdad. Upon his arrival, the inhabitants of the Kāẓemein quarter[96] all of a sudden took offense at him, and raising a clamor they shouted: "Haji Mirzā Moḥammad is a nonbeliever, a distorter of truth and a damned heretic!"[97] Haji Mirzā Moḥammad, sitting in his house and not knowing of the uproar, said to his friends: "Before one hour has passed I shall be murdered." Then people entered the house and killed him."

The author of this book has been told by old people from Firuzābād and Fārs the following story: About the year 1215/16[98] Haji Mirzā Moḥammad-e Akhbāri-ye Nishāpuri stayed at Firuzābād. He used to preside over the daily prayers. In those days Egyptian locusts had devoured the crops in most of the districts of Fārs, and had then devastated the district of Firuzābād, too. Within one day much harm was done. The inhabitants of Firuzābād asked the Mirzā for a prayer to drive away the locusts. He wrote some words on a piece of paper, and ordered the paper to be fixed to a long pole which was to be put up on a hill overlooking the whole plain. The people then should cry at the top of their voices: "Moḥammad-e Nishāpuri says: 'Go away!'" When they did this, all the locusts flew up and disappeared in so

96. The inhabitants of Kāẓemein were in the main adherents of the Shia faith. In addition, there are in Kāẓemein the burial places of two Emāms of the Shia, which are counted among the Holy Places of Mesopotamia and are visited by Shii pilgrims.

97. As an "akhbāri," Mirzā Moḥammad acknowledged in religious matters the traditions (akhbār) handed down from the imams of the Shia only, and was, therefore, an opponent of the mojtaheds, who employed analogy in arriving at their conclusions. According to what is told in the Qeṣaṣ ol-ʿOlamā, he had collaborated in destroying Ishpokhdur on condition that the shah would "abrogate and abandon the mojtaheds, extirpate and eradicate them root and branch, and make the akhbari doctrine current throughout all the lands of Persia," see Browne, IV, 374 seq.

98. 1800/1.

great a swarm that the sun grew dark. They flew away and did not return.

DEPOSAL OF CHARĀGH ᶜALI KHĀN, VIZIER OF FĀRS. In that year, too, Charāgh ᶜAli Khān-e Navā'i was removed from the vizierate of Fārs, having held this office for seven years. The reason for his removal was this: After he had been vizier for a long time, some officials of Fārs became angry with him and took their complaints to the court. As the secretary in charge of the letters (monshi-ye rasā'el), Mirzā Reżā Qoli Navā'i, was a cousin and father-in-law of Charāgh ᶜAli Khān and of the deputy-governor of Fārs, he submitted the petitions of the people from Fārs to the shah in a distorted form. The stay of those people was protracted. One of the plaintiffs against Charāgh ᶜAli Khān was Āqā Jāni-ye Qiri, former governor (żābeṭ) of the district of Qir va-Kārzin, who as a poet had the pen-name Sā'el.[99] In order to obtain the removal of Charāgh ᶜAli Khān he invited all the people from Fārs who were staying in Tehran to a banquet in his house, from the mighty emirs and merchants down to the clay workers, binding them by an oath to be his helpers. The following day 200 people or more assembled on the Meidān-e Ark, raising an uproar and clamor which reached the ears of the shah. Inquiring after the reason for this tumult he was answered that people from Fārs wanted to submit a petition to him without a mediator. When they were admitted into the shah's presence, they reported to him many stories of Charāgh ᶜAli Khān's tyranny and injustice. As proof for their accusations they said that for a time Mirzā Reżā Qoli had not admitted the petition of the people from Fārs to be submitted to the shah. Then by order of the shah, Charāgh ᶜAli Khān was removed from his office, and Naṣrollāh Khān-e Qaraguzlu, who was an efficient emir and [255] a competent vizier, was appointed vizier of Fārs.

The deposition of the vizier Chadrāgh ᶜAli Khān has also been

99. Āqā Moḥammad Saᶜid; his family had been holding the governorship of Qir va-Kārzin since the time of the Zand, see *FNN*, II, 254.

reported in a different manner.[100] After the death of ᶜAbdollāh Khān-e Qiri, his two sons, Moḥammad Taqi Khān and Āqā Moḥammad Saᶜid, known as Āqā Jāni-ye Qiri with the pen name "Sā'el" were both governors (żābeṭ) of Qir for several years and ruled in harmony. Āqā Jāni used to stay at Shiraz, Moḥammad Taqi Khān in the district of Qir. Several years went by in this manner. They accomplished great perfection and showed benevolence and benignity to all. When in the year 1215[101] Charāgh ᶜAli Khān was appointed vizier of the province of Fārs, he removed Moḥammad Taqi Khān and Āqā Jāni-ye Qīrī from the governorship of Qir va-Karzin and appointed another governor. In this way he proceeded in most of the districts of Fārs; those who had been removed from their posts went to Tehran and complained about Charāgh ᶜAli Khān. Since Haji Mirzā Reżā Qoli Navā'i, a nephew of Charāgh ᶜAli Khān, was vizier at the court, he prevented the petitions of the people of Fārs from being presented to the shah. Some years went by in this manner and the patience of these people was exhausted. Then the ministers issued a farmān containing regulations for the population of the whole Persian empire with regard to the dress to be assumed, of which material, and how it was to be made for the different classes of people. A specimen for each class was made in Tehran and sent to the provinces. When this farmān was issued, Āqā Jāni-ye Qiri conceived a remarkable idea and worked out a very good plan: he invited all the people of Fārs staying in Tehran, officials removed from their offices, merchants, dealers, and other men who had complaints, to his house and said to them that on a certain day, for three or four hours, they had to do what he would tell them; that he would remove the evil of Charāgh ᶜAli Khān from Fārs. They said that they were willing

100. The following account is taken from the second volume of the *Farsnama*, from the chapter which deals with the district of Qir va-Kārzin, see *FNN*, II, 76.

101. 1800/1.

to do what he said and swore an oath to do so. On the morning of the day which had been fixed, about 250 people of Fārs assembled in Āqā Jāni-ye Qiri's house. According to his orders they took off their clothes, except headgear and shoes, and put on a cloak. Then they marched in procession to the palace and burst into the government building with great clamor. Fatḥ ᶜAli Shāh said: "What has happened for the people of Fārs to make such a riot?" Then Āqā Jāni-ye Qiri submitted the following statement: "Charāgh ᶜAli Khān, the vizier, has decreed a dress for the inhabitants of Fārs which we all have to wear. He has sent us 200 garments as samples so that we might present them to the ministers." Then they all dropped the cloaks from their shoulders. The shāh said to Haji Mirzā Reżā Qoli Navā'i: "We must remove Charāgh ᶜAli Khān from the vizierate of Fārs. He has to come to Tehran as soon as possible!"

Charāgh ᶜAli Khān was a perfect master of literature, the Arabic language, and the interpretation of difficult passages in Persian poetry. At Shiraz he spent many nights in discussions with learned men. Mirzā Yusof and Mirzā Abu'l-Qāsem-e Hamadāni, both of them eminent scholars and efficient savants of their age, came as his boon companions from Esfahan to Shiraz. Mirzā Abu'l-Qāsem, the younger brother of Mirzā Yusof, some years later took off the scholar's gown and was appointed vizier to Moḥammad Ḥosein Mirzā Ḥeshmat od-Doula, governor of Kermānshāh. He received the title "Dhu'r-Reyāsatein." The "Caravanserei of Charāgh ᶜAli Khān" at Shiraz is one of the reminders of that vizier of Fārs; originally it had belonged to the Pious Foundation of the late Emām Verdi Beg and his son, but now was dilapidated. By permission of the administrator (motavalli), Charāgh ᶜAli Khān undertook the repair of the building, which then was known by his name, as has been reported under the events of the year 1094.[102]

102. "In the year 1094 (1683) Emām Verdi Beg, son of Begi, the governor of Fārs, built a madrasa in the Darb-e Kāzerun quarter of Shiraz,

REFORMS IN THE CENTRAL GOVERNMENT. The New Year fell on 1st Moḥarram of the year 1221.[103] Changing his vestment of state into that of mourning, the shah celebrated the ᶜĀshurā feast in memory of the murder of Emām Ḥosein. After the celebrations he selected four intelligent Persian men and appointed them members of the body called the "Four Viziers." To each of them a special task and a specified rank was allotted. Then he conferred important functions of the state, such as the appointment and removal of governors, emirs, and generals, upon Mirzā Shafiᶜ-e Māzandarāni, appointing him prime minister (vazir-e avval va-ṣadr-e aᶜzam). The financial affairs and the inspection of the peshkash to be paid by the governors of the provinces he entrusted to Haji Moḥammad Ḥosein Khān, governor of Esfahan, appointing him minister of finance (mostoufi ol-mamālek) with the title "Amin od-Doula." Although he could neither read nor write, he was able to keep in his memory the accounts, from the toman up to the crore, by means of digital computation.[104] He was able to add, to subtract, to multiply, and to divide faster than the accountants (arbāb-e dafāter). The writing of the royal decrees, letters, diplomatic missives, and official correspondence he conferred upon Mirzā Reżā Qoli Navā'i, appointing him chancellor of the empire. The payment of pensions, emoluments, and sums for the maintenance

---

which now is known as Sang-e Seyāh quarter; the madrasa was called 'Madrasa-ye Emāmiya.' . . . Today it is known by name only and from old inscriptions. Its Pious Foundations have been incorporated into the crown property (khāleṣa-ye divān-e aᶜlā) and claimed by usurpers, except the village of Bābā Eiyub in the district of Seyākh in the province of Fārs, the Bāzār-e Āqā, which lies between the shrine of Shāh Charāgh and the shrine of Seiyed Mirzā Moḥammad, and the Kāravānserā-ye Emāmiya which is situated at Shiraz, in the Bāzār-e Morgh. This karavanserei which had gone out of repair, was renovated by the late Charāgh ᶜAli Khān-e Navā'i, vizier of the province of Fārs, in the year 1216 (1801/02); now it is called 'Karavanserei of Charāgh ᶜAli Khān.'" See *FNN*, I, 154.

103. March 21, 1806.

104. In Arabic Ḥisāb al-ᶜaqd, see EI[1] III, s.v. Ḥisāb al-ᶜaqd (Ch. Pellat).

of the army, and the registration of the soldiers as to name, presence, absence, and death was entrusted to Mirzā Hedāyatollāh Tafashi, a seiyed of noble birth. He was appointed minister of the army.

NAPOLEON OFFERS A TREATY OF FRIENDSHIP. This having been done, orders were issued for the army to assemble, and they arrived at the court in due course. On 25th Rabiᶜ I of that year[105] the shah departed for the pasture of Solṭāniya in order to march against the Russian troops. Some days after the departure of the army from Solṭāniya, envoys arrived carrying a letter of friendship in the name of Emperor Napoleon to the following effect: "We and you are enemies of the Russians. As normally the enemy of one's enemy is one's friend, a treaty of friendship must be concluded between us and you. Moreover, we demand that the title 'Emperor' be accorded to the French kings by the kings of Persia and Turkey. We ask you to put at the head of your reply the words: 'Napoleon, Emperor.'" Then a correctly written letter of reply was handed over to the French envoy and a robe of honor and royal favors were bestowed upon him.

At that time happy news arrived from Ādherbāyjān and accounts of a series of victories which had been gained by Crown Prince ᶜAbbās Mirzā in that region.

SOLEIMĀN PASHA TAKEN PRISONER BY THE PERSIANS. Also, at that time, Soleimān Pasha, known as Kahyā,[106] arrived at the royal camp. He was commander of the Turkish troops which by permission of ᶜAli Pasha, governor of Baghdad, had marched through the latter's territory and then by way of

105. June 12, 1806.

106. *Kahyā* is the Turkish version of the Persian katkhodā, "lord of the house" or "major-domo," a title accorded to various officials in the Ottoman administration, see H. A. R. Gibb and Harold Bowen, *Islamic Society and the West* (London; New York; Toronto, 1950), I, 60*n*3.

the plain of Zohāb-e Kermānshāh to Ṭāq-e Gerrā.[107] After their defeat by Moḥammad ᶜAli Mirzā, governor of Kermānshāh, the latter had taken prisoner Soleimān Pasha and sent him to the royal camp. The shah ordered his swordstraps and his dagger to be taken away and his billeting in the prime minister's tent. Having been reassured of Ādherbāyjān and Kermānshāh, the shah departed from the pasture of Solṭāniya and arrived at Tehran on 22th Jomādi II.[108] Then ᶜAli Pasha, governor of Baghdad, summoned the learned mojtahed, Sheikh Jaᶜfar-e Najafi, from Najaf to Baghdad; having asked him to mediate for the liberation of Soleimān Pasha, he sent him to Tehran. On the latter's arrival and mediation, the shah set Soleimān Pasha free, presented him with a robe of honor and handed him over to the sheikh, and they both departed for Baghdad.

WAR WITH RUSSIA CONTINUED. In that year, after the shah's return from the pasture of Solṭāniya and Crown Prince ᶜAbbās Mirzā's return from the borders of Ādherbāyjān, a Russian corps which was staying in the region of Tiflis and Shervān availed themselves of the opportunity to occupy Baku, Darband, Shakki, Ganja, Sālekhān,[109] and the whole region on this side of the river Araxes except Erevan.

The New Year fell on 12th Moḥarram of the year 1222.[110] After the feast the shah summoned the whole army of the Persian empire to the court; in order to protect the border provinces and to keep in check the enemies of the dynasty he marched off from Tehran and put up his camp on the pasture of Solṭāniya. Then he dispatched several detachments of horse and

107. Zohāb is the frontier region west of Kermānshāh, near the "Gate of Asia." Tāq-e Gerra is the Tak-i Girra of archaeology, a site explored by E. Herzfeld and others, see Gabriel, *Die Erforschung Persiens*, p. 240*n*13.

108. September 6, 1806.

109. The region east of Baku, between the Caucasus in the north and the river Kura in the south, see EI¹ IV, s.v. Shekki (V. Minorsky).

110. March 22, 1807 (should be March 21).

foot soldiers and several pieces of artillery as reinforcements of the crown prince in Ādherbāyjān.

Czar Alexander,[111] being informed of the death of the Russian commander in chief, Ishpokhdur [256], appointed without delay in his stead Count Gudovich,[112] an aged and experienced man. As Russia was on hostile terms with both Persia and Turkey, Count Gudovich decided cunningly to open peace negotiations with Persia and to deal with Turkey separately. Accordingly, he sent his adjutant with a letter announcing his intentions to the court of the Persian shah. The adjutant brought also a letter addressed by the Russian emperor to the prime minister, Mirzā Shafiᶜ, and some of the presents sent by the czar. On his arrival, the envoy of Count Gudovich was put up in the prime minister's tent; then he submitted his proposals. The shah answered: "With regard to a combined action of the two powerful empires I do not see any difficulties. However, as long as one square inch of Persian soil remains in the possession of the Russian empire, we shall be enemies." After the departure of the envoy, the shah paid no attention to Gudovich's unusual proposal. Having sent some additional detachments to Ādherbāyjān, he returned to Tehran.

ARRIVAL OF GARDANE, CONCLUSION OF A TREATY WITH FRANCE. In the month of Shavvāl of that year, the French ambassador, Brigadier-General Gardane,[113] arrived in Tehran, with 70 artisans, master artisans, army instructors, and engineers,

111. Alexander I, r. 1801–25.

112. Ivan Vasilevich Gudovich, general and commander of the Caucasian line since 1792, governor general of Caucasia as successor of Zizianov in 1806, see Lang, *The Last Years of the Georgian Dynasty*, pp. 213, 223, 260.

113. The month of Shavvāl of 1222 began on December 2, 1807. Claude-Matthieu Gardane (also written Gardanne), 1766–1817, was promoted to the rank of a brigadier in 1799 and appointed *aide-de-camp* of Napoleon and *gouverneur des pages* in 1804. He was accompanied to Persia by his brother, Paul-Ange-Louis de Gardane, who wrote an account of his travels in the East, see Bibliography at the end of this book.

and bearing a treaty and presents from Napoleon. He was honorably received and put in the prime minister's palace. Having received the letter, the gifts, and messages, the shah bestowed honors upon all the members of the mission and granted Gardane the title "Khān." Then he ordered the party to stay in Tehran. Now in 1218 Moḥammad Nabi Khān-e Shirazi[114] had been sent on a mission to India. He had submitted to the governor general of India that an article should be included in the treaty between Persia and England according to which England, in conformity with her capacity, was obliged to put money and troops at the disposal of Persia in case Russia intended to invade the territory belonging to Persia from time immemorial. Since at that time the friendly alliance between Russia and England was undisturbed, the governor general of India had shown reserve and coolness with regard to accepting this request. When the Persian ministers heard of the governor general's reserve concerning this question, they admitted the establishment of friendly relations with France. On General Gardane's arrival they accepted his demand, and a contract was drawn up. Its main substance was this: By means of war or peace, the French Emperor Napoleon shall try to push the Russian troops out of Tiflis, the provinces of Georgia, and the districts of Ādherbāyjān. Each year he shall put at the disposal of the Persian government instructors, engineers, and war matériel in accordance with what is needed. Whenever troops are required for the defense against enemies at home and from outside, they shall be sent by the French emperor without hesitation, provided the Persian government annuls the treaty with the English government. Having expelled the Russians from Georgia and the Persian districts, French troops aiming at the conquest of India shall have permission to march through Persian territory and Khorasan. As these terms meant peace for Persia, the shah accepted them all.

114. His mission to India is reported under the events of the year 1217:1802/3, see above, p. 106.

The treaty was committed to writing by the chancellor, Mirzā Reżā Qoli, and sealed by the prime minister and the minister of finance, Haji Moḥammed Ḥosein Khān Amin od-Doula. The conveyance of the treaty was entrusted to ᶜAskar Khān-e Afshār Orumi[115] who was appointed envoy to the French court. He departed with precious gifts and the royal missive.

In that year, under the supervision of Napoleon's representatives, reforms were introduced into the Persian army. A royal decree was issued to the effect that half the army was to fight after the French model as infantry and that the use of artillery and muskets was to be increased. The first to introduce these reforms was Crown Prince ᶜAbbās Mirzā in Ādherbāyjān. Mirzā Bozorg Qā'em Maqām, the distinguished vizier of Ādherbāyjān, excelled in zeal and knowledge. By order of the shah this reform was also introduced in the other provinces of Persia. The disciplined troops (neẓām) of Ādherbāyjān were called "Sarbāz," those of ᶜErāq and Māzandarān, "Jānbāz." Yusof Khān-e Gorji,[116] who had made his career under the Qājārs, was appointed commander in chief of the Jānbāz of ᶜErāq with the rank of a Sepahdār.

MISCELLANEOUS EVENTS. On 6th Dhu'l-Qaᶜda of that year[117] the daughter of Amir-e Kabir Moḥammad Khān-e Qājār Devehlu presented Crown Prince ᶜAbbās Mirzā with a son. In accordance with the last will and testament of Āqā Moḥammad Shāh he was called Moḥammad Mirzā.[118] He was to ascend the throne and display the virtues of an enlightened statesman. Also in that year Moḥammad Nabi Khān-e Shirāzi, ambassador to India, returned to Tehran.[119]

115. That is, from Urmia in Ādherbāyjān.

116. He was a Georgian by birth, and had probably come to Persia as a prisoner of war and made his career in the famous body of slave soldiers (qullar).

117. January 5, 1808. 118. See below, p. 160.

119. On his mission to India see above, p. 106.

The New Year fell on 20th Moḥarram of the year 1223.[120] The shah celebrated the feast in a befitting manner. Naṣrollāh Khān-e Qaraguzlu was removed from the vizierate of Fārs. In his place Moḥammad Nabi Khān, the former ambassador to India, was appointed vizier of the province of Fārs.

DIPLOMATIC ACTIVITIES IN TEHRAN. In the meantime, a representative of Count Gudovich, the commander in chief of the Russian troops, arrived from Tiflis at the court of Fatḥ ᶜAli Shāh in Tehran, carrying an *aide-mémoire*. He brought, too, a message for Gardane, the French ambassador staying in Tehran, which contained the following information: "The shah may send an ambassador to the Russian emperor, asking for an agreement and [257] a peace treaty." Endeavoring to refute this fantastic proposal the shah answered: "If we had started enmity and war it would be incumbent on us to send an ambassador and to ask for peace. Since, however, hostilities were begun by the other side, there will be not an ambassador but muskets and the sharp sword of the valiant Persian warriors." And the representative of Count Gudovich was ordered to depart. On 10th Rabiᶜ II of that year[121] the shah marched off to the pasture of Solṭāniya with a big army. Having put up his camp there he was waiting for news from Ādherbāyjān. Count Gudovich had again sent a messenger to Ambassador Gardane: "As in these days the emperors of Russia and France are negotiating a peace treaty,[122] I wrote to Napoleon telling him to persuade the Russian emperor to hand over Tiflis, Armenia, and Ādherbāyjān (to Persia). I am sure that orders to this effect will arrive shortly." Informing the Persian ministers of this message, Gardane said: "What is the sense, under these circumstances, of sending an army to Ādherbāyjān, and what is the sense of the shah's presence on the pasture of Solṭāniya?" Then he wrote a letter, which he sealed with his seal, to the following effect: "If Gudovich moves

120. March 21, 1808. 121. June 5, 1808.
122. The peace treaty of Tilsit, concluded in July, 1807.

from his place and starts a war, this will be his fault." He further requested that the Persian ministers, too, were to enter into an agreement according to which Mirzā Bozorg, the deputy (qā'em maqām) and vizier to Crown Prince ᶜAbbās Mirzā, should be responsible in case the army of Ādherbāyjān took up hostilities against the Russian troops. Then they wrote a letter to this effect and handed it over to Gardane Khān. Some days later an envoy arrived in the name of Gudovich with the following message: "Thanks be to God! A peace treaty has been concluded between France and Russia. It is my desire that by our mediation an agreement comes about between Persia and Russia. I cannot, however, avoid the occupation of Erevan, which up to now has remained in the possession of Persia—as an order to this effect has been issued by the Russian emperor. When the restitution of the Russian possessions in Karabagh and Armenia is taken in hand, I shall include in this restitution Erevan. For the time being I am, however, obliged to effect this order. If you know a loop-hole to get out of this, show it to me!" Alarmed at the breach of the agreement by Gudovich, Gardane sent his adjutant to Gudovich requesting him to desist from his march on Erevan. Before Gardane's representative arrived, Gudovich had departed for Erevan. On his way he had encounters with the Persian troops at several places, with varying success. On his arrival he laid siege to the citadel and launched several attacks. About 3,000 Russian soldiers were killed, and Gudovich returned to Georgia without success. Concerning Gudovich's tactics it became known that Napoleon in the course of the peace negotiations with the Russian empire had not uttered a word regarding Persia and that he had simply forgotten the agreement (concerning Persia). These proceedings, though they do not fall within the scope of this book, have only been described in detail to make known the cause of the breach of the treaty between Persia and France and the cause of the strengthening of the friendship with the British empire.

TREATY OF FRIENDSHIP CONCLUDED WITH ENGLAND. The royal court was still staying on the pasture of Solṭāniya when General Sir John Malcolm Bahādor arrived again at Bandar Bushehr to cement the friendship; the first time he had come to Tehran in 1215 to conclude a treaty of friendship between Persia and England.[123] He informed the Persian ministers that he had settled himself at Bandar Bushehr, waiting to be summoned to the court and for the arrival of the mehmāndār; that he expected Gardane to be expelled from the Persian empire, since France had not complied with the treaty. When Gardane heard of this, he made strenuous efforts to have the Russian troops removed from Georgia and Ādherbāyjān. The ministers sent Page of the Presence (gholām-e pishkhedmat) Esmāᶜil Khān-e Dāmghāni from Solṭāniya to Bushehr. On his arrival at Shiraz he sent a message to Sir John Malcolm that the French ambassador was making efforts to have the Russian troops removed from Persian territory at some suitable time; that as long as Gardane was doing this, he (Malcolm) had to stay at Bandar Bushehr. In the meantime Sir John Malcolm received a letter from the governor general of India saying that there was no sense in his staying at Bandar Bushehr, since Sir Harford Jones[124] had been appointed English ambassador to Persia. On the arrival of this letter Sir John Malcolm departed from Bandar Bushehr for Calcutta, while Esmāᶜil Khān-e Dāmghāni returned from Shiraz to Solṭāniya.

At the end of the month of Ramażān of that year[125] the royal court left Solṭāniya for Tehran. Gardane Khān continued his efforts to remove the Russian troops from Georgia and Karabagh

123. See above, p. 94.

124. Sir Harford Jones Brydges (1764–1847) began his career in the service of the East India Company and was envoy extraordinary and minister plenipotentiary to the court of Persia from 1807 to 1811. After his return to England he translated part of a Qājār chronicle (see Introduction, p. vi) and wrote an account on his mission to Persia which was published in 1834, see Bibliography at the end of this book.

125. About the middle of November, 1808.

for some time, but without success; when he asked for a new delay in this matter, the ministers decided to send ᶜAli Moḥammad Khān-e Astarābādi from Tehran to Fārs as mehmāndār of Ambassador Sir Harford Jones; he was to convey the ambassador from Bandar Bushehr to Shiraz where the latter should stay for a while and rest before proceeding to Esfahan. If Gardane's efforts were to continue without success, the English ambassador was to enter Tehran; in case of Gardane's being successful, the English ambassador would be asked to return home. When Mehmāndār ᶜAli Moḥammad Khān arrived at Shiraz, the governor of Fārs, Ḥosein ᶜAli Mirzā, sent Page of the Presence Moḥammad Zaki Khān-e Nuri, an eloquent, intelligent, and shrewd man, to Bandar Bushehr to welcome the English ambassador to escort him from Bandar Bushehr to Shiraz, doing him all the honors. There he was treated for some time to all sorts of entertainment. Then he was escorted with all honors to Esfahan. Gardane, seeing that in spite of his efforts he had no success, gave up hope and left Tehran without the permission of the Persian ministers. He returned with haste to the French court in Paris. The Persian ministers now summoned the English ambassador [258], Sir Harford Jones, from Esfahan to Tehran, where he arrived on 28th Dhu'l-Ḥejja of that year.[126] He was put up in the house of Haji Moḥammad Ḥosein Khān Amin od-Doula. On 3d Moḥarram of the year 1224[127] he was received in audience. He brought a letter of friendship with the seal of the English king and European gifts. He presented the shah with a piece of jewelry worth 25,000 toman, and the shah bestowed favors and honors upon him. To Haji Moḥammad Ḥosein Khān Amin od-Doula he handed over a treaty, written in London and sealed with the seals of the ministers of the British empire, concerning the cooperation of the two governments, their mutual protection, the friendly relations between the merchants of both countries, and the assistance in all things necessary to

126. February 14, 1809. 127. February 18, 1809.

fight the Russian troops. The ambassador was given rich and comfortable lodgings.

HOLY WAR DECLARED ON RUSSIA. In order to excite the enthusiasm of the Moslem army to do battle with the Russian troops, the shah ordered Mirzā ᶜIsā-ye Farāhāni, known as Mirzā Bozorg and vizier to Crown Prince ᶜAbbās Mirzā, a virtuous and highly religious man, to ask the ulema for a fetvā.[128] The fetvās of the ulema were to be made known to high and low in the Islamic countries. Accordingly, he sent Haji Mollā Bāqer-e Salmāsi and Mollā Ṣadr od-Din Moḥammad-e Tabrizi to Qom, Najaf, and Kerbelā.[129] They requested Mirzā Abu'l-Qāsem-e Gilāni, known as Qomi, Āqā Seiyed ᶜAli-ye Ṭabāṭabā'i-ye Esfahāni, known as Kerbelā'i, and Sheikh Jaᶜfar-e Najafi, all of whom had the degree of a "Ḥojjat ol-Eslām," to issue a fetvā on the following question: "Is the fighting between the Islamic army and the Russian troops who have invaded the Persian territory setting up the banner of disbelief, in accordance with the injunctions of the Sharia and religious law, and the assistance and protection of that army with money and men an obligation incumbent on all Moslems individually?" In the same way Mollā Aḥmad-e Narāqi, Haji Mir Moḥammad Ḥosein Solṭān ol-ᶜolamā, imam of prayers at Esfahan, Haji Moḥammad Ḥasan-e Qazvini at Shiraz, and Haji Mirzā Ebrāhim, mojtahed at Shiraz, grandson of the late Seiyed ᶜAli Khān-e ᶜAllāma,[130] were requested to answer this question in writing. After a short time numerous letters arrived from Persian and Arabic ᶜErāq and from Fārs and Esfahan to the following effect: "The king of the Moslems is, in this battle, a ghāzi fighting the Holy War. To

128. A fetvā contains the mofti's answer to questions on religious matters, in this case, whether the declaration of the Holy War on Russia was allowed or not.

129. That is, the main centers of Shii theology and learning.

130. Hāji Mirzā Ebrāhim was a cousin of Ḥasan-e Fasā'i, the author of this chronicle, see Genealogical Tables at the end of this book.

fight the nonbelief of the Russians as best as he can is an obligation incumbent on the individual Moslem. There is no doubt about the legal permission that taxes (kharāj) collected in accordance with the injunctions of the Sharia may be spent for this purpose. The participants in this war will merit remission of their sins on the Day of the Last Judgment, provided the participation is based on religious and sincere motives. The Moslems, high and low, are obliged to be ready to fight for the strengthening of their religion, the exaltation of the true word, and the protection of Islamic territory, and to engage busily and attentively in fighting the infidels when this is required by circumstances." When these fetvās arrived, Mirzā Bozorg wrote a treatise summing up the statements of the mojtaheds. This treatise was entitled *Resāla-ye jehādiya.*[131] Then the Persians became enthusiastic over the defense of Islam, and everybody, from craftsman up to theologian, prepared for war waiting for the time of attack.

The New Year fell on Tuesday, 4th Ṣafar of that year.[132] From Armenia news arrived that the Russian emperor had removed Count Gudovich from the office of commander in chief in Georgia because of Gudovich's defeat in the battle of Erevan, and that in his stead he had appointed and dispatched a man named Tormasov.[133] Thereupon Fatḥ ᶜAli Shāh mobilized the army of the Persian provinces and ordered it to gather on the pasture of Solṭāniya at a fixed time.

APPOINTMENT OF A PERSIAN AMBASSADOR TO LONDON. Because the English ambassador, Sir Harford Jones, had received from his government a letter that he should put at the disposal of the Persian ministers the sum of 120,000 toman as a subsidy for

131. The *Resāla-ye jehādiya* was one of the first books to be printed in Persia.

132. March 21, 1809.

133. Alexander Tormasov, governor general of Caucasia since 1809, see Lang, *The Last Years of the Georgian Monarchy*, p. 261.

the war with Russia (which sum was to be drawn on the East India Company) and the governor general of India refused to assign this sum, Sir Harford Jones requested the Persian ministers to send an envoy to the government in London to learn the reason of the governor general's treachery. As the talk of a mission to England sounded strange in the ears of the Persians, nobody was willing to go until the lot fell on the name of Haji Mirzā Abu'l-Ḥasan. He was granted the title "Khān," and from then on was called Haji Mirzā Abu'l-Ḥasan Khān. He was a son of Mirzā Moḥammad ᶜAli from the region of Esfahan. For a reason unknown he was living far from his home. In the time of Karim Khān Vakil he was appointed intendant of the army (sar reshta-dār). He was married to a daughter of the lord mayor of Shiraz, Haji Hāshem, father of the grand vizier, Haji Ebrāhim, and Mirzā Abu'l-Ḥasan Khān was their son. As a nephew of the grand vizier he had gained rank and authority so that he was appointed deputy governor of Shoshtar. After the arrest of the Haji Hāshem family[134] he had gone to India and established himself in Hyderabad/Deccan. Owing to the Persian grand vizier's prestige, he advanced to the rank of a boon companion of the ruler of that country.[135] He received a monthly salary of 200 rupees and wasted this money for four years on a handsome boy named Feiż Bakhsh. When he learned that Fatḥ ᶜAli Shāh had pardoned the offspring of the grand vizier, he came from India to Shiraz and was appointed life guardsman (yasāvol) of Ḥosein ᶜAli Mirzā Farmān-Farmā. Haji Moḥammad Ḥosein Khān Amin od-Doula being son-in-law of the grand vizier, Haji Ebrāhim, Mirzā Abu'l-Ḥasan Khān was not satisfied with the office of a life guardsman and entered the service of Amin od-Doula. Through the latter's mediation he was appointed ambassador to London.

134. The arrest took place on 1st Dhu'l-Ḥejja 1215: April 15, 1801, see above, p. 99.

135. The Nezam of Hyderabad, Skandar Shāh (1803–29), see EI² III s.v. Ḥaydarābād (J. Burton-Page).

NEW CAMPAIGN TO ARMENIA AND GEORGIA. The shah departed from Tehran and mustered the army assembled on the [259] pasture of Solṭāniya. After several days' stay he marched off and put up camp at Ujān in Ādherbāyjān[136] on 22d Jomādi II.[137] On being informed that Tormasov, commander in chief of the Russian troops, was encamping 1 parasang from Tiflis and that he had dispatched several detachments of his army to Karabagh, the shah after some deliberation sent Moḥammad ᶜAli Mirzā, governor of ᶜErāq and Kermānshāh, with 2,000 horsemen and infantry to Tiflis, and Crown Prince ᶜAbbās Mirzā with a corps of his army to Ganja. The shah himself departed and put up his camp in the region of Sarāb,[138] waiting there for news from the princes. Having marched through the region of Tiflis and having come out of each encounter victorious, Moḥammad ᶜAli Mirzā made his way back, reaching the royal court at Sarāb, while the crown prince remained solid as a mountain in the vicinity of Erevan, guarding the districts of that region.

Russia's General Tormasov, undertaking no campaign in that year, sent his nephew to Crown Prince ᶜAbbās Mirzā carrying a letter with the following contents: "In case you renounce the Iranian territories which are in the possession of the Russian empire, the provinces of Erzerum and Baghdad and several other Turkish districts bordering the Persian territory may be occupied in their place by the combined forces of the two empires, Persia and Russia, and added to the Persian empire. If a Persian envoy would proceed to the Russian emperor, a peace treaty could be concluded." The crown prince sent this letter to the shah. As

136. Ujān is now a dehestan east of Tabriz, see *Farhang*, IV, 54.

137. August 4, 1809.

138. There are three places named Sarāb in Ādherbāyjān, the most important being Sarāb west of Tabriz, see above, p. 40, note 187; a village named Sarāb lies 3½ miles east of Khoy, see *Farhang*, IV, 263 seq., another village of the same name south of Marāgha, see l. c., p. 264. It is difficult to decide which Sarāb is meant here; Sarāb west of Tabriz was often visited by the Qājār rulers.

things were going smoothly and the winter was near, the royal court departed from Sarāb and arrived in Tehran in the last third of the month of Ramażān.[139]

APPOINTMENTS IN THE CENTRAL GOVERNMENT AND IN FĀRS. In that year Chancellor Mirzā Reżā Qoli, head of the royal chancellery, renounced his office and was appointed vizier to Prince Moḥammad Vali Mirzā, governor of Khorasan. The royal chancellery was entrusted to Mirzā ᶜAbd ol-Vahhāb-e Esfahāni, with the penname "Nashshāt."[140] He was granted the title "Moᶜtamad od-Doula." Also, in that year the title "Ṣadr-e aᶜẓam" was bestowed upon the prime minister, Mirzā Shafiᶜ, on the model of the Ottoman empire in which the grand vizier is styled "ṣadr-e aᶜẓam." From then on Mirzā Shafiᶜ was called "Ṣadr-e aᶜẓam." And that year Mirzā Bozorg, vizier to Crown Prince ᶜAbbās Mirzā, was appointed deputy of the prime minister; and the title "Qā'em Maqām" was granted him, in the same way as the crown prince is called "Nā'eb os-Salṭana."

At the end of that year Ḥosein ᶜAli Mirzā, governor of Fārs, deposed his vizier, Moḥammad Nabi Khān-e Shirāzi, because the administration of the finances was in a state of confusion. Then by order of the shah, Minister of Finance Haji Moḥammad Ḥosein Khān Amin od-Doula arrived from the court at Shiraz to settle the finances. He inquired into the revenues and expenditure of the province of Fārs and of the army and the subjects, and after one year he returned to Tehran. Old people from Shiraz tell the story that the followers of the minister of finance reproached the handling of the financial affairs before he took them in hand, while the followers of the vizier of Fārs, Moḥammad Nabi Khān, reproached the handling of the financial

139. Beginning of November, 1809.

140. "He was celebrated as a calligraphist as well as a poet, and master of the three languages, Arabic, Persian and Turkish. . . . He excelled in the gazel, and his best-known work is entitled 'Ganjina' ('Treasury')," see Browne, IV, 311.

affairs before the latter's appointment to the vizierate. Because of this, enmity arose between the minister of finance and Moḥammad Nabi Khān. Proud of the services which he had rendered Persia as ambassador to India, Moḥammad Nabi Khān did not care for the minister's ideas. The minister, who supervised the financial administration of the provinces of the empire, made Moḥammad Nabi Khān, vizier of the province of Fārs, responsible for the excessive expense of various sums, and came in person from Tehran to Shiraz to recover these sums. He recovered—through the application of various kinds of torture—the whole sum from both Moḥammad Nabi Khān and his brother, Moḥammad Jaᶜfar Khān, governor of Dashtestān and Bandar Bushehr. At the end of Yunat Yil[141] he entrusted the vizierate of Fārs to Mirzā Yusof-e Ashrafi-ye Māzandarāni and returned to Tehran. As is known at Shiraz, about 150,000 toman in cash, kind, and estates were extorted. Moḥammed Nabi Khān delivered quietly all the wealth which he had acquired his life long by trade and through his post as ambassador to India. He was a son of Āqā Kuchek, a merchant from Shiraz. His sister was married to Haji Khalil Khān-e Koroghlu Malek ot-Tojjār-e Qazvini. As has been reported, after the murder of Haji Khalil Khān in the year 1218, Moḥammad Nabi Khān had been appointed ambassador to India in the latter's place.[142] He stayed there for a time, and after his return he was vizier of Fārs for two years. Then he lived in misery and died after a short time. He was buried in the shrine of Seiyed Mir Moḥammad.[143]

RUSSIAN PEACE OFFER. The New Year fell on 15th Ṣafar of the year 1225.[144] After the feast an envoy arrived from the Crown Prince in Ādherbāyjān, bringing an offer of the Russian

141. That is, in the spring of the year 1810. 142. See above, p. 106.
143. Mohammad was a son of the seventh Emām, Musā ol-Kāẓem, see *FNN*, II, 154.
144. March 21, 1810.

General Tormasov which Tormasov had made to Crown Prince ᶜAbbās Mirzā, to the following effect: "Since the Russian empire has only suffered detriment and losses by the continual wars with the Persian empire, the Russian emperor, being inclined to an agreement and a peace treaty, has ordered me to put this into execution by an interview with a plenipotentiary appointed by that government. Accordingly, the prime minister, Mirzā Shafiᶜ, or Mirzā Bozorg Qā'em Maqām, might be appointed for the conclusion of the peace treaty. By the negotiations taking place in one of the districts of Ādherbāyjān, the enmity should be turned into friendship." Realizing the deceitful basis of this proposal, the shah answered: "The prime minister, Mirzā Shafiᶜ, is to remain at my disposal at all costs. Concerning a meeting with Mirzā Bozorg, there is no hesitation."

According to his practice of the previous years [260] the shah, together with the army, departed for the pasture of Solṭāniya on 27th Rabiᶜ II of that year,[145] arriving there on the 8th Jomādi II.[146] A courier arrived from Ādherbayjān announcing that Mirzā Bozorg Qā'em Maqām had met Tormasov in the latter's camp, but aware of Tormasov's machinations, he had returned without paying attention to Tormasov's false talk.

SIR JOHN MALCOLM AT SOLṬĀNIYA. In that year Sir John Malcolm Bahādor arrived at Bandar Bushehr in the name of the governor general of India. On behalf of the royal court Meḥrāb Khān was sent to Bandar Bushehr as mehmāndār. Upon his arrival at Shiraz, Ḥosein ᶜAli Mirzā, governor of Fārs, appointed Moḥammad Zaki Khān-e Nuri his own mehmāndār, and the latter proceeded to Bandar Bushehr together with Meḥrāb Khān. They escorted Sir John Malcolm to Shiraz, showing him all respect. Upon his arrival at Shiraz, Sir John presented the governor of Fārs with the gifts sent by the governor general of India.

145. June 1, 1810. 146. June 11, 1810.

Then Sir John and Meḥrāb Khān departed from Shiraz and arrived by way of Esfahan at the pasture of Solṭāniya on 15th Jomādi I.[147] Together with several gentlemen—his deputy, physician, and interpreter—the ambassador was received in audience, and favors exceeding all bounds were bestowed upon them. They presented the shah with the gifts from India. Some time later a letter arrived from Haji Mirzā Abu'l-Ḥasan Khān, the Persian ambassador to London, saying that by decision of the English government Sir Harford Jones was to continue as the English ambassador at the court, while Sir John Malcolm, being ambassador in the name of the governor general of India, was to return to Calcutta. Accordingly, Sir John Malcolm departed without delay for his place of destination by way of Baghdad.

The royal court left the pasture of Solṭāniya for Ujān in Ādherbāyjān. And Crown Prince ᶜAbbās Mirzā, fighting the Russians at several places with varying success, restored order to the districts of Ādherbāyjān. As the weather grew cold, the royal court departed from Ujān and arrived in Tehran on 1st Shavvāl of that year.[148]

PERSIAN TROOPS ASSIST THE IMAM OF MASQAṬ AGAINST VAHHĀBIS. Also in that year Solṭān Seiyed Saᶜid, Imam of Masqaṭ and ᶜOman, who, being a vassal of the Persian empire, had been paying tribute to the governor of Fārs for ages,[149] complained before Ḥosein ᶜAli Mirzā Farmān-Farmā of Fārs, of the encroachment of Sheikh Saᶜud, head of the Vahhābis, who lived in the desert of Najd. The Imām asked for troops to be sent from Fārs. Ṣādeq Khān-e Qājār Devehlu was appointed commander in chief in ᶜOmān by the governor of Fārs and arrived with several thousand musketeers from Lārestān, Dashti and Dashtestān at Bandar Bushehr by way of Fasā, Dārāb, and

147. June 18, 1810. 148. October 30, 1811.

149. In 1794 Bandar ᶜAbbās had been ceded to Seiyed Solṭān ibn Aḥmad (r. 1792–1804), the father of Seiyed Saᶜid, for a yearly rent of 6,000 toman, see Miles, *Persian Gulf*, p. 287.

Sab^{c}a. Then they boarded ships from Masqaṭ, crossed the Persian Gulf, and entered Masqaṭ. Some days later they departed for Najd with troops from ^{c}Oman. Sheikh Sa^{c}ud Vahhābi appointed Sheikh Moḥammad ibn Seif and Sheikh Seif ibn Mālek commanders in chief and marched with a detachment of Bedouin Arabs against the army of Fārs and ^{c}Omān. The troops of Najd having drawn up for battle opposite the troops of Ṣādeq Khān, several crossbowmen (charkhchis) from both sides began the fighting by attacking each other. When the Persian troops were pushed back, the Bedouins got the upper hand, drove the enemy out of the camp, and took to plundering. Then a quarrel over the partition of the booty turned into a fight. At this moment Ṣādeq Khān attacked the Bedouins and killed most of them. Moḥammad ibn Seif and Seif ibn Mālek, having received painful wounds, took to flight. Advancing as far as the region of Der^{c}iyya, the army of Fārs and ^{c}Omān plundered the districts of Najd and then returned to Masqaṭ. Seiyed Sa^{c}id Khān, the Imam of Masqaṭ, being thankful for this generosity, presented the governor of Fārs with rich presents and gave Ṣādeq Khān and the officers of the musketeers a large sum of money. They all returned to Bandar ^{c}Abbās with their wishes fulfilled.

THE SHAH TRAVELS TO ESFAHAN. In that year the shah proceeded to Qom, Kāshān, and Esfahan to inquire into the conditions of his subjects. Because of the famine and the misery of the subjects he released Esfahan and Kāshān from the payment of taxes amounting to 100,000 toman in cash and granted the deserving people rest. On 23rd Ṣafar of the year 1226[150] he returned to Tehran.

ARRIVAL OF AN OTTOMAN EMBASSY IN TEHRAN. The New Year fell on 25th Ṣafar of that year,[151] in which Seiyed ^{c}Abd ol-Vahhāb Efendi, ambassador of Solṭān Maḥmud, the Ottoman sultan, entered Tehran with all honors on 14th Rabi^{c}

150. March 19, 1811. 151. March 21, 1811.

II[152] carrying rich presents and gifts. He was put up in the house of Prime Minister Mirzā Shafiᶜ. After recovering from the hardships of his voyage, he was received in audience by the shah and submitted a letter from the sultan and presents in the latter's name, and royal favors were bestowed upon him. He carried, too, a letter which the sultan had addressed to the prime minister. The request of both letters, as it became known, was this: "The pashas of Van are continually the cause of trouble between the governments of Persia and Turkey. The responsible officials of Persia must renounce protecting them; they must even punish them in a fitting manner. Furthermore, the frontier guards of this government are incessantly engaged in fighting the Russian troops in the region of Kars. The responsible officials of that empire should not, in accordance with their capacity, consider themselves freed from the defense (of the frontier), and they should never give the Russians respite." The shah answered as follows: "As God imposed on the leaders of this state the duty to take care of the Islamic community, there are no difficulties concerning the defense (of the frontier). However, the appointment of the pashas of Shahrazur[153] has always to take place by permission and assent of this government. Furthermore, the vizier of Baghdad[154] must from now on keep up friendly relations with this government just as former viziers have done. He has to treat the pilgrims to the holy places indulgently and patiently, and they shall perpetrate no hostile action against the vizier. If they act [261] contrary to this agreement, they shall be punished." Then he delighted the ambassador by several kinds of courtesies and assigned him Tabriz as his domicile.

THE SHAH AT SOLṬĀNIYA. On 9th Jomādi II of that year[155] the shah departed with the army from Tehran and encamped on

152. May 8, 1811.
153. The region south of the upper course of the Little Zab River, northwest of Kirkuk.
154. That is, the Ottoman governor of Baghdad.
155. July 1, 1811.

the pasture of Solṭāniya on 1st Rajab.[156] He sent the Dāmghāni commander Esmāᶜil Khān to Ādherbayjān, placing him under the command of Crown Prince ᶜAbbās Mirzā for the battle with the Russians. And happy news arrived from Moḥammad ᶜAli Mirzā, governor of ᶜErāq and Kermānshāh, with regard to the settling of affairs of the Two ᶜErāqs.[157] As autumn was drawing near and with it the cold season, the royal court departed from the pasture of Solṭāniya and arrived in Tehran on 7th Shavvāl.[158]

SIR GORE OUSELEY APPOINTED AMBASSADOR TO PERSIA.

It has been reported under the events of the year 1224 that Haji Mirzā Abu'l-Ḥasan Khān had been sent on a mission to London to effect the payment of the subsidy.[159] Upon his arrival he was welcomed by a mehmāndār in the name of the English government and escorted to London with all honors, and they observed everything which was due him. The sum of 120,000 toman which had been accorded by the ambassador, Sir Harford Jones, and was to be paid every year in times of war with Russia, was increased by 80,000 toman. When the ambassador, Haji Mirzā Abu'l-Ḥasan Khān, realized that in England unusual honors were bestowed upon him, his avidity increased and he became a docile disciple of that country. As he demanded a regular salary, the administration of the East India Company assigned him monthly emoluments to the amount of 1,000 rupees, which is 250 toman of Persian value, to be paid for a lifetime. Along with him, Sir Gore Ouseley[160] was sent as

156. July 22, 1811.

157. That is, ᶜErāq-e ᶜArabi (Mesopotamia) and ᶜErāq-e ᶜAjami (the central part of western Persia).

158. October 25, 1811. 159. See above, p. 129.

160. Sir Gore Ouseley (1770–1844) went to India in 1787 as a merchant and then took up Oriental studies. He was the mehmāndār of the Persian ambassador mentioned above and was appointed ambassador extraordinary and minister plenipotentiary to the Persian court on March 10, 1810. He is the author of *Biographical Notes of Persian Poets, with Critical and Explanatory Remarks*, London, 1846.

ambassador to Persia. Both departed for their destination by way of the Atlantic Ocean; because of opposing winds blowing on the high sea the captain and steersman lost control of the ship. Without choice, they sailed about for some days and nights and eventually found themselves on the shore of the New World. They disembarked by means of small boats and established themselves; in the vicinity was a town named Rio de Janeiro, which belonged to Brazil, a possession of the Portuguese king. The king,[161] having fled out of aversion for the French emperor, was staying in Brazil (a country which included in its natural resources a diamond mine). Having learned of their arrival, the king sent a group of nobles to welcome the two ambassadors, and they were escorted to Rio de Janeiro with all honors. There they rested for some days. During this time a great snake was killed by chance in the jungle and brought before the Portuguese king. The snake was 16 shāhi cubits long,[162] its nape having a width of 1 shāhi cubit and its skin being as thick as cowhide. The skin was brought by the ambassador, Mirzā Abu'l-Ḥasan Khān, to Persia. Until now, which is the year 1303,[163] this skin has been kept in a state of perfect preservation in the royal treasury.

Haji Mirzā Abu'l-Ḥasan Khān and the English ambassador having arrived happily at Bandar Bushehr, Mirzā Moḥammad Zaki Mostaufi-ye Nuri-ye Māzandarāni was dispatched as mehmāndār in the name of the Qājār court to Bandar Bushehr. Upon his arrival he showed the English ambassador all honors, escorting him from Bandar Bushehr as far as Tehran, where he was put up in the house of Haji Moḥammad Ḥosein Khān Amin od-Doula. On 27th Shavval of that year[164] he was received in

161. John IV, prince regent of Portugal from 1799 onward, left Portugal for Brazil in November, 1807, when Napoleon invaded the Iberian Peninsula. He returned to Portugal in 1821.

162. The dirāᶜ al-malik was about 95 cm. long, see Hinz, *Masse und Gewichte*, p. 62.

163. 1885/86. 164. November 14, 1811.

audience. Sir Gore Ouseley was an ambassador who possessed perfect intelligence, knowledge, shrewdness, and a striving for felicity. He had mastered several languages and spoke English, French, Russian, Arabic, Persian, and Hindustani well. In all these languages he wrote well also. He was perfectly acquainted with the history of the world, and in discussions of certain sciences and fine arts, he proved an asset at all the social gatherings. His perfection was without equal. The shah held him in such esteem that the other ambassadors hated him. Sir Gore submitted a letter from the English king in a manner pleasant to the shah, by presenting him with, apart from other gifts, a diamond worth 25,000 toman. In the name of the English queen, his wife was appointed ambassadress to the shah's spouse and was permitted entrance to the inner palace by mediation of Mirzā ᶜAli Reżā, son of Haji Ebrāhim Khān Eᶜtemād od-Doula, guard of the royal Harem.[165] Upon meeting the Bānu—the daughter of Ebrāhim Khalil Khān-e Javānshir, governor of Karabagh—and after the exchange of courtesies, she presented her with a perfume bottle studded with jewels worth 20,000 toman, as a gift from the English queen. By royal order the ambassador built a house in Tehran with a garden in the Frankish style, near the ᶜErāq gate in the bazaar quarter. He handed over to the Persian ministers the subsidy for three years, that is, from the arrival of the former ambassador, Sir Harford Jones, to one year in advance, the sum of 600,000 toman. Apart from that he brought 3,000 pieces of select English muskets, 20 pieces of artillery, 40 cartridge wagons, and 30 instructors and engineers. Then Sir Harford Jones departed for London by way of Istanbul.

ARGHUN KHĀN'S TOMB DISCOVERED. In that year the tomb of the Chingizid Arghun Khān, who had died in the year

165. What happened to him after his father's deposition is mentioned above, p. 99.

690 of the hegira,[166] was discovered. It happened thus: Sojās Rud, 6 parasangs from Solṭāniya,[167] is a district of the province (velāyat) of Khamsa, which belongs to ᶜErāq, and one where several Mongol rulers had had their residence.

[262] On one mountain of this district is buried Kedar, son of Ishmael, son of Abraham.[168] Half a parasang from the shrine of Kedar lies a village known by the name of Arghun,[169] and above this village there is a fountain known by the name of Arghun Bolāqi. South of this village and fountain lies the mountain. One day a shepherd of a man named Kerbelā'i Fatḥ ᶜAli Shāhsevan was leading his sheep to pasture at the foot of that mountain. Lying down to rest he saw all of a sudden a mouse that was fetching some white grains from a hole putting them into the sun. The shepherd took the grains and gave some of them to his betrothed, a daughter of his master, Kerbelā'i Fatḥ ᶜAli, and some he kept for himself. Kerbelā'i Fatḥ ᶜAli, seeing his daughter with those grains, wanted to know what was going on and asked the shepherd. When he went with him to the mousehole and dug up the earth, a vault appeared; he found several objects of gold studded with jewels. That same night, he brought them to his house and buried them. A man named Majid, from Garrus,[170] heard of the occurrence; he was in the possession of a book in which was written the history of the Mongols, especially those

166. 690:1291. A mausoleum was built over his tomb by Maḥmud Ghāzān (r. 1295–1304), see EI[1] I, s.v. Arghun (W. Bartold). Uljāitu Khātun, Arghun's daughter, added to the mausoleum a khāngāh, or convent for dervishes, see Le Strange, *Lands*, p. 223.

167. A village named Sojās is to be found on the 1:500,000 map, about 19 miles southwest of Solṭāniya.

168. The first-born son of Ishmael, see Genesis 25:13. The mountain 25 miles southwest of Solṭāniya which is 9,500 feet high is called Kuh-e Qaidār; this is probably the mountain that Ḥasan-e Fasā'i mentions further on in the text.

169. The village of Arkin marked on the 1:500,000 map on the northern slope of the Kuh-e Qaidār, is probably the village of Arghun.

170. The *Farhang*, IV, 450, cites three places with this name: near Mārand, Marāgha and Kāghadhkonān; see also above, p. 24, note 110.

who had resided in the province of Khamsa. This book also exactly described the tomb of Arghun Khān at the foot of that mountain. Proceeding to that place Majid dug with great accuracy at the spot which still bore traces of the former digging, and he found some more objects. Because of his fear of the governor of that region he escaped, making his way to Shirvān. Thence he proceeded to the province of Haji Tarkhān [that is, Astrakhān]. And the shepherd, for the services he had rendered to Fatḥ ᶜAli, demanded his betrothed in marriage and preparation of the wedding feast without delay. Fatḥ ᶜAli, however, refused, using abusive language. Giving up his hope of becoming son-in-law, the shepherd reported the occurrence to ᶜAbdollāh Mirzā, governor of Khamsa. With the help of several reliable men the governor took away from Fatḥ ᶜAli all the things of Arghun Khān. These were in detail: a tuft of feathers of a strange make to which fragments of rubies, emeralds, and turquoises were attached; a girdle adorned in the same manner; a dagger with a gilt handle and sheath; some other objects of gold that as far as one could see were horse ornaments, the wood of which had vanished whereas the gold had remained; a square water bottle of gold studded with jewels, and full of water; a goblet of gold studded with rubies and emeralds; swordstraps with golden glowworms (kermakhā); rubies some bigger, some smaller than almonds; about 25 nut-size pearls. One could see that the rubies formed a turban decoration and the pearls a necklace. ᶜAbdollāh Mirzā sent another group who examined the vault and found some golden nails, the weight of each being 25 miskal,[171] and some black, white, and red hairs that looked like hair from a beard. All was brought to Tehran, handed over to the shah and put into the treasury, and by these measures Kerbelā'i Fatḥ ᶜAli was reduced to misery. When this became known in Fārs, Ḥosein ᶜAli Mirzā Farmān-Farmā gave orders to pierce the lids of the stone coffins of the Kayānids at Takht-e Jamshid in the

171. 115 grams (1 miskal = 4.6 grams).

district of Marvdasht,[172] so that a man might enter. They did not find anything except a handful of fine dust of the bodies of Jamshid, Kāvus, and Qobād.

HAJI EBRĀHIM KHĀN'S SON RESTORED TO OFFICE IN SHIRAZ. And that year, the shah, by mediation of Haji Moḥammad Ḥosein Khān Amin od-Doula, entrusted the office of lord mayor of the province of Fārs to Mirzā ᶜAli Akbar, son of the late Haji Ebrāhim Khān Eᶜtemād od-Doula Shirāzi, the former grand vizier of Persia, as this office belonged by law of inheritance to Mirzā ᶜAli Akbar and suited his talents. Shokrollāh-e Nuri, being son-in-law of Mirzā Ebrāhim, the lord mayor of Shiraz, and having a confidential post in the service of Ḥosein ᶜAli Mirzā Farmān-Farmā, objected to Mirzā ᶜAli Akbar's appointment as lord mayor. Also, Mirzā Hādi-ye Fasā'i, who had an influential post in the administration of Fārs, advised the governor to call a gathering of the people of Shiraz in order to inquire into their opinion, as to their assent or dissent to the appointment of either Mirzā ᶜAli Akbar or Mirzā Ebrāhim. When the inhabitants of Shiraz had gathered it became known that they demanded from the bottom of their hearts the appointment of Mirzā ᶜAli Akbar. Accordingly, the governor confirmed in the same gathering the royal decree, appointing Mirzā ᶜAli Akbar lord mayor of the province of Fārs and presenting him with the robe of honor due him.

THE SHAH AT SOLṬĀNIYA. The New Year fell on 7th Rabiᶜ I of the year 1227.[173] After the celebration of the feast the shah turned to governing the affairs of the empire. The royal court departed from Tehran and encamped on the pasture of Solṭāniya on 12th Jomādi II.[174] There, he appointed a prince and an emir

172. Takht-e Jamshid ("Throne of Jamshid") is the palace of Persepolis. The coffins of the Kayānids mentioned in the text are very likely the Achaemenian tombs at the slope behind and above the palace.

173. March 21, 1812. 174. June 23, 1812.

to each part of the empire. After staying for some time on the pasture of Solṭāniya, he departed for a change of air and encamped in the district of Sojās Rud in the province of Khamsa. When the autumn grew cold he departed from Sojās Rud and arrived in Tehran on 9th Shavvāl of that year.[175]

THE PEACE TREATY OF GOLESTĀN. The New Year fell on 17th Rabīᶜ I of the year 1228.[176] The shah celebrated the feast in Tehran and then ordered the army to assemble. They arrived in due course at the court. In order to take vengeance on the Russian troops, the shah departed from Tehran on 19th Jomādi I of that year[177] and put up his camp at Ujān in Ādherbāyjān. When the Russian commander in chief heard of the shah's arrival with a big army at Ujān, he also received news that the French emperor, Napoleon, had again broken with the Russian empire and was endeavoring to conquer Russia. Shocked by the two terrible messages, he sent one of his confidants to the ambassador, Sir Gore Ouseley, [263] asking for a peace treaty with the Persian empire. When the English ambassador had fulfilled his mission and consultation had taken place, the officials in charge of the matter decided to conclude a peace treaty. To settle this affair Mirzā Abu'l-Ḥasan Khān was sent to Karabagh, and upon his arrival the treaty was concluded. The treaty was written on two sheets of paper, containing eleven articles of considerable length. As this treaty is not so related to the subject of the Fārsnāma, the reader is referred to the detailed Qājār chronicles for its full contents. The date of the treaty is the 29th Shavvāl of that year.[178] Since the shah now had nothing to fear from the Russian troops, he left Ujān for Tehran.

175. October 16, 1812. 176. March 21, 1813.
177. May 20, 1813.
178. October 25, 1813. According to article 3 of the treaty, "His Majesty, the King of Persia, in demonstration of his amicable sentiments towards the Emperor of Russia, acknowledges in his own name and that of his heirs the sovereignty of the Emperor of Russia over the provinces of Karabagh and Georgia, now called Elizabeth Paul, the districts of

A PERIOD OF NEGOTIATIONS FOREIGN AND CONSOLIDATION HOME

APPOINTMENTS AND PROMOTIONS. At the beginning of that year, before the departure of the royal court, Haji Moḥammad Ḥosein Khān Amin od-Doula Mostoufi ol-Mamālek was sent to settle the affairs of the provinces of Fārs and ᶜErāq. And his son ᶜAbdollāh Khān, beglerbegi of Esfahan, proceeded to the court, taking the place of his father. He was appointed mostoufi ol-mamālek (minister of finance) and granted the title "Amin od-Doula"; and Haji Moḥammad Ḥosein Khān was granted the title "Neẓām od-Doula."

ENVOYS FROM THE ARABIAN PENINSULA IN TEHRAN. In that year two Arabs well versed in the art of rhetoric arrived at the court in the name of the Imam of Yemen, carrying a humble petition to the effect that the Imam complained to the shah of hostile actions committed by Saᶜud, king of Najd. Moreover, three Bedouin-Arabs arrived in the name of Sheikh Saᶜud, son of Sheikh ᶜAbd ol-ᶜAziz Vahhābi, carrying a petition and presents, one of which was an emerald the size of the palm of the hand, very pure, clear, and transparent. In the petition it was requested that in future the shah might induce the pilgrims to prefer traveling through Najd, as this way was shorter. The townspeople would minister to the needs of each pilgrim. Then a man named Sheikh ᶜAli arrived at the court in the name of the governor (ḥākem) of Baḥrein with a petition, and several pearls and precious objects from India, requesting the following:

Shekie, Shiriwan, Kobek, Derbend, Bakoobeh, and such part of Talish as is now possessed by Russia, the whole of Dagestan, Georgia, the tract of Shoorgil, Achook, Bash, Gooreea, Mingrelia, Abtichar, the whole country between the boundary at present established and the line of Caucasus, and all the territory between the Caucasus and the Caspian Sea," see Hurewitz, I, 84–86, dated September 30/October 12 (ratifications exchanged, Tiflis, September 3–15, 1814).

"Upon the death of Nāder Shāh Afshār some ᶜOṭubi Arabs,[179] inhabitants of the islands in the Persian Gulf, have occupied the province of Baḥrein. Furthermore, some Javāshem tribesmen,[180] inhabitants of the island of Qeshm and of Bandar Ra's ol-Kheima belonging to ᶜOmān,[181] have taken to piracy on the sea, plundering the ships of Persian merchants and killing the passengers and crews." When the friendship between Persia and England was firmly established, the Persian ministers considered it advisable for both sides to undertake the extermination of the Javāshem, who had become a nuisance on the sea. After consideration of the petitions of the envoys from Yemen, Najd, and Baḥrein, all three were answered in writing, in Arabic, by Mirzā ᶜAbd ol-Vahhāb Moᶜtamad od-Doula Eṣfahāni, and all returned home.

THE SHAH PAYS DEBTS OF A COURTIER. In that year the shah bestowed a gift upon Moᶜtamad od-Doula,[182] such as had never before been bestowed upon a courtier by the rulers. The *Tārikh-e Dhu'l-Qarnein* states in detail the following:

While engaged in the acquisition of spiritual perfection, Moᶜtamad od-Doula had few ties to the corporeal world. Apart from his confidential intercourse with matters of the most sublime nature he never dealt with any affair of this world requiring practical knowledge. To him gold and dust, jewels and rubbish were all the same. All through the year he wasted his precious time on unimportant people and satisfied the needs of his stomach by eating just enough not to die. Although he lived only on bread and lemonade and all the year over wore only the clothes given

179. The Bani ᶜOtub are said to have gone from Najd to Kuweit in 1716; they captured Bahrein from the Persians, who had been ruling it for the previous century and a half, see Winder, *Saudi Arabia*, p. 30.

180. The Javāshem were engaged in pearl fishery and took to piracy from 1770–1820, when they were subdued by British forces from India, see Miles, *Persian Gulf*, p. 430.

181. The island of Qeshm lies off Bandar ᶜAbbās, Ra's ol-Kheima on the southern coast of the Persian Gulf. Thus the Javāshem were enabled to control the entrance to the Gulf.

182. Moᶜtamad od-Doula, chancellor of the empire.

him by the court, his agents began closing the accounts with a deficit; gradually their huge spending required the borrowing of money, and in this year his liabilities amounted to the sum of 30,000 toman. When the shah heard of this, he ordered the servants of the harem to disburse the amount of 30,000 toman from his private purse to Mo^{c}tamad od-Doula, and with this money he paid his debts.

APPOINTMENT OF A NEW VIZIER IN SHIRAZ. The New Year fell in the month of Rabi^{c} I of the year 1229.[183] At the beginning of that year, Mirzā Yusof-e Ashrafi-ye Māzandarāni, vizier of Fārs, was removed from his office. One of his accomplishments in Shiraz is the bazaar known as "Bazār-e Mirzā Yusof." It lies in the vicinity of the Esfahan gate at Shiraz and is an enlargement of the Bazār-e Karim Khān Vakil. The exterior was made in the same fashion exactly as the Bazār-e Vakil. According to the proverb "What has the surface of the earth to do with the Pleiades," the difference between the two bazaars is exactly the same as that between the two builders. At the beginning of that year the vizierate of the province of Fārs was entrusted to Mirzā Zein ol-^{c}Ābedin-e Kāshāni. After the calligrapher Mir ^{c}Emād od-Din[184] nobody has written as beautiful nasta^{c}liq as he.

FOREIGN RELATIONS. In that year Haji Mirzā Abu'l-Ḥasan Khān was appointed ambassador to Russia; he was to demand by all means the restitution of the territory on this side of the river Araxes that had been occupied by the Russians. The presents for the Russian emperor and the nobles of the Empire handed over to the ambassador were: 10,000 toman in cash, 2 elephants, 10 select horses, 100 Kashmir shawls, 10 incom-

183. March 21, 1814.

184. A famous calligraphist from Qazvin who flourished in the sixteenth and seventeenth centuries, see Qāżi Aḥmad (c. 1615–16), *Calligraphers and Painters*, translated from the Persian by V. Minorsky (Washington, D.C.; Freer Gallery of Art Occasional Papers, Vol. III, Part 2 [1959]), p. 167.

parable strings of pearls, several rubies from Badakhshān,[185] pomegranate-colored hyacinths,[186] swords from Khorasan, brocaded silk from Esfahan, boxes studded with jewels and filled with bezoar stones from Shabānkarā,[187] and carpets from Herāt. After his departure, another 40,000 toman were sent to him to be spent on the restitution of the provinces; the end, however, proved a disappointment.

In that year the English ambassador, Sir Gore Ouseley, went to England, at his own request. Mr. Morier[188] was appointed his deputy, with the title "envoy." Sir Ouseley traveled by way of Istanbul.

ARREST OF THE GOVERNOR OF ASTĀRABĀD. On the 11th Rabi^{c} II of that year[189] the shah departed from Tehran and set up his camp on the pasture of Firuzkuh.[190] [264] After sufficient recreation and hunting the shah proceeded to Chashm-e ^{c}Ali, in the region of Dāmghān, called ^{c}Ali Bolāgh by the Turks.[191] In this camp, Mohammad Zamān Khān-e Qājār ^{c}Ezz od-Dinlu, governor of Astarābād, who for a time had been disobedient, was caught by bailiffs sent by the shah. He was brought before the shah and then deprived of sight in both eyes. Shortly after,

185. Badakshān on the upper Oxus was famous for its jewels in the Middle Ages, see Le Strange, *Lands*, p. 436.

186. "Rommāni" means pomegranate-colored hyacinth, see E. Wiedemann, *Über den Wert von Edelsteinen bei den Muslimen*, in: Der Islam 2 (1911), pp. 345–58, esp. p. 348 (according to Biruni).

187. Shanbānkāra is a region in the southeastern part of Fārs, stretching from Niriz down to Ṭārom. Their Bezoar stones came from goat stomachs and were used for medical purposes.

188. James Justinian Morier (c. 1780–1849), is the famous author of *The Adventures of Hajji Baba of Isfahan*, 1824. He left Tehran on October 6, 1816. He is also the author of a most instructive account of his travels, see Bibliography at the end of this book.

189. April 2, 1814.

190. Famous summer resort of the Persian rulers, situated about 80 miles east of Tehran in the valley which now is used by the railway line ending at Bandar Shahpur on the Caspian Sea.

191. For ^{c}Ali Bolāgh, see above, p. 16, note 73.

the royal court departed from Chashm-e ᶜAli in the region of Dāmghān and returned to Tehran at the end of Ramażān.[192]

A CASE OF BLOOD REVENGE. That year, Mirzā Bāqer-e Fāmuri, intendant of the province of Fārs and governor of Kāzerun, maternal cousin of the author of this book, and son of Haji Seiyed Yusof Mojtahed-e Thoranjāni Kāzeruni, proceeded from Shiraz to Fāmur[193] to settle agricultural affairs. However, between Fāmur and Dāyen near Kāzerun,[194] Mir Shams od-Din-e Noudāni Kāzeruni, a servant (noukar) of Mirzā Bāqer, killed this noble seiyed by a shot from his musket. Two months later Mollā Shāh Moḥammad, another servant of Mirzā Bāqer, killed Mir Shams od-Din; and on the threshold of the "New Mosque" at Shiraz a black slave of Mir Shams od-Din killed Mollā Shāh Moḥammad. The same day the governor of Fārs, Ḥosein ᶜAli Mirzā, killed the black slave of Mir Shams od-Din.

SUPPRESSION OF A LOCAL REVOLT. The New Year fell on 9th Rabiᶜ II of the year 1230.[195] There are three Qājār chronicles; the authors were contemporaries of Fatḥ ᶜAli Shāh and have reported the events day by day: 1) *Tārikh-e Dhu'l-Qarnein*, by Mirzā Fażlollāh-e Khāveri Monshi-ye Shirāzi, 2) *Roużat oṣ-Ṣafā-ye Nāṣeri*, by Amir-e Kabir Reżā Qoli Khān-e Māzandarāni with the penname Hedāyat, and, 3) *Tārikh-e Nāsekh ot-tavārikh*, by Mirzā Moḥammad Taqi Mostaufi-ye Kāshāni with the penname Sepehr.[196] In all three chronicles it is stated that Amir Abu Dolaf, a ruler during the time of the Abbasids,[197]

192. About September 10, 1814.
193. 19 miles southeast of Kāzerun.
194. *FNN*, II, 185 mentions Dāyen-e ᶜolyā and Dāyen-e soflā in the district of Jira, south of Fāmur. A Dāyen near Kāzerun is unknown.
195. March 21, 1815.
196. These chronicles are discussed in the Introduction.
197. Abu Dolaf (d. 225:839/40) was the founder of a principality in the region east of Nehāvand between Hamadān and Esfahan, his capital was Karaj (near the modern town of Arāk). The power of the Dulafids came to an end at the close of the ninth century, see EI² II, s.v. Dulafids (E. Marin).

had in the district of Farāhān near Qom built two towns, one below ground, and the other above. For the town he built below ground, he had a big hole dug, with a circumference of 3 parasangs, and in this he built mosques, bazaars, streets, and baths and other buildings of bricks and plaster. To get light, each building had a hole the size of the opening of a well. Above this subterranean town another town of the same shape and size was built. The name of both these towns, the visible and the invisible, was Dolafābād. In the course of time it became known by the name Zolfābād.[198] In olden times, when the inhabitants of Zolfābād were afflicted by misfortune, they left the visible town and took refuge in the invisible town. All the people of that town who are living in the invisible town will disappear until the day of the Last Judgment. Nowadays only a few traces of that town have survived; from these one can guess its width and length. And the inhabitants of Zolfābād brought their belongings into that subterranean town and rose in revolt against the governor of Farāhān. That year they mocked Imāni Khān, governor of Farāhān; they stole the possessions of the merchants, hid during the day in the subterranean town, and came out by night to plunder the possessions of the Moslems. This state of affairs was submitted to the shah by Yusof-e Gorji, commander in chief of the army corps of ʿErāq. The shah sent a body of troops to ʿErāq to smoke out the hiding place. Hearing of this, the inhabitants of Zolfābād marched against the troops; they were, however, defeated within a short time and hid in the subterranean town. Then strong forces occupied the surroundings of the town and cut off provisions. After a few months the people grew weary and asked for pardon. On receiving pardon, they took their belongings and their families and were expelled from that region, and Zolfābād was destroyed.

198. Zolfābād lies 31 miles north of Arāk/Solṭānābād, and about 70 miles west of Qom (not mentioned in the *Farhang*).

THE SHAH TRAVELS TO DIFFERENT PARTS OF THE COUNTRY. In the middle of the month of Rabiᶜ I of that year,[199] mountains and plains were covered with snow, so the royal court departed from Tehran for Shekār Masila, a winter habitation on low ground in the region of Qom.[200] Then, when finished hunting gazelles, they encamped in Qohestān near Qom[201] and the other districts. On 12th Rabiᶜ II the court returned to Tehran.[202]

On 17th Rajab of that year[203] the royal army marched off to settle affairs in the province of Khorasan. After some days they encamped in a district of the province of Kabud Jāma near Astarābād.[204] An ᶜErāqi and Bakhteyāri detachment of the regular army (fouj-e jānbāz) was dispatched to establish order in each of the districts and completed this within a short time. The royal court then departed and arrived in Tehran on 22d Shavvāl.[205]

The New Year fell on 21st Rabiᶜ II of the year 1231.[206] On 7th Rajab of that year[207] the royal court departed from Tehran for the pasture of Solṭāniya. Upon the court's arrival, Crown Prince ᶜAbbās Mirzā and Prince Qavām ol-Khelāfa Moḥammad ᶜAli Mirzā arrived from Ādherbāyjān and Kermānshāh at the pasture of Solṭāniya, and royal favors were bestowed upon them. When the weather grew cold, the royal court departed and arrived in Tehran at the end of Shavvāl.[208]

199. February 25, 1815. 200. Not mentioned in our sources.

201. The region south and southwest of Qom, as a Rostāq already mentioned by Ḥasan-e Qomi, *Tārikh-e Qom*, p. 56; for the modern district with its center Kahak, see Keihān, *Joghrāfiyā-ye mofaṣṣal-e Irān*, II, 396.

202. March 24, 1815.

203. June 25, 1815. In the original text this paragraph is erroneously placed behind the story about Zolfābād.

204. The modern Gorgān; Kābud Jāma is not mentioned in the *Farhang*.

205. September 27, 1815. 206. March 21, 1816.

207. June 3, 1816. 208. About September 20, 1816.

THE PERSIAN AMBASSADOR'S NEGOTIATIONS IN ST. PETERSBURG. As has been reported under the events of the year 1229, Haji Mirzā Abu'l-Ḥasan Khān had been appointed ambassador to Russia.[209] He was treated with due respect everywhere. When he arrived in Saint Petersburg, the capital of the Russian empire, the emperor was not there. The ambassador received lodgings in a palace outside the city, and there he waited until the emperor, having fulfilled his aim, the destruction of Napoleon, returned to Saint Petersburg. During the several audiences to which the emperor invited the ambassador, he was very friendly to the ambassador. In the last audience the ambassador's demand for the restitution of the territories occupied by Russia was openly answered by the emperor in the following manner: "We have not conquered Armenia, Georgia and Karabagh in battle; the inhabitants have surrendered to us of their own desire.[210] That man does not act chivalrously who destroys the hopes of those who have surrendered to him. This is a final answer."

Concerning Ganja, Shirvān and Ṭālesh, there are no difficulties. However, our ambassador, the new governor general of Georgia, has to proceed to that region [265] to inquire into the wishes of the inhabitants." At that time, Alexander Yermelov, a Russian prince, was granted the title "ambassador to Persia" and appointed governor general of the province of Caucasia.[211] Numerous presents were given him, and he was sent to Persia with the Persian ambassador, Mirzā Abu'l-Ḥasan Khān. After his arrival in Tiflis he stayed for some time to settle the affairs of that province and sent three of his followers with Haji Mirzā Abu'l-Ḥasan Khān to the Persian court to inform the shah of his appointment and of his forthcoming departure from Tiflis and

209. See above, p. 146 seq.
210. Concerning Georgia, see above, p. 66, note 261.
211. Governor general of Caucasia 1816–27, see Sarkisyanz, *Geschichte der orientalischen Völker Rußlands*, p. 84.

arrival at the court in the middle of spring. When Haji Mirzā Abu'l-Ḥasan Khān and Yermelov's envoys arrived in Tehran and handed over this information, Alexander was asked in the reply note to meet the court on the pasture of Solṭāniya at a fixed time.

ANOTHER CHANGE IN THE VIZIERATE OF SHIRAZ. The New Year fell on 2d Jomādi I of the year 1232.[212] At the beginning of that year Mirzā Zein al-ᶜĀbedin-e Kāshāni was removed from the vizierate of the province of Fārs. The vizierate was entrusted to Āqā Moḥammad Bāqer-e Kāshāni, who was a confidant of Ḥosein ᶜAli Mirzā Farmān-Farmā.

A RUSSIAN AMBASSADOR SENT TO PERSIA. And at the beginning of that year, a royal decree was issued to Crown Prince ᶜAbbās Mirzā, governor of Ādherbāyjān, and ᶜAbdollāh Mirzā, governor of Khamsa, to the effect that on the arrival of the Russian ambassador they were to escort him with all honors from the border of the Persian territory as far as the province of Zenjān. Furthermore, Mirzā ᶜAbd ol-Vahhāb Moᶜtamad od-Doula was sent to the province of Khamsa to prepare lodgings upon the Russian ambassador's arrival, a parasang from the pasture of Solṭāniya, and to entertain him and inquire into his opinions.

The royal court departed from Tehran on 27th Shaᶜbān of that year[213] and encamped on the pasture of Solṭāniya on 17th Ramażān.[214] On the following day a delegation was sent to welcome the Russian ambassador, and he was escorted to the camp with all honors. After entering the enclosure of the royal pavilion, he prostrated himself at four spots and was granted permission to enter the royal pavilion. Since an ambassador has royal rank, he was allowed, in honor of the Russian emperor, to sit down, but knowing etiquette, he sat for a short while and then rose. The prime minister, Mirzā Shafiᶜ, accepted the letter from

212. March 20, 1817 (should be March 21).
213. July 12, 1817. 214. July 31, 1817.

the Russian emperor and put it on the jewel-studded throne. The shah then ordered the ambassador's followers to be introduced. Upon their entering the ambassador introduced each of them to the shah, and they all received a royal favor according to rank. After receiving permission to leave the audience, the ambassador returned and established himself in the tent of the prime minister. Three days later he presented the shah with the gifts from the Russian emperor, among them a mechanical elephant with a litter of gold. In the elephant's left side was a key which could be turned like that of a clock. The elephant's limbs would then move and from inside the elephant came beautiful sounds.

All the Persian ministers tried to learn the ambassador's opinion concerning the restitution of the provinces occupied by the Russians. They heard exactly the same answer which the Russian emperor had given to Haji Mirzā Abu'l-Ḥasan Khān. After some time the Russian ambassador was allowed to leave the pasture of Solṭāniya, and he returned to Tiflis. And the royal court departed from Solṭāniya and arrived in Tehran on 11th Dhu'l-Qa^{c}da.[215]

THE GOVERNOR OF FĀRS UNDERTAKES CAMPAIGN TO THE PERSIAN GULF. In that year Naṣir Khān, governor of Lārestān, sent a letter of complaint to the governor of Fārs, Ḥosein ^{c}Ali Mirzā, concerning the hostile actions of Sheikh Vahhābi, governor of Bandar Maghu.[216] At the beginning of autumn that year the governor of Fārs departed from Shiraz with several detachments of Nuri musketeers, Lors, Turks, and men recruited from the districts (boluki), in order to defeat Sheikh Vahhābi; he marched through Firuzābād to the town of Galladār, the governor's residence in the district of Bikha-ye Fāl.[217] When the

215. September 22, 1817.

216. Bandar Maghu lies near the southern-most point of the Persian Gulf coast, about 80 miles southeast of Lār.

217. Fāl is the ancient name of the district of Galladār, see *FNN*, II, 285. In the *Farhang*, VII, 161, a village *Fāl*, 50 miles southeast of Bandar Kangān, is mentioned. Bikha is unknown to both authors.

auxiliary forces of Galladār joined the other detachments, Moḥammad Zaki Khān-e Nuri was appointed commander in chief of all these troops. Then news arrived from Bandar Maghu that most of the people of Shib Kuh[218] in Lārestān, to which the village of Bandar Maghu belongs, not only had refused obedience to the governor of Fārs and asked for the assistance of the Javāshem tribesmen, the inhabitants of the island of Qeshm and of Bandar Ra's ol-Kheima on the coast of ᶜOmān, who like themselves professed the faith of the Vahhābiya; but they had sent for several large and small vessels which had transported their families to the islands, whilst the men remained for battle. Troops, under the command of Moḥammad Zaki Khān-e Nuri were dispatched to Shib Kuh by the governor of Fārs, who stayed at Galladār. When Moḥammad Zaki Khān arrived at Shib Kuh, the Arabs from the ports and islands and Bandar Ra's ol-Kheima, about 10,000 men, marched against the musketeers, and Moḥammad Zaki Khān engaged them in battle at two or three places in the mountains and on the plain. Moḥammad Zaki Khān carried the day everywhere. Then Sheikh-e Maghu'i[219] entrenched himself with his followers in the fortress.[220] Laying siege to that fortress, the regular troops engaged in heavy fighting for three days without interruption. On the fourth day, on the advice of Moḥammad Zaki Khān, they made an assault and captured the fortress easily. After killing all the soldiers they could find, they piled up the skulls in a pyramid on the seashore. The governor of Fārs departed from Galladār and Bikha-ye Fāl victorious and marched by way of Lār, Jahrom, Khafr, and Kavār to Shiraz, arriving there in the month of Rabiᶜ II of the

218. Shib Kuh is the name of the coastal area stretching from Bandar Dayyer as far as Bandar Charak, see *Farhang*, VII, 145.

219. The name is not given in full; this Sheikh-e Maghu'i is probably identical with Sheikh Vahhābi mentioned above.

220. The name of the fortress is omitted in the text; as one can conclude from the details reported further down, it was situated on the seashore.

year 1233.[221] Several people from Bandar Maghu and Shib Kuh who after their escape from the battle had been taken prisoner were sent in fetters to Tehran. After their arrival they renounced the Vahhābiya faith and were released by the mercy of the shah.

MOVEMENTS OF THE ROYAL COURT. The royal court departed from Tehran on 3d Rabi[c] II of that year[222] to seek recreation in the mountains and plains of Māzandarān and on the shores of the Caspian Sea. The shah visited Bārforush, [266] Sāri, Āmol, and Ashraf for entertainment and hunting and then returned to Tehran.

PERSIAN AMBASSADORS SENT TO SEVERAL EUROPEAN COUNTRIES. The New Year fell on 13th Jomādi I of that year.[223] And in that year, Ambassador Mirzā Abu'l-Ḥasan Khān was sent on a mission to Turkey, France, and England to strengthen the friendship between the shah and the rulers of those countries. Mirzā ᶜAbd ol-Ḥosein Khān-e Shirāzi, the ambassador's nephew, was appointed ambassador to Austria (velāyat-e Nemsa), and was given presents befitting kings. In the middle of Rajab of that year[224] they departed for their places of destination.

THE SHAH UNDERTAKES CAMPAIGN TO KHORASAN. The Afghan emirs and the khāns of Khvārezm and Turkestan had no sooner removed themselves from his presence, than the shah made up his mind to proceed to Khorasan and punish them. Orders for the assembling of the army were issued, and the soldiers arrived at the court in due course. On 18th Rajab of that year[225] the royal court departed from Tehran marching by way of Firuzkuh. When news of Ḥasan ᶜAli Mirzā's victory and the defeat of the Afghans had come to the ears of the shah, he turned towards Khvārezm and marched to Khorasan by way of Jājarm

221. Began on February 8, 1818. 222. February 10, 1818.
223. March 21, 1818. 224. May 21, 1818. 225. May 24, 1818.

and Esfarā'en.[226] On 3d Ramażān of that year[227] he arrived in the district of Bām.[228] Mortażā Qoli Khān, the lord of Bām, fled to the strong fortress of Bām, closed the gates, and entrenched himself behind the walls. After two or three days a detachment of brave soldiers made an assault and took the fortress, and Mortaża Qoli Khān took refuge in the royal stable.[229] Since it was the month of Ramażān, the shah forbade plundering and slaughtering in the fortress of Bām, but in compensation he gave the soldiers a sum of money.

An unusual incident occurred: one day before the capture of the fortress of Bām, the shah had proceeded to a hill to observe the fortress. A shot was fired at him from the fortress which hit a slave in the forehead, killing him on the spot. Upon the capture of the fortress it became known that the shooter had been a man named Moḥammad and that he had made his escape. The shah, however, never inflicted a punishment on the man's family.

The royal court then proceeded to Khabushān.[230] Upon the arrival the shah ordered the siege of the fortress of Khabushān. The commanders of the army had an entrenchment dug around the fortress and established themselves comfortably. A satisfac-

226. Jājarm lies about 110 miles east of Gorgān, Esfarā'en about 50 miles east-northeast of Jājarm. Accordingly, he used the northern route to Mashhad.

227. Began July 5, 1818.

228. The *Farhang*, IX, 61, mentions Bām 62 miles northeast of Ṭabas; however, this town cannot be meant here, as the Bām of the text probably lies on the northern side of the Kuh-e Shāh Jahān, either on its northern slope or in the valley in which Shirvān and Khabushān, mentioned in the text further down, are situated.

229. This is to be understood as a symbolic action: the refugee puts himself at the disposal of the owner of the stable, as a beast. According to Euan Smith, "the stable of the Shah and the British Minister at Tehran are, for instance, privileged places where all criminals can securely take bast or refuge," see *Eastern Persia, an Account of the Journeys of the Persian Boundary Commission 1870–71–72*, London 1876, Macmillan and Co., I 182.

230. Khabushān is about 10 parasangs away from Shirvān, mentioned below.

tory camp was put up on the plain and in the desert, and orders were issued to the people of the camp that they should prepare for a stay of three months. Within a short time they erected a new fortress around the old fortress of Khabushān. When Reżā Qoli Khān-e Kord Za^cfarānlu, the lord of Khabushān, who was staying at Torbat-e Ḥeidari, heard of the shah's arrival with 50,000 men and the siege of Khabushān, he could not but move off. Since he could not enter Khabushān, he established himself at Qal^ca-ye Shirvān, 10 parasangs from Khabushān.[231] Then Prince Moḥammad Taqi Mirzā was ordered to lay siege to the fortress of Shirvān. Aware of his great difficulties, Reżā Qoli Khān saw no remedy but to implore the mediation of the prime minister, Mirzā Shafi^c, and, as a reassurance, he asked Mirzā Shafi^c to come and see him. The ministers were of the opinion that it would be useful for the prime minister to proceed, so he departed with several of his confidants from Khabushān and after marching 10 parasangs arrived at Shirvān. There he stayed for eight days. His advice, threats, and promises made no impression upon Reżā Qoli Khān. However, the latter's aged father, Amir Guna Khān, imprisoned in the fortress of Shirvān by his son's own tyranny, said to his son in paternal affection: "To win the favor of the prime minister you must do this: Put your head on the palm of your hand and proceed to the royal camp. If they kill you, it will cover that dynasty with shame. If they let you live, it will be for you the foundation of your fame." Reżā Qoli Khān did not heed the advice of this old man either, and the prime minister returned to the camp. On the following day, by order of the shah, the districts of Khabushān were devastated, the houses burned down. Then Reżā Qoli Khān implored the mediation of the theologians and seiyeds and sent his son, daughter, and wife as hostages that his appearance before the

231. Probably the same as Shirvān, about 40 miles northwest of Quchān. According to the *Farhang*, IX, 252, Shirvān lies about 45 miles west of Quchān.

shah might be postponed to the following year. Complying with the mediation of the theologians and seiyeds, the shah sent Reżā Qoli Khān's hostages to Mashhad. When Moḥammad Raḥim Khān, king of Khvārezm[232] heard of this, he retreated from the vicinity (of the shah) to the remotest part of his own country.

THE SHAH VISITS THE SHRINE AT MASHHAD. In the middle of the month of Shavvāl of that year[233] the shah departed from Khabushān and went on a pilgrimage to the shrine of Emām Reżā at Mashhad. Upon his arrival at the Kheyābān gate of Mashhad, he dismounted and prostrated himself on the ground every few steps. From excessive observation of the custom he did not proceed beyond the Dār ol-Ḥoffāẓ;[234] assuming the attitude of devotion, at a place in the shrine where he could look at the sacred sepulcher, and shedding tears, he performed the rites of the pilgrimage. He remained six days outside the town of Mashhad and ordered the building of a new courtyard at the foot of the blessed tomb. For this purpose he disbursed the sum of 10,000 toman. Then he departed for Tehran, arriving there on 17th Dhu'l-Ḥejja of that year.[235]

THE VIZIER OF SHIRAZ MURDERED. At the end of that year an agent of the Divan, not having received his pay in accordance with the rule, and incited by agitators, plunged his dagger into the chest of Āqā Moḥammad Bāqer-e Kāshāni, vizier of the governor of Fārs, killing him on the spot. This happened on the Meidān-e Ark at Shiraz, when the vizier left his house to see the governor. During these days Haji Mirzā Reżā Qoli Navā'i, the former chancellor of the empire, an aged

232. Khān of Khiva of the Inakide line, reigned 1221:1806–1241:1826, see Zambaur, *Manuel*, p. 275 seq.

233. August 18, 1818.

234. "House of the Koran reciters," that is, a building adjacent the sepulcher in which continuous recital of the Koran is performed by officials paid from the regular income of the shrine.

235. October 18, 1818.

and senile man, arrived at Shiraz coming from Mecca and Medina by way of Baḥrein and Bushehr. The governor, making favorable use of this opportune arrival, appointed him vizier of Fārs.

DIPLOMATIC RELATIONS WITH AUSTRIA. And that year there arrived in Tehran Mirzā ᶜAbd ol-Ḥosein Khān-e Shirāzi (son of Ambassador Mirzā Abu'l-Ḥasan Khān's sister) who had been sent on a mission to Austria,[236] [267] carrying a letter of friendship and presents from the Austrian emperor.

MOVEMENTS OF THE ROYAL COURT. The New Year fell on 24th Jomādi I of the year 1234.[237] On 12th Jomādi I[238] Fatḥ ᶜAli Shāh left Tehran for Qom and Kāshān and returned on 2d Jomādi II.[239] On 27th Shaᶜbān[240] the shah departed from Tehran for the pasture of Solṭāniya. Some days later he encamped at Solṭāniya; the inhabitants of Ādherbāyjān, Kurdistan, and Kermānshāh offered prayers on behalf of the perpetuity of the dynasty and for the efficiency of the princes, namely Crown Prince ᶜAbbās Mirzā and Moḥammad ᶜAli Mirzā, in establishing order and security.

DEATH OF THE PRIME MINISTER. In that year the prime minister, Mirzā Shafiᶜ, was taken ill during his journey with the court to the pasture of Solṭāniya and died on arriving at Qazvin. His body was brought to Solṭāniya and then transferred to Kerbelā. The office of prime minister was bestowed upon Haji Moḥammad Ḥosein Khān Neẓām od-Doula Eṣfahāni; he was granted the title "Ṣadr-e aᶜẓam." Mirzā Fażlollāh-e Khāveri-ye Shirāzi writes in his *Tārikh-e Dhu'l-Qarnein*:

> I found the words *vazir-e aᶜẓam* as a chronogram for the date of the death of Mirza Shafi-e Māzandarāni and the appointment of Haji Moḥammad Hosein Khan-e Eṣfahāni, and for this I was praised.

236. See above, p. 155.
237. March 17, 1819 (should be March 21).
238. March 5, 1819.
239. March 29, 1819.
240. June 21, 1819.

MARRIAGE OF CROWN PRINCE MOḤAMMAD MIRZĀ. Since autumn was drawing near, the Shah departed from Solṭāniya and arrived in Tehran on 19th Dhu'l-Qaᶜda of that year.[241] At that time Moḥammad Mirzā, the second crown prince and son of Crown Prince ᶜAbbās Mirzā, was received in audience, and a wedding feast was celebrated for him when he was married to the daughter of Moḥammad Qāsem Khān-e Qājār Qoyunlu, son of the shah's daughter. Both royal children were happy when they saw each other. One of the remarkable stories which are told in the Qājār chronicles is this: "One day, the late Āqā Moḥammad Shāh said in a conversation with Fatḥ ᶜAlī Shāh: 'I have united the Qājār Devehlu with my dynasty.[242] You must marry the daughter of Mirzā Moḥammad Qājār Devehlu to your crown prince, ᶜAbbās Mirzā. Their child, Devehlu by the mother and Qoyunlu by the father, will also be crown prince. When he has grown up and if you are still alive, choose for him a girl from the Qoyunlu, then their son will be a Qoyunlu from both sides. When he ascends the throne, the shah will be totally Qoyunlu.' Having said this, Āqā Moḥammad Shāh, overwhelmed with joy, shouted ecstatically several times: 'All shall be Qoyunlu, all shall be Qoyunlu.'" (Perhaps inspiration, peculiar to a ruler, made him say this; for it is said that "statesmen are inspired" and that saying seems to prove true by the existence of Nāṣer od-Din Shāh.)

APPOINTMENT OF A "CHIEF OF THE TRIBES" OF FĀRS. In that year [1234], by mediation of Haji Mirzā Reżā Qoli Navā'i, vizier of Fārs, the title "Ilkhāni" was bestowed upon Jāni Khān-e Qashqā'i, ilbegi of Fārs. His son Moḥammad ᶜAli he appointed ilbegi. Up to that year nobody in Fārs had been called by the title "Ilkhani." The head of the tribes in Khorasan used to be called "Ilkhani."

241. September 9, 1819.

242. By marrying Fatḥ ᶜAli Khān to the daughter of Fatḥ ᶜAli Khān-e Qājār Devehlu, see above, p. 16.

THE SHAH RECEIVES GIFTS FROM THE RUSSIAN EMPEROR. The New Year fell on 8th Jomādi II of the year 1235.[243] On 26th Shaᶜbān[244] the royal court departed for the pasture of Solṭāniya. Envoys from the Russian emperor arrived at the station of Karaj,[245] carrying a letter of friendship and European presents. Among the presents was a crystal basin of octagonal shape, each side measured 2 cubits in width and length, the depth was 1 cubit; the fountain piece was also 1 cubit high. The basin and its fountain piece were cut like beautiful diamonds. In addition there were several large mirrors, a good 2 or 3 cubits high, and a luster. The shah was impressed by the presents and sent them to Tehran. Then he departed for Solṭāniya, where he arrived on 12th Ramażān.[246] When the summer had passed and all the districts had been put in order he departed for Tehran, arriving there on 11th Dhu'l-Qaᶜda of that year.[247]

MEASURES TAKEN AGAINST A SUFI ORDER. The Sufi order of Shāh Neᶜmatollāh-e Mahāni Kermāni[248] had already spread before the time of the Safavids in the provinces of Persia; its profession of the Shia faith is generally known. Many theologians and sheikhs of the Twelver-Shia have praised this order and have become adherents of its leaders. In those years Haji Moḥammad Ḥosein-e Eṣfahāni, descendant of Sheikh Zein od-Din,[249] and

243. March 23, 1820 (should be March 21).

244. June 8, 1820.

245. About 18 miles west of Tehran.

246. June 23, 1820.

247. August 20, 1820.

248. One of the three Sufi orders of Persia, besides the Dhahabi and the Khāksār; the Neᶜmatollāhi trace their origin back to Maᶜruf al-Karkhi, a famous mystic and ascetic of the eighth to ninth century, see Richard Gramlich, *Die schiitischen Derwischorden Persiens*. Erster Teil: Die Affiliationen, Wiesbaden, 1965 (Abhandlungen für die Kunde des Morgenlandes, Vol. XXXVI, Part 1).

249. Ḥosein ᶜAli Shāh Eṣfahāni, "Pole" (qoṭb) of the order since 1212:1797/98; he left Esfahan in 1233:1817/18 and settled down at Kerbelā, see Gramlich, *Derwischorden*, p. 40.

Haji Moḥammad Jacfar-e Karaguzlu Hamadāni[250] were renowned for mystical exercise and asceticism. Several people joined them as disciples, among them cAli Khān-e Eṣfahāni, vizier to Prince Moḥammad Reżā Mirzā, governor of Gilān and Rasht.[251] By mediation of this vizier, Moḥammad Reżā Mirzā, too, considered becoming a follower of Haji Moḥammad Ḥosein, Sheikh Zein od-Din and Haji Moḥammad Jacfar-e Qaraguzlu. A group of adherents of this order who had gathered together in Gilān were favored by the prince, and other people, totally destitute, joined this group and spent the money gained from the donations of the prince on pleasure. The theologians of Gilān assumed that those ignorant fools were actually adherents of the Necmatollāh order and that they did this with the permission of their *pir* und *morshed*. Under this erroneous assumption they complained about the prince and submitted petitions to the court. The shah left Tehran to hunt and amuse himself at Ṭārom[252] and to investigate this affair. Upon his arrival at Ṭārom [268] he summoned Prince Moḥammad Reżā Mirzā and the officials of Gilān. cAli Khān-e Eṣfahāni was then removed from the vizierate of the prince and the group of corrupted followers was expelled from Gilān, some of them in fetters. Since the corrupted group allied itself with Haji Moḥammad Jacfar-e Karaguzlu Kābudārahangi-ye Hamadāni, the shah ordered Chief Courier (jārchi bāshi) Fāżel Khān-e Garrusi, an educated and irreproachable man, to proceed to Hamadān and to confiscate the sum of 1,000 toman, as a punishment for the crimes of the Gilānis, from Haji Moḥammad Jacfar.[253] Fāżel Khān

250. Moḥammad Jacfar Kābudarāhangi Hamadāni Qaraguzlu "Maḥjub" cAli Shāh," disciple of Ḥosein cAli Shāh, was "Pole" after the latter's death in 1234:1818. The modern Dervishes consider him the greatest Sufi of the nineteenth century, see *ibid.*, pp. 43 seq.

251. He was a son of Fatḥ cAli Shāh, see Genealogical Tables at the end of this book.

252. For Ṭārom, see above, p. 14, note 60.

253. He was punished in his capacity as "Pole" of the whole order (not mentioned by Gramlich); three or four years later he died at Tabriz.

executed this order, and the shah returned to Tehran on 27th Jomādi I of the year 1236.[254]

TRIBAL QUARRELS IN FĀRS SETTLED. At the end of spring and the beginning of summer of that year quarrels and fighting concerning summer quarters and pasture grounds arose between the Qashqā'i and Bakhteyāri tribesmen of Fārs, on the plain of Falā Rad and Khān Mirzā, in the district of Sarḥadd-e Shesh Nāḥeya, which adjoins the district of the Bakhteyāri near the Sabz-e Kuh and Chaghākhur.[255] On both sides several people were killed. In the end the Qashqā'i came out victorious. When news of this was heard at Shiraz by Ḥosein ᶜAli Mirzā Farmān-Farmā, he sent Jāni Khān-e Qashqā'i, the ilkhani of the tribes of Fārs, to Falā Rad to reconcile both parties. The Bakhteyāri, not content with the peace concluded by the ilkhani, appealed to the shah. Amir-e Kabir Moḥammad Qāsem Khān, son of Amir-e Kabir Soleimān Khān Neẓām od-Doula Qājār Qoyunlu, was then ordered to effect the reconciliation. Upon his arrival he conferred successfully with both sides. He then proceeded to Shiraz, paid Farmān-Farmā a visit and was granted honors, and returned to Tehran.

DIPLOMATIC RELATIONS WITH ENGLAND AND EGYPT. And that year Ambassador Haji Mirzā Abu'l-Ḥasan Khān-e Shirāzi, who in the year 1233[256] had been sent on a mission to the king of England to strengthen the friendship between Fatḥ ᶜAli Shāh and the king of England, completed his mission and returned to Tehran by way of Istanbul.

Some years earlier the Ottoman sultan had bestowed the government of Egypt and the Holy Places of Mecca and Medina upon Moḥammad ᶜAli Pasha.[257] Since Moḥammad ᶜAli Pasha

254. March 28, 1821.
255. Chaghākhur lies about 90 miles southwest of Esfahan. For the "Six Districts" (Sarḥadd-e shesh nāḥeya) see below, p. 225, note 485.
256. See above, p. 155.
257. The appointment had taken place in 1220:1805.

treated the Persian pilgrims and merchants exceedingly well, the shah that year decided to bestow a royal favor upon him, which was to be conveyed by Ḥeidar ᶜAli Khān, son of Moḥammad ᶜAli, the brother of Haji Ebrāhim Khān Eᶜtemād od-Doula, who was treasurer (sonduqdār) in the service of Ḥosein ᶜAli Mirzā Farmān-Farmā. As a gift (khalᶜa) he sent a sword from Khorasan, studded with hyacinth from Rommān. In the appendix of the royal decree the following was stated: "Sheikh ᶜAbdollāh ibn Saᶜud Vahhābi[258] deserves severe punishment, because he oppresses and fights not only opponents but pilgrims and neighbours. Since the desert of Najd belongs to the Ottoman empire, our sending of an army against ᶜAbdollāh ibn Saᶜud without the permission of the sultan would be contrary to the agreement and friendship. Therefore the Persian ministers hesitate to punish ᶜAbdollāh. The army from Fārs, having crossed the sea, will certainly root out ᶜAbdollāh and destroy Derᶜiyya." When Ḥeidar ᶜAli Khān arrived in Egypt and Moḥammad ᶜAli Pasha realized the situation, he sent Ebrāhim Pasha[259] with a large army to subdue ᶜAbdollāh and to destroy Derᶜiyya. ᶜAbdollāh was taken prisoner and sent in fetters to Istanbul. He was put to death in the presence of the Ottoman Sultan Maḥmud Khān. Having completed his mission, Ḥeidar ᶜAli Khān proceeded to Mecca and Medina and performed the rites of the ḥājj and pilgrimage. In accordance with the usage of the Persian Moslems he became "Haji" Ḥeidar ᶜAli Khān. He returned then to Tabriz by Syria.

THE SHAH TRAVELS TO KHORASAN. The New Year fell on 16th Jomādi II of that year.[260] Since the khāns of Khorasan had

258. ᶜAbdollāh I ibn Saᶜud, ruler since 1229:1814. The incident reported here must have taken place before 1233:1818, when Derᶜiyya was occupied by Ebrāhim Pasha and ᶜAbdollāh brought to Istanbul.

259. Son of Moḥammad ᶜAli Pasha; the campaign was undertaken in 1233:1818.

260. March 21, 1821.

become negligent in their obedience toward Ḥasan ᶜAli Mirzā Shojāᶜ os-Salṭana,[261] the shah departed to see to their punishment on 11th Shaᶜbān.[262] After marching through Firuzkuh,[263] he put up his camp on the pasture of Khosh Yeilāq.[264] Within a short time most of the khāns appeared at the court, surrendered hostages, and returned to their places. Several of them who had exceeded all bounds were subdued by Shojāᶜ os-Salṭana, and dispersed in all directions, and on 16th Shavvāl of that year[265] a set of two pearls surrounded with jewels, worth 10,000 toman and made in Tehran, was sent to Mashhad together with ᶜAbdollāh Khān Amin od-Doula. On 1st Dhu'l-Qaᶜda,[266] Shojāᶜ os-Salṭana and the theologians, seiyeds and servants of the shrine, and the nobles of the town welcomed ᶜAbdollāh Khān and escorted him into the town with all honors. A banquet was celebrated in the Dār ol-Ḥoffāẓ, and Mojtahed Mirzā Hedāyatollāh attached the pearls to the foot of the holy sepulcher.[267] The court departed from Khosh Yeilāq on 26th Shavvāl[268] and took up residence in the Negārestān palace outside Tehran on 11th Dhu'l-Qaᶜda of that year.[269]

THE ROYAL COURT AT SOLṬĀNIYA. The New Year fell on 26th Jomādi II of the year 1237.[270] The court departed for Solṭāniya on 5th Shavvāl,[271] arriving and encamping there on 15th

261. Governor of Khorasan, see above, p. 155.
262. May 14, 1821.
263. The mountain range north of Tehran.
264. It was 40 miles northeast of Shahrud, near the Kuh-e Qāsem (2,800 m.), 5 miles from the highway Gorgān-Shahrud, see *Farhang*, III, 132. The 1:500,000 map has "Khāsh-Āylān" by mistake.
265. July 17, 1821.
266. July 31, 1821.
267. The ornaments at the foot of the sepulcher are shown in a photograph in Sykes, *The Glory of the Shia World*, p. 225.
268. July 27, 1821.
269. August 10, 1821.
270. March 20, 1822 (should be March 21).
271. June 25, 1822.

of that month.[272] Every day news of victory over the Ottoman Turks arrived from Crown Prince ᶜAbbās Mirzā.[273]

PERSIA RAVAGED BY PLAGUE. That year plague invaded Persia from China and India. Within five or six days 6,000 people died at Shiraz, and the disease continued to spread. On 3d Dhu'l-Ḥejja of that year[274] the shah broke camp at Solṭāniya and marched to Esfandābād.[275] Outside Hamadān, at the foot of the Kuh-e Alvand, the royal court was infected by the plague. Several people died. The court encamped then at Nehāvand,[276] [269] and the shah spent the days from 1st Moḥarram 1238[277] until the 13th in mourning over Emām Ḥosein. He arrived in Tehran on 24th of that month.[278] And that year Mirzā ᶜIsā-ye Farāhāni, known by the name of Mirzā Bozorg and the title "Qā'em Maqām-e Ṣadārat-e ᶜOẓmā," died from plague. His office and title were conferred upon his son, Mirzā Abu'l-Qāsem.

A REVOLT PLANNED BY THE GOVERNOR OF KHORASAN. In that year, the khāns of Khorasan secretly informed the Persian ministers that Ḥasan ᶜAli Mirzā Shojāᶜ os-Salṭana was planning to rise in revolt and seize the rule, but the shah put no faith in this malicious talk and these obscure insinuations. However, Shojāᶜ os-Salṭana informed Ḥosein ᶜAli Mirzā Farmān-Farmā, governor of Fārs and his full brother, of this story, sending the letter by a courier who traveled through the desert of Lut. Farmān-Farmā wrote in answer: "We must travel to the court, I

272. July 5, 1822.

273. While Turkey, from 1820 onward, was engaged on the Balkan in fighting the Greek revolution, ᶜAbbās Mirzā undertook a successful campaign on the Kurdish frontier; the war ended with the peace treaty of Erzerum, see below, p. 169.

274. August 21, 1822.

275. Esfandābād lies in the region of Razan, 50 miles northeast of Hamadān; the shah took the eastern road leading from Solṭāniya to Hamadān.

276. About 50 miles south of Hamadān.

277. September 18, 1822.

278. October 11, 1822.

from Shiraz and you from Mashhad, in order to free ourselves from the impurity of this inculpation." Farmān-Farmā departed from Shiraz in the company of Haji Akbar Navvāb-e Shirāzi, a man of outstanding learning[279] and arrived in Tehran on 22d Rabiᶜ I of that year.[280] Shojāᶜ os-Salṭana arrived at the court on 5th Rajab[281] and obediently and readily renounced the governorship of Khorasan. Though he did not feel well, he accompanied Farmān-Farmā as far as Esfahan, and then stayed on to be cured. Farmān-Farmā returned to Shiraz at the beginning of the month of Ramażān.[282]

The New Year fell on 8th Rajab of that year.[283] As that year the inhabitants of the Persian empire were in a state of perfect tranquillity and comfort and the court had no motive to proceed anywhere, the shah spent his time hunting.

DEATH OF THE PRIME MINISTER. In the middle of the month of Moḥarram of the year 1239[284] the prime minister, Haji Moḥammad Ḥosein Khān, was taken ill in Tehran. His condition grew worse all the time, until he died on 13th Ṣafar.[285] He was an offspring of the Kadkhodā family from Esfahan. By reason of his sagacity and ingenuity in the handling of affairs and in bargaining with the landowners and his capacity to derive advantage from everything, he was superior to most learned men. Although he could neither read nor write, he was not in need of a scribe or accountant in his transactions and administrative affairs. Step by step he advanced: he was appointed lord mayor of Esfahan; then he advanced further and became beglerbegi of that province; next he was promoted to the governorship of the same region; later he became minister of finance of the

279. Author of the *Tārikh-e Delgoshā*, which contains biographies of prominent citizens of Shiraz; the author of the Fārs-nāma quotes from it, see below, p. 192, note 360.

280. December 7, 1822. 281. March 18, 1823.

282. Began on May 12, 1823. 283. March 21, 1823.

284. September 21, 1823. 285. October 19, 1823.

empire; finally the office of prime minister of the Persian empire was bestowed upon him.[286] When he reached that position, he was truly a third Ma^{c}an and Ḥātem in generosity;[287] his court was a refuge to mankind. After his death the office of prime minister was bestowed upon his son ^{c}Abdollāh Khān Amin od-Doula. However, he was not granted the title "Ṣadr-e A^{c}ẓam"; until the end of his life he was simply called "Amin od-Doula."

After the death of the prime minister, the shah performed a pilgrimage to Qom, to the shrine of Fāṭema, in order to relieve his sadness. Upon his return, out of a desire for a visit of the Ka^{c}ba and in honor of the grave of the Prophet Moḥammad, he gave Haji ^{c}Abdollāh-e Eṣfahāni, the chief eunuch, and the ascetic Ḥāji ^{c}Ali Moḥammad-e Kāshāni the sum of 2,000 toman from the English subsidy, since that money, from the point of view of the Sharia, was lawfully acquired.[288] Since he could not

286. In the year 1234:1818/19, see above, p. 159.

287. Ma^{c}an ibn Zā'edāt (see Steinggass, Persian English Dictionary, s.v.) and Ḥātem oṭ-Ṭāy, two Arabs of pre-Islamic times, were famous for their liberality. The "second" Ḥātem was ^{c}Ali ibn Abi Ṭāleb, mentioned together with Abraham and Ḥātem as an example of liberality by Neẓām ol-Molk, *Siyāsat-nāma*, German translation by Schabinger Freiherr von Schowingen, p. 227.

288. The same is reported by an English merchant who traveled to Persia at the end of the sixteenth century: "One thing somewhat straunge I thought good in this place to remember, that whereas hee (that is, the shah) purposed to send a great summe of money to Mecca in Arabia, for an offering to Mahomet their prophet, hee would not send any money or coine of his owne, but sent to the English merchants to exchange his coine for theirs, according to the value of it: yeelding this reason for the same, that the money of the merchants was gotten by good meanes and with good consciences, and was therefore woorthie to bee made an oblation to their holy prophet, but his owne money was rather gotten by fraud, oppression, and unhonest meanes, and therefore was not fit to serve for so holie a use," see *Early Voyages and Travels to Russia and Persia by Anthony Jenkinson and other Englishmen*, ed. by E. Delmar Morgan and C. H. Coote, New York, N.Y., Burt Franklin (n.d.). Works issued by the Hakluyt Society, First Series, No. LXXIII, Vol. II, p. 426.

go on the pilgrimage himself,[289] he sent the two men mentioned above, appointing them his deputies. Haji ᶜAbdollāh was given a marble block into which was cut a gazel by Mirzā Fażlollāh-e Khāveri-ye Shirāzi, that had impressed the shah.

TREATY CONCLUDED WITH TURKEY. In the middle of the month of Jomādi II of that year,[290] a noble Turk named Najib Efendi arrived in Tehran as ambassador of the sultan. He was received with all honors and put up in the house of the prime minister, Amin od-Doula. On the next day, he was received in audience, and a letter of friendship sealed with the seal of Sultan Maḥmud Khān, submitted with perfect courtesy, was graciously accepted. In the course of several sittings he negotiated the conclusion of a peace treaty with Mirzā Abu'l-Qāsem Qā'em Maqām. Finally they committed to writing the peace treaty concerning the peace between the two governments, and it was sealed with the shah's seal. Then it was handed over to Qāsem Khān, commander of the Special Detachment (fauj-e khāṣṣ) at Tabriz, who was appointed ambassador to Istanbul. Together with Najib Efendi he traveled to Turkey. Upon his arrival a copy of the treaty was to be sealed with the seal of the sultan and brought back to Tehran by Qāsem Khān. After some time the latter returned to Tehran, having attained his end. A copy of this treaty has been inserted in the Qājār chronicles.[291]

289. Visits of the shah to foreign countries were not yet possible (as in the game of chess "two kings cannot stay on the same field," see Ibn al-Athir, *al-Kāmil fi't-ta'rikh*, Vol. IX, under the year 419:1028). In the peace treaty of Erzerum, concluded between Persia and Turkey in the year 1239:1823, provisions were made for the visit of the wives of the shah and of high dignitaries to the Holy Places in Mesopotamia and Arabia, see Noradounghian, II, 95–99.

290. February 16, 1824.

291. The peace treaty of Erzerum, concluded on 19th Dhu'l-Qaᶜda 1238:July 28, 1823, is reproduced in Noradounghian, II, 95–99. Some of the stipulations of this treaty were: free access for the Persians to the Holy Places in Mesopotamia and Arabia; prevention of the Kurds from plundering on Persian territory by the Ottoman authorities; release of the possessions of Persian merchants in Turkey; and the exchange of embassies.

EARTHQUAKES IN SOUTHERN PERSIA. The New Year fell on the evening of 19th Rajab of that year.[292] In the month of Shavvāl,[293] a heavy earthquake occurred at Kāzerun. Some days later, at the time between sunrise and morning prayer, an earthquake of greater intensity occurred at Shiraz, in which most of the old and new buildings, such as mosques, colleges, shrines and houses, were destroyed. As it was the end of spring and all the people were either in the courtyards or on the roofs, only a few thousand people perished. Some days later, another earthquake occurred at Shiraz, less severe, however, than the first. All the people, shocked by the first earthquake, were staying on the roofs, and when they jumped to the ground they broke their bones.

THE SHAH TRAVELS TO ESFAHAN AND ESTABLISHES ORDER THERE. [270] The New Year fell on the evening of 1st Shaᶜbān of the year 1240.[294] After the celebration of the feast the Shah departed from Tehran for the punishment of the evildoers at Esfahan. The best condensed report of what happened is this: Haji Hāshem Khān, son of Haji Rajab ᶜAli-ye Bakhteyāri, inhabitant of the Lombān quarter at Esfahan, who was a brother of the wife of ᶜAbdollāh Khān Amin od-Doula,[295] in his depravity had assembled a group of Lors from the Lombān quarter and criminals from Esfahan. By night they invaded without permission the houses of the wealthy and demanded money. If the landlord did not accede to their demand, they extorted the money by cruel tortures. If the unfortunate man could not afford to hand over the sum requested, he was killed. By day Haji Hāshem Khān, quite publicly and without the permission of the government, ran a tax office (divān khāna) and a guardroom (farrāsh khāna). After arresting guilty or innocent people in the streets under false charges, he brought them to his

292. March 20, 1824 (should be March 21).
293. Began on May 30, 1824. 294. March 21, 1825.
295. Grand vizier since October, 1823, see above, p. 168.

office and gave them the bastinado in order to extort money from them. As long as the late prime minister, Haji Moḥammad Ḥosein Khān, was alive,[296] the latter was able to calm down people who complained; employing his sagacity and patience and using a thousand means, he prevented reports of these occurrences from coming to the ears of the shah. After the prime minister's death the governorship of Esfahan was given to Mirzā ᶜAli Moḥammad Khān, son of ᶜAbdollāh Khān Amin od-Doula.[297] Because Mirzā ᶜAli Moḥammad Khān's mother was a sister of Haji Hāshem Khān-e Bakhteyāri, the latter's misbehavior was not efficiently dealt with by the new governor. Then, one day, Haji Hāshem Khān punished a young Hāshemi Seiyed, shedding the blood of that seiyed of noble birth. By mediation of several pious theologians from Esfahan the latter's mother complained about the treatment of the young man to the shah. The shah proceeded to Esfahan in order to take vengeance for the seiyed's blood. Haji Hāshem Khān, nourishing false hopes because of his pride and his relations to Amin od-Doula and considering his dishonorable actions as correct, welcomed the shah with a group of his assistants and helpers. Upon the arrival of the shah he was, however, arrested and deprived of his sight. By the application of painful tortures to him and his followers everything was extorted from them that over a long period of time they had taken away from the people by oppression and tyranny. The governorship of Esfahan was bestowed upon Solṭān Moḥammad Mirzā, whose mother, Tāj od-Doula, came from Esfahan and was the favorite wife of the shah.[298] Solṭān Moḥammad Mirzā was granted the title "Seif od-Doula." And General (sepahdār) Yusof Khān-e Gorji was appointed vizier of Esfahan.

In those days Ḥosein ᶜAli Mirzā Farmān-Farmā and the nobles of Fārs, namely Moḥammad Zaki Khān-e Nuri, the lord

296. He had died in October, 1823, see above, p. 167.
297. ᶜAbdollāh Khān was the new grand vizier.
298. Probably the "Eṣfahāniya" mentioned above, p. 35.

mayor of Shiraz, Mirzā ᶜAli Akbar, the intendant Mirzā Moḥammad ᶜAli known as Khafrki, Moḥammad ᶜAli Khān-e Eṣfahāni, and Mirzā Moḥammad Ḥosein, vakil of the province of Fārs and son of the late Mirzā Hādi-ye Fasā'i, were received in audience. Each of them was granted a royal favor, according to rank and family. On 1st Shavvāl of that year,[299] having completed the fasting of the month of Ramażān, the royal court departed from Esfahan for Tehran, and Farmān-Farmā and the nobles of Fārs returned to Shiraz.

APPOINTMENTS AND PROMOTIONS. Since Amin od-Doula had for a long time concealed the depravity and tricks of Haji Hāshem Khān-e Bakhteyāri, not reporting this affair to the shah, he was ordered either to pay the sum of 50,000 toman to the treasurers of the shah or to renounce his office. Amin od-Doula, however, considered this a measure which was to be disapproved in a powerful monarch. Accordingly, he was removed from his office. For the administration of important affairs, Allāh Yār Khān-e Qājār Devehlu, a mighty emir and distinguished by being the son-in-law of the shah, was appointed prime minister. He was addressed by the title "Āṣaf od-Doula." And that year Haji Mirzā Abu'l-Ḥasan Khān, the ambassador, was granted the title "minister of the foreign powers" (vazir-e doval-e khāreja).

That year, too, the office of chancellor of the empire was conferred upon the physician in ordinary to the shah (ṭabib-e khāṣṣa), Haji Mirzā Raḥim-e Shirāzi, an elegant writer and sagacious poet,[300] since the rank of Mirzā ᶜAbd ol-Vahhāb Moᶜtamad od-Doula had grown beyond the title and the task of chancellor of the empire. Haji Mirzā Raḥim was granted the title "Monshi ol-Mamālek."

THIRTIETH ANNIVERSARY OF THE SHAH'S ACCESSION TO THE THRONE. The New Year fell on 12th Shaᶜbān of the

299. May 19, 1825.
300. His biography is given below, p. 191, note 360.

year 1241,[301] and Fatḥ ᶜAli Shāh celebrated the feast. Since that year was the thirtieth anniversary of the shah's accession to the throne, new silver and gold coins, the "Ṣāḥeb qerān," was struck by his order: 18 nokhud of pure gold were worth 9,000 dinar of pure silver, and 36 nokhud of pure silver, the equivalent of 1 miskal and half a ṣirafi, were worth 1,000 dinar. The nominal value of the new coins was fixed at 1 toman. On one side of the gold coin was put: "Fatḥ ᶜAli Shāh Khosrou Keshvar-setān," on one side of the silver coin: "Fatḥ ᶜAli Shāh Khosrou Ṣāḥeb qerān." On the other side of both coins the name of the mint town was struck. The silver coins were called "Ṣāḥeb-qerān," the gold coins "Keshvar-setān."[302] The coins from the beginning of Fatḥ ᶜAli Shāh's rule up to that time on which the legend "Solṭān ibn Solṭān Fatḥ ᶜAli Shāh Qājār" was put (the gold coin being called "ashrafi," [271] the silver coin "reyāl"), and having a weight of 2 miskals[303] were abolished.

MISCELLANEOUS EVENTS. And that year Moḥammad Zaki Khān-e Nuri, vizier of Fārs, was granted the privilege of becoming brother-in-law of the shah; he married a sister of Ḥosein ᶜAli Mirzā Farmān-Farmā. And Ilkhāni-e Moḥammad ᶜAli Khān Qashqā'i became son-in-law of Farmān-Farmā, marrying a daughter of His Highness.

Also, in that year a number of gold and silver coins fell into the hands of the inhabitants of Varāmin, a district belonging to Reiy, and of the highland of Dāmghān. Several of the coins bore the name and portrait of Shāpur Dhu'l-Aktāf, the portrait of the coins bore a striking resemblance to the portrait of Shāpur cut

301. That is, 1241: March 22, 1826 (should be March 21).

302. According to Rabino di Borgomale, *Coins, Medals and Seals of the Shahs of Iran*, p. 64, the keshvarsetān was struck from 1246 to 1250, the ṣāḥeb-qerān from 1240 (or 1241) to 1245. The ṣāḥeb-qerān weighed 108 grains.

303. The ashrafi weighed 1 miskal, which equals 72 grains, see Rabino, *Coins, Medals and Seals*, p. 64.

in rock in the vicinity of Kāzerun.[304] The other coins were in the name of the "Four Caliphs" and the Umaiyads, Abbasids, and Mongols. All the coins were delivered to Ḥosein ᶜAli Khān, master of the imperial mint (moᶜeiyer ol-mamālek).

LAST ATTEMPT TO RECOVER ARMENIA AND ĀDHERBĀYJĀN

HOLY WAR DECLARED ON RUSSIA. The Russian troops who were occupying the provinces of Ganja, Karabagh and Shirvan, raped some Moslem women. By mediation of the theologians of that region this affair was reported to Mojtahed Āqā Seiyed Moḥammad, son of the late mojtahed from Esfahan, Āqā Seiyed ᶜAli, who was living in the Holy Places (of Mesopotamia). The aforementioned mojtahed considered the Holy War with the Russians a duty incumbent upon the Moslems according to the laws of the Sharia. Realizing that the shah was inclined to conclude a peace treaty and an agreement with the Russians, he sent at the beginning (of that year) the theologian Mollā Reżā-ye Khoyi Mohammad one of his confidents and an eloquent man, to the court with the order to wage the Holy War. The shah consented to the order and sent Moḥammad Reżā back to Āqā Seiyed Moḥammad, assuring the latter of his benevolence. At the beginning of Shavvāl of that year,[305] Āqā Seiyed Moḥammad arrived in Tehran with a group of theologians. They were highly honored by the shah, the emirs, and the nobles. Then the shah ordered letters to be addressed to all the mojtaheds of the Islamic countries, summoning all the Moslems to the Holy War. In addition to the ordinary expenditure for the army, the shah assigned the sum of 300,000 toman to be spent on the Holy War and appointed ᶜAbdollāh Khān Amin od-Doula, who at that time was being removed from the vizierate,

304. That is, the colossal statue of King Shapur near the ruins of Bishapur.

305. Beginning of May, 1826.

mehmāndār to Āqā Seiyed Moḥammad and the other theologians.

VAIN EFFORTS OF THE RUSSIAN AMBASSADOR TO STOP HOSTILITIES. On 26th Shavvāl of that year,[306] the shah departed from Tehran and encamped on the pasture of Solṭāniya on 6th Dhu'l-Qaᶜda.[307] Crown Prince ᶜAbbās Mirzā proceeded to that place, too. Then the Russian ambassador arrived on the pasture of Solṭāniya. He brought as a present a bed to which bars of crystal were attached; the bed was 3 shāhi cubits long and 2 shāhi cubits wide.[308] Apart from this the ambassador brought a letter of friendship. Having delivered the gifts to the shah he was granted royal favors. On the 17th of that month,[309] Mojtahed Āqā Seiyed Moḥammad, Haji Mollā Moḥammad Jaᶜfar-e Astarābādi, Āqā Seiyed Naṣrollāh-e Astarābādi, Haji Seiyed Moḥammad Taqi-ye Qazvini, and Mojtahed Seiyed ᶜAzizollāh-e Tāleshi arrived in the vicinity of the royal camp. Having been welcomed by all the princes, emirs, and nobles and even all the people of the camp, the mojtaheds entered the royal pavilion with all honors. On the 18th of that month Haji Mollā Aḥmed Narāqi-ye Kāshāni, the highest in rank of all the mojtaheds, Haji Mollā ᶜAbd ol-Vahhāb-e Qazvini and a group of theologians arrived in the vicinity of the camp and were escorted into the camp with all honors by a huge crowd of high and low. Those mojtaheds pronounced a fetvā according to which everybody who did not take part in the Holy War, in accordance with his capacity, was to be considered as one who refused to obey God and joined the followers of Satan. The shah and the crown prince confirmed this statement. Among the nobles, Mirzā ᶜAbd ol-Vahhāb Moᶜtamad od-Doula and Haji Mirzā Abu'l-Ḥasan Khān, minister for the foreign powers, were

306. June 3, 1826. 307. June 12, 1826.

308. 1 shāhi cubit (derāᶜ-e pādeshāh ?), which equals 81.28 centimeters, see Hinz, *Masse und Gewichte*, p. 64.

309. June 24, 1826.

of the opinion that the war with Russia was not promoting the interests of Religion and Empire. In unfriendly messages sent to both of them, the mojtaheds convinced them by religious arguments. When the Russian ambassador became aware of the commotion, he tried to establish peace, but was not listened to. He tried to convene a gathering of the mojtaheds in order to conclude by their mediation a treaty concerning the restitution of the occupied provinces and the withdrawal of the Russian troops from Persian territory. Again this proposal was not taken seriously. The shah informed the ambassador by word of mouth: "The prosperity of the Empire is founded on agreement and peace; it is, however, our religious duty to comply with the orders of the mojtaheds and to wage the Holy War." Seeing that peace was irretrievably lost, the Russian ambassador departed.

THE PERSIAN ARMY LAYS SIEGE ON SHUSHĀ. After the departure of the Russian ambassador the shah dispatched several thousand Māzandarāni horsemen and infantry to Ādherbāyjān, putting them under the command of Prince Esmāᶜil Mirzā. The following day another thousand men under the command of Moḥammad Qoli Khān-e Qājār Devehlu, a son of Prime Minister Allāh Yār Khān-e Astarābādi, were dispatched. On 4th Dhu'l-Ḥejja of that year[310] Crown Prince ᶜAbbās Mirzā departed from the pasture of Solṭāniya for Tabriz. The shah did not go out for the Holy War himself,[311] whereas the mojtaheds, who were models for the people, proceeded with all their followers to Ādherbāyjān in order to incite the civilians and the army. They joined the main body under the command of the crown prince. With their approval the crown prince marched on Shushā and laid siege to the fortress. Every day people from the provinces joined the mojtaheds and put themselves at their dis-

310. July 10, 1826.

311. Literally: "he put the Holy War in his heart," that is, he performed this religious duty mentally, which was one possibility to comply with the orders of the religious authorities.

posal for the Holy War. On the 21st of that month[312] the shah departed from the pasture of Solṭāniya and encamped outside the town of Ardebil. He sent each of the commanders who were in his company with several detachments of Holy War fighters and with several pieces of artillery to Karabagh, Ganja, and Shirvān. After a short time news of victory [272] gained by the Islamic forces arrived from everywhere. On 11th Moḥarram of the year 1242[313] about 1,000 prisoners of war and 500 skulls stuck on lances, taken from the Russian troops and sent by the crown prince were brought before the shah outside Ardebil. And each day several skulls stuck on lances and Russian prisoners of war, sent by the emirs, were brought into the camp of the shah. On the 21st of that month[314] the royal court departed from outside Ardebil for the fortress of Shushā. They encamped on the bank of the river Ṭavila Shāmi[315] on the 24th of that month.[316] The shah ordered Āṣaf od-Doula with 20,000 men and two pieces of artillery to join the crown prince and to endeavor to capture the fortress of Shushā. On 2d Ṣafar of that year,[317] he joined the crown prince in front of the fortress of Shushā. The religious leaders were inciting the people for the Holy War everywhere, and stretch by stretch the territories occupied by the Russians for fourteen years were added to the Persian Empire by the bravery of the army and the incitement of the mojtaheds. And in those days the new ambassador from England[318] arrived at the royal camp. He was welcomed by a group of emirs and put up in a suitable tent.

312. July, 27, 1826. 313. August 15, 1826.

314. August 25, 1826.

315. A tributary of the Araxes River which passes about 45 miles west of Ardebil and flows into the Araxes about 40 miles southeast of Shushā.

316. August, 28, 1826.

317. September 5, 1826.

318. Sir John Macdonnald Kinneir (1782–1830) had made a military career in India and was attached to Sir John Malcolm's mission to Persia, 1808–9.

PERSIAN DEFEAT NEAR GANJA. As has been reported, Crown Prince ᶜAbbās Mirzā aided by the mojtaheds laid siege to the fortress of Shushā. Then the defenders asked for pardon deceitfully protracting the negotiations for some days. The crown prince sent Second Crown Prince Moḥammad Mirzā, with troops of Khvāja Vand[319] and ᶜAbd ol-Maleki[320] to Ganja to guard the fortress which had passed into the possession of the Persian army. The crown prince himself, in agreement with the mojtaheds, and Āṣaf od-Doula remained before Shushā in order to occupy the fortress (as soon as the negotiations with the Russians were finished). Whereupon the Russian General Madatov[321] sent several detachments to conquer Ganja. The commander, Amir Khān-e Qājār, maternal uncle of Crown Prince ᶜAbbās Mirzā, being on his guard, entrusted the protection of the fortress of Ganja to ᶜAli Khān-e Marandi and marched against Madatov, accompanied by Second Crown Prince Moḥammad Mirzā. When they started fighting, the commander, Amir Khān, was killed by a Russian musket ball. The Persian troops were dispersed, and Madatov, marching with great haste to Ganja, occupied the fortress. At the same time Crown Prince ᶜAbbās Mīrzā had the fortress of Shushā firmly in his grip. When news of the capture of Ganja arrived, he left the fortress of Shushā without delay and marched hastily on Ganja, taking with himself, with the approval of the theologians, the whole army. Madatov came out of the town and encamped with the Russian troops and the artillery opposite the Persian troops. In the first night a Russian general named Paskevich[322] arrived with

319. They probably belonged to the Lak, a Kurdish tribe in the region of Kermanshah, see above, p. 52, note 218.

320. Concerning the ᶜAbd ol-Maleki, see above, p. 46.

321. Valerian Grigorievich Madatov (1782–1829), see *Enziklopedichesky slovar'* (1896), XVIII, 339.

322. Ivan Fedorovich Paskevich (1782–1856), Count of Erevan, became more famous for his suppression of the revolt of Poland in 1831 and was granted the title "Prince of Warsaw."

several detachments and cannon and joined the camp of Madatov. On 28th Ṣafar of that year,[323] the troops of both sides lined up for battle. The crown prince entrusted the center of his lines to the soldiers from Ādherbāyjān, putting them under the command of Prince Khosrou Mirzā and two of his other sons. At the beginning of the battle the Persian troops were victorious and pushed the Russians back a little. When the Russian artillery gave fire, the crown prince, fearing lest the princes—God forbid! —got confused in the thick of the battle, sent a horseman to inform the tutor (lala) and the servants to bring out the princes. Accordingly, they brought them out of the thick of the battle, helping them imprudently to retreat from the battle line before the eyes of the soldiers. The captains, seeing their leaders in full flight, sounded to retreat, and the whole Ādherbāyjāni army, the center of the line, was defeated without giving battle. Falling back near the horses of the ᶜErāqi and Bakhteyāri soldiers, who had dismounted and were fighting on foot, the Ādherbāyjāni soldiers mounted the horses and made their escape. Having noticed this, the ᶜErāqi and Māzandarāni soldiers stopped fighting and entrenched themselves on top of a small hill. In the space of twenty-four hours the Ādherbāyjānis hurried from the region of Ganja as far as the river Araxes.[324] The mojtaheds and theologians, the instigators of this war, made good their escape faster than all the others. The next day the Russians took prisoner the ᶜErāqis and Māzandarānis who had entrenched themselves on top of the hill after they had offered to surrender. Crown Prince ᶜAbbās Mirzā and Āṣaf od-Doula afflicted with grief and repentance gathered together their defeated army on the bank of the river Araxes.

RETURN OF THE ROYAL COURT TO TEHRAN BY WAY OF TABRIZ. When the shah heard of this, he sent Crown Prince

323. October 1, 1826.

324. The distance between Ganja/Kirovabad and the Araxes River was about 125 miles.

ᶜAbbās Mirzā and Āṣaf od-Doula affectionate messages. During the night of 1st Rabiᶜ I of that year,[325] so much snow fell on the camp of Ṭavila Shāmi as to make any further stay unthinkable. The court departed with haste from this camp and hurried to Tabriz. Āqā Seiyed Moḥammad and the rest of the theologians had already arrived at Tabriz. The inhabitants of Tabriz were angry with them for several reasons, one being that in the battle of Ganja a noble seiyed and preacher from Tabriz and a group of men waging the Holy War had been killed. Since the people of Tabriz considered Āqā seiyed Moḥammad the propagator of the war and of the breach of the peace treaty with the Russians, they planned his downfall. This state of affairs was reported to the shah by ᶜAbdollāh Khān Amin od-Doula, the mehmāndār of the mojtaheds. One day the shah, out of concern for the Sharia, paid a visit to Āqā Seiyed Moḥammad, showing the latter great respect. The people of Tabriz, seeing this affectionate treatment, gave up their intentions on the seiyed. After three days the royal court departed from Tabriz; marching by way of Marāgha, the shah arrived in Tehran on 22d Rabiᶜ II.[326] After the departure of the royal court Mojtahed Āqā Seiyed Moḥammad departed for the Holy Places (in Mesopotamia). On the way he was taken ill with diarrhea and died.

A NEW PERSIAN CAMPAIGN OPENED. [273] The New Year fell on 22d Shaᶜbān of that year.[327] After the celebration of the feast, the shah issued orders to the army concerning the continuation of the war with the Russians. Within a short time the surroundings of Tehran were crowded with troops. On 8th Dhu'l-Ḥejja of that year,[328] the shah departed from Tehran for Ādherbāyjān. In the camp of Meyāna, 500 Russian skulls stuck on lances were brought up before the shah by Ḥasan Khān-e Sāru Aṣlān. Then the shah arrived at Tabriz, whence he departed after

325. October 2, 1826. 326. November 23, 1826.
327. March 21, 1827. 328. July 3, 1827.

some days for the pasture of Qebla.[329] Some days later he encamped outside the town of Khoy, then on the pasture of Marand,[330] and then he departed for the pasture of Mehrebān.[331] On 17th Ṣafar of the year 1243,[332] news arrived at the pasture of Mehrebān that the princes and emirs sent against the Russians had gained victories, and the shah was delighted. Some days later news arrived of Crown Prince ᶜAbbās Mirzā's victory near Üch Kilise.[333] The following day several hundred prisoners and skulls were brought before the shah. Then the shah departed from the pasture of Mehrebān and encamped in the region of Sarāb.[334] The next day news arrived of the crown prince's victory in the region of Nakhechevān, and about 2,300 skulls stuck on lances and 1,500 Russian prisoners of war and 5 pieces of artillery were brought before the shah. A group of prisoners with 2 cannons were sent to Esfahan, the rest to Tehran. The royal court departed from Sarāb and arrived in Tehran on 12th Rabiᶜ I of that year.[335]

TABRIZ OCCUPIED BY RUSSIAN TROOPS. When the royal court had returned from Ādherbāyjān to Tehran, the Russian General Paskevich became insolent, assembled his dispersed army, and occupied Erevan.[336] Then he decided to march on Tabriz.

329. According to the *Farhang*, a village called Qebla-ye Masjed lies about 45 miles southeast of Tabriz; this would mean that the court first moved in a south-eastward direction and then traveled in a circle around Tabriz, as is suggested by the other stations mentioned in the text.

330. 40 miles northwest of Tabriz, west of Khoy.

331. 45 miles east of Tabriz ("Mehrevan" on the 1:500,000 map), north of Qebla-ye Masjed, the station mentioned first.

332. September 9, 1827.

333. The famous Armenian monastery Echmiadzin ("Unigenitus descendit") near the village of Vagarshapat, 12 miles west of Erevan, called Üch Kilise ("Three Churches") by the Turks.

334. 25 miles southeast of Mehrebān, see also above, p. 130, note 138.

335. octber 3, 1827.

336. For this accomplishment Paskevich received the honorific name "Erivansky."

He was guided by a group of people from Ādherbāyjān who were angry with Crown Prince ᶜAbbās Mirzā. Then Paskevich tried to win over the inhabitants of Tabriz. And Mir Fattāḥ, unworthy son of the Mojtahed Haji Mirzā Yusof-e Tabrizi, a young man addicted to pigeon-playing, a ruffian, cheat, and disobedient son of an honorable father, who after his father had taken over the office of imam of prayers, seduced the inhabitants of Tabriz to obey the Russians and on the pulpit raised his voice offering prayers for the prosperity of the Russian emperor. Taking the ruffian rabble of the town he plundered the garrison of the citadel of Tabriz and threw the soldiers out. Āṣaf od-Doula, who at that time was staying in Tabriz, not being able to calm down the populace and hearing of Paskevich's encamping 2 or 3 parasangs from the city, sent the family of the crown prince from Tabriz to Hamadān. He himself returned and in vain undertook efforts to advise the people of Tabriz. Notwithstanding his lack of authority he remained in the city. When the roar of the Russian cannons was 2 parasangs from the city, Mir Fattāḥ put up a standard and went to meet the Russians with the nobles of the city. On 3d Rabiᶜ II[337] the Russians entered the city with all honors. Āṣaf od-Doula, who was helpless in the citadel, was arrested and honorably imprisoned. Two days later the Russian General Paskevich arrived in Tabriz. Then the command over the city was entrusted to Mir Fattāḥ.

PEACE NEGOTIATIONS AT KHĀRQĀN. When a few days had passed, a number of Russian soldiers had disappeared during those days. What happened was that the people of Tabriz seized them, put them to death, and interred them in the cellars of the houses. Paskevich despaired of establishing order in the city and of protecting the Russian troops by his sagacity. He asked Crown Prince ᶜAbbās Mirzā for a meeting in the village of Khārqān,[338]

337. October 24, 1827.

338. Not mentioned in the *Farhang*. Probably northwest of Marāgha, on the highway Marāgha-Tabriz.

8 parasangs from Marāgha, in order to negotiate the peace between the two governments and to establish quiet and tranquillity. Commending himself to God's decree and making himself a sacrifice for the shah's prosperity, the crown prince departed with several confidants to the village of Khārqān. When he was near the Russian camp, he was welcomed by Paskevich and all the generals. In their custom, they honored him by taking off their headgear. The crown prince treated each of them courteously, according to rank, while Paskevich performed the duties of hospitality befitting such a guest. By order of Paskevich, Āṣaf od-Doula, who was imprisoned in Tabriz, was conveyed to the Russian camp. After some days of negotiations Paskevich stated that the officials of the emperor, when there was still peace between the two governments, had established stores of grain and fodder and stocks of war materiel and provisions for the troops in the region of Karabagh and the other districts of Ādherbāyjān occupied by Russia; that the Russian emperor, after the reconquest of this region by the Persian army, had had to spend about 10 million in gold (20 crore) on repairing the loss; that now, both governments being inclined toward peace, the Persian government had two choices: either to pay 10 million in gold to compensate for the damages suffered by Russia or to deliver the territories Russia had occupied after the last peace treaty in a manner enabling it to collect taxes from this province worth 10 million; after that this province was to be given back to Persia.

The crown prince, accordingly, sent Fatḥ ᶜAli Khān-e Rashti to Tehran to submit these proposals. On 10th Rabiᶜ II of that year,[339] Fatḥ ᶜAli Khān arrived in Tehran and reported the matter to the shah. Getting angry the shah declared in the public assembly: "God willing, I shall spend half of the sum on repairing the victorious army and leave not a span of Persian soil to the Russians." Then he ordered [274] all the commanders and the

339. October 31, 1827.

army to assemble and to depart from Tehran and to wait at Qazvin for further orders. When Paskevich heard of this harsh answer, he gave up his intransigent position. By mediation of the crown prince, the deputy of the prime minister, Mirzā Abu'l-Qāsem, and an envoy versed in languages, in the name of Paskevich, proceeded to the court. Upon their arrival the sum to be paid according to the peace treaty was fixed at 5 million in gold. Minister for the Foreign Powers Mirzā Abu'l-Ḥasan Khān was sent to the village of Khārqān in order to settle the articles of the peace treaty. Then a group of intriguers spread the rumor of the shah's having removed ᶜAbbās Mirzā from the office of crown prince and having appointed Ḥasan ᶜAli Mirzā Shojāᶜ os-Salṭana crown prince. When Paskevich heard of the rumor, he did not negotiate with Haji Mirzā Abu'l-Ḥasan Khān, the minister for the Foreign Powers, declaring that one had to wait for the succession to the throne to be settled.

In the meantime, the English ambassador, an intelligent and wise man, who was staying in Tabriz,[340] had come to the village of Khārqān and advised Paskevich not to forget the agreement of the European rulers according to which all the monarchs in a combined action had to push back any ruler who had crossed the border of his territory;[341] if the Russian troops did not retreat now from the province of Ādherbāyjān, England together with the other powers would destroy the Russian empire just as they had destroyed Napoleon. By these remonstrances the English ambassador succeeded in mitigating Paskevich. After proceeding to Tehran, the English ambassador was received in audience and submitted the following proposal:

In most cases when in Europe or Turkey a state was all of a sudden occupied by an enemy, according to circumstances, 20 or 30 crore were

340. Sir John Macdonald Kinneir, ambassador 1824–30, see above, p. 177, note 318.

341. An allusion to the Congress of Vienna.

paid and the property returned. This is not considered dishonorable; it is on the contrary praiseworthy behavior. If this, however, seems harsh to the Persian government, the shah may allow the English government to pay the sum from their pocket and to extinguish the fire of discord.

Having made the shah inclined to peace, the ambassador hurried to Ādherbāyjān.

CONCLUSION OF A PEACE TREATY AT TORKMĀNCHĀY. Crown Prince ᶜAbbās Mirzā proceeded to the village of Torkmānchāy[342] belonging to Tabriz; the English ambassador, too, was present. Paskevich and Āṣaf od-Doula arrived from Tabriz. Ich Āqāsi Manuchehr Khān departed from Tehran with 8 crore of coined money, the sum agreed upon in the peace treaty. Minister for the Foreign Powers Haji Mirzā Abu'l-Ḥasan Khān traveled from Zenjān together with Manuchehr Khān to the village of Torkmānchāy. Crown Prince ᶜAbbās Mirzā and Paskevich exchanged their credentials, and in the night of 5th Shaᶜbān of that year,[343] a treaty of friendship was committed to writing, sealed by the crown prince and Minister for the Foreign Powers Haji Mirzā Abu'l-Ḥasan Khān, and handed over to Paskevich. Another copy corresponding exactly to the first was written, sealed by Paskevich and handed over to the crown prince. Then Paskevich proceeded to Tabriz, removed his troops from the city, and sent them to Karabagh. A copy of the peace treaty has been inserted in the Qājār chronicles.[344]

CONCENTRATION ON INTERNAL POLICY

A NEW PRIME MINISTER APPOINTED. The New Year fell on 5th Ramażān of that year.[345] Since Āṣaf od-Doula Allāh Yār

342. About 80 miles southeast of Tabriz. 343. February 21, 1828.

344. By the treaty, the territories north of the Araxes River were ceded to Russia. Russia received preferential trade terms, together with the exclusive right to sail her warships on the Caspian Sea; apart from that, Persia had to pay a 20-million ruble indemnity, see Hurewitz, II, 96–102.

345. March 21, 1828.

Khān-e Qājār Devehlu had spent some of the war in Ādherbayjān and as a prisoner of Paskevich in the city of Tabriz, and the financial administration of the Persian empire had been thrown into confusion, the office of prime minister was at the beginning of that year again bestowed upon ᶜAbdollāh Khān Amin od-Doula, in accordance with the law of inheritance and the latter's merits.

THE SHAH TRAVELS TO QOM AND SOLṬĀNĀBĀD. The shah spent the summer in Tehran in the gardens of Shemrān. In the middle of Jomādi I of the year 1244,[346] the royal court departed for Qom. After a four days' stay, the court departed for Solṭānābād, which belongs to the district of Kazzāz,[347] and was a new foundation (mostaḥdath) of the corps commander, Yusof Khān-e Gorji. Upon the shah's arrival at Solṭānābād, Gholām Ḥosein Khān, the second corps commander and governor of ᶜErāq, son of the first corps commander, presented the shah with all his possessions in cash and kind, including even the title deeds of his inherited and acquired property, and royal favors were bestowed upon him.[348] He also provided the court with victuals and fodder from his own big storehouses,[349] and was honored accordingly. Having settled the affairs of ᶜErāq, the shah departed for Tehran, arriving there on 27th Jomādi II.[350]

346. November 23, 1828.

347. Solṭānābād, the capital of the modern province of ᶜErāq, is now called ᶜErāq (or Arāk). The district of Kazzāz lies southwest of Arāk, see EI[1] IV, s.v. Sulṭānābād (V. Minorsky), see also above, p. 20, note 85.

348. There can be no doubt that the shah had forced the governor of Solṭānābād/Arak to deliver his possessions to him. For similar incidents in Safavid times, see H. Braun, "Das safavidische Königtum und der Niedergang des Reiches im 17. Jahrhundert," in *ZDMG, Supplementa I: XVII. Deutscher Orientalistentag vom 21. bis 27. Juli 1968 in Würzburg, Vorträge Teil 3*, Wiesbaden, 1969, pp. 941–47.

349. This was in accordance with the old custom of soyursāt, by which the shah and the officials were entitled to accommodation and provisions free of charge.

350. January 4, 1829.

THE RUSSIAN AMBASSADOR GRIBOYEDOV MURDERED IN TEHRAN. When the peace treaty between the governments of Persia and Russia was submitted to the shah for confirmation, a man named Griboyedov, a noble prince and nephew of Paskevich,[351] traveled from Saint Petersburg to Tehran in order to obtain the ratification of the treaty. At each halting place he was befittingly honored. Three days after his arrival in Tehran he was received in audience, according to the etiquette to be observed with an ambassador. He submitted to the shah a letter of friendship and presented him with the gifts of the Russian emperor. He established himself in the lodging house of the Russian envoys.[352] Because of the great honors which were shown him and which are part of the courtesy befitting a guest, he became arrogant, addressing high and low without their titles and talking in an unfriendly manner. The ministers answered his insolence with softness in order to turn his thought from disdain and abusive talk, but without success. Since the treaty included articles concerning the exchange of old and new prisoners on both sides,[353] he claimed with excessive arrogance the release of

351. Alexander Sergeyewich Griboyedov (1795–1829), was known in the history of Russian literature as a leading playwright of the early nineteenth century. After military service, he was sent to Persia in 1818 as a secretary to the Russian Mission. From 1827 onward he had a diplomatic post in the Caucasus, see William E. Harkins, *Dictionary of Russian Literature* (London, 1957), pp. 147–49.

352. The house was situated southwest of the Sepahsālār Mosque, see Litten, *Persien*, map 7 in the Appendix.

353. According to Article XIII "All prisoners of war made in one way or another, whether in the course of the last War, or before, as well as the subjects of the Governments reciprocally fallen into captivity, at no matter what time, will be freed within a period of four months and, after having been provided with food and other necessary objects, they will be directed to Abbas Abbad in order to be turned over there into the hands of the Commissioners, respectively charged with receiving them and to decide upon their eventual return to their homes. . . . The two Governments reserve expressly the unlimited right to reclaim them (i.e., those who have not been freed within the four months mentioned above) at no matter what time, and they obligate themselves to restore them mutually in the

the Georgian and Armenian prisoners who were serving since time immemorial in the royal harem and had acquired high ranks and founded families. Among them were two Georgians in the palace of Āṣaf od-Doula Allāh Yār Khān-e Qājār Devehlu who had been there for many years. Griboyedov made such an uproar for their release that Āṣaf od-Doula sent both of them to Griboyedov's lodging house, because he was afraid of destroying the agreement between the two governments if he did not release them. When the other classes of prisoners saw this but had not the boldness to submit a request to the shah, they out of sheer necessity sent a gentle message to Griboyedov [275] asking him to leave the prisoners the choice of their being released or not. Griboyedov answered again unseemingly. Accordingly, the prisoners, men and women, sent the theologians of the city the following message:

> All of us have had the honor to embrace the faith of Islam and have become parents of children. The ministers are not willing to break the treaty which they have concluded with the Russian empire. The theologians, sitting on the throne of the religious law, will bring about our salvation.

Having received this message, the theologians convened a gathering in the Friday mosque in Tehran to which they invited all the inhabitants. They were of the opinion that Griboyedov had to release all the prisoners who were firm in their profession of Islam. The crowd, behaving like a herd of cattle, without regard to the aim and end of the theologians, were of the opinion that the prisoners had to be removed from Griboyedov's house. Accordingly, they proceeded, weapons in hand, to his house. The ministers were informed only when the matter was finished. And an unruly mob of more than 100,000 people gathered. Seeing this, Griboyedov sent several Georgian men and

---

measure that they may present themselves for that purpose, or in the measure that they may reclaim them," see Hurewitz, I, 99.

women out of the house. Having closed the doors he took to defending the house from the roof. During the fighting a youth of fourteen from Tehran was killed by a musket ball which had come out of Griboyedov's house. The fury of the Moslems increased; climbing up the walls on to the roof they broke into the courtyard like a sudden disaster. Killing all the Russians they found and finally Griboyedov, too, they plundered the house. Thirty-seven Russians perished; their lodging house was destroyed. Then the mob dispersed into all directions. Amidst the turmoil Griboyedov's deputy managed to flee and, after some time, informed the ministers of his escape. He was then fetched from the ruined house and conveyed to Tabriz with all honors.

When Crown Prince ᶜAbbās Mirzā heard of the occurrence, he ordered all the soldiers and the nobles to put on black dress as a sign of mourning, all the bazaars to be closed for three days, and all the people to stop working. Then he sent Griboyedov's deputy to Tiflis with all honors. To Paskevich he sent an explanation of the occurrence, referring to the testimony of Griboyedov's deputy. Having arrived at Tiflis, the deputy mentioned the innocence of the Persian ministers and Griboyedov's violent procedure. Paskevich having been informed of the real facts immediately sent the deputy to Saint Petersburg, addressed a letter on the incident to the Russian emperor, and requested the Persian ministers to expedite a letter of excuse. He suggested that the crown prince should send a shrewd ambassador in the name of the Persian ministers to the Russian emperor in order to beg the latter's pardon for the occurrence as long as it was in fresh remembrance; further, that the mollās involved should be exiled to satisfy the emperor. Accordingly, the crown prince addressed a letter concerning these questions to the shah.

A SON OF THE CROWN PRINCE SENT TO SAINT PETERSBURG. The New Year fell on the evening of 15th Ramażān of that year.[354] After celebrating the feast in a befitting manner, the shah received a letter from Crown Prince ᶜAbbās Mirzā that upon the arrival of Griboyedov's deputy in Saint Petersburg the Russian emperor had written Paskevich a letter to the effect that a son of the crown prince was to proceed to Saint Petersburg to offer excuses; having strengthened the bond of friendship between the two governments he was to return with all honors; that accordingly the crown prince had appointed Khosrou Mirzā on that mission; that together with the latter he had sent Amir-e Neẓām Moḥammad Khān-e Zangana, a shrewd man. The shah approved the crown prince's proposals and sent 100,000 toman in cash for the equipment of Khosrou Mirzā's mission, together with Mirzā Nabi Khān-e Qazvini, vizier ṯo ᶜAli Naqi Mirzā, the governor of Qazvin.

Before the arrival of those 100,000 toman the crown prince had sent his son Khosrou Mirzā to Saint Petersburg who received high honors everywhere. He arrived in the vicinity of Saint Petersburg and, outside the city, was welcomed by all the generals of the army and the nobles of the empire, who performed everything which is done on the day of arrival of the emperor. Every morning and evening the Russian emperor proceeded to Khosrou Mirzā's lodging and had supper and dinner with him. Of exquisite tact and courtesy, the emperor did not mention a word of Griboyedov's murder. Upon Amir-e Neẓām Moḥammad Khān he bestowed honors exceeding the usual. As has been reported,[355] the sum to be paid to the Russians was fixed at 10 crore, according to the peace treaty, of which 8 crore had been paid. Of the 2-crore balance the emperor gave Prince Khosrou Mirzā 1 crore for his endeavors, and prolonged the term of payment of the other crore by five years. After the completion of their mission, he sent the prince and Moḥammad Khān back to Tabriz.

354. March 21, 1829. 355. See above, p. 184 seq.

APPOINTMENTS TO HIGH POSITIONS IN THE GOVERNMENT. Mirzā ᶜAbd ol-Vahhāb Moᶜtamed od-Doula Eṣfahāni had spent about thirty years in the service of Fatḥ ᶜAli Shāh and obtained the rank and the title "Chancellor of the Empire." Because of his efficiency he devoted his time to the handling of affairs which normally would have come within the competence of the prime minister. Out of his great humility, however, he did not call himself "Prime Minister." The title "Chancellor of the Empire" had been conferred upon Haji Mirzā Raḥim-e Shirāzi, the Shah's physician in ordinary.[356] When this arrangement had lasted for a long time, the official correspondence was again taken care of by Mirzā ᶜAbd ol-Vahhāb. Haji Mirzā Raḥim was distantly related to Mirzā ᶜAbd ol-Vahhāb. That year the latter was taken ill from consumption and died on 5th Dhu'l-Ḥejja[357] in Tehran. The title "Muᶜtamad od-Doala" was conferred upon Manuchehr Khān Ich Āqāsi-ye Gorji. [276] The office of chancellor of the empire was entrusted to Mirzā Khān-e Lor Māzandarāni.

The family of Mirzā ᶜAbd ol-Vahhāb Moᶜtamad od-Doula comes from the town of Jahrom in Fārs. The latter's ancestor Haji Ḥakim Salmān-e Musavi-ye Ḥoseini, by order of Shah ᶜAbbās,[358] proceeded from Jahrom to Esfahan and occupied for many years the office and rank of physician in ordinary (ḥakim bāshi) to the Safavids. Up to the end of Nāder Shāh's rule,[359] this office was held by the family of the late Ḥakim Salmān. The physician in ordinary to the shah, Haji Mirzā Raḥim, is one of the descendants of the late Ḥakim Salmān; his biography is given in the second volume of this book, in the chapter dealing with the Meidān-e Shāh quarter of Shiraz.[360]

356. See above, p. 172. 357. June 8, 1829.
358. Reigned 1588–1629. 359. About 1736–47.
360. *FNN*, II, 114: "Hāji Mirzā Ḥakim Bāshi-ye Fakhr od-Doula, with the pen-name 'Bidel' is the leading scholar in philosophy and medicine and the first writer of the age in literature and poetry; in medicine he is known as 'Hakim Bāshi' and in poetry as 'Bidel,' besides that he bears the title

RISE AND DOWNFALL OF THE NURI FAMILY IN SHIRAZ. That year Ḥosein ᶜAli Mirzā Farmān-Farmā deposed Moḥammad Zaki Khān-e Nuri, who had been vizier for ten years.[361] In the latter's place he appointed Mirzā Moḥammad ᶜAli-ye Shirāzi, known as Khafrki, intendant of the province of Fārs and son of the late Mirzā Ebrāhim Mostoufi-ye Shirāzi. All the

---

'Fakhr od-Doula.' As a young man he studied philosophy and medicine with the famous scholar Ḥasan ᶜAli Ṭabib. From Shiraz he proceeded to Tehran and started to practice as a doctor. Because he was praised by the officials of the state, he became known at the court within a short time and was commissioned to cure the members of the royal harem; he treated especially the Princess Fakhr od-Doula, the sixth of the forty-eight daughters of the shah, and he was called 'Hakim Bāshi [Chief Physician] of Fakhr od-Doula.' Daily he attended the general audience together with the chief physicians of the shah. Since he was a relative of the chancellor of the empire, Moᶜtamad od-Doula, he wrote letters and decrees as the latter's deputy. Eventually, after the latter's death, he was appointed chancellor of the empire. In about 1245 (1829/30) he returned to Shiraz and died at Qom in 1248 (1832/33). The late Haji Akbar Navvāb-e Shirazi writes in his *Ketāb-e Delgoshā*: 'Bidel' is the pen-name of Mirzā Raḥim, a Musavi-Seiyed. His ancestor was from Jahrom in Fārs. He was a learned physician, proceeded to Esfahan at the time of the Safavids and became physician in ordinary to the Safavid rulers. Mirzā Raḥim's father came to Shiraz at the time of Karim Khān-e Zand and settled down there. Then he entered the service of the late Qājār ruler [that is, Āqā Moḥammad Shāh] and later returned to Shiraz. Haji Mirzā Raḥim is a seiyed of noble birth and a high-ranking scholar. In the sciences he excelled especially in medicine, wrote numerous books, and composed poems which sound nice and are easily comprehensible."

His father, Mirzā Moḥammad Hakim Bāshi, died at Shiraz in 1215: 1800/1; his grandfather, Mirzā Moḥammad Ḥosein, had come to Shiraz (from Esfahan ?) at the time of the Afshār war and entered the service of the beglergebi of Fārs, Moḥammad Taqi Khān-e Shirāzi, see *FNN*, II, 113. Two brothers of Haji Mirzā Raḥim are mentioned in the *FNN*, II, 113: Mirzā Moḥammad Bāqer Mollā Bāshi (d. 1240:1824/25), and Mirzā Moḥammad Ḥosein, that is, Haji Āqā Mollā Bāshi (d. 1265:1848/49). Moḥammad Bāqer wrote several books on theology and mysticism and was mollā bāshi to Ḥosein ᶜAli Mirzā Farmān-Farmā. ᶜAli (born 1230:1814/15), a son of Haji Mirzā Raḥim, lived at Mashhad and became known as a poet with the pen name "Fakhri."

361. This is not quite clear, see the list of viziers at the end of this book.

relatives of Moḥammad Zaki Khān were expelled from Shiraz and sent back to Māzandarān, their original home.

Their story runs in detail as follows: As has been reported, in the year 1214,[362] several hundred musketeers together with their families had been sent from the district of Nur to Fars and entered the service of Ḥosein ᶜAli Mirzā Farmān-Farmā; they were put under the command of Naṣrollāh Khān, a brother of the minister of the army, Mirzā Asadollāh Khān-e Nuri. They had established themselves in the quarter of Murdestān, which since the end of the Zand rule had fallen into disrepair, each of them building a house in accordance with his rank. Three or four years later Naṣrollāh Khān died in Shiraz. Then the command of the Nuri soldiers was conferred upon Shokrollāh Khān, son of Mirzā Asadollāh Khān, the former being a young man. Moḥammad Zaki Khān-e Nuri, the other brother of Mirzā Asadollāh Khān, the minister of the army, was appointed page of the presence to Farmān-Farmā. The whole time he was endeavoring to satisfy the wishes of the aforementioned excellency. Accordingly, his reputation at the court of Farmān-Farmā increased rapidly. In order to strengthen the position of the Nuris he gave, in about the year 1223,[363] the daughter of Mirzā Ebrāhim, the lord mayor of Shiraz, in marriage to the commander Shokrollāh Khān, his maternal nephew. In about the year 1234,[364] the daughter of the late commander Naṣrollāh Khān, the eldest brother of Moḥammad Zaki Khān, was married to the lord mayor of Shiraz, Mirzā ᶜAli Akbar. And in about the year 1243,[365] the daughter of Lord Mayor Mirzā ᶜAli Akbar was given in marriage to Kheirollāh Khān, son of Moḥammad Zaki Khān-e Nuri. During that time Moḥammad Zaki Khān was continually being promoted at the court of Farmān-Farmā until he obtained a position which enabled him to appoint and depose the viziers; the last year he had deposed a vizier and appointed

362. See above, p. 92. 363. 1223:1808. 364. 1234:1818/19.
365. 1243:1827/28.

another vizier inside the space of a short time. Finally, in the year 12—,[366] he brought his scheming to light and assumed himself the administration of the vizierate. Because of the influence of Moḥammad Zaki Khān, the Nuris oppressed the inhabitants of Shiraz. Finally, in the year 1240,[367] the princess, Hamdam os-Solṭān, a sister of Farmān-Farmā, was given in marriage to Moḥammad Zaki Khān, and the daughter of Farmān-Farmā to Shokrallāh Khān. By these marriages their rank was promoted, and the brutality of the Nuris toward the inhabitants of Shiraz, the tribes, and the districts exceeded all bounds. In accordance with the saying "Everything exceeding the bounds will be turned into the opposite," murders were being committed among the Nuris, the inhabitants of Shiraz, the tribes, and in the districts. In the course of time several people on both sides were killed, vendettas being practiced on both sides. Finally they were trying to kill each other in the streets and the bazaars. One day a group of Nuris killed a man from the Qashqā'i tribe in the city of Shiraz. When Farmān-Farmā made Moḥammad Zaki Khān and Shokrollāh Khān responsible for the murder, they pleaded not guilty, saying that once a Turk had killed a Nuri and that the Turk was killed in retaliation. Then the tribes gathered together, entered into an agreement with the inhabitants of Shiraz, and occupied the surroundings of the Nuri-quarters. To stamp out this evil, Farmān-Farmā saw no other possibility but to expel the Nuris from Shiraz. Accordingly, that year he ordered them, old and young, high and low, after so many years of stay, to leave the city with all their belongings, and sent them back to Māzandarān.

THE SHAH TRAVELS TO FĀRS TO SETTLE THE AFFAIRS OF THAT PROVINCE. And Moḥammad Zaki Khān's vizierate

366. The exact date is not given in the text; according to what is mentioned at the beginning of this paragraph, he should have assumed the duties of a vizier in about 1234:1818/19.

367. 1240:1824/25.

came to an end. In order to induce the royal court to proceed to Fārs, he mentioned something with regard to irregularities in the payment of taxes due to the court, which had become known in Fārs. On 24th Jomādi I of the year 1245[368] Fatḥ ᶜAli Shāh departed from Tehran and arrived at Esfahan on 10th Jomādi II.[369] After some days' rest he departed for Shiraz. [277] Ḥosein ᶜAli Mirzā Farmān-Farmā together with the nobles of Fārs was received in audience at the station of Shulgestān near Ābāda;[370] having made the necessary arrangements for the reception of the royal court at the station of Eqlid near Ābāda,[371] Farmān-Farmā returned to Shiraz. On 3d Rajab of that year,[372] the shah put up his quarters in the Bāgh-e Nou 1,500 cubits east of Shiraz, which had been founded by Farmān-Farmā.[373] In the courtyard of the pavilion (eiwān) of the Bāgh-e Nou, Farmān-Farmā presented the shah with the sum of 200,000 toman in cash out of his own treasury, precious carpets, Kashmir-shawls, and brocaded silk from Gojarat. During his four days' stay in that garden, the shah dispatched detachments of horse and foot belonging to his escort to the southern districts of Fārs. Then he entered Shiraz with the splendor of Jamshid and the retinue of Kāvus[374] and established himself in the Vakili palace. As host, Farmān-Farmā paid for ten days' provisions and expenditure of the court and the retinue, then by order of the shah the costs of the stay were debited to the ordinary budget (az bābat-e māleyāt-e mostamerra). During this stay snow and rain fell daily. In spite of heavy rain the shah was daily taking care of the oppressed, issuing orders, and giving the officials instructions (dastur ol-ᶜamal). The 200,000 toman Farmān-Farmā had given him as a gift he acknowledged as a compensation for the tax arrears

368. November 21, 1829. 369. December 7, 1829.

370. About 19 miles northwest of Ābāda, north of the Shiraz-Esfahan highway.

371. About 19 miles northwest of Ābāda. 372. December 29, 1829.

373. See also below, p. 241.

374. Jamshid and Kāvus are famous heroes of Persian epics.

(bāqayā-ye māleyāt). And Ḥasan ᶜAli Mirzā Shojāᶜ os-Salṭana, governor of Kerman, proceeded to Shiraz because it was very close, and Moḥammad Zaki Khān-e Nuri, who after his removal from the vizierate of Fārs was serving at the court as a page of the presence, was appointed administrator (pishkār) to Shojāᶜ os-Salṭana and vizier of Kerman. In the meantime, Moḥammad ᶜAli Khān, ilkhāni of Fārs, had seized several Bakhteyāri robbers and brought them before the shah; they were all punished.

And the title "Qavām ol-Molk" was bestowed upon Mirzā ᶜAli Akbar, lord mayor of Shiraz;[375] and Mirzā Moḥammad ᶜAli, vizier of Fārs, received the title "Moshir ol-Molk." Āqā Bābā Khān-e Bārforushi-ye Māzandarāni, who at the beginning of his career had the office of deputy in the wardens' room (farrāsh khāna) of Ḥosein ᶜAli Mirzā Farmān-Farmā and then, because of his efficiency had been appointed chief warden (farrāsh bāshi), was promoted to the rank of chief tutor (lala bāshi) for the education of the Farmān-Farmā's children. In those days he was appointed commander in chief of the province of Fārs. And Mirzā Moḥammad Ḥosein, deputy of the subjects (vakil or-raᶜāyā) of the province of Fārs, and Mirzā Moḥammad, governor of the districts of Dārābgerd, and Mirzā Abu'l-Ḥasan Khān, son-in-law of Ḥosein ᶜAli Mirzā Farmān-Farmā, all of them sons of the late Mirzā Hādi, son of the late Mirzā Jāni-ye Shirāzi known as Fasā'i, received royal favors as a remuneration of the merits of their fathers and grandfathers which exceeded the merits of all the inhabitants of Fārs. Then Mirzā Abu'l-Ḥasan Khān, because of his being son-in-law, his noble birth as a seiyed, the reputation of his fathers and forefathers and his family, was granted the title "Farzand Maqām,"[376] and in the royal decrees and orders he was styled "Farzand Maqāmi

375. He was the eldest son of Haji Ebrāhim, the late Grand vizier of Persia, who had been lord mayor of Shiraz before his appointment to the grand vizierate.

376. Meaning "adopted son."

Navvāb-e Mirzā Abu'l-Ḥasan Khān." During his stay at Shiraz, the shah paid a visit to the houses of the following persons only: Mojtahed Mirzā Ebrahim, son of the aforementioned late Mirzā Jāni, uncle of the author of this book and grandson of the late Seiyed ᶜAli Khān-e ᶜAllāma-ye Madani-ye Shirāzi, and Haji Akbar Navvāb-e Shirāzi.

AN ATTEMPT AT THE SHAH'S LIFE; THE COURT RETURNS TO TEHRAN. On 15th Shaᶜbān of that year,[377] the shah left Shiraz for ᶜArabestān and Lorestān, marching by way of Shulestān[378] and Behbehān. Proceeding by way of Zenyān[379] and Dasht-e Arjon, the birthplace of Salmān-e Fāresi,[380] he visited Kāzerun, putting up his camp in the Bāgh-e Naẓar. After a rest he marched through Chenār-e Shāhejān[381] and Sarāb-e Bahrām[382] and put up his camp near Fahleyān,[383] the capital of the district of Mamasanni. It happened by chance that the shah on that day had no appetite. Contenting himself with sherbet, he distributed the food for the whole day to his retinue. About fifty people, eating more than was good for them, vomited. They vomited so much as to lose consciousness. Inspector (nāẓer) Ebrāhim Khān, son of the late Grand Vizier Haji Moḥammad Ḥosein Khān-e Eṣfahāni, and son of the daughter of the late Haji Ebrāhim Khān Eᶜtemād od-Doula Shirāzi and son-in-law of the shah, who had the office of steward of the royal household (khāna sālār), having eaten of that food, too, vomited like the others and leaned against a wall. The chief physician of the

377. February 9, 1830.

378. ᶜArabestān is the province of Khuzestān, Lorestān the mountainous country to the east; Shulestān is the region north of Kāzerun, also called Mamassani.

379. Khān-e Zenjān, about 22 miles west of Shiraz.

380. About 10 miles west of Khān-e Zenjān. Salmān-e Fāresi was of Persian origin, a famous follower of the Prophet, and an expert in military affairs. His grave is venerated at Salmān Pāk, south of Baghdad.

381. About 16 miles north-northwest of Kāzerun, see *Farhang*, VII, 76.

382. About 12 miles north of Chanār-e Shāhejān.

383. 12 miles north-northwest of Sarāb-e Bahrām.

ordinary to the shah, Mirzā Moḥammad Ḥosein, suspected that deadly poison had been added to the food; as the quantity had been small compared to the quantity of the cooking, no greater damage was done. The testimony of a group of people confirmed that there was a spring near Sarāb-e Bahrām, the water of which made people vomit; that the previous night the servants of the kitchen had cooked the meals for the day using water from that spring. I, the author of this book, have to state the following:

Having made inquiries, I learned that in that region a spring of this kind is not known by name nor has it been seen. Old people say that the royal servants had planned evil; not having reached their end, they had obscured this by false testimony.— God knows best!

At the station of Fahleyān Farmān-Farmā was granted leave, and he returned to Shiraz. Then the court departed, marched by Sarāb-e Seyāh,[384] passed the village of Bāsht,[385] the stations Do Gombadān[386] and Lishtarr[387] and the plain of Kheirābād,[388] and put up camp 1 parasang north of the town of Behbehān. On 1st Ramażān[389] they were still there; then the tents were pulled down, and on 9th Ramażān[390] the shah arrived at the town of Shoshtar. He departed, marched through the town of Dezful and other places and put up his camp at Khorramābād. [278] The New Year fell on 25th Ramażān of that year.[391] The court proceeded by way of Borujerd and Hamadān and arrived happily in Tehran on 8th Dhu'l-Qaᶜda of that year.[392]

ARRIVAL OF AN AMBASSADOR FROM SIND. The days of the month of Moḥarram of the year 1246[393] were passed in

384. Not mentioned in our sources.
385. 22 miles northwest of Fahleyān, the center of Mamassani.
386. 12 miles west of Bāsht.
387. 16 miles northwest of Do Gombadān.
388. About 10 miles northwest of Lishtar.
389. February 24, 1830. 390. March 4, 1830.
391. March 21, 1830. 392. May 1, 1830.
393. Began on June 22, 1830.

mourning over Emām Ḥosein. That year Mir Morād ᶜAli, governor of Sind,[394] who considered himself a vassal of the royal court, sent a man named Mirzā Moḥammad ᶜAli-ye Shirāzi as ambassador to Tehran, carrying a message of devotion and bringing three elephants and precious objects. Marching through the desert of Beluchistan to Bandar ᶜAbbās, the ambassador went by way of Ṭārom,[395] Forg,[396] Dārābjerd, Fasā, and Sarvestān,[397] arriving at Shiraz at the end of the month of Ṣafar of that year.[398] After a rest he departed for Tehran. On 11th Rabiᶜ II of that year,[399] he arrived in Tehran and was granted royal favors.

THE SHAH TRAVELS TO KERMĀNSHĀH AND ESFAHAN TO SETTLE AFFAIRS THERE. The New Year fell on 6th Shavvāl of that year.[400] Since Prince Moḥammad Taqi Mirzā Ḥosām os-Salṭana, governor of Borujerd, and Moḥammad Ḥosein Mirzā Ḥeshmat od-Doula, governor of Kermānshāh, were bitter enemies, the shah departed on 6th Dhu'l-Qaᶜda of that year[401] from Tehran in order to bring about the reconciliation of the two princes. Having visited those regions and reconciled the princes, he departed and put up his camp on the pasture of Qahnir, one of the districts of Chahār Maḥāll of Esfahan,[402] on

394. Mir Morād ᶜAli was a nephew of Mir Fatḥ ᶜAli Khān of the Talpor dynasty of Sind, who ruled over Sind with its capital Hyderabad from 1783 onward. Mir Morād ᶜAli and his brothers were Shiis, while Sobodār Khān, son of Fatḥ ᶜAli Khān, was a Sunni, see *The Cambridge History of the British Empire*, Vol. IV: *British India 1497–1858*, p. 522 seq. In 1843, Sind passed into the possession of the British (Hyderabad, founded in 1182:1768, was named after ᶜAli ibn Abi Ṭāleb, see EI² III, 323).

395. About 75 miles north-northwest of Bandar ᶜAbbās, in the valley of the Rud-e Shur.

396. About 37 miles northwest of Ṭārom.

397. About 50 miles southeast of Shiraz.

398. About August 15, 1830. 399. September 29, 1830.

400. March 21, 1831. 401. April 18, 1831.

402. The "Four Districts," the region west of Esfahan; the name has now become obsolete.

1st Moḥarram of the year 1247.[403] To settle the accounts of the province of Fārs, he sent ᶜAbdollāh Khān Amin od-Doula to Shiraz. In the town of Qomesha the latter met Ḥosein ᶜAli Mirzā, the governor of Fārs, who was on his way to the shah, and both returned to the pasture of Qahnir. On the ᶜĀshurā feast[404] the shah attended the commemoration (dhekr) of the murder of Emām Ḥosein. On 4th Ṣafar,[405] the royal court departed from the pasture of Qahnir; marching through the hilly country and along the Zāyanda Rud River, they put up their camp at the village of Deh Kord,[406] which belongs to the district of Chahār Maḥāll of Esfahan.

BIRTH OF NĀṢER OD-DIN MIRZĀ. On 6th Ṣafar of that year,[407] Nāṣer od-Din Qājār was born of the queen mother, who was a daughter of Amir-e Kabir Moḥammad Qāsem Khān, son of Amir-e Kabir Soleimān Khān Neẓām od-Doula, son of Amir Moḥammad Qājār.

CROWN PRINCE ᶜABBĀS MIRZĀ SENT TO KHORASAN. By order of the shah the crown prince, ᶜAbbās Mirzā, having settled the affairs of the districts of Yazd and Kerman, arrived from Kerman at Deh Kord on 1st Rabiᶜ II.[408] He was granted royal favors and ordered to settle the affairs of the province of Khorasan. The sum of 50,000 toman was disbursed from the treasury to his servants to be spent on the equipment of the soldiers, the horsemen, and the artillery. The governorship of Kerman was bestowed upon Seif ol-Moluk Mirzā, son of ᶜAli Shāh Ẓell os-Solṭān, son-in-law of the crown prince.

ALLEVIATION OF TAXES GRANTED TO THE GOVERNOR OF FĀRS. Then the court entered Esfahan. Having rested for a

403. June 12, 1831. 404. That is, 10th Moharram: June 21.

405. July 15, 1831.

406. The village (not mentioned in the *Farhang* and not shown on the map) probably lies west of Jolfa, where the Zāyanda Rud flows from west to east.

407. July 17, 1831. 408. September 9, 1831.

while, Amin od-Doula settled the accounts of Fārs for all those years. He ascertained a deficit of 200,000 toman in the ordinary budget (aṣl-e māleyāt). Ḥosein ᶜAli Mirzā Farmān-Farmā, being asked about the deficit, confirmed by oath the correctness of the budget, adducing as evidence the devastation of the province of Fārs by epidemics and Egyptian locusts. The shah graciously granted the whole sum of 200,000 toman as an alleviation of taxes (takhfif) to the province of Fārs. Farmān-Farmā was accorded all his wishes, and by order of the shah the princes Holāgu Mirzā, Arghun Mirzā, Abāqā Khān Mirzā and Ögetei Qā'ān Mirzā, sons of Ḥasan ᶜAli Mirzā Shojāᶜ oṣ-Salṭana, and Shokrollāh Khān-e Nuri, who for a time had been away from Fārs, were given in company to Farmān-Farmā and sent to Shiraz. By order of Farmān-Farmā, Shokrollāh Khān summoned his family and followers from Tehran, and they returned to Shiraz.[409] On 8th Jomādi I,[410] the court departed from Esfahan and arrived in Tehran on 1st Jomādi II.[411]

TROUBLES IN FĀRS

SHEIKH ᶜABD OR-RASUL KHĀN EXPELLED FROM BUSHEHR. The sons of Ḥosein ᶜAli Mirzā Farmān-Farmā were quarreling with each other, the younger not being willing to obey the older and neither their father. The nobles of Fārs, accordingly, each attached themselves to one of the princes, and as a result of this the payment of taxes (woṣul-e māleyāt) was thrown into confusion. Sheikh ᶜAbd or-Rasul Khān Daryābegi-ye Bushehri attached himself to the mother of Keikhosrou Mirzā, known as "Sepahsālār" and son of Farmān-Farmā. She was a daughter of Amir Khān-e Kord Zaᶜfarānlu-ye Khorāsāni. In the year 1237,[412] the daughter of Moḥammad Qoli Khān-e Afshār Oromi,

409. The Nuri family had been expelled from Fārs, see above, p. 194.
410. October 15, 1831. 411. November 7, 1831.
412. 1237:1821/22.

spouse of Farmān-Farmā and mother of Reżā Qoli Mirzā Nā'eb ol-Eyāla and of Timur Mirzā Ḥosām od-Doula, left Shiraz to go on a pilgrimage. When she arrived at Masqaṭ, Seiyed Sa^{c}id Khān, Imam of Masqaṭ, welcomed her with all the nobles at the anchorage of her ship, escorted her with all honors into Masqaṭ and fulfilled the duties of devotion. He presented her with a sum of money, pearls, and jewels. Then he asked her by mediation of her servants for intercession with Farmān-Farmā that the latter might grant him new honors befitting the services he was rendering him, and give him a princess in marriage, namely the sister of Reżā Qoli Mirzā; [279] that he was willing to give her (the spouse of Farmān-Farmā) a certain sum of money as a peshkash. The mother of Reżā Qoli Mirzā accepted his petition and departed from Masqaṭ for the Holy Places. Having performed the pilgrimage she returned to Masqaṭ. The Imam of Masqaṭ, increasing his services to her, repeated his petition. When the lady returned to Shiraz, she was called "Hajiya."

In the year 1238[413] another spouse of Farmān-Farmā, the mother of Sepahsālār, departed from Shiraz to go on a pilgrimage and arrived at Bushehr. Sheikh ^{c}Abd or-Rasul Khān-e Bushehri, too, was going to perform the pilgrimage. In order to please Farmān-Farmā he made preparations for the voyage befitting the travels of rulers, and covered the costs out of his own purse. He put at her disposal two ships of his own, of which one was named *Noṣrat Shāhi.*[414] After loading the equipment and provisions for the voyage out and back on one of the ships, he himself, the lady, and her servants went on board the *Noṣrat Shāhi*. Then they sailed through the Persian Gulf and the Sea of ^{c}Omān and Yemen to the Holy Places. Sheikh ^{c}Abd or-Rasul Khān served her everywhere like one of the servants and distributed so much gold and silver among the Arabs as to surpass Ḥātem oṭ-Ṭa'i.[415] When

413. 1238:1822/23. 414. That is, "Royal Victory."

415. The model of liberality in pre-Islamic Arabic poetry, see also above, p. 168.

Hajiya heard of this, she grew jealous and sent the Imam of Masqaṭ the following message:

When Sheikh ᶜAbd or-Rasul Khān arrives in Masqaṭ, arrest him and put him in prison. Do not interfere with the mother of Sepahsālār. Send her with all honors to Shiraz. Then I shall make good my promise and give you the princess in marriage.

When Sheikh ᶜAbd or-Rasul Khān's ship came near Masqaṭ, the Imam of Masqaṭ sent several ships with cannons and musketeers. They beset the ship of the sheikh on all sides, and he engaged in fighting until the powder of the musketeers from Bushehr was consumed. Looking death in the face, Sheikh ᶜAbd or-Rasul Khān ordered the sailors at the top of his voice to perform the ritual washing and to put on the shroud, and the captain, Moḥammad, to set fire to the ship, lest he himself and the spouse of Farmān-Farmā be disgracefully imprisoned. When the spouse of Farmān-Farmā perceived his intention, she threw herself unveiled at the feet of Sheikh ᶜAbd or-Rasul Khān: "If he takes us prisoner, Farmān-Farmā will inflict the deserved penalty on Seiyed Saᶜid, destroy Masqaṭ and put the population in prison. The delight of retaliation will be greater than the fear of a captivity of a few days." By this argument she calmed down the fury of Sheikh ᶜAbd or-Rasul Khān. The people from Masqaṭ went on board the *Noṣrat Shāhi*, did not interfere with the spouse of Farmān-Farmā, and brought Sheikh ᶜAbd or-Rasul Khān to Masqaṭ. About one year he remained in prison. Seiyed Saᶜid Khān sent his vizier and a group of other people to Shiraz and Hajiya made good her promise. By permission of Farmān-Farmā Hajiya's daughter was married to the Imam of Masqaṭ and sent to Masqaṭ.

And Sheikh ᶜAbd or-Rasul Khān was released from prison at Masqaṭ and returned to Bushehr. He insulted Hajiya in harsh words without regard to Reżā Qoli Mirzā and Timur Mirzā, the sons of Hajiya. Then, in the year 1246,[416] Timur Mirzā

416. 1246:1830/31.

Ḥosām od-Doula entered into an agreement with the khāns of Dashtestān, such as Sālem Khān-e Borāzjāni, Ra'is Moḥammad Bāqer, son of Ra'is Ḥosein-e Tangestāni, Mirzā Jaᶜfar Khān-e Khormuji, and the other kalāntars from Dasht and Dashtestān. They laid siege to Bushehr with several thousand musketeers. After two days' siege they occupied the town. Sheikh ᶜAbd or-Rasul Khān fled on board his ship and from the sea watched the plundering of Bandar Bushehr. The wares of all the merchants, foreign and indigenous, were carried away as booty. Two days later, having finished the breaking up of vaults and storehouses, they left with Timur Mirzā Bushehr and returned to Dashtestān.

THE GOVERNOR OF FĀRS GOES TO BUSHEHR AND ESTABLISHES ORDER THERE. The merchants from different countries with stock-in-trade at Bushehr took their complaints to the Persian government, and by a royal decree Ḥosein ᶜAli Mirzā Farmān-Farmā was made responsible for the restitution of the plundered stores. When the people of Dashtestān refused the restitution of the goods, Farmān-Farmā tried to win over Sheikh ᶜAbd or-Rasul Khān and to engage him in clearing up this affair. The sheikh answered in writing: "If you arrest and deliver the khāns of Dashtestān, the originators of this encroachment, to me, I shall compensate the losses of the merchants from my purse, and the merchants will write you a letter of agreement." At the beginning of winter of the year 1247[417] Farmān-Farmā departed from Shiraz under the pretext of recreation for Kāzerun and the region of Dashtestān, accompanied by Reżā Qoli Mirzā Nā'eb ol-Eyāla, Timur Mirzā Ḥosām od-Doula, Holāgu Mirzā, son of Shojāᶜ os-Salṭana, Mirzā Moḥammad ᶜAli Moshir ol-Molk, vizier of the province of Fārs, Shokrollāh Khān-e Nuri, Āqā Bābā Khān Sardār-e Māzandarānī, the writer Reżā Qolī Khān-e Māzan-

417. Winter 1831/32.

darāni with the pen name Hedāyat,[418] special page of the presence (gholām-e pishkhedmat-e khāṣṣa) and companion of Reżā Qoli Mirzā, and a group of other courtiers. Upon his arrival at Kāzerun, Farmān-Farmā took up quarters in the Bāgh-e Naẓar and stayed there for a few days. Then he proceeded from Kāzerun to Khesht, Dālaki, and Borāzjān and tried to win over the khāns of Dashtestān. To Reżā Qoli Mirzā he gave cannons and soldiers and sent him to the plain of Samal and Ābād[419] which belonged to the eastern districts of Dashtestān. Because Sheikh ᶜAbd or-Rasul Khān was angry with the princes, he boarded ship and set sail. From Borāzjān Farmān-Farmā proceeded with a small host, Moshir ol-Molk and Sālem Khān-e Borāzjāni to Bushehr and established himself in the house of Sheikh ᶜAbd or-Rasul Khān [280]; the house is known as "Ark." Reżā Qoli Mirzā arrested Ra'is Moḥammad Bāqer, son of Ra'is Ḥosein-e Tangestāni, and sent him to Bushehr. The governorship (żabṭ) of the districts of Tangestān he conferred upon Moḥammad ᶜAli Khān and Bāqer Khān, sons of Aḥmad Shāh Khān, a brother of Ra'is Ḥosein. He also seized Mirzā Jaᶜfar Khān-e Khormuji and the other khāns and sent them to Bushehr. Sālem Khān-e Borāzjānī, too, was imprisoned at Bushehr. Moshir ol-Molk boarded the ship, captured Sheikh ᶜAbd or-Rasul Khān, and returned to Bushehr. The following day, Farmān-Farmā put in fetters Ra'is Moḥammad Bāqer, Sālem Khān, Mirzā Jaᶜfar Khān, and the other instigators of the plundering of Bushehr, and delivered them to Sheikh ᶜAbd or-Rasul Khān. Putting the end of the chain on his shoulders, the sheikh conducted them right through the bazaar of Bushehr to a ship and brought them to the island of Khārk. Some time

418. 1800–72. Mainly known as prose writer and historian; he was tutor (lala bāshi) to Prince Nāṣer od-Din Mirzā, see Browne, IV, 344. Ḥasan-e Easā'i quotes from his Roużat oṣ-Ṣafā-ye Nāṣeri. See Introduction above, p. xvii.

419. Samal lies about 25 miles east of Bushehr, Abād 6 miles south of Samal, see *Farhang*, VII, 16.

later he drowned all but Mirzā Ja^cfar Khān, who escaped from the prison and went to Shiraz. For a long time after, Mirzā Ja^cfar Khān devoted himself to studies. He is the author of *Tārikh-e Nozhat ol-Akhbār* and *Āthār-e Ja^cfari*.[420]

RIVALRIES IN SHIRAZ. During Farmān-Farmā's absence from Shiraz, Mirzā ᶜAli Akbar Qavām ol-Molk quarreled with Moḥammad ᶜAli Khān Ilkhāni-ye Qashqā'i, against whom he had had a grudge for a long time, while Moshir ol-Molk because of the enmity between the two was living at ease.[421] Since both were angry at Moshir ol-Molk, they came to terms; to strengthen their union they agreed to give the daughter of Qavām ol-Molk in marriage to Moḥammad Qoli Khān, the brother of the ilkhāni; the daughter of the ilkhāni was married to Mirzā Fatḥ ᶜAli Khān, the son of Qavām ol-Molk. When Moshir ol-Molk, who was staying at Bushehr, heard of this, he realized that the harmony had been established at his expense. He then found a solution and submitted to Farmān-Farmā that the aim of this union was separation from Farmān-Farmā and attachment to Crown Prince ᶜAbbās Mirzā. His talk to Farmān-Farmā was such that the latter at once made up his mind to entrust Bushehr to Jamāl Khān-e Shirāzi, administrator (pishkār) of Sheikh ᶜAbd or-Rasul Khān, and to hurry to Shiraz to settle the affairs of the province of Fārs; he appointed Sheikh ᶜAbd or-Rasul Khān to his company. Upon his arrival at Shiraz, Qavām ol-Molk, in

420. In 1276:1860, Mirzā Jaᶜfar Khān proceeded to Tehran and was ordered by Nāṣer od-Din Shāh to write a history of the Qājārs; the result was *Ḥaqā'eq ol-akhbār*, see Storey, p. 344 (No. 443), one of the few really critical works on the Qājārs, which therefore was confiscated. The work was recently edited by Ḥosein Khadiv-Jām, Tehran 1345:1966. *Āthār-e Jaᶜfari*, a work on the topography and history of Fārs, is mentioned in the Introduction, see above, p. xv.

421. Qavām ol-Molk was lord mayor, Moshir ol-Molk vizier of Shiraz. The incident illustrates the tensions between three authorities: the central government, represented by the vizier, the local government, and the tribal forces.

order to obtain the benevolence of Farmān-Farmā, stated that the aim of these marriages had been the strengthening of mutual obligation between him and the ilkhāni and that the tie could easily be untied in case Farmān-Farmā did not approve of it. After demanding a suitable peshkash they dissolved both marriages by divorce.

BEHBEHĀN OCCUPIED BY MIRZĀ MANṢUR KHĀN. At the the end of that year Mirzā Manṣur Khān-e Behbehāni, who for a certain space of time had been excluded from the inherited governorship of Kuh-e Giluya,[422] assembled a group of Lors and marched to Behbehān, assisted by Reżā Qoli Mirzā Nā'eb ol-Eyāla. Najaf Qoli Mirzā, governor of Behbehān, sent a detachment of troops against him and at 2 parasangs east of Behbehān they engaged in fighting. Mirzā ᶜAbdollāh Khān, son of Mirzā Manṣur Khān, who had the strength of Rostam and the vigor of Esfandeyār,[423] was killed. In the end the troops sent by the governor were defeated but made their escape. The next day when the town was occupied by Mirzā Manṣur Khān, the governor hurried to Shiraz.

APPOINTMENT OF NEW GOVERNORS TO SEVERAL DISTRICTS OF FĀRS. And that year Farmān-Farmā deposed Mirzā Moḥammad Ḥosein, vakil of the province of Fārs, from the governorship of Fasā and Dārāb which since olden times had been held by the latter's family. The governorship of Dārāb was entrusted to Farmān-Farmā's son Jahāngir Mirzā, who was granted the title "Ṣāḥeb Ekhteyār-e Dārāb." The governorship of Fasā was bestowed upon Mirzā Abu'l-Ḥasan Khān, the younger brother of Mirzā Moḥammad Ḥosein Vakil and son-in-law of Farmān-Farmā. The legend of Mirzā Abu'l-Ḥasan

422. In 1237:1821/22 Ḥosein ᶜAli Mirzā, the governor of Fārs, had appointed his own son, Najaf Qoli Mirzā, to Kuh-e Giluya, see *FNN*, II, 268.

423. Rostam and Esfandeyār were legendary heroes of Persian epics.

Khān's seal was this: "A rose whose natural fragrance is the recreation of the meadow—the qualities of Ḥasan and the descent from Ḥosein: Abu'l-Ḥasan."[424]

In that year Ḥosein ᶜAli Mirzā Farmān-Farmā deposed the beglerbegi of Lārestān, Naṣir Khān-e Lāri, governor of Lār and Sabᶜa. The governorship of Lārestān was entrusted to Aḥmad Khān-e Bastaki,[425] maternal uncle of the aforementioned Naṣir Khān. The governorship of Sabᶜa he conferred upon his own son Emām Qoli Mirzā Ghażanfar od-Doula.

And at the beginning of that year Farmān-Farmā appointed his son Naṣrollāh Mirzā governor of Shulestān and Mamassani. Upon the latter's arrival on the plain of Nurābād in the district of Shulestān,[426] Vali Khān-e Mamassani, kalāntar of the Bakash Mamassani tribe, revolted against the prince. When Yusof Khān-e Gorji, vizier to Naṣrollāh Mirzā, rebuked Vali Khān harshly in the assembly, he was killed by Vali Khān without hesitation.

THE QASHQĀ'I AND OTHER TRIBES MOVE FROM FĀRS TO KERMAN. The New Year fell on the evening of 17th Shavvāl of that year.[427] The shah celebrated the feast in Tehran in good health. And from the southern districts of Fārs, Farmān-Farmā was informed that Ilbegi Mortażā Qoli Khān was about to move to the districts of Kerman. Farmān-Farmā sent Ilkhāni Moḥammad ᶜAli Khān from Shiraz in order to give the ilbegi good news. A few days later the ilkhāni sent the following message:

The ilbegi of the Qashqā'i tribes, Mortażā Qoli Khān, moved off to Kerman before my arrival. ᶜAli Akbar Khān-e Nafar with the Nafar and

424. Abul'l-Ḥasan means "father of Ḥasan." Mirzā Abu'l-Ḥasan Khān was a near relative of the author of the *Fārs-nama*, see Genealogical Tables at the end of this book. The family was allegedly sprung from Ḥosein, the second Emām of the Shia.

425. The town of Bastak lies about 30 miles south of Lār.

426. Nurābād lies at the foot of the Qalᶜa-ye Safid, 1 parasang east of Fahleyān, see below, p. 244, note 44.

427. March 21, 1832.

Bahārlu tribe and Ma^cṣum Khān-e Inālu with the Inālu tribe have entered into an agreement with the ilbegi. I went to Kerman in order to bring them back. However, because of their anger at Mirzā Moḥammad ᶜAli Moshir ol-Molk[428] they are not willing to return to Fārs.

And Mirzā Moḥammad Ḥosein Vakil, who had been removed from the governorship of Fasā and Dārāb, fled from Shiraz and proceeded to the ilkhāni in the districts of Qir va-Kārzin[429] and thence to Kerman. Then the ilkhāni and the ilbegi in the district of Fasā divided the tribes in two, one half marched by way of Tang-e Karam,[430] Rouniz,[431] and Niriz[432] to Sirjān,[433] the other half by way of Sheshdeh[434] and Seh Chāh[435] and the districts of Dārāb, Forg, and Ṭārom to Sirjān in the province of Kerman. Having joined there they dispersed in the province of Kerman. The governor of Kerman, Seif ol-Moluk Mirzā, son of ᶜAli Shāh Ẓell os-Solṭān and [281] son-in-law of Crown Prince ᶜAbbās Mirzā, was delighted with their coming and assigned them pasture for summer and winter for 100,000 families in the northern and southern regions of Kerman. He invited Ilkhāni Moḥammad ᶜAli Khān, Vakil Mirzā Moḥammad Ḥosein, and Mirzā Qāsem Khān-e Khalaj, son-in-law of the ilkhāni, to the city of Kerman and treated them with the utmost respect. Upon deliberation he ordered Mirzā Moḥammad Ḥosein Vakil and

428. See above, p. 206.

429. Two formerly distinct districts which had been united to form one; the town of Qir lies about 31 miles west of Jahrom, the town of Kārzin 5 miles east of Qir, on the banks of the Mānd Rud.

430. 12 miles north of Fasā, see above, p. 57, note 230.

431. About 9.5 miles east of Tang-e Karam.

432. About 31 miles east of Rouniz.

433. One of the southwestern districts of the province of Kerman, the center of which is now called Saᶜidābād, 80 miles east-northeast of Niriz, see also p. 37, note 180.

434. "Six villages," about 25 miles east of Fasā.

435. "Three wells," not mentioned in the *Farhang*. From the stations mentioned it is clear that one half of the tribes first marched in a southern direction and then turned off to the north, while the other half marched directly to Sirjān.

Mirzā Qāsem Khān to march by way of Yazd and Ṭabas to Khorasan and to obey the orders of the crown prince.[436] Accordingly, they both departed the following day.

NAṢIR KHĀN REAPPOINTED GOVERNOR OF LĀRESTĀN. In the month of Shavvāl of that year,[437] Farmān-Farmā deposed Aḥmad Khān-e Bastaki from the governorship of Lārestān and Emām Qoli Mirzā Ghażanfar od-Doula from the governorship of Sabᶜa. Naṣir Khān-e Lāri was again appointed beglerbegi of Lārestān and Sabᶜa.

THE GOVERNOR OF FĀRS UNDERTAKES CAMPAIGN TO KERMAN. After the ᶜĀshurā feast in the month of Moḥarram of the year 1248,[438] Farmān-Farmā entrusted the city of Shiraz to Reżā Qoli Mirzā Nā'eb ol-Eyāla and put the commander, Āqā Bābā Khān, under the latter's orders. Sheikh ᶜAbd or-Rasul Khān, who sometimes stayed at Shiraz, was granted a robe of honor and sent back to Bushehr. Then Farmān-Farmā ordered his sons and nephews and Sheikh Moḥammad Amin, sheikh ol-eslām of Fārs, Qavām ol-Molk, Moshir ol-Molk, and Āqā Mirzā Moḥammad-e Fasā'i, the younger brother of Mirzā Moḥammad Ḥosein Vakil, to march off from Shiraz with 15,000 musketeers from the districts and 8 pieces of artillery, and bring back the tribes of Fārs from Kerman. Having arrived in Sarvestān, 14 parasangs to the southeast of Shiraz, Farmān-Farmā sent Sheikh Moḥammad Amin and Qavām ol-Molk through Rouniz, Niriz and Sirjān to Kerman in order to win over the ilkhāni and the other nobles. He himself proceeded to the town of Fasā. For some days he was the guest of Mirzā Abu'l-Ḥasan Khān, his son-in-law. Then he marched by way of Noubandagān[439] and Seh Chāh[440] to the plain of Dārāb. About forty

436. Crown Prince ᶜAbbās Mirzā was governor of Ādherbāyjān and Khorasan.

437. Began on March 4, 1832.

438. Began on May 31, 1832.

439. 12 miles southeast of Fasā.

440. See above note 435.

days he enjoyed himself in the districts of Fasā and Dārāb. Every day he waited for the return of Sheikh Moḥammad Amin and Qavām ol-Molk. Then he hurried from Dārāb by way of Niriz and Bavānāt[441] to Shahr Bābak[442] in Kerman, the fief of his sister.

MURDER OF SHEIKH ᶜABD OR-RASUL KHĀN AT DĀLAKI. When Farmān-Farmā was staying at Shahr Bābak, news arrived of the murder of Sheikh ᶜAbd or-Rasul Khān. This happened as follows: When Sheikh ᶜAbd or-Rasul Khān after his departure from Shiraz for Bandar Bushehr arrived at the village of Dālaki[443] in the district of Dashtestān, the khāns of Dashtestān, such as Haji Moḥammad Khān-e Borāzjāni, Moḥammad Amin Khān-e Shabānkāra, Moḥammad ᶜAli Khān, and Bāqer Khān, sons of Aḥmad Shāh Khān-e Tangestāni who all were longing to revenge the blood of their tribe on Sheikh ᶜAbd or-Rasul Khān, occupied the surroundings of his house and killed all his servants and retinue, except the sheikh himself and a black Swahili slave; then they fled. The sheikh and the slave retreated to the shelter of a tower. The slave loaded the musket and gave it to the sheikh who with each shot killed one of his opponents, until the powder and the balls were exhausted and only one shot was left. Then the sheikh pointed the musket at his chest and killed himself, thereby evading disgraceful captivity.

THE DEPUTY GOVERNOR OF FĀRS MARCHES TO BUSHEHR. When news of this arrived at Shiraz, Reżā Qoli Mirzā departed from Shiraz for Dashtestān with great haste. Upon his arrival at Borāzjān he reassured several khāns of Dashtestān, and about 5,000 musketeers assembled around him. Then he de-

441. See above, p. 57, note 228.

442. About 130 miles west of Kerman, at the southern slope of the Kuh-e Masāhem.

443. About 12 miles north-northeast of Borāzjān, on the highway to Kāzerun.

parted for Bushehr. The inhabitants of Bushehr and the merchants were shocked at this measure; fearing lest the plundering of the past year be repeated they loaded as much as they could carry on ships and took refuge on the sea. Sheikh Naṣr Khān, son of Sheikh ᶜAbd or-Rasul Khān, and Jamāl Khān-e Shirāzi went on board a small vessel (zauraq) and sailed for Qāvi,[444] an anchorage of big ships, where they took refuge on board an English ship. Reżā Qoli Khān entered Bushehr without doing harm to anybody. Because the administration of Bushehr in the absence of Sheikh Naṣr Khān and Jamāl Khān-e Shirāzi did not function properly, Reżā Qoli Mirzā sent the writer Reżā Qoli Khān with the pen name Hedāyat together with the English physician on board the English ship in order to reassure Sheikh Naṣr Khān. The sheikh, however, remained on the ship, whereas Jamāl Khān went to Bushehr. Notwithstanding the extreme heat at Bushehr, Reżā Qoli Mirzā remained there in order to settle the affairs of the district (velāyat) of Dashtestān.

THE GOVERNOR OF FĀRS RECONCILES THE QASHQĀ'I TRIBE AND SETTLES AFFAIRS IN KERMAN. As has been reported, Ḥosein ᶜAli Mirzā Farmān-Farmā, the governor of Fārs, arrived at Shahr Bābak and was staying there a few days waiting for the sheikh ol-eslām and Qavām ol-Molk.[445] The princess, his sister, who was in the possession of Shahr Bābak as her fief, received him as a guest. ᶜAbdollāh Khān, major (yāver) of the Hamadāni Qaraguzlu detachment who with a detachment of Qaraguzlu and two hundred regular soldiers (sarbāz) was in charge of the citadel of Shahr Bābak in the name of Seif ol-Moluk Mirzā, the governor of Kerman, had no choice but to open the gate, and Farmān-Farmā entered the house of his sister. ᶜAbdollāh Khān and the two hundred soldiers were deprived of their

444. The name is not mentioned in our sources. When James Morier arrived at Bushehr, the ship had to cast anchor 4 miles off shore, see Morier, *A Second Journey*, p. 36.

445. See above, p. 210.

weapons and sent to Shiraz with 400 musketeers. The following day the sheikh ol-eslām and Qavām ol-Molk returned from their mission to the ilkhāni, carrying the following letter: "As long as Mirzā Moḥammad ᶜAli Moshir ol-Molk remains vizier of Fārs, none of the tribes will return to Fārs." In order to win the benevolence of the ilkhāni and his followers, Farmān-Farmā sent Moshir ol-Molk from Shahr Bābak to Fārs; he was not to stay at Shiraz but to proceed to Kāzerun and Bandar Bushehr to put in order the administration of that region in the service of Reżā Qoli Mirzā. Then the vizierate of the province of Fārs was conferred upon Mirzā Ḥāsan Neẓām ol-ᶜOlamā, son of Mollā Bāshi Mollā ᶜAli Aṣghar-e Hezār Jaribi Māzandarāni. [282] Moshir ol-Molk did not stay at Shiraz but hurried to Kāzerun. Reżā Qoli Mirzā sent Reżā Qoli Khān Hedāyat from Bushehr to Kāzerun to entertain Moshir ol-Molk. Upon the latter's arrival he reassured him in the name of Reżā Qoli Mirzā and returned to Bushehr, carrying a petition for Moshir ol-Molk.

Having sent Moshir ol-Molk to Kāzerun, Ḥosein ᶜAli Mirzā Farmān-Farmā sent the sheikh ol-eslām and Qavām ol-Molk again to the ilkhāni in order to reassure him and bring him before Farmān-Farmā. Then the ilkhāni sent a letter to the ilbegi, Mortażā Qoli Khān, his younger brother, and ᶜAli Akbar Khān-e Nafar and Maᶜṣum Khān-e Inālu, ordering them to return to Fārs from the districts of Bam and Narmāshir in Kerman, with all the tribes of Fārs. When Seif ol-Moluk Mirzā, the governor of Kerman, heard of this, he ordered a detachment to march to the tribes of Fārs and to prevent them from departing. When Farmān-Farmā received news of this, he at once ordered Naṣir Khān, beglerbegi of Lārestān, to come with 5,000 musketeers from Lārestān. When the order arrived in the region of Lār, Naṣir Khān dispatched his younger brother with 5,000 musketeers to Kerman. And Farmān-Farmā sent Sheikh ol-Eslām Moḥammad Amin and Qavām ol-Molk to Shiraz; a report on the latter's hostility to Moshir ol-Molk is given below.[446] Āqā Mirzā Moḥammad-e Fasā'i, the younger brother of Mirzā Moḥammad Ḥosein Vakil, was sent with a letter to the city of Kerman, to Seif ol-Moluk Mirzā. The letter contained advice and admonition and threats of the shah's indignation. Farmā-Farmā himself departed from Shahr Bābak and proceeded to Bam and Narmāshir. When Āqā Moḥammad arrived at the city of Kerman, Seif ol-Moluk had departed for a few days' hunting, and when he returned, the inhabitants of the city of Kerman closed the gates and entrenched themselves behind the ramparts. A group of them proceeded to Farmān-Farmā in order to complain of Seif ol-Moluk's bad behavior. Seeing no other remedy, Seif ol-Moluk went to the camp of Farmān-Farmā, his mighty uncle, and was graciously received. Because the complaints of the people were overwhelming, Farmān-Farmā, in order to calm them down, sent Seif ol-Moluk off under the pretext of being brought to Shiraz in the company of ᶜAli Naqi Khān-e Qājār Qoyonlu; at his arrival in the district of Bavānāt he was to be released. ᶜAli Naqi Khān did as ordered. And Mortażā Qoli Khān, the ilbegi, left the districts of Bam and Narmāshir with all the tribes of Fārs and marched to Fārs; he put his younger brother Moṣṭafā Qoli Khān with 2,000 fully equipped horsemen in the service of Farmān-Farmā. When Farmān-Farmā was about to return to Fārs, the nobles of the city of Kerman lamented:

Because of our complaints you have deposed Seif ol-Moluk Mirzā and sent him to Shiraz. Now the citadel of the city of Kerman is in the possession of the princess, the spouse of Seif ol-Moluk Mirzā and daughter of Crown Prince ᶜAbbās Mirzā, with the Qaraguzlu general (sartip), ᶜAli Naqi Khān, and 1,000 soldiers from Hamadān under her command. Either you evacuate the nobles from Kerman, bringing them to Shiraz or you remove from us the calamity of ᶜAli Naqi Khān's presence!

446. See below, p. 219 seq.

Taking into consideration the proposals of the inhabitants of Kerman, Farmān-Farmā sent ᶜAli Naqi Khān the following message: "You must send the spouse of Seif ol-Moluk Mirzā to Yazd!" ᶜAli Naqi Khān did not obey Farmān-Farmā's order and prepared the defense of the citadel. In the meantime ᶜAli Khān had arrived with 4,000 musketeers. The army of Farmān-Farmā now numbered more than 15,000 men. The following day the inhabitants assembled for the capture of the citadel and started shouting. Arghun Mirzā, son of Ḥasan ᶜAli Mirzā Shojāᶜ os-Salṭana, and Moṣṭafā Qoli Khān-e Qashqā'i, the younger brother of the ilkhāni of Fārs, considered it shameful that the citadel should be conquered by craftsmen and merchants. Accordingly, the two valiant warriors attacked the citadel. By God's decree these two famous young men fell victim to the muskets of the Qaraguzlu Hamadāni soldiers within two hours. At the moment when the wounded Arghun Mirzā, half dead, was wrapped in a carpet, he said in a feeble voice: "Who are you that you dare to wrap the sword of the shah of Persia in a carpet?" Then the Qashqā'i Turks, in order to revenge their commander, took the citadel from the Qaraguzlu soldiers by force, gave them pardon, and did not harm anybody. Farmān-Farmā approved of the temerity of ᶜAli Naqi Khān and the killing of Arghun Mirzā and Moṣṭafā Qoli Khān, received graciously the daughter of the crown prince and her retinue, and sent them with suitable equipment to Yazd. The inhabitants of Yazd submitted a petition to Farmān-Farmā complaining about the bad behavior of Seif od-Doula Mirzā, the younger brother of Seif ol-Moluk Mirzā, and requesting Farmān-Farmā to come to Yazd. He answered them in writing: "We were entitled to the occupation of Kerman because of the relations of the city with our brother Shojāᶜ os-Salṭana. Without the permission of the Persian government we cannot put our foot on the soil of Yazd."[447]

447. A few years ago, an attempt of the governor to conquer Yazd had failed, see Vaziri, *Tārikh-e Kermān*, p. 376 seq.

Farmān-Farmā reported all the events to the shah and sent Haji Moḥammad Ṣādeq Khān, son of the late Ḥosein Qoli Khān, the younger brother of the shah, to Tehran. He appointed Holāgu Mirzā, son of Shojā^c os-Salṭana, governor of Kerman. And Lindsay John,[448] an Englishman, instructor of a detachment of Qaraguzlu soldiers, and Bardi Khān, lieutenant (nā'eb) [283] of the artillery of Crown Prince ^{c}Abbās Mirzā, entered the service of Farmān-Farmā. Their salary was fixed at a sum higher than normal, and they came to Shiraz in the company of Farmān-Farmā.

At the end of Jomādi II of that year,[449] Farmān-Farmā returned from Kerman to Shiraz by way of Sirjān, Niriz, Khir,[450] Korbāl[451] and Dāryān.[452] He entered Shiraz in the middle of Rajab of that year.[453] He entrusted the governorship of Ḥuma-ye Shirāz,[454] Sarvestān, Eṣṭahbānāt, and Fasā to Āqā Mirzā Moḥammad-e Fasā'i because he had removed Mirzā Abu'l-Ḥasan Khān from the governorship when the population of those districts had risen in revolt against the latter.

UNSUCCESSFUL ATTEMPT OF SHEIKH ^{c}ABD OR-RASUL KHĀN'S SON TO CONQUER BUSHEHR. As has been reported, Reżā Qoli Mirzā Nā'eb ol-Eyāla arrived at Bushehr after the murder of the governor of Bushehr, ^{c}Abd or-Rasul Khān.[455] Reżā Qoli Mirzā undertook nothing against the

448. John Lindsay (?), not the same "Mr. Lindsay" mentioned further down. It seems that all Englishmen are called "John" in the Persian sources.

449. Began on October 26, 1832.

450. About 19 miles east of Niriz, on the southern fringe of the Daryācha-ye Bākhtegān, see *Farhang*, VII, 94.

451. The region which is bordered by Persepolis in the north, Zarqān in the west and the Daryācha-ye Bākhtegān in the east, irrigated by several branches of the Kur River.

452. About 19 miles east of Shiraz, see *Farhang*, VII, 96.

453. December 8, 1832.

454. That is, the city of Shiraz and the surrounding area.

455. See above, p. 211.

governor's murderers. Sheikh Naṣr Khān, son of Sheikh ᶜAbd or-Rasul Khān, had boarded a ship with his family and sailed out for Baḥrein, Qaṭif, and Ra's ol-Kheima in order to implore the Arabs for assistance. When news of the death of Arghun Mirzā and Moṣṭafā Qoli Khān arrived at the ports of the Persian Gulf, Sheikh Naṣr Khān entered into an agreement with several thousand ᶜOtubi Arabs from Baḥrein, Javāshem Arabs from Ra's ol-Kheima,[456] and Arabs from Najd. At the beginning of Jomādi II of that year,[457] he arrived at Bushehr with several ships and cast anchor at Bushehr; he claimed his inherited property and wanted to avenge his father's blood. At nightfall they went ashore and attacked Bushehr from the waterfront. About 650 Shirazi soldiers and musketeers from Dashtestān who were placed in the towers on one side of the town and around the palace of Sheikh ᶜAbd or-Rasul Khān, lined up opposite them and engaged in fighting. Moḥammad ᶜAli Khān-e Tangestāni and Moḥammad ᶜAli Solṭān-e Shirāzi fought bravely. Because the relation of numbers was like that of one drop to the ocean, all the towers and ramparts of Bushehr, except the palace, the residence of Reżā Qoli Mirzā, fell into the hands of the Arabs. At daybreak the Arabs by order of Sheikh Naṣr Khān attacked the palace. When they were fighting fiercely an Arab entered bringing Reżā Qoli Mirzā a head. He said: "I am a Damukhi Arab living at Chāh Kutāh[458] belonging to Bushehr, and a servant of your servant Ḥosein, sheikh of the Damukhi Arabs. This is the head of Sheikh ᶜAbdollāh, the commander of the Arab army." Then Reżā Qoli Mirzā ordered the drummers to beat the drum of victory and joy. The head of Sheikh ᶜAbdollāh was suspended from the lintel of the palace gate. The musketeers from Dashtestān and the Shirazi soldiers who had fled the previous night, assembled near the palace. After the death of Sheikh

456. See above, p. 145. 457. Began on October 26, 1832.

458. The Damukhi Arabs had come from Najd and settled at Chāh Kutāh, north of Bushehr, see *FNN*, II, 331.

ᶜAbdollāh, the new commander of the troops, Sheikh Naṣr Khān, despaired of capturing Bushehr and fled with all the Arabs to the ships and returned home. About forty ᶜOtubi and Javāshem Arabs were taken prisoner in this battle and put in prison. After some time they were released by mediation of Seiyed Saᶜid, Imam of Masqaṭ, a son-in-law of Farmān-Farmā,[459] and were returned home.

HOLĀGU MIRZĀ'S APPOINTMENT TO THE GOVERNORSHIP OF KERMAN CONFIRMED BY THE SHAH. As has been reported, Haji Moḥammad Ṣādeq Khān was sent to Tehran in the name of Ḥosein ᶜAli Mirzā Fermān-Farmā.[460] Upon his arrival in Tehran he was graciously received and was given a certificate of the appointment of Holāgu Mirzā to the governorship of Kerman. He then returned to Shiraz.

AN UNUSUALLY COLD WINTER. In the whole of Persia the winter 1832/33 was much colder than in all the preceding years, and in the harbors of the Persian Gulf and the southern districts of Fārs where snow and ice were known by name only, both were seen with the eyes. The author Reżā Qoli Khān Hedāyat writes in his *Roużat oṣ-Ṣafā-ye Nāṣeri*:

That winter I was going to travel with a group of people from the village of Dasht-e Arjan in the region of Kuh-i Marra,[461] 11 parasangs to the west of Shiraz, to the station Khān-e Zenjān,[462] 8 parasangs to the west of Shiraz, the distance between the two places being 3 parasangs. In the village of Dasht-e Arjan snow was falling; because of uninterrupted snowing, the blocking of the pass, and the sinking of horseman and horse into the snow, we had a stay of forty days. We could neither return to Kāzerun, which was 3 parasangs away and snowed-in, nor

459. See above, p. 203. 460. See above, p. 216.
461. Dasht-e Arjan lies about 31 miles west of Shiraz.
462. About 9.5 miles east of Dasht-e Arjan; the pass between the two villages—more than 2,000 meters high—is called Kotal-e Dokhtar (the map shows on the western slope of the pass the village of Meyān Kotal, "Middle of the Pass").

could we proceed to Khān-e Zenjān. One group of travelers had departed before me for Kāzerun and Khān-e Zenjān; of them nothing was ever heard again.

MEASURES TAKEN AGAINST MOSHIR OL-MOLK, THE FORMER VIZIER OF FĀRS. As has been reported, Farmān-Farmā during his stay at Shahr Bābak, in order to obtain the benevolence of the ilkhāni and the nobles of Fārs, had deposed Mirzā Moḥammad ᶜAli Moshir ol-Molk from the vizierate of Fārs and sent the latter to the southern districts of Fārs, to Kāzerun and Bandar Bushehr, for the settling of the administrative affairs of Reżā Qoli Mirzā Nā'eb ol-Eyāla.[463] When Moshir ol-Molk arrived at Kāzerun, the fief of the mother of Reżā Qoli Mirzā, Moshir ol-Molk was enjoying the protection of that lady. Two days after Moshir ol-Molk's departure from Shahr Bābak, Mirzā ᶜAli Akbar Qavām ol-Molk submitted to Farmān-Farmā the following request:

> Moshir ol-Molk and his followers and agents have embezzeled the sum of 120,000 toman, even more, from the public treasury and taken it as their property. If you leave this immense sum as a gift to him and his followers, you grant them a favor of unusual liberality. If you do not grant them the money as a gift, there is not much hope, taking into consideration the strictness of the royal agents, regarding the collection of taxes. By the grace of God, I shall take this enormous sum from the deceivers of Farmān-Farmā. I shall prove their fraud. If not, I shall pay the sum of 120,000 toman to the treasury from my own pocket.

Farmān-Farmā granted this request. Then Qavām ol-Molk, taking ᶜAli Akbar Khān-e Nafar and a hundred Bahārlu and Nafar horsemen from Shahr Bābak for the collection of the tax arrears (vajh-e molzami) from Moshir ol-Molk, departed with great haste to meet Moshir ol-Molk at Shiraz. Moshir ol-Molk, however, [284] after spending but one hour at Shiraz, had proceeded to Kāzerun. When Qavām ol-Molk arrived at the Bāgh-e

463. See above, p. 212.

Delgoshā, 0.5 parasang to the east of Shiraz, and heard of the departure of Moshir ol-Molk, he recited the following verse: "How often have I undertaken useless endeavors of searching, running behind the fluttering sparrow like a child!" Mirzā Esmāᶜil, son of Moshir ol-Molk's sister, not suspecting anything, came out to the Bāgh-e Delgoshā with all pomp in order to welcome Qavām ol-Molk. Several of his retinue, hearing the rumors of the people of Shiraz, returned hastily to the city. Mirzā ᶜAli Naqi Mostoufi, son of Moshir ol-Molk's brother, and Mirzā Moḥammad ᶜAli Khān, son of Haji Ḥeidar ᶜAli Khān-e Shirāzi,[464] son-in-law of Moshir ol-Molk, betook themselves from their houses to the shrine of Emāmzāda Seiyed Mir Moḥammad. Mirzā Esmāᶜil was arrested in the Bāgh-e Delgoshā and requested to pay the sum of 20,000 toman. The next day Qavām ol-Molk entered Shiraz; he posted policemen as guards at the doors of the houses of Moshir ol-Molk and his relatives. They were requested to pay the sum of 100,000 toman, and within about three or four months they produced the whole sum. Then Qavām ol-Molk, the ilkhāni, and a group of nobles of Fārs submitted to Farmān-Farmā the following request: "You must expel Mirzā Moḥammad ᶜAli Moshir ol-Molk from the province of Fārs and send him to Kerbelā.[465] If you do not do that, and as long as he stays at Kāzerun, the disorder of the administration of Fārs will not be settled." And they won over the vizier, Mirzā Ḥasan Neẓām al-ᶜOlamā, and by order of Farmān-Farmā the followers and family of Moshir ol-Molk, including the daughter of Farmān-Farmā, the spouse of Mirzā Abu'l-Ḥasan Khān, son of Moshir ol-Molk, were sent from Shiraz to Kāzerun. Upon their arrival at Kāzerun, Moshir ol-Molk sent them from Kāzerun by way of Shulestan-e Mamassani, Behbehān, and Shoshtar to Kerbelā. When they arrived at

464. He was a cousin of Qavām ol-Molk.

465. That is, he should not be given another office in the government, Kerbelā being one of the Holy Places in Mesopotamia.

Sarāb-e Seyāh in the region of Mamassani,[466] they were attacked suddenly by a group of Lors who plundered all their belongings. In great distress, Moshir ol-Molk proceeded with his family to the town of Behbehān. Mirzā Manṣur Khān, governor of Behbehān, treated him with great respect, procured the necessities for the journey from his own property, gave them money to cover the expenses as far as Kerbelā, and sent them off. Arriving at Shoshtar, Moshir ol-Molk exchanged his destination, Kerbelā, for Esfahan and proceeded to Esfahan through the Bakhteyāri region. He took up quarters in the neighborhood of Ḥojjat ol-Eslām Haji Seiyed Moḥammad Bāqer.[467]

MILITARY REFORMS IN FĀRS. Mirzā Ḥasan Neẓām al-ᶜOlamā was plenipotentiary vizier of the province of Fārs. Just as Crown Prince ᶜAbbās Mirzā had put up several detachments of soldiers under the command of Mirzā Abu'l-Qāsem Qā'em Maqām-e Farāhāni, who were daily trained on the Meidān of the city of Tabriz by French and English instructors, Neẓām ol-ᶜOlamā induced Farmān-Farmā to recruit three detachments of soldiers from the city of Shiraz, the districts, and the tribes and to garrison them in Shiraz. Each detachment was fixed to number 800 men. Nāder Mirzā, son of Farmān-Farmā, was appointed commander (sarhang) of the Shirazi detachment, his major being Fatḥollāh Khān, son of the former lord mayor of Shiraz, Mirzā Ebrāhim. Jahāngir Khān, son of the ilkhāni, Moḥammad ᶜAli Khān, was appointed commander of the Qashqā'i, ᶜArab, Nafar, and Bahārlu detachment. His major was Reżā Qoli Khān, son of Āqā Khān and alderman of the Arabs. Mirzā ᶜAbdollāh Khān, younger brother of Āqā Mirzā Moḥammad-e Fasā'i, was appointed commander of the detachment from the districts of Ḥuma-ye Shirāz, Sarvestān, Fasā, Dārāb and Eṣṭaḥbānāt; his

466. See above, p. 198.
467. That is, near the sepulcher of Moḥammad Bāqer-e Majlisi, famous theologian of Safavid times who died in 1111:1699/1700.

major was Mirzā Moḥammad Reżā, son of Mirzā ᶜAbd ar-Raḥim Mostoufi-ye Shirāzi, son of the maternal aunt of Mirzā ᶜAbdollāh Khān.[468] An Englishman named John Walter[469] trained these three detachments daily on the Meidān-e Tubkhāna ("Square of the Cannons") at Shiraz and outside the Bāgh-e Shāh Gate.

And Mirzā Moḥammad Ḥosein, vakil of the province of Fārs, and Mirzā Khān-e Khalaj, who at the beginning of that year had gone from Kerman to Khorasan and were received in audience by Crown Prince ᶜAbbās Mirzā, returned to Shiraz.

DEATH OF CROWN PRINCE ᶜABBĀS MIRZĀ. The New Year fell on the evening of 28th Shavvāl of that year.[470] Having settled the affairs of the whole province of Kerman and every emir being at his place, Crown Prince ᶜAbbās Mirzā left Khorasan for Tehran to be received in audience by the shah. When he arrived in the vicinity of Tehran, all the princes, emirs and nobles, the artillery and the arsenal, and the inhabitants of the city came out to welcome him by order of the shah. On 23d Moḥarram of the year 1249,[471] he entered Tehran with great pomp. He was granted royal favors exceeding the usual. On 19th Rabiᶜ I of that year,[472] he returned from Tehran to Khorasan for the attack of Afghanistan. Then he was stricken with several diseases and died on 10th Jomādi II[473] in the citadel of Mashhad. He was buried in the shrine of ᶜAli ibn Musā or-Reżā. He had been born in 1203 and died in 1249.[474] Mirzā Fażlollāh-e Khāveri-ye Shirāzi writes:

468. She was a daughter of Haji Ebrāhim Khān Eᶜtemād od-Doula, see the Genealogical Tables at the end of this book.
469. See above, p. 216, note 448.
470. March 20, 1833 (should be March 21).
471. June 12, 1833.
472. August 6, 1833.
473. October 25, 1833.
474. 1203:1788/89; 1249:1833/34.

Two of the younger princes informed the shah of these sad news. The shah suffered the same fate as had befallen Feridun by the murder of Iraj, and Shāh Goshtāsp by the death of Esfandeyār.[475]

And a royal decree was issued with the appointment of the second crown prince, Moḥammad Mirzā, son of the first crown prince, ᶜAbbās Mirzā Nā'eb os-Salṭana, as governor of Ādherbāyjān and Khorasan.

THE GOVERNOR OF FĀRS SUBDUES THE QASHQĀ'I KHĀNS. [285] In the middle of the winter of that year,[476] Farmān-Farmā of Fārs decided to subdue the Qashqā'i khāns, who secretly were inclining to the second crown prince. He ordered the commander, Āqā Bābā Khān-e Māzandarāni, with a hundred Shirāzi and Nuri horsemen of the bodyguard (mulāzem) to undertake this mission. And letters of honor were addressed to the khāns of the southern districts, who were angry at the bad behavior of the tribes. Āqā Bābā Khān departed from Shiraz under the pretext of settling the affairs of the districts of Galladār and the harbors of ᶜAsluya,[477] Ṭāheri,[478] and Kangān.[479] After arriving on the plain of Qir va-Kārzin, he encamped in the fortress of Parkān, 2,000 cubits to the east of the town of Qir,[480] which had towers and rampart and was the residence of Karim Khān-e Bidshehri.[481] The next day he rested and sent an eloquent servant to the ilbegi, Mortaẓā Qoli Khān, who had his winter quarters 2 or 3 parasangs from the fortress of Parkān, telling the

475. Feridun and Shāh Goshtāsp were legendary kings of Persian antiquity. This and similar remarks show that the Qājārs (or at least their chroniclers) considered the heroes of Persian epics as their prototypes.

476. That is, winter 1833/34.

477. About 12 miles south of Galladār.

478. About 25 miles northwest of Bandar ᶜAsluya.

479. About 25 miles northwest of Bandar Ṭāheri.

480. A fortress about 1 mile east of Qir (which lies about 31 miles west of Jahrom) is shown, without name, on the 1 : 500,000 map.

481. Bidshehr, the center of the united districts of Juyom and Bidshehr, lies about 50 miles southeast of Qir, see *FNN*, II, 182.

ilbegi that it was foolish not to meet, given the nearness and the good relations between them. Karim Khān, who inwardly was an enemy of the ilbegi, outwardly, however, showed him friendship, was informed of this message to the ilbegi. Karim Khān brought 200 musketeers from Bidshehr in great secret and hid them in the towers of the fortress of Parkān. Then the ilbegi, who out of pride considered nobody to be a match for himself, arrived at the fortress of Parkān with 40 horsemen. One hour later, Āqā Bābā Khān produced the order of Farmān-Farmā for the ilbegi's arrest. After reading the order, he said to Āqā Bābā Khān: "High Heaven cannot put my hands in fetters. If I was not obliged to you by true friendship, I should smash your head with a blow of my fist," then he rose. When he came out of the house, they were shooting at him from the tower and rampart and several of his followers were killed. When he walked into the gateway, the gate was closed and fastened with bolt, and the musketeers made holes through the roof of the gateway and covered him with a shower of bullets. A black slave named Khosrou, who threw himself as a protection in front of the ilbegi, was killed. Then the ilbegi was hit by the shower of bullets, and the whole upper part of his body was wounded. All his followers were killed. The wounded ilbegi was arrested and a chain was put round his waist; the occurrence was then reported to Farmān-Farmā. Farmān-Farmā ordered his son Emām Qoli Mirzā to proceed to the ilkhāni, Moḥammad ᶜAli Khān, to arrest him and his son-in-law Mirzā Qāsem Khān-e Khalaj, and to bring them before him. Mirzā Qāsem Khān was at once deprived of his sight, and the house of the ilkhāni was plundered. His possessions, which had been amassed in the course of several centuries, were carried away as booty. The ilkhāni himself was put in fetters and imprisoned. Mirzā ᶜAli Akbar Qavām ol-Molk cautiously withdrew and took refuge[482] in the shrine of Emāmzāda Seiyed ᶜAlā od-Din Ḥosein. Since Farmān-Farmā did not

482. On his agreement with the ilkhāni, see above, p. 206.

consider it advisable to leave Qavām ol-Mulk in the shrine, he ordered Emām Qoli Mirzā to proceed to the shrine. Violating the sanctuary, the latter drew Qavām ol-Molk and his son Mirzā Moḥammad Khān out of the shrine and brought them before Farmān-Farmā. This bad behavior bore no blessing to Farmān-Farmā and his sons; before one year had elapsed they were arrested in retribution for this action. The next day about 60,000 toman in cash were unearthed and brought before Farmān-Farmā from a grave in front of the Bāgh-e Eram, 0.25 parasang to the north of Shiraz, which belonged to the ilkhāni and wherein were several graves of the Qashqā'i family. The office of lord mayor of Shiraz was entrusted to Hādi Khān, son of the former lord mayor, Mirzā Ebrāhim. And Āqā Bābā Khān brought the ilbegi, Mortażā Qoli Khān, to the city of Shiraz with all caution. Forty days later the ilbegi died from his terrible wounds.

When news of this arrived at Bushehr, Reżā Qoli Mirzā Nā'eb ol-Eyāla appointed Shokrollāh Khān-e Nuri his deputy and proceeded to Shiraz. Because he was a close friend to Qavām ol-Mulk, he mediated every day upon his arrival with Farmān-Farmā. At the beginning of the month of Shavvāl of that year,[483] Farmān-Farmā released Mirzā ᶜAli Akbar Qavām ol-Molk and Moḥammad ᶜAli Khān, the ilkhāni, from prison and appointed Mirzā Moḥammad Khān, son of Qavām ol-Molk, lord mayor of Shiraz as before. The governorship of the Qashqā'i tribes and the districts of Sarḥadd-e Chahār Dānga,[484] Sarḥadd-e Shesh Nāḥeya,[485] Firuzābād,

483. Began on February 11, 1834.

484. Region on the upper course of the Kur River, the center of which was the small town of Āsopās, 80 miles north of Shiraz.

485. The mountainous region of difficult access south of Shahreżā (Qomisha), which had been in the possession of the Qashqā'i tribe ever since. The most important peaks are the Kuh-e Dinār and Kuh-e Seyāh. The name of the region, "Six Districts," reminds one that there were originally six distinct regions: Pādonā (with Khour, 7 parasangs south of Samirom), Ḥannā (with Ḥannā, 4 parasangs south of Samirom), Samirom (in Qājār times the center of the whole region, 22 miles southwest of

Farrāshband,[486] Khonj,[487] Afzar,[488] and Navāḥi Arba^c[489] was entrusted to the ilkhāni as before.[490] The title "Ilbegi" was given to Moḥammad Qoli Khān, the younger brother of the ilkhāni, and he became ilbegi of the Qashqā'i tribes.

MOSHIR OL-MOLK REAPPOINTED VIZIER OF FĀRS. Because Mirzā Ḥasan Neẓām ol-ᶜOlamā, vizier for a year, had several times shown bad behavior, Farmān-Farmā was angry with him. Upon deliberation with Qavām ol-Molk and the ilkhāni and with the permission of Reżā Qoli Mirzā Nā'eb ol-Eyāla, Farmān-Farmā apologized to Mirzā Moḥammad ᶜAli Moshir ol-Molk, who for nearly a year had been living at Esfahan in retreat, and tried to win Moshir ol-Molk over. Farmān-Farmā sent Haji Darvish Nadim, known as "Naqqāl,"[491] one of his most reliable men, [286] secretly to Esfahan. Upon his arrival Haji Darvish handed over to Moshir ol-Molk the letter of Farmān-Farmā and Reżā Qoli Mirzā and the assurances of Qavām ol-Molk and the ilkhāni; after receiving assurances in writing for Qavām ol-Molk and the ilkhāni, Haji Darvish secretly returned to Shiraz and brought the letter of acceptance.

Izadkhvāst), Falārod (with Falārod, 5 parasangs west of Samirom), Vardasht (with Garmābād, 7 parasangs north of Samirom), and Vanak (with Vanak, 80 miles west of Izadkhvāst, on the western slope of the Kuh-e Nākhodā), see *FNN*, II, 220.

486. About 60 miles southwest of Shiraz.

487. The region south of Firuzābād; the center is Khonj, which lies 38 miles northwest of Lār, see *Farhang*, VII, 90.

488. The region southwest of Jahrom, the center, Nim Deh, is 17.5 miles south of Qir, see *Farhang*, VII, 237.

489. "Four Districts," the region south of Firuzābād, composed of the four districts (nāḥeya): Deh Ram, Deh Rud, Hangām (approximately 30 miles south of Firuzābād) and Rudbāl (or Rudbār ?), see *FNN*, II, 172 (s.v. Arbaᶜa); now Arbaᶜa bālā and Arbaᶜa pā'in, see *Farhang*, VII, 7.

490. The districts in the northern and southern part of Fārs enumerated in this list from the summer and winter quarters of the Qashqā'i tribes.

491. That is, "narrator," a man employed by the governor as boon-companion ("nadim") for entertainment.

Neẓām ol-ᶜOlamā, who was a shrewd man, perceived what was going on and hurried from Shiraz to Kerman to enter the service of Ḥasan ᶜAli Mirzā Shojāᶜ os-Salṭana. At the beginning of the month of Dhu'l-Qaᶜda of that year,[492] Moshir ol-Molk proceeded from Esfahan to Shiraz and established himself in the Vakili palace, the residence of Farmān-Farmā. Upon his arrival he was granted the insignia of the vizierate and was inducted into his office.

ARRIVAL OF AN ENGLISH MILITARY MISSION. At the end of that year, 40 officers and instructors, whose leader was called Kinneir,[493] arrived at Bushehr and entered Shiraz with all honors; they had been sent by the English government as a token of friendship toward the shah for the instruction of the soldiers of Ādherbāyjān. They traveled from Shiraz by way of Esfahan to Tehran.

LAST MEASURES

MOḤAMMAD MIRZĀ APPOINTED CROWN PRINCE. The New Year fell on Friday, 10th Dhu'l-Qaᶜda of that year.[494] The shah summoned Second Crown Prince Moḥammad Mirzā, governor of Khorasan and Ādherbāyjān, from Khorasan, and by order of the shah the prince departed from Mashhad. When he arrived in the vicinity of Tehran, all the viziers, emirs, and princes, except ᶜAli Shāh Ẓell os-Solṭān,[495] welcomed him with royal pomp. On 6th Ṣafar of the year 1250,[496] he entered Tehran and was received in audience. On the 12th of that month a royal banquet was celebrated in the Bāgh-e Negārestān.

492. Began on March 12, 1834.

493. Not the Ambassador Kinneir mentioned above, p. 184.

494. March 21, 1834.

495. He claimed succession to the throne for himself or one of his sons. For marriage relations to ᶜAbbās Mirzā, see Genealogical Tables at the end of this book.

496. June 14, 1834.

By order of the shah, the leading theologians, emirs, viziers, and officials and nobles of the country were summoned, and the jewel-studded objects appropriate to the crown prince were sent to Moḥammad Mirzā: a sword and girdle studded with jewels, the Order of the Lion and Sun, a robe of honor and the certificate of appointment to crown prince and Nā'eb os-Salṭana. In an hour of happy augury he put on the robe of honor and the jewel-studded objects and put the royal farmān like a crown on his head. Gold and silver were distributed to the assembly and the prayer of the crown prince was said in his name. Then the second crown prince left for Tabriz to settle affairs in Ādherbāyjān and to proceed thence to Khorasan.

THE SHAH TRAVELS TO ESFAHAN TO SETTLE AFFAIRS IN SOUTHERN PERSIA. On 3d Jomādi I of that year,[497] the shah, left Tehran for Esfahan in order to punish the Bakhteyāris, who were assaulting their neighbors, committing highway robbery, and perpetrating a new act of violence every day; furthermore, he was going to collect 600,000 toman in cash, which is a crore and 100,000 toman, the taxes of four years of the province of Fārs, which under the pretext of disturbances in the province and the calamity of locusts had not been paid by Farmān-Farmā. On 4th Jomādi II,[498] the royal court put up camp in the Bāgh-e Saᶜādatābād at Esfahan. On the 10th of that month Farmān-Farmā and Mirzā ᶜAli Akbar Qavām ol-Molk arrived from Fārs. When they were admitted to audience, the shah ordered Moḥammad Taqi Mirzā Ḥosām os-Salṭana[499] to collect the tax arrears of Fārs of four years, to escort Farmān-Farmā back to Shiraz and to collect from him 600,000 toman in full. ᶜAbdollāh Khān Amin od-Doula and Haji Mirzā Abu'l-Ḥasan Khān, minister of the foreign powers, were ordered to march behind Farmān-Farmā to Shiraz with 7,000 horsemen and

497. September 7, 1834. 498. October 8, 1834.
499. A son of Fatḥ ᶜAli Shāh.

infantry. They were to chastise Vali Khān-e Mamassani, the Bakhteyāris, and the other rebels of Fārs. Farmān-Farmā and Ḥosām os-Salṭana were dismissed on the 17th of that month[500] and departed for Shiraz. Qavām ol-Molk remained at Esfahan in order to march from Esfahan to Shiraz together with ᶜAbdollāh Khān Amin ad-Doula and Haji Mirzā Abu'l-Ḥasan Khān.

DEATH OF FATḤ ᶜALI SHĀH. On the 19th of that month, a Thursday,[501] three hours before sunset, as the shah was changing his dress in order to proceed to the government building, he fainted and fell to the ground. He gasped for breath several times, then stopped breathing, and died. In order to conceal the event from the court, the princes refrained from lamentation, washed the corpse right in the palace, wrapped it in a shroud, and performed the funeral prayers. Then all hurried away, harboring irrational ideas. Until sunset they kept the shah's death secret. At nightfall the secret was divulged and because of the commotion at the court an uproar arose among the inhabitants of Esfahan. At daybreak the corpse of the shah was put on a traveling litter as though he was alive. Together with the royal harem, ᶜAli Naqi Mirzā Rokn od-Doula[502] departed for Kāshān and Qom. Upon arrival at Qom, the corpse was buried in a grave which had been prepared previously for this ruler in the vicinity of the sepulcher of Ḥażrat-e Maᶜṣuma.[503]

In *Tadhkera-ye Mojmaᶜ ol-Foṣahā*,[504] two verses (robāᶜi) are ascribed to Fatḥ ᶜAli Shāh. [287] Some state that he reached the age of sixty-seven, others that he was aged seventy, others give sixty-four years and four months. According to the last of these

500. October 21, 1834. 501. October 23, 1834 (a Friday!).

502. Son of Fatḥ ᶜAli Shāh.

503. That is, Fāṭema, sister of ᶜAli ibn Musā or-Reżā, the Eighth Emām, whose burial place is Mashhad.

504. The author of this anthology of contemporary Persian poetry was the famous Reżā Qoli Khān Hedāyat; the book was printed in Tehran in 1295:1878.

statements he was born in the year 1185.[505] He was buried in the vicinity of the shrine of Ḥażrat-e Maᶜṣuma in the town of Qom. He ruled thirty-eight years and five and a half months. Mirzā Fażlollāh-e Khāveri-ye Shirāzi writes in his *Tārikh-e Dhu'l-Qarnein* (which is preserved in his handwriting): "At the time of his death the shah left 53 sons and 46 daughters. The number of grandchildren is beyond count. By estimation one comes to 784 persons, not reckoning the grandchildren of the princes."

505. 1185:1771/72.

CHAPTER 3

Moḥammad Shāh

THE STRUGGLE FOR SUCCESSION

THE PRIME MINISTER INCITES ḤOSEIN ᶜALI MIRZĀ FARMĀN-FARMĀ, THE GOVERNOR OF FĀRS, TO ASSUME RULERSHIP. The day upon Fatḥ ᶜAli Shāh's death, Allāh Yār Khān Āṣaf od-Doula and Gholām Ḥosein Khān Sepahdār and the other emirs sent Amin od-Doula the following message: "Since things have changed, you must proceed from your camp to the court in order to do what you consider advisable, until upon deliberation we remove the army (which has come with the deceased shah) from Esfahan." Since Amin od-Doula sympathized with Farmān-Farmā, he wrote in answer: "When the shah was alive I entered into an agreement with him that after him I shall not serve any other shah. Therefore I shall renounce my office." And to Farmān-Farmā he sent a courier:

Return without delay so that I may deliver Esfahan to you without difficulty. The army which is with me I put under your command as your retinue. If you take up your residence at Esfahan, your orders will be obeyed better at Shiraz. The army of Fārs will come to you without hesitation. Ḥasan ᶜAli Mirzā Shojāᶜ os-Salṭana, too, will come from Kerman, and most of the princes from ᶜErāq will come to you, for you are the eldest brother[1] and you can put yourself in your father's place. March to Tehran with 100,000 soldiers and put yourself in your father's place, and you will be king of the whole of Persia.

Farmān-Farmā, however, not being hot-tempered, did not care for the words of Amin od-Doula. He realized that he would be happier if he stayed at Shiraz in the company of his men.

1. After ᶜAbbās Mirzā's death, Ḥosein ᶜAli Mirzā Farmān-Farmā was Fatḥ ᶜAli Shāh's eldest son born from a Qājār princess, see above, p. 36.

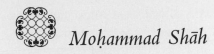

From Qomesha[2] he sent Moḥammad Taqi Mirzā Ḥosām os-Salṭana to Borujerd,[3] and he himself hurried to Shiraz. And Amin od-Doula gave up his hope in Farmān-Farmā, sent the whole army home and went to Esfahan.

MOḤAMMAD SHAH ASCENDS THE THRONE IN TABRIZ AND TEHRAN. Moḥammad Reẓā Mirzā, son of the deceased shah, proceeded from Esfahan to Tabriz and informed the second crown prince, Moḥammad Mirzā Nā'eb os-Salṭana, of the shah's death. The prince had been sad at the death of his father; now, at the death of his grandfather, he was afflicted by deep melancholy. He took counsel with Mirzā Abu'l-Qāsem Qā'em Maqām and the emirs of the court, and they all said that in accordance with the last will and testament of the late shah[4] nobody was to take over the government except him; and that he had to proceed to Tehran in order to bring the affair to a happy conclusion, since he was the father's and the grandfather's heir. For his preparations the English ambassador put the sum of 70,000 toman at the disposal of the crown prince, who then decided to depart for Tehran with a well-organized army. On 7th Rajab,[5] at the urging of the ambassadors of England and Russia, he ascended the throne with royal splendor. On this accession the following chronogram has been composed: "At his accession he was like the 'light of truth'—the words *ẓohur ol-ḥaqq* ('the appearance of truth') became the date (of his accession)." Putting his trust in God he departed for Tehran with 6,000 men of the disciplined army (lashgar-e neẓām), 24 pieces of artillery, and 3,000 horsemen in the middle of the month of Rajab.[6] On 22d Shaᶜbān of that year[7] he entered

2. The governor was on his way back from Esfahan to Shiraz, see above, p. 229.

3. Borujerd, south of Hamadān, did not belong to Farmān-Farmā's government; it seems that he tried to extend his rule to Kurdistan.

4. See above, p. 160. 5. September 9, 1834.

6. September 17, 1834. 7. December 24, 1834.

Tehran with royal pomp. The accession to the throne was celebrated in the Bāgh-e Negārestān with imperial splendor. On 2d Ramażān of that year[8] he proceeded to the palace and met the harem. On 14th Ramażān,[9] the solemn accession to the throne was performed in the government building of the citadel of Tehran. He sat on the throne of his grandfather and put the crown of the Kayānids on his head. A general audience was held with great splendor, gold and silver were distributed, and the ceremony of enthronement was brought to a happy conclusion. Then he devoted himself to the affairs of the state and the people were at ease.

THE GOVERNOR OF FĀRS CLAIMS THE THRONE. When the governor of the province of Fārs, Ḥosein ᶜAli Mirzā Farmān-Farmā, was informed from Qomesha of the shah's departure, he sent two couriers on horseback to Kerman informing his younger brother, [288] Ḥasan ᶜAli Mirzā Shojaᶜ os-Salṭana, of the event and summoning him to Shiraz. He himself proceeded with great haste to Shiraz. After the arrival of Shojāᶜ os-Salṭana, they had the name of Farmān-Farmā mentioned on the pulpits and put on the coins.[10] When Farmān-Farmā summoned Qavām ol-Molk, who was staying at Esfahan, he refused to come. Then Farmān-Farmā arrested Qavām ol-Molk's eldest son, Mirzā Moḥammad Khān, and ordered him to be executed. By intercession of Shokrollāh Khān,[11] he was saved from death and imprisoned in the palace of Shiraz. Then Farmān-Farmā started preparing and assembling the army of Fārs. Shojāᶜ os- Salṭana and several other princes, together with 5,000 horsemen and infantry recruited from the tribes and the city, were sent from Shiraz to Esfahan.

FIRUZ MIRZĀ APPOINTED GOVERNOR OF FĀRS; THE REBELS SUFFER DEFEAT NEAR IZADKHVĀST. At the end

8. January 2, 1835. 9. January 14, 1835.
10. That is, Farmān-Farmā assumed independent rule.
11. He was the maternal uncle of Mirzā Moḥammad Khān.

of the month of Shavvāl,[12] the shah made up his mind to subdue Farmān-Farmā and Shojā^c os-Salṭana and to conquer the province of Fārs. He appointed his younger brother, Firuz Mirzā, governor of the province of Fārs and made Manuchehr Khān-e Gorji Mo^ctamad od-Doula responsible for the conquest of that province. Mirzā Abu'l-Qāsem Dhu'r-Reyāsatein, former vizier of Kermānshāh, Lorestān, and ^cArabestān, and a man of great efficiency, and Moḥammad Ṭāher Khān-e Qazvini, a famous emir, were ordered to accompany Mo^ctamad od-Doula. The following persons were put under the command of Firuz Mirzā and Mo^ctamad od-Doula: Mr. Lindsay and Sheil Ṣāḥeb[13] and several other English officers, and 6,000 men of the disciplined army (sepāh-e neẓām) and several pieces of artillery together with Mirzā Moḥammad Khān, son of Amir Khān-e Qājār Devehlu, maternal uncle of the late crown prince, ^cAbbās Mirzā, and the Māku'i general Moḥammad Khān, the Qarācha Dāghi general Ja^cfar Qoli Khān, the Khoy'i colonel Maḥmud Khān, Manṣur Khān-e Farāhāni, and Sālem Khān-e Chagani. When these troops arrived at Kāshān, one half under the command of Firuz Mirzā and Mo^ctamad od-Doula marched by way of Ardestān[14] to the region of Yazd, the other half under the command of Lindsay to Esfahan. At Esfahan, Lindsay heard that Shojā^c os-Salṭana, the princes Ḥeidar Qoli Mirzā and Soleimān Mirzā and the sons of Farmān-Farmā had marched off with a

12. That is, end of February, 1835.

13. Henry Lindsay, afterwards Sir Henry Lindsay Bethune (1787–1851), had come to Persia for the first time in 1810 with Sir John Malcolm's mission; until 1821 he was instructor of the Persian army, together with captain Christie. By order of the English government, he returned to Persia in 1834 and left for England shortly after the events described here. His third mission to Persia in 1836 was repudiated by the shah.

J. Sheil had come to Ādherbāyjān as an instructor in 1830; he and his wife, Lady M. L. Sheil, have contributed much to our knowledge of Persian geography and folklore, see Bibliography, and Gabriel, *Die Erforschung Persiens*, p. 145.

14. About 170 miles southeast of Kāshān.

big army from Shiraz to Esfahan and put up their camp near Ābāda. Accordingly, Lindsay hurried with several detachments of experienced troops and the Afshār horsemen to Izadkhvāst. He blocked the road and encamped, ready for battle. Then Shojāᶜ os-Salṭana left Ābāda and entered Shulgestān, 5 parasangs from Izadkhvāst.[15] The following day, Lindsay marched with strong detachments from Izadkhvāst in the direction of Shulgestān, while Shojāᶜ os-Salṭana marched from Shulgestān in the direction of Izadkhvāst. When they saw each other, they drew up for battle. Shojāᶜ os-Saltana, a long spear in hand, ran along the front and the rear of his lines, reciting the half verse "No army will subsist without an experienced leader."[16] On both sides the artillery opened fire. The royal artillery fired at the artillery of Fārs in such a manner that pieces of it weighing 300 mann[17] were thrown from the gun carriages and Shojāᶜ os-Salṭana's troops became discouraged. Several other cannons were firing at the horse and foot of Fārs, and a number of them were killed. Shojāᶜ os-Salṭana fought bravely; he advanced several times as far as the cannons of the shah and urged his troops on to fight. This was, however, useless; the troops of Fārs were defeated; stumbling across the plain covered with snow, using the roads or not using them, they retreated to the hills. After resting for an hour they had no other choice but to return to Shiraz.

INDECISION AND UPROAR IN SHIRAZ. When news of the defeat arrived at Shiraz, the ministers of Farmān-Farmā hesitated to take measures. The nobles of Fārs, who in the previous year had all been deceived by Farmān-Farmā financially and morally, held grudges against Farmān-Farmā and were willing to submit

15. Shulgestān lies about 19 miles southeast of Izadkhvāst, see also above, p. 195.
16. That is, he tried to encourage his men in the traditional manner of Persian warfare.
17. About 1,000 kilograms.

to Moḥammad Shāh. Firuz Mirzā, Manuchehr Khān Moᶜtamad od-Doula, Mirzā Abu'l-Qāsem Dhu'r-Reyāsatein-e Hamadāni, and Moḥammad Ṭāher Khān-e Qazvini marched off from Ardestān and the region of Yazd and joined Lindsay's troops at the camp of Ābāda. The defeated troops of Fārs did not march as far as Shiraz, but all went home. When they arrived at Shiraz, Shojāᶜ os-Salṭana, Reżā Qoli Mirzā, and Timur Mirzā suggested to Farmān-Farmā that he flee from Shiraz. Since he considered flight dishonorable, Reżā Qoli Mirzā Nā'eb ol-Eyāla, Timur Mirzā, and Najaf Qoli Mirzā Vāli, the sons of Farmān-Farmā, took their mother and their wives and children and the gold and jewels which they had amassed during a lifetime, mounted their horses, and left Shiraz in the early morning. They hurried through the Bāgh-e Shāh Gate by way of Shulestān in Mamassani, Zeidun in the district of Behbehān, Jarrāḥi and Falāḥi to Moḥammar;[18] there they went on board a ship and sailed to Basra. After resting from the hardship of the voyage, they went to Baghdad and established themselves comfortably.[19]

On the same day that the princes left Shiraz, the wives of Farmān-Farmā with the help of their servants brought their treasures to the houses of the theologians and nobles of Shiraz. When the rabble of the city heard of this, they took away from them most of the treasures, and all the poor became rich and

18. Shulestān is an old name of the region of Mamassani, north of Kāzerun, Moḥammara—the modern Khorramshehr.

19. From Baghdad they went to London, but returned to ᶜErāq again, see *FNN*, II, 110. Later on, they were apparently confined at Bursa, for the treaty of Erzerum of 1263:1847, concluded between Persia and Turkey, contains an article according to which the Turks were obliged to hold the princes who had fled from Persia in custody at Bursa, see Noradounghian II, 95–99. Only Timur Mirzā eventually returned to Tehran and died there. The adventures of the princes have been described by J. Frazer, *The Narrative of the Residence of the Persian Princes in London*, London, 1836. See also Aṣghar Farmān-Farmā'i Qājār, "Safar-e pasarān-e Farmān-Farmā," in: *Rāhnamā-ye Ketāb*, 12 (1969), pp. 125–33, 241–50, and 355–70, and the journal written by Prince Najaf Qoli Mirzā translated into English by Assaad Y. Kayat, Bibliography at the end of this book.

wealthy. Then the rabble, not satisfied with this, hurried to the houses of Farmān-Farmā's sons and family, which were outside the Vakili palace, and carried away as booty everything they found. When Farmān-Farmā heard of the riot, he repented of having stayed at Shiraz and of refusing the advice of his sons; with great difficulty he seized 3 or 4 horses and departed with Shojāᶜ os-Salṭana and several other people to catch up with the princes. When they arrived at the Bāgh-e Shāh Gate, they were stopped and pushed back by ᶜAli Akbar Khān-e Nafar,[20] who [289] was guarding the gate with tribal musketeers. They could not but return to the palace.

The next day, rumors spread at Shiraz that Moḥammad Shāh's army was composed of Turks from Ādherbāyjān who did not speak Persian; that their general was a European; that they killed the people everywhere and plundered their belongings. The rabble and the craftsmen of Shiraz were alarmed by this news, caused a riot, and shouted: "We do not want any other shah but our Ḥosein ᶜAli Shāh!" They assembled in vast numbers on the Meidān-e Ark, and Farmān-Farmā came out of the palace in ceremonial dress and sat with royal splendor in the government building. Mirzā Moḥammad Khān, son of Qavām ol-Molk, who had been imprisoned for some time, was brought before Farmān-Farmā, a robe of honor was bestowed upon him to win his friendship, and he was appointed lord mayor of Shiraz as before. The ilkhāni, Moḥammad ᶜAli Khān, too, was summoned; however, he was angry and refused to come. When Shojāᶜ os-Salṭana together with several people went to the ilkhāni's house, the latter made his escape and took refuge in the house of Sheikh Abu Torāb, imam of Prayers of Shiraz. Shojāᶜ os-Salṭana proceeded to the imam's house and drew his sword to kill the ilkhāni. The imam forbade this, gave Shojāᶜ os-Salṭana good advice, and the latter went away without having attained

20. The Nafar tribe was allied with the Qashqā'i tribes, see above, p. 208 seq.

his end. The rabble, however, plundered the ilkhāni's house and carried away what was to be found, including the door wings, the window grates, and the columns of the gateway.

SHIRAZ OCCUPIED BY THE ROYAL ARMY; THE GOVERNOR ARRESTED. Moᶜtamad od-Doula reassured Farmān-Farmā by friendly messages in such a way that the latter made arrangements for the reception and entertainment of him and his retinue; he appointed a mehmāndār and hoped for a peace treaty and an agreement. On 28th Dhu'l-Qaᶜda,[21] Firuz Mirzā and Moᶜtamad od-Doula, buffeting snow and cold, marched quite confidently from Ābāda through Tang-e Allāh Akbar to the region of Shiraz and encamped in the Bāgh-e Nou and its surroundings, 0.25 parasang north of Shiraz. Most of those who had been followers of Farmān-Farmā from the beginning and all the nobles of Fārs came out of the city to welcome them. On 29th Dhu'l-Qaᶜda they entered the city through the Esfahan Gate with artillery and soldiers. They laid siege to the palace and sent Farmān-Farmā the following message:

It is not wise to entrench behind the walls of the citadel, to close the gate, and to acquire a bad reputation by not obeying the shah. What preparations did you make for such a day while your rule extended from Khuzestān as far as the remotest borders of Beluchistān?[22] If you do not open the gate of the citadel, the rampart will be leveled to the ground by the fire of the artillery and the attack of the soldiers. If you allow me to come to you, I shall reassure you regarding the shah!

As Farmān-Farmā was considering this proposal with benevolence, Shojāᶜ os-Salṭana tried to persuade his brother: "Our salvation will be this: As soon as Moᶜtamad od-Doula comes, I shall cut him in two with my sword. Once his army is without leader, it will obey us." Farmān-Farmā approved this proposal and arranged with Shojāᶜ os-Salṭana that the latter was to execute

21. March 28, 1835.

22. Allusion to the inclusion of the province of Kerman into Farmān-Farmā's government, see above, p. 238.

his plan upon a certain signal. When Firuz Mirzā and Mo^{c}tamed od-Doula entered the citadel, the guards did not stop them, and a detachment of the newly arrived troops entered, too. Farmān-Farmā was sitting in a portico, while Shojā^c os-Salṭana was standing opposite him, sword in hand. Firuz Mirzā and Mo^{c}tamad od-Doula saluted Farmān-Farmā reverently and discussed several topics with him, while Shojā^c os-Salṭana waited for Farmān-Farmā's signal. When the officers had drawn up the lines outside the citadel, Firuz Mirzā and Mo^{c}tamad od-Doula left, put Farmān-Farmā and Shojā^c os-Salṭana under arrest, and completed the arrangements for encamping and provisioning the troops. Firuz Mirzā and Mo^{c}tamad od-Doula put up their quarters in the Bāgh-e Naẓar adjoining the citadel. Mirzā Moḥammad Khān-e Qājār Devehlu established himself in the house of Reżā Qoli Mirzā,[23] Mirzā Abu'l-Qāsem Dhu'r-Reyāsatein in the "small courtyard" (enderun-e kuchek) of Karim Khān, known as "House of Abu'l-Fatḥ Khān," son of the late Vakil Karim Khān Zand,[24] and Moḥammad Ṭāher Khān-e Qazvini was put up in the house of Āqā Bashir, eunuch of Farmān-Farmā's harem. At nightfall of the same day Farmān-Farmā and Shojā^c os-Salṭana were brought out of the citadel and sent to Tehran under the custody of Manṣur Khān-e Farāhāni.

THE GOVERNOR OF FĀRS IS BROUGHT TO TEHRAN AND DIES THERE. The New Year fell on 21st Dhu'l-Qa^{c}da of that year.[25] The shah celebrated the feast in Tehran. On 11th Dhu'l-Ḥejja,[26] the Farāhāni general Manṣur Khān, arrived with Ḥosein ^{c}Ali Mirzā Farmān-Farmā, and Shojā^c os-Salṭana Ḥasan ^{c}Ali Mirzā at the station of Kenāra Gerd,[27] one march from Tehran, and reported his arrival to the shah. By order of

23. Son of Farmān-Farmā and deputy governor of Fārs, who had fled to Baghdad, see above, p. 236.

24. He reigned for only a short time after his father's death in 1779, see above, p. 6.

25. March 21, 1835. 26. April 10, 1835.

27. 21 miles southwest of Reiy.

the shah, Moḥammad Bāqer Khān, beglerbegi of Tehran, proceeded with several executioners to Kenāra Gerd and deprived Shojāᶜ os-Salṭana of the sight of both eyes. The next day the two brothers were separately brought into Tehran and put in two different lodgings. On 26th Rabiᶜ I of the year 1251,[28] Farmān-Farmā was taken ill with plague and died. Until his death nobody was with him except Haji Mirzā Ḥasan Nāẓer-e Māzandarāni and the chief eunuch, Haji Āqā Jouhar. Shojāᶜ os-Salṭana lived several years as a blind man and died in the year 1269.[29]—Farmān-Farmā had ruled over the province of Fārs without interference from anybody and completely undisturbed from the year 1214[30] until five months before his death. He had nineteen sons: 1) Reżā Qoli Mirzā [290] Nā'eb ol-Eyāla, 2) Emām Qoli Mirzā Ghażanfar od-Doula, 3) Najaf Qoli Mirzā Vāli, 4) Naṣrollah Mirzā, 5) Timur Mirzā Ḥosām od-Doula, 6) Shāhrokh Mirzā, 7) Jahāngir Mirzā, 8) Akbar Mirzā, 9) Keikhosrou Mirzā, 10) Eskandar Mirzā, 11) Moḥammad Mirzā, 12) Nāder Mirzā, 13) Moḥammad Kāẓem Mirzā, 14) Dārāb Mirzā, 15) Kāmrān Mirzā, 16) Iraj Mirzā, 17) Manuchehr Mirzā, 18) Ṭahmāsp Mirzā, 19) Solṭān Ebrāhim Mirzā.[31] The marks

28. July 22, 1835. 29. 1269:1852/53.

30. 1214:1799/1800, see above, p. 91 seq.

31. The fate of the princes (Nos. 1, 2, and 5) has been briefly described above, p. 236, note 19. The princes who remained in Persia no longer had any political influence. Emām Qoli Khān died in 1270 (1853/54); Naṣrollāh was known for his accomplishments in the field of calligraphy. Shāhrokh was a student of philosophy and theology and for a short time (1265/66:1848/49) governor of Kāshān; he died in 1290 (1873/74) at Shiraz. Kei Khosrou lived after his father's death as an ascetic and died about 1270 (1853/54) at Mashhad. Eskandar died in Kerman. Ṭahmāsp was employed in the Tubkhāna at Shiraz and died after 1270. Reżā Qoli Mirzā's (No. 1) son, Noudhār Mirzā, returned from Baghdad to Tehran in 1265 (1848/49) and was granted a pension by the shah. In 1266 he went to Shiraz and was installed in the estate of his father. In 1276 (1859/60) he was appointed governor of Galladār, Asīr and ᶜAlā Marvdasht. In 1278, he fought the Turkomans in Khorasan and was appointed Sepahsālār-e Khorasan; in 1282 (1865/66), he returned to Shiraz and was appointed chief magistrate of Fārs. In 1300 (1882/83) he was again governor of Galladār and became governor of the district Qir va-Kārzin in 1301, see *FNN*, II, 110 seq.

Farmān-Farmā has left at Shiraz are the Bāgh-e Nou, which was completed in the year 1225,[32] and the hall of the mirrors in the Bāgh-e Naẓar-e Vakili.

After Farmān-Farmā had been brought to Tehran, Moᶜtamad od-Doula used his sagacity to settle the administrative affairs of the province of Fārs within a short time, established his rule, and reassured the shah on this quarter.

HAJI MIRZĀ ĀQĀSI APPOINTED PRIME MINISTER. The shah was angry with Mirzā Abu'l-Qāsem Qā'em Maqām, as the latter, since his appointment to the vizierate of Ādherbāyjān,[33] did not do anything in accordance with the wishes of the shah and, after the shah's accession to the throne, doubted whether the shah was true and benevolent towards him. Finally the shah decided to arrest him. In the night of 24th Ṣafar of the year 1251,[34] he summoned him to the Bāgh-e Negārestān in Tehran and had him arrested upon his arrival. In the night of the last day of the month of Ṣafar—a Saturday[35]—Qā'em Maqām was strangled and buried in the vicinity of the shrine of ᶜAbd ol-ᶜAẓim. Then the office of prime minister was entrusted to Haji Mirzā ᶜAbbās-e Erevani, known as Haji Mirzā Āqāsi, whom the shah esteemed as an excellent lawyer and outstanding ascetic. Haji Mirzā Āqāsi was a son of the late Mirzā Moslem-e Erevani. He was born in 1198[36] and had traveled, when still a young man, with his father, a renowned theologian, to the Holy Places in Mesopotamia. He studied with Ākhund Mollā ᶜAbd oṣ-Ṣamad-e Hamadāni, one of the most renowned theologians and scholars, and, after the latter's death, with other outstanding scholars. He grew up to be a man of fine qualities and was acknowledged by

32. 1225:1810. The pavilion in this garden, built of hewn stones, was destroyed in the earthquake of the year 1269 (1852/53) and not repaired, see *FNN*, II, 167.

33. He had succeeded his father in the vizierate of Ādherbāyjān in 1247 (1831/32), see Browne, IV, 311 seq.

34. June 20, 1835. 35. June 26, 1835. 36. 1198:1783/84.

the scholars. Then he traveled for a long time in the garb of poverty and mystics, visited Mecca and Medina, and returned to Ādherbāyjān. In the service of the princes and nobles of Ādherbāyjān, he won a high reputation. The second crown prince, Moḥammad Mirzā, put his trust in him, studied under his guidance some of the current sciences (ᶜolum-e rasmi)[37] and acquired from him fear of God, piety, and devotion. It is known that his accession to the throne was predicted by Haji Mirzā Āqāsi. Upon his accession to the throne, the shah appointed him prime minister, bestowed more and more honors upon him and exempted him from the duties of the vizierate. He preferred conversation with him to that of anyone else and agreed with all his statements.[38]

NĀṢER OD-DIN MIRZĀ APPOINTED CROWN PRINCE. And that year the shah, in accordance with the suggestion of the late Āqā Moḥammad Shāh,[39] appointed his son Nāṣer od-Din Mirzā crown prince and bestowed upon him the diadem, the jewel-studded dagger, the cloak of the Kayānids studded with jewels, the bracelet and belt and the Order of the Lion and the Sun; with these privileges of the crown prince he was decorated from head to foot. And royal banquets befitting kings were celebrated in Tehran and Tabriz.

REORGANIZATION OF THE PROVINCE OF FĀRS. When Firuz Mirzā, the governor of Fārs, and Manuchehr Khān Moᶜtamad od-Doula had sent Farmān-Farmā and Shojāᶜ os-Salṭana to Tehran and had subdued all the inhabitants of Fārs, they summoned the governors of the districts to Shiraz and

37. The "ᶜolum-e rasmi" are listed above, p. 101.

38. Concerning him, Browne, IV, 147, writes: "He (the qā'em maqām) was succeeded as prime minister by the notorious Ḥāji Mirzā Āghāsi, concerning whom many ridiculous anecdotes are still current in Persia." In a poem composed after his death, Qā'āni calls him "a vile tyrant," see, Browne, IV, 329; a portrait of the grand vizier facing p. 328.

39. See above, p. 160.

fixing the latters' taxes and tributes sent them home. They summoned Mirzā Moḥammad ^{c}Ali Moshir ol-Molk, the chief of the registers (ra'is-e daftar-khāna), and entrusted the account books (moḥāsabāt va-ḥavālajāt) to him. The government of the district of Fasā was taken from Mirzā Abu'l-Ḥasan Khān, the son-in-law of Farmān-Farmā, and entrusted to Mirzā Moḥammad Ḥosein, vakil of the province of Fārs, the elder brother of Mirzā Abu'l-Ḥasan Khān. In Ṣafar of that year,[40] there arrived at Shiraz Naṣir Khān, beglerbegi of the district (khaṭṭa) of Lār, son of ^{c}Abdallāh Khān-e Lāri, and in Rabi^{c} I,[41] Mirzā Manṣur Khān-e Behbehāni, governor of the districts of Kuh-e Giluya, son of Mirzā Solṭān Moḥammad Khān. They were graciously received and confirmed in their offices.

In the middle of Rajab of the year 1251,[42] Mo^{c}tamad od-Doula arrested the ilkhāni, Moḥammad ^{c}Ali Khān, and Āqā Mirzā Moḥammad, known as Fasā'i, governor of Ḥuma-ye Shiraz, Niriz, Eṣṭahbānāt, and Dārāb; both were arrested on mere suspicion. After spending ten and a half months in prison, they were sent to Tehran guarded by 100 horsemen. When they arrived at the station of Deh Bid in the district of Qunqari, six marches north of Shiraz,[43] a courier arrived on behalf of the shah with the order for their release, and they were dismissed. As they had been planning to present themselves before the shah, they hurried to Tehran. Upon their arrival they were graciously received. The ilkhāni bought a house and established himself in Tehran, while Āqā Mirzā Moḥammad was appointed mostoufi and entered into the service of the court. When Mirzā Moḥammad Ḥosein, vakil of Fārs, heard of this, he proceeded from Fasā to Tehran. Upon his arrival the very important office of [291]

40. Began on May 29, 1835. 41. Began on June 27, 1835.

42. November 6, 1835. The text has 1252; however, in Rajab, Mo^{c}tamad od-Doula had already been removed from his office, see below, p. 251.

43. Deh Bid lies about 80 miles north-northeast of Shiraz, on the highway to Esfahan.

a mostoufi of the Divān and vakil of Fārs was entrusted to him, and he entered into the service of the court, too.

VALI KHĀN, CHIEF OF THE MAMASSANI LORS, SUBDUED. Vali Khān, son of Khub Yār Khān-e Bakash Mamassani, had been assaulting the caravans of Bandar Bushehr, Behbehān, and Shoshtar and plundering the neighbors far and near; once he had even plundered Kāzerun. When there was any danger, he retreated to the fortress of Safid (Qalᶜa-ye Safid), which is dealt with in the second part of this book, in the chapter on the fortresses of Fārs.[44] To win him over, Ḥosein ᶜAli Mirzā Farmān-

44. See *FNN*, II, 335: "The Qalᶜa-ye Safid in Mamassani is also called Dez-e Sapid. It lies more than a parasang east of the town of Fahleyān. Farhād Mirzā Moᶜtamad od-Doula writes in his *Jām-e Jam*: 'The Qalᶜa-ye Safid is an isolated mountain which is surpassed by no other mountain in its vicinity. The circumference at its foot is about 4 parasangs. There are 4 known accesses by which one can climb up to the summit. The southern access is called Seyāh Shir; here one could climb up on foot, but now it is blocked. When Vali Khān-e Mamassani was besieged in the fortress, he built a wall of stone and mortar and thus blocked the path. The eastern access is called Zarrin Kolāh, it is on the way to Shiraz. One can walk on it. The northern access is called Golestān. One can go on it by horseback from Fahleyān up to the summit. The western access is called Shatr Khvāb, it is near Nurābād; one can ride on it by horseback up to the summit. The Qalᶜa-ye Safid is about 0.5 parasang (3,000 meters) high. The summit forms a platform, which makes cultivation possible. There are many trees, such as oaks, fig trees, mountain almonds, olive trees, pomegranates, grapes, etc. In winter the whole mountain is covered with snow, which, however, does not last long. There is much fodder and mountain game. There are 5 springs on the mountain, of which 3 dry up in summer. On the platform are several water basins filled with water. There is a water basin below each spring, in which the water is stored. At the time of the Persian kings, huge stones were put up around the mountain which were arranged in such a manner that they could be moved in a short space of time; in this way the mountain was made inaccessible. By the moving of these solid rocks such protection was effected that the enemy had no possibility of attack. In the course of time the stones have been dispersed during the sieges; only a few have been left as samples in several places. Besides the ways of access mentioned above, there are several other paths on which one can climb up with great difficulty. There are numerous springs at the foot of the mountain.

Farmā had given Vali's daughter in marriage to his own son Timur Mirzā Ḥosām od-Doula. This was, however, of no use; Vali Khān stole from his neighbors and molested them more than before. When that year all the nobles of Fārs came to Shiraz and returned home, all their wishes having been granted by Farmān-Farmā, Vali Khān-e Mamassani, lord of the Qal^{c}a-ye Safid, came to Shiraz like the others in the month of Jomādi II of that year[45] and was courteously treated by Mo^{c}tamad od-Doula. A group of flatterers who knew of Mo^{c}tamad od-Doula's avidity submitted the following:

Vali Khān-e Mamassani himself and his father Khub Yār Khān have been plundering the caravans for years and stored up different kinds of precious textiles from India and Kashmir shawls. At the beginning of this year, the princes Reżā Qoli Mirzā Nā'eb ol-Eyāla, Timur Mirzā Ḥosām od-Doula, and Najaf Qoli Mirzā Vāli took the jewels collected by Farmān-Farmā over many years;[46] when they traveled through the region of Mamassanī, Vali Khān obtained from them half the jewels as a transit duty and added them to his treasures.

In accordance with the saying "Love makes a man blind and deaf," Mo^{c}tamad od-Doula was overwhelmed by avidity and demanded the sparkling jewels and glittering diamonds of Vāli Khān. The latter repented of having come to Shiraz and admitted that these jewels were in his possession, as he realized that he was lost unless he confessed the crime. He told the officials:

I am a nomad without abode. I am not an expert on jewels; however, there are round and flat, long and black, red and yellow stones which have come into my possession and which I have hidden in the ravines of the mountains and hills. Nobody knows of these treasures except me. If you send a trustworthy man with me, I shall hand over to him the

---

In Dhu'l-Ḥejja of the year 1257 (January/February, 1842), when I was engaged in punishing the Lors, I examined this fortress thoroughly. Nobody except Timur Gurkān (Timur Leng) has occupied this fortress by force."

45. Began on August 25, 1835. 46. See above, p. 236.

colored stones which have no value for a man like me. I shall surrender the Qal^{c}a-ye Safid, give up doing evil and be satisfied to toil like other people in the fields and live in tranquillity.

Mo^{c}tamad od-Doula selected Moḥammad Ṭāher Khān-e Qazvini to collect these jewels, and, in the middle of the month of Rajab of that year,[47] he sent with Vali Khān a group of cavalry and infantry commanders and officers and several pieces of artillery under the pretext of settling the affairs of the region of Shulestān and Kuh-e Giluya. Upon their arrival on the plain of Nurābād in the district of Mamassani,[48] Vali Khān made good his promise. He summoned his garrison from the Qal^{c}a-ye Safid and surrendered the fortress to Moḥammad Ṭāher Khān. Ḥasan ^{c}Ali Khān-e Bayyāt Zarandi climbed up to the fortress where he established himself with a group of Zarand warriors.[49] When Moḥammad Ṭāher Khān saw that Vali Khān was deprived of the Qal^{c}a-ye Safid he became insolent and raised difficulties with regard to the latter, harshly demanded the jewels and precious objects from him, showed less respect for him, talked badly of him, and planned his imprisonment. A fair youth, a relative of Vali Khān, was passionately regarded by the people of the camp, and eventually this affair passed from fun to reproaches and fighting. Then the officers interfered in the fighting between the soldiers, and in that same dark night a group of Lors covered the camp with a shower of bullets; the soldiers and gunners, drowsy and not knowing what had happened, opened fire without hitting their goal. Moḥammad Ṭāher Khān, Ja^{c}far Qoli Khān-e Qarāchi Dāghi, Colonel Reżā Qoli Khān-e Qājār, Sālim Khān-e Chagani, and the officers of the tribes from Qazvin came out of their tents and tried to push back the Lors. Having no success, they made their escape into the mountain and the plain. During

47. About November 6, 1835.

48. Nurābād lies at the western foot of the Qal^{c}a-ye Safid, see above, p. 244, note 44.

49. Zarand is a town and district about 50 miles northwest of Kerman.

that night nearly 1,000 men of the camp were killed. Moḥammad Ṭāher Khān and the commanders of the detachments were taken prisoner by the Lors. At daybreak the people of the leaderless camp reported the occurrence to Moᶜtamad od-Doula. When the latter heard of this, he slapped his thighs at the bad behavior of the officers and recited a poem by the late Mirzā Abu'l-Qāsem Qā'em Maqām Farāhāni: "Oh these dishonorable and religiousless people! Turks from Reiy, Kurds from Khamsa and Qazvin: against cucumbers and pumpkins you fight like Rostam, when you face the foe, you run away like Gorgin!"[50] Some days later Vali Khān released Moḥammad Ṭāher Khān and the commanders, and they returned to Shiraz. Moᶜtamad od-Doula appointed Moḥammad Ṭāher Khān deputy governor (nā'eb ol-hoḳuma) of Shiraz and ordered the dispersed troops and the auxiliary forces of Fārs to come together, and within a short time they assembled. At the beginning of Dhu'l-Qaᶜda of that year,[51] Firuz Mirzā and Moᶜtamad od-Doula marched off from Shiraz to Shulestān in Mamassani and Kuh-e Giluya. And the deputy governor of Fārs, Moḥammad Ṭāher Khān, entrusted the governorship of the district of Fasā to Mirzā ᶜAbdollāh Khān, the younger brother of Moḥammad Ḥosein Khān Vakil-e Fārs.

After storming the camp and the capture of the commander and the officers, Vali Khān attacked the Qalᶜa-ye Safid several times; he was, however, pushed back by the commander, Ḥasan ᶜAlī Khān, and the Zarand detachment. When he despaired of capturing the fortress and heard of the army's departure from Shiraz, he retreated to Māhur-e Milāti, which is dealt with in the second part of this book, in the chapter on the districts of Fārs.[52]

50. Rostam and Gorgin are famous opponents in Persian epics.

51. Began on February 18, 1836.

52. *FNN*, II, 292: "Māhur-e Milāti is a district (nāḥeya) to the northwest of Shiraz; it belongs to the hot region (garmsirāt) of Fārs. Its length, from the Kuh-e Pari Kadah in the east to the western border, the beginning of Lirāvi-ye Dasht in Kuh-e Giluya, is 20 parasangs, its width, from the north to the southern border, 16 parasangs. On its eastern side lie the

He changed his encampment every day, entrusted his family to Bāqer Khān and sent them to the fortress of Gol and Golāb [292] in Kuh-e Giluya, which is described in the second part of this book.[53] Vali Khān put his trust in Khvāja Ḥosein-e Qal^ca-ye

---

district (boluk) Kāzerun and the district Mamassani, on its northern and western side the region Kuh-e Giluya, on its southern side the districts Khesht and Dashtestān. The relation of mountain and plain ground is 20:1 or even 30/40:1. One should say Māhur-e Milāti consists proverbially of deep valleys and stony hills. In the province of Fārs one calls 'Māhur' a place which has high hills and deep valleys. There are in Māhur-e Milāti numerous springs of block naphtha and foul smelling, sulphuric water. If somebody examined the ground, he would undoubtedly find mines of mineral coal. In summer the air is very hot and disagreeable. It is the winter camp of the Qashqā'i tribes who come to these valleys when the rainy season begins; they stay there until about Nouruz (New Year), then they flee from the multitude of flies and gnats. There is no cultivation irrigated by rain water or underground water, except in 6 places which have little water and stony ground. The center of this district, i.e., the fortress in which the nobles of the tribes stay during winter, is Bābā Monir, 37 parasangs from Shiraz. The district has 5 villages: Bābā Monir, the central place, Bigard, 5 parasangs west of Bābā Monir; Tavvaj (also spelled Tavvaz, Touz, Touf-e Milāti or Tavah) was a town in Māhur-e Milāti, 2 parasangs north of Jamāl Gerd and 12 parasangs west of Kāzerun. As has been reported in the first part of this book, the Moslems occupied this town by force in the year 18 of the Hegira (A.D. 639). It has been lying in ruins for many years and is only known from books and poetry."

Bābā Monir lies about 16 miles west of the Qal^ca-ye Safid, Bigard 10 miles southwest of Bābā Monir.

53. *FNN*, II, 335 seq.: "The Qal^ca-ye Gol lies in Kuh-e Giluya. It is an isolated mountain 2 parasangs east of the village of ^cAskari in the district of Zeidun which forms part of Kuh-e Giluya. Its water comes from springs. There are several accesses to the fortress, which is not very strong. The Qal^ca-ye Golāb in Kuh-e Giluya, about 1,000 cubits west of the Qal^ca-ye Gol, about 6 parasangs south of Behbehān, the center of Kuh-e Giluya, is completely isolated. There is space for 1,000 families on the summit of the mountain; about 300 houses are inhabited now. The fortress has one access only, and this can be defended by two men. The mountain is more than 1,000 cubits high. The water comes from springs. There is a cave in the fortress, in which a water basin is cut into the rock. Several hundred drops of water flow each minute from the roof into the cave, are stored in the basin, and provide the inmates of the fortress with drinking

Golābi, and the latter put the family up in the fortress of Gol, which was not very strong.

The New Year fell on 2d Dhu'l-Ḥejja of that year.[54] Moḥammad Shāh celebrated the New Year feast and distributed so much gold and silver that the treasury was emptied.

When Firuz Mirzā and Mo^c^tamad od-Doula arrived at Shulestān and found no trace of Vali Khān, they ordered Esmā^c^il Khān-e Qarāchlu to proceed to Māhur-i Milāti and arrest Vali Khān. They sent the army by way of Shulestān to the fortress of Gol and Golāb in order to capture Vali Khān's family. When they arrived at Do Gombadān, 12 parasangs east of Behbehān,[55] they were welcomed by Mirzā Manṣur Khān, the governor of Kuh-e Giluya and Behbehān. The governor brought Khvāja Ḥosein-e Qal^c^a-ye Golābi before them, and the khvāja was graciously received. When the army arrived in the vicinity of the fortress of Golāb, Khvāja Ḥosein sent for his family and surrendered the fortress of Golāb, which lies above the fortress of Gol, the abode of Bāqer Khān and Vali Khān's family, to the people of the camp, and 300 soldiers ascended to the fortress. The army occupied the sides of the fortress of Gol, while the soldiers of the fortress of Golāb leveled their muskets at the fortress of Gol and thus confined the movements of Bāqer Khān and his detachment. When Bāqer Khān's men saw themselves faced with captivity, the young women out of fear of dishonorable captivity tied themselves together by their hair and threw themselves down from the fortress of Gol, the height of which is at least 500 cubits. The rest were taken prisoner. Bāqer Khān and his followers were bound with fetters. At the beginning of the month of Ṣafar of the year 1252,[56] Firuz Mirzā and Mo^c^tamad od-Doula, having attained their end, entered Shiraz.

---

water. I, the author of this book, climbed up the fortress in the year 1284 (1867/68), in the company of Eḥteshām od-Doula Solṭān Oveis Mirzā."

54. March 21, 1836. 55. About 40 miles southeast of Behbehān.

56. Began on May 18, 1836.

Outside the Bāgh-e Shāh Gate they erected a tower; about 70 to 80 members of Vali Khān's tribe and people from Shul-e Jouzag in the region of Kām Firuz,[57] friends and followers of Vali Khān, were put alive into the tower, their heads sticking out of the holes of the tower. People of the city brought them bread and water, and they lived for several days.

And every day Esmāᶜil Khān-e Qarāchlu, the leader of the Qarāchlu horsemen, searched everywhere in Māhur-e Milāti for Vali Khān without finding a trace of him. When at the beginning of the month of Rabiᶜ I,[58] he arrived at the top of a small hill, he saw Vali Khān with 5 or 6 horsemen asleep there and took them prisoner without difficulty. The next day Esmāᶜil Khān entered Kāzerun and sent the happy news to Moᶜtamad od-Doula. Vali Khān was brought to Shiraz with two other people, namely his sons Bāqer Khān and Hādi Khān. Thence they were sent to Tehran, thence to Ardebil, thence to Tabriz. There they died several years later.

ATTEMPT TO ESTABLISH PERSIAN SUPREMACY OVER AFGHANISTAN

ATTEMPT TO CONQUER HERĀT FAILS. The Shah mobilized the army of the empire for the conquest of Herāt; the troops assembled in the surroundings of Tehran in due course. On Sunday 18th Rabiᶜ I of that year[59] the court departed from the Bāgh-e Negārestān in Tehran. At the first halting place, Moḥammad Qoli Khān Ilbegi, the youngest brother of the ilkhāni, Moḥammad ᶜAli Khān, arrived from Fārs and took refuge in the stable of the prime minister, Haji Mirzā Āqāsi. After several days a report arrived from Moᶜtamad od-Doula stating that the ilbegi, Moḥammad Qoli Khān, was engaged all day long in stealing and

57. According to the *Farhang*, VII, 142, a village named Shul lies 16 miles northeast of Ardekān, in the valley of the Kur River, see also *FNN*, II, 256.

58. Began on June 16, 1836.

59. July 3, 1836.

causing disorder in the districts of Fārs. The shah summoned the ilkhāni, Moḥammad ᶜAli Khān, Mirzā Moḥammad Ḥosein Vakil-e Fārs, and Āqā Mirzā Moḥammad-e Fasā'i and interrogated them rigorously. They stated that Moᶜtamad od-Doula had not told the truth, because the ilbegi, Moḥammad Qoli Khān, had fled from the tyranny of Moᶜtamad od-Doula some time ago, had taken refuge in the stable of the prime minister, and consequently was present at the camp. Haji Mirzā Āqāsi confirmed the truth of the statement of these people from Fārs. The same day a royal farmān was issued for the removal of Manuchehr Khān Moᶜtamad od-Doula from the vizierate of Fārs and the appointment of Mirzā Moḥammad Taqi Qavām od-Doula to the vizierate in Moᶜtamad od-Doula's place. The former vizier was summoned to the court and the new vizier ordered to proceed to Fārs.

When the army was encamping on the pasture of Firuzkuh, a messenger arrived on behalf of Allāh Yār Khān Āṣaf od-Doula, governor of Khorasan, announcing that plague had broken out in that region and that the troops had dispersed; that it was advisable to postpone the conquest of Herāt to another time. Reciting the words "I acknowledge God as the destroyer of (human) intentions," the shah changed the conquest of Herāt to the chastisement of the Tekke, Yomut, and Göklen Turkomans.[60] He stayed on the pasture of Firuzkuh for nearly forty days.

MOᶜTAMAD OD-DOULA SUMMONED FROM SHIRAZ TO TEHRAN. Moᶜtamad od-Doula appeared at the court in

60. The Tekke had begun to move from the Balkhan mountains (on the eastern shore of the Caspian Sea) to the east towards the end of the eighteenth century; pushing as far as Sarakhs and Marv, they expelled other Turkoman tribes from that area. The Yomut and Göklen were less powerful than the Tekke. The Göklen live in the valley of the Atrāk and Gorgān rivers as farmers; their relations to the Yomut west of them were not always friendly. The national poet of the Turkomans, Makhdum Qoli, was a Göklen (eighteenth-nineteenth century). In the second half of the nineteenth century, the Turkomans were subdued by Russia; see EI[1] I, s.v. Ā*kh*āl Tekke, EI[1] IV, s.v. Teke and Turkmenen (W. Barthold).

accordance with the summons. Several months later he was ordered to arrange the affairs of the regions of the Two ᶜEraqs and appointed governor of Kermānshāh, Khuzestān, Lorestān, and the Bakhteyāris. Within a short space of time he established order in these districts. And the ilkhāni, Moḥammad ᶜAli Khān, and the ilbegi of Fārs, Moḥammad Qoli Khān, and Mirzā Moḥammad Taqi Qavām od-Doula were allowed to leave Firuzkuh. The ilkhāni remained in Tehran, while the ilbegi and Qavām od-Doula went to Fārs. Mirzā Moḥammad Ḥosein Vakil-e Fārs and Āqā Mirzā Moḥammad-e Fasā'i, the latter's younger brother, were ordered to stay in the service of the court.

THE SHAH SETTLES THE AFFAIRS OF TURKOMAN TRIBES IN KHORASAN. On 3d Jomādi I,[61] the court departed [293] from Firuzkuh, marched through the region of Kuh-e Safid,[62] and stopped only at the station of Shāhkuh.[63] At this station several nobles of the Yomut and Göklen appeared at the court and were graciously received. After several halts the court marched along the bank of the Āb-e Gorgān River and encamped near the Gombad-e Qābus[64] amidst the Göklen tribes. Their nobles brought provisions and fodder to the camp, using their saddle horses for transportation. In order to obtain the favor of the shah, they surrendered 500 people as hostages. Then the court proceeded to the Yomut tribes and marched to Bibi Shirvān,[65] which is one of the buildings erected by Qābus-e

61. August 16, 1836.

62. The Kuh-e Safid, about 2,800 meters high, lies 9 miles west of Dāmghān.

63. The Shāh Kuh lies 25 miles north of Dāmghān; its peak reaches a height of nearly 3,800 meters. The 1:500,000 map shows the villages of Shāh Kuh pā'in and Shāh Kuh bālā at the northern foot of the mountain.

64. Now the second town of Gorgān province, 70 miles northeast of Gorgān/Astarābād, the capital of the province. The town is named after the mausoleum of the Ziyarid ruler Qābus ibn Voshmgir, see EI² II, s.v. Gunbad*h*-i Ḳābūs.

65. 16 miles west of Gombad-e Qābus, on the road to Gorgān, on the Gorgān River, see *Farhang*, III, 54.

Voshmgir, king of Gorgān.[66] When the Yomut tribe fled, their belongings and cattle came into the possession of the court. The shah then ordered the return to Tehran.

FIRUZ MIRZĀ SENT TO KERMAN; FARIDUN MIRZĀ FARMĀN-FARMĀ APPOINTED GOVERNOR OF FĀRS. A royal decree (manshur) with the appointment of Faridun Mirzā, the younger brother of the shah, to the governorship of Fārs was issued. He was granted the title "Farmān-Farmā." Firuz Mirzā, governor of Fārs, was appointed governor of Kerman. Mirzā Muḥammad Taqi Qavām od-Doula remained vizier as before. In the month of Shaᶜbān of that year[67] Faridun Mirzā entered Shiraz and treated the people of Fārs with kindness. And the treasurer, Mirzā Aḥmad Khān, enjoying full confidence of Farmān-Farmā, interfered with the affairs of the vizierate. Qavām od-Doula became angry at this and renounced his office; from Tehran arrived the appointment of Mirzā Jaᶜfar Mostoufi-ye Savādkuhi to the vizierate of Fārs. The latter arrived at Shiraz, was, however, unable to take up his post. And Mirzā Aḥmad Khān entrusted the governorship of Fasā, Dārāb, Niriz, and Eṣṭaḥbānāt to Mirzā Ebrāhim-e Tabrizi, one of his followers. When a year had elapsed and Āqā Mirzā Moḥammad-e Fasā'i returned from the court to Shiraz, Farmān-Farmā entrusted all the united districts of Mirzā Aḥmad Khān to him. And in the month of Dhu'l-Qaᶜda,[68] Naṣir Khān-e Lāri, beglerbegi of Lārestān, and Mirzā Manṣur Khān-e Behbehāni, governor of Kuh-e Giluya and Behbehān, arrived at Shiraz. Both were graciously received and returned to their governorships, having realized their aims.

THE SHAH UNDERTAKES CAMPAIGN TO AFGHANISTAN. The New Year fell on the evening of 13th Dhu'l-Ḥejja of that year.[69] When Moḥammad Shāh celebrated the feast, he decided

66. Shams ol-Maᶜāli Qābus, reigned over Gorgān 367–402:978–1012.
67. Began on November 11, 1836.
68. Began on February 7, 1837. 69. March 21, 1837.

to conquer Herāt and, therefore, mobilized the army of the empire. On 14th Ṣafar of the year 1253,[70] the shah proceeded from Tehran to the Bāgh-e Negārestān.[71] Then 80,000 horsemen and infantry and 80 pieces of artillery were gathered together within a short space of time. On 19th Rabiᶜ II,[72] the court departed from the Bāgh-e Negārestān and stayed twenty days on the pasture of [Khosh Yeilāq][73] and twenty days on the plain of Sabzavār.[74] After completing the preparations for the campaign, the shah departed to Herāt by way of Torbat-e Sheikh Jām.[75] On 7th Shaᶜbān of that year,[76] he encamped near the fortress of Ghureyān,[77] which belongs to Herāt. After several days of siege Shir Moḥammad Khān-e Afghān asked for pardon. On 14th Shaᶜbān,[78] he appeared at the court and was graciously received, and Asadollāh Khān-e Qā'eni was placed with a detachment of Khorāsāni soldiers in the fortress of Ghureyān. On 23d Shaᶜbān,[79] the royal army entered the region of Herāt and encamped on the northern side near the Moṣallā.[80] The

70. May 20, 1837.

71. The Negarestān ("Picture Hall," because of its rich decoration with wall paintings) was a royal palace 0.5 mile to the northeast of nineteenth-century Tehran, see Dubeux, *La Perse*, p. 15, and Curzon, *Persia and the Persian Question*, I, 336 seq.

72. July 23, 1837.

73. The name of the pasture is left blank in the text, it is very likely Khosh Yeilāq, see above, p. 165, note 264.

74. About 120 miles east-southeast of Khosh Yeilāq.

75. About 90 miles southeast of Mashhad, on the Jām River, named after the mausoleum (torbat) of the saint and mystic Sheikh Aḥmad-e Jāmi (d. 536:1142); the medieval name of the town was Buzjān, see EI[1] IV, s.v. Turbat-i *Shaikh*-i *Dj*ām (V. F. Büchner).

76. November 6, 1837.

77. About 44 miles west of Herāt, probably named after the Ghurids, who ruled over Afghanistan in the twelfth century.

78. November 13, 1837. 79. November 22, 1837.

80. The Moṣallā ("Place of prayers") of Herāt lies opposite the citadel, which forms part of the northern defenses of the city, see Alexander Lézine. "Herāt, notes de voyage," in *Bulletin d'ètudes Orientales*, XVIII (1963–64), 127–45, plate facing p. 145.

Afghans came out of the city, engaged in battle, were defeated, and returned to the city. The next day the royal army departed and encamped on the pasture of Sang-e Safid.[81] The same day, the Afghans again came out of the city, attacked the camp, and returned to the city. The next day, by order of the shah, siege was laid to the city of Herāt. Every emir was given one side of the city, and every day saw fighting. Amidst these occurrences the mostoufi of Herāt, Mirzā Jān, fled from Kāmrān Mirzā, governor of Herāt,[82] and took refuge in the shah's camp. The following day, General Shams od-Din Khān-e Afghān, angry with Yār Moḥammad Khān, vizier to Kāmrān Mirzā, appeared before the shah and was graciously received. In the night of 15th Ramaẓān,[83] the vizier proceeded, when both sides were engaged in fighting, to a tower and shouted: "Stop fighting. Tomorrow one of the Persian nobles shall come into the city and pardon us on behalf of the shah, so that we may surrender!" The next day, by order of the shah, ᶜAziz Khān-e Mokri,[84] commander of a detachment of soldiers, entered the city. After two days' stay, he returned to the camp, bearing a petition from Kāmrān Mirzā and Yār Moḥammad Khān. It became known that the latter wanted to persuade the shah to raise the siege of the city on the presentation of a peshkash and the payment of a sum of money. The shah, however, paid no attention to their proposal and ordered the siege to be continued with more vigor. Since winter was approaching, the shah ordered the people of the camp to build houses of stones, clay, and wood outside the city. Within a short time they erected a new town opposite the old one. Then siege

81. "White Rock," not mentioned in our sources.

82. Kāmrān was a son of Maḥmud, the last Sadozay (Dorrāni) ruler of Afghanistan, who in the year 1818 had taken refuge at Herāt. Kāmrān ruled over Herāt and the western part of Afghanistan from 1245:1829 to 1258:1842/43, see Zambaur, *Manuel*, p. 304.

83. December 13, 1837.

84. From Mokrān in Ādharbāyjan, Commander of Ādharbayjāni detachment. See below, p. 276.

guns were cast; each piece of artillery was to fire at the fortifications of Herāt.

HERĀT BELEAGUERED BY THE PERSIAN ARMY. The New Year fell on the night of 24th Dhu'l-Ḥejja of that year.[85] The shah [294] celebrated the feast before the city of Herāt. Several days after the feast Ambassador MacNeill of England,[86] arrived at the court from Tehran. He considered the following problems: If the city of Herāt is incorporated in the Persian empire, the inhabitants of Kābol and Kandahar will without hesitation submit to the orders of the Persian shah, and the frontiers of the Persian empire will border on India. The Indians will turn to the Persian empire; they will show contempt for the English agents and expel them from India. Moved by these considerations the English ambassador tried to remove the shah from Herāt before he had occupied the city. Then he proposed to the ministers that they might allow him to enter the city in order to reassure Kāmrān Mirzā and bring the latter before the shah. With permission, he entered the city and encouraged Kāmrān Mirzā to defend the city and promised him subsidies, war materiel, and troops on behalf of the English government so that the defenders should offer brave resistance. Leaving Herāt he told the ministers that as long as he went on offering both threats and hopes to Kāmrān Mirzā, the latter would not surrender the fortress; that there was no sense in negotiating in this manner. The shah

85. March 21, 1838.

86. Sir John MacNeill (1795–83); he served as surgeon in the East India Company's service since 1816. In 1824–36, he was attached to the East India Company's legation in Persia, first in medical charge, then as a political assistant to the envoy. In June 1835, he was appointed secretary of the mission sent to Tehran under Sir Henry Ellis, to congratulate Moḥammad Shāh on his accession to the throne; on February 9, 1836, he was appointed minister plenipotentiary. He arrived in the Persian camp before Herāt on April 6, 1838, see *National Biography*, s.v. MacNeill.

became angry with this and ordered the siege to be continued with greater force. Huge cannons, brought to the top of hills, opened fire on the fortifications.

At the beginning of Ṣafar of the year 1254,[87] famine and poverty broke out in the city of Herāt; Yār Moḥammad Khān expelled about 12,000 people who had taken refuge from the surroundings of the city. When the shah heard of this, he ordered them to be fed and distributed gold and silver among them. Then they were sent to Khorasan. The governor, Kāmrān Mirzā, took counsel with his vizier, Yār Moḥammad Khān, and sent a petition to the shah. At the head of the petition was written: "Oh you gardener, when you expel the birds from the garden, spare the nests of the nightingales which have been there for a long time!" He asked for one of the officials of the court to enter the city and pardon him; only then would he appear at the court. In accordance with the decision of the ministers, Haji Mollā ᶜAbd ol-Moḥammad-e Maḥallāti[88] was ordered to enter the city and assure Kāmran Mirzā that the next day he would be received in audience together with himself. When English Ambassador MacNeill heard of this, he sent somebody to Kāmrān Mirzā telling him that he should never surrender the city; that he, MacNeill, would settle the affair in accordance with Kāmrān's wishes. Then the ambassador submitted the following proposal to the Persian ministers: "The conquest of Afghanistan by Persia is causing disquietude to India. With regard to the harmony between Persia and England it would be better to raise the siege of Herāt, leave the city to Kāmrān Mirzā, and return to Tehran." The shah was astonished at this proposal

87. Began on April 26, 1838.

88. From Maḥallāt, the region south of Qom, the center of which is now the town of Maḥallāt. After two unsuccessful attempts, a religious authority in the person of Mollā ᶜAbd ol-Moḥammad was sent into the city of Herāt.

and said that MacNeill was an inexperienced ambassador and did not know the requirements of religion and state[89] and that no attention was to be paid to him. Because Kāmrān Mirzā became haughty as a result of MacNeill's advice, Haji Mollā ᶜAbd ol-Moḥammad returned from Herāt without result.

At the end of the month of Ṣafar of that year,[90] Moḥammad ᶜOmar Khān, son of Kohan Del Khān-e Afghān-e Kandahāri,[91] appeared with 4,000 Afghan horsemen at the court, offered his submission, and was accepted into the retinue. Several days later, he was ordered to march against Jalāl od-Din Mirzā, son of Kāmrān Mirzā, who was staying in the region of Farāḥ.[92] He subdued these regions for the shah. Jalāl od-Din Mirzā had no choice but to proceed to the shah's camp and take refuge in the shah's stable. By order of the shah, he was brought by Prince Moḥammad Reżā Mirzā into the shah's tent, and he agreed.

The gunners greatly reduced the quarters of the inhabitants, and most of the high buildings of Herāt were razed by cannon balls. The surrounding gardens, stretching 20 to 30 parasangs in each direction, had their trees destroyed, and the villages and fields were devastated. The inhabitants of Herāt suffered these tribulations on the advice of English Ambassador MacNeill. The ambassador presented himself before the shah and said that if he entered the city he would bring Kāmrān Mirzā and Yār Moḥammad Khān before the shah. After entering the city, he gave them the sum of 10,000 toman in cash and said:

89. The capture of Herāt was a matter of religion in so far as the Afghans were, in general, adherents of the Sunni faith, opposed to the Shia creed of the Persians.

90. About May 20, 1838.

91. Kohandel was the brother of the Barakzay ruler Dust Moḥammad; four years before the events described here, Kohandel was defeated by the fourth Dorrāni ruler, Shāh Shojāᶜ.

92. A town in southwestern Afghanistan, 140 miles south of Herāt, on the Farāḥ River, where the trade routes from Herāt, Kandahar and Sistan join, see EI^2 II, s.v. Farāḥ (R. N. Frye).

Repair the damages of the fortifications in these days during which the fighting has come to a stop. Withstand another two months; then our battleships from the Indian Ocean will arrive at the coast of Fārs. The shah will march off and send his whole army to Fārs to fight the English troops. Then you will be left alone!

When MacNeill returned from Herāt, he repeated his former words, stating that there was no hope of capturing Herāt. The shah became angry and ordered Ambassador MacNeill to be removed from the camp. Complying with the order, the ambassador hurried to Tehran.[93] He received [295] a letter from London ordering him to return to London and to send his deputy to the shah's camp to report on the events.[94]

Upon Ambassador MacNeill's departure, the shah ordered 2 bastions to be erected which were to be higher than the fortifications of the city. Then by means of cranes 4 siege guns the projectiles of which weighed 82 pounds, were raised on to those 2 bastions. Each pound corresponds to 96 miskal.[95] Then day and night the city was covered with a shower of fire from these guns. Houses were destroyed, people killed. The next day the shah summoned the commanders and took counsel with them regarding the assault of Herāt. All agreed and attacked the following day. Through the deep trench, 50 cubits wide, they advanced to the foot of the wall and put up ladders; in the middle of the trench the Afghans had built 3 breastworks, which they, too, called "shir-ḥāji,"[96] and placed a detachment of Afghan soldiers with scimitars and muskets behind them. Having set up the

93. On June 7, 1838, see *National Biography*, s.v. MacNeill.

94. That is, Colonel Stoddard, who succeeded in persuading the shah to raise the siege, see *National Biography*. MacNeill returned to London only in August 1842.

95. The measure 96 miskal (at 4.6 grams each) corresponds to 441.6 grams, a little less than the English pound which weighs 453.5 grams.

96. The word is not listed in the dictionaries. Shir means "lion," ḥāji "pilgrim," that is, "lion's pilgrimage": one needs the courage of a lion for passing the trench.

ladders, several Persian soldiers climbed up the tower. Several thousand of the bravely fighting Afghan and Persian soldiers were killed. Eventually the Afghans gained the upper hand and dislodged the Persians from the tower and rampart.

SIEGE OF HERĀT RAISED AFTER ENGLISH INTERVENTION IN THE PERSIAN GULF. Amidst the battle, news arrived from Fārs that: English warships had entered the Persian Gulf and 1 ship had appeared before Bushehr; 500 soldiers had gone ashore and established themselves in a fortalice, the house of the English consul; Sheikh Ḥasan, the mojtahed of the ᶜOṣfur tribe,[97] and Sheikh Salmān, nephew of the mojtahed, and Bāqer Khān-e Tangestāni had risen in rebellion with the inhabitants of Bushehr[98] and expelled the regular soldiers and the consul from the town; several people had been killed on both sides; and the crew of the English ship then had occupied the island of Khārk,[99] had bought every mann of grain and fodder at the fourfold price, and stored it on the island. The English general was reported as having said: "If the Persian army does not raise the siege of Herāt, we shall occupy the whole coast of Fārs, even the whole province. We shall change the friendship between Persia and England to enmity and do what will be appropriate and suitable." When the Persian ministers balanced the friendship with England and the profit of possessing the region of Herāt on the scales of reason, they found a relation like that of a mountain to straw and submitted the calculation of gain and loss to the shah. On 19th Jomādi II of that year[100] the shah ordered the army before Herāt to withdraw. About 3,000 Afghans from Kabol, Kandahar, and Herāt, who had submitted, were assigned

97. An Arabic tribe of the Persian Gulf region.

98. The collaboration of religious and secular authorities gave the "rebellion" the character of a Holy War.

99. The big island northwest of Bushehr; for a description, see below, p. 400.

100. September 9, 1838.

domiciles in the districts of Khorasan. For each a salary was fixed. Moḥammad ᶜOmar Khān, son of Kohan Del Khān, the commander of Kandahār, and Shams od-Din Khān, commander of Herāt, entered the service of the Persian court. On 8th Rajab,[101] the shah entered Mashhad and performed the pilgrimage to the shrine of ᶜAli ibn Musā or-Reżā. Then he departed from Mashhad and arrived in Tehran on 19th Shaᶜbān.[102]

Upon the return of the court from Herāt, all the English warships that had cast anchor in the Persian Gulf and whose crews were staying on the islands of Khārk and of Derāz[103] returned to India. The same year the districts of Eṣṭaḥbānāt and Niriz, both flourishing regions of Fārs, were bestowed upon the commander of Herāt, Shams od-Din Khān-e Afghān, as a fief. He sent several people of his tribe and his family to those 2 districts, while he himself remained in Tehran in the service of the shah.

POLICY IN SOUTHERN PERSIA

MISCELLANEOUS EVENTS IN THE PROVINCE OF FĀRS. That year, Naṣir Khān, beglerbegi of Sabᶜa and Lārestān, dispatched 500 Lāri musketeers to the village of Bahādorān in the district of Dārāb,[104] the possession of which he claimed for himself. He was opposed by Āqā Mirzā Moḥammad-e Fasā'i, whose family had been holding the governorship of the Dārāb district for generations. Hostile actions were committed on both sides and several people from Lārestān, Fasā, and Dārāb were killed. A month later the Lāri musketeers left the fortress of Bahādorān and fled to Lārestān in the middle of the night.

The New Year fell on 5th Moḥarram of the year 1255.[105]

101. September 27, 1838. 102. November 7, 1838.

103. Derāz ("long" sc. "island") is another name for Qeshm, the biggest island in the Persian Gulf, off Bandar ᶜAbbās.

104. About 14 miles west-southwest of Dārāb.

105. March 21, 1839.

Instead of celebrating the New Year, the shah mourned over Emām Ḥosein, the grandson of the Prophet. In the month of Rabiᶜ I,[106] Haji Seiyed Mirzā Ebrāhim the mojtahed, paternal cousin of the author of this book, died at Shiraz. He was eighty-two years old. The funeral procession from his house to the shrine of Shāh Charāgh was attended by Faridun Mirzā Farmān-Farmā II, and the theologians and emirs. For three days, all the bazaars and caravanserais of Shiraz were closed. The theologians, seiyeds, nobles, merchants, and craftsmen were in mourning and recited the Koran in all the mosques and in the streets of the bazaars. The late mojtahed has left *Ketāb-e Baḥr ol-Ḥaqā'eq*, a book on jurisprudence. In each of the four parts are contained the Koran verses and Traditions which pertain to that particular part, the teachings of the theologians, and the most preferable Traditions and doctrines; *Hāsheya bar Ketāb-e Sharḥ-e Lomᶜa* and *Hāsheya-ye mabsuṭa bar Ketāb-e* [296] *Maᶜālem-e Oṣul-e Feqh.*[107] To this day the scholars and students of the different branches of learning are happy to have these writings. The corpse of the late mojtahed was transferred to Najaf.

DISTURBANCE AND CIVIL WAR IN SHIRAZ. Farmān-Farmā II had entrusted the entire administration of Fārs to Mirzā Aḥmad Khān-e Tabrizi, who from his early youth had been in the service of Farmān-Farmā II; thus Mirzā Jaᶜfar-e Savādkuhi, vizier of the province of Fārs on behalf of the shah, had this

106. Began on May 15, 1839.

107. *Ketāb-e sharḥ-e lomᶜa* is a commentary on *Kitāb al-lumᶜa ad-Dimashqiya*, written by Abu ᶜAbdullāh al-ᶜĀmili in the fourteenth century, see Brockelmann, *Geschichte der Arabischen Litteratur, Supplementband* II, 131, also mentioned in *Fehrest-e ketābkhāna-ye dāneshgāh-e Tehrān*, p. 1903, No. 299. *Ḥāsheya-ye mabsuṭa* is a commentary on *Maᶜālim ad-din wa-malādh al-mujtahidin fi uṣul ad-din*, written by Ḥasan ibn Zain ad-Din al-ᶜĀmili (d. 1011:1602), see Brockelmann, *ibid.* II, 321, *Supplementband* II, 450, and Spies/Pritsch, *Klassisches islamisches Recht*, p. 265. Three commentaries were written in the time of the Safavids; there exist more than ten commentaries on *Kitāb al-lumᶜa.*

office in name only.[108] Furthermore, the people from Ādherbāyjān who had fled from their respective towns and had come to Shiraz,[109] oppressed the inhabitants of Shiraz and of the districts and in doing this enjoyed the protection and assistance of Mirzā Aḥmad Khān. When people took their complaints to Farmān-Farmā, the latter referred the plaintiff to Mirzā Aḥmad Khān. As long as Mojtahed Haji Mirzā Ebrāhim was alive, Mirzā Aḥmad Khān, out of respect for him, did not oppress the people. After his death, however, the gunners and soldiers from Ādherbāyjān connected with Mirzā Aḥmad Khān caused disturbances every day, while Mirzā Aḥmad Khān distorted the affair before Farmān-Farmā. When Mirzā ᶜAli Akbar Qavām ol-Molk, to whom the shah had entrusted the establishing of order at Shiraz, saw this state of affairs, he deemed it best to leave Shiraz for the Holy Places to perform the pilgrimage. At the beginning of Jomādi I of that year[110] he departed from Shiraz for Mecca and Medina and the Holy Places in Mesopotamia. Traveling by way of Bushehr and Basra, he proceeded to Najaf and Kerbelā and the other Holy Places, then he went along the bank of the Euphrates River and through Syria to Medina and Mecca. In the month of Jomādi I of the following year,[111] he returned by way of Masqaṭ, Bandar ᶜAbbās, Lār, Jahrom, and Khafr to Shiraz.

In the middle of the month of Rajab of the year 1255,[112] a gunner was joking with a woman on the Meidān-e Ark at Shiraz; from joking the affair developed in such a manner that the woman started screaming at the top of her voice. The people of the Bazār-e Vakili came running to assist the woman and several gunners and soldiers from Ādherbāyjān came along to help the gunner; the affair then turned into a brawl. Several

108. See above, p. 253.

109. After the peace treaty of Torkmanchay, by which the territories north of the Araxes River had been ceded to Russia, see above, p. 185.

110. Began on July 13, 1839. 111. Began on July 1, 1840.

112. About September 20, 1839.

people were wounded and the inhabitants of Shiraz shouted in unison: "If Farmān-Farmā wants Mirzā Aḥmad Khān, he does not want us!" The next day they went into the mosques and the houses of the theologians and confirmed their desire to have Mirzā Aḥmad Khān removed. Most of the men were armed. Mirzā Jaᶜfar-e Savādkuhi, vizier of Fārs on behalf of the shah, was taking pains secretly and publicly to inflate this affair by joining the men in their resistance against Mirzā Aḥmad Khān and inciting the bazaar people from Shiraz and the gunners and soldiers from Ādherbāyjān to hostile actions. When Farmān-Farmā despaired of imposing his rule on the inhabitants of Shiraz, he ordered breastworks to be installed on the roof of the government buildings and soldiers and servants of the Divān to be placed behind them. Two cannons were placed on the Meidān-e Naqqāra Khāna[113] opposite the main entrance of the Masjed-e Vakil. When the inhabitants of Shiraz saw this, they banded together and entered the Masjed-e Jāmeᶜ Nou, known as "Masjed-e nou." All the theologians, nobles, and merchants assembled willy-nilly to deliberate. Despite many differences, opinion to resist Faridun Mirzā Farmān-Farmā II was unanimous. Since each group needed a leader to obey, Āqā Moḥammad Ḥasan, alderman (kadkhodā) of the Sang-e Seyāh quarter, a man combining liberality with boldness, was appointed leader of the inhabitants of the 5 Neᶜmati Khāna quarters of Shiraz. The quarters are explained in the second part of this book, in the chapter on the city of Shiraz.[114] Mirzā ᶜAli Torāb Khān, Āqā

113. The Naqqāra Khāna is the establishment of the ceremonial band of musicians, a prerogative of kings and governors.

114. See *FNN*, II, 22: "As to the eleven quarters of Shiraz, five of them are called Ḥeidari Khāna, such as the quarters (maḥalla) Esḥāq Beg, Bazār-e Morgh, Bālā Keft, Darb-e Shāhzāda, Meidān-e Shāh, and five of them Neᶜmati Khāna, such as Darvāza-ye Masjed, Sarbāgh, Sar Dazak (or Dezak), Sang-e Seyāh, and Labb-e Āb. The quarter of the Jews (maḥalla-ye Yahudān) is to be added to them [as the eleventh quarter]. One says that at the time of the Safavids, because of internal strife, the inhabitants of Shiraz, even of the hamlets and villages, were ordered to assume these

Moḥammad Ḥosein Kamāl Khān, ᶜAli Moḥammad Khān-e Fili Sang-e Seyāhi, Akbar and Bāqer, sons of Ḥosein the son of Mo'men Khān-e Saruzaki, and Bāqer Solṭān, all of them respectable men with a large number of followers, put themselves under the command of Āqā Moḥammad Ḥasan. The inhabitants of the 5 Ḥeidari Khāna quarters appointed Aḥmad Solṭān, son of Haji ᶜAbd ol-Ḥosein, major of a detachment of Shirāzi soldiers,[115] their leader. The following persons put themselves under the command of Aḥmad Solṭān: Haji Asad the sword cutler; Moḥammad Raḥim the dyer; Esmāᶜil Beg, son of Gholām Ḥosein-e Bālā Kefti; Karim, son of Ḥasan Khān-e Darb Shāhzāda'i; Morād-e Meidān-e Shāhi; Reżā the musket maker; and Kāẓem-e Bazār-e Morghi. They erected breastworks on the roof of the Masjed-e Vakil, which is adjacent to the government buildings, and on the roof of the Madrasa-ye Khān. A number of Shirāzi musketeers were placed on the roof and at the entrance of the Masjed-e Vakil, and other Shirāzi musketeers under the command of Haji Asad the sword cutler and Moḥammed Raḥim the dyer were placed on the roof and at the entrance of

names: those of the eastern quarters were to call themselves Ḥeidari, that is, followers of Solṭān Ḥeidar, the ancestor of the Safavids and their mystical sheikh, whilst the inhabitants of the western quarters were to call themselves Neᶜmati, after the Sheikh of the Neᶜmatollāhi order. The people of Ḥeidari Khāna had to gather at times prepared to fight the people of Neᶜmati Khāna. The people of Neᶜmati Khāna were to do the same. The blood of those who were killed on both sides was to be considered as a gift (hadiya). This custom was observed at Shiraz; three or four times every year the people of Ḥeidari Khāna used to fight those of Neᶜmati Khāna. Each time several people were killed, others lost an eye, a hand, or a leg. By the endeavors of the Qājār government this foolish custom was abolished about forty years ago [that is, forty years before the composition of the Fārs-nāma-ye Nāṣeri]. The number of houses in the eleven quarters which were counted in 1301 (1883/84) was 6,327, the inhabitants numbered 25,284 people, men and boys, and 28,323 women and girls."

115. The Shirazi detachment had been established in the year 1248:1832/33, see above, p. 221.

the Madrasa-ye Khān; all of them established themselves behind the breastworks. Moḥammad Raḥim the dyer and 9 men with crossbows (shamkhalchi) were placed on the 2 minarets of the Madrasa-ye Khān, which overlooked all the buildings of Shiraz. For some time, fighting went on between the inhabitants of Shiraz and the soldiers and gunners from Ādherbāyjān. The gunners fired several shots at the entrance of the Masjed-e Vakil, damaging it in several spots; the base table of the entrance of this mosque, consisting of a single stone 3 cubits long, 2 cubits wide, and half a cubit thick, was destroyed. (Six years later Ḥosein Khān Neẓām od-Doula, governor of the province of Fārs,[116] ordered the destroyed parts of this stone to be taken away and a stone of one piece, corresponding to the length of the base table, to be put in their place.) Nearly every day the inhabitants of the quarters of Shiraz fought with the Divan servants in various ways, and, every day two, several people on both sides were hit by musket balls; the fighting went on for some time. Because the prime minister, Haji Mirzā Āqāsi, [297] was a close friend of Faridun Mirzā Farmān-Farmā, the former prevented the shah from being informed of the occurrence. He wanted the subjects to make peace with the governor by entering into an agreement.

The New Year fell on 15th Moḥarram of the year 1256.[117] The shah wanted to stay in Tehran. When news of the rebellion of the inhabitants of Shiraz spread and reached the ears of the shah, he ordered Mirzā Nabi Khān-e Qazvini, the chief magistrate (amir-e divān-khāna-ye ᶜadliya), to proceed to Fārs and to inquire into this unfortunate affair. In the month of Shaᶜbān,[118] the chief magistrate arrived at Shiraz. Seeing that it was not possible to reconcile the two parties, he sent Farmān-Farmā perforce to Tehran and took the administration of the province of

116. See below, p. 274.
117. March 19, 1840 (should be March 21).
118. Began on September 28, 1840.

Fārs into his own hands; the rebels then were calmed down. The shah left Tehran for Esfahan in order to chastise the evildoers of that city and arrived there in the month of Dhu'l-Ḥejja of that year.[119] A number of inhabitants of Esfahan were punished.

NĀṢER OD-DIN MIRZĀ APPOINTED PRINCE GOVERNOR, FARHĀD MIRZĀ DEPUTY GOVERNOR OF FĀRS. The New Year fell on the evening of 27th Moḥarram of the year 1257.[120] Having settled the affairs of the districts of Fārs and Kerman, the shah departed from Esfahan and, traveling by way of Khvānsār and Golpāygān,[121] arrived in Tehran in the month of Rajab.[122] At Golpāygān, news arrived that the people of Fārs did not agree with Amir-e Kabir Mirzā Nabi Khān's measures. The shah bestowed the title of "Ṣāḥeb Ekhteyār-e Fārs" upon Naṣrollāh Khān-e Qājār Devehlu, Sar Keshik Bāshi of the court, a man combining cleverness in politics with sagacity, and he departed for that province. Upon his arrival at Shiraz he turned chaos into order within the space of four months. Because he allowed himself no rest, he fell ill and died on 28th Rajab at Shiraz.[123] Then the shah appointed the crown prince, Nāṣer od-Din Mirzā, prince governor of Fārs and entrusted the governorship of that province to his younger brother, Farhād Mirzā, giving him the title "Nā'eb ol-Eyāla." Mirzā Fażlollāh Naṣir ol-Molk, son of the former vizier of the province of Fārs, Mirzā Naṣrollāh-e ᶜAliābādi Māzandarāni, whose biography is given under the year 1212,[124] was appointed vizier of Fārs and arrived at Shiraz in the month of Ramażān[125] in the company of Nāṣer od-Din Mirzā.

119. Began on January 24, 1841.
120. March 20, 1841 (should be March 21).
121. Two districts northwest of Shiraz. This means that the shah deviated from the direct route to Tehran.
122. Began on August 19, 1841.
123. September 15, 1841. 124. See above, p. 64.
125. Began on October 17, 1841.

FARHĀD MIRZĀ SUBDUES THE CHIEFS OF THE MAMASSANI LORS. Because all the Lori Khāns of Mamassani were rebellious, were driving away and stealing the cattle of the Qashqā'i, and were firmly established in mountain fortresses, such as the Qalᶜa-ye Safid and the Qalᶜa-ye Ṭus[126] and in the mountains of Fahleyān and Shulestān, Farhād Mirzā departed from Shiraz in the middle of winter—the climate of that region being like that of Paradise—with 4,000 horsemen and infantry and 4 pieces of artillery to chastise the Lors. Upon his arrival in the plain of Shulestān, Khān ᶜAli Khān, the mayor of the tribe of Rostam[127] in Mamassani, made his escape from the fortress of Ṭus. ᶜAli Veis Khān-e Kur, the latter's brother, was arrested and executed. Upon his arrest, ᶜAli Veis Khān stated in writing the persons with whom his huge fortune was deposited. After his execution, Farhād Mirzā summoned these people, demanding of them the delivery of ᶜAli Veis Khān's money. One of them said:

> If ᶜAli Veis Khān was a just man telling the truth, why then has he been punished? If he was a liar and a criminal, we have been put under suspicion by him because of his enmity towards us, and this could cause Farhād Mirzā to oppress the subjects and to be blamed!

On this argument, to which no answer could be found, the governor released all of them.

As the inhabitants of Kuh-e Giluya, Behbehān, Rāmhormoz, Falāḥi, and Moḥammara[128] were neglecting the payment of

126. The Qalᶜa-ye Safid is described above, p. 244, note 44. The Qalᶜa-ye Ṭus lies 1 parasang north of the village of Māl-e Qā'ed, see *FNN*, II, 335. According to *FNN*, II, 304, Māl-e Qā'ed lies 7 parasangs (about 30 miles) north of Fahleyān, on the Faryāb River; this is perhaps the upper course of the Āb-e Khersān which flows in the valley southwest of the Kuh-e Dinār, in a northwestern direction.

127. One of the four Lorish tribes of Mamassani (Shulestān); The Rostam occupy the northern part of Mamassani, stretching from Fahleyān to the Kuh-e Dinār in the north, see EI[1] III, s.v. Lur, and *ibid.* IV, s.v. *Sh*ūlistān (both articles by V. Minorsky).

128. That is, from the western part of Fārs as far as the Shaṭṭ al-ᶜArab.

taxes, the governor ordered Manṣur Khān-e Farāhāni with soldiers from Farāhān to collect the taxes. When the latter arrived at Behbehān, Mirzā Qavāmā, governor of that region, fled from Behbehān and hurried to Esfahan to Manuchehr Khān Mo^ctamad od-Doula and established himself there. Within a short space of time, Manṣur Khān collected the taxes of Kuh-e Giluya, Rāmhormoz, and Falāḥi and subdued the rebels. Sheikh Sāmer Khān, chief sheikh of the Banu Ka^cb[129] and governor of Falāḥi, was fittingly punished. When the governor of Fārs heard of this, he appointed the Farāhāni commander Manṣur Khān governor of Kuh-e Giluya, Behbehān, Rāmhormoz, and Falāḥi, from Bandar Hendiyān[130] as far as the region of Moḥammara. However, the latter had little profit from his great luck: in the month of Ramażān of that year,[131] he died at Deh Dasht in the district of Kuh-e Giluya.

FARHĀD MIRZĀ SETTLES AFFAIRS IN THE COASTAL AREA OF THE PERSIAN GULF. After settling the affairs of the region of Mamasanni, Farhād Mirzā appointed Major Mirzā Kuchek governor of this region, departed from Fahleyān and marched by way of Kamārej, Khesht, and Dālaki to Borāzjān. Having subdued the rebels of the region of Dashtestān, he proceeded to Bandar Bushehr. There he stayed for several days, then departed from Bandar Bushehr in order to settle the affairs of the region of Dashti, Bandar Kangān, ^cAsluya, and Galladār.[132] He marched through each district, established order, [298] and had Ḥasan Khān-e Galladāri, Sheikh Jabbāra Khān-e Kangāni, and Sheikh Khalfān Khān-e ^cAslu'i put in fetters. The other sheikhs of the region were graciously received.

129. For the Bani Ka^cb, see above, p. 26, note 116.
130. Moḥammara is now Khorramshehr. By "from Bandar Hendiyān . . . to Moḥammara" the extent of Falāḥi is indicated.
131. Began on October 17, 1841.
132. The coastal area on the Persian Gulf, stretching from Bushehr to the southeast.

The New Year fell on 8th Ṣafar of the year 1258.[133] In the middle of that month, Farhād Mirzā arrived in the district of Khonj and heard of the strong fortress of Shahreyāri, which is dealt with in the second part of this book, in the chapter on the fortresses.[134] Hearing of this fortress, Farhād Mirzā ordered a group of soldiers of the vanguard (sarbāz-e qarāvol) to fill up the well of that fortress with stones; the well was more than 100 cubits deep and had a width of 4 cubits; the garrison of the fortress got its drinking water from it. By blocking the well, the rebels of the region lost their stronghold. Then Farhād Mirzā marched through the districts of Afzar, Qir va-Kārzin, Jahrom, and Fasā and arrived at Shiraz in the month of Rabiᶜ I.[135]

SEVERAL DISTRICTS SEPARATED FROM THE PROVINCE OF FĀRS. And that year, the districts of Rāmhormoz and Falāḥi, from the border of Bandar Hendiyān as far as the town of Moḥammara, were separated from the province of Fārs, added to ᶜArabestān and Shoshtar and put under the administration of Manuchehr Khān Moᶜtamad od-Doula.

Also, in that year, ᶜAli Khān-e Lāri went to Tehran, and the district of Lārestān and the districts of Sabᶜa were exempted from the taxes to be paid to the governor of Fārs. As a compensation for the taxes, several loads of powder for the musketeer detach-

133. March 21, 1842.

134. See *FNN*, II, 235: "The Qalᶜa-ye Shahreyāri is a mountain which lies slightly more than 1 parasang west of the village of Makuy in the district of Khonj. On three sides it is surrounded by the water of the Bāz River. From the top of the fortress a well with a diameter of more than 4 cubits and a depth of more than 100 cubits has been dug to reach the water of that river. Twenty musketeers can defend themselves against as many as 1,000 enemies."

The *Farhang*, VII, 224, mentions a village Kakuya, 80 miles northwest of Lār, near the Qara Aghach River, or Makku on the 1:500,000 map, 20 miles southwest of Jahrom. The Rudkhāna-ye Bāz of this text is probably a tributary of the Qara Aghach River; there is a nameless peak on the 1:500,000 map, about 4 miles northwest of Makku, 1,466 meters high, which is perhaps the fortress described in the text.

135. Began on April 12, 1842.

ments and the artillery were to be delivered each year. When Ḥabibollāh Khān, commander of the artillery, was appointed governor of Kerman that year, he was ordered to chastise the Beluchs and to conquer the fortress of Bampur in Beluchistan.[136] ᶜAli Khān-e Lāri, according to the arrangements of the ministers, was ordered to accompany the former with 3,000 musketeers. He arrived there, captured the fortress of Bampur, and returned to Lārestān. The following year he died in the town of Lār.

NEW GOVERNOR OF KUH-E GILUYA AND BEHBEHĀN APPOINTED BY FARHĀD MIRZĀ. When Manṣur Khān, the Farāhāni commander, died in the month of Ramażān of that year,[137] Farhād Mirzā appointed Shokrollāh Khān-e Nuri governor of Kuh-e Giluya and Behbehān.

FARHĀD MIRZĀ'S SUCCESSFUL ADMINISTRATION OF FĀRS. In the same year, Farrokh Khān-e Kāshāni, special page of the presence to the shah, came to Shiraz to collect taxes in the amount of 100,000 toman. Within a few days, this sum was handed over to him through the assistance of the governor's agents. And Seiyed Ḥasan Khān, commander of the Firuzkuh detachment,[138] arrived with his troops at Shiraz.

Also, in that year, Khān ᶜAli Khān, kalāntar of the tribe of Rostam in the region of Mamassani, who for some time had been wandering in the mountains and on the plains, came to Shiraz and established himself in the arsenal (tub-khāna). After several

136. A town, chiefly remarkable for its strong fortress, which lies about 260 miles east of Bandar ᶜAbbās, near the border of Afghanistan. "After the assassination of Nādir *Sh*āh in 1160:1747, Naṣīr *Kh*ān, the governor of Balōčistān, transferred his allegiance to Aḥmad *Sh*āh Durrānī, of Afghanistan, but later became independent. Persian authority over Bampūr was not restored until 1849," see EI² I, s.v. Bampūr (L. Lockhart).

137. See above, p. 269.

138. Thereby, the tradition of earlier Qājār times to send troops from Māzandarān, the homeland of the Qājārs, to southern Persia was continued. The first to be sent were the Nuri soldiers, see above, p. 92.

days he was graciously received and confirmed in his office as kalantār of the Rostam tribe.

FARHĀD MIRZĀ SUMMONED TO TEHRAN. And, Farhād Mirzā was removed from the governorship of Fārs and proceeded to Tehran. The detailed story of the event runs as follows: Since the inhabitants of Fārs had taken their complaints about Faridun Mirzā Farmān-Farmā to the court in the year 1256,[139] and the prime minister, Haji Mirzā Āqāsi, though one of his protectors had not been able to cover up the misdeeds, the shah deposed Faridun Mirzā without the prime minister's consent. The latter was always longing for discontent in Fārs, so that the shah might appoint Faridun Mirzā governor of Fārs a second time. Although the prime minister deemed Farhād Mirzā the youngest and least experienced of the princes,[140] he appointed him governor of Fārs in order to incite riots by such an appointment. When Farhād Mirzā came to Fārs, he united the different parts of the province of Fārs, which had not been united for fifty years, although the new governor was not yet thirty years of age; he made the roads and paths safe against robbery and other crimes and collected the taxes, even the arrears of many years. He combined dexterity in politics with wisdom, added to these virtues perserverance and made wolf and sheep drink from the same water. Because his nature was formed of pure clay and not soiled by hypocrisy and avidity, he suspected no one of hypocrisy and avidity. During the time of his governorship he did not cater to swindlers. These people who were earning a bare livelihood by bribing and avidity reported affairs to the court with regard to Farhād Mirzā in which he was not at all involved; and they were listened to in accordance with the proverb "They are deaf when they hear something good about me, and they listen attentively when they hear something bad;" and they claimed

139. 1256:1840.

140. Farhād Mirzā and Faridun Mirzā were brothers of Moḥammad Shāh.

that if he was summoned to Tehran he would not come. Then the shah summoned him experimentally. Having received the summons, he proceeded to Tehran without hesitation. When upon his arrival he was told to return, he did not do so. (He left his mark at Shiraz in such things as: the Bāgh-e Farhādābād, 1 mile east of Shiraz, the trees of which are all orange trees. In the upper part of the garden he built a pavilion, the ceiling of which was decorated with paintings representing the signs of the zodiac taken from *Ketāb-e Ṣowar* by ᶜAbd or-Raḥmān.[141] Mirzā Kuchek Vaṣṣāl-e Shirāzi[142] composed a chronogram about this ceiling, "If Paradise is in Heaven, look at the Heaven in this garden!" Another landmark of his is the mirror mosaic in the shrine of Shāh Charāgh Seiyed Mir Aḥmad, and a special mosque for the Shiis in the town of Galladār, most of the inhabitants of which are Sunnis.)

MIRZĀ NABI KHĀN'S UNSUCCESSFUL GOVERNMENT OF FĀRS. The New Year fell on 19th Ṣafar of the year 1259.[143] Moḥammad Shāh celebrated the feast. The governorship of Fārs was entrusted to Mirzā Nabi Khān-e Qazvini from Māzandarān, [299] chief magistrate of the empire, who went with great haste to Shiraz and established himself in the governorship.[144] Since this appointment was not approved by the prime minister, Haji Mirzā Āqāsi, Mirzā Nabi Khān had no success. In the month of Shaᶜbān,[145] he departed for the southern districts of Fārs with a detachment of soldiers and 2 pieces of artillery to settle the administrative affairs of that region. When he arrived in the districts of Lārestān, all the nobles of Fārs departed from Shiraz,

141. ᶜAbd or-Raḥmān oṣ-Ṣufi, the famous astronomer who lived in the tenth century.

142. Died 1262:1846. "He is generally regarded by his countrymen as one of the most eminent of the modern poets . . . said to have written twelve thousand verses," see Browne, IV, 315–19.

143. March 21, 1843.

144. For his earlier activities in Shiraz, see above, p. 266 seq.

145. Began on August 27, 1843.

such as, Mojtahed Āqā Loṭf ᶜAli-ye Shirāzi, Seiyed Āqā Mir Mo'men-e Reżavi, Haji Qavām ol-Molk, Moḥammad Qoli Khān Ilbegi, and the governor and alderman of those regions, Mirzā ᶜAli Akbar, chief alderman of the Neᶜmati Khāna quarters of Shiraz, and Haji Moḥammad Kāẓem, alderman of the Darb-e Shāhzāda quarter. Upon their arrival in Tehran, they complained about Mirzā Nabi Khān, governor of the province of Fārs, and praised Faridun Mirzā, the former governor of Fārs. As the shah did not want to appoint Faridun Mirzā governor, he paid no attention to their petition. The nobles of Fārs stayed in Tehran for a while in a state of amazement and hopelessness.

ḤOSEIN KHĀN APPOINTED GOVERNOR OF FĀRS. The New Year fell on the last day of Ṣafar of the year 1260.[146] That year the shah entrusted the governorship of Fārs to Ḥosein Khān, chief (moqaddam) of Marāgha and chief adjutant (ajudan bāshi)[147] of the army (afwāj-e qāhira); he was granted the title "Ṣāḥeb Ekhteyār." The latter took all the nobles of Fārs with himself, except Haji Qavām ol-Molk and the ilbegi, Moḥammed Qoli Khān, who were ordered to stay in Tehran. Upon his arrival at Shiraz, he entrusted the vizierate of the province of Fārs to Mirzā Moḥammad ᶜAli Moshir ol-Molk, the former vizier of Fārs, who for many years had been living without office in retirement. The office of lord mayor of Shiraz, he entrusted to Hādi Khān-e Beiżā'i, son of Haji Mirzā Ebrāhim, the former lord mayor of Shiraz.[148] Then he prevented the evildoers (ashrār) from committing crimes and punished them. A group of them, such as Aḥmad Solṭān, who had been chief of the trouble makers of the

146. March 20, 1844 (should be March 21).

147. The nomenclature indicates the overwhelming French influence in the reorganization of the Persian army, although, later on, the instructors were mainly English.

148. Author of "Rūznāma," see above p. 9, note 44; it seems that the family had acquired estates at Beiżā, a small town north of Shiraz.

Esḥāq Beg quarter,[149] and his servants were executed. All of them were cut in two and suspended at the gateway of the Meidān. Several evildoers of each quarter were punished in the same manner. By these measures, the governor reassured the people of Shiraz who had been molested by the evildoers; he ordered the shops to be kept open for four nights, while the owners were ordered to sleep without worry.

IRRIGATION WORK UNDERTAKEN IN THE SHIRAZ AREA. The New Year fell on 12th Rabiᶜ I of the year 1261.[150] Ḥosein Khān Ṣāḥeb Ekhteyār-e Fārs submitted the following petition to the Persian ministers:

The Shesh Pir River,[151] which has sufficient water to keep 50 mills going, flows through the districts of Ardekān[152] and the region of Doshman Zeyāri[153] in Mamassani, Shulestān, Māhur-e Milāti, and Zeidun in Kuh-e Giluya and flows into the Persian Gulf near Bandar Hendeyān, its water being used for agriculture in a few places only. In the time of previous rulers a barrier was constructed across that river. An expert built a subterranean canal and a water conduit through flat and hilly ground covering a distance of 14 parasangs and brought the water to the plain of Shiraz. Thereby the cultivation and agriculture of Shiraz was increased equally. Nowadays, the foundations of the water conduit and the holes of the subterranean canal are still visible at several points of this line. If the inhabitants of Shiraz are granted royal favors, this will be most beneficial.

The shah answered that he had no objections to spending the revenue of one year of the province of Fārs for that purpose.

149. He was one of the chiefs of the uproar five years ago, see above, p. 265.

150. March 21, 1845.

151. Named on the 1:500,000 map Rud-e Shul, Rud-e Fahleyān and Zohreh Rud successively; its springs are southeast of Ardekān. For a description of its course see also *Farhang*, VII, 147, s.v. Shiraz. Shesh Pir means "Six Saints," probably the name of a sanctuary in that region.

152. About 60 miles northwest of Shiraz, at the southern foot of the Kuh-e Barm Firuz.

153. A district southeast of Fahleyān, see *FNN*, II, 304.

Thereupon the governor made arrangements for the execution of this plan. At the beginning of that year, he confirmed Āqā Mirzā Moḥammad-e Fasā'i, whose family had held the governorship of Ḥuma-ye Shiraz, Fasā, and Dārāb for years, in the governorship of these districts, adding the governorship of the region (maḥāll) of Sab^ca, Rudān, and Aḥmadi to the latter's office. ^cAziz Khān-e Mokri, commander of the Ādherbāyjāni detachment, was put under the former's command and sent to him. ^cAziz Khān eventually became commander in chief of the Persian empire.

The New Year fell on the evening of 23d Rabi^c I of the year 1262.[154] The shah celebrated the feast in Tehran. After settling the affairs of the districts of Fārs, the governor turned his attention to diverting the course of the Shesh Pir River to Shiraz. He summoned several thousand workers from the adjacent and remote districts and sent architects, cement workers, and stone cutters to the site. They leveled the ground for several parasangs and built a water conduit of stone and cement.

A CHANGE IN THE VIZIERATE OF FĀRS. That year Mirzā Moḥammad ^cAli Moshir ol-Molk died at the age of more than eighty years. Ḥosein Khān Ṣāheb Ekhteyār transferred the title "Moshir ol-Molk" and the vizierate of Fārs to Mirzā Moḥammed ^cAli's son Mirzā Abu'l-Ḥasan Khān, in accordance with the law of inheritance and merit; he was to administrate this office for no less than thirty years.[155]

QUARRELS AMONG THE QASHQĀ'I KHĀNS. [300] Moḥammad Qoli Khān, the ilbegi, was staying in Tehran according to orders, and again a quarrel arose among the sons of the khāns of the Qashqā'i. They were all ambitious, obstinate, and proud and thus fought against each other several times, and a number

154. March 20, 1846 (should be March 21).

155. His death is one of the last events recorded in the *Fārs-nāma-ye Nāṣeri*, see below, p. 419.

of their followers were killed. Ḥeidar Qoli Khān, too, son of Mortażā Qoli Khān, the ilbegi, was killed. Things went so far that the unity of the tribes was destroyed. The ilkhāni and the ilbegi, Moḥammad Qoli Khān, who were staying in Tehran were unable to do anything, though they tried to reconcile the sons of the khāns by sending messengers. Then the ilbegi, Moḥammad Qoli Khān departed from Tehran without the permission of the courtiers and arrived at Shiraz in the autumn of that year; he was, however, unable to calm the turbulence of the tribes.

ḤOSEIN KHĀN GOES TO TEHRAN TO CLOSE THE ACCOUNTS OF FĀRS. At the end of that year,[156] Ḥosein Khān Ṣāḥeb Ekhteyār appointed Seiyed Ḥasan Khān-e Firuzkuhi, commander (sartip) of the Firuzkuh detachment, deputy governor of Fārs and left Shiraz for Tehran to close the accounts of the province of Fārs. He spent several months there, and royal favors and the title "Neẓām od-Doula" were bestowed upon him.

FOUNDATION OF THE BĀBI FAITH. That year the civil war of the Bābis broke out; they considered themselves followers of the merchant Mirzā ᶜAli Moḥammad, son of Mirzā Bazzāz-e Shirāzi. Since the chronicles and journals are full of descriptions of this occurrence, we have not inserted it in this book.[157] May the Almighty God grant strength and power to the Moslem faith and the Moslem king and humiliate and reject the heretics and rebels!

ḤOSEIN KHĀN RETURNS TO FĀRS AND SETTLES AFFAIRS IN THE QASHQĀ'I REGION. The New Year fell on 4th Rabiᶜ II of the year 1263.[158] The shah celebrated the feast according to the Persian custom. Ḥosein Khān Neẓām od-Doula,

156. Autumn 1846.

157. A full account of the Bābis has been given by Browne, see Bibliography, and now also A. Bausani, EI² I, s.v. Bābīs.

158. March 22, 1847 (should be March 21).

Ṣāḥeb Ekhteyār-e Fārs, was allowed to depart from the court; accordingly, he left Tehran for Fārs. Because in the autumn of the last year,[159] Moḥammad Qoli Khān, the ilbegi, had come to the tribes of Fārs without official permission, Neẓām od-Doula proceeded to the district of Sar-ḥadd-e Shesh Nāḥeya in order to punish the ilbegi. Neẓām od-Doula spent several days at Garmābād[160] and some time on the pasture of Ḥannā[161] and sent messengers and letters to the ilbegi, until he received a sum of money as peshkash and the ilbegi ceased encroaching. In the month of Shᶜbān of that year,[162] Neżām od-Doula arrived at Shiraz and turned his attention to the renovation of the river bed of the Shesh Pir River.

ḤOSEIN KHĀN FINISHES IRRIGATION WORK IN THE SHIRAZ AREA. The New Year fell on 14th Rabiᶜ II of the year 1264.[163] Neẓām od-Doula proceeded to the plain of Homā'ejān in Ardekān[164] and encamped there to inspect the diversion of the course of the Shesh Pir River. With great seriousness he inspected daily, even by night, the performance of the architects, canal builders and pick- and shovel-workers. They built a river bed of stone and cement for a length of nearly 3.5 parasangs and dug a subterranean canal 1 parasang long in the plain of Khallār,[165] the ground of which was above the river; in the technical terminology of the people of Fārs such a subterranean canal is

159. Autumn 1846.

160. A distance of 7 parasangs north of Samirom, see *FNN*, II, 221. For comments on the district of Sarḥadd-e Shesh Nāḥeya, see above, p. 225, note 485.

161. Located 4 parasangs south of Samirom, see *FNN*, II, 221, and above, p. 225, note 485.

162. Began on July 15, 1847.

163. March 20, 1848 (should be March 21).

164. Now a dehestān south of Ardekān, see *Farhang*, VII, 242.

165. About 30 miles southeast of Ardekān, 4.5 miles off the Ardekān–Shiraz highway, see *Farhang*, VII, 89. The 1:500,000 map shows Shul and Tang-e Shul to be in that area and an irrigation canal which is cut into the hills in a southeastern direction.

called "Navāmdar tufeyāt."[166] They made the water run through this canal. Five parasangs farther, they cemented at several spots the wide river bed, which ran through flat and hilly ground and brought the water as far as the plain of Qaṣr-e Qomesha, 2 parasangs from Shiraz. There a field was laid out which yielded more than 2,000 mann of wheat, and a vegetable culture of melons, watermelons, and pumpkins. By order of Neẓām od-Doula, all the nobles of Fārs planted gardens outside the Bāgh-e Shāh Gate of Shiraz. Four roads, each 30 cubits wide, were built, stretching from the gate to a certain point; they were covered with vaults built of stone and cement from beginning to end. At the crossing of those 4 roads a huge water basin was installed, at the 4 corners of which 4 minarets were erected. Then pavilions and tents were put up around the basin, and a painting of the shah was put up at the entrance of the courtyard. On 4th Shaᶜbān of that year,[167] all the nobles of religion and empire were invited to a banquet. The evening before, the water of the Shesh Pir River flowed into the bed of the Nahr-e Aᶜẓam, so that it was to come to the "Basin of the Four Roads" on the fourth day of that month. That day all the nobles of the city came to the tents, proceeding according to the rules of a royal reception; the theologians sat down in front of the painting of the shah according to their rank, then the officials in official dress with sword; then the viziers, the officers of the chancery, and the governors of the districts (żābet-e bolukāt) approached the painting. All of them put a sum of money as a peshkash in front of the painting, inclining their heads and bowing from the hips. Standing under the splendid painting, Neẓām od-Doula inquired about their welfare. Then the artillery and two detachments of

166. The term is not to be found in the dictionaries. For the terminology used, for instance, in Kerman, see Philip Becket, "Qanats around Kirman," *Journal of the Royal Central Asiatic Society*, XL (1953), 47–58. Becket gives a list of terms, in which the term used by Ḥasan-e Fasā'i is not included.

167. July 6, 1848.

soldiers with drums and trumpets were ordered to go meet the water, and carpets were spread on the four sides of the basin. When the participants of the reception finished saluting the painting of the shah, they sat down around the basin, and the water of the Shesh Pir River ran into the basin, while the sound of the trumpets and drums which had been sent to meet the water became louder. Then the dishes were brought in and distributed among the participants of the meeting, 4,000 to 5,000 people or more.

DEATH OF MOḤAMMAD SHĀH. It is a strange fact that this banquet and the coming of the water bore [301] no blessing to the people of Fārs, nay Persia, and that this water was not brought to Shiraz a second time.[168] The water conduits and subterranean canals were destroyed completely. A detailed story of what happened is this: For nearly ten years Moḥammad Shāh Ghāzi[169] had been suffering from gout, his condition getting worse year by year, even day by day; the Persian and European physicians were not able to cure the shah and admitted their inability. In the night of 6th Shavvāl of that year,[170] the shah died in the Qaṣr-e Jadid ("New Palace") near Tehran. After some time his corpse was transferred to Qom and buried in the vicinity of Ḥażrat-e Maᶜṣuma. He was born in the month of Dhu'l-Qaᶜda of the year 1222[171] and died at the age of forty-two. Being one of the powerful monarchs, this king did not soil his hands with things forbidden or his lips with intoxicating liquors. He complied with the injunctions of the religious law of the Prophet and

168. According to the traditional ideas of Persian kingship, the welfare of the country depends upon the king's virtues; If the king is a good and just Ruler, rain will be abundant. On the other hand, the construction of irrigation canals is one of the highest accomplishments of a king, recompensed by long life and divine favor.

169. He is styled "Ghāzi" ("Fighter in the Holy War"), because he had taken part in the Russian War, see above, p. 178.

170. September 4, 1848.

171. Began on December 31, 1807.

observed the laws of friendship with the Prophet's successors.[172] His high rank in the mathematical sciences and his perfection in writing Nastaᶜliq has been mentioned by Reẓā Qoli Khān Hedāyat, author of the *Roużat oṣ-Ṣafā-ye Nāṣeri*,[173] in the latter's elegy composed on the shah's death. On his coins were put the words: "Shāhanshāh-e anbeyā Moḥammad,"[174] and the legend of his seal was: "Moḥammad Shāh Ghāzi became owner of crown and ring, and there came greatness of kingship and nation and splendor of law and religion."[175] At the time of his death the shah had five sons: 1) Nāṣer od-Din Shāh, the ruling monarch. His mother is the daughter of Moḥammad Qāsem Khān-e Qājār Qoyonlu. He was born on 6th Ṣafar of the year 1247;[176] 2) ᶜAbbās Mirzā Molk Ārā; 3) ᶜAbd oṣ-Ṣamad Mirzā ᶜEzz od-Doula; 4) Moḥammed Taqi Mirzā Rokn od-Doula; and 5) Abu'l-Qāsem Mirzā.

172. That is, the seiyeds, the descendants of the Prophet through Fāṭema and ᶜAli. The author was a seiyed too.

173. See above, p. xvii.

174. "Moḥammad (that is, the Prophet Moḥammad, the shah's namesake) is king of kings of the prophets." See also Rabino di Borgomale, *Coins, Medals and Seals*, p. 70. Moḥammad Shāh introduced the Lion and the Sun on his coinage.

175. Rabino, *ibid.*, p. 70, mentions two other seals: one has the inscription: os-Solṭān ibn os-Solṭān Moḥammad Shāh Ghāzi, the third has a Lion and Sun, and on the lion's body the words: "Solṭān Moḥammad Shāh—1255."

176. See above, p. 200.

CHAPTER 4

Nāṣer od-Din Shāh

INTERNAL DIFFICULTIES

NĀṢER OD-DIN SHĀH ASCENDS THE THRONE. The nobles of the empire sent word of Moḥammad Shāh's death to Tabriz, the capital of Crown Prince Nāṣer od-Din Mirzā's governorship. Then the crown prince, in accordance with the decision of the astrologers of Tabriz, selected an hour of lucky augury,[1] ascended the throne, and put the crown on his head in the city of Tabriz on the evening of 14th Shavvāl of that year.[2] The theologians, emirs, and nobles of that city were present and congratulated the shah on his succession to the throne. On the 19th of that month,[3] he departed from Tabriz with 10,000 soldiers and Mirzā Fażl-ollāh Naṣir ol-Molk, the former vizier of Fārs, who had been appointed vizier to the shah.[4] After several stops, the office of grand vizier was conferred upon Mirzā Taqi-ye Farāhāni, who, up to that time, had been a commander of the regular army (amir-e neẓām). On 21st Dhu'l-Qaᶜda of that year,[5] the court entered Tehran. On the evening of the 22d of that month,[6] the shah, in accordance with the law of inheritance and on account

1. Fixing the time of enthronement according to the rules of astrology has a long tradition in Persian history: the Safavid ruler Soleimān I (r. 1666–94) repeated the ceremony and even changed his name from Ṣafi II to Soleimān, when several years later it was discovered that the first enthronement had taken place at a time of unlucky augury, see E. Kaempfer, *Am Hofe des Persischen Grosskönigs (1684–85). Das erste Buch der Amoenitates exoticae in deutscher Bearbeitung*, ed. W. Hinz, Leipzig, 1940, p. 42.

2. September 12, 1848. 3. September 18, 1848.

4. That is, vizier of Ādherbāyjān, the crown prince's province.

5. October 19, 1848.

6. That is, on the evening of October 19, because in Persia, as in the other Oriental countries, the date was not reckoned from midnight, but from the evening.

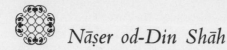

of his merits, donned the royal vestment, put the crown of the Kayānids on his head, and sat on the jewel-studded throne. Those who were present offered congratulations and received royal favors in a most distinguished manner. The same night the grand vizier, Mirzā Taqi Khān, received the honorific title "Atābeg." The meaning of this term is explained in the second part of this book under the heading "The Atābegs of Fārs."[7] The administrative decisions were to be confirmed by his signature and seal.

THE PEOPLE OF SHIRAZ RISE IN REBELLION AGAINST ḤOSEIN KHĀN NEẒĀM OD-DOULA. On 11th Shavvāl[8] news of the Moḥammad Shāh's death reached Shiraz. When the governor of Fārs, Ḥosein Khān Neẓām od-Doula, heard of this, he summoned the nobles of Fārs and informed them of the occurrence. He spent that day in mourning. The next day the legend "os-Solṭān Nāṣer od-Din Shāh" was put on the dinars and dirhems, an audience of felicitation was held, and gold and silver in new coins were distributed among the people. A suitable peshkash of new and old coins was sent to the royal court. As the grand vizier, Mirzā Taqi Khān Amir-e Atābeg, had been a bitter enemy of Ḥosein Khān Neẓām od-Doula—as it happens in this world—he prevented the gift from being accepted, and the governor's envoy returned to Shiraz without having accomplished his mission. When the people of Fārs heard of the atābeg's attitude, they united in enmity against Neẓām od-Doula, [302] though not even four of them were able to agree upon doing the same thing, and all of a sudden rose in rebellion against him. At that time, Neẓām od-Doula commanded two detachments of regular soldiers of Ādherbāyjān and 16 pieces of artillery with 100 gunners who were staying in Shiraz. ᶜAziz Khān-e Mokri—soon to become commander in chief of the whole army—[9] was commander of a detachment in Shiraz. Hāji

7. See *FNN*, I, 30–42 (an historical account of the Atabegs only). Originally, the Atabegs were tutors of the princes of royal blood.
8. September 10, 1848. 9. See above, p. 276.

Mirzā ᶜAli Akbar Qavām ol-Molk, who exercized a great influence at Shiraz and Fārs, entered into an agreement with the ilbegi of the tribes, Moḥammad Qoli Khān,[10] and within a short space of time gathered together nearly 15,000 men of the auxiliary forces among the tribes and from the districts. In full rebellion they marched to the plain of Delgoshā, 0.5 parasang to the east of Shiraz. In addition to this host Hāji Qavām ol-Molk summoned to Shiraz the auxiliary forces from Shiraz and the districts belonging to him, and the next day he left Shiraz with great pomp in order to meet the ilbegi. All night they deliberated with each other upon the measures to be taken against Neẓām od-Doula, and the next day Qavām ol-Molk returned to Shiraz and sent the following message to Neẓām od-Doula: "The nobles of the city and of the districts and tribes are holding a meeting outside the city and are deliberating upon your going or staying. You may join the meeting or else send somebody as your deputy to be informed of the outcome of the affair!" Accordingly, Neẓām od-Doula dispatched Mirzā ᶜAbdollāh Monshi-ye Māzandarāni and ᶜAziz Khān Sarhang-e Mokri as his deputies to the meeting. Upon their arrival, the people of Fārs said to them:

> The shah who appointed Neẓām od-Doula our governor has bidden farewell to throne and crown. We do not know whether the king of Persia considers Neẓām od-Doula to be our governor. The best thing for him to do is to go to Tehran and leave us alone, so that we might be able to obey the decisions of the shah. If Neẓām od-Doula does anything else, he will be the target of shooting!

Haji Qavām ol-Molk did not say a word at this meeting. After his return to the city he sent Neẓām od-Doula a message that he would not soil himself with treachery towards the government; that the latter, if he was able to do so, should defy the ilbegi. Since Neẓām od-Doula with only 3,000 men was not able to

10. The lord mayor of Shiraz was, in general, not living on good terms with the tribal chiefs, see above, p. 206. The aim of this alliance was to avoid a civil war, which had happened after Fatḥ ᶜAli Shāh's death.

fight and could not go to Tehran without the permission of the ministers, he gave an evasive reply:

What you have said is true, and I am preparing my journey to Tehran. However, you have to give three-months' pay to my soldiers and gunners who are present and who have to go to Tehran with me. Give us a voucher of the Divan, so that we may receive the equivalent in case we do not get provisions on the journey. You have to give back our 200 camels which you have driven away, for the transport of my luggage. Furthermore, you have to grant a delay of eight days!

At night ᶜAziz Khān-e Mokri left the city for the camp of the ilbegi and said to him:

The message you have sent to Neẓām od-Doula, telling him to depart with haste or else be attacked, is altogether unwise, as to this date he is a servant of the state. If you kill him or his men, you will be inevitably punished by the state. Accordingly, give the soldiers three-months' pay, and Neẓām od-Doula will march off within eight days!

The ilbegi agreed with ᶜAziz Khān's proposal and gave the soldiers three-months' pay. Then ᶜAziz Khān returned to Neẓām od-Doula, and they prepared the palace and the government buildings for defense. When eight days had elapsed without anything having become known of Neẓām od-Doula's departure, the people of Fārs repented granting a delay and giving three months' pay to the two detachments, and they engaged in civil war. The musketeers of the city, nearly 2,000 men, climbed on the roof of the Masjed-e Vakil and the high buildings and opened fire. The Ādherbāyjāni soldiers installed breast works on the roofs of the government buildings and posted themselves behind them, fully prepared. The connections between the Divan servants and the inhabitants were intercepted. The next day the evildoers of 10 quarters of Shiraz gathered together, plundered the square of the Bazār-e Vakili, and carried away wares from India, Turkey, China, and Europe as booty.[11] The people of the

11. In those days, Shiraz was still a center of some importance for the overland trade from the East to Turkey and Europe.

Vakili storehouses, which are high like fortresses, took pains to defend themselves and were not molested by the trouble-makers. The day after that, ᶜAziz Khān engaged in fighting the people of Fārs with great bravery and ordered the gunners to place 4 pieces of artillery on the Meidān-e Naᶜlbandān[12] opposite the entrance of the Masjed-e Vakil. They fired many shots that damaged the entrance of the Masjed-e Vakīl, a solid structure, at several spots. Then the Ādherbāyjānī soldiers of the Shaqāqi detachment made an assault and took the Masjed-e Vakil from the Shirāzi musketeers. Three soldiers and 4 citizens of Shiraz were killed. The fourth Tabrizi detachment climbed on the roof of the Bazār-e Vakil, which is connected with the Masjed-e Vakil, and installed breastworks there. A small piece of artillery was brought up on the roof of the bazaar. Within two or three days, the people of the districts and tribes and the citizens erected 25 breastworks opposite the government buildings and the bazaar and the Masjed-e Valkil and placed 100 men behind each of them. The distance between the breastworks of the people of Fārs and those of the soldiers was not more than 5 to 6 cubits, and during that time several people on each side were killed. Then the elders of the city asked Neẓām od-Doula if ᶜAziz Khān might come to the Tekke of Ḥāfeẓ[13] for peace negotiations. When ᶜAziz Khān went to the Tekke of Ḥāfeẓ, he took with himself several hundred soldiers, [303] and the inhabitants of Shiraz suspected him of planning to take the elders prisoner—If this was not his intention, then why so many soldiers? The elders prudently took several soldiers with them. They had not yet arrived at the Tekke when the soldiers committed encroachments, and there was fighting halfway between the Tekke and the city. When the citizens heard of this, the people of the Fārsi breastworks attacked the breastworks of the soldiers at the same time. Neẓām od-Doula ordered the artillery to open fire, and

12. "Square of the Shoemakers."

13. Burial place of the famous poet Ḥāfeẓ, outside the city.

nearly 40 Fārsis were killed by the cannon balls, while 10 or 12 soldiers were killed by the musket fire of the Fārsi musketeers. When ᶜAziz Khān, who was going to take the elders prisoner, heard the sound of the cannons and muskets, he led his soldiers with great haste and without delay back to the breastworks, and the crews of the entrenchments were bent on fighting more than ever.

When the grand vizier heard of this, he sent Amir Aṣlān Khān, page of the presence of the shah, to Shiraz to quench the flames of the civil war. Upon his arrival, the fighting calmed down; the flames were, however, not extinguished. After a short while the ministers sent Aḥmad Khān-e Navā'i, deputy chamberlain (eshiq āqāsi bāshi), a wise emir, to Shiraz to inquire into the reasons of the civil war and to find out the instigators. Upon Aḥmad Khān's arrival and by order of the nobles of Fārs, the citizens and people from the districts desisted from fighting, and Aḥmad Khān took up his quarters in the house of Āqā Bābā Khān-e Bavānāti in the center of Shiraz. By promises and threats he calmed the people.

BAHRĀM MIRZĀ MOᶜEZZ OD-DOULA APPOINTED GOVERNOR OF FĀRS. In Dhu'l-Ḥejja of that year,[14] the governorship of the province of Fārs was entrusted to Bahrām Mirzā Moᶜezz od-Doula, uncle of the shah. The vizierate was bestowed upon Mirzā Fażlollāh Naṣir ol-Molk ᶜAliābādi, the former vizier of Fārs,[15] and the Ilkhāni Moḥammad ᶜAli Khān, who had been in Tehran for nearly thirteen years,[16] returned to Shiraz in the former's company. On 24th Dhu'l-Ḥejja,[17] the new governor and his retinue departed from Tehran and arrived at Shiraz on 9th Ṣafar of the year 1265;[18] and Bahrām Mirzā subdued the rebels of the province.

14. Began on October 29, 1848.
15. See above, p. 267, year 1257.
16. See above, p. 252, year 1252.
17. November 21, 1848.
18. January 4, 1849.

SHEIKH NAṢR KHĀN APPOINTED GOVERNOR OF BUSHEHR AND DEFENDS HIMSELF SUCCESSFULLY AGAINST A PRETENDER. The New Year fell on the evening of 25th Rabiᶜ II of the year 1265.[19] Moᶜezz od-Doula entrusted the governorship of Bandar Bushehr and its dependencies to Sheikh Naṣr Khān, son of Sheikh ᶜAbd or-Rasul Khān, in accordance with the laws of inheritance and on account of his father's merits.

That year, too, Mirzā Moḥammad ᶜAli Khān Nāẓem ol-Molk returned from Tehran to Shiraz. His biography is given in the second part of this book, in the chapter on the Bālā Keft quarter of Shiraz, under the Hāshemi family.[20] He took over part of the Divan affairs. Since Sheikh Naṣr Khān during his stay in Tehran had borrowed money from Nāẓem ol-Molk and the latter claimed this money now and Sheikh Naṣr Khān displayed negligence in returning the sum, Nāẓem ol-Molk asked the court for the governorship of Bandar Bushehr. After obtaining the certificate and the appointment, Nāẓem ol-Molk appointed his younger brother Mirzā Mahdi Khān deputy governor and sent him to Bushehr; Nāẓem al-Molk entered into an agreement with

19. March 19, 1849 (should be March 21).

20. See *FNN*, II, 52: "Mirzā Moḥammad ᶜAli Khān Nāẓem ol-Molk was born in the year 1220 (1805/6). After being educated by his noble father and attaining perfection, he wrote Shekasta beautifully, stayed for some time in Ādherbāyjān with Crown Prince ᶜAbbās Mirzā and was intendant (mostaufi) of that province. In the year 1257 (1841/42), he was granted the title 'Nāẓem ol-Molk.' In the year 1271 (1854/55), he was sent from Tehran to Shiraz to levy the taxes of Fārs. In 1271, 1272, and 1273 (1854–57), he was governor of the districts (bolukāt) of Dārāb, Jahrom, Qir va-Kārzin, Juyom and Bidshehr; he granted the landowners a respite for the payment of taxes (māleyāt-e divāni-ye molzami) at the beginning of the year, payed the installments month by month out of his own pocket and collected the money from the landowners at the end of the year. Until now, although many years have elapsed in the meantime, the inhabitants of those regions hold his name in high esteem. After the year 1284 (1867/68), he held no governmental office, stayed one year at Mashhad and one year at the Holy Places in Mesopotamia. He died in the year 1288 (1871/72) at Shiraz; he left no children."

his brother that he should arrest Sheikh Naṣr Khān and put him in prison as soon as he met him. When Sheikh Naṣr Khān was informed of Nāẓem ol-Molk's intention, he brought his belongings on board a ship and sent them to the island of Khārk. He himself remained at Bushehr with a number of musketeers in order to defy Haji Mirzā Mahdi Khān. He placed several pieces of artillery belonging to the Divan which had been brought to Bandar Bushehr on the towers of the harbor. When Haji Mirzā Mahdi Khān arrived at Borāzjān, 10 parasangs from Bushehr, and heard of Sheikh Naṣr Khān's behavior, he summoned Bāqer Khān-e Tangestāni, who was on hostile terms with Sheikh Naṣr Khān,[21] and the former arrived at Borāzjān with 1,000 musketeers. The next day, he departed with Haji Mirzā Mahdi Khān to conquer Bandar Bushehr. At each station a detachment of Tangestānti musketeers joined them. When they arrived on the plain of Rishehr,[22] 1 parasang from Bushehr, the auxiliatory forces of Haji Mirzā Mahdi Khān numbered 4,000 men. The next day they assaulted Bushehr. The guns which Sheikh Naṣr Khān had placed on the rampart and the towers of the fortress of Bushehr, prevented the musketeers from approaching. In this manner some time elapsed and Bāqer Khān-e Tangestāni, the commander of these troops, despaired of capturing Bushehr. He sent a messenger to Behbehān summoning Mirzā Solṭān Moḥammad Khān, the governor of Behbehān, to join him. Accordingly, Mirzā Solṭān Moḥammad Khān came with 2 pieces of artillery and 2,000 horsemen and infantry to the plain of Rishehr, and Haji Mirzā Mahdi Khān's vigor grew threefold. As Bandar Bushehr is encircled by water on three sides, it can be assaulted only on the fortified side. This fortification was enforced by fortress artillery; accordingly, the siege of Bushehr

21. For the reason of the hostility between the two, see above, p. 211. As a Persian, Bāqer Khān was backed by the other local rulers against Sheikh Naṣr Khān who was an Arab.

22. 6 miles south of Bushehr.

grew lengthy. [304] News of this arrived in Tehran through the English courier mail.[23] The ministers ordered Nāẓem ol-Molk in writing to raise the siege of Bushehr and to hand the town over to Sheikh Naṣr Khān. Nāẓem ol-Molk complied with this order and summoned Haji Mirzā Mahdi Khān from Bushehr. Sheikh Naṣr Khān won his independence anew.

At the end of that year the governorship of Kuh-e Giluya and Behbehān was entrusted to Moḥammad Karim Khān-e Qājār.

FIRUZ MIRZĀ NOṢRAT OD-DOULA APPOINTED GOVERNOR OF FĀRS. The New Year fell on the evening of 6th Jomādi I of the year 1266.[24] At the beginning of that year, Bahrām Mirzā Moᶜezz od-Doula proceeded from Shiraz to Tehran, and the governorship of Fārs was conferred upon Firuz Mirzā Noṣrat od-Doula.[25]

BĀBI DISTURBANCES AT FASĀ AND NIRIZ. At the beginning of Moḥarram,[26] Seiyed Yaḥyā, son of Āqā Seiyed Jaᶜfar from Dārāb, known as "Eṣṭahbānāti," who in the name of Mirzā ᶜAli Moḥammad "Bāb" had invited people to embrace the newly invented religion, was welcomed with great honors at each place he came to, because his father was Āqā Seiyed Jaᶜfar. At the end of the previous year, he had come from Yazd to Fasā, apparently to preach, teach, and explain the laws of the religion of the Prophet Moḥammad, actually, however, to spread the religion of Mirzā ᶜAli Moḥammad "Bāb." The governor of Fasā, Āqā Mirzā Moḥammad, welcomed him with honors and assigned him suitable lodgings. He tried in various manners to win sympathies and spent the nights in discussions (mosāmara)

23. It seems that the local authorities tried by all means to keep the central government out of the dispute.

24. March 20, 1850 (should be March 21).

25. Bahrām Mirzā and Firuz Mirzā were paternal uncles of Nāṣer od-Din Shāh.

26. That is, Moḥarram 1265 which began on November 27, 1848, see Bausani, EI² I, s.v. Bābīs, and further down in the text.

and the days preaching, and eventually several people accepted his teachings. Then he propagated his teachings in public. When Āqā Mirzā Moḥammad was informed of the latter's faith, he summoned him and said:

The inhabitants of this district are firm in their profession of Islam and immovable in their faith. When they get knowledge of your profession, it might happen that they would stain their hands with your blood. The best thing you can do is to leave this town and proceed to another place.

And he sent a report on this occurrence to Shiraz. Because Moᶜezz od-Doula had left Shiraz and Noṣrat od-Doula had not yet arrived, the responsibility was with Mirzā Fażlollāh Naṣir ol-Molk, and Āqā Mirzā Moḥammad was given no clear reply. At his wit's end, he sent Seiyed Yaḥyā a large sum of money as a gift and ordered a group of people to proceed at the end of the night to the latter's house and to threaten him with death. At the end of Ṣafar of the year 1266,[27] Seiyed Yaḥyā went from Fasā to Eṣṭaḥbānāt. The inhabitants of this town, too, were not willing to have anything to do with him, and since he did not know what to do, he chose as his abode the town of Niriz, where the evildoers[28] had risen in rebellion against their governor, Haji Zein ol-ᶜĀbedin Khān. Seiyed Yaḥyā won the evildoers as his friends and made his intentions public without reserve. All the evildoers, about 500 people, accepted his teachings. He wiped out the injunctions of the Islamic religion, and his reputation increased every day. Then he chose a ruined fortess outside Niriz as his abode and repaired its defense works. He moved to that fortress and decided to wage a religious war (jang-e madhhabi)[29] with Haji Zein ol-ᶜĀbedin. Every day his followers brought the people of the bazaar forcibly before him, and he would demand

27. About January 10, 1850.

28. "Ashrār"; the term comprises different kinds of opponents of the Qājār rule, without clear definition of their political aims.

29. A war fought between the adherents of different sects (madhhab) as opposed to Holy War (jehād), which is fought against nonbelievers.

a sum of money from them before releasing them. After some time all had been brought before him.[30] Those who were not willing to pay homage to him had either to pay a large sum of money as a ransom or to prepare to be executed. This procedure was applied to a number of people. One day a man was brought before him; when he crossed the courtyard and saw Seiyed Yaḥyā, he fell down and died on the spot. When Haji Zein ol-ᶜĀbedin Khān saw things going on in this manner, he gathered an army and prepared for battle with Seiyed Yaḥyā. Seiyed Yaḥyā's men, however, anticipated the attack and threw themselves at midnight, sword in hand, upon Haji Zein ol-ᶜĀbedin Khān's host and killed about 150 people, sparing neither men nor women. Among those killed was ᶜAli Aṣghar Khān, the eldest brother of Haji Zein ol-ᶜĀbedin Khān. His body was brought to the fortress and thrown into a water conduit. Three of the governor's sons were taken prisoner and brought to the fortress. Haji Zein ol-ᶜĀbedin with great effort mounted an unsaddled horse and hurried to the village of Qaṭru,[31] 9 parasangs north of Niriz, and informed Naṣir ol-Molk in writing of the occurrence. Upon this victory the inhabitants of Niriz and the villages had no choice but to join Seiyed Yaḥyā and accept his teachings. The houses of Haji Zein ol-ᶜĀbedin Khān and ᶜAli Aṣghar Khān and their followers were plundered and the booty was distributed among the adherents of Seiyed Yaḥyā. The inhabitants were so afraid of the Bābis that they delivered everything they were asked for without delay. The Bābis were firmly convinced that they would subdue Fārs or even more within a short space of time and that they would destroy the religion and the state. Their power was increasing every day, the unflinching warriors numbered more than 3,000 men. Noṣrat od-Doula was informed of this before his arrival at Shiraz. Four stations from Shiraz, he

30. As newly established religious and secular authority, Seiyed Yaḥyā claimed the right of collecting taxes.

31. 31 miles east of Niriz, see *Farhang*, VII, 172.

wrote to Naṣir ol-Molk saying that Mehr ᶜAli Khān Shojāᶜ ol-Molk Nuri, commander of the Shirazi horsemen, [305] was to march with great haste, together with the commander, Moṣṭafā Qoli Khān Eᶜtemād os-Salṭana Qaraguzlu and two detachments of Qaraguzlu soldiers, and to attack Seiyed Yaḥyā. Accordingly, Naṣir ol-Molk supervised the preparations of these troops and made them march off with 2 pieces of artillery. Haji Zein ol-ᶜĀbedin Khān, upon his arrival at the village of Qaṭru, summoned the aldermen of the mountains (Kuhestān) and the districts of Niriz, and about 2,000 men came to his support. Near Rostāq,[32] 3 parasangs from Niriz, he joined the troops of Shojāᶜ ol-Molk and Eᶜtemād os-Salṭana; together they marched to Niriz and encamped opposite the fortress of Sayyid Yaḥyā. Five days elapsed without any fighting. On the sixth night, Seiyed Yaḥyā wrote a few words on scraps of paper and fixed them at the belts of his men and said: "This scrap of paper will protect you from the fire of muskets and guns." Then he selected 300 of them for a night attack on Eᶜtemād os-Salṭana's camp. He gave each of them a scimitar, and at midnight they came out of the fortress, hurried to the camp with great clamor, and invaded the breastworks without fear. They killed several people and caused Eᶜtemād os-Salṭana and Shojāᶜ ol-Molk much trouble. They fought in the camp until sunrise. Several Bābis were killed by the spears and muskets of the soldiers. The rest of them returned to the fortress. Then it became known that 160 Bābis and 300 men of the camp had been killed during the night. When the Bābis realized that the paper scraps were of no use, their faith dwindled; groups of 5 or 10 people deserted from Seiyed Yaḥyā's camp, at first in secret, then quite openly, and his army was diminished. Three days after this event, Seiyed Yaḥyā made new preparations and selected 300 men for another night attack, and they assaulted the camp making a lot of noise. The people of the camp leveled their guns at them, and about

32. It is 2 parasangs northwest of Niriz, see *FNN*, II, 308.

50 Bābis were killed by cannon and musket fire. However, the rest of them invaded the breast works with great bravery, and about 100 men of the camp were killed. Eʿtemād os-Salṭana and Shojāʿ ol-Molk fought back bravely and threw the Bābis out of the camp. During this battle another group of Seiyed Yaḥyā's followers went their way. When he saw that his army was diminishing, he began peace negotiations. After the exchange of messengers and letters, Seiyed Yaḥyā, five days later, came out of the fortress with 12 of his adherents, entered the camp with all honors, and was put up in Eʿtemād os-Salṭana's tent. After spending one night with honors, he and his adherents were arrested and killed the next day by the heirs of ʿAli Aṣghar Khān;[33] 2 of Seiyed Yaḥyā's sons and 30 of his followers were put in fetters and sent to Shiraz. The 30 persons were executed, the 2 sons of Seiyed Yaḥyā, who were not yet grown up, were sent to Borujerd and surrendered to their grandfather, Āqā Seiyed Jaʿfar.

APPOINTMENTS IN SHIRAZ. Upon his arrival at Shiraz, Noṣrat od-Doula conferred the vizierate of the province of Fārs upon Mirzā Abu'l-Qāsem-e Tafrishi, one of his old servants. The office of intendant was conferred upon Mirzā Abu'l-Ḥasan Khān Moshir ol-Molk.

SHEIKH NAṢR KHĀN OF BUSHEHR SUMMONED TO SHIRAZ AND SENT TO TEHRAN. Sheikh Naṣr Khān was summoned from Bushehr; upon his arrival at Shiraz, he was sent to Tehran. The governorship of Bushehr, its dependencies, and Dashtestān was entrusted to Mirzā Ḥasan ʿAli Khān, son of Haji Mirzā ʿAli Akbar Qavām ol-Molk, and he was granted the title "Daryābegi." When Sheihk Ḥosein Khān, uncle of Naṣr Khān and deputy governor of Bushehr, heard of this, he gathered together a host of Arabs and Lors and reinforced the fortifications of Bushehr. He placed several pieces of artillery on the bastions and

33. This is a typical mixture of official measures and blood revenge.

sent for several ships so that he might board ship and make his escape in case things went wrong. When Mirzā Ḥasan ᶜAli Khān Daryābegi arrived at Rishehr and heard of Sheikh Ḥosein Khān's resistance, he reported to Noṣrat od-Doula. The latter sent Moṣṭafā Qoli Khān Eᶜtemād os-Salṭana to Bushehr with two detachments of Qaraguzlu soldiers who were under his command and two pieces of artillery. Eᶜtemād os-Salṭana marched off by way of Firuzābād[34] and joined the daryābegi at Rishehr. When he saw with his own eyes that Sheikh Hoṣein Khān was not giving in and that the affair was not to be cleared up without attack and assault, he sent a letter to the inhabitants of Bushehr, most of whom were merchants and craftsmen and foreigners saying:

Because Sheikh Ḥosein Khān has not complied with the royal decree and as it is incumbent upon the government to wage war with him and this affair will not be finished without killing and plundering the inhabitants of Bushehr, everybody may take his family and his belongings and spend several days in the villages, until the affair of Sheikh Hosein Khān is finished. If you do not do this, you shall be informed in writing that nobody [306] will be entitled to indemnification if he has suffered damage of money and life during the capture of Bushehr.

When this letter became known to the inhabitants of Bushehr, Sheikh Ḥosein Khān saw their trouble. Accordingly, he summoned the nobles and said to them: "You may be sure that I shall not fight with the servants of the shah; tonight I shall depart across the sea!" Then he summoned the customhouse officers in the same manner, took the money of the custom house, went with his family on board a ship, and sailed for Basra. The next day Mirzā Ḥasan ᶜAli Khān Daryābegi and Moṣṭafā Qoli Khān Eᶜtemād os-Salṭana entered Bushehr.

34. This means that he took the southern route to Bushehr, probably in order to avoid a clash with the local rulers of Kāzerun and Dashtestān, who claimed Bushehr for themselves.

QUARRELS ABOUT THE GOVERNORSHIP OF KUH-E GILUYA AND BEHBEHĀN. One of the occurrences in the province of Fārs is: Several years ago Mirzā Qavām od-Din-e Behbehāni, known as "Mirzā Qavāmā"—details on his family are given in the second part of this book, in the chapter on the district of Kuh-e Giluya and Behbehān—[35] was expelled from Kuh-e Giluya and Behbehān. The previous year he had come to Behbehān without the permission of the government. He asked the governor, Moḥammad Karim Khān,[36] for pardon and sent him away. When news of this arrived at Shiraz, Bahrām Mirzā Mo^{c}ezz od-Doula sent a certificate appointing Mirzā Solṭān Moḥammad Khān, nephew and son-in-law of Mirzā Qavāmā, governor of Kuh-e Giluya and Behbehān. Mirzā Qavāmā paid

35. The author writes Qoumā and Qavāmā. Some details have already been given above, p. 36, note 176. Here some additions from the same passage of *FNN*, II, 267 seq.: Mirzā Solṭān Moḥammad Khān, the father of Mirzā Qavāmā, was governor of Kuh-e Giluya from 1200 (1785/86) onward. In 1213 (1798/99), the governorship was conferred upon Moḥammad Ḥosein Khān, the younger brother of the powerful grand vizier Ebrāhim Khān E^{c}temād od-Doula, while Solṭān Moḥammad became the new governor's deputy. Two years later, when the grand vizier was deposed, Solṭān Moḥammad assumed independent rule again. In 1217 (1802/3), Ṣādeq Khān Āqā-ye Qājār was appointed governor, and Solṭān Moḥammad became his vizier. A year later, Ṣādeq Khān was deposed for having Solṭān Moḥammad blinded. Upon Solṭān Moḥammad's death, his son, Mirzā Manṣur Khān, took over and appointed Mirzā Qavāmā his vizier. In 1237 (1821/22), Ḥosein ^{c}Ali Mirzā Farmān-Farmā appointed his son Najaf Qoli Mirzā governor of Kuh-e Giluya, who married a daughter of Mirzā Manṣur Khān and appointed his father-in-law vizier. The next year, however, the vizier was deposed and sent to Shiraz with his family. In 1249 (1833/34), he was again governor of Kuh-e Giluya and died in 1255 (1839/40) at Behbehān. Then his son, Mirzā Solṭān Moḥammad Khān, became governor and appointed Mirzā Qavāmā vizier. Later on, a quarrel arose between the two. In 1265 (1848/49), ^{c}Abbās Qoli Khān-e Lārijāni came to Behbehān and sent Mirzā Qavāmā to Tehran, while Mirzā Solṭān Moḥammad Khān was removed from the governorship; Mirzā Qavāmā died in Tehran.

36. His appointment to Kuh-e Giluya and Behbehān is mentioned above, p. 290.

no attention to Mirzā Solṭān Moḥammad Khān and spent the state revenue on preparing the defense works and to pay his soldiers (noukarhā). Mirzā Solṭān Moḥammad Khān was not pleased with these measures and wrote a letter of complaint to Shiraz. Then Mirzā Qavāmā repaired the fortress of Nārin at Behbehān, which lies in the outskirts of the town, and stored sufficient provisions there. He occupied the districts of Rām-hormoz and Falāḥi and repaired the fortress of Cham Mollā,[37] which belongs to Rāmhormoz. There he stored plenty of provisions; and his harmony with Mirzā Solṭān Moḥammad Khān turned to enmity. Every day groups of both sides fought each other, and every day 2 or 3 people were killed. Since the Arab sheikhs of the Sharifāt tribe[38] were on Mirzā Qavāmā's side and did not obey Mirzā Eḥteshām od-Doula, the governor of ᶜArabestān,[39] the governor ordered Soleimān Khān Sehām od-Doula Armani, nephew of Manuchehr Khān Moᶜtamad od-Doula, to settle the affairs of Falāḥi and the Sharifāt Arabs. Because Mirzā Qavāmā was the refuge of the Sharifāt Arabs and Sehām od-Doula was not ordered to ruin the former, he took counsel with the ministers. Having obtained the permission of the ministers, he started his inquiries with the Sharifāt Arabs. In order to offer them protection, Mirzā Qavāmā went with 1,000 horsemen and infantry to the fortress of Cham Mollā, which lies on the bank of the Kordestān River and is encircled by water on three sides. He sent his grown-up son Mirzā Moḥammad Reżā Khān with a group of horsemen and infantry as reinforcements to the Arabs. When they arrived opposite Sehām od-Doula's camp, a fierce battle was fought; however, Mirzā Moḥammad Reżā Khān was defeated and Mirzā Qavāmā came to the assistance of his son from the fortress of Cham Mollā. He gathered

37. It was 8 parasangs southeast of Rāmhormoz, see *FNN*, II, 216.

38. The Sharifāt Arabs were farmers and cattle breeders and lived at Bandar Hendeyān, on the banks of the Zeidun River, see *FNN*, II, 331.

39. That is, the province of Khuzestān.

together the defeated men and put up his camp opposite Sehām od-Doula. Then Sehām od-Doula ordered ʿAli Reżā Khān-e Bakhteyāri to undertake a night attack on the fortress of Cham Mollā. The Bakhteyāri horsemen crossed the Kordestān River and lost several men who drowned; then they laid siege to the fortress. Although the people of the fortress fought fiercely, killing 10 Bakhteyāri horsemen with musket shots and wounding 25 of them, the Bakhteyāris did not slacken but captured the fortress by force. They destroyed the defense works and seized several small cannons. A big cannon which had been in the fortress since the times of Nāder Shāh, was knocked to pieces, as its transport would have been too difficult. After the capture of the fortress of Cham Mollā, Mirzā Qavāmā, and Mirzā Moḥammad Reżā Khān returned with their horsemen and infantry without delay from Kuh-e Giluya to Behbehān and stayed in the fortress of Nārin. Sehām od-Doula entered Behbehān with 4,000 or 5,000 horsemen and infantry after Mirzā Qavāmā and laid siege to the fortress of Nārin. Mirzā Solṭān Moḥammad Khān, governor of Behbehān, who was not pleased with the behavior of Mirzā Qavāmā, put himself with his auxiliary forces from Kuh-i Giluya under the command of Sehām od-Doula. The siege lasted four months, every day the defense works were shattered by cannon balls. As Mirzā Qavāmā was finding the going difficult, he made his escape one midnight and took refuge in the fortress of Golāb, 7 parasangs south of Behbehān.[40] And Sehām od-Doula destroyed the fortress of Nārin at Behbehān. When he heard of Mirzā Qavāmā's situation, he proceeded without delay to the fortress of Golāb in the company of Mirzā Solṭān Moḥammad Khān and laid siege to that sky-high fortress. And a man named Morād ʿAli, a relative of the castellan (kalāntar) of the fortress of Golāb, was taken prisoner by the horsemen of the camp as he was returning from the tribes of Mamassani to the fortress. When they identified him, he was

40. See above, p. 248, note 53.

brought before Sehām od-Doula, who said: "Your salvation is to show a way to capture the fortress!" Morād ᶜAli complied with this demand and sent somebody to the fortress informing his relatives of his situation. Several of them came to the camp and remained there as hostages. Morād ᶜAli promised that the fortress would be surrendered without difficulty if Mirzā Solṭān Moḥammad Khān went there at midnight. Accordingly, Morād ᶜAli proceeded to the fortress and made good his promise. And Mirzā Qavāmā made his escape to the district of Mamassani. On his way he was taken prisoner by Lārijāni horsemen, who at this time were coming from Shiraz under the command of ᶜAbbās Qoli Khān Sardār-e Lārijāni. ᶜAbbās Qoli Khān ordered him to be honored and brought him to Behbehān. [307] Then Mirzā Solṭān Moḥammad Khān arrested the governor and sent him from Behbehān to Shiraz, thence he was sent to Tehran, where he was put in prison. Three months later, ᶜAbbās Qoli Khān by order of the grand visier arrested Mirzā Qavāmā and sent him to Tehran, where he was put in prison and died of cholera. Two months later ᶜAbbās Qoli Khān arrested Mirzā Solṭān Moḥammad Khān and sent him to Shiraz. Now ᶜAbbās Qoli Khān was the independent governor of Kuh-e Giluya and Behbehān. He entrusted each district to one of the Lārijāni officers and acted himself as administrator (ᶜāmil). And Moḥammad Bāqer Khān, son of Moḥammad Shafi ᶜKhān, alderman of the Jāvi tribe, one of the four tribes of Kuh-e Giluya,[41] did not comply with ᶜAbbās Qoli Khān's orders. For some time Moḥammad Bāqer Khān behaved in this manner. Then ᶜAbbās Qoli Khān sent Lārijāni soldiers and horsemen and auxiliatory forces from Kuh-e Giluya, and they captured the fortress of Poli, 9 parasangs east of Behbehān,[42] the camp of Moḥammad Bāqer

41. The Mamassani group of Lors comprised these four tribes: Bakash, Jāvidi (Jāvi), Doshmanzeyāri, and Rostam, see above, p. 268, note 127.

42. About 30 miles northwest of Behebhān, on the sourthern outskirts of the Kuh-e Nil (Qalᶜa-ye Pili on the 1:500,000 map).

Khān. They sent the latter in fetters to Behbehān, where he was tried and executed.

POLICE STATIONS ESTABLISHED IN THE PERSIAN CITIES AND TOWNS. That year a royal decree was issued to the effect that in Tehran and the other cities of Persia police stations were to be established at the main thoroughfares and that to each station several soldiers were to be assigned as guards.

THE SHAH TRAVELS TO ESFAHAN. The New Year fell on Friday, 17th Jomādi I of the year 1267.[43] The shah celebrated the feast after the model of Faridun and Jam.[44] The viziers, emirs, and commanders of the detachments were ordered to accompany the shah on his journey of Esfahan. The court departed from Tehran on 1st Rajab,[45] marched by way of Qazvin, Sāva, and Borujerd and arrived at Esfahan on 15th Ramażān.[46] On 22d Ramażān,[47] Firuz Mirzā Noṣrat od-Doula, governor of the province of Fārs, and Moḥammad Qoli Khān, ilbegi of the tribes of Fārs, arrived at Esfahan and were granted royal favors beyond the usual. On 25th Shavvāl,[48] the court departed from Esfahan, marched by way of Kāshān and Qom and arrived in Tehran on 8th Dhu'l-Ḥejja.[49]

THE GOVERNOR OF FĀRS SETTLES AFFAIRS IN BEHBEHĀN AND MAMASSANI. Noṣrat od-Doula proceeded through the district of Sarḥadd-e Shesh Nāḥeya and the districts of Kuh-e Giluya and Deh Dasht to Behbehān and conferred the governorship of Behbehān upon Mehr ᶜAli Khān Shojāᶜ ol-Mulk. Having settled the affairs of those regions and of the district of

43. March 20, 1851 (should be March 21).

44. First remark of this kind in this chronicle in connection with the New Year feast. It seems that the Qājār dynasty was more and more seen in the light of Persian legendary history of pre-Islamic times.

45. May 2, 1851. 46. July 14, 1851. 47. July 21, 1851.

48. August 23, 1851. 49. October 4, 1851.

Mamassani, he returned to Shiraz by way of Kāzerun at the end of Dhu'l-Ḥejja of that year.[50]

In the same month of Dhu'l-Ḥejja, Mirzā Moḥammad Taqi Kāshāni with the pen name Sepehr completed his *Tārikh-e Qājāriya.*[51]

A NEW PRIME MINISTER APPOINTED. On 18th Moḥarram of the year 1268,[52] Mirzā Moḥammad Taqi Khān-e Farāhāni Amir-e Atābeg, vizier of the Persian empire, was removed from his office and assigned Kāshān as his abode. His illustrious office was conferred upon Mirzā Āqā Khān-e Nuri E^c^temād od-Doula, vizier of the army (vazir-e lashgar). He was called "Grand Vizier" (vazir-e a^c^ẓam).

FIRUZ MIRZĀ SETTLES AFFAIRS IN THE SOUTHERN DISTRICTS OF FĀRS. In the month of Ṣafar of that year,[53] Firuz Mirzā Noṣrat od-Doula departed from Shiraz to settle the affairs of the southern districts of Fārs. He marched by way of Firuzābād and then through the districts of Ṣimekān, Qir va-Kārzin, Afzor, Khonj, Galladār, and Bikh-e Fāl in Lārestān and entered Lār. He arrested Mirzā Hāshem-e ^c^Evażi-ye Lāri, who had risen in rebellion some time ago, did not care for the governor of Lārestān, and put him in prison. In the month of Rabi^c^ II,[54] Noṣrat od-Doula left Lār for Bandar ^c^Abbās. That town had been in the possession of the people of Masqaṭ for many years;[55] each year they had paid taxes amounting to 5,000 toman to the governor of Fārs. The governor entered the districts of Sab^c^a (maḥāll-e Sab^c^a), which lies near Bandar ^c^Abbās, with two detachments, one detachment of Arab soldiers from Fārs under the command of Reżā Qoli Khān-e ^c^Arab, and one detachment of Qashqā'i soldiers under the command of Loṭfi Khān, son of the

50. About October 25, 1851.
51. See above, p. xvii.
52. November 13, 1851.
53. Began on November 26, 1851.
54. Began on January 24, 1852.
55. To be precise, since 1794, see above, p. 134, note 149.

ilkhāni, Moḥammad ᶜAli Khān-e Qashqā'i. Two days after his arrival he executed Mirzā Hāshem-e ᶜEvażi in the town of Forg. The latter's body was quartered and each part sent to one of the officials. Noṣrat od-Doula stayed on in the town of Ṭārom and sent two detachments of soldiers with 2 pieces of artillery to Bandar ᶜAbbās. Upon negotiations a certain sum was added to the taxes to be paid, and Sheikh Seif Masqaṭi[56] was confirmed in the governorship of Bandar ᶜAbbās and its dependencies as before. In the month of Jomādi II,[57] Noṣrat od-Doula returned to Shiraz.

BĀBIS' ATTEMPT AT THE SHAH'S LIFE. The New Year fell on 28th Jomādi I of that year.[58] The shah celebrated the feast. One remarkable event occurred when the heretical sect of the Bābis, who consider themselves as community of Mirzā Reżā Bazzāz-e Shirāzi, rose in rebellion in Tehran. They assembled in order to form a plot; in their strange imagination which sprang from stupidity and ignorance they thought of becoming leaders and seizing power. They convened a meeting in the house of Soleimān Khān, son of Yaḥyā Khān Mir Ākhur-e Tabrizi, who was enjoying the profits of this God-given state. [308] Having entered into an agreement, they selected 12 people to sacrifice their lives and to proceed to the vicinity of Neyāvarān-e Shemrān near Tehran.[59] As soon as an opportunity presented itself, they were to make an attempt on the shah's life. On Sunday, 28th Shavvāl of that year,[60] two hours after sunrise, when the shah

56. The name *Seif* (meaning "sword") is very frequent in Oman; this is perhaps Seif, son of Badr, a cousin of Seiyed Saᶜid and Seiyed Sālem. However, in this case one should expect him to bear the title *Seiyed*, not *Sheikh*, see Zambaur, *Manuel*, p. 129, and Miles, *Persian Gulf*, Index (Seif ibn Badr is not mentioned there). According to Miles, *ibid.*, p. 351, the governor was Seif ibn Nebhān; he was not called back to Masqaṭ by the Imam, as stated below, p. 304 but expelled from Bandar ᶜAbbās by the Persians.

57. Began on March 23, 1852.

58. March 21, 1852.

59. 2 miles east of Tajrish (9 miles north of Tehran), see *Farhang*, I, 226.

60. August 15, 1852.

had mounted his horse to hunt and relax and was riding through the narrow streets of Neyāvarān accompanied by a number of grooms on foot, 3 of the 12 Bābis made a rush for the shah and approached like people who have suffered an injustice. They bowed and came near, putting their hands into their pockets and under their armpits like people who are going to present a petition. The shah stopped his horse in order to inquire into their complaint. When they had come near, they "complained about injustice" and attacked the shah from three sides. Instead of a petition they produced fire-spitting pistols from their armpits, and one of them rushed forward and discharged his pistol at the shah. The ball and shot missed the target and did no visible harm. Then another of them discharged his pistol, and again the shah remained under the protection of God; the chief groom (shāṭer bāshi) and one of the servants rushed upon both of them with dagger and knife and killed them with several thrusts. Then the third Bābi discharged his pistol at the shah; the horse shied, the shah got out of the firing line and the bullet failed. Ten grains of shot penetrated the skin of the shah's shoulder blade and stuck without wounding the bone. When the grooms arrested this coward and the shah ordered him to be spared for the inquiry another of the 12 Bābis was arrested. When news of the occurrence spread in Tehran, the people grew restless; they calmed down when news gradually arrived of the shah's being safe and sound. When the 2 arrested Bābis were put on trial, it became known that 70 or more Bābis were assembled in Soleimān Khān's house and that they had prepared weapons for the revolt. Then a group of emirs and nobles went to that house and arrested Soleimān Khān and 12 Bābis. The rest of the Bābis made their escape. They were arrested one by one and punished in accordance with their plot. Decrees of the Sharia courts were issued to the effect that the Bābis were to be executed;[61] Soleimān Khān

61. According to Islamic law, death sentence could not be passed except where the delinquents were convicted of defection from the Islamic

was made a candlestick (sham[c] ājin), that is to say, holes were made in the flesh of his body and candles stuck into them and lit; then he was taken round the city and the bazaar, until the candles had burnt down. Then each of the Bābis was surrendered to a group of nobles, to different classes of the servants and craftsmen of the bazaar, and they executed them. Mollā Sheikh [c]Ali for example, one of the religious leaders of the Bābis, was handed over to the scholars and students of the religious sciences, and they put him to death.[62] The other Bābis were treated accordingly.

On 17th Dhu'l-Qa[c]da of that year,[63] the shah proceeded from Neyāvarān-e Shemrān to Tehran and brightened the outlook of all the people of Persia.

FIRUZ MIRZĀ SETTLES AFFAIRS AT BUSHEHR AND SURROUNDINGS. In the month of Rabi[c] I of the year 1269,[64] Noṣrat od-Doula, governor of the province of Fārs, departed from Shiraz to settle the affairs of the districts of Dashtestān and Dashti, he marched to Borāzjān by way of Kāzerun and Khesht. After settling the affairs of the districts of Dashtestān, he spent several days at Bandar Bushehr. Then he left Bushehr to settle the affairs of the district (maḥāll) of Dashti. He stayed for a while in the district of Dashti and established order there.

---

faith; otherwise, the normal penalty for murder was payment of blood money (or blood revenge, which was, however, officially not allowed). Therefore, in this case a decree of the Sharia court was issued declaring the delinquents enemies of the faith.

62. In Persian administrative practice, "solidarity groups," such as the inhabitants of a certain place or the members of a guild, not the individuals, were made responsible, for instance, for the payment of taxes. The same seems to apply in this case; on the other hand, the execution of criminals by particular groups was apt to prove their solidarity as a group towards the ruler.

63. September 2, 1852.

64. Began on December 13, 1852.

EARTHQUAKE IN SHIRAZ. In the night of 25th Rajab of that year,[65] on 15th Ordibehesht,[66] when the sun was 13° 46′ in the Zodiacal sign of Taurus,[67] about one hour before sunrise, a heavy earthquake occured at Shiraz. Several hundred houses were ruined and several thousand damaged. Several thousand people died under the ruined buildings. Most of the mosques and madrasahs were destroyed, all of them needed repair.

TAHMĀSP MIRZĀ MO'EIYED OD-DOULA APPOINTED GOVERNOR OF FĀRS. In the month of Shacbān,[68] Noṣrat od-Doula returned by way of Firuzābād; he did not enter Shiraz but stayed in the Bāgh-e Nou in the shadow of the trees and the pavilion. He asked to be dismissed from the governorship of Fārs and asked the ministers for permission to go to Tehran. This he demanded with great perseverance. To close the accounts, he brought Mirzā Abu'l-Ḥasan Khān Moshir ol-Molk, the vizier of Fārs, with him to Tehran. The governorship of Fārs was conferred upon Mo'eiyed od-Doula Ṭahmāsp Mirzā, son of the late Moḥammad cAli Mirzā Kermānshāhi, son of the late Fatḥ cAli Shāh. In the middle of the month of Dhu'l-Ḥejja of the year 1269,[69] the latter entered Shiraz. He entrusted the vizierate of Fārs to Mirzā Moḥammad Taqi-ye Āshteyāni. On behalf of the ministers he gave the sum of 5,000 toman to the aldermen for the repair of the thoroughfares and streets of Shiraz.

QUARREL WITH THE IMAM OF MASQAṬ ABOUT THE POSSESSION OF BANDAR cABBĀS

PERSIAN ATTEMPT TO OCCUPY BANDAR cABBĀS FAILS. The New Year fell on 21st Jomādi II of the year 1270.[70] During

65. May 3, 1853.
66. Second month (April 22–May 21) of the Persian solar year, which begins on Nouruz (March 21).
67. The exact position is given because of the belief in the influence of the stars on the events in the sublunar sphere.
68. Began on May 10, 1853.
69. About September 20, 1853.
70. March 21, 1854.

the previous year Seiyed Soveini, son of Seiyed Sa^c^id Khān, the Imam of Masqaṭ,[71] summoned Sheikh Seif Masqaṭi, governor of Bandar ^c^Abbās, to Masqaṭ, and the latter died upon his arrival at Masqaṭ. Since Bandar ^c^Abbās was without a governor, Firuz Mirzā Noṣrat od-Doula sent several musketeers from Lārestān with two groups of soldiers to protect Bandar ^c^Abbās. Haji Moḥammad Raḥim Khān-e Shirāzi, chief of the merchants (malek ot-tojjār) who had lived as a merchant in Bombay [309] for many years and was now staying in Tehran, rented the custom house of Bandar ^c^Abbās, Shamil, and Mināb[72] from the agents of the Divan, took over the governorship of those regions, and arrived at Bandar ^c^Abbās. With the assistance of the soldiers and musketeers of the garrison, he established his rule. However, Sheikh ^c^Abd or-Raḥmān-e Qeshmi, a man of great wealth, deceived Haji Moḥammad Raḥim Khān, saying that Bandar ^c^Abbās did not need soldiers and musketeers. Thereupon the soldiers and musketeers were dismissed and marched off. After several days Seiyed Soveini, Imam of Masqaṭ, sent Sheikh Sa^c^id, the nephew of Sheikh Seif, the former governor of Bandar ^c^Abbās, to Bandar ^c^Abbās. Upon his arrival, he pretended for the space of several days to be the deputy of Haji Moḥammad Raḥim Khān. Then, one midnight, he brought the khān on board a ship and imprisoned him in the house of Sheikh ^c^Abd or-Raḥmān-e Qeshmi on the island of Qeshm, which lies several parasangs southeast of Bandar ^c^Abbās. Then Sheikh Sa^c^id Masqaṭi and Sheikh ^c^Abd or-Raḥmān Khān were independent governors.

71. Soveini acceded to the throne in 1273:1856/57 only, see Zambaur, *Manuel*, p. 129.

72. Shamil lies about 45 miles northeast of Bandar ^c^Abbās, Mināb 50 miles east of Bandar ^c^Abbās. Thus Moḥammad Raḥim Khān secured for himself not only the customs of the harbor but also those of the overland trade from Bandar ^c^Abbās to the north. The appointment of the Bombay merchant is typical for the combination of government office and commercial interests, which was a salient feature of later Qājār times.

BANDAR ᶜABBĀS CONQUERED BY PERSIAN TROOPS. That year Ṭahmāsp Mirzā Mo'eiyed od-Doula, governor of Fārs, was ordered to conquer Bandar ᶜAbbās and to liberate Haji Moḥammad Raḥim Khān. In the month of Ṣafar of the year 1271,[73] the governor appointed his son ᶜAbd ol-Bāqi Mirzā deputy governor of Fārs and left the latter back at Shiraz together with the vizier, Mirzā Moḥammad Taqi-ye Āshteyāni. He appointed Mirzā Bozorg Mostoufi-ye Dashtaki his procurator and departed from Shiraz with a big army and 4 pieces of artillery. He dispatched Reżā Qoli Khān, commander of the Arab and Bahārlu detachment, with 1 piece of artillery by way of Fasā, Dārāb, and Sabᶜa to capture the fortress of Kamiz,[74] which belongs to the district of Rudān and Aḥmadi and lies in the vicinity of the dependencies of Bandar ᶜAbbās; its chief (ra'is), Gholām Reżā-ye Aḥmadi had risen in revolt. Mo'eiyed od-Doula himself marched from Fasā to Dārāb. There he was entertained for several days by Mirzā Moḥammad ᶜAli Khān Nāẓem od-Doula, the governor of Jahrom and Dārāb, until the preparations for the campaign had been completed. Then Mo'eiyed od-Doula and the whole army departed from Dārāb and entered Lār. ᶜAli Reżā-ye Garāshi, the governor of Lārestān, gave him a befitting welcome. Mo'eiyed od-Doula spent some time at Lār and sent messengers and letters to Sheikh Seif Masqaṭi and Sheikh ᶜAbd or-Raḥmān-e Qeshmi. Seeing that this was of no use, he made up his mind to attack. Then he sent Naṣrollāh Khān Sartip, son of the late Mirzā Nabi Khān, the chief magistrate of the empire and former governor of Fārs, with the Golpāygān detachment and 1 piece of artillery and the arsenal and Prince Abu'l-Qāsem Khān, his son, to Bandar ᶜAbbās. He put them under the command of ᶜAbbās Khān-e Shirāzi, known as Hamadāni, maternal cousin of Mo'eiyed od-Doula, an efficient man.

73. Began on October 24, 1854.

74. In the dehestān of Rudān, 22 miles north of Mināb, see *Farhang*, VII, 329 seq.

Two days later he sent Loṭf ᶜAli Khān Sartip, son of Moḥammad ᶜAli Khān Ilkhāni, with the Qashqā'i detachment and a cannon after Naṣrollāh Khān. One dark night when the Golpāygān detachment was searching for an encampment on top of a hill, 0.5 parasang from Bandar ᶜAbbās, the Masqaṭ Arabs suddenly fired their muskets at the soldiers and killed several of them. Although the soldiers had marched a distance of 6 parasangs, they were not exhausted and fought until the following night. They took away 14 breastworks from the Arabs and killed a group of them. When it began to grow dark, all the officers and soldiers remained in their positions and advanced on Bandar ᶜAbbās step by step. At daybreak they found themselves at the edge of the ditch of the town, erected breastworks at the same spot, and settled down behind them. News of this occurrence was sent to Mo'eiyed od-Doula within forty-eight hours at Lār, over a distance of 30 parasangs. Two days after this battle Loṭf ᶜAli Khān and the Qashqā'i detachment joined the Golpāygān detachment at Bandar ᶜAbbās. The fighting at the edge of the ditch of Bandar ᶜAbbās went on for six full days. The seventh day the flower of the army made up their mind to capture the town, and they ordered the trumpets to be blown and the drums to be beaten. In the first phase, the Golpāygān detachment assaulted the Maghrebi Gate[75] and took several towers from the Arabs. The Qashqā'i detachment attacked with much noise from the other side and occupied several other towers. Then all the towers were occupied by the royal troops. Now the gates were opened, and the whole army entered the town and took to killing and plundering. Sheikh ᶜAbd or-Raḥmān and Sheikh Saᶜid and the rest of the Arabs went on board a ship, sailed off to the island of Qeshm, and remained there. Bandar ᶜAbbās was occupied by the victorious army. After this victory a Persian trading vessel passing by Masqaṭ was stopped by Seiyed Soveini. When news of this victory arrived in Tehran, the

75. That is, the "Western Gate" of Bandar ᶜAbbās.

ministers [310] conferred upon Mo'eiyed od-Doula the Order of the Effigy of the Shah, which was studded with jewels. And all the officers of the victorious army were granted orders and robes of honor, according to their rank.

ṬAHMĀSP MIRZĀ RETURNS TO SHIRAZ. As the weather grew hot and the affairs of those districts had been settled, Mo'eiyed od-Doula entrusted the governorship of Bandar ᶜAbbās to ᶜAbbās Khān, his maternal cousin, left 200 soldiers, 1,000 musketeers from Lār, 2 cannons and the arsenal at Bandar ᶜAbbās and returned to Shiraz on 16th Shaᶜbān.[76] He brought Moṣṭafā Khān-e Bastaki, whom he had taken prisoner, to Shiraz. As ᶜAbd ol-Bāqi Mirzā, the deputy governor, during Mo'eiyed od-Doula's absence had displayed great zeal in guarding the town and making safe the roads and the streets, he was granted royal favors and a robe of honor.

Upon his arrival at Shiraz, Mo'eiyed od-Doula ordered the reconstruction of streets and shrines and the renovation of the mosques to be taken in hand. Within three or four months the damages which had been caused everywhere by the earthquake[77] were being repaired.

And at the end of this year,[78] Āqā Mirzā Moḥammad-e Fasā'i grew very uneasy of the governor's officials; he went to Tehran and took refuge at the shrine of Emāmzāda ᶜAbd ol-ᶜAzim. One and a half years later he returned to Shiraz. During his absence the governorship of Fasā was entrusted to Mojtahed Mirzā Abu'l-Ḥasan Khān, brother of Āqā Mirzā Moḥammad. The former divided the regions (nawāḥi) of Fasā and entrusted each division to the chief of the landowners (ra'is-e arbāb-dārān).

BANDAR ᶜABBĀS LOST AND RECONQUERED. As Seiyed Saᶜid Khān, Imam of Masqaṭ, had several years ago entrusted the governorship of Masqaṭ to Seiyed Soveini, his eldest son, he

76. May 4, 1855. 77. See above, p. 305. 78. That is, spring 1855.

himself used to stay in the coastal area of Africa[79] which he had recently occupied. Having heard of the occurrences at Bandar ᶜAbbās and its dependencies, he returned immediately from the coast to Masqaṭ. As the summer drew near—the heat at Bandar ᶜAbbās resembles the heat of the Barhut Valley,[80] nay, it is like that on the first floor of Hell—and the soldiers and musketeers of the garrison at Bandar ᶜAbbās either died or ran away, the Imam of Masqaṭ ordered his eldest son, Seiyed Soveini, to capture Bandar ᶜAbbās. The latter put 3,000 Arab musketeers from ᶜOmān, who considered Bandar ᶜAbbās a summer camp, on board a ship and sent them off. Upon their arrival in the bay of Bandar ᶜAbbās the governor, ᶜAbbās Khān, and the rest of the soldiers and musketeers of the garrison fled immediately, and Seiyed Soveini entered Bandar ᶜAbbās without difficulty. Faridun Khān-e Tavalloli, who had been sent to Bandar ᶜAbbās as an officer in charge of over 100 Shirazi cavalry, arrived at Shiraz with 3 or 4 sick horsemen and reported what had happened. Mo'eiyed od-Doula decided to take measures and ordered his son ᶜAbd ol-Bāqi Mirzā to conquer Bandar ᶜAbbās. In the month of Ṣafar of the year 1272,[81] he sent his son to Bandar ᶜAbbās by way of Fasā, Dārāb, and Sabᶜa, together with 2 detachments of Arab and Hamadāni soldiers and 4 pieces of artillery under the command of ᶜAbdollāh Khān Ṣārem od-Doula Qaraguzlu and Režā Qoli Khān-e ᶜArab. By order of the ministers, Moḥammad Ḥasan Khān Sardār-e Erevani, governor of the province of Kerman, sent his son ᶜAbd ol-Ḥosein Khān

79. Navāḥe-ye savāḥel-e Afriqa, as the eastern coast of Africa was called by the Moslem geographers; Seiyed Saᶜid, since 1832, used to stay on the island of Zanzibar, see Miles, *Persian Gulf*, p. 333, which, however, does not fit the description in this passage. The residence in question might be Mogadishu, now the capital of Somali.

80. A valley in Hadhramout, with the Bi'r Barhut ("Well of Barhut"), according to early Islamic tradition the worst well on earth, haunted by the souls of infidels, see EI² I, s.v. Barhūt (G. Rentz).

81. Began on October 13, 1855.

Mir Panj and Emām Qoli Khān and Rostam Khān Sarhang and 2 detachments of Qaraguzlu Hamadāni scouts (mokhber) and 300 loads of grain as provisions from Kerman to Bandar ᶜAbbās. They marched through the districts of Isin and Tāzyān[82] and joined the troops of ᶜAbd ol-Bāqi Mirzā. At the beginning of Rabiᶜ I,[83] they put up their camp 0.5 parasang from Bandar ᶜAbbās. They sent Seiyed Soveini a message that they would not attack him and that he should leave Bandar ᶜAbbās and return to Masqaṭ. However, Seiyed Soveini was enticed by the money, the men and the strength of the defense works of Bandar ᶜAbbās and paid no attention to the message. He placed 26 large and small cannons which he had brought from Masqaṭ on the rampart and towers, positioned 4 big vessels with 20 cannons each opposite Bandar ᶜAbbās and prepared for battle. On the 8th of that month,[84] ᶜAbd ol-Bāqi Mirzā ordered the assault on the town. From sunrise to sunset he made vain efforts. As he was going back to the camp a soldier lost his way; seeing himself in front of the enemy's breastwork, he started to run and a group of soldiers who saw him running followed him and ran too, assuming that an attack was going on. When ᶜAbd ol-Bāqi Mirzā saw this, he too assumed that it was an attack and hurried up to the soldiers. From the fortifications of Bandar ᶜAbbās the Arabs fired with cannons and muskets. The fighting went on until four o'clock in the evening, and the Isin Gate was occupied. The Arabs who were guarding the gate and the rampart made their escape and ran to the Dutch building which belongs to the Dutch Company and is like the citadel of Bandar ᶜAbbās. The soldiers who followed at their heels killed a number of them and wounded others. Two pieces of artillery and a European ammunition carriage were seized by Rostam Sarhang. The soldiers surrounded the Dutch building on three sides, and Seiyed

82. Both towns lie about 9 miles northwest of Bandar ᶜAbbās; accordingly, the troops passed Bandar ᶜAbbās in the north.

83. Began on November 11, 1855.

84. November 18, 1855.

Soveini came out of the gate of the building with a group of his special servants and went from the building, which is near the sea, to his ship, where he was in safety. About 300 Arabs were enclosed in the Dutch building. The next day the victorious army occupied the building by force and killed all 300 men, except a few who made their escape to the sea and were drowned. More than 3,000 men of the army of Masqaṭ were killed. [311] The Arabs who were staying at Shamil and Mināb took Aḥmad Shāh Khān, the mayor of Mināb, to the island of Qeshm; then ᶜAbd ol-Bāqi Mirzā appointed Raᵓis Moḥammad Ṣāleḥ-e Minābi mayor of those regions. When by order of Mo'eiyed od-Doula 400 Tangestāni musketeers who where famous for their toughness and used to the heat arrived across the sea under the command of Bāqer Khān-e Tangestāni at Bandar ᶜAbbās, ᶜAbd ol-Bāqi Mirzā and the soldiers departed from Bandar ᶜAbbās in the month of Ramażān[85] and entered Lār by way of Bastak.[86] There they saw themselves in the promised Paradise and said: "Ask people in Hell, [and they will tell you] that Purgatory is Paradise!" When news of this arrived in Tehran, the shah sent ᶜAbd ol-Bāqi Mirzā a robe of honor, granted him the title "Sartip-e avval" and appointed him governor of Lārestān and Bandar ᶜAbbās.

ṬAHMĀSP MIRZĀ APPOINTS HIS SON GOVERNOR OF KUH-E GILUYA AND BEHBEHĀN. In the same year Mo'eiyed od-Doula conferred the governorship of Kuh-e Giluya and Behbehān upon his son Loṭf ᶜAli Mirzā, a youth of about fifteen. Mirzā Bozorg Mostoufi, a Seiyed of the illustrious family Dashtaki at Shiraz, was appointed the former's vizier.

FRENCH AMBASSADOR ARRIVES AT BUSHEHR. The same year the French ambassador residing in Tehran arrived at

85. Began on May 6, 1856.

86. They took the southern road of the two which lead from Bandar ᶜAbbās to Lār; normally it would have been the northern road, see Gabriel, *Die Erforschung Persiens*, Table facing p. 72.

Bushehr.[87] ᶜAli Khān Noṣrat al-Molk Sartip, son of Rostam Khān-e Qaraguzlu, was sent from Tehran to welcome the ambassador and arrived at Shiraz. Mo'eiyed od-Doula sent Mirzā ᶜAli Moḥammad Khān-e Nuri, chief registrar of the army, to Bushehr to welcome the ambassador. Then the ambassador departed from Bushehr for Shiraz in the company of the two men mentioned above and, on his way, was welcomed and entertained everywhere by the governors and mayors. ᶜAli Khān Noṣrat al-Molk met the ambassador in the vicinity of Kāzerun. Thence they traveled together and entered Shiraz with all honors on 6th Ramażān.[88] The ambassador was welcomed by Mo'eiyed od-Doula and spent several days at Shiraz with all honors. Then he departed for Tehran together with Mehmāndār ᶜAli Khān Noṣrat al-Molk.

THE IMAM OF MASQAṬ CONFIRMED IN THE POSSESSION OF BANDAR ᶜABBĀS. The birthday of ᶜAli and the New Year both fell on 13th Rajab of the year 1272.[89] The shah celebrated both feasts suitably. On escaping Bandar ᶜAbbās, Seiyed Soveini had come to Masqaṭ. Then Seiyed Saᶜid Khān, Imam of Masqaṭ, realized that it was impossible to maintain the possession of Bandar ᶜAbbās and its dependencies by force; accordingly, he was ready for negotiations. He sent for Haji ᶜAbd ol-Moḥammad Malek ot-Tojjār-e Bushehri[90] and pointed out to him:

The trading vessels of the merchants in the ports of Fārs cannot avoid sailing by way of Masqaṭ. I shall inevitably seize the vessels, the money and the merchandise at Masqaṭ, as long as Bandar ᶜAbbās is not in my possession. This will cause harm to the custom houses in the ports and losses of merchandise. The Persian empire cannot exercise any power on

87. The famous Joseph Arthur Comte de Gobineau (1816–82); he was to stay in Persia for three years, see also the Bibliography at the end of this book.

88. May 11, 1856. 89. March 20, 1856 (should be March 21).

90. He was a prominent merchant of Bushehr with trading relations to Oman.

Masqaṭ as long as it has no warships. It will take several years to have warships ready.[91] The best thing you can do is to persuade the Persian ministers to leave Bandar ᶜAbbās to me as before. I shall pay the agents of the governor of Fārs each year the double rent (muqāṭaᶜa), even more.

Then Seiyed Saᶜid, Imam of Masqaṭ, upon the advice of Haji ᶜAbd ol-Moḥammad Malek at-Tojjār-e Bushehri, sent Sheikh ᶜAbdollāh Masqaṭi to Tehran with a large string of pearls, several Arab horses from Najd, muskets overlaid with gold, and a humble petition written in friendly terms. Upon the latter's arrival at Bushehr, Haji ᶜAbd ol-Moḥammad sent a separate letter, containing benevolent wishes for the empire, the prosperity of the subjects, and to the ministers in Tehran, with one of his trustworthy men who arrived in Tehran after Sheikh ᶜAbdollāh Masqaṭi. After Sheikh ᶜAbdollāh's and Haji ᶜAbd ol-Moḥammad-e Bushehri's departure from Masqaṭ, the Imam of Masqaṭ, reflecting upon the negotiations, sent Haji Moḥammad ᶜAli, known as "Tājer-e Kabāb,"[92] vizier of Masqaṭ and the mainland of ᶜOmān and the Imam's confidant, to Mirzā Āqā Khān, grand vizier of Persia, with a suitable gift, and this envoy departed for Bushehr. Again by mediation of Haji ᶜAbd ol-Moḥammad the Imam's petition and desire was submitted to the court. The grand vizier submitted Seiyed Saᶜid's petition to the court; it was accepted and a treaty containing 16 articles was concluded.

Copy of the treaty (qarār-nāma) by which Seiyed Saᶜid, Imam of Masqaṭ, was appointed governor of Bandar ᶜAbbās:

In accordance with the orders and permission of the dignitaries of the empire, the governorship of Bandar ᶜAbbās and its dependencies,

91. Since Nāder Shāh, no efforts had been made to establish a Persian naval force in the Gulf, see above, p. 32, note 143. The only remembrance of Nāder Shāh's unsuccessful attempt to establish a naval base at Bushehr was the title *Daryābegi* ("Sealord") which was traditionally bestowed upon the governor of that port.

92. "Kabab merchant," probably a nickname, *kabab* being a dish of roasted meat.

which are in the possession of the Persian empire, has been conferred upon the agents of Seiyed Saᶜid, Imam of Masqaṭ and ᶜOmān, on the basis of a treaty containing sixteen [16] articles:

1) The governor of Bandar ᶜAbbās, like the other governors, shall render to the governor of Fārs obedience.

2) [312] Each year he shall pay in two [2] installments: 1,200 toman of taxes, 2,000 toman as a peshkash for the grand vizier, 1,000 toman as a gift (peshkash) for the governor of Fārs, 1,000 toman as a gift (hadiya)[93] for Mehr ᶜAli Khān Shojāᶜ ol-Molk Nuri-ye Shirāzi.

3) He shall fill up the ditch around Bandar ᶜAbbās.

4) The governorship of Bandar ᶜAbbās shall be at the disposal of the Imam of Masqaṭ and the Imam's sons for the space of twenty [20] years. Then they shall restore in flourishing condition Bandar ᶜAbbās and dependencies to the Persian empire.

5) The flag of the empire shall remain at Bandar ᶜAbbās with several standard-bearers and a diplomatic representative (tadhkera-dār).

6) Those of the inhabitants of Bandar ᶜAbbās and its dependencies who have served the Persian empire for the past three [3] or four [4] years shall not be molested.

7) The governor of Bandar ᶜAbbās shall not extend the districts of Isin, Tāzyān, Bandar Khamir, Shamil, Mināb, and Jāshk[94] beyond the borders which were in the possession of the Imam of Masqaṭ at the time of the late Fatḥ ᶜAli Shāh.

8) When the governor (vāli) of the province of Fārs and the governor (ḥākem) of Lārestān proceed to the region of Bandar ᶜAbbās for hunting and recreation, the governor of Bandar ᶜAbbās shall welcome them as they are welcomed by the other governors of Fārs.[95]

9) If the governors of Fārs and Kerman send an army to settle the

93. For the difference between peshkash and hadiya see EI² III, s.v. Hiba (H. Busse).

94. According to this statement, the district of Bandar ᶜAbbās covered the whole coastal area from Khamir in the west (about 45 miles west of Bandar ᶜAbbās: *Farhang*, VII, 32: Bandar Khamirān) as far as Jāshk (140 miles southeast of Bandar ᶜAbbās). The most northern point was Shamil, which is about 30 miles from the coast.

95. That is, they must be given accommodation and provisions free of charge (soyursāt), see also above, p. 186, note 349.

affairs of Beluchistan,[96] the governor of Bandar ᶜAbbās shall not be negligent in delivering provisions and matériel necessary for the campaign. The expenditure shall be put down to the account of his yearly payments.

10) If the governor of Fārs complains about the governor of Bandar ᶜAbbās, the Imam of Masqaṭ shall remove the governor without excuse and appoint another governor.

11) If the subjects of Lārestān or Sabᶜa and other people move to the districts of Bandar ᶜAbbās to settle there, the governor of Bandar ᶜAbbās shall send them back to their homes as soon as he learns of this.[97]

12) This treaty has been concluded with Seiyed Saᶜid Khān and his sons. If somebody else seizes power at Masqaṭ, the Persian government will not be bound to him by this treaty.

13) So long as the districts of Bandar ᶜAbbās are in the possession of the Imām of Masqaṭ, no agent of any foreign power shall have permission to settle there, except in transit.

14) The Imam of Masqaṭ shall not have the right to transfer any districts of Bandar ᶜAbbās to foreign powers.

15) The title on vessels and Persian merchandise which pass through Masqaṭ shall be levied at Bandar ᶜAbbās, because they might sink or be burned on the way.

16) The belongings of Persian merchants which were confiscated in the last three [3] or four [4] years by Seiyed Soveini on the island of Qeshm, shall be handed over to Haji ᶜAbd ol-Moḥammad Malek ot-Tojjār; he, in turn, shall hand them over to the agents of the merchants.

Written on 20th Shaᶜbān of the year 1272.[98]

Copy of the letter of obligation (taᶜahhod-nāma) of Sheikh Saᶜid Masqaṭi:

96. The conquest of Belochestan was not completed until 1870, when the famous Persian-English Boundary Commission settled the boundary question between the Persian and English sphere of influence in that region.

97. This article aims at the nomad population of Fārs, which supplied a good deal of the military forces to the governor of Fārs and was, therefore, not allowed to leave the province. On the other hand, the sedentary population was by this article prevented from evading the paying of taxes to the authorities of Fārs by moving to Bandar ᶜAbbās.

98. April 26, 1856.

I, Sa^c^id ibn Aḥmad, governor of Bander ^c^Abbās, consider myself as a subject of the Persian empire. In my capacity as governor of Bandar ^c^Abbās and dependencies, which office has been conferred upon me, a servant of the Persian court, I shall be obliged to pay the installments in accordance with what I have promised, and I shall display zeal in fostering the prosperity of the subjects and the cultivation of the country. I will not undertake anything which is contrary to the opinion of the government. Written on 20th Sha^c^bān of the year 1272.

Seiyed Soveini and Seiyed Moḥammad, sons of the Imam of Masqaṭ, affixed their seals to the document, and on 11th Ramażān,[99] the citadel of Bandar ^c^Abbās was occupied by Sheikh Sa^c^id. Jn the 25th of that month,[100] Seiyed Sa^c^id Khān, Imam of Masqaṭ, arrived at Bandar ^c^Abbās, put his seal to the treaty and signed the letter of Sheikh Sa^c^id. The belongings of the merchants on the island of Qeshm were handed over to Haji ^c^Abd ol-Moḥammad without diminution. Seiyed Sa^c^id Khān, Imam of Masqaṭ, was happy about the acceptance of the 16 articles; however, he pointed out: "When Āqā Moḥammad Shāh conferred the governorship of Bandar ^c^Abbās upon my father, Seiyed Solṭān,[101] I conquered the islands of Qeshm and Hormoz and expelled the Banu Mo^c^in[102] from those two islands. I would be delighted if those two islands were entered in my name in the treaty." From this statement of the Imam of Masqaṭ, one can draw the conclusion that at that time he was at least ninety years of age. The Imam of Masqaṭ submitted an obedient and humble petition to the Qājār court and sent 12,000 toman in cash and other precious objects as a peshkash together with Seiyed ^c^Ali,

99. May 16, 1856.
100. May 30, 1856.
101. See above, p. 134, note 149.
102. Miles, *Persian Gulf*, writes "Beni Naeem" (the text has a clear "Bani Mo^c^in"). At the end of the eighteenth century, the Bani Mo^c^in (Beni Naeem) played an important part in the internal policy of Oman, see Miles, *ibid.*, p. 334.

one of his relatives,[103] and Sheikh ᶜAbdollāh Masqaṭi and Aḥmad Shāh Khān, the mayor of Mināb. He himself departed for Masqaṭ on 5th Shavvāl.[104] The envoys arrived at Shiraz by way of Bushehr and were put up in the house of Mehr ᶜAli Khān Shojāᶜ al-Molk. The next day Mo'eiyed od-Doula sent for them and tried to win their sympathies. They presented the gifts which the Imam of Masqaṭ had sent to Mo'eiyed od-Doula and ᶜAbd ol-Bāqi Mirzā, and the following day they departed for Tehran. Upon their arrival they presented the gifts and were granted royal favors. A royal decree with the bestowal of the Order of the Effigy of the Shah (neshān-e timthāl-e homāyun) was issued and sent to Masqaṭ. Seiyed Saᶜid Khān, the Imam of Masqaṭ, died in the month of Jomādī II of the following year,[105] at the age of more than ninety years.

APPOINTMENTS IN THE PROVINCE OF FĀRS. In the same year, Mirzā Abu'l Ḥasan Khān Moshir ol-Molk, who spent nearly three years in Tehran closing the accounts of [313] Noṣrat od-Doula Firuz Mirzā, the former governor of Fārs, brought his activities to an end and returned to Shiraz in the company of Mirzā Moḥammad-e Fasā'i.[106] Several months later he was appointed vizier of the province of Fārs.

That year the governorship of the districts of Dārāb, Jahrom, Qir va-Kārzin and Bidshehr was taken from Mirzā Moḥammad ᶜAli Khān Nāẓem ol-Molk and conferred upon Mirzā Naᶜim-e Nuri, chief registrar of the army, in addition to the latter's governorship of the district of Niriz.

And that year the governorship of Lāristān was entrusted to Jalāl od-Doula Mirzā, son of Mo'eiyed od-Doula. The latter's

103. Possibly ᶜAli ibn Saᶜid, who later on ruled Zanzibar (1307–10: 1890–93), see Bosworth, *The Islamic Dynasties*, p. 78.

104. June 9, 1856.

105. January/February 1857, see Zambaur, *Manuel*, p. 129.

106. He had gone to Tehran in 1271:1854/55, see above, p. 307.

office of deputy governor was conferred upon Moṣṭafā Qoli Khān-e Qaraguzlu Eᶜtemād os-Salṭana Mir Panj.

QUARREL BETWEEN LOR AND BAKHTEYĀRI TRIBES SETTLED. Also, Khodā Karam Khān-e Bavir Aḥmadi of Kuh-e Giluya with 2,000 cavalry and infantry assaulted the Bakhteyāri tribe in his vicinity and plundered the belongings of more than a thousand families; according to a statement of the Lors he carried away all the goods and chattels which he found. When the government heard ot this, Mo'eiyed od-Doula dispatched Āqā Mirzā Moḥammad-e Fasā'i, an efficient man and usually sent on all the difficult missions, to take away the booty from Khodā Karam Khān-e Bavir Aḥmadi and to punish him; 500 regular horsemen, 2 detachments of Qaraguzlu soldiers from Shiraz, and 1,000 men of auxiliary forces from Fasā were put under his command. At the beginning of autumn of that year[107] they marched off. Upon their arrival in the plain of Sarāb,[108] the Mamassani troops of Khodā Karam Khān presented themselves with their weapons before Āqā Mirzā Moḥammad, and Khodā Karam Khān set about restoring the belongings of the Bakhteyāris and gave his son as a hostage. Then he handed over the belongings worth nearly 5,000 toman to the chiefs of the Bakhteyāris and turned his enmity to friendship. By mediation of the Bakhteyāri khāns the punishment of Khodā Karam Khān was suspended.

NEW ATTEMPT TO ESTABLISH PERSIAN SUPREMACY OVER AFGHANISTAN AND ENGLISH INTERVENTION IN THE PERSIAN GULF

BUSHEHR OCCUPIED BY ENGLISH TROOPS UPON PERSIAN CAMPAIGN TO AFGHANISTAN. When in the month of Ṣafar of the year 1273,[109] the city of Herāt in Afghanistan was captured

107. Autumn 1856.
108. That is, Sarāb-e Bahrām, 30 miles north of Kāzerun.
109. Began on September 1, 1856.

by Ḥosām os-Salṭana Solṭān Morād Mirzā, the uncle of the shah, the English agents who were staying in all the towns of the Persian empire became angry and left the country; the English ambassador, too, left Tehran.[110] When Captain Jones, the English consul at Bushehr, received news that English warships had put to sea, he wrote, on 11th Rabiᶜ I of that year,[111] a letter to Mirzā Ḥasan ᶜAli Khān Daryābegi, governor of Bushehr, to the following effect: "Today I have been ordered by my government to leave Bushehr. I deposit in your house several pieces of furniture which would be too difficult to transport." The daryābegi complied with the demand, and the furniture was handed over. On the 17th of that month the consul took leave of the daryābegi and returned to his house. He hauled down the flag of his government, boarded ship, and left Bushehr. The inhabitants of Bushehr were confounded and regretted the occurrence. On the 21st of that month,[112] 3 English warships entered the bay, that is, the anchorage of Bushehr. Until 4th Rabiᶜ II,[113] 30 warships arrived in the bay of Bushehr and dropped anchor. Several other ships were sent to Basra and Baghdad to buy wheat, fodder, and sheep. The commander in chief of all the English warships was Outram.[114] The troops were composed of 2,270 gunners and soldiers from London, called "whiteskins," 3,400 Indian soldiers, 3,750 men of auxiliary forces and servants, 1,150 horses, and 450 oxen to draw the carriages. Of the aforementioned ships, 8 were steamships belonging to the government, and 7 steamships were rented

110. The English ambassador in question was Sir Justin Sheil (1803–71), who had been appointed MacNeill's successor in 1844, see *National Biography*, s.v. Sheil.

111. November 9, 1856. 112. November 19, 1856.

113. December 2, 1856.

114. Sir James Outram (1803–63), lieutenant general in the Indian army; he left Bombay on January 15, 1857, and arrived at Bushehr on January 27, see *National Biography*, s.v. Outram. For his personal account of the Persian campaign, see Bibliography at the end of this book.

from the merchants. Through this assembly a new town sprang up on the surface of the water. Since the English warships arrived without warning, the Persian government had no troops at its disposal for its defense, except Moḥammad ᶜAli Khān, commander (sartip) of the Qarācha Dāghi detachment,[115] who was staying at Bushehr with 2 or 3 groups of soldiers. On 5th Rabiᶜ II,[116] Moḥammad ᶜAli Khān died, and the soldiers were without leader. Then Rostam Khān, his brother, took over. Staying at Bushehr was Mahdi Khān, commander (sarhang) of the Nehāvandi detachment; however, he had no complete detachment at his disposal. Then Madhi Khān and the daryābegi sent Mo'eiyed od-Doula the following report: "The English troops are staying on steamships and sailships in the Bay of Bushehr, 1 parasang from the town, ready for battle. We have neither an army which deserves this name nor the permission of the government to wage war." Accordingly, Mo'eiyed od-Doula made preparations for battle and dispatched the ilkhāni of Fārs, Moḥammad Qoli Khān, and Loṭf ᶜAli Khān, commander of the Qashqā'i detachment, nephew of the ilkhāni, with 1 detachment of soldiers and 1,000 Qashqā'i horsemen and 4 pieces of artillery to the districts of Dashti; they were to stay in that region to be ready at the time they were needed. On 8th Rabi ᶜII,[117] Shojāᶜ ol-Molk marched from Shiraz to wage war with the English and put up his tent in the Bāgh-e Jahān-Nomā. The special detachment (khāṣṣa),[118] the fourth detachment, half of the Shirazi detachment,[119] 100 horsemen in the service of the Divan (gholām-e divāni),[120] 4 pieces of artillery and 1 mortar

115. That is, troops from Ādherbāyjān. 116. December 3, 1856.

117. December 6, 1856.

118. The commander of this detachment was Moḥammad Qoli Khān-e Javānshir, see below, p. 328.

119. Probably part of the local regiments established in the last years of Ḥosein ᶜAli Mirzā Farmān-Farmā, see above, p. 221.

120. These horsemen served normally for administrative purposes, tax collecting, etc

(araba-ye khompāra), and the arsenal were put under the command of Shojā^{c} ol-Molk and sent to Bushehr; part of them marched by way of Kāzerun, part Firuzābād.[121] Then the generals of the English troops wrote a letter to the daryābegi to the following effect:

The English warships and guns are staying on the outskirts of Bushehr. It is within their power to reduce this town to ashes and to scatter the ashes to the wind. From now until tomorrow [314] we offer a delay to evacuate the women and children, craftsmen and merchants from the town. If they stay, they will be safe on condition that you obey our orders and haul down the Persian flag. If they obey, we shall not molest them with regard to their families and their property. You have to hand over the provisions of the arsenal and the war matériel belonging to the government in accordance with the registers. Another condition is that the Persian troops in garrison at Bushehr deliver their drums, standards, and trumpets. The officers will have to deliver their scimitars and orders, then they may go wherever they like, for we are enemies of the Persian government, not of the servants of the Almighty God.

As the daryābegi had not permission to wage war and no soldiers, he was completely without hope. He sent Mahdi Khān Sarhang to the fortress of Bahman, 1 parasang from Bushehr,[122] which had nothing but a ruined rampart and a dried-up ditch. Furthermore, he summoned Bāqer Khān-e Tangestāni with 400 musketeers to Bushehr; and Mahdi Khān sent Bāqer Khān a message: "You must come to the fortress of Bahman, for I must guard the tower of Khal^{c}at Pushān, 0.25 parasang from Bushehr."[123]

121. By using the northern and southern route to Bushehr, it was easier to provision the troops from the country they marched through.

122. *Farhang*, VII, 42, mentions a village Bahmani 5 miles south of Bushehr; the English attack was expected from this side. According to *FNN*, II, 210, Qal^{c}a-ye Bahmani was also the name of a small fortress of Rishehr, 1.5 parasangs south of Bushehr.

123. *Khal^{c}at Pushān* means "the place where the governor puts on the dress of honor" (khal^{c}at) sent at certain occasions from the capital as a token of the shah's grace.

Bāqer Khān complied with the order and the next day sent a message to the daryābegi: "If Mahdi Khān had given me permission to proceed to Bushehr, I should have installed 10 breastworks on the outskirts of the town last night."

On 9th Rabi^{c} II,[124] the English troops landed at Holeila,[125] 2 parasangs south of Bushehr; they brought 30 pieces of artillery, 4, 5, 6, and 9 pounders, ashore. Eight detachments of Indians, Sindis, Beluchis, Arabs, and Englishmen encamped at Holeila. They stayed there on the 10th, and in the night of the 11th they sent 6 detachments of soldiers and 30 cannons to the fortress of Bahman. At sunrise they arrived in the vicinity of the fortress. Bāqer Khān and Aḥmad-e Tangestāni, his grown-up son, and Sheikh Ḥasan-e ^{c}Arab Damukh-e Chāh Kutāhi,[126] in spite of their small number and the superior forces of the enemy, were established behind the rampart of the fortress. At daybreak the battle began; 60 pounders opened fire on the fortress from the sea, and 30 pieces of artillery from the land. The Tangestāni musketeers withstood bravely and replied with their muskets. The fighting went on from sunrise to noon without either side yielding. The distance between the two became so small that a group of Tangestānis, putting aside their muskets, continued fighting with scimitar and dagger and killed a number of Englishmen. The number killed came up to 740 men and 50 engineers; and news spread that the English commander and the surgeon were among those killed and that a large number had been wounded. When the gunners of the English warships saw the bravery of the Persians, they leveled their guns at that small number of men, and 70 Tangestānis were killed by the ships' gunfire. Aḥmad Khān, who had fought bravely, was among the dead. Bāqer Khān sat down in mourning over his son, the rest of the Tangestānis dispersed and the fortress of Bahman was

124. December 7, 1856.
125. About 9 miles southeast of Bushehr.
126. Chāh Kutāh lies about 19 miles east of Bushehr.

occupied by the English. They stayed in the fortress and its vicinity for forty-eight hours; and Outram, the English commander in chief, sent a message to the daryābegi asking him to surrender or prepare for battle. The daryābegi answered that he did not have permission to fight; that a delay should be granted until the arrival of Shojāᶜ ol-Molk with the Persian troops and the opening of negotiations. The commander in chief paid no attention to this reply and at sunrise marched on Bushehr. Moḥammad Khān-e Dashti and Moḥammad Ḥasan Khān-e Borāzjāni stayed with their musketeers in the tower of Khalᶜat Pushān and the entrenchment near that tower, 0.25 parasang from Bushehr. They had several gunners and 3 pieces of artillery at their disposal. Then the English commander in chief, Outram, arrived with 8 detachments of soldiers and 30 guns in order to destroy the tower. When 2 of the gunners were killed by the English cannon balls, the other gunners went to Bushehr. Moḥammad Khān-e Dashti, Moḥammad Ḥasan Khān-e Borāzjāni, and Moḥammad Reżā Beg-e Zeyārati fled with their followers. Some of them threw themselves into the sea, others went to Bushehr. The Qarācha Dāghi soldiers who were guarding the towers and ramparts of Bushehr left their positions when they saw the flight of the soldiers of the fortress of Bahman. Mirzā Ḥasan ᶜAli Khān Daryābegi was in a state of confusion and distress. At this moment the Persian flag was hauled down, and Moḥammad Reżā Beg-e Zeyārati and 4 hoursemen dashed out of the gate of Bushehr and rode right through the English troops. Moḥammad Reżā Beg, with his scimitar, killed 2 English horsemen who were on his heels, and a group of English horsemen fired at him jointly. He was hit by 35 bullets and killed on the spot. Moḥammad Khān-e Dashti and a group of Dashti soldiers got into a boat and escaped over the sea to Dashti. Moḥammad Ḥasan Khān-e Borāzjāni spent two days in a hiding-place and went in disguise to Borāzjān.

When the English occupied Bushehr, the commander in chief,

Outram, ordered the Persian soldiers to deliver their muskets at the gate to the English policemen; after that they could go wherever they liked. The sick and wounded were to stay at Bushehr and leave after they had been cured. When the soldiers dismissed from Bushehr arrived at Borāzjān, they demanded bread and fodder of Moḥammad Ḥasan Khān. He replied that on such a day he was not able to impose anything on the subjects. [315] Having no other choice, the soldiers proceeded to Kāzerun. Upon their arrival, Mirzā ᶜAli Moḥammad Khān, son of Haji Qavām, then governor of Kāzerun, displayed mercy, gave them provisions, and entertained their nobles. He gave them money to buy fodder for their horses (mal-e sovari) and sent them to Shiraz.

Outram, the English commander in chief, appointed policemen (sheḥna) and night-guards (dārugha) at Bushehr and ordered the people of the bazaar to open their shops and caravanseries and go back to work. The daryābegi, Mirzā Ḥasan ᶜAli Khān, and the intendant (kār-pardāz), Mirzā Reżā, were put on a ship and brought to Bombay. Then 700 cows, 2,000 sheep, and 500 bags (jeld) of dates which had been bought at Basra arrived at Bushehr. And Outram wrote the following proclamation, which was sealed by him and affixed to the gate of Bushehr:

In the name of the Queen,[127] I have conquered the town of Bushehr within four hours by the strength of the English sea- and land-forces. As the Persian flag has been hauled down, I have hoisted the English flag. In order to inform the people (of this event), the English ships at sea have been decorated. Written on 11th December, A.D. 1856.

And a poster was affixed to the gate of Bushehr to the following effect:

1) Since the town of Bushehr has come under English administration, the inhabitants must behave in accordance with the English laws.

2) As long as no order has been issued, the craftsmen and merchants shall be free of the tithe (ᶜashur).

127. That is, Queen Victoria Alexandrina (r. 1837–1901).

3) Any weapons found shall be confiscated. Without official permission no intoxicating liquor shall be bought or sold.

4) Except intoxicating liquors, everything may be brought into the town or taken out.

5) It shall be forbidden to buy or sell female and male slaves. All people are free.

6) Everybody staying in the town will be under the protection of the English government if he wants so.

7) Except the soldiers and the policemen, nobody will be allowed to bear weapons. Travelers who come to the gate may enter the town after they have surrendered their arms. Having finished their business, they may get back what they have delivered at the gate and go where they like.

8) Everybody under the protection of the English government may worship in accordance with his faith and religion.

9) Nobody who has debts in this town will be allowed to pass through the gate without bail.

The English generals were staying at Bushehr and placed 2 detachments of soldiers in the center of the town. Every day they employed 2,000 workmen and made them dig entrenchments and a ditch. Sixty pieces of artillery were placed in the entrenchments. At the two sides of Bushehr which border on the sea, they moored big ships and leveled the guns at the streets. Then they ordered grain and fodder to be stored. The aldermen and mayors of the villages of Dashtestān and Dashti were sent robes of honor.

THE GOVERNOR OF FĀRS PREPARES CAMPAIGN TO BUSHEHR. On 16th Rabi^{c} II,[128] news of the capture of Bushehr by the English troops came to the ears of Mo'eiyed od-Doula. At that time Shojā^{c} ol-Molk and his followers had departed from Shiraz in order to fight the English army, and were staying at Chenār Rāhdār, 2 parasangs from Shiraz.[129] The governor sent him a

128. December 14, 1857.
129. 5 miles west of Shiraz, see *Farhang*, VII, 76.

message that he was to hurry to Bushehr by way of Firuzābād, and Reżā Qoli Khān, commander of the Arab detachment, who was staying at Kāzerun, was put under the command of Shojāᶜ ol-Molk. In addition, the ilkhāni, Moḥammad Qoli Khān, was ordered to join Shojāᶜ ol-Molk with the Qashqā'i detachment and the Qashqā'i cavalry, who were staying in the districts of Dashti. A report on the occurrence was sent to Tehran. The governor himself paid attention to the gathering of the army and the storing of provisions. The inhabitants of Fārs were not in the least upset by these news. Haji Qavām ol-Molk and the nobles of Fārs asked Mo'eiyed od-Doula to be allowed to wage war with the English army, stating that they were prepared to fight for religion and empire and that, in accordance with the exigencies of the time, they were not willing to comply with the demands of the English. They confirmed further that on other occasions they had exerted themselves on behalf of religion and empire. Ḥāji Qavām ol-Molk, Āqā Mirzā Moḥammad-e Fasā'i, and the chief magistrate of the empire, Haji Moḥammad Hāshem Khān, and Āqā Mirzā Naᶜim-e Nuri-ye Shirāzi obliged themselves, each according to his rank, to put at the disposal of the Persian army a quantity of grain and fodder. And they made good their promise.

Moṣṭafā Qoli Khān Eᶜtemād os-Salṭana Mir Panj was staying with 2 detachments of Qaraguzlu soldiers and 4 pieces of artillery at Bandar Kong, 1 parasang from Bandar Langa.[130] When on 20th Rabiᶜ II[131] the English warship bringing the daryābegi and his retinue from Bushehr to Bombay sailed by the camp of Moṣṭafā Qoli Khān and fired several gunshots at the camp, he moved his camp from opposite the ship behind a hill and settled down there.

Upon the advice of the ministers, the command of the whole Persian army was conferred upon Amir ol-Omarā Mirzā

130. Bandar Kong lies about 4 miles northeast of Bandar Langa.
131. December 18, 1856.

Moḥammad Khān-e Qājār Sar Kashik Bāshi. In his company Fażl ᶜAli Khān Amir-i Tumān-e Karabaghi, who was incomparable in the affairs of war and had taken part in numerous wars, was sent to Bushehr. On 4th Jomādi I of that year,[132] 4 pieces of artillery, 6 [316] detachments of soldiers, and a large number of Shāhsevan horsemen from Shakki, Nānkoli, and the other tribes departed from Tehran for Bushehr and arrived at Shiraz in the month of Jomādi II.[133] Since it was the time of snow and rain, they encamped, by the permission of the theologians, in the mosques.[134] Moḥammed Ebrāhim Khān Sehām ol-Molk Miri Sartip joined the army with 3 detachments from Esfahan.

When Mehr ᶜAli Khān Shojāᶜ ol-Molk had marched through Firuzābād, he encamped for several days at the station of Farrāshband.[135] The ilkhāni joined the army of Shojāᶜ ol-Molk with 1,000 horsemen and the Qashqā'i detachment under the command of Loṭf ᶜAli Khān-e Qashqā'i. Then they departed for Bushehr with all pomp. On 7th Jomādi I,[136] they arrived on the plain of Nanizak, several parasangs from Borāzjān.[137] The ilkhāni remained there with his cavalry. Shojāᶜ ol-Molk went to Borāzjān, arranged the troops, and ordered them to encamp. Among the nobles who were staying at Borāzjān were Mirzā Solṭān Moḥammad Khān, the governor of Kuh-e Giluya and Behbehān, Moḥammed Qoli Khān-e Javānshir, commander of the special detachment, Loṭf ᶜAli Khān, commander of the Qashqā'i, and Reżā Qoli Khān, commander of the Arab detachment. In the night of the 14th of that month,[138] Reżā Qoli Khān-e ᶜArab

132. December 30, 1856.
133. Began on January 27, 1857.
134. This permission implies that the campaign was considered as a Holy War against unbelievers, a religious duty; consequently, the mosques were put at the disposal of the warriors.
135. About 30 miles west of Firuzābād.
136. January 3, 1857.
137. 7.5 miles southeast of Borāzjān, about 25 miles from Bushehr.
138. January 9, 1857.

left the camp with 2 pieces of artillery and 400 Arab soldiers to collect provisions. He was joined by 300 Qashqāʾi soldiers and a cannon. They transported the grain collected at the village of Chāh Kutāh[139] to the camp.

PERSIAN ATTACK ON THE ENGLISH CAMP NEAR BORĀZJĀN.
Shojāʿ al-Molk remained at Borāzjān for one month without going out to fight. Then Moḥammad Ṣādeq Khān, scout (qalāwuz) of the Persian army, sent a report to the effect that the English troops had marched from Bushehr to Chāh Kutāh and were advancing to Borāzjān to make a night attack. Shojāʿ ol-Molk agreed with the proposal of the leaders that they were to anticipate the night attack. When they had come to an agreement, 3 detachments of soldiers, 500 horsemen, and 12 pieces of artillery were sent from Borāzjān to Chāh Kutāh before sunset; Chāh Kutāh was 4 parasangs from Borāzjān. When they had covered 1 parasang, such a rain set in that it soaked their war matériel, such as guns, muskets, and the arsenal, and put it out of order. Torrents spread in the hills and the plains and made hills and plains one, and the road became invisible. Then news arrived from Bāqer Khān-e Tangestāni that the English commander was with his troops on the way to make a night attack on the camp. Accordingly, Shojāʿ ol-Molk returned to protect the camp. Then the English troops encamped at their intended stopping place. The next day Moḥammad Qoli Khān Ilkhāni sent 2 English skulls stuck on lances to the Persian camp and admonished the Persians to fight bravely and not to yield. Shojāʿ ol-Molk and the other leaders preferred staying on to marching off to keep the English from the camp. Then he sent the train and the baggage away and marched without baggage several parasangs from Borāzjān to Dālaki[140] to wait for the arrival of the enemy. The English troops marched as far as

139. 14 miles southwest of Borāzjān.
140. 12 miles north of Borāzjān; this means that they retreated!

Borāzjān, encamped at the site of the Persian camp, and took possession of the arsenal which had been left behind. Shojā^c ol-Molk wrote a letter to the ilkhāni telling him to leave his camp, Nanizak, on the night of 12th Jomādi II,[141] for Borāzjān and put his troops into an ambush, 0.5 parasang from the English camp; that upon hearing the sound of the Persian guns, Shojā^c ol-Molk would start the night attack from the north and the ilkhāni from the south. The English spies heard of this agreement between Shojā^c ol-Molk and the ilkhāni and informed their leaders of it. Accordingly, the English commander made arrangements to anticipate the Persians and to fire a gunshot, so that the ilkhāni, thinking the shot was fired by a Persian gun, would start his night attack from the south and would be routed completely. Shojā^c ol-Molk marched off from Dālaki before sunset with 3,000 cavalry and infantry and 8 pieces of artillery in the direction of Borāzjān for the night attack, without having the slightest notion that the enemy was informed of his intention the day before and was ready for battle. When part of the night had passed, the sound of a cannon was heard from the English camp. When Shojā^c ol-Molk heard this, he realized that his plan had failed and that the ilkhāni, having heard the gunshot, would rush, without having any suspicion, upon the English camp and perish in battle. In order to caution the ilkhāni, he attacked the Englishmen. When he came near the English camp and fired 3 gunshots to caution the ilkhāni, the English soldiers thought from the sound of the cannon that a big army had arrived from Shiraz; being caught in this fancy, they set fire to the arsenal which they had taken away from the Persians and left Borāzjān for Bushehr. They took Moḥammad Ḥasan Khān, the mayor of Borāzjān, who was staying with them, to Bushehr. The Persian troops caught up with the English in the vicinity of the village of Chāh Kutāh, and they fought with each other for three hours. The ilkhāni came from the direction of Nanizak and attacked

141. February 7, 1857.

the English troops on the other side. In this dark night [317] a number of soldiers on both sides were killed by cannon balls, musket shots, and scimitars. The English troops left the ordinary road to Bushehr and marched by way of Shif,[142] which lies several parasangs nearer to Bushehr. They fired a series of gunshots to attract the attention of the troops staying at Bushehr. Since no trace was to be seen of troops coming to their assistance, they withdrew to the shore by way of Shif. Towards sunrise a group from Bushehr joined them. General Outram is said to have sent 5 pieces of artillery and 2 detachments of soldiers to their assistance. At sunrise it was realized that the distance between the English troops and the Persians placed on the hills and in the dales was not more than a gunshot. The English numbered 11 detachments of soldiers, 1,000 horsemen (sovār-e neẓām), and 800 gunners; they had 25 pieces of artillery at their disposal. The whole assembly, being placed on ground not easy to survey, was not seen by the Persians. Accordingly, the Persians were deceived and rushed upon the English without the permission of the officers. When they arrived at the hills and mounds, they saw themselves amidst a shower of bullets and made a headless attack. The ilkhāni and the Qashqā'i horsemen, being less timid, killed a number of the enemy's horsemen and returned to their positions without haste. When the Arab detachment, the Qashqā'i and Shirazi detachments, the special detachment, and the Qaraguzlu detachment and the Persian gunners saw the bravery of the Qashqā'i cavalry, they attacked the English irregularly, and the English fired a shower of bullets at the Persian troops. Because the Persians had taken courage and remained in their places, many of them were hit. The English, who outnumbered the Persians 5 to 1, discharged their guns from all sides at the Persians and scattered them. When they fled, the English did not follow, but returned to Bushehr and stopped fighting. It has

142. Shif lies on the bay of Bushehr, about 9 miles north of the town; the English troops deviated to the west.

been said that on the way from Bushehr to Borāzjān and back the English lost nearly 1,500 horsemen and infantry. The losses of the Persians were about 500 to 600 men. God, the Knowing, knows best! On their forced march to Bushehr, the English threw away a good deal of their baggage; it was collected by the inhabitants of Dashtestān.

THE PERSIAN TROOPS RALLY AT NANIZAK. The Persian troops marched through the plain of Borāzjān and Dālaki and encamped on the plain of Khesht. The ilkhāni with the detachment of Qashqā i soldiers returned to Nanizak, his first camp. When Mo'eiyed od-Doula, who was staying at Kāzerun, heard of this, he hurried with 400 Kāzeruni and Kheshti musketeers through the plains of Khesht and marched to the village of Dālaki. He summoned the ilkhāni from Nanizak and gave him the pieces of artillery left at Dālaki. The latter brought them to Nanizak, which was designated as the camp of the Persian army. Mehr ᶜAli Khān Shojāᶜ ol-Molk moved his camp from Khesht back to Dālaki, marched through Borāzjān, and joined the camp of the ilkhāni at Nanizak. All this happened in the month of Jomādi II of that year.[143] On 5th Rajab,[144] Fażl ᶜAli Khan Amir-e Tumān-e Karabaghi arrived at Nanizak with the Afshār and Nānkoli cavalry and the regular soldiers (gholām-e neẓām), and joined the main body of the army. Amir ol-Omarā Mirzā Moḥammad Khān-e Qājār, commander in chief of the whole Persian army, departed from Shiraz and going by way of Firuzābād arrived at Nanizak on 12th Rajab.[145] Then he summoned the Persian nobles and deliberated with them on the war with the English. When the divergent opinions were united and an official agreement was established, the nobles took it upon their oath to defend themselves against the English as long as they were alive. They entered into an agreement with the khāns

143. Began on January 27, 1857. 144. March 1, 1857.
145. March 9, 1857.

of Dashtestān and bound the latter by a solemn oath. Haji Moḥammad Hāshem Khān-e Kheshti and Ḥosein Khān-e Dashti, who were always negligent in paying taxes, now paid what was expected of them for the previous year and the coming year with great zeal and benevolence to the treasurer of the army. It was included in the agreement that the grain which was on stock in that region was to be handed over: half as victuals for the inhabitants and half as provisions for the army. About 3,000 musketeers from Dashti, Dashtestān, Khesht, and Tangestān assembled, according to the summons, at Nanizak under the command of Bāqer Khān-e Tangestāni, Haji Moḥammad Hāshem Khān-e Kheshti, Ḥosein Khān-e Dashti, ᶜAli Moḥammad Khān-e Zeyārati, and Sohrāb Khān-e Shabānkāra;[146] they were put up on the outskirts of the camp. Mirzā Solṭān Moḥammad Khān-e Behbehāni, although several years removed from the government of Behbehān and staying at Shiraz, gathered together by the orders of Mo'eiyed od-Doula about 1,500 horsemen and musketeers from Kuh-e Giluya and joined the army.

While this was going on, news arrived that the rabble of Dashti had gone to Bushehr in order to do business with the English troops who were paying the threefold or fourfold value for everything. Mo'eiyed od-Doula dispatched 60 horsemen [318] who arrested those people and brought them to the camp. They were found carrying 2,000 hens and cocks and 10 loads of watermelons. The governor ordered 6 of them to be executed and their wares to be divided among the horsemen.

PERSIAN ADVANCE TO THE VICINITY OF BUSHEHR. When the Persian army gathered at Nanizak, part of it marched on 1st Sha'bān of that year[147] to the vicinity of the village of Chaghādak, 4 parasangs from Bushehr,[148] namely: Fażl ᶜAli

146. The list comprises all the local rulers of the Bushehr area, who were always eager to lay hands on the town.

147. March 27, 1857.

148. About 14 miles from Bushehr, on the Borāzjān-Bushehr highway.

Khān Amir-e Tumān and Soleimān Khān Mir Panj-e Afshār with the Qarācha Dāghi detachment, the fourth detachment, the Qaraguzlu detachment, the Chahār Maḥāll-e Eṣfahān detachment, 6 pieces of artillery, and the Afshār, Shāhsevan, Nānkoli, and Mokri horsemen, and the ilkhāni with the Qashqā'i cavalry under the command of ᶜAli Qoli Khān, Sohrāb Khān, Dārāb Khān and Qobād Khān, nephews of the ilkhāni, and the Qashqā'i detachment and 4 pieces of artillery. Much as they defied the English troops, they elicited no response and returned to Nanizak.

PEACE TREATY CONCLUDED IN PARIS. The New Year fell on the evening of 24th Rajab of that year.[149] As the weather grew hot at Nanizak and nothing became known with regard to war or peace with the English, the nobles of the Persian army, having made the camp as safe as possible, proceeded with a number of trustworthy men to the summer camps of the Kuh-e Kisakān near Borāzjān. (The Kuh-e Kisakān is dealt with in the second part of this book, in the chapter on the mountains of Fārs.[150]) They were all staying at a fountain and in the shadow of trees and tents, waiting for news of war or peace. On 7th Rajab of that year,[151] by mediation of Farrokh Khān Amin ol-Molk Kāshāni,[152] the peace treaty between Persia and England was concluded in Paris, according to which the Persian army was to return from Herāt and the English army from Bushehr. When the treaty arrived in Tehran, both armies returned accordingly, and the Persian troops of Nanizak returned to

149. March 19, 1857 (should be March 21).

150. See *FNN*, II, 338: "A high mountain 3 parasangs east of Borāzjān. In summer, the climate on top of this mountain is similar to summer in the districts of Khaft and Fasā." The mountain (Kuh-e Gisakan on the 1 : 500,000 map) is 1,794 meters high. Nanizak lies at its western foot.

151. March 3, 1857 (peace treaty of Paris).

152. A report on Farrokh Khān's mission to Paris was written by Ḥosein ibn ᶜAbdollah Sarābi, *Makhzan ol-vaqā'i*, ed. Karim Eṣfahāniyān and Qodratollāh Roushani, Tehran 1344:1966 (Enteshārāt-e Dāneshgāh-e Tehrān, No. 1020).

Shiraz at the end of the month of Dhu'l-Qaᶜda.[153] The nobles of the Persian troops who were staying in the summer camp on the Kuh-e Kisakān returned home, too, except Suleimān Khān-e Afshār, who was sent to Behbehān to settle the affairs of the region of Kuh-e Giluya. Upon his arrival, on the advice of Loṭf ᶜAli Mirzā, governor of Behbehān and son of Mo'eiyed od-Doula, he settled the affairs of the mayors of Kuh-e Giluya and calmed down the rebels within a short space of time.

APPOINTMENTS AND PROMOTIONS. In the month of Shavvāl of that year,[154] Mehr ᶜAli Khān Shojāᶜ ol-Molk was promoted to the rank of Amir-e Tumān, and the title and signs of an Amir Panj were bestowed upon the ilkhāni Moḥammad Qoli Khān-e Qashqā'i.

Also in that month Mirzā Shafiᶜ Ṣāḥeb Divān died in Tehran. The title "Ṣāḥeb Divān"[155] was bestowed upon Mirzā Fatḥ ᶜAli Khān Mostoufī, son of Haji Mirzā ᶜAli Akbar Qavām ol-Molk Shirazi, a man of great efficiency and noble birth.[156] He gave his signature in the place of Mirzā Shafiᶜ Ṣāḥeb Divān and affixed his seal to the decisions of the grand divan (divān-e aᶜlā).

FĀRS IN A STATE OF UNREST

MISCELLANEOUS EVENTS. That year Mirzā Moḥammad Ḥosein Vakil died, son of the cousin of the author of this book, who had been granted the title "Vakil" more than forty years ago.[157] His title was bestowed upon Mirzā ᶜAli Moḥammad Khān, another son of Haji Qavām ol-Molk, and he was styled "Mirzā ᶜAli Moḥammad Khān Vakil."

153. About July 20, 1857. 154. Began on May 25, 1857.

155. "Chief of the Divān," which may be compared with the modern office of minister of Finance.

156. Fatḥ ᶜAli Khān was a grandson of the famous Haji Ebrāhim, the grand vizier of early Qājār times.

157. He is first mentioned under the year 1241:1825/26, see above, p. 172.

And that year the government of Bandar Bushehr, Dashti, and Dashtestān was separated from the province of Fārs and entrusted to Aḥmad Khān ᶜAmid ol-Molk Navā'i. He was styled "Daryābegi." In that year, too, Mirzā Ḥasan ᶜAli Khān, the former daryābegi of Bushehr, who had been taken prisoner in the English war and brought to Bombay, was released and entered Shiraz with all honors.

FĀRS HAUNTED BY PLAGUE; GOVERNOR OF LĀRESTĀN SUBDUED. In the month of Moḥarram of the year 1274,[158] plague broke out at Shiraz and in the province of Fārs; a number of people died. Ṭahmāsp Mirzā Mo'eiyed od-Doula departed from Shiraz with his retinue and his family and established himself in the village of Pas Kuhak, 4 parasangs northwest of Shiraz;[159] the air of that village is cool and the water fresh.

While the plague raged, Naṣrollāh Khān-e Lāri, the former governor of Lārestān who because of a sum of money belonging to the Divān was imprisoned in the arsenal at Shiraz, made his escape and established himself in the region of Lārestān and Sabᶜa. The inhabitants of those regions joined him, since his family had been governor of Lārestān and Sabᶜa from time immemorial, and sent Mirzā Loṭfollāh Mostoufi-ye Shirazi, governor of Sabᶜa, to Shiraz, begging his pardon. Naṣrollāh Khān put up his standard in the region of Sabᶜa. When Mo'eiyed od-Doula heard of this, he entrusted the governorship of Sabᶜa to Reżā Qoli Khān-e ᶜArab Fārsi, commander of the detachment of the Bahārlu, Inālu, and Arabs[160] and sent him to Sabᶜa with

158. Began on August 22, 1857.

159. About 20 miles northwest of Shiraz, *Farhang*, VII, 47 seq., on the northeastern slope of the Kuh-e Sorkh-e Kalāta (2,981 meters high).

160. The Inālu and Bahārlu were Turks. The Inālu had their winter quarters in the districts of Khafr, Dārāb, and Fasā, their summer quarters in the districts of Rāmjerd and Marvdasht (on the Kur and Polvār Rivers). The winter quarters of the Bahārlu were in the districts of Izadkhvāst, Lārestān, and Dārāb; their summer quarters were in the districts of Rāmjerd and Marvadasht and, too, in Kamin (north of Marvdasht). The Arab

2 pieces of artillery and the Shirazi detachment to defeat Naṣrollāh Khān. ᶜAli Naqi Khān-e Qaraguzlu, commander of the Dargezin detachment,[161] and Jaᶜfar Qoli Khān, commander of the artillery, were sent to Lārestān. When these troops were not successful, Mo'eiyed od-Doula sent his son ᶜAbd ol-Bāqi Mirzā, a man of intelligence and political dexterity, to settle the affairs of Sabᶜa and Lārestān. The latter departed from Shiraz in the month of Jomādi II of that year[162] with an Ādherbāyjāni detachment and 2 pieces of artillery; [319] marching by way of Sarvestān, Fasā, and Dārāb to Forg, he encamped in the Bāgh-e ᶜAliābād.[163] Reżā Qoli Khān Sartip with an Arab detachment erected a breastwork in the ruined fortress of Bahmani which lies on top of a hill 2 parasangs southeast of Forg, and settled down there. ᶜAli Naqi Khān-e Qaraguzlu came with the Dargezin detachment from Lārestān and established himself in the region of Bikhu.[164] When Naṣrollāh Khān saw that he could not escape the anger of the shah, he marched by way of Ṭārom, and his troops dispersed and hid in the mountains of the region of Fin.[165] Supposing Naṣrollāh Khān to have gone from the region of Sabᶜa to Lārestān, ᶜAbd ol-Bāqi Mirzā marched through the region of Forg to the town of Lār.

MISCELLANEOUS EVENTS. The New Year fell on the evening of Sunday, 5th Shaᶜbān.[166] That same year ᶜAbd ol-Vahhāb

---

tribes of Fārs had their winter quartes in Sabᶜa, Rudān, and Aḥmadi; their summer quarters in Bavānāt, Qunqari and Sar-e Jahān (that is, north of the winter quarters of the two Turkish tribes mentioned above), see *FNN*, II, 309 seq.

161. Dargezin near Hamadān (?), see above, p. 84, note 17.

162. Began on January 17, 1858.

163. The town of Forg had many gardens; a place called ᶜAliābād, 4 parasangs south of Forg, is mentioned in the *FNN*, II, 217.

164. According to the *Farhang*, VII, 42, about 70 miles northeast of Lār (that is, near Forg).

165. About 60 miles southeast of Forg; accordingly, Naṣrollāh Khān had been encircled on three sides and escaped to the south.

166. March 21, 1858.

Khān-e Shirāzi was granted the title and office of deputy minister of foreign affairs.

That year, too, a telegraph line was experimentally installed from Tehran to the outskirts of the city. After this experiment, orders were issued to the effect that a telegraph line was to be installed from Tehran to Bushehr.[167]

By order of the shah, the 15th Sha^{c}bān was decreed to be celebrated as the birthday of the Twelfth Emām,[168] which was to be celebrated every year like the birthdays of Moḥammad and ^{c}Ali in the Persian towns.

And that year Naṣrollāh Khān-e Lāri, who had hidden himself in the mountains of Fin, sent a message to Shojā^c ol-Molk that he would come to Shiraz if the latter was ready to mediate for him and give him a guarantee. Accordingly, Shojā^c ol-Molk sent Shir Khān-e Nuri to Fin to reassure Naṣrollāh Khān. The latter was brought to Shiraz and granted a pension (mavājeb-e divāni) of 1,000 toman.

REORGANIZATION OF THE CENTRAL GOVERNMENT. On 20th Moḥarram of the year 1275,[169] on the strength of a personal letter from the shah, the grand vizier, Āqā Khān-e Nuri and his family and tribe were removed from all the offices they held. Six efficient viziers were appointed for the administration of all the important affairs of the king, the state, and the court. At Shiraz, Mirzā Na^{c}im-e Nuri, cousin of the grand vizier, and Mehr ^{c}Ali Khān Shojā^c ol-Molk and Haji Hāshem Khān, chief magistrate of the province of Fārs, both of them nephews of the

167. Persia and England entered into an agreement "for the construction of a line of telegraph from Khanakeen to Bushire via Teheran" on December 17, 1862. The text of the agreement is reproduced in W. Litten, *Persien*, p. 5 seq. Accordingly, the "orders" mentioned by Ḥasan-e Fasā'i were not issued before 1862.

168. Moḥammad ol-Montaẓar ("The Expected") disappeared mysteriously on July 24, 874, in a cave near Sāmarrā, at the age of five, and is expected to appear at the end of times to establish the divine kingdom.

169. August 30, 1858.

grand vizier, were arrested. They were all sentenced to pay a certain sum of money in cash for bad behavior and to stay in their houses.

SOLṬĀN MORĀD MIRZĀ ḤOSĀM OS-SALṬANA APPOINTED GOVERNOR OF FĀRS. The New Year fell on 16th Shaᶜbān of that year.[170] In the same month Ṭahmāsp Mirzā Mo'eiyed od-Doula was removed from the governorship of Fārs. The governorship of this province was conferred upon Solṭān Morād Mirzā Ḥosām os-Salṭana, uncle of the shah. News of the removal and the appointment arrived at Shiraz in the night of 1st Ramażān.[171] Mo'eiyed od-Doula summoned ᶜAbd ol-Bāqi Mirzā, the governor of Sabᶜa and Lārestān and the ports and shores of the Persian Gulf, who was staying at Galladār, and Loṭf ᶜAli Mirzā, the governor of Kuh-e Giluya, to Shiraz. Ḥosām os-Salṭana arrived at Shiraz at the end of the month of Shavvāl of that year.[172] Upon the news of his removal, Mo'eiyed od-Doula spent three months in the Bāgh-e Nou, half a mile east of Shiraz, without doing anything.

APPOINTMENTS AND PROMOTIONS. In that year the governorship of the province of Yazd was entrusted to Fatḥ ᶜAli Khān Ṣāḥeb Divān-i Shirazi; Mirzā Shafiᶜ-e Shirazi, secretary to the grand vizier, was appointed mostoufi-ye divān; and Ḥosām os-Salṭana appointed Mirzā Moḥammad Ḥosein-e Hamadāni, one of his oldest and most loyal servants, vizier of the province of Fārs. Mirzā Abu'l-Ḥasan Khān Moshir ol-Molk was removed from the vizierate. When he resisted, he was arrested and put in prison and fined about 18,000 toman on a charge of treachery; then he was sent to Tehran.

NEW GOVERNORS APPOINTED TO SEVERAL DISTRICTS OF FĀRS. Also, in that year, the governorship of Lārestān and the

170. March 21, 1859. 171. April 3, 1859.
172. About June 1, 1859.

region of Sab^{c}a, Bandar ^{c}Asluya, and Bandar Langa was conferred upon Mirzā Ḥasan ^{c}Ali Khān Daryābegi. The governorship of Kuh-e Giluya and Behbehān was entrusted to Ebrāhim Khān-e Qājār Joveini-ye Khorasani, an aged man. Mirzā Solṭān Moḥammad Khān-e Behbehāni was appointed the latter's deputy. The districts of Dashti, Dashtestān, and Bandar Bushehr were given to Ḥasan Khān-e Qarāchadaghi Ādherbāyjāni. The governorship of Jahrom, Qir va-Kārzin, and Eṣṭaḥbānāt was conferred upon Moḥammed ^{c}Ali Khān-e Tabrizi, maternal cousin of Ḥosām os-Salṭana. Since the latter lived in the town of Jahrom, he appointed his brother Āqā Qoli governor of those districts. The governorship of Kāzerun was conferred upon Mir Ḥeidar Khān-e Ṭālesh. Mirzā ^{c}Ali Moḥammad Khān, son of Mirzā Na^{c}im-e Nuri, was appointed governor of the region of Galladār, Asir, ^{c}Alā Marvdasht, and Bandar ^{c}Asluya. At the beginning of autumn of that year he deposed Bāqer Khān-e Galladāri, in whom he had no trust, and appointed Noudhār Mirzā, grandson of the late Ḥosein ^{c}Ali Mirzā, the former governor of Fārs, governor of Galladār and the adjoining districts.

THE BAHĀRLU AND INĀLU TRIBES SUBDUED. [320] At the end of the previous year Aḥmad Khān, chief of the Bahārlu and Nafar[173] had died. Then unusual quarrels arose among the Bahārlu; they did not shrink from violating each others' possessions, lives, and women. The Inālu, neighbors of the Bahārlu, rose in rebellion, devastated the districts of Dārāb and Sab^{c}a and infested the roads and paths. Then Ḥosām os-Salṭana entrusted the governorship of Dārāb to Mahdi Qoli Mirzā, and the governorship of the tribes of Bahārlu, Nafar and Inālu to Ja^{c}far Qoli Mirzā; both were sons of Haji Moḥammad Vāli Mirzā, the uncle of Ḥosām os-Salṭana. He ordered them to

173. The Nafar were Turks, too (on the Bahārlu see above, p. 336, note 160). Sometimes the Nafar and Bahārlu were united under one chief (kalāntar), see *FNN*, II, 310.

subdue the tribes of Bahārlu and Inālu and to settle the affairs of the districts. Upon their arrival in the districts of Dārāb, they won over several branches of the Bahārlu tribes, and they submitted. Several of them remained in rebellion and did not care for the governor's orders. The governor subdued the rebellious tribes with a loyal group and sent 40 men of the Bahārlu in fetters to Shiraz. At Shiraz 24 of them were executed; 16 were sent to Tehran and put in prison.

THE SHAH TRAVELS TO KURDISTAN AND SOLṬĀNIYA. That year the royal court departed from Tehran and marched by way of Qom and Hamadān to Kurdistan. The shah stayed for three days in the town of Senānda, known as Senna.[174] Because the governor of Kurdistan was not able to satisfy the wishes of the shah's retinue and several of them were getting angry, the court departed from Kurdistan, marched through the districts of Garrus and encamped on the pasture of Solṭāniya on 2d Dhu'l-Ḥejja.[175] The shah spent the ᶜĀshurā days of the year 1276[176] on the pasture of Solṭāniya in mourning over Emām Ḥosein. On 3d Ṣafar,[177] the court encamped at Tabriz; then it marched from Tabriz to Marāgha, thence to Tehran, arriving there on 22d Rabiᶜ I.[178]

THE GOVERNOR OF FĀRS SETTLES AFFAIRS AT BUSHEHR. The New Year fell on 27th Shaᶜbān.[179] Ḥosām as-Salṭana appointed his nephew Asadollāh Mirzā deputy governor and granted him the title "Nā'eb ol-Eyāla." The governor himself departed from Shiraz to settle the affairs of the districts of Dashti and Dashtestān and arrived by way of Kāzerun and Borāzjān at Bandar Bushehr. He established complete order in those regions.

174. Now Sanandaj, 90 miles northwest of Hamadān.
175. July 3, 1859. 176. Began on July 31, 1859.
177. September 1, 1859. 178. October 19, 1859.
179. March 21, 1860.

STREET RIOTS IN SHIRAZ. A remarkable occurrence was the quarrel between Haji Reżā-ye Qāsi and Mollā ᶜAli Akbar. Haji Reżā, son of Qāsi, was a man of the Lor tribes who at the time of Karim Khān Vakil had come from Lorestān-e Fili[180] to Shiraz and established themselves there. Mollā ᶜAli Akbar, son of Mollā Moḥammad ᶜAli, was a maternal brother of Sheikh Abu Torāb, imam of the prayers at Shiraz. Since Mollā ᶜAli Akbar deviated from the path of virtue, his family was angry with him. During the time of the interregnum,[181] Haji Reżā and Mollā ᶜAli Akbar had each assembled a group of the rabble and perpetrated evil acts. According to the saying "The souls of two wolves and dogs are discordant," they were always suspecting each other. In the month of Ramażān of that year,[182] when Ḥosām os-Salṭana was staying at Bandar Bushehr, Haji Reżā and Mollā ᶜAli Akbar turned the dispute in the Masjed-e Nou of Shiraz to a fight, and the followers of both came running along, muskets and scimitars in hand. Several people on both sides were wounded. The fighting lasted three days, and the judicious citizens were not able to put an end to the civil war. Then Haji Reżā, by mediation of several people, pleaded "not guilty" with Nā'ib ol-Eyāla Asadollāh Mirzā, and took refuge in the coffee-house of the palace. Mollā ᶜAli Akbar, however, did not yield. Asadollāh Mirzā demanded of Haji Qavām ol-Molk the surrender of Mollā ᶜAli Akbar. Haji Qavām ol-Molk, however, did not come up to his obligations and considered himself excused. Asadollāh Mirzā did not acknowledge Haji Qavām ol-Molk's excuses and wrote a letter of complaint to Ḥosām os-Salṭana, and was considered as the originator of the revolt.

180. The western part of Lorestān (or Posht-e Kuh), see EI[1] III, s.v. Luristān (V. Minorsky). The article "Pusht-i Kūh," announced by Minorsky in the article "Luristān," never appeared.

181. Mo'eiyed od-Doula had been removed on 16th Shaᶜbān, 1275: March 21, 1859, see above, p. 339; his successor, Ḥosām os-Salṭana, arrived at Shiraz only at the end of Shavvāl 1275: June 1859.

182. Began on March 23, 1860.

Several days later Mollā ᶜAli Akbar took refuge in the house of Asadollāh Mirzā, too; however, this proved futile. Ḥosām os-Salṭana entrusted the governorship of Bushehr, Dashti, and Dashtestān to Soleimān Mirzā, son of the late Faridun Mirzā, the former governor of Fārs, and returned with great haste to Shiraz by way of the districts of Dashti and Firuzābād, in the month of Shavvāl of that year.[183] Upon his arrival he sent Haji Qavām ol-Molk perforce to Tehran.This he did on the strength of a report submitted by Asadollāh Mirzā, stating that Haji Qavām ol-Molk originated the troubles at Shiraz in order to win influence by shaking the foundations of the government. [321] Since Ḥosām os-Salṭana several months after his arrival at Shiraz had sent Moshir ol-Molk, the vizier of Fārs, in fetters to Tehran and appointed Mirzā Moḥammad Ḥosein-e Hamadāni vizier and, now, had sent Haji Qavām ol-Molk to Tehran, too, he was afraid lest both assembled arguments for his own removal from the governorship of Fārs. Having no other choice, he summoned Mirzā Abu'l-Ḥasan Khān Moshir ol-Molk from Tehran and conferred upon him the administration of all the affairs connected with the vizierate.

MAHDI QOLI MIRZĀ SUBDUES LOCAL RULER OF BASTAK. That year the governorship of Lārestān was conferred upon Mahdi Qoli Mirzā.[184] Upon his arrival in the town of Lār, Mahdi Qoli Mirzā marched to Bastak with a detachment of soldiers and a group of musketeers and 2 pieces of artillery, to chastise Moṣṭafā Khān-e Bastaki[185] who, putting his trust in the inaccessible mountains of Bastak in the course of the last years paid no attention to the orders of the governor of Lārestān. When Mahdi Qoli Mirzā arrived in the plain of Bāgh,[186] he

183. Began on April 22, 1860.
184. A son of Moḥammad Vāli Mirzā and grandson of Fatḥ ᶜAli Shāh.
185. A few years ago, he had been brought to Shiraz in fetters, see above, p. 309, but evidently managed to return to Bastak.
186. About 37 miles southwest to Lār, see *Farhang*, VII, 21.

realized that Moṣṭafā Khān had fortified the pass of Anvah[187] by placing musketeers on it and had blocked the road. The other passes of the region of Bastak had been put under the custody of the Farāmorzi and Lāvari tribes.[188] Since Mahdi Qoli Mirzā despaired his ability to invade the region of Jahāngiriya[189] and Bastak, he left the camp in the company of a horseman. When he arrived at the pass of Anvah, he said to the road guards: "I am an agent sent on behalf of the prince to conclude a peace treaty." The same he said to the musketeers of the Farāmorzi tribe. After arriving at the gate of Bastak, he sent a message to Moṣṭafā Khān, saying: "I am Prince Mahdi Qoli Mirzā and come as a guest." When Moṣṭafā Khān found this to be true, he came out of the gate, kissed the prince's stirrup, brought him to his house, and prepared a banquet suitable for such a guest. He surrendered the seal bearing his name to the prince, saying: "Whatever you demand in cash and kind, fill in a check, and everything will be remitted to you!" The prince displayed liberality and demanded not a dinar, then he returned to Lār. Several days later Moṣṭafā Khān sent a seeming peshkash. Then he presented himself in person before the prince at Lār; having reached his aim, he returned to Bastak.

A CHANGE IN THE GOVERNORSHIP OF BANDAR ᶜABBĀS. That year the Imam of Masqaṭ conferred the governorship of Bandar ᶜAbbās and dependencies upon Haji Aḥmad Khān, son of Haji Moḥammad ᶜAli Tājer, known as "Kabābi,"[190] vizier of Masqaṭ and the mainland of ᶜOmān.

THE GOVERNOR OF FĀRS SENT TO KHORASAN. In the month of Moḥarram of the year 1277,[191] the shah spent the ᶜĀshurā

187. Anvah lies 16 miles northwest of Bastak (26 miles on the road), see *Farhang*, VII, 16 (on the 1:500,000 map: Naweh).

188. Perhaps branches of the Arab tribes who had their winter quarters in this region, see above, p. 336, note 160.

189. Bastak was the center of this region (nāḥeya), see *FNN*, II, 228.

190. For him, see above, p. 312.

191. Began on July 20, 1860.

days mourning over Emām Ḥosein. In the month of Rabiᶜ I,[192] several revolts occurred in the province of Khorasan; the government knew nobody who was able to settle the affairs except Ḥosām os-Salṭana. So, at the beginning of Rabiᶜ I, he was summoned from Fārs to Tehran, and the governorship of Khorasan was bestowed upon him. On 12th Jomādi I,[193] he left Shiraz for Tehran and ordered Haji Moḥammad Kāẓem, kadkhodā of the Darb-e Shāhzāda quarter of Shiraz, and Haji Mirzā Aḥmad, kadkhodā of the Meidān-e Shah quarter, both of whom had special offices in the service of the governor, to prepare their journey to Khorasan and to leave for their place of destination. When they arrived at Khorasan, Haji Moḥammad Kāẓem was appointed mayor of Mashhad and Haji Mirzā Aḥmad chief magistrate of Khorasan.

ṬASMĀSP MIRZĀ MO'EIYED OD-DOULA AGAIN APPOINTED GOVERNOR OF FĀRS. In the month of Rabiᶜ I of that year,[194] the governorship of Fārs was again entrusted to Ṭahmāsp Mirzā Mo'eiyed od-Doula, the former governor of Fārs.[195] He appointed his son ᶜAbd ol-Bāqi Mirzā deputy governor (nā'eb ol-ḥokuma). The son arrived at Shiraz in the middle of Rabiᶜ I,[196] and Mo'eiyed od-Doula arrived at Shiraz at the beginning of Jomādi I.[197] He entrusted the governorship of Bandar Bushehr, Dashti, Dashtestān, Galladār, Asir, ᶜAlā Marvdasht,[198] Bandar Kangān, and Kuh-e Giluya and Behbehān to Mehr ᶜAli Khān Shojāᶜ ol-Molk Nuri, and the governorship of the regions of Lārestān and Sabᶜa to Mirzā Ḥasan ᶜAli Khān Daryābegi, son of Haji Qavām ol-Molk. Mirzā Moḥammad ᶜAli Jāberi Anṣari

192. Began on September 17, 1860. 193. November 26, 1860.
194. Began on September 17, 1860.
195. He had been governor from 1269:1852/53 onward, see above, p. 305.
196. About the end of September 1860.
197. Began on November 15, 1860.
198. Center of a district (boluk), 16 miles east of Galladār, see *FNN*, II, 227.

Eṣfahāni was appointed chief of the district of Fasā, and Ṭahmāsp Qoli Khān-e Qazvini, chief of Dārāb. Bandar ᶜAbbās remained in the possession of Haji Aḥmad Khān-e Masqaṭi as before. Shojāᶜ ol-Molk bound himself by a solemn oath and upon his arrival at Behbehān arrested Mirzā Solṭān Moḥammad Khān-e Ṭabāṭabā'i, the governor of Kuh-e Giluya and Behbehān, whose family had held the governorship of that region from time immemorial.[199] Solṭān Moḥammad Khān was arrested on the basis of an injust imputation with regard to an administrative affair and on account of Shojāᶜ ol-Molk's desire to seize his possessions. He was put in prison and sent to Shiraz. Upon his arrival at Shiraz he was sent to Tehran. This evil act bore no blessing to Shojāᶜ ol-Molk; one year later, he failed to obtain another governorship.

ṬAHMĀSP MIRZĀ CONSTRUCTS BRIDGE ACROSS THE PARVĀB RIVER. The New Year fell at sunset of 8th Ramażān.[200] The governorships of Fārs were confirmed as in the year before. [322] In this year Ṭahmāsp Mirzā, the governor of Fārs, had a solid bridge constructed across the Parvāb River, known as the "Sivand-e Marvdasht River," 12 parasangs to the northwest of Shiraz;[201] this bridge was to facilitate the traffic of the caravans. By order of the shah, 6,000 toman were spent on repairing the government buildings at Shiraz. That year, too, Mirzā Moḥammad ᶜAli, agent of the foreign affairs of the province of Fārs, was granted the title "Khān."

199. See above, p. 36, note 176. 200. March 21, 1861.

201. See *FNN*, II, 323: "Where the Rudkhāna-ye Kamin reaches the village of Sivand, it becomes the Rudkhāna-ye Parvāb; this river flows into the Rudkhāna-ye Rāmjerd [or Kur River] below the village of ᶜEmāda Deh, in Khafrak-e soflā belonging to the district of Marvdasht, and becomes the Rudkāna-ye Korbāl." According to this statement, the Parvāb River is a section of the river called Polvār on the map. A place named "Pol-e Khān" ("Khan's Bridge") is to be found on the 1:500,000 map, near the confluence of the Polvār River and the Kur River; according to the text, however, the bridge in question must have been further up the Polvār River.

PROCEEDINGS AT THE ROYAL COURT; MOẒAFFAR OD-DIN MIRZĀ APPOINTED CROWN PRINCE. When the ᶜĀshurā days of the month of Moḥarrem of the year 1278[202] came near, the shah, because of the heat, held the audience in the summer camp in Tehran, cut short his mourning for Emām Ḥosein, postponing full mourning to the month of Ṣafar in the city of Tehran.

The New Year fell on the evening of 20th Ramażān.[203] That year the regions of Bushehr, Dashti, and Dashtestān were separated from the province of Fārs and entrusted to ᶜAmid ol-Molk Aḥmad Khān, who arrived at Bandar Bushehr in the month of Dhu'l-Qaᶜda.[204]

At the end of the month of Dhu'l-Ḥejja,[205] Prince Moẓaffar od-Din Mirzā was appointed crown prince of the Persian empire.[206]

SOLṬĀN MASᶜUD MIRZĀ YAMIN OD-DOULA ẒELL OS-SOLṬĀN APPOINTED GOVERNOR OF FĀRS. The New Year fell on 1st Shavvāl of the year 1279.[207] [843] At the beginning of that year Mo'eiyed od-Doula Ṭahmāsp Mirzā, Haji Mirzā ᶜAli Akbar Qavām ol-Molk, Mirzā Abu'l-Ḥasan Khān Moshir ol-Molk, Moḥammed Qoli Khān Ilkhāni, and Mirzā Moḥammad Reżā Mostoufi were summoned from Shiraz to Tehran; they arrived there at the end of Shavvāl.[208] Several days later the governorship of the province of Fārs was conferred upon Solṭān Masᶜud Mirzā Yamin od-Doula Ẓell os-Solṭān.[209] Moḥammad Nāṣer Khān Ẓahir od-Doula Qājār was appointed administrator and vizier of the whole province. In the month of Dhu'l-Ḥejja

202. Began on July 9, 1861.
203. March 20, 1862 (should be March 21).
204. Began on April 30, 1862.
205. About June 20, 1862.
206. He ascended the throne in 1896 as Nāṣer od-Din Shāh's successor, and died in 1907.
207. March 22, 1863 (should be March 21).
208. About April 15, 1863.
209. Grand uncle of Nāṣer od-Din Shāh, son of Fatḥ ᶜAli Shāh.

of the year 1279,[210] both were sent from Tehran to Shiraz and arrived there at the end of Dhu'l-Ḥejja. Haji ᶜAli Akbar Qavām al-Molk was appointed administrator of the shrine of Emām Reżā at Mashhad and sent from Tehran to his place of destination. Aḥmad Khān ᶜAmid ol-Molk Navā'i was established in the governorship of Bandar Bushehr, Dashti, and Dashtestān. And that year a telegraph line was installed from the Araxes river in Ādherbāyjān to Bushehr.[211]

A CHANGE IN THE VIZIERATE OF FĀRS. The New Year fell on 12th Shavvāl of the year 1280.[212] Ẓahir od-Doula was removed from the vizierate of Fārs; Mirzā Moḥammed Qavām od-Doula Farāhāni-ye ᶜErāqī was appointed in his place and arrived at Shiraz in the month of Dhu'l-Qaᶜda.[213]

SOLṬĀN OVEIS MIRZĀ EḤTESHĀM OD-DOULA'S SUCCESSFUL ADMINISTRATION OF KUH-E GILUYA AND BEHBEHĀN. That year the governorship of the region of Kuh-e Giluya and Behbehān was conferred upon Eḥteshām od-Doula Solṭān Oveis Mirzā, son of Haji Farhād Mirzā Moᶜtamad od-Doula; he arrived at Shiraz in the company of Qavām od-Doula. Mirzā Solṭān Moḥammad Khān, the former governor of Behbehān, because of the difficulties of life and out of disdain, had fled from Shiraz the previous year without the permission of the government and had occupied Kuh-e Giluya and Behbehān. When Qavām od-Doula reassured him, he returned to Shiraz and was granted a suitable pension. In the month of Rabiᶜ I of the year 1281,[214] Eḥteshām od-Doula left Shiraz for Kuh-e

210. Began on May 20, 1863.

211. That year Persia and England entered into an agreement concerning the Tehran–Bushehr line; telegraph lines connecting Jolfa (on the Araxes River) with Tehran were only installed later, namely, three lines: 1. Line of the Indo-European Telegraph Company (1868), 2. a Persian line under Russian control, and 3. a line operated by the Persian government, see Litten, *Persien*, Map 1 in the Appendix.

212. March 21, 1864. 213. Began on April 8, 1864.

214. Began on August 4, 1864.

Giluya and Behbehān, together with Commander Asad Khān, a detachment of Qashqā'i soldiers, and with ᶜAli Khān and Moḥammad Ṣādeq Khān from Marāgha in Ādherbāyjan—both captains of 300 horsemen of the Ādherbāyjāni vanguard. Upon his arrival, Eḥteshām od-Doula calmed down the people by doing good and talking gently; he united the Lors of Kuh-e Giluya and allowed no encroachments. If in a tribe two men were enemies, he would inquire into their behavior, remove one of them, and assign him a living, because most depravities and most cases of disobedience were the outcome of financial troubles. By these means he calmed all the rebels of the Lors within a short space of time; the tribes of the region, such as the tribes of Ḥuma-ye Behbehān, Zeidun, and Lirāvi[215] who had been dispersed by the unseemly behavior of the governor, were united by persuasion and promises of tax remittance and subsidies and became engaged in agriculture. At the end of that year, Eḥteshām od-Doula paid a sum of money which the districts owed the Divān out of his own pocket to the treasury and thus became creditor of the districts.

PROCEEDINGS AT THE ROYAL COURT. The New Year fell on 23d Shavvāl;[216] the shah celebrated the feast in the most perfect manner. [323] The province of Fārs was well arranged in the shadow of Ẓell os-Solṭān,[217] and the inhabitants lived in tranquillity.

The shah spent the ᶜĀshurā days of the month of Moḥarram of the year 1282[218] in mourning over Emām Ḥosein. On 25th Moḥarram,[219] the court departed for Firuzkuh.

DEATH OF QAVĀM OL-MOLK; HIS SONS PROMOTED TO HIGH OFFICES. In the same month Haji Mirzā ᶜAli Akbar

215. For Lirāvi, on the coast northwest of Bushehr, see above, p. 25, note 112.

216. March 21, 1865.

217. The meaning of "Ẓell os-Solṭān" is "shadow of the solṭān."

218. Began on May 27, 1865. 219. June 20, 1865.

Qavām ol-Molk Shirazi at Mashhad died at the age of eighty years; he had been appointed deputy administrator of the shrine of Emām Reżā at Mashhad. The title "Qavām ol-Molk" was conferred upon his son, Mirzā ᶜAli Moḥammad Khān-e Shirāzi. Another son, Mirzā Fatḥ ᶜAli Khān Ṣāḥeb Divān, was appointed governor of Shoshtar, Dezful, and the region of ᶜArabestān-e ᶜajam. Mirzā Ḥasan ᶜAli Khān Daryābegi was granted the title "Naṣir ol-Molk."

SOLṬĀN OVEIS MIRZĀ ESTABLISHES ORDER IN KUH-E GILUYA. That year, when the sun entered the sign of Gemini,[220] Eḥteshām ol-Doula, governor of Kuh-e Giluya and Behbehān, departed from Behbehān to settle the affairs of the tribes, to collect taxes in Posht-e Kuh,[221] and to escape the heat; he took with him the Qashqā'i detachment and the horsemen of the Ādherbāyjāni vanguard. They put up camp in the plain of Ṭassuj, a district of Chorām in Posht-e Kuh,[222] the fountains of which have drinkable water and the air of which is cool. The camp was at the foot of the Kuh-e Ashkar[223] and the Kuh-e Sāvorz,[224] which most of the time are covered with snow. By these means he established complete order in the region of Posht-e Kuh.

UPROAR IN SHIRAZ, UPON WHICH THE VIZIER IS DEPOSED. In the month of Ṣafar of that year,[225] the nobles of Fārs grew angry at the shameless talk of the vizier of Fārs, Mirzā Moḥam-

220. That is, June/July 1865.

221. For Posht-e Kuh, see above, p. 342, note 180. The *FNN*, II, 271, mentions a village called Posht-e Kuh 2.5 parasangs south of Bāsht.

222. The center of the district of Chorām was Tell Gerd, 10 parasangs northeast of Behbehān, see *FNN*, II, 273.

223. According to *FNN*, II, 336, the Kuh-e Ashkar lies between the village of Ṭassuj and the village of Pichāb, in the nāḥeya of Bāvi (on the 1:500,000 map: Kuh-e Eshger, 2,700 meters high).

224. Southeast of the Kuh-e Dinār, 3,22 meters high, and northeast of the Kuh-e Ashkar.

225. Began on June 26, 1865.

mad Qavām od-Doula, while the craftsmen and merchants were irritated by the poor conduct of the said vizier's officials; they crowded together and occupied the house of Qavām od-Doula. Things passed to the discharging of muskets, until prudent citizens sent for several men, such as Haji Sheikh Yaḥyā, imam of the prayers, Haji Sheikh Moḥammad Ḥosein Sheikh ol-Eslām, and Mirzā Ḥasan ᶜAli Khān Naṣir ol-Molk, who calmed down the anger of the people. Qavām od-Doula considered Mirzā ᶜAli Khān, the beglerbegi of Shiraz, to be the originator of the trouble; he reported this to the government and called Mirzā ᶜAli Khān an enemy (moqaṣṣer) of the state. Ḥāji Reżā-ye Qāsi[226] was not at all involved in this civil war; however, Mirzā Abu'l-Ḥasan Khān Moshir al-Molk, who at that time was staying in Tehran and had for a long time harbored hatred towards the beglerbegi, Mirzā ᶜAli Khān, and Haji Reẓā-ye Qāsi, reported the affair in the most disparaging manner to the government. Accordingly, the shah ordered both men to be executed under the responsibility of Ḥosām os-Salṭana. Mirzā Qavām od-Doula Farāhāni was removed from the vizierate of Fārs.

SOLṬĀN MORĀD MIRZĀ ḤOSAM OS-SALṬANA AGAIN GOVERNOR OF FĀRS, EXECUTES HEAD OF THE REBELS. Then Ẓell os-Solṭān left Shiraz for Tehran to celebrate his marriage there. The governorship of Fārs was entrusted to Solṭān Morād Mirzā Ḥosām os-Salṭana. On 14th Rabiᶜ II of the year 1282,[227] Ḥosām os-Salṭana and Mirzā Abu'l-Ḥasan Khān Moshir ol-Molk left Tehran for Fārs. Upon their arrival at Eṣfahan the following information (eᶜlām-nāma) was sent to Eḥteshām od-Doula, who was a nephew and in addition to this son-in-law of Ḥosām os-Salṭana: "By order of the government you have been established in the governorship of Kuh-e Giluya

226. For his former activities, see above, p. 343.
227. September 6, 1865.

and Behbehān. Entrust your affairs to your agents and join us with your family, wherever this is possible!" Eḥteshām od-Doula, accordingly, proceeded from Kuh-e Giluya to Shiraz, left his wife, a daughter of Ḥosām os-Salṭana, back at Shiraz, and met Ḥosām os-Salṭana in the district of Mashhad-e Omm on-Nabi.[228] Because Haji Reẓā-ye Qāsi considered himself free from the crime of being involved in the civil war, he arrived confidently at the foot of the Takht-e Jamshid;[229] the next day he climbed the hill joyfully, being sure of Ḥosām os-Salṭana's sympathy and benevolence. When he had entered the prince's pavilion, he was arrested and executed. His body was suspended two nights and a day at the Takht, his goods and chattel were plundered and carried away as a booty by Moḥammad Qāsem Khān-e Beiżā'i. Ḥosām os-Salṭana arrived at Shiraz on the 19th of that month.[230] Having inquired into the affair of the beglerbegi, Mirzā ᶜAli Khān, he announced that the beglerbegi had fallen incurably ill and had been bedridden for several days; he canceled the execution and left him to his fate. Then he conferred the vizierate of Fārs upon Mirzā Abu'l-Ḥasan Khān Moshir ol-Molk and made him independent holder of this office. The governorship of Sabᶜa and Lārestān was entrusted to Mahdi Qoli Mirzā, Ḥosām os-Salṭana's cousin. Soleimān Mirzā, Ḥosām os-Salṭana's nephew, was appointed governor of Kāzerun. The governorship of Bandar Bushehr, Dashti, and Dashtestān was conferred upon Asadollāh Mirzā Nā'eb ol-Eyāla, Ḥosām os-Salṭana's nephew.

SOLṬĀN OVEIS MIRZĀ CONSTRUCTS WATER CONDUIT AT BEHBEHĀN. The governorship of the region of Kuh-e Giluya remained with Eḥteshām od-Doula Solṭān Oveis Mirzā as

228. Mashhad-e Mādar-e Soleimān, about 25 miles northeast of Persepolis, see above, p. 29, note 132.

229. The palace of Persepolis. Apparently, the governor had set up camp on the hill behind the palace.

230. September 11, 1865.

before. The latter arrived by way of Kāzerun and Mamassani at Behbehān in the month of Rajab.[231] Because there had never been running water in the town of Behbehān, outside [324] its eastern gate 3 water basins were constructed which were supplied with water from the irrigation canals of the surrounding region. From those basins the water was carried to the town by water carriers. During summer and autumn, when the water was needed for agriculture, the farmers prevented the water from flowing into the basins. Three or four months each year the inhabitants of Behbehān had to drink the bitter and brackish water of the wells in their houses. When Eḥteshām od-Doula saw this state of affairs the previous year, he made up his mind to supply Behbehān with drinking water. When the flat and hilly ground stretching between the Kordestān River, 2 parasangs away, and the town had been examined, it was realized that it would be possible to supply the town with water by digging a subterranean water canal and constructing a water conduit. The conduit would bring the water of the Kordestān River (the digestibility of this water rates next to that of the Euphrates and Tigris)[232] to the southern gate of the town; flowing out of the town through the northern gate, the water could be used for the irrigation of the fields which were not now irrigated. That year Eḥteshām od-Doula submitted a new petition to the government. Accordingly, the construction was put under his responsibility. Since there were no canal builders and no tools for this purpose at Behbehān, the governor selected, when he passed through Kāzerun, 3 canal builders and brought them to Behbehān. Ḥosām os-Salṭana ordered Haji Moḥammad Kāẓem-e Shirāzi, known as "Kadkhodā," who for many years had been mayor of Mashhad and had complete knowledge of canal

231. Began on November 20, 1865.

232. The praise of the Euphrates and Tigris goes back the medieval times, when Mesopotamia was the seat of the Caliphate and therefore, a country of blessing; al-Furāt ("Euphrates") is a synonym of "very fine, sweet water," see Steingass, *Persian-English Dictionary*, s.v. Furāt.

building, to settle in Behbehān. In the month of Shaᶜbān,[233] the kadkhodā arrived at Behbehān with 12 experienced canal builders from Kāzerun, and they engaged in digging the subterranean canal and the water conduit. After more than three years, the construction was completed, and the water flowed into Behbehān through the southern gate and out of the town through the northern gate. The canal was called "Qanāt-e Nāṣeri."[234] When in 1286,[235] Eḥteshām od-Doula left Kuh-e Giluya for Tehran, the Divan agents of Behbehān diverted the water of the canal from its mouth (az dam-e kat) to the agricultural irrigation canals and increased the taxes levied from the irrigated fields. Thus the whole system of the Qanāt-e Nāṣeri was disrupted, and the inhabitants of Behbehān during three of four summer months had to drink bitter and brackish water as before.

THE SHAH TRAVELS TO MĀZANDARĀN. The New Year fell on the evening of 3d Dhu'l-Qaᶜda.[236] The shah celebrated the feast and held the private and public audience and granted each courtier a special favor. At the end of Dhu'l-Qaᶜda,[237] the shah departed from Tehran to go to Māzandarān. On the Feast of Sacrifices,[238] he encamped at Sāri in Māzandarān. On the 13th of that month,[239] he departed for the town of Ashraf and set up camp in the Bāgh-e Shah ᶜAbbās.[240] Two days later he set out

233. Began on December 20, 1865.

234. In honor of Nāṣer od-Din Shāh, the ruling monarch; at that time, it was quite common to name things in honor of the king, as, for example, the *Fārs-nāma-ye Nāṣeri* itself.

235. 1286:1869/70, see below, p. 366.

236. March 19, 1866 (should be March 21).

237. About April 15, 1866.

238. April 26, 1866 (ᶜId ol-ażhā, that is, 10th Dhu'l-Ḥejja).

239. April 29, 1866.

240. The new town of Ashraf, 35 miles east of Sāri on the road to Astarābād, had been built by Shāh ᶜAbbās I (r. 1588–1629) in 1021:1612/13 and consisted of a series of splendid palaces; having suffered heavily under Nāder Shāh, the town was rebuilt by Āqā Moḥammad Shāh in 1193:

for a visit of Ṣafiābād,[241] which was built by Shāh Ṣafi Safavi[242] on top of a high hill and overlooked a wide stretch of the country. On 16th Dhu'l-Ḥejja,[243] the shah encamped in the outskirts of ᶜAbbāsābād,[244] 4 parasangs from Ashraf. ᶜAbbāsābād is the name of a small lake. Shāh ᶜAbbās[245] had constructed a solid dam of stones and mortar across the Farākhi valley[246] by which the winter water was dammed; through a series of holes, one above the other, several villages were provided with water at the time of cultivation. On the 21st of that month,[247] the shah proceeded to Farākhābād[248] and encamped at the shore of the Caspian Sea. The next day the court boarded some small boats to visit the Russian ships anchored there to welcome the shah and his retinue.[249] On the 24th[250] the shah departed from Farākhābād and encamped on the 26th at the town of Bārforush in Māzandarān. On the 28th he arrived at Āmol and on 1st Moḥarram of the year 1283[251] at Soula Deh.[252] Then he decided to return to Tehran and arrived at the summer camp of Shemrān

---

1779/80. The Bāgh-e Shāh ᶜAbbās is perhaps the same as the Bāgh-e Shāhi, mentioned in the EI² I, s.v. A*sh*raf (R. M. Savory); see also above, p. 12, note 52.

241. Neither is mentioned in the *Farhang*, nor shown on the map; probably located in the hilly region south of Ashraf.

242. The successor of Shāh ᶜAbbās I, Shāh Ṣafi I, who reigned 1629–42.

243. May 2, 1866.

244. The *Farhang*, III, 194, mentions a village ᶜAbbāsābād, 12 miles northeast of Sāri.

245. He reigned 1588–1629.

246. The Valley of Farakhi is most probably named after Farakhābād at its mouth, mentioned a few lines further down.

247. May 7, 1866.

248. 16 miles north of Sāri according to the *Farhang*, III, 203. The 1:500,000 map shows Farahābād on the Caspian Sea, north of Sāri.

249. The peace treaty of Torkmānchāy, concluded in 1828, granted Russia free seafaring on the Caspian Sea.

250. May 10, 1866.

251. May 16, 1866.

252. 27 miles northwest of Āmol, on the shore of the Caspian Sea, see *Farhang*, III, 165.

on the 23d of that month.[253] On 10th Jomādi II,[254] he settled down in Tehran.

FAMINE IN SHIRAZ. That year the governorships of the districts of the province of Fārs remained as before. On 2d Shaᶜbān,[255] at sunrise, there was a hail-storm at Behbehān and 2 miles around; the hailstones were bigger than oranges. In the winter of that year[256] the prices of grain and victuals went up at Shiraz and in the districts of Fārs. The merchants and inhabitants of Shiraz together with the widows, orphans, and gossipy women complained and crowded together on the Meidān and at the entrance of the government buildings, demanding Ḥosām os-Salṭana to lower the price of bread and to increase provisions. The governor ordered several loads of the wheat and barley in the government stores to be put aside for the daily allowances of the soldiers and the Divan horsemen and the rest to be sold at half of the actual price to the bakers. When [325] forty to fifty days had elapsed and the prices increased slightly, the inhabitants gathered together, causing a riot and a hunger revolt. The first day the people were calmed down and dispersed. Two or three days later, the riots and troubles increased, and people were groaning at the entrance of the government buildings. The governor sent to high and low the following message:

> I have no land in the province of Fārs the grain of which I could store. I have given the grain which was held in the government stores to the merchants, and you have been living on it for some time. God willing, I shall put at your disposal the camels, mules, and beasts of burden which are in my possession, and in addition I shall rent beasts near and far; I shall buy grain in the region of Fārs and transport it to Shiraz without any charge.

That day he calmed down the people by these means. The next day he assembled a number of donkeys, camels, and mules and

253. June 7, 1866. 254. October 20, 1866.
255. December 10, 1866. 256. That is, winter 1866/67.

sent some to the southern districts of Fārs, some to Esfahan, to buy grain. Three or four days later the people crowded together again, assembled at the entrance of the government building, shouting at the top of their voices: "Ḥosām os-Salṭana is the cause of the high price of bread. We are not content with him. He must leave the town!" A renowned person in the service of the governor suggested that the civil war had been caused by Beglerbegi Mirzā ᶜAli Khān. The governor paid no attention to this talk, sent for several of the rioters and said to them: "I shall send beasts of burden to the surroundings in order to alleviate your condition. There will be plenty of grain after two or three days." Having said this, he ordered the people to disperse. When a quantity of grain arrived at Shiraz, it was distributed among the bakers free of charge. The next day the people crowded together again, shouting at the top of their voices: "We want neither grain and bread nor the governorship of Ḥosām os-Salṭana!" The renowned person repeated his suggestion that Beglerbegi Mirzā ᶜAli Khān and his followers and the sons of Haji Qavām ol-Molk were the instigators of the riot; that he had to do one of two things: either fire a gun loaded with lead at these people or send for Mirzā ᶜAli Khān and make him silence those people. The governor replied: "Those ignorant people demand bread of me. It would be inhuman to kill them with shrapnel. The beglerbegi, though bedridden, must come!" The beglerbegi appeared, although he was feeble and sick.[257] Having heard the orders of the governor, the beglerbegi left the government building and distributed a sum of money out of his own pocket among the people. He promised to distribute bread among the inhabitants of Shiraz every day, according to the demand. The next day he installed bread shops at different spots and provided them with plenty of bread. As the grain and the victuals which Ḥosām os-Salṭana brought from the surroundings were distributed at low prices among the inhabitants of Shiraz,

257. See above, p. 351 seq.

the year of famine came to an end with low prices. At the beginning of the following year,[258] Mirzā ᶜAli Khān, the beglerbegi, died, though still a young man.

THE SHAH TRAVELS TO MASHHAD. The New Year fell on the evening of Thursday, 14th Dhu'l-Qaᶜda.[259] On 15th Dhu'l-Qaᶜda the shah departed from Tehran and made the pilgrimage to Mashhad. On 9th, 10th, and 11th Moḥarram of the year 1284,[260] he stayed at Dāmghān and spent his time in mourning the family of the Prophet. Then he departed from Dāmghān and arrived at Mashhad on 14th Ṣafar.[261]

When the shah was crossing the courtyard of the shrine of Emām Reẓā, he took off the jewel-studded clasp which is the prerogative of the reigning monarch and presented it as a gift to the shrine.[262] On 18th Rabiᶜ I[263] he bade the shrine farewell and left for Tehran going by way of Quchān and Bojnurd.[264] He arrived in Tehran on 15th Jomādi II.[265]

FINAL SETTLEMENT OF THE BANDAR ᶜABBĀS QUESTION

SOLṬĀN MORĀD MIRZĀ ḤOSĀM OS-SALṬANA OCCUPIES BANDAR ᶜABBĀS. As has been reported under the events of the year 1272,[266] the governorship of Bandar ᶜAbbās, Shamil, and Mināb had been restored by the Persian ministers to Seiyed Saᶜid Khān, Imam of Masqaṭ. Each year he was to pay taxes amounting to 16,000 toman to Tehran or to the governor of

258. May/June 1867. 259. March 19, 1867 (should be March 21).
260. May 13–15, 1867. 261. June 17, 1867.
262. This might be explained as a symbolic action, by which Emām Reżā was declared ruler of Persia.
263. July 20, 1867.
264. Quchān lies about 95 miles northwest of Mashhad, Bojnurd about 60 miles northwest of Quchān. This means that he traveled to Tehran through Gorgān.
265. October 14, 1867. 266. See above, p. 313 seq.

Fārs. Several years passed with this regulation in force. Then the Imamate of Masqaṭ was transferred to Seiyed Sālem Khān, son of Seiyed Soveini, son of Seiyed Saᶜid Khān.[267] The agents of Seiyed Sālem collected double taxes from the subjects of those regions. When the Persian ministers heard of this, they ordered Ḥosām os-Salṭana to depart from Shiraz and to take away Bandar ᶜAbbās and dependencies from the agents of the Imam of Masqaṭ and to occupy that region. If they refused, pointing out that tax arrears for a certain space of time were still to be collected and that they would not surrender Bandar ᶜAbbās and dependencies before that space of time had elapsed,[268] the governor was to reply:

In accordance with the treaty concluded with the late Imam of Masqaṭ, Seiyed Saᶜid, two conditions are in force: 1) The governor of Bandar ᶜAbbās shall comply with the orders of the governor of Fārs and must not act contrary to the latter's orders. 2) The governor shall not [326] be tyrant over the subjects and shall not double the taxes. However, the governor of Bandar ᶜAbbās has in the last years oppressed the subjects beyond bounds and not complied with the orders of the governor of Fārs; he has sent no report and rendered no service.

Ḥosām os-Salṭana was ordered to occupy Bandar ᶜAbbās by force in case they started quarreling and then to transfer it to a man of his confidence. Accordingly, Ḥosām os-Salṭana departed from Shiraz at the end of Ramażān[269] to occupy Bandar ᶜAbbās. He marched to Dārāb by way of Sarvestān and the district of Fasā and established himself at Dārāb. Then he summoned Mahdi Qoli Mirzā, the governor of Lārestān, and ordered him to conquer Bandar ᶜAbbās. Mahdi Qoli Mirzā returned to Lār and sent for a number of aldermen and nobles

267. This happened in 1282:1866, see Bosworth, *The Islamic Dynasties*, p. 78 (in 1283 according to Zambaur, *Manuel*, p. 129).

268. According to the agreement of 1272:1855/56, Bandar ᶜAbbās was rented to the Imam of Masqaṭ for twenty years, see above, p. 315.

269. About January 20, 1868.

of Lār. He gave them the following order: "A group of you will go to Bandar ᶜAbbās under the pretext of lodging complaint against me and take up quarters in different houses. Another group will eventually join you under the pretext of giving you good words in my name. Their arrival will be reported to me." When the second group had arrived at Bandar ᶜAbbās, Mahdi Qoli Mirzā proceeded with two horsemen to the region of Bandar ᶜAbbās and told the road guards: "I am riding ahead of a caravan and in a great hurry, as I have to receive a shipment which has arrived at the port, so as not to lose time until the arrival of the caravan." With this ruse he managed to pass the police stations and to enter Bandar ᶜAbbās. When those who had arrived before him heard of his arrival, they joined him, and answering no questions they entered the Dutch building, the seat of the governor. The agents of the Imam of Masqaṭ had no choice but to surrender.

THE BAHĀRLU AND INĀLU TRIBES COMPLAIN ABOUT QAVĀM AL-MOLK'S OPPRESSION. Two or three days after Ḥosām os-Saltana's arrival at Dārāb, petitions arrived from the mayor and the aldermen of the Bahārlu and Inālu tribes, complaining about Mirzā ᶜAli Moḥammad Khān Qavām ol-Molk and stating that they were not content with him. They demanded of Ḥosām os-Salṭana: that he should send a deputy to Izadkhvāst, their winter camp which was several parasangs from Dārāb;[270] that the deputy could draft a record on Qavām ol-Molk's oppression and tyranny; and that they would present themselves before that deputy. The governor sent Eshiq Āqāsi Bashi Haji Mirzā Aḥmad-e Shirazi. When he arrived at the camp, he gave the aldermen guarantees and asked them to proceed to Dārāb and to settle affairs with Qavām ol-Molk. Because Moshir ol-Molk, vizier and chief of Fārs, continuously quarreled with

270. The governor of Dārāb was Qavām ol-Molk, see below, p. 364. Izadkhvāst is now called Oulād-e ᶜAli and lies 38 miles south of Dārāb, see *Farhang*, VII, 16.

Qavām ol-Molk and knew that if the Bahārlu did come to Dārāb, the governor, willing or not, would surrender them to Qavām ol-Molk, Moshir ol-Molk hastily sent a man to Izad-khvāst telling him that they would be arrested and handed over to Qavām ol-Molk if they came to Dārāb. Accordingly, upon the arrival of Moshir al-Molk's messenger, they postponed their going to Dārāb to another time. When the governor heard of this, he said: "I shall not hesitate to punish the Bahārlu who have deviated from the path of obedience. I shall not go to Bandar ᶜAbbās before having subdued them." And Qavām ol-Molk promised that he would either persuade them or fight and exterminate them.

OFFER TO THE IMAM OF MASQAṬ CONCERNING THE POSSESSION OF BANDAR ᶜABBĀS. When news of the capture of Bandar ᶜAbbās arrived from Mahdi Qoli Mirzā, Ḥosām os-Salṭana departed from Dārāb, marched by way of Forg and Ṭārom to Sabᶜa and arrived at Bandar ᶜAbbās on 3d Dhu'l-Qaᶜda of that year.[271] He sent for the officials and agents of Seiyed Sālem, the Imam of Masqaṭ, who were staying at Bandar ᶜAbbās, and told them:

> It is not our intention to take Bandar ᶜAbbās and its dependencies away from the Imam of Masqaṭ. It shall remain in his possession until the lease has elapsed. However, the oppression of and tyrannical rule over the inhabitants of Bandar ᶜAbbās and its dependencies must stop, and a governor must be appointed whom we can accept!

A letter containing these conditions was sent to Seiyed Sālem and the English consul, the protector (ḥāmi) and deputy (jāneb-dār) of the Imam of Masqaṭ.[272] Some time elapsed without reply to the letter.

271. February 26, 1868.

272. "Political resident on the Persian Gulf" was Lewis Pelly, from 1862 onward, see below, p. 365, note 277. British influence in Oman was increasing from the beginning of the nineteenth century onward; the division of Seiyed Saᶜid's territory after his death in 1856 was effected

THE SHAH ORDERS NEW DISTRIBUTION OF THE GOVERNMENT SCHEDULES. The New Year fell on the 25th Dhu'l-Qa^c^da.[273] The shah ordered the government schedules to be distributed for the week, the month, and the whole year and a strict observation of the new arrangements:

Saturday. Special and public audiences
Sunday. Sessions of the court of complaints (divān-e maẓālem) and inquiries into the petitions submitted by the chief magistrates court (divān khāna-ye ᶜadliya)
Monday. Day of rest
Tuesday. Government decrees (baravāt-e divāni) and official diplomas
Wednesday. Special accounts of the treasury and account books of the provinces of the empire (kitābchahā-ye dastur ol-ᶜamal)
Thursday. Special proposals of the ministry of war and of foreign affairs
Friday. Day of worship, free of all other occupations

NEW GOVERNOR APPOINTED TO DĀRĀB AND THE BAHĀRLU AND INĀLU TRIBES. When Ḥosām os-Salṭana stayed at Bandar ᶜAbbās for a while and no reply arrived from the Imam of Masqaṭ and the English consul, the governorship of the whole of Bandar ᶜAbbās, Shamil, and Mināb and all the dependencies was added to the governorship of Lārestān and Sabᶜa and conferred upon Mahdi Qoli Mirzā. Ḥosām os-Salṭana departed from Bandar ᶜAbbās and marched by way of Lār to Jahrom. [327] Mirzā ᶜAli Moḥammad Khān Qavām ol-Molk, who during Ḥosām os-Salṭana's stay at Dārāb had been ordered to settle the affairs of the Bahārlu and Inālu tribes, despairing of the

---

through British mediation. A British formal protectorate was not established until 1890; it did not include Oman, but was restricted to Zanzibar and Pemba. Thus the term *ḥāmi* used by Ḥasan-e Fasā'i should not be interpreted as meaning a 'protectorate' in the strict sense of the word.

273. March 20, 1868 (should be March 21).

possibility to persuade them, gathered together after Ḥosām os-Salṭana's departure from Dārāb to Bandar ᶜAbbās auxiliary forces from the district of Dārāb, added his own servants to them, and marched off to subdue the tribes by threats. Because the Bahārlu had been secretly ordered by Moshir ol-Molk to refuse obedience to Qavām ol-Molk, they were waiting to open battle and drew up their lines opposite Qavām ol-Molk. After a few skirmishes, Qavām ol-Molk, seeing that fighting was futile, returned to Dārāb. Since he could not expect to be protected by Moshir ol-Molk, he did not consider it useful to stay with Ḥosām os-Salṭana, according to the proverb: "If your enemy is the vizier, the emir is of no use." So he gave up his endeavors and returned to Tehran. When Ḥosām os-Salṭana, who at that time was staying at Bandar ᶜAbbās, heard of this master stroke, he conferred the governorship of Dārāb upon Mirzā ᶜAli Akbar Khān-e Fasā'i, governor of the district of Fasā, whose family had been holding the office of governor of the district of Fasā for generations; the governorship of the Bahārlu and Inālu tribes was added to the governorship of those districts. And Hosām os-Salṭana departed for Shiraz by way of Jahrom.[274]

QAVĀM OL-MOLK'S MACHINATIONS IN TEHRAN WITH REGARD TO THE GOVERNORSHIP OF DĀRĀB AND FASĀ. When Qavām ol-Molk arrived in Tehran and heard of the transfer of the governorship to Mirzā ᶜAli Akbar Khān, he gave the ministers a sum of money as a peshkash and won their sympathies. At the displeasure of Mirzā ᶜAli Akbar Khān, son-in-law of Moshir ol-Molk, the principal taxes (aṣl-e māleyāt) of the districts of Fasā which amounted to 8,160 toman, were increased by 12,000 toman, and the governorship of that district was added to Dārāb and the tribes of Bahārlu and Inālu, and a royal decree on this matter was issued. Since Qavām ol-Molk

274. By mistake the author (or the copyist) placed this sentence at the end of the following paragraph.

knew that Moshir ol-Molk, as long as he was alive, would not desist from trying to destroy him, he persuaded Haji Mirzā Zamān Khān, paternal uncle of Farrokh Khān Amin od-Doula Kāshāni,[275] to depart with him from Tehran to strengthen his position and to arrange his affairs. They appeared before Ḥosām os-Saltana at Jahrom. The governorship of Dārāb and Fasā and the Bahārlu and Inālu tribes was taken away from Mirzā ᶜAli Akbar Khān and conferred upon Qavām ol-Molk. Because about four-fifths of all the lands of the district of Fasā were the hereditary possessions of Mirzā ᶜAli Akbar Khān and his cousins and they were prejudiced by Qavām ol-Molk's increasing of the taxes, Mirzā ᶜAli Akbar Khān hastily left Jahrom for Tehran; immediately upon his arrival he made a statement with regard to the oppression and the injustice of the taxes imposed on the district of Fasā. After he had stayed in Tehran for one year, the ministers diminished the taxes, which had been fixed at 20,000 toman, by 8,000 toman and fixed the taxes to be paid by the district of Fasā at 12,000 toman. Mirzā ᶜAli Akbar Khān was granted the title "Khān" and appointed vakil of the province of Fārs. He was called "Mirzā ᶜAli Akbar Khān Vakil" and appointed governor of the district of Fasā.

APPOINTMENT OF NEW GOVERNORS TO BANDAR ᶜABBĀS, LĀRESTĀN, AND BUSHEHR. The shah spent the ᶜĀshurā days of the month of Moḥarram of the year 1285[276] in mourning the family of the Prophet. Ḥosām os-Salṭana took the governorship of Lārestān, Sabᶜa, and Bandar ᶜAbbās away from Mahdi Qoli Mirzā and appointed Asadollāh Mirzā Nā'eb ol-Eyāla governor in his stead. The governorship of Bandar Bushehr was taken away from Asadollāh Mirzā Nā'eb ol-Eyāla and conferred upon Mirzā Ḥasan ᶜAli Khān Naṣir ol-Molk. The other governorships were not altered.

275. Farrokh Khān was a man of great influence; he was Persian plenipotentiary for the peace treaty of Paris, see above, p. 234.

276. Began on April 24, 1868.

BANDAR ᶜABBĀS RESTITUTED TO THE IMAM OF MASQAṬ. When part of this year had elapsed and Asadollāh Mirzā had been established in his governorship, Ḥosām os-Salṭana received letters from Seiyed Sālem, the Imam of Masqaṭ, and Pelly Ṣāḥeb, consul of the British empire,[277] to the effect that the Imam of Masqaṭ asked to be pardoned for not having replied to the honorable letter; that the delay had been caused by a revolt in ᶜOmān. Pelly Ṣāḥeb, the English consul, wrote:

> If the governor gives his permission, I shall come to Shiraz in the company of the son of the vizier of Masqāṭ and a Persian by birth, Haji Aḥmad Khān. If Bandar ᶜAbbās was entrusted to the latter, the subjects of Bandar ᶜAbbās had no reason to complain about tyranny and oppression exercized by that official.

Accordingly, Ḥosām os-Salṭana summoned Pelly Ṣāḥeb, the English consul, and Haji Aḥmad Khān from Bushehr. Upon their arrival their desires were fulfilled and they returned. The negotiations went on until the month of Jomādi II of that year.[278] When Asadollāh Mirzā Nā'eb ol-Eyāla, governor of Lārestān, Sabᶜa, and Bandar ᶜAbbās, heard of the restitution of the region of Bandar ᶜAbbās, he renounced the governorship of Lārestān and Sabᶜa and returned to Shiraz. His governorship was conferred upon Soleimān Mirzā, nephew of Hosām os-Salṭana.

FINAL SETTLEMENT OF THE POSSESSION OF BANDAR ᶜABBĀS. When the nobles of Masqaṭ saw that Seiyed Sālem was under the protection of the British empire,[279] they entered into an agreement and laid siege to the Imam's palace. Seiyed Sālem left the palace through a secret door, went with his family

277. Lewis Pelly (1825–92); 1858–60 in Persia, first secretary of legation, then *chargé d'affairs*. At the end of 1861, he was appointed political agent at Zanzibar. In 1862, he was transferred to the post of political resident on the Persian Gulf and took part in a long series of difficult negotiations with the Arabs near the coast. In 1865, he undertook his famous journey to Riyādh; see *National Biography*, Vol. XV, s.v. Pelly.

278. Began on September 19, 1868.

279. See above, p. 361.

on board a ship, and left Masqaṭ [328] for Bandar ᶜAbbās. Several days later, realizing that he was not safe at Bandar ᶜAbbās, he proceeded to the island of Qeshm, which belongs to Bandar ᶜAbbās, and established himself there. The English government dropped Seiyed Sālem, the Imam of Masqaṭ, and withdrew its protection from him. Then they summoned Haji Aḥmad Khān, governor of Bandar ᶜAbbās in the name of Seiyed Sālem, to Bombay and gave him instructions for the governorship of Bandar ᶜAbbās, and he returned. When Ḥosām os-Salṭana heard of the Imam's overthrow and stay on the island of Qeshm, and Haji Aḥmad Khān's journey to Bombay, he sent orders to Bandar ᶜAbbās to the effect that nobody was allowed to pay a dinar from Bandar ᶜAbbās and its dependencies to Seiyed Sālem. When Haji Aḥmad Khān heard of this order, he sent a letter to Ḥosām os-Salṭana, saying:

> Formerly I administered the districts of Bandar ᶜAbbās in the name of the Imam of Masqaṭ; now I have quit the Imam's service and consider myself a servant and agent of your excellency. I shall increase the taxes collected from Bandar ᶜAbbās and pay them to you.

The governor complied with the petition and appointed him governor of Bandar ᶜAbbās. That year all the districts of Fārs were well arranged and its inhabitants were living in tranquillity.

SOLṬĀN MASᶜUD MIRZĀ ẒELL OS-SOLṬĀN AGAIN APPOINTED GOVERNOR OF FĀRS. The New Year fell on Saturday, 6th Dhu'l-Ḥejja,[280] 10 hours, 30 minutes, and 43 seconds after sunrise. The feast was celebrated in the presence of the shah. On the 14th of that month,[281] news arrived of Ḥosām os-Salṭana's removal from the governorship of Fārs. These reports were sent from Shiraz to Behbehān on the 19th of that month. On the 23d,[282] Eḥteshām od-Doula Solṭān Oveis Mirzā, governor of Kuh-e Giluya and Behbehān, left Behbehān for the

280. March 20, 1869 (should be March 21).
281. March 28, 1869. 282. April 9, 1869.

province of Kurdistan, the governorship of his father, Moᶜtamad od-Doula Farhād Mirzā, who was an uncle of the shah. He traveled by way of Rāmhormoz, Shoshtar, Dezful, Khorramābād-e Fili, Borujerd, Nehāvand, and Kermānshāh to Sanandej, capital (balada) of Kurdistān, and rested there.

When the month of Moḥarram of the year 1286[283] came near, the shah spent the ᶜĀshurā days in mourning the family of the Prophet. Then he conferred the governorship of Fārs upon Solṭān Masᶜud Mirzā Ẓell os-Solṭān. Haji Moḥammad Qoli Khān-e Qājār Āṣaf od-Doula was appointed vizier and chief of Fārs. They arrived at Shiraz in the month of Ṣafar.[284] The governorship of Kuh-e Giluya was entrusted to Amir ol-Omarā Abu'l-Fatḥ Khān Ṣārem od-Doula, son of Amir-e Kabir Khān Bābā Khān Sardār. The governorship of Lār, Bushehr, Dashti, and Dashtestān remained with Ḥasan ᶜAli Khān Naṣir ol-Molk.

In the same year, Mirzā Fatḥ ᶜAli Khān Ṣāḥeb Divān-e Shirazi, who the previous year had been appointed vizier and chief of the province of Esfahan, was appointed independent governor of that province.

SHIRAZ AND FĀRS INFESTED WITH PLAGUE. From the beginning of the month of Jomādi I to the beginning of the month of Rajab,[285] Shiraz and the province of Fārs were infested with plague; a number of people died.

MISCELLANEOUS EVENTS. On 20th Shavvāl,[286] the shah departed for Gilān and encamped at Rasht on 11th Dhu'l-Qaᶜda.[287] On 1st Dhu'l-Ḥejja,[288] he departed from Rasht and arrived in Tehran on 15th Dhu'l-Ḥejja.[289]

The governorship of Bandar ᶜAbbās remained with Haji

283. April 21, 1869. 284. Began on May 13, 1869.
285. August 1869 to October 1869. 286. January 20, 1870.
287. February 12, 1870. 288. March 4, 1870.
289. March 18, 1870.

Aḥmad Khān as the year before. By the zeal of Ẓell os-Solṭān the whole province of Fārs was well arranged and the inhabitants were living in tranquillity and offering prayers on behalf of the stability of the dynasty.

The New Year fell on the evening of 18th Dhu'l-Ḥejja.[290]

The New Year feast and the Ghadir feast[291] fell together on a Monday. The special and public audiences, which are necessities in both feasts, were held in the presence of the shah. The shah spent the ᶜĀshurā days of the month of Moḥarrem of the year 1287[292] in mourning the family of the Prophet, as in the years before. Ẓell os-Solṭān remained governor of the province of Fārs and Haji Moḥammad Qoli Khān Āṣaf od-Doula vizier and chief to the aforementioned excellency. They did not alter the governorships of the districts and regions of Fārs.

COEXISTENCE WITH OTTOMAN TURKEY ADOPTED

THE SHAH'S PILGRIMAGE TO THE HOLY PLACES IN MESOPOTAMIA. It is a remarkable fact that from the beginning of Islam until now no Persian shah has been known to have traveled to Iraq which belongs to the Ottoman empire, except at the time of enmity and war with the Ottoman soltans.[293] The first shah to travel peacefully from Persia to Iraq, [329] to perform the pilgrimage to the shrines of the Emāms and without the intention of conquering that region, was Nāṣer od-Din Shāh. He departed from Tehran, the capital of the Persian empire, on 20th Jomādi II,[294] and arrived at Hamadān on 13th Rajab.[295] A strange story is told by Eḥteshām od-Doula Solṭān Oveis Mirzā, governor of Hamadān:

290. March 20, 1870 (should be March 21).
291. For this feast, see above, p. 103, note 70.
292. Began on April 3, 1870.
293. Visits of state had not yet been the custom, see above, p. 169, note 289.
294. September 17, 1870. 295. October 9, 1870.

Before the arrival of the court at Hamadān a merchant from Shoshtar had died at Hamadān. The judge of Hamadān had no hesitation about confiscating the merchant's belongings and declared the heir as being excluded from the heritage. When the governor asked the judge to give over the money to the heir, the judge uttered unjustifiable excuses. Two or three days after the court's arrival at Hamadān, the theologians and nobles of Hamadān were received in audience on the 15th of that month.[296] When it was the judge's turn to be introduced to the shah, the shah said: "He is the judge of Hamadān!" This was an allusion to a story told by Sheikh Saᶜdi in the *Golestān*: "The judge of Hamadān had fallen in love with a farrier's apprentice, and his heart's own horseshoe was in the fire. For a while he was distraught searching, observing, and questioning—like the one in the story which goes: Nothing can temper my thoughts of you—I am a snake whose head has been smashed, I cannot help writhing.—When the apprentice heard of this, he became very angry and ruthlessly started cursing the judge, and throwing stones at him; his anger knew no restraint. The judge said to himself: Without a doubt! His insolence bears the scent of yielding. Kings talk harshly, when perhaps in secret they are waiting for peace. New grapes have a sour taste, but wait two or three days, then they are sweet!"

At sunset (Eḥteshām od-Doula continued) the judge came to my house asking the meaning of the shah's utterance. I said to him: "The shah may have heard rumors of your treatment of the merchant of Shoshtar's heir. He wants to punish you for that." The judge was very upset about that conversation. The next day he handed the merchant's possessions over to the heir.[297]

On 10th Shaᶜbān,[298] the shah arrived at Kermānshāh; on 21st Shaᶜbān,[299] at Khāneqin, the first town of Iraq. That day he was welcomed by Medḥāt Pasha, the governor of Baghdad,[300] who

296. October 11, 1870.

297. There are many stories told about deceitful judges in Persian literature; mocking at the handling of affairs by the Sharia courts was universal, see for instance Ḥasan-e Fasā'i's remarks, above, p. 98 sec.

298. November 5, 1870.   299. November 16, 1870.

300. Midḥāt Pasha was governor of Baghdad from 1869 to 1872; he was a statesman of great efficiency and introduced modern ideas into the administration of the province of which he was governor. Later on, he

had come with the other pashas of Iraq and several thousand Turkish horsemen and soldiers. On 28th Sha^{c}bān[301] the shah arrived in Baghdad. The inhabitants of Baghdad behaved in a most friendly manner. The shah was put up in a palace suitable to him. On 29th Sha^{c}bān he performed the pilgrimage to Kāẓemein.[302] The inhabitants of Kāẓemein and servants of the shrine welcomed the shah. The shah writes in his *Safar-nāma-ye Shāhenshāhi ba-^{c}atabāt-e ^{c}āliyāt*:[303] "We entered the shrine of Kāẓemein. It is part of Paradise and a sign of God's mercy." When he returned to Baghdad, he prayed the Fāteḥa[304] at the sepulcher of the great Imām Abu Ḥanifa.[305] On the last day of Sha^{c}bān, he went with his retinue on board a merchant ship to visit the sepulcher of Salmān ol-Fāresi[306] and to see the ruins of Madā'en.[307] On 4th Ramażān[308] he departed from Baghdad and

---

was twice invested with the grand vizierate. It would be interesting to know whether the shah's journey to Mesopotamia was directly or indirectly connected with the fact that the governor of Baghdad was Midḥāt Pasha, who was remarkably tolerant in religious questions, see EI[1] III, s.v. Midhat Pa*sh*a (Fr. Babinger).

301. November 23, 1870.

302. A small town north of Baghdad, where Musā ol-Kāẓem and Moḥammad Javād, the seventh and ninth Emām of the Shia, are buried, one of the important places of pilgrimage of the Shia, see also above, p. 113, note 96.

303. Browne, IV, 155, passes the following judgment on this book: "though it is doubtful whether he or his attendant derived more advantage from what they saw in the course of their peregrinations than Persian literature did from his accounts of his experiences." Rypka, *Iranische Literaturgeschichte*, p. 322, too, points out the importance of the book for the creation of a new style in Persian literature.

304. Sura I of the Koran, a prayer comparable to the Christian "Pater noster."

305. The famous founder of the Ḥanafiya, one of the four rites of the Sunna; the grave is one of the few remnants of ancient Baghdad.

306. Salmān Pāk, about 19 miles southeast of Baghdad, near the ruins of al-Madā'in (Seleucia/Ktesiphon).

307. The capital of the Sassanian kings, the predecessors of the shahs of Persia!

308. November 28, 1870.

visited the shrine at Kāẓemein. The theologians, seiyeds, and servants of the shrine were received in audience, and each of them was granted a royal favor according to his rank. On 5th Ramażān the shah traveled to the village of Moseiyeb[309] and put up his camp on the bank of the Euphrates. He remained there on the 6th, too. That day the theologians and mojtaheds of Kerbelā were received in audience. On the 7th the shah departed for Kerbelā and entered the town through the gate called "Gate of Najaf." From the entrance to the Holy Courtyard (ṣaḥn-e moqaddas) to the shrine of Ḥosein he went on foot, displaying utmost humility, and shed tears in remembrance of the adversities which befell the family of the sinless and pure house.[310] Then he performed the pilgrimage in accordance with the custom. Having finished the pilgrimage, he proceeded to the shrine of ᶜAbbās.[311] On the 12th of that month[312] he departed to visit the shrine of ᶜAli.[313] On the 13th he arrived outside Najaf. In the *Safar-nāma-ye Shāhenshāhi*, the entering of the town is described in the following manner:

When we arrived in the vicinity [330] of the gate of Najaf, we dismounted from the carriage and entered the town on foot in the company of all the servants and pashas. The ear of my soul heard a voice: "Behold, you are in the sacred valley of Ṭawā,"[314] and the tongue of my heart was singing: "O Lord, let me enter the truth, for this pure soil and this

309. About 19 miles northeast of Kerbelā.

310. Ḥosein, son of ᶜAli ibn Abi Ṭāleb, was killed with his followers in the year 61:680, when he tried to establish his rule in opposition to the Omaiyads.

311. He was a half-brother of Ḥosein; the shrine lies 600 meters northeast of Ḥosein's shrine.

312. December 6, 1870.

313. The shrine of ᶜAli ibn Abi Ṭāleb, son-in-law of the Prophet, fourth caliph (r. 656–61); first of the twelve Emāns of the Shia and father of Ḥosein. ᶜAli was murdered at Kufa and buried at Najaf (near the ancient Kufa).

314. Koran XX, 12; the context refers to God's revelation to Moses on Mount Sinai.

sacred ground must be considered as part of God's throne and as a sign of the promised Paradise, the home of the soul and the house of the heart." And I felt a spiritual tranquillity whose description is not in my power.

Then he kissed the shrine and the spot of the Prince of Believers. Having accomplished the duties of the pilgrimage, he proceeded to the sepulcher of Āqā Moḥammad Shāh Shahid[315] and prayed the Fāteḥa. He then went on foot to the gate. On 14th Ramażān the royal camp was put up on the bank of the Lake of Najaf. On the 15th the shah visited the sepulcher of Moslem ibn ᶜAqil[316] and the sepulcher of the other nobles of the religion; then he returned to the camp. On the 19th,[317] he performed the farewell pilgrimage at the shrine and departed for Kerbelā where he arrived on the 20th and stayed for three days. On the 24th[318] he departed for Baghdad. On the 27th he visited the shrine at Kāẓemein. On 2d Shavvāl[319] he proceeded to Sāmarrā. There he arrived on 6th Shavvāl and performed the pilgrimage to the shrine of the two ᶜAskari.[320] On 8th Shavvāl he departed for Tehran and arrived there on 1st Dhu'l-Ḥejja of that year.[321]

A SON BORN TO SOLṬĀN MASᶜUD MIRZĀ. That year a son was born to Solṭān Masᶜud Mirzā Ẓell os-Solṭān, governor of the province of Fārs.[322] He was called Solṭān Ḥosein Mirzā Jalāl od-Doula.

THE AUTHOR'S PILGRIMAGE TO MECCA AND MEDINA. That year I, the author of this book, departed from Shiraz to

315. See above, p. 80. He is styled "Shahid," because he was murdered when engaged in the Holy War.

316. A cousin of Ḥosein; executed by the Omaiyad governor of Kufa shortly before Ḥosein's arrival at Kufa.

317. December 13, 1870.

318. December 18, 1870.

319. December 26, 1870.

320. ᶜAli ol-Hādi (also called ol-ᶜAskari) and his son Ḥasan ol-ᶜAskari, tenth and eleventh Emām of the Shia (died A.D. 868 resp. 874); Ḥasan was buried in Sāmarrā, in his house beside his father.

321. February 22, 1871.

322. His marriage is mentioned above, p. 351.

perform the pilgrimage to Mecca and Medina and to the shrines of the Emāms. From 2 parasangs from Shiraz as far as half a parasang from the caravanserai of Meyān Kotal,[323] which is a distance of about 14 parasangs, we traveled in the midst of snow and ice. On the 23d of that month,[324] we arrived at Kāzerun, and on the 28th, at Bushehr. On 15th Dhu'l-Qaᶜda[325] we went on board a steamship and arrived at Masqaṭ on the 20th. On the 26th we arrived at Aden, and on 3d Dhu'l-Ḥejja, at Jidda. On 8th Dhu'l-Ḥejja, six hours after sunset, we arrived at Mecca.[326] After performing the pilgrimage, we departed from Mecca for Medina on 28th Dhu'l-Ḥejja.[327] We arrived at Medina on the ᶜĀshurā day of the month of Moḥarram of the year 1288.[328] Having performed the pilgrimage to the sepulcher of the Prophet and the graves of the Emāms,[329] we departed from Medina for Jidda on 17th Moḥarram.[330] In the 28th we arrived at Jidda. On 14th Ṣafar,[331] we boarded a steamship and arrived at Bandar Ḥodeida[332] on 18th Ṣafar, at Masqaṭ on 1st Rabiᶜ I.[333] On 7th Rabiᶜ I[334] we arrived at Bushehr. On the 25th[335] we returned to Shiraz sound and safe.

APPOINTMENTS AND PROMOTIONS. The New Year fell on 29th Dhu'l-Ḥejja.[336] The shah spent the ᶜĀshurā days of the

323. 16 miles east of Kāzerun, on the western slope of the Kotal-e Dokhtar, see above, p. 218, note 462.

324. January 16, 1871. 325. February 6, 1871.

326. February 28, 1871. 327. March 21, 1871.

328. Began on April 1, 1871.

329. That is, the graves of Ḥasan ibn ᶜAli ibn Abi Ṭāleb (brother of the second Emām), of ᶜAli ibn Ḥosein Zein ol-ᶜĀbedin (fourth Emām), of Moḥammad ol-Bāqer (fifth Emām) and of Jaᶜfar oṣ-Ṣādeq (sixth Emām), see ᶜAli al-Haravi, *Guide des lieux de pélerinage*, p. 92 (translation p. 210 seq.). Apart from that, the house of ᶜAli ibn Abi Ṭāleb and the school (maktab) of Ḥasan and Ḥosein were visited by the Shiis.

330. April 8, 1871. 331. May 5, 1871.

332. The main port of Yemen, about 95 miles north of Bāb al-Mandeb.

333. May 21, 1871. 334. May 27, 1871. 335. June 14, 1871.

336. March 22, 1871 (should be March 21).

month of Moḥarram of the year 1288[337] in mourning the "Family of Pureness." That year Haji Moḥammad Qoli Khān Āṣaf od-Doula, vizier and chief of the province of Fārs, was summoned to Tehran. The vizierate of that province and the office of pishkār to Ẓell os-Solṭān was conferred upon Moḥammad Qāsem Khān Vāli, an uncle of the assayer of the empire (moᶜeiyer ol-mamālek), Dust ᶜAli Khān. Moḥammad Qāsem Khān arrived from Tehran at Shiraz in the month of Ṣafar of that year.[338]

And that year: Mirzā Fatḥ ᶜAli Khān Ṣaḥeb Divān-e Shirazi was appointed chief of the province of Ādherbāyjān and vizier to Moẓaffar od-Din Mirzā, the crown prince of Persia. And Mirzā ᶜAbd ol-Vahhāb Khān-e Shirazi was granted the title "Naṣir od-Doula."

MOḤAMMAD QĀSEM KHĀN VĀLI APPOINTED GOVERNOR OF FĀRS. In the month of Jomādi I[339] Solṭān Masᶜud Mirzā Ẓell os-Solṭān left Shiraz for Tehran and arrived there on 15th Rajab.[340] The independent governorship of Fārs was entrusted to Moḥammad Qāsem Khān Vāli.

A STEP TOWARD REFORMS AND MODERNIZATION

PRIME MINISTER HAJI MIRZĀ ḤOSEIN KHĀN ANNOUNCES REFORMS IN THE CIVIL SERVICE. [331] On 29th Shaᶜbān[341] Haji Mirzā Ḥosein Khān, who had been granted the title "Sepahsālār," was appointed grand vizier, which is the highest office of the state. Haji Mirzā Ḥosein Khān Ṣadr-e aᶜẓam was a son of the late Mirzā Nabi Khān-e Qazvini, chief magistrate of the empire, who was governor of Fārs in 1256 and 1259.[342] Upon his investitute, the grand vizier wrote a letter, containing hopes and threats, to the governors of the provinces. The main contents of the letter are:

337. Began March 23, 1871.
338. Began on April 22, 1871.
339. Began July 19, 1871.
340. September 30, 1871.
341. November 13, 1871.
342. See above, p. 266, 273.

It is a fact of principal importance that the existence of the state is bound to the prosperity of the country and the tranquillity of its inhabitants. The decline of prosperity and tranquillity is caused by greed and avidity. Those who are kindly disposed to the welfare of the state must eradicate the evil of these two illnesses, so as to render the royal favors palatable to those who are afflicted by them. It is an age-old custom for the nobles of Persia to call the illness of avidity those "revenues" which they collect from the subjects of the state by three different means: The first of them is bribery: they pay a sum of money (ḥaqq-e maẓlumi) to an official (ẓālem)[343] and receive something in return. There is a saying in Fārs: "The teeth become blunt from eating anything acid, the teeth of the judge and governor become blunt from eating sugar cane." The second is peshkash: the governorship of a district is conferred upon a deceitful man, and one closes one's eyes to his oppression and tyranny. The third is presents (hadiya): timid people, out of fear of the officials, send the governor the first-born of cattle, well-tasting dishes, or horse outfits as a tribute. Further on, the leopardlike Persians call the illness of avidity "punishment" (seyāsat) and "official fine" (mo'ākhadha-ye doulati): if they are nursing a hatred against somebody, they accuse the unfortunate man falsely of treachery (kheyānat-e doulati) and bring him into a situation from which he does not find a way out. The shah has become attentive to these two widespread illnesses. When he conferred upon me the high office of grand vizier, he first of all ordered me to eradicate both fatal illnesses which have become universal in Persia. Thank God! one can say that in this short space of time bribery and gifts have disappeared at the royal court and are not even known by name. However, up to now the suspicion has remained that the governors, proud of their relationship to the royal family or of their ancient services, consider themselves exempt from punishment. In the same way it is known that they do not care for the saying "Kingship is barren"; accordingly, this rule has no connection with children, relations, servants and friends, but the children (farzand) of the rule (salṭanat) are the trained army and the reliable subjects. Everybody who oppresses those two classes of people has to risk punishment by the king, as the shah has

343. To show the injustice of the methods, the author calls the official "ẓālem," oppressor, and the fee "ḥaqq-e maẓlum," extorted money.

stated in the audience on 25th Shavvāl of that year[344] making a solemn vow that he would destroy the possessions, life, and existence of any governor who oppresses the subjects by increasing the taxes fixed by the Divan or demanding something in another way, and likewise of any officer who is a tyrant in the service of the army and dares to shorten the rations and pay of a single soldier.

FAMINE IN SEVERAL PARTS OF FĀRS. That year the governorships of the province of Fārs were not altered. Hunger and epidemics spread among the inhabitants of several parts of Fārs. The price of 1 mann of wheat weighing 720 miskal—this mann is called "Nine ᶜAbbāsi"[345]—reached the sum of 2 reyāls, which corresponds to 2 miskal and 17 nokhud of coined money.[346] Moḥammad Qāsem Khān, the governor of Fārs, installed several alms houses, each of which accommodated 50 to 60 poor people. He entertained 6 alms houses himself and gave the poor people living in them victuals. Several other alms houses were put under the responsibility of the nobles of Shiraz, and the poor people were provided for in every respect. May God allot benefits to him! However, among the tribes and in the districts many people died from hunger.

SOLṬĀN MASᶜUD MIRZĀ ẒELL OS-SOLṬĀN APPOINTED GOVERNOR OF FĀRS A THIRD TIME. The shah spent the ᶜĀshurā days of the month of Moḥarram of the year 1289[347] in mourning over Emām Ḥosein. On the evening of 11th Moḥarram,[348] Moḥammad Qāsem Khān, governor of the province of Fārs, died at Shiraz from the illness of lethargy.

344. January 7, 1872.

345. 720 miskal (4.6 grams each) would be 3.322 kilograms, a "big" mann, see Hinz, *Masse und Gewichte*, p. 18 seq.; the ᶜAbbāsi is not mentioned by Hinz.

346. 2 miskal equals 9.2 grams; 17 nokhud are 3.335 grams. Accordingly, 2 reyāls make 12.535 grams of coined money, see Hinz, *Masse und Gewichte*, p. 24.

347. Began on March 11, 1872.

348. March 20, 1872 (should be March 21).

The New Year fell on 11th Moḥarram.[349] The governorship of Fārs was bestowed upon Solṭān Masᶜud Mirzā Ẓell os-Solṭān. Haji Moḥammad Naṣir Khān Ẓahir od-Doula Qājār Devehlu was appointed chief and vizier of the province of Fārs. They arrived at Shiraz in the month of Rabiᶜ I.[350]

CHANGE IN THE GOVERNORSHIP OF BANDAR ᶜABBĀS. And that year Haji Aḥmad Khān, son of Haji Moḥammad ᶜAli Kabābi, the former vizier of Masqaṭ, was removed from the governorship of Bandar ᶜAbbās and its dependencies, and Aḥmad Shāh Khān-e Minābi, whose family had been holding the office of mayor of the district of Mināb from time immemorial, was appointed governor of Shamil, Mināb, and the whole region of Bandar ᶜAbbās.

THE SHAH TRAVELS TO THE SHORES OF THE CASPIAN SEA. On 1st Jomādi I[351] the shah departed for Nur and Kojur on the Caspian Sea.[352] He returned to Tehran on 14th Shaᶜbān of that year.[353] Praise be to the foresight of the shah the whole population of Persia was living in prosperity [332] and tranquillity. The shah spent the ᶜĀshurā days of the month of Moḥarram of the year 1290[354] in mourning the family of the Prophet as usually. The New Year fell on the evening of 21st Moḥarram,[355] and the feast was celebrated in the usual manner.

THE SHAH'S FIRST VISIT TO EUROPE. A remarkable event of that year was the shah's trip to Europe. When the time of departure came near, the army was drawn up outside the Doulat Gate of Tehran, and the shah inspected the army. Grand Vizier Haji Mirzā Ḥosein Khān read, in a loud voice, a royal decree

349. March 21; the date is left blank in the text.
350. Began on May 9, 1872. 351. July 7, 1872.
352. Two districts west of Āmol, see above, p. 92, note 39.
353. October 17, 1872. 354. Began on March 1, 1873.
355. March 21; the date is left blank in the text.

which had been issued to the army. A brief copy of the decree follows:

All the officers and soldiers of the army of the capital shall know: The day of departure of the shah to Europe in order to visit the powerful and mighty rulers and kings who are related in friendship to us has arrived. Today, on 14th Ṣafar of the year 1290,[356] I have come here to see you. It is our royal intention to promote the affairs of the army and your welfare. In the same way as you received your pay in the last year at the given time, without delay, so it will happen in the next year. Our royal heart is delighted at your assiduity in fulfilling the duties of your service. Trusting in your firm friendship and perfect zeal, we expect every soldier during our absence to climb upon the steps of our service and to protect the order of the empire under the command of our officers. We shall use the time of our journey to satisfy the needs of the army with regard to weapons and instructors. Our royal heart will not desist from remembering you. For the time of our absence we have appointed our dear son, Crown Prince Moẓaffar od-Din Mirzā,[357] deputy and commander in chief. Because the grand vizier will be in our company, we put our uncle Moᶜtamad od-Doula[358] as plenipotentiary, at the side of the aforementioned son. You shall listen to this royal decree and not act contrary to it. 14th Ṣafar of the year 1290.

Copy of the royal autograph to Moᶜtamad od-Doula:

Because of the full confidence which we have in the benevolence, efficiency, and sagacity of our honored uncle, we consider it superfluous to put down the regulations point by point in writing. We leave our uncle a free hand. God willing, on the basis of the royal decree which has been issued to the whole Persian empire, and on the basis of the prescriptions which have been given in writing and by word of mouth, he will devote himself with all the power of his heart to the settling of the affairs of the state and the empire and report the daily events by telegraph to us.

356. April 13, 1873.

357. Moẓaffar od-Din Mirzā, appointed crown prince and governor of Ādherbāyjān in about 1867.

358. Farhād Mirzā, later on governor of Fārs.

Everybody who acts contrary to your orders and interdictions, will definitely incur our royal displeasure.

On 21st Ṣafar of that year,[359] the shah departed from Tehran. On 12th Rabiᶜ I[360] he arrived at Rasht. On the 14th he went on board a merchant ship in the harbor of Enzeli, which had been put at his disposal by the Russian government. The ship's name was *Constantinople*. In the afternoon of the 16th of that month the shah arrived at Haji Tarkhān.[361] [The shah visited Moscow, St. Petersburg, Berlin, Cologne, Bonn, Frankfurt, Baden-Baden, Spa, Brussels, London, Manchester, Paris, Geneva, Turin, Salzburg, Vienna, Brindisi, Istanbul, Poti, Tiflis, and Baku and arrived][362] [334] on 14th Rajab[363] at Bandar Enzeli. The whole population of the Persian empire was happy to see the shah return in good health. The same day Grand Vizier Haji Mirzā Ḥosein Khān asked to be dismissed from his office and to be appointed governor of Gilān. Then he settled down at Rasht. The shah arrived in Tehran on the last day of the month of Rajab.[364]

MIRZĀ FATḤ ᶜALI KHĀN-E SHIRAZI APPOINTED PRIME MINISTER. That year: the governorships of Fārs remained the same as the years before; and too, Mirzā Fatḥ ᶜAli Khān-e Shirazi Ṣāḥeb Divān, vizier of the province of Ādherbāyjān, was promoted to the high office of grand vizier, and Mirzā ᶜAbd ol-Vahhāb Khān-e Shirazi Naṣir od-Doula was appointed minister of commerce of the Persian empire.

The Shah spent the ᶜĀshurā days of the month of Moḥarram of the year 1291[365] in mourning Emām Ḥosein. The New Year

359. April 20, 1873. 360. May 10, 1873.
361. That is, Astrakhan.
362. The dates of arrival and departure at each station of the journey enumerated by the author have been omitted in the translation.
363. September 7, 1873. 364. September 23, 1873.
365. Began on February 18, 1874.

fell on 2d Ṣafar.[366] The feast and the private and public audiences were held in the presence of the shah.

SOLṬĀN MORĀD MIRZĀ ḤOSĀM OS-SALṬANA'S THIRD TERM OF OFFICE AS GOVERNOR OF FĀRS. At the beginning of that year Ẓell os-Solṭān Mas^c^ud Mirzā and Haji Ẓahir od-Doula Moḥammad Naṣir Khān-e Qājār Devehlu, vizier of the province of Fārs, went from Shiraz to Tehran. The governorship of Fārs was conferred upon Ḥosām os-Salṭana Morād Mirzā. On 17th Rabi^c^ I of that year,[367] Ḥosām os-Salṭāna arrived at Shiraz and appointed Mirzā Abu'l-Ḥasan Khān Moshir ol-Molk vizier of Fārs. The governorship of Kuh-e Giluya and Behbehān was entrusted to Moḥammad Taqi Khān, whose mother was a niece of Ḥosām os-Salṭana; Moḥammad Taqi Khān was sent to Behbehān. A few days after his arrival Moḥammad ^c^Ali, son of Āqā Abu'l-Ḥasan Khān, the former mayor of Behbehān, killed Mirzā Ṭāher Khān, son of Mirzā Manṣur Khān, the former governor of Behbehān; as he was passing by Moḥammad ^c^Ali's house, he was killed by a musket shot fired from behind the wall. Since Moḥammad Taqi Khān, contrary to what would have been his duty, did not arrest the murderer, his weakness and complete inability in matters of government became evident, and a number of people prepared to revolt. Ḥosein Khān-e Bavir Aḥmadi, lord of the fortress of Āru, 8 parasangs east of Behbehān[368] refused obedience to the governor. Moḥammad Taqi Khān laid siege to the fortress with 400 soldiers and 1 piece of artillery. The next day a number of musketeers came down from the fortress and dispersed the governor's troops. When Moḥammad Taqi Khān entered Behbehān with the defeated army, his authority dwindled away. When news of this arrived at Shiraz, Ḥosām os-Salṭana asked the ministers to send Eḥteshām

366. March 21; the day is not given in the text.
367. May 4, 1874.
368. 28 miles east of Behbehān (shown on the map).

od-Doula, a prudent leader who combined political dexterity with justice and had been governor of Kuh-e Giluya and Behbehān for ten years,[369] from Tehran to Fārs. He arrived at Shiraz in the month of Jomādi II.[370] On 20th Sha^cbān[371] he left Shiraz for Behbehān. Upon his arrival he established order in all the districts of Kuh-e Giluya and Behbehān. He united the dispersed people, offered them assistance and help, and brought the ruined districts under cultivation. He paid special attention to the reconstruction of the districts of Zeidun and Lirāvi, turning a region of wasteland into a flourishing country.

THE "CHEST OF JUSTICE": A NEW EXPERIMENT OF INTERNAL REFORMS. The governorships of Fārs were not altered. That year the ministers sent a chest with padlock and key and 3 trustworthy servants from Tehran to Shiraz. [335] It was called the "Chest of Justice" (ṣonduq-e ᶜadālat) and was placed in the Masjed-e Vakil at Shiraz. Every oppressed person was to describe his situation in a petition, affix his seal to it, and put it into the "Chest of Justice."[372] Each week the petitions were taken out of the chest and sent by couriers to Tehran. The ministers put short and sufficient replies at the head and in the margin of the petitions and sent them back to Shiraz. One of the petitions put into the "Chest of Justice" was that of the farmers of the surroundings of Shiraz and the garden owners of Masjed-e Bardi, 1 parasang northwest of Shiraz. They had written:

At the time of the Kayānid kings[373] a ditch was dug which was nearly 2 parasangs long and 100 cubits wide. The bottom reached down to the level of the underground water, and several springs appeared, which were called "Chashma-ye Jushak." Several subterranean canals were dug on both sides of that ditch and connected to the latter. There was

369. See above, p. 348 seq. 370. Began on July 16, 1874.
371. October 2, 1874.
372. The idea was to allow everybody free access to the ruler, which was one of the traditional ideals of Islamic and Persian political ethics.
373. That is, in pre-Islamic times.

enough water in the ditch to run several mills. At the end of the ditch a solid dam had been constructed from the top of which the water was conducted to several canals for the irrigation of fields and gardens. A few years ago the agents of Mirzā Abu'l-Ḥasan Khān Moshir ol-Molk constructed 2 or 3 subterranean canals which were connected to that ditch; they have been taking away all the water from the ditch and selling it at a high price to owners of fields and gardens. In this manner several gardens have been destroyed and a number of fields have gone out of cultivation for lack of water.

In reply to this petition the ministers ordered Ḥosām os-Salṭana to inspect the water conduits and subterranean canals in person and to pronounce a just decision. The governor acted in accordance with the orders and had Moshir ol-Molk's subterranean canals obstructed. All the water of the ditch was divided up and everybody conducted the water to his canal according to his needs. To this day, the year 1300,[374] a number of gardens and fields are under cultivation because of this water.

Once the followers of Moshir ol-Molk realized that the originator of that quarrel and that infamy had been ᶜAli Moḥammad Khān Qavām ol-Molk, the tax agent for the guilds (vojuhāt-e aṣnāf) of the city of Shiraz, Moshir ol-Molk incited the master craftsmen to complain about excessive taxes and to put the petition containing the complaint into the "Chest of Justice." Upon the arrival of the reply to that petition the governor convened several meetings to inquire into the accusation, and he inquired thoroughly into the affair on the basis of the account books of the guilds. Then the taxes and fees (māleyāt va-vojuhāt) to be paid by the guilds were fixed. A sum to cover the expenses of the lord mayor was allowed to be added to the Divan fees (vojuh-e divāni) and the principal taxes; an assessment (sar khaṭṭ) was drawn up and handed over to the master craftsmen and Qavām ol-Molk's agents were ordered to levy the taxes in accordance with the assessment. As a result of the care taken by

374. 1300:1882/83, that is, when those lines were written by the author.

the aforementioned governor the whole province of Fārs was safe. The governorships were not altered.

YAḤYĀ KHĀN MOᶜTAMAD OL-MOLK APPOINTED GOVERNOR OF FĀRS, GIVES MOSHIR OL-MOLK PLENIPOTENTIARY POWER. The shah spent the ᶜĀshurā days of the month of Moḥarram of the year 1292[375] in mourning over the misfortune of the family of the Prophet. The New Year fell on 13th Ṣafar.[376] The shah celebrated the feast in a befitting manner. That year Ḥosām os-Salṭana was removed from the governorship of Fārs. The governorship of that province was conferred upon Yaḥyā Khān Moᶜtamad ol-Molk, the son of Amir-e Kabir Mirzā Nabi Khān-e Qazvini, chief magistrate of the empire, who in the years 1256 and 1259 had been sent to Fārs as agent (mobāsher) in the name of the shah.[377] In Jomādi I of that year[378] the new governor arrived at Shiraz. He gave Mirzā Abu'l-Ḥasan Khān Moshir ol-Molk plenipotentiary power over the whole province and established himself comfortably.

ADMINISTRATIVE DIFFICULTIES IN SEVERAL DISTRICTS OF FĀRS. By order of the shah, the governorship of Kuh-e Giluya and Behbehān remained with Eḥteshām od-Doula Solṭān Oveis Mirzā on condition that the latter settled the financial affairs (moᶜāmalāt-e divāni) in collaboration with Moᶜtamad ol-Molk. In the month of Rajab,[379] Eḥteshām od-Doula came to Shiraz to be confirmed in his office. When the governor wanted to increase the taxes to be paid by Kuh-e Giluya, Eḥteshām od-Doula refused and asked to be removed from his office. Then a royal decree was issued to the effect that Eḥteshām od-Doula was entitled to claim the money he had spent as a subsidy[380] and that he should receive the sum and

375. February 7–16, 1875.
376. March 21, 1875.
377. See above, p. 266, 273.
378. Began on June 5, 1875.
379. Began on August 3, 1875.
380. See above, p. 349, 381.

hand over Kuh-e Giluya to the governor of Fārs. When this was examined it was found that about half of the taxes of Kuh-e Giluya were due to Eḥteshām od-Doula. The governor of Fārs had no choice but to entrust the governorship of Kuh-e Giluya to Eḥteshām od-Doula.

The governorship of Bandar Bushehr, Dashti, and Dashtestān was conferred upon ᶜAbd ol-Ḥosein Khān, son of the late Khān Bābā Khān. The other governorships of Fārs were not altered.

That year the governorship of the district of Khesht was entrusted to Ḥosein Qoli Khān-e Kort Beglu Mir Panj. This is a detailed story of the occurrence:

A man who was enriching himself at the expense of other people and thereby won a reputation with the viziers (pishkārān) of Fārs, affirmed for his own profit that the revenues of the district of Khesht were five times more than the sum at which the taxes of the district were farmed out by the Divan (moqāṭaᶜa-ye divāni). His scheming for the acquisition of the tax farming of the district aimed only at the ruin of Ḥasan ᶜAli Khān-e Kheshti, the governor of Khesht, as all the landed property and the palm groves had for generations been in the hereditary possession of the governor's family. [336] In order to escape the impending reassessment, Ḥasan ᶜAli Khān had most of the years added to the taxes of the district a peshkash and thus avoided having to appear before the governor. When the governorship of Khesht was entrusted to Ḥosein Qoli Khān he had bound himself to seize Ḥasan ᶜAli Khān dead or alive. Then he sent Ḥasan ᶜAli Khān a message in which he confirmed by a solemn oath that he had demanded the governorship and the financial administration (ᶜāmeli) of the district of Khesht to Ḥasan ᶜAli Khān's profit. Several months later Ḥosein Qoli Khān proceeded from Shiraz to Khesht under the pretext of coming as a guest. Having lulled Ḥasan ᶜAli Khān into a false sense of security, he arrested him, took him to Shiraz, and killed him between Khesht and Kāzerun in order to do a favor to those who wanted to seize the possessions of the khāns of Khesht.[381] However, Ḥosein Qoli Khān got his just deserts in this world: One year later he was killed by his own brothers with the sword because of an inheritance quarrel.

THE SHAH TRAVELS TO THE SHORE OF THE CASPIAN SEA. The shah departed for Māzandarān for the sake of recreation. He arrived in the district of Nur va-Kojur on 1st Ramażān.[382] On 9th Shavvāl,[383] he encamped at the town of Ashraf; on the 13th, at Bārforush; on the 23d, at Āmol; and returned to Tehran on 5th Dhu'l-Qaᶜda of that year.[384]

INCREASE OF CRIME AND HIGHWAY ROBBERY IN FĀRS. In the middle of that year,[385] everywhere in the province of Fārs, except Kuh-e Giluya,[386] criminals began to rob the highways; wide stretches of the province were alarmed about stealing, raping, and plundering, and guilty and innocent people earned a bad reputation. The governorships of the districts of Fārs were not altered. The governorship of Bandar ᶜAbbās remained with Aḥmad Shāh Khān as before.

PROCEEDINGS AT THE ROYAL COURT. The Shah spent the ᶜĀshurā days of the month of Moḥarram of the year 1293[387] in mourning the family of the Prophet. The New Year fell on 23d Ṣafar of that year:[388] 3 hours, 38 minutes, and 40 seconds after sunrise. The shah celebrated the feast in accordance with the rules of the previous years.

381. The same story is told by F. Stolze/F. C. Andreas, "Die Handelsverhältnisse Persiens, mit besonderer Berücksichtigung der deutschen Interessen", in *Petermanns Mitteilungen aus Justus Perthes' Geographischer Anstalt* (Gotha, Justus Perthes, 1885), XVII, 2*n*1.

382. October 1, 1875. 383. November 8, 1875.

384. December 3, 1875. 385. About August 1875.

386. The district was governed by Eḥteshām od-Doula, the son of Ḥasan-e Fasā'i's patron!

387. January 28–February 6, 1876. 388. March 21, 1876.

FĀRS RULED BY EFFICIENT AND ENLIGHTENED GOVERNOR

FARHĀD MIRZĀ MOᶜTAMAD OD-DOULA APPOINTED GOVERNOR OF FĀRS. When Haji Farhād Mirzā Moᶜtamad od-Doula returned from Mecca and Medina to Tehran on 1st Rabiᶜ II of that year,[389] the shah, several days later, bestowed the governorship of the province of Fārs upon him and ordered him to put an end to the depravity and to punish the criminals of the districts and tribes of that province. In the month of Rajab,[390] Moᶜtamad od-Doula departed for Shiraz to take over the governorship. The former governors of Fārs had had no full knowledge of the financial administration and no power to settle quarrels about ownership, owing to the overwhelming influence exercised by Mirzā Abu'l-Ḥasan Khān Moshir ol-Molk in all the districts and tribes. Consequently they had no other choice but to exercise a rule without supervision and a leadership without punishment. Secretly they informed the shah of what was going on. When the shah made a governor of Fārs responsible for the seizure and arrest of Moshir ol-Molk, that governor postponed the arrest, giving unjustifiable reasons. Consequently, the disorder of the province of Fārs increased year by year. Several years passed in that manner. When the governorship of that province was entrusted to Haji Moᶜtamad od-Doula, he arrived at Shiraz in the middle of the month of Shaᶜbān[391] on the birthday of the Twelfth Emām.[392] Having held a public audience, he addressed Moshir ol-Molk, reproached him, and enumerated his peculations (taqṣirāt) year by year. Then Moshir ol-Molk received the bastinado and was put in prison for some time. The day after Moᶜtamad od-Doula's arrival, from sunrise to noon and from afternoon to sunset, the oppressed were liberated from their

389. April 26, 1876. 390. Began on July 23, 1876.

391. October 5, 1876.

392. That is, Ḥasan ol-Montaẓar, the "Expected Emām," see above, p. 338, note 168.

oppressors and the arrangement of the disordered affairs of the province was entrusted to experienced men who were bound to act with integrity. The notorious thieves were handed over to them and punished in accordance with their crimes. Within a short space of time danger was turned into safety and chaos into order.

MO^c^TAMAD OD-DOULA APPOINTS NEW GOVERNORS TO SEVERAL DISTRICTS OF FĀRS. The governorship of Lārestān and the districts of Sab^c^a and Bandar ^c^Abbās was conferred upon Mirzā Ḥasan ^c^Ali Khān Naṣir ol-Molk, that of Jahrom and Qir va-Kārzin upon Moḥammed Bāqer Khān-e Eṣfahāni, and Mirzā ^c^Ali Moḥammad Khān Qavām ol-Molk was appointed governor of Dārāb, Ḥuma-ye Shiraz, and the Five Tribes, that is, the Nafar, Bahārlu, Inālu, and Bāṣeri,[393] and was ordered to conquer the fortress of Tebr, which is dealt with in the second part of this book, under the heading on the fortresses of Fārs.[394] The

393. The Bāṣeri are a Persian-speaking tribe; their winter quarters are in the districts of Sarvestān, Korbāl, and Kavār (east and southeast of Shiraz), their summer quarters in the districts of Arsenjān and Kamin (north of Korbāl). Since the time of the Safavids, they have been governed by Arab sheikhs. For the other tribes mentioned in the text, see above, p. 336, note 160.

394. See *FNN*, II, 333 seq.: "The fortress lies in the district of Jahrom, 8 parasangs east of the town of Jahrom. It is a steeple-like hill, 350–460 cubits high, its circumference measuring 1 parasang. It lies on top of a mountain which is called Rag-e avval. The distance from the foot of the hill to the foot of the basic mountain is about half a parasang. On the western side of the mountain is a spring called Āb-e Del Seyāhān; during the dry season it provides three or four people with drinking water. From this spring a winding path leads up on which one has to crawl on one's hands and feet; then one comes to a tower (borj) which is called "gate," which can be defended against many people by two musketeers. East of the spring Del Seyāhān, less than a quarter of a parasang away, is another access, formed by steps which are cut into the rock; this is called the "Eastern Gate" and "Rāh-e dālān." On the southern side of the Rag-e avval, 500 to 600 steps away, is a mountain which is higher than the Rag-e avval; it is called "Qal^c^a-ye Deh Morda ("Fortress of the Ten Dead"). On the Rag-e avval, on the side of the Deh Morda, is an entrenchment, called "Sangar-e Eskandari" ("Entrenchment of Alexander"). If this entrenchment was not there, one could pass from the Deh Morda to the Rag-e avval. Except for these accesses, there is no path on which one could

governorship of Bandar Bushehr was conferred upon Haji Mirzā Esmāʿil Vazir, who had been vizier to Moʿtamad od-Doula

---

climb up. On top of the Rag-e avval is a steeple-like hill, smaller than the Rag-e avval. Its height is assessed at 300 to 350–60 cubits. This hill is called "Rag-e dovom" ("Second Rag"), its top Nāranj-e Qalʿa." Round the foot of the Rag-e dovom, on top of the Rag-e avval, is a terrace which is 50–60 cubits wide. On this terrace, 16 water basins which are coated with mortar are cut into the rock. They are filled with rain water. On the side of the Gate, a passage, one should say a well which is turned upside down, is cut into the slope of the Rag-e dovom, 15–16 cubits long, and wide enough for a man to pass. Having passed through this upside down well—only few people can do it without a rope—one comes to a difficult pass which winds around the hill, about 100 cubits long, along which one has to crawl on hands and feet to the top of the Rag-e dovom, the Nāranj-e qalʿa. There is a water basin on the top, 30 cubits long, 15 cubits wide, and 3 to 4 cubits deep, which is filled with rain water. Near the water basin is a small spring which at the end of summer and in autumn provides drinking water for two or three men, in winter and spring more. Except for the "well," there is no access to the Nāranj. On the Nāranj, near the "well," are three small springs side by side, one of which contains salt water. These three springs are especially (khāṣṣa) for the people of the Nāranj.

"In the year 458 (A.D. 1066) Fażluya Shabānkāra fled from the Saljuqid Solṭān Alp Arslan to the fortress of Tebr. In the year 1275 (1858/59), when the Bahārlu of Fārs rose in rebellion, a man named Fażl ʿAli, who was connected with the Bahārlu, took refuge with his family and three or four of his cousins in the fortress of Tebr; he passed through the "well" and established himself on the Nāranj-e qalʿa. In the course of time, groups of the rabble joined Fażl ʿAli, took refuge with him and put up their quarters on the Rag-e avval, at the foot of the Rag-e dovom. Then they took to stealing in the surrounding villages and to highway robbery. Later they came to friendly terms with their neighbors and stopped attacking them; the inhabitants of the villages gave them gifts (toḥfa va-hadiya) and were safe. The followers of Fażl ʿAli took to highway robbery in Bandar ʿAbbās, Kerman, Lārestān and other regions. All the measures of the governors of Fārs for their punishment proved useless; Fażl ʿAli's temerity still increased. His followers numbered more than 500 men. Only he and his cousins had access to the Nāranj-e qalʿa. In the year 1293 (1876/77) Moʿtamad od-Doula Farhād Mirzā put horsemen and infantry of the regular army (neẓām) and auxiliary forces, artillery, and the arsenal and the contributions in kind of that year (soyursāt-e sālāna) at the disposal of Mirzā ʿAli Moḥammad Khān Qavām ol-Molk-e Shirazi and ordered him to occupy the fortress of Tebr."

for many years. [337] Kuh-e Giluya and Behbehān were given again to Eḥteshām od-Doula. The other governorships were not altered. The leadership of the Qashqā'i tribe was entrusted to Dārāb Khān Ilbegi.

REFORMS OF TAXATION AND CIVIL SERVICE IN FĀRS. Oppressive taxes and taxes that could be considered oppressive were abolished and a new assessment was introduced in the province of Fārs. The practice of peshkash [present], reshva [bribery], and hadiya [gift] were abolished. When somebody received pay (ḥaqq-e maẓlumi) from an official (ẓālem)[395] a tenth was deducted from the sum (woṣuli). This procedure (moᶜāmala) was called "Ḥokm-e ᶜarab shāhi."

Another usage which was abolished was this: When the taxes to be paid by a district did not come in at the fixed term or somebody was summoned from one of the districts of Shiraz, a man of high standing was sent with 5 or 6 servants and 7 or 8 horses to settle the affair. He was granted a sum of money which covered the expenses of a whole year, the amount of which was fixed in the decree (raqam). Upon his arrival, the official in question, not being content with that sum (aṣl-e khedmatāna), received from the governor of the district a sum of money under the name of reshwa [bribery] and mohletāna [delay]. Thus a large sum of money was spent on the daily expenditure of that man. At the end of the year, the financial agents did not put that sum of money down to the account of the governor of the district. The governor had no choice but to collect the sum from the subjects who, not being able to raise the money, made their escape to Basra and India. In this manner every year, 2 or 3 districts decreased in population; their taxes were entered into the books of the Divan as arrears and alleviations (takhfif). Having abolished this usage, Moᶜtamad od-Doula sent a single

395. Concerning "ḥaqq-e maẓlumi" and "ẓālem," see above, p. 375, note 343.

messenger on foot to collect the tax installments (aqsāṭ) and to summon people to Shiraz; the allowances (khedmatāna) were fixed with regard to the distance: For instance, the allowance of a messenger ranged from 1 to 10 toman, while the allowances of the tax collectors of the former governors ranged from 50 to 1,000 toman, not including the expenses called: shām [dinner]; nāhār [supper]; jira [tips]; ᶜaliq [fodder]; reshva [bribery]; and peshkash [gift]. In reality those expenses were paid out of the pocket of the shah.

THE FORTRESS OF TEBR, STRONGHOLD OF HIGHWAY ROBBERS CONQUERED. Having issued those regulations, Moᶜtamad od-Doula decided to conquer the fortress of Tebr. That fortress had for many years been in the possession of Fażl ᶜAli Beg-e Bahārlu. A number of people (of that fortress) were engaged in highway robbery and plundering the wares of the caravans traveling on the roads in the vicinity of and some distance from the fortress; then the robbers retreated to the fortress and lived there comfortably. For about ten or fifteen years things had been going in this way. The governors of Fārs, seeing that the capture of the fortress was not within their power, treated the ugly affair as nonexistent. Haji Moᶜtamad od-Doula, however, declared the capture of the fortress, which was very difficult, a matter of primary importance and ordered Qavām ol-Molk to execute it. The governor concentrated on everything that was needed, whether money or men. Qavām ol-Molk was sent on the mission in the month of Ramażān of that year.[396] (Because the beginning of the third decade of the month of Dhu'l-Qaᶜda was the beginning of the thirtieth year of the shah's rule,[397] the bazaars of the city of Shiraz were decorated by order of Moᶜtamad od-Doula and lamps and candles were lit during three nights.) When Qavām ol-Molk arrived with siege matériel

396. Began on September 20, 1876.

397. That is, the thirtieth lunar year, from the year 1246 onward; the lunar year has eleven days less than the solar year.

at the foot of the fortress of Tebr and put up his camp and realized the strength of the fortress—a high mountain between the districts of Jahrom, Dārāb, Juyom and Fasā, with three successive terraces, one smaller than the other—he despaired of the capture and sent the governor a message. In reply he received harsh orders, the gist of which went something like this: "Either Qavām ol-Molk will capture the fortress or he will be killed at the foot of it. Otherwise he will be executed!" Since Qavām ol-Molk had no hope of being relieved of the orders, he established himself, trusting in God, at the foot of the fortress and waited for divine consolation. By the good fortune of the shah, the zeal of Moᶜtamad od-Doula, and the endeavors of Qavām ol-Molk, the fortress of Tebr was captured on 4th Moḥarram of the year 1294.[398] The commander of the fortress, Fażl ᶜAli Beg, and his followers perished. The capture of that fortress is dealt with in detail in the second part of this book, in the chapter on the fortresses of Fārs.[399]

398. January 19, 1877.

399. See *FNN*, II, 334: "Four months went by without result, as before. Then the governor wrote a letter to Qavām ol-Molk saying that he should: either admit his inability by leaving the camp and returning so that another man might be appointed in his place or oblige himself to pay two-months' salary as a fine in case he did not conquer the fortress; that he should expose himself either to the projectiles of Fażl ᶜAli or to the anger of the governor. In the first decade of the month of Moḥarram of the year 1294, Qavām ol-Mol put his soul on the palm of his hand and advanced, though lame on one leg, at the head of his troops. A small piece of artillery with ammunition and the auxiliary forces of the Arabs and Bahārlu, all of them holding death in contempt, followed him. The cannon was tied to a rope and drawn to the top of the Deh Morda. At once they installed an entrenchment opposite the Sangar-e Eskandari. After sunrise they fired several cannon shots. Fażl ᶜAli, not suspecting a cannon to have been brought on the top of the Deh Morda, descended from the Nāranj-e qalᶜa through the "well" to the Rag-e avval, inspected the entrenchment and his men, and proceeded to the gate. Then several cannon shots were fired at the gate. Part of the tower of the gate was destroyed and three or four men killed by the cannon balls. By chance Fażl ᶜAli was among those killed. Then the men in the Sangar-e Eskandari were put to flight by

EḤTESHĀM OD-DOULA, GOVERNOR OF KUH-E GILUYA AND BEHBEHĀN, SUBDUES REBELS IN THE COASTAL AREA OF THE PERSIAN GULF. That year, praise be to Moᶜtamad od-Doula's efficiency, all the inhabitants of the province of Fars lived in peace, except Sheikh Madhkur Khān-e Kangāni, Moḥammad Ḥasan Khān-e Borāzjāni, and Moḥammad Ṭāher Khān-e Galladāri, who harbored foolish ideas and did not submit to the orders of Moᶜtamed od-Doula; their ruin was postponed to another time.

The New Year fell on Tuesday, 4th Rabiᶜ I:[400] 3 hours, 37 minutes, and 36 seconds after sunrise. The shah celebrated the feast in a royal manner. Haji Moᶜtamad od-Doula ordered his son Eḥteshām od-Doula, governor of Behbehān, to deal with Sheikh Madhkur Khān-e Kangāni, Moḥammad Ṭāher Khān-e Galladāri, and Moḥammad Ḥasan Khān-e Borāzjāni. In the month of Moḥarram of that year[401] Eḥteshām od-Doula [338] proceeded by way of the district of Lirāvi and Dashtestān to Bandar Bushehr. Because he was suffering from gout, he summoned me, the author of this book, from Shiraz to cure his illness. I arrived at Bandar Bushehr on 19th Ṣafar.[402] After his gout was cured, Eḥteshām od-Doula summoned Moḥammad Ḥasan Khān-e Borāzjāni and Ḥeidar Khān, the latter's son, from Borāzjān to Behbehān, arrested both of them and put them in prison. On 1st Rabiᶜ I,[403] Eḥteshām od-Doula left Bandar Bushehr for Bandar Kangān. At the time of the barley harvest he

---

cannon shots. The auxiliary forces advanced from the Deh Morda to the Sangar-e Eskandari on the Rag-e avval. When they found the body of Fażl ᶜAli, they cut off his head and sent it to Shiraz within three days. Fażl ᶜAli's family, his son and five or six of his cousins, seeing that he was dead, asked for pardon. From that time until now, the year 1304 (1891/92), a hundred regular soldiers are stationed in the fortress of Tebr as a guard (kotvāl)."

400. March 19, 1875 (should be March 21).

401. Began on January 16, 1877.

402. March 5, 1877. 403. March 16, 1877.

arrived in the district of Tangestān, 4 parasangs from Bushehr. He marched through Tangestān by way of Khormuj, Kāki, Ābavān, and Bardestān[404] and through the districts of Dashti and arrived at Bandar Kangān on 7th Rabi^c II of that year.[405] After eight-days' stay he arrested Sheikh Madhkur Khān-e Kangāni and Moḥammad Ṭāher Khān-e Galladāri and put them in fetters. On the 17th of that month he left Bandar Kangān for Shiraz and arrived at Bandar Dayyer in the region of Dashti.[406] He entrusted the governorship of the district of Galladār and Bandar Kangān, Bandar Ṭāheri, Bandar Nakhl-e Taqi and dependencies, Bandar ^{c}Asluya, and the district of Gāvbandi[407] to Moḥammad Ḥasan Khān-e Māfi, the brother of Ḥosein Qoli Khān Sa^{c}d ol-Molk. Having settled the affairs of the districts of Dashtestān and Dashti, Galladār and the ports of the Persian Gulf, he arrived at Shiraz by way of Qarya-ye Riz, Dezgāh, Dehram, Firuzābād, and Kavār[408] on 10th Jomādi I of that year.[409]

I was in his company all this time. Upon his arrival he handed the prisoners over to Haji Mo^{c}tamad od-Doula. Ḥeidar Khān-e Borāzjāni and Moḥammad Ṭāher Khān-e Galladāri, who were found to deserve death, were executed. Sheikh Madhkur Khān and Moḥammad Ḥasan Khān-e Borāzjāni were imprisoned in the Karim Khāni Prison.

404. Khormuj lies 38 miles southeast of Bushehr; Kāki (center of the district of Dashti) 28 miles southeast of Khormuj. Ābdān lies 45 miles southeast of Khormuj (see *Farhang*, VII, 4), and Bardestān 90 miles southeast of Khormuj (see *Farhang*, VII, 26).

405. April 21, 1877.

406. About 9 miles west of Kangān.

407. Gāvbandi, center of the district of the same name, lies 120 miles southwest of Lār, about 6 miles from the coast of the Persian Gulf.

408. Riz, a small village, is 7 parasangs northeast of Bandar Dayyer (see *FNN*, II, 212); Dezgāh lies 65 miles southwest of Firuzābād (see *Farhang*, VII, 100); Dehram lies 38 miles southwest of Firuzābād, see *Farhang*, VII, 108. Kavār is a small town 25 miles southeast of Shiraz.

409. May 23, 1877.

That year Mirzā ᶜAli Moḥammad Khān Qavām ol-Molk was ordered to settle the affairs of the districts of Lārestān. Upon his arrival, he established order in the district of Shib Kuh in Lārestān and returned to Shiraz.

In the month of Shaᶜbān,[410] Eḥteshām od-Doula returned from Shiraz to Kuh-e Giluya, the seat of his governorship.

THE SHAH'S SECOND VISIT TO EUROPE. All that year the inhabitants of Fārs lived in safety and performed prayers for the welfare of the shah. The shah spent the ᶜĀshurā days of the month of Moḥarram of the year 1295[411] in mourning over Emām Ḥosein. The New Year fell on the evening of 16th Rabiᶜ I[412] at 3:15. The feast was celebrated on the 17th of that month, the birthday of the Prophet. The private and public audiences were held in the presence of the shah and performed in a most befitting manner.

A remarkable event of that year was the Shah's departure for Europe, to learn the new rules (rosum) and laws (qavāᶜed) which were introduced and whose practice was useful for the development of the countries and the prosperity of the inhabitants. The shah departed from Tehran on the last day of the month of Rabiᶜ I[413] and encamped outside Qazvin on 4th Rabiᶜ II. He arrived at Tabriz on the 25th.[414] On the 29th he departed from Tabriz and encamped on 3d Jomādi I[415] on the bank of the Araxes River, the actual border between Persia and Russia. On the 7th he arrived at Erevan, on the 11th at Tiflis. On the 13th he departed from Tiflis and arrived on the 14th in the town of Vladikavkaz;[416] on the outskirts of the town he boarded a train. On the 19th of that month[417] he arrived at Moscow.

410. Began on August 11, 1877. 411. January 5–14, 1878.
412. March 21, 1878. 413. April 4, 1878. 414. April 28, 1878.
415. May 5, 1878.
416. Vladikavkaz was renamed Ordshonikidse under Soviet rule; the town lies on the northern slope of the Caucasus range and is terminal of the railway line from Rostov.
417. May 21, 1878.

When he left the train at Saint Petersburg on the 20th, he was welcomed by the emperor[418] and the Russian princes who had come out to meet such a great guest. Then both monarchs mounted a carriage and went to the palace. The shah spent the 21st in Saint Petersburg and paid a visit to the emperor. On the 25th he took leave of the emperor at the summer palace at Peterhof and arrived in Berlin on the last day of Jomādi I.[419] The same day the German emperor[420] came from Berlin to see the shah. They proceeded together to the residence (manzel-e doulati). After half an hour the shah took leave of the emperor, and on the last day of the month of Jomādi I he departed for Baden-Baden; he arrived there on 2d Jomādi II[421] and stayed for five days. On the 7th he departed by train for Paris and arrived there on the 8th. There he took up residence in the Grand Hotel, the abode of kings. The president of the French republic[422] paid him a visit. The shah stayed in Paris for twenty-two days. On Tuesday, 1st Rajab of that year[423] he departed for Persia and arrived at Bandar Enzeli on 25th Rajab.[424] On 9th Shaᶜbān[425] he arrived in Tehran.

REPAIR OF IRRIGATION CANALS IN THE SHIRAZ AREA. [339] In the years before Haji Moᶜtamad od-Doula's governorship most of the Karim Khāni irrigation canals of the city of Shiraz either had disappeared or had been obstructed with mud. Several of them had been conducted by the nobles of Fārs to the waters of the Jushak fountain (chashma-ye Jushak), which is dealt with in the second part of this book.[426] The irrigation

418. Czar Alexander II (r. 1855–81). 419. June 1, 1878.

420. Wilhelm I (r. 1861–88).

421. June 3, 1878, shortly before the opening of the Congress of Berlin (June 13–July 13), by which Russia was deprived of part of its acquisitions through the Turkish war (1877–78).

422. Mac Mahon (1873–79). 423. July 1, 1878.

424. July 25, 1878. 425. August 8, 1878.

426. See *FNN*, II, 319: "It is situated in the district of the city of Shiraz (Ḥuma-ye Shiraz), slightly more than 2 parasangs northwest of Shiraz.

canals, which got their water from the Nahr-e Aᶜẓam River and were claimed by the gardeners of Masjed-e Bardi and the farmers in the surroundings of Shiraz, had been cut off from the water. When the nobles were blamed by the governor, they replied: "The water of the Karim Khāni irrigation canals belongs to the landowners, as the irrigation canals are out of repair."[427] At the beginning of that year Moᶜtamad od-Doula proceeded to the plain of Qomesha and ordered an inquiry into the renovation of the Karim Khāni irrigation canals. With the best of intention and hoping for reward in the next life, he spent a large sum on the repair, and the irrigation canals were renovated. Then he distributed the water of those canals and the Jushak fountain in a just and befitting manner among those who were entitled to it.

That year, too, Moᶜtamad od-Doula ordered the construction of an irrigation canal in the uncultivated ground on the bank of the Nahr-e Aᶜẓam River, whose water was sufficient to turn 1 mill. The water of the irrigation canal was divided into 14 parts:[428] 4 parts were made a Pious Foundation (vaqf) the revenues of which were to be spent on the repair of the Takya of the wife of Amirzāda ᶜAbd ol-ᶜAli Mirzā, son of the governor, and on the pay of the Koran readers in that Takya, who read the Koran day and night.[429] The Takya lies on the eastern side of

---

It irrigates the gardens of Masjed-e Bardi and the fields in the surroundings of the city." See also above, p. 381 seq.

427. Normally, water and arable land were in the hands of different owners; the owners of the irrigation canals were responsible for the repair, otherwise they lost ownership of the water.

428. In honor of the "Fourteen Saints," that is, the Prophet Moḥammad, his daughter Fāṭema, and the twelve Emāms of the Shia.

429. The Takya was most probably the burial place of the prince's wife, as can be inferred from its situation near the Takya of Ḥāfeẓ and the employment of Koran reciters.

the Takya of Khvāja Ḥāfeẓ. Ten parts of the water were given free of charge to 10 nobles of Shiraz, of whom I, the author of this book, was one.

EḤTESHĀM OD-DOULA UNDERTAKES ANOTHER CAMPAIGN TO THE COASTAL AREA. That year, too, Eḥteshām od-Doula was ordered to settle the affairs of the ports of the Persian Gulf, the regions of Dashti, Dashtestān, and Galladār and the southern districts of Fārs. He departed from Behbehān and arrived at Bandar Bushehr on 17th Moḥarram.[430] Sheikh Madhkur Khān-e Kangāni was imprisoned at Shiraz; Haji ᶜAbd on-Nabi Khān Tājer-e Bushehri came as his mediator from Shiraz to Bushehr. The governorship of Bandar Kangān, Bandar Ṭāheri, Gāvband, and the districts of Galladār, Asir, and ᶜAlā Marvdasht was conferred upon Sheikh Madhkur Khān. Eḥteshām od-Doula was ordered to return after the settling of the affairs of Dashtestān, Dashti, Kangān, and Galladār; accordingly, he arrived at Shiraz by way of Firuzābād in the month of Jomādi I.[431]

Owing to Moᶜtamad od-Doula's efficiency, the affairs of the whole province of Fārs were settled that year, and the inhabitants were safe from oppression. The governorship of Dashti, Dashtestān, and Bushehr was with Haji Moḥammad Bāqer Khān, grandson of the late Haji Moḥammad Ḥasan Khān Ṣadr-e Eṣfahāni.

PROCEEDINGS AT THE ROYAL COURT. The shah spent the ᶜĀshurā days of the month of Moḥarram of the year 1296[432] in mourning over the family of the Prophet. The New Year fell on the evening of Friday, 27th Rabiᶜ I,[433] at 11:39 P.M. The feast and the private and public audiences were celebrated in the presence of the shah in a most befitting manner.

430. January 17, 1878. 431. Began on May 3, 1878.
432. December 26–January 4, 1879. 433. March 21, 1879.

AN ECLIPSE OF THE SUN. On 28th Rajab[434] an eclipse of the sun occurred; a third of the solar disc was obumbrated. Remarkable occurrences were these: a dog brought forth 15 puppies; and the young of a cat was without 2 paws up to the age of three or four months; the 2 paws were not fully developed, instead of running the cat jumped from one spot to the other.

QAVĀM OL-MOLK REPAIRS IRRIGATION CANALS NEAR SHIRAZ. That year Mirzā ᶜAli Moḥammad Khān Qavām ol-Molk had cleaned the obstructed vaults of the irrigation canals known as "Limak," 3 parasangs to the northwest of Shiraz. The canal had been obstructed for many years; Qavām ol-Molk bought it from the owners, renewed the stones of the ceiling (sang-e posht) and repaired the parts which were ruined. After a year the water was made to flow and brought to the vicinity of Shiraz. Half the water was made a Pious Foundation for the inhabitants of the Labb-e Āb and Bālā Keft quarters of Shiraz.[435] The quantity and digestibility of the water saved a number of people from thirst and other people benefited from it, too. This irrigation canal had enough water to turn one mill.

EḤTESHĀM OD-DOULA SENT TO THE COASTAL AREA A THIRD TIME. Haji Moᶜtamad od-Doula ordered his son, Eḥteshām od-Doula, to settle the affairs of the region of Dashti and Dashtestān. On 9th Ṣafar[436] the latter departed from Behbehān and arrived at Bandar Bushehr by way of Lirāvi, Ganāva, and Ḥayyāt-e Dā'ud[437] on the 29th of that month.[438] Dashti, Dashtestān, and Bushehr were in the possession of

434. July 18, 1879.
435. On the quarters, see above, p. 264, note 114.
436. February 2, 1879.
437. Lirāvi is the region of Bandar Deilam. Ganāva lies about 37 miles southeast of Bandar Deilam. Ḥayyāṭ-e Dā'ud is now a dehestān of 44 large villages, southeast of Lirāvi, stretching from the coast of the Persian Gulf as far as the mountains of Māhur-e Milāti, see *Farhang*, VII, 84.
438. February 22, 1879.

Moḥammad Bāqer Khān as before. On 3d Rabiᶜ II,[439] Eḥteshām od-Doula departed from Bandar Bushehr and marched through Tangestān and Ahrom[440] to the village of Khormuj, the residence of Moḥammad Khān-e Dashti. Having settled the affairs and collected the taxes, Eḥteshām od-Doula departed from Khormuj on 27th Rabiᶜ II[441] and arrived at Shiraz by way of Borāzjān, Khesht, and Kāzerun on 9th Jomādi I.[442]

The governorship of Lārestān and the districts of Sabᶜa, Dārāb, and the Five Tribes[443] remained with Qavām ol-Molk Mirzā ᶜAli Moḥammad Khān as before.

MISCELLANEOUS EVENTS. On the evening of 24th Rabiᶜ II of that year[444] the daughter of the late Haji Mollā Āqā Bābā Tājer-e Shirazi bore the author of this book a son; he gave him the name Mirzā Seiyed Moḥammad—May God grant him a long life and happiness!

That year the governorships of Fārs remained with efficient men as before.

The shah spent the ᶜĀshurā days of the month of Moḥarram of the year 1297[445] in mourning Emām Ḥosein. The New Year fell on 8th Rabiᶜ II[446] at 2:30 A.M. The feast and the private and public audiences were held in the presence of the shah.

THE AUTHOR ACCOMPANIES EḤTESHĀM OD-DOULA ON THE FOURTH CAMPAIGN TO THE COASTAL AREA AND VISITS THE ISLAND OF KHĀRK. As in the previous years, Moᶜtamad od-Doula again ordered his son Eḥteshām od-Doula to settle the affairs and to collect the taxes of the region of Dashti and Dashtestān, the ports of the Persian Gulf, and Galladār.

439. March 27, 1879.

440. Tangestān is the coastal area southeast of Bushehr. Ahrom, center of the same district, lies 34 miles east of Bushehr.

441. April 20, 1879. 442. May 1, 1879.

443. See above, p. 387. 444. April 17, 1879.

445. December 15–24, 1879.

446. March 20, 1880 (should be March 21).

Eḥteshām od-Doula departed from Behbehān on 27th Rabiᶜ I;[447] he passed Lirāvi and Ganāva and arrived at Bandar Bushehr on 9th Rabiᶜ II[448] in the company of the author of this book. On the 20th of that month,[449] they went on board a steamship to visit the island of Khārk, which lies 12 parasangs to the northwest of Bushehr. The passage lasted five hours. The next day I examined the island thoroughly. It is about 5 miles long and 2 miles wide. A Dutch building, nearly razed to the ground, is still to be seen on that island; there are, too, about 400 human dwellings, though most of them are uninhabited. There are several wells for agricultural purposes (gāv chāh-e zerāᶜati), whose water is sweet and digestible, and several irrigation canals which are cut into the rock right down to their springs. Each has a quantity of water amounting to a well (gāv-e chāhi). If the canals were cleaned, there would be even more water. In addition to the canals, there are about 500 to 600 wells, each with a diameter of 2 shāhi cubits. In the plain and on the hills one can still see the vines planted in former times, each of which produced 200 mann of grapes and wine or more. The vines have been cut down and are of no use any more. There is a high and solid cupola on the island; the interior is built of hewn stones and mortar. Inside is a vault (ṭāq), from the middle of which a door leads to another room. The floor of that room consists of a single piece of rock. There is a fissure in that rock which is known to hide Moḥammad ibn Amir ol-Mo'menin,[450] known as Moḥammad ibn Ḥanafiya.[451] On the front of the vault,

447. March 10, 1880. 448. March 21, 1880. 449. April 1, 1880.

450. "Prince of Believers," that is, ᶜAli ibn Abi Ṭāleb.

451. He was a son of ᶜAli ibn Abi Ṭāleb, his mother descended from the Bani Ḥanifa tribe. After Ḥosein's murder, he was considered by the Alids as protagonist of their claims, but he adopted strict neutrality. He died at Medina in 81:700/01; however, extremist Shiis believe him to have retreated to a mountain west of Medina whence he will, one day, return as a victorious leader. The alleged hiding place on the island of Khārk is just a variant of the mountain west of Medina, see also EI[1] III, s.v. Muḥammad b. al-Ḥanafīya. (Fr. Buhl).

decorated with tiles, is written in white characters on blue tiles: "In the name of God! Peace to the inhabitant of this place (mashhad), Amir ol-Mo'menin Moḥammad ibn Amir ol-Mo'menin ᶜAli, God bless them both![452] This has been written by Ḥosein ol-Bokhāri (?) in the year 740."[453] The interior wall of that cupola is covered to a height of 1 cubit with small glazed octagonal tiles. At the edges of these tiles are written poems from *Leilā and Majnun*,[454] in Persian. Most of them are broken and scattered on the floor. We stayed on that island until the 12th of that month.[455] Every day the governor, in my company, mounted his horse and visited the plains and the hills of the island. On the hills we saw 12 gazelles, partridges, quail, pigeons, hoopoes, and many other kinds of birds. Wild beasts, such as leopards, wolves, jackals, and foxes there are none. We saw no dogs on the island. When we asked the reason of this, people replied: "Each dog we bring to the island inevitably becomes crazy after two or three summer months." On the 27th[456] we boarded the steamship and arrived at Bushehr five hours later.

SHEIKH MADHKUR KHĀN-E KANGĀNI SUBDUED. Sheikh Madhkur Khān-e Kangāni, who had been in revolt for many years and had been arrested by Eḥteshām od-Doula and sent to Shiraz, as has been reported,[457] was again appointed governor of Bandar Kangān, Galladār, and dependencies by mediation of Haji ᶜAbd on-Nabi Tājer-e Bushehri in the year 1295.[458] In the first year, he behaved in accordance with the laws. In the year 1296, he became proud because of the inaccessibility of the fortress of Qalāt-e Sorkh—it is dealt with in the second part of

452. That is, Moḥammad and ᶜAli (father and son).

453. 740:1339/40.

454. A famous epical tale of Arabic origin which was chosen as *sujet* by many Persian poets, among them Neẓāmi.

455. A mistake for the twenty-seventh, see the following note.

456. April 7, 1880. 457. See above, p. 397. 458. 1295:1878.

this book, in the chapter on the fortresses of Fārs[459]—stopped paying taxes and administrating the districts, brought his possessions and his family to the fortress of Qalāt-e Sorkh, and entrenched himself there. Eḥteshām od-Doula sent Moḥammad Ebrāhim Beg, one of his oldest and most trustworthy servants, with 400 horsemen and infantry from Kuh-e Giluya under the command of Khodā Karam Khān-e Bavir Aḥmadi Kuh-e Gilu'i and 400 soldiers and 2 pieces of artillery to capture the fortress of Qalāt-e Sorkh and arrest Sheikh Madhkur Khān. [341] He himself remained at Bushehr, waiting for news. When news of the capture of the fortress arrived, he departed from Bushehr on 9th Jomādi II of that year[460] and marched by way of Borāzjān and Khesht to Kāzerun. When Moḥammad Ebrāhim Beg arrived at the foot of the fortress of Qalāt-e Sorkh, he captured it within a few days, arrested Sheikh Madhkur Khān, put him in fetters, and brought him by way of Dashti and Dashtestān, Khesht and Kāzerun to Eḥteshām od-Doula's camp. The latter arrived at Shiraz on the 22d of that month.[461] The same day Sheikh Madhkur Khān, by orders of Haji Moᶜtamad od-Doula, was hung. When news of this arrived in Tehran, the ministers promoted Moḥammad Ebrāhim Beg in reward for his services to the rank of sarhang without a detachment (khārej az fouj) and granted him the title "Khān," and he was styled "Moḥammad Ebrāhim Khān Sarhang." The governorship of the districts of Kangān, Galladār, and Gāvbandi was bestowed upon him.

THE SHAH TRAVELS TO MĀZANDARĀN. On 18th Rajab of that year[462] the shah departed for the summer camp in Māzandarān. On 25th Shaᶜbān[463] he returned to the summer camp in

459. See *FNN*, II, 335: "The fortress of Qalāt-e Sorkh is a mountain 2 parasangs south of the village of Gāvbandi, in the region of Fumestān belonging to the district of Lārestān. The drinking water comes from rain water basins. The fortress can be defended by 50–60 musketeers."

460. May 19, 1880. 461. June 1, 1880. 462. June 26, 1880.

463. August 2, 1880.

Tehran. He spent the ᶜĀshurā days of the month of Moḥarram of the year 1298[464] in mourning Emām Ḥosein.

THE PROVINCE OF FĀRS IN PERFECT ORDER. That year all the districts of Fārs were safe, from Moghestān-e ᶜAbbāsi[465] as far as the district of Bahmani in Kuh-e Giluya,[466] and from Kheirābād near Niriz[467] as far as Bandar Bushehr. The inhabitants were not molested by oppressors and prayed for the shah, wishing him a long life and happiness.

MOᶜTAMAD OD-DOULA RETURNS TO TEHRAN: EXAMPLES OF HIS WISE GOVERNMENT OF THE PROVINCE OF FĀRS. The New Year fell on 19th Rabiᶜ II:[468] 8 hours and 17 minutes after sunrise. The feast was celebrated in the presence of the shah. On the 20th of that month Haji Moᶜtamad od-Doula was summoned to Tehran; he stayed a few days, waiting for Eḥteshām od-Doula's arrival from Bushehr. Upon the latter's arrival, Haji Moᶜtamad od-Doula departed from Shiraz on 5th Jomādi II[469] and arrived safe and sound in Tehran on 14th Rajab.[470] Since he attended to the office of governor of Fārs every day in the expected manner, abolished undesirable laws, educated the subjects in a new manner, and showed them benevolence beyond bounds, it has become necessary to decorate this book with his virtues as far as my weak memory remembers them, so that it might be a source of information for the readers and a reminder to those who listen to it.

In short: Upon his arrival at Shiraz, Moᶜtamad od-Doula convened a governmental meeting. When high and low had

464. December 4–13, 1880.

465. The region is east of Bandar ᶜAbbās, stretching from Mināb in the north to Jāshk in the south, see *FNN*, II, 224.

466. Bahman is the western part of Kuh-e Giluya, the region west of Behbehān, see *FNN*, II, 263.

467. About 60 miles east-northeast of Niriz, at the western outskirts of a salt desert.

468. March 21, 1881. 469. May 5, 1881. 470. June 12, 1881.

assembled, he saluted them in the following manner: "I like true and upright men and consider liars and people of ambiguous talk enemies, as the saying goes: 'Lies are the beginning of each fault, and hypocrisy the origin of all evil.'" Then he appointed an experienced writer secretary of petitions (ᶜariża-negār), who was to write down the petitions of plaintiffs in a concise manner; for each petition he was to receive as reward the sum of 10 shāhi, which corresponds to half a miskal of coined money. Then he summoned the guards and watchmen to the doors and ordered them to prevent nobody from going to see him; when a plaintiff brought a petition written by the secretary of petitions, the plaintiff was to be admitted to the governor by mediation of the chief chamberlain (eshik āqāsi bāshi) and he (Moᶜtamad od-Doula) would write the answer in the margin of that petition. Then he summoned the members of the chief magistrate's court and addressed Amir ol-Omarā Haji Moḥammad Hāshem Khān-e Nuri, chief of the magistrate's court, in the following manner:

If somebody appeals to the magistrate's court and his claim (maṭlab) is found to be justified beyond any doubt, the documents (sanad) of the plaintiff, the defendant, and the witness (dalil-e ḥaqqiyat) shall be submitted in the afternoon of the same day and a decision shall be passed, and I shall write in the margin of the decision "all right" (ṣaḥiḥ ast). We shall demand 10 percent of the plaintiff as a fee (ḥokm-e ᶜarab-shāhi) and divide it between the two. If the claim is not clear, you shall refer the matter to a judge of the religious law (ḥākem-e sharᶜ) acceptable to both parties, and at the same time you shall impose on both parties a sum of money to be paid as a pledge; then you shall execute the decision of the judge. If a liar commits a base action against him who says the truth, the liar shall pay an indemnification.

The next day he summoned the night watches and the guards of the city of Shiraz and said to them:

If you carry out the duties of your office in a satisfactory manner, you shall receive a robe of honor and continue to attend to your office. If a theft occurs in the city, you either have to arrest the thief within ten days or pay a fine and compensation for the stolen goods out of your own pocket.

Since the pay of the night watches was not much—How then could they pay compensation?—their pay was increased accordingly. The next day he settled the affairs of the financial administration (daftar-e ḥesāb-e divāni) of Fārs and the proceedings (moᶜāmalat) of the taxation agents (ᶜommāl) and established perfect order. The next day he inquired into the affairs of the government servants (noukarhā-ye divān), such as gunners, horsemen, and soldiers, and fixed their daily allowances (jira), pay (mavājeb), and fodder (ᶜaliq). From the secretary of the army and the officers (ṣāḥeb mansabān), he took a written obligation in which they promised integrity. Then he appointed honest men financial agents and governors of the districts and tribes [342] and took from them a written statement in which they promised to pay the taxes and to administrate the affairs of the subjects in an orderly manner. He then committed each road to a number of musketeers for protection against thieves and robbers and fixed for the musketeers a suitable pay, and they signed a pledge to pay a fine and compensation for goods stolen from travellers. From the day of his arrival in Fārs onwards, he ordered independent people to inquire into the oppression of thieves and highway robbers and took notes of their names and features in his own handwriting; he appointed governors of the districts and tribes on the principal condition that they seize the thieves and evildoers. Every governor who arrested a thief or an evildoer was granted special favors and a robe of honor. When a wrongdoer (moqaṣṣer) was brought before him, he was punished in accordance with his crime; once the wrongdoer was convicted of the crime, nobody's mediation was accepted. By these means thefts, lies, crime, and oppression were eradicated in the province of Fārs within a short period. The revenues collected from the oppressed people were taken away from the oppressors.

Four days each week, Moᶜtamad od-Doula sat from sunrise to noon in the assembly settling the affairs of the state and the subjects in a most accurate manner. He never postponed a matter from one day to the next, because other matters were to be taken care of then. He made arrangements by which everybody was easily enabled to submit a matter to him by word of mouth, day or night, without mediator, because until sunrise there was no guard at his door and nobody who prevented people from having access to him. At nightfall an old and tireless Kurdish woman named "Parijān" watched at the door of the inner palace. Each occurrence in the city of Shiraz was immediately submitted to the governor and a decision was passed. Three hours before sunset he held in the palace the second audience, which was attended by all the theologians, scholars, and outstanding people; they passed the time in discussing scientific questions. In most of the ordinary (rasmiya) sciences,[471] the governor surpassed most of the scholars of his age. He surpassed scholars of profound learning in mathematics and its branches, such as arithmetic, geometry, astronomy, astrology, spherical geometry, and the science of astrolabes, and in letters, such as lexicography, grammar, morphology, etymology, semantics, rhetoric, and interpretation of the Koran. When he discussed a problem he did not lack proof and arguments and put forward the different opinions with the right and wrong arguments. He never treated a question in a summary manner. He made profit of the teachings of every scholar whom he met. Haji Sheikh Yaḥyā, imam of the prayers at Shiraz, an encyclopaedia of learning, stated repeatedly on the pulpit:

I never went away from His Excellency without having profited in a scholarly problem. For instance, in my presence he asked the others who were present: "How do you read the word *habbu* in that poem by

471. From the ᶜolum-e rasmiya ("ordinary sciences") listed a few lines below it seems that these sciences are opposed to the ᶜolum-e ilāhiya ("theological sciences") which are based on revelation and tradition.

Ḥāfeẓ: 'Last night the nightingale sang beautifully in the circle of the rose and the wine: Let the sun rise, *habbu*, oh you inebriate'?" Some said: "With *yā* and two dots under the *tashdid*,[472] i.e., well then!," others said: "With *hā* without a dot and *yā* with two dots under the tashdid,[473] i.e., come near!" His Excellency said: "Neither, it is *hā-ye havvaz* and *bā* without *shadda*, the imperative of *habba*, *yohibbu*, i.e., *istaiqiz*, which means 'wake up and pay attention!'"

Whenever he received a letter from a scholar, he examined the beauty or ugliness of the handwriting, secondly he directed his attention to the orthography, pointed out the blunders and as a punishment demanded a book of the writer, and accepting even books like *Ketāb-e Taṣrif* or *Ketāb-e Amthela*.[474] Three or four months later there was nobody among the scholars of Shiraz who made a blunder.

To the best of his ability, the governor attended to the administrative affairs in accordance with the religious law. One day, a man brought a letter from Mirzā Moḥammad Ḥasan-e Lārijāni, a scholar from Shiraz. Reading the letter, the governor learned that the man had received a garden as a gift from his father and that the father had some time later sold that garden to a merchant. The man then proved his claim before Mirzā Moḥammad Ḥasan. By order of the governor, the merchant and the man's father were summoned, and the governor ordered the merchant to return the garden in accordance with the decision based on the religious law. The government agents were ordered to collect from the vendor the actual price of the garden, which was double the former price, and to hand this sum over to the merchant as indemnification. Then the governor passed a governmental decision (ḥokm-e doulati) to the effect that the hand of the vendor was to be cut off, because he had sold the

472. A sign which indicates reduplication of a consonant. In this case, one would say "hayyā" in stead of "habbu."

473. That is, ḥayya.

474. Books on elementary grammar as used in the schools.

garden by a theft, which was worse than highway robbery.[475]

When the governor referred an obscure case to the judge of the religious law who was acceptable to both parties and an oath had to be taken, the theologians of that time used to be cautious and did not impose the oath. Thus the cases remained without decision. Therefore Emām Haji Mollā Āqā Bozorg, an experienced scholar, was appointed "Official of the Oath." A large square marble seal with carved writing was made and handed over to the aforementioned Haji to seal the evidence (qasam-nāma).[476] Until today, the year 1305, Haji Mollā Āqā Bozorg's seal is acknowledged on the witness documents of the chief magistrate's court.

One day an intoxicated man [343] was brought before the governor. The governor said to him: "You are drunk. Why have you gone out of the house and not done according to the saying 'Put your head where you have drunk wine'?"[477] The man replied: "I was a guest in a friend's house. When part of the night had passed, my host threw me out of the house, and I was arrested by the night watch." Then the governor sent for the host and asked him: "Why have you not honored your guest?" The host replied: "He flirted with my wife." The governor said: "An intoxicated man cannot avoid having

475. The religious law required simple restitution of the garden to the son, without indemnification of the merchant, because the selling was illicit and therefore invalid. The governor, having a strong sense of justice, went beyond the requirements of the religious law and had an indemnification paid to the merchant; in addition to that, he punished the father for theft, which was outside the scope of the religious law, too. In that way justice was done to all persons involved. "Ḥokm-e doulati," a decision passed by a secular authority, is opposed to "ḥokm-e sharʿi," a decision passed by a religious authority.

476. The inscription on the seal contained probably the formula of oath; by these means, the persons involved were not obliged to take an oath by word of mouth; the written or printed oath was less delicate than the spoken oath.

477. Islamic law persecutes only what happens in public; the private sphere remains outside the competence of the religious authorities.

treachery in his eyes." Then he ordered the host whipped twice as much as the guest.[478]

Moᶜtamad od-Doula never disappointed anybody who asked him for something. In the last two or three years the secret alms which he distributed among the poor amounted to more than 15,000 toman. The same amount or more was given as open gifts to indigent people in the name of emoluments (mavājeb), pay (vaẓifa) and pension (mostamarri). When an unfortunate man of high standing had to stay in bed, the governor sent an official every day to ask about his condition. If he was indigent, he was given the money for medicine, food, and the doctor's fee. When he died, the governor paid for the shroud, the funeral, prayers and sermon in the mosque, and water and provisions for the first three days and even the tombstone.

At each meeting the governor would inspire those who were present to act ethically and used to say: "The former governors of Fārs considered themselves as being committed to collect the taxes, and that was all. I consider myself in addition to that as being committed to induce the people, willy-nilly, to doing good."

In the year 1295,[479] there was a drought in Fārs; the prices of victuals were going up and the people complained. Haji Moᶜtamad od-Doula—God nourish him with His grace!—summoned the nobles of Shiraz and said to them:

The Lord of the Islamic Religious Law has ordered His community to turn their attention to acts of beneficence, that is, the rich shall assist the poor with their possessions. You shall know that the price of grain has gone up and that the lamentations about hunger have become overwhelming with the merchants. Until the harvest, there are four months left. We must examine the quantity of victuals of the inhabitants of the

478. The host had committed a double crime: he brought his guest into a situation to flirt with his wife and then threw him out of his house in a state of intoxication.

479. 1295:1878.

city and of the owners of the storehouses. We must fix the price of bread so as to enable the poor to buy it.

Then he ordered an assessment of the grain stored up in the storehouses of Shiraz to be drawn up, and the owners of the storehouses were informed that in case their assessment was not true, all their grain would be confiscated. After the examination it was realized that all the provisions of grain in the city of Shiraz amounted to a quantity of 1 crore and 400,000 mann in the Shirazi weight[480] and that the population of Shiraz needed on the average each day 7,000 to 8,000 mann of bread. About 3,000 mann of the whole quantity were stored up as contribution in kind (jens) in the government storehouses, which was the property of the governor. Then he ordered the bakers' guild to sell 1 mann of grain out of the government storehouses, the price of which was 900 dinar, at the price of 600 dinar and to take that grain into their stores. The owners of the storehouses showed patience and justice, too, and continued selling their grain at the same price until the end of the year. On account of these laudable measures the following saying was applied to many people: "He nourished them when they were hungry and protected them when they were anxious—May God reward him with beneficence!"

From the second year of his governorship onward, he summoned at the beginning of each year the brick makers, stucco workers, and mortar workers and fixed the size of the bricks and of the stucco work. The costs of 1,000 bricks, 1,000 stucco pieces, and 1,000 mann of mortar were assessed and a fee was

480. That is, 1 crore (or 500,000 mann) plus 400,000 mann equals 900,000 mann; since the eighteenth century the mann-e shirāzi (also called mann-e shāhi) weighed 6 kilograms, see Hinz, *Masse und Gewichte*, p. 21; accordingly, the stores of grain amounted to 5,400,000 kilograms. Each day 8,000 mann or 48,000 kilograms were needed, which seems reasonable for a population numbering 53,607 people, see above, p. 264, note 144.

fixed for the master. And a decree was issued to the effect that they were not allowed to sell their products at a price higher than had been fixed.

From the year of his arrival in Fārs onward, he inquired successfully into the conditions of all the inhabitants of the city of Shiraz and the districts and knew everybody's virtues and vices much better than the families and clans of the persons in question knew them. Every day he learned new details about the people of the city that the mayor and the superintendent (moḥtaseb)[481] did not know. Things went so far that nobody dared say a harsh word. When a debate between husband and wife degenerated into using bad language, they were punished the next day. The governor was so well informed because everybody who brought true information was admitted without mediator and granted a special reward. The governor knew the families of Shiraz by their names and characteristics.[482]

One day two children playing the nut game got into a quarrel. It became known to the governor that the bigger child had maltreated the smaller one. The governor gave the maltreated child 1,000 nuts and pulled the other child by the ears until the child started screaming.

One day a man tied like a corpse to 4 pieces of wood was brought before the governor. The man had been beaten by somebody and was not able to feel or to move and near to death. The man who had beaten him was brought before the governor, and when questioned he answered: "I have a claim against him, therefore he was brought before Your Excellency in such a state." Then the governor ordered the beaten man's pulse and state of health to be examined, and both were found

481. The moḥtaseb supervises the markets (measures and weights) and, in general, the behavior of people in public, whether they comply with the prescriptions of the religious law.

482. Ḥasan-e Fasā'i may have used the material collected by the governor for Vol. II of his *Fārs-nāma-ye Nāṣeri* which contains a large amount of biographical data.

to be all right. The governor then ordered him to be left alone for two hours, and the latter remained lying in the sun without moving about. Then the governor ordered a jar to be filled with lemon juice and snow and to put it quietly near the man's mouth and nose. When he smelled the cool lemon juice, he took quite unaware, because of the great heat, the jar with lemon juice and got on his feet. The governor ordered the sum claimed to be taken from him and handed over to the claimant.

One day the governor said: "Somewhere I read the name 'Masjed-e Ṭāheri-ye Shiraz.'" Nobody replied. Then he ordered old people to be questioned. Several days later, it was stated that Haji Mirzā Moḥammad ᶜAli, chief servant (khādem bāshi) of the Masjed-e Vakil, had torn down that mosque and built a stable in its place. The governor sent several architects to search for the foundations and old parts of that mosque. Then the stable was torn down [344] and the governor spent about 500 toman of legal money[483] on the renovation of the mosque, and the mosque was restored to holy service. The Masjed-e Ṭāhiri is situated at the southern side of the Masjed-e Jāmiᶜ ᶜAtiq of Shiraz.

To this governor belongs credit for the renovation of the palace-like building in the courtyard of the shrine at Kāẓemein, which both tongue and hand fail to describe. It is widely known that he spent 200,000 toman of Persian value on that building.

MOᶜTAMAD OD-DOULA'S ACTIVITIES IN THE FIELD OF SCHOLARSHIP AND WRITING. Among the scholarly works of the governor is *Ketāb-e Kanz ol-Ḥesāb*, a commentary on *Kholaṣā-ye Ḥesāb* by the late Sheikh Bahā' od-Din ᶜĀmeli.[484]

483. "Vajh ol-ḥalāl," that is, money acquired in accordance with the prescriptions of the religious law, which alone it was allowed to spend on such an object, see also above, p. 168, note 288.

484. Bahā' ad-Din Moḥammad ibn Ḥosein b. ᶜAbd aṣ-Ṣamad al-Ḥārithi al-Jabā'i al-ᶜĀmili al-Bahā'i died in 1030:1621; the full title of his book is *Kholāṣat al-ḥisāb al-Bahā'iya*; it has been preserved in numerous manuscripts; fourteen commentaries in Arabic are mentioned by Brockelmann, *Geschichte der Arabischen Litteratur*, Supplementband II, 595 seq.

It was completed in the month of Rajab of the year 1256.[485] Furthermore, there is *Ketāb-e Jām-e Jam*, which is a treatise on the science of geography; nothing comparable has been written in Arabic and Persian; several hundred copies of it have been printed and spread all over the world. Its composition was started in the year 1270.[486] Furthermore, *Ketāb-e Qamqām* is a treatise on the misfortunes of the family of the Prophet, especially that of Abu ᶜAbdollāh Ḥosein, the fifth of the "Family of the Cloak."[487] Until today no other book like this has been written on the subject. Doubtful traditions which cannot be accepted by sound reason have not been included, but only the traditions of the old authorities, and no more. The book was completed on 25th Dhu'l-Ḥejja of the year 1304.[488] Several hundred copies were printed and became the model of the recital (on the ᶜĀshurā days). "Qamqām" means "a great thing" and "ocean." And finally there is *Ketāb-e ruznāma-ye safar-e Madinat os-Salām va-Beit Ollāh ol-ḥarām*.[489] In this book all the occurrences of each day and night are noted, from the departure from Tehran up to the return to Tehran. The date of departure is given as the last day of the month of Rajab of the year 1292;[490] the day of

485. September 1840.

486. 1270–72: 1853–55/56; a translation of W. Pinnock's *Geography* (see Rypka, *Iranische Literaturgeschichte*, p. 334), with additions on the geography of Persia, especially Fārs. The book is quoted by the author of the *FNN*, see above, p. 244, note 44. The title "Jām-e Jam" refers to the magic cup (jām) in which the Iranian hero Jamshid (Jam) saw the universe.

487. The "Holy Family" of Islam, that is, the Prophet Moḥammad, his daughter Fātema, her husband ᶜAli, and the latter's sons Ḥasan and Ḥosein.

488. September 14, 1887; see Storey, p. 204: "*Qamqām-i zakhkhār va-ṣamṣām-i battār*, notices of Moḥammad, the Caliphs and the Imāms, followed by a list of works on the subject (713 folio pp.) Edition: Tihran 1305: 1887."

489. "Diary of a Travel to Medina and Mecca." According to Storey, p. 204 (also p. 1157) the title of this book is *Hedāyat os-sabil va-kefāyat od-dalil*, of which two editions, Shiraz 1294: 1877 and Tehran 1294: 1877, have appeared.

490. Began on August 3, 1875.

arrival, as the 2d Rabi^c II of the year 1293.[491] He traveled from Tehran to Medina and Mecca by way of Rasht, Baku, Tiflis, Trapezunt, Istanbul, Izmir, Alexandria, Suez, and Yambo^c, and returned to Tehran by way of Jidda, Port Said, Beirut, Istanbul, Trapezunt, Baku, and Rasht.

In short, Mo^ctamad od-Doula did not spend his life in vain endeavors, from the beginning of the age of discernment until today, when he is more than 70 years old, as he writes at the beginning of his book *Jām-e Jam*:

In olden times the frontiers and the army were to be taken care of. Nowadays travels are to be undertaken[492] and books to be studied. Formerly, one dealt with white leaves, now with black leaves.[493] First come the years of play, then one has to engage in the study of the Koran and the Sunna, finally, one has to sit on the throne of governorship to settle disputes. Again one has to seek solitude and to close the door to people known and unknown. The result of the endeavors of throne and Divan is the prosperity of the subjects and the peace of the countries, the profit of retreat and sitting in the eivān is the acquiring of knowledge and abundance of honors; the impious will be unhappy in any case, people thinking of the good—happy and successful. It is better to acquire perfection than money; it is dangerous to pile up money in the treasury, but what misfortune can attain you when you disburse perfection?

In addition to his theoretical and practical accomplishments, his efficiency in ethical education, administering the household, ruling the state,[494] giving laws to the province, and inflicting punishment, Farhād Mirzā Mo^ctamad od-Doula was a gifted

491. April 27, 1876. Immediately upon his return, Farhād Mirzā was appointed governor of Fārs.

492. That is, war has given place to peaceful relations, see also above, p. 368.

493. In former times, the scholars wrote books, but did not read books (because there were none, or at least not many books), now one has to read books before one starts writing oneself.

494. The list enumerates the three subdivisions of practical ethics in the traditional manner.

poet. He had a wide-ranging knowledge of Arabic and Persian poetry, and sometimes he composed poems as a proof of his talent.

[345] However, let us return to our subject: During his second five-year term as governor of Fārs, Farhād Mirzā Mo^c^tamad od-Doula educated the inhabitants of the province of Fārs, eradicated the depravities of the vicious, and introduced good behavior in their stead. All the people offered prayers to God during his lifetime and the time of his governorship. When he left Shiraz for Tehran on 5th Jomādi II of that year,[495] the whole population of Shiraz, masters and servants, high and low, assembled to see him to the gate; they closed the halls and the caravanserais, the colleges and the bazaars and left the city, and horsemen and pedestrians followed the wise, just, and generous prince. When they arrived at the Teppe-ye Salām,[496] a small mound made of clay and stones 1.5 miles east of Shiraz, the governor dismounted from his horse, turned in the direction of the Qebla, and gave with great eloquence a farewell sermon in Arabic. Then he took leave of all who had accompanied him, allowed them to return to the city, mounted a carriage drawn by horses, and departed. Those who had seen him off recited, tears in their eyes, the following verse from the Koran: "He Who has made the Koran binding on thee will certainly bring thee Back."[497]

ADMINISTRATIVE REORGANIZATION OF SOUTHERN PERSIA; SOLṬĀN ḤOSEIN MIRZĀ JALĀL OD-DOULA APPOINTED GOVERNOR OF FĀRS. On 20th Rabi^c^ II of that year,[498] the governorship of Fārs was added to the governorships of the province of Esfahan, Borujerd, Khvānsār, ^c^Eraq-e ^c^ajam, ^c^Arabestān-e Irān, Kermānshāh, Golpāygān, Kurdistan, and Yazd and conferred upon Solṭān Mas^c^ud Mirzā Ẓell os-Solṭān. The latter appointed his son, Solṭān Ḥosein Mirzā Jalāl od-Doula,

495. May 5, 1881. 496. "Hill of Farewell."
497. *Koran* XXVIII, 85. 498. March 22, 1881.

governor of Fārs. The office of vizier and chief was entrusted to Mirzā Fatḥ ᶜAli Khān Ṣāḥeb Divān-e Shirazi, son of the late Haji Qavām ol-Molk. By telegraph, Ẓell os-Solṭān appointed Mirzā ᶜAli Moḥammad Khān Qavām ol-Molk, the younger brother of Ṣāḥeb Divān and disciple of Haji Moᶜtamad od-Doula, whose efficiency and sagacity had been made known at the court by the latter's mediation, deputy governor.

PANJ ᶜALI BEG OF THE INĀLU TRIBE SUBDUED. In the years before Haji Moᶜtamad od-Doula's governorship, Panj ᶜAli Beg of the Abu'l-Vardi branch of the Inālu tribe[499] had gathered together several families of the dispersed tribes and plundered the caravans and taken to encroaching on the districts of Jahrom, Qir va-Kārzin, Khafr, and Ṣimekān.[500] Since he realized that after Moᶜtamad od-Doula's appointment to the governorship things had changed, he and his brother did not revolt against the governor, but took refuge in the governor's stable and signed a pledge of good behavior by the mediation of the master of the stable (mir ākhur). For five years he and his followers earned their livelihood by trade and agriculture. When a new governor of Fārs was appointed, Qavām ol-Molk in wise forethought decided to ruin Panj ᶜAli Beg. On the evening of 12th Jomādi I of that year,[501] when the Panj ᶜAli Beg's clan was staying in the vicinity of Pol-e Fasā, 3 parasangs southeast of Shiraz,[502] he ordered a number of cavalry and infantry to surround their houses. Panj ᶜAli Beg made his escape and took refuge in the

499. One of the 23 branches of the Inālu, enumerated in *FNN*, II, 310, see also above, p. 336, note 160.

500. That is, the region south of Fasā and Firuzābād, see above, p. 87, note 25.

501. May 12, 1881.

502. A small village 11 miles southeast of Shiraz (see *Farhang*, VII, 47), probably so-called from the bridge crossing the river which flows into the Daryācha-ye Bākhtegān. The bridge (or the village) has been known since medieval times.

shrine of Shāh Charāgh. Three or four days later, he was given a guarantee and returned home.

ADMINISTRATIVE ACTIVITIES OF GOVERNOR AND VIZIER OF FĀRS. At the end of the month of Rajab of that year,[503] the governor, Solṭān Ḥosein Mirzā Jalāl od-Doula, and the vizier, Ṣāḥeb Divān, arrived at Shiraz to take over their posts. The governorship of Lārestān and the districts of Sab^{c}a, Dārāb, and the Five Tribes[504] remained added to the district of Fasā as before and were entrusted to Qavām ol-Molk. The office of financial agent and governor of Dashti and Dashtestān and the governorship of Bandar Bushehr were conferred upon Mirzā Moḥammad Mostoufi-ye Neẓām. The governorship of Kuh-e Giluya and Bandar ^{c}Abbās was entrusted to Haji Naṣir ol-Molk.

When Ṣāḥeb Divan examined the emoluments of the 10 aldermen of the quarters of Shiraz, which were 12 toman for each, [346] he fixed them at 50 toman each; and it was entered into the account book of Fārs, that the emoluments were to be paid to them every year.

CAVALRY DETACHMENT FROM FĀRS STATIONED IN TEHRAN. Nāṣer od-Din Shāh spent the ^{c}Āshurā days of the month of Moḥarrem of the year 1299[505] in mourning the family of the Prophet. In the same month, Ẓell os-Solṭān ordered Mirzā ^{c}Ali Moḥammad Khān Qavām ol-Molk[506] by telegraph, to go to Shiraz with 500 horsemen selected from the tribes of Fārs. On 19th Ṣafar of that year,[507] when the sun had passed half the sign of Capricorn, Qavām ol-Molk departed from Shiraz to Esfahan; from Esfahan he accompanied Ẓell os-Solṭān to

503. The end of July 1881.
504. That is, the Inālu, Bāṣeri, Bahārlu, Arabs, and Nafar, see above, p. 387.
505. December 23–January 2, 1882.
506. He was deputy governor of Fārs, see above, p. 416.
507. December 30, 1881.

Tehran. On 8th Rabiᶜ I,[508] they arrived in Tehran. When Ẓell os-Solṭān presented the horsemen to the shah, he was granted royal favors. Of the 500 horsemen, 150 were of the Arab tribes of Fārs, 50 of the Bahārlu tribe, 50 of the Inālu tribe, and 50 of different tribes that had settled at Shiraz, and 200 of the Qashqā'i tribes. The command over them was conferred upon Ḥabib-ollāh Khān, the actual beglerbegi of Shiraz and grandson of Mirzā ᶜAli Moḥammad Khān Qavām ol-Molk. The pay of each horseman was fixed at 20 toman after deductions (noqṣān), the victuals (jira) at 0.5 mann of bread, the fodder at 2 mann of straw and 1 mann of barley.[509]

MISCELLANEOUS EVENTS. Up to the spring of the year 1298,[510] the province of Fārs was tranquil, owing to the administration (tadbir) of Ṣāḥeb Divān and the carefulness of Qavām ol-Molk who followed closely the instructions given by Haji Moᶜtamad od-Doula.

The New Year fell on the evening of Tuesday, 1st Jomādi I:[511] 2 hours and 4 minutes after sunset. The feast was celebrated in the presence of the shah in a befitting manner. On the 28th of that month,[512] Soltan Masᶜud Mirzā Ẓell os-Solṭān, governor of the provinces of Yazd, Fārs, Esfahan, ᶜErāq-e ᶜajam, ᶜArabestān, Borujerd, Kermānshāh, Kurdistan, Lorestān, Khvānsār, and Golpāygān, left Tehran for Esfahan, and Mirzā ᶜAli Moḥammad Khān Qavām ol-Molk arrived in his company at Esfahan. After resting from the exertions of the journey the governor gave him permission to return to Shiraz at the end of the month of Jomādi II of that year.[513] On the 29th of that month[514] a full eclipse occurred in the sign of the dragon.

508. January 28, 1882.

509. They were stationed in Tehran in the shah's special service and were, at the same time, as hostages, a pledge for the good behavior of the unruly tribes of southern Persia.

510. Spring 1881. 511. March 21, 1882. 512. April 17, 1882.

513. The middle of May 1882. 514. May 18, 1882.

The governorship of Bandar Bushehr, Dashti, and Dashtestān was added to that of Kuh-e Giluya and Bandar ᶜAbbās and conferred upon Mirzā Ḥasan ᶜAli Khān Haji Naṣir ol-Molk.

That year, by order of Ṣāḥeb Divān, all the streets of the 10 quarters of Shiraz were paved with mortar and stones; henceforth they were free from clay and mud in winter and from dust in summer. According to the orders of Qavām ol-Molk, the Bazār-e Mesgerān,[515] which had a roof of reeds and rush mats, was covered with a vault of mortar and bricks, like the Bazār-e Vakili. The shops from the Esfahan gate as far as the Bazār-e Vakili were covered with vaults of bricks and mortar.

During the time of the summer heat, the court proceeded from the city of Tehran to Shemrān, and a little later to Māzandarān. Having finished relaxing and hunting, the shah returned to Tehran.

That year the governorship of Kuh-i Giluya, Bandar Bushehr and Bandar ᶜAbbāṣ was with Mirzā Ḥasan ᶜAli Khān Naṣir ol-Molk, that of Lārestān, Dārāb, Fasā, and the Five Tribes[516] with Mirzā ᶜAli Moḥammad Khān Qavām ol-Molk, and that of the Qashqā'i tribe with Solṭān Moḥammad Khān Ilkhāni as before. The province of Fārs was as safe as in the previous years.

DEATH OF MOSHIR OL-MOLK AND QAVĀM OL-MOLK. The shah spent the ᶜĀshurā days of the month of Moḥarram of the year 1300[517] in the Takya Doulati in mourning the family of the Prophet. At the end of that year,[518] Mirzā Abu'l-Hasan Khān Moshir ol-Molk died. At the beginning of Ṣafar,[519] Mirzā ᶜAli Moḥammad Khān Qavām ol-Molk died, too. The two men had been bitter enemies during their lifetime. Since there were only a few days between their death, the poet Farazdaq's saying is

515. The coppersmith bazaar.
516. See above, p. 386.
517. November 12–21, 1882.
518. That is, September/October 1882.
519. Began on December 12, 1882.

confirmed: When the latter heard of the poet Jarir's death[520] and uttered lamentations, somebody said to him: "Jarir's death must cause you joy." He replied: "I lament my own death."

520. Farazdaq and Jarir were two famous Arabic poets of the early eighth century; they were bitter rivals and died in about 728/29, the one shortly after the other.

APPENDIX I

THE QĀJĀR RULERS

1. Āqā Moḥammad Shāh
   Crowned in spring 1210/1796
   Murdered on 21 Dhu'l-Ḥejja 1211/17 June 1797
2. Fatḥ ʿAli Shāh
   Crowned on New Year 1212/21 March 1798
   Died on 19 Jomādi II 1250/23 October 1834
3. Moḥammad Shāh
   Died on 6 Shavvāl 1264/4 September 1848
4. Nāṣer od-Din Shāh
   Crowned in Tabriz on 14 Shavval 1264/12 September 1848, in Tehran on 22 Dhu'l-Qaʿda 1264/19 October 1848
   Murdered 1313/1896

THE PRIME MINISTERS

1. Haji Ebrāhim Khān Eʿtemād od-Doula
   Appointed Jomādi II 1209/January 1795
   Deposed 1 Dhu'l-Ḥejja 1215/15 April 1801
2. Mirzā Shafiʿ Māzandarānī
   Died 1234/1819
3. Haji Moḥammad Ḥosein Khān Neẓām od-Doula Eṣfahānī
   Died 13 Ṣafar 1239/19 October 1823
4. ʿAbdollah Khān Amin od-Doula (son of the preceding)
   Until 1240/1824–1825
5. Allāh Yār Khān-e Qājār Devehlu Āṣaf od-Doula
   Until Ramażān 1243/March–April 1828
6. Abdollāh Khān Amin od-Doula, second term
   Until 1834 (?)
7. Abu'l-Qāsem Qā'em Maqām
   Executed 29 Ṣafar 1251/26 June 1835
8. Haji Mirzā ʿAbbās-e Erivani "Haji Mirzā Āqāsi"
   Until 1264/1848 (?)
9. Mirzā Taqi Farahāni Amir-e Atabeg
   Appointed after Shavvāl 1264/September–October 1848
10. Mirzā Āqā Khān-e Nuri Eʿtemād od-Doula
    Appointed 18 Moḥarram 1268/13 November 1851
11. Appointment of six ministers
    20 Moḥarram 1275/30 August 1858

12. Haji Mirzā Ḥosein Khān Sepahsālār
Appointed 29 Shaᶜbān 1288/13 November 1871
13. Mirzā Fatḥ ᶜAli Khān-e Shirāzi Ṣāḥeb Divān
Appointed Rajab 1290/September 1873
Appointed vizier of Fārs after 20 Rabiᶜ II 1298/22 March 1881

THE GOVERNORS OF THE PROVINCE OF FĀRS

1. Haji Ebrāhim Khān (see Prime Minister, No. 1)
Appointed Beglerbegi of Fārs in 1206/1791–1792
2. Fatḥ ᶜAli Mirzā Johānbāni (later Fatḥ ᶜAli Shāh)
Appointed Jomādi II 1209/December–January 1794/1795
(governor of Fārs, Kerman, and Yazd)
3. Moḥammad ᶜAli Mirzā (son of the preceding)
Appointed 1212/1798
4. Ḥosein Qoli Khān
Appointed 1212/1797–1798
5. Moḥammad ᶜAli Khān-e Qājār Qoyunlu
Appointed 1213/1798–1799
6. Ḥosein ᶜAli Mirzā Farmān-Farmā (I) (son of No. 2)
Deposed on 29 Dhu'l-Qaᶜda 1250/29 March 1835
7. Firuz Mirzā Noṣrat od-Doala (brother of Moḥammad Shāh)
Appointed end of Shavval 1250/end of February 1835
8. Faridun Mirzā Farmān-Farmā (II) (brother of Mohammad Shāh)
Appointed Shaᶜbān 1252/November–December 1836
9. Mirzā Nabi Khān-e Qazwini
Appointed Shaᶜbān 1256/October 1840
10. Naṣrollāh Khān-e Qājār Devehlu Ṣāḥeb Ekhteyār-e Fārs
Appointed Rajab (?) 1257/August–September 1841
Died 28 Rajab 1257/15 September 1841
11. Nāṣer od-Din Mirzā, together with Farhād Mirzā Moᶜtamad od-Doala
Appointed after Rajab 1257/September–October 1841
12. Mirzā Nabi Khān-e Qazwini, second term
Appointed after Ṣafar 1259/March–April 1843
13. Ḥosein Khān Ṣāḥeb Ekhteyār
Appointed after Ṣafar 1260/March–April 1844
Received title "Neẓām od-Doula"
14. Bahrām Mirzā Moᶜezz od-Doula
Appointed Dhu'l-Ḥejja 1264/November 1848
15. Firuz Mirzā Noṣrat od-Doula
Appointed beginning of 1266/end 1849
16. Ṭahmāsp Mirzā Mo'eiyed od-Doula (cousin of Moḥammad Shāh)
Appointed after Shaᶜbān 1269/May–June 1853

17. Solṭān Morād Mirzā Ḥosām os-Salṭana (uncle of Nāṣer od-Din Shāh)
Appointed beginning of 1275/August 1858
18. Mo'eiyed od-Doula, second term (see No. 16)
Appointed Rabiᶜ I 1277/September–October 1860
19. Solṭān Masᶜud Mirzā Yamin od-Doula Ẓell os-Solṭān (son of Naṣer od-Din Shāh)
Appointed Dhu'l-Qaᶜda 1279/May 1862
20. Ḥosām os-Salṭana, second term (see No. 17)
Appointed after Ṣafar 1282/June–July 1865
21. Ẓell os-Solṭān, second term (see No. 19)
Appointed Moḥarram 1286/April–May 1869
22. Moḥammad Qāsem Khān Vāli
Appointed Jomādi I 1288/July–August 1871
Died 11 Moḥarram 1289/21 March 1872
23. Ẓell os-Solṭān, third term (see No. 19, 21)
Appointed March–April 1872
24. Ḥosām os-Salṭana, third term (see No. 20)
Appointed Rabiᶜ I 1291/April–May 1874
25. Yaḥyā Khān Moᶜtamad ol-Molk
Appointed Jomādi I 1292/June 1875
26. Farhād Mirzā Moᶜtamad od-Doula, second term (see No. 11)
Appointed Rabiᶜ II 1293/April–May 1876
Summoned to Tehran on 20 Rabiᶜ II 1298/22 March 1881
27. Ẓell os-Solṭān, fourth term (see No. 23)
Appointed 20 Rabiᶜ II 1298/22 March 1881, appointed his son Solṭān Ḥosein Mirzā Jalāl od-Doula deputy-governor of Fārs

THE VIZIERS OF THE PROVINCE OF FĀRS

1. Mirzā Naṣrollāh-e ᶜAliābādi Māzandarāni
Appointed Jomādi II 1209/December–January 1794/1795
2. Mirzā Moḥammad Khān (son of Prime Minister Haji Ebrāhim)
Appointed 1213/1798–1799
3. Charāgh ᶜAli Khān-e Navā'i
Appointed 1214/1798–1799
4. Naṣrollāh-e Khān Qaraguzlu
Appointed 1220/1805–1806
5. Moḥammad Nabi Khān-e Shirāzi
Appointed 1223/1807–1808
6. Mirzā Yusof-e Ashrafi Māzandarāni
Appointed end 1224/January–February 1810
7. Mirzā Zein ol-ᶜĀbedin-e Kāshāni
Appointed beginning of 1229/January 1814
8. Āqā Moḥammad Bāqer-e Kāshāni
Appointed beginning of 1232/December 1816
Murdered end of 1233/October 1818

9. Haji Mirzā Reżā Qoli Navā'i
Appointed end of 1233/October 1818
Still as Vizier mentioned in 1234/1819–1820
10. Moḥammad Zaki Khān-e Nuri
Deposed 1244/1828–1829
11. Mirzā Moḥammad ᶜAli Shirāzi Khafrki Moshir ol-Molk (I)
Appointed 1244/1828–1829
Receives title "Moshir al-Molk" in 1245/1829–1830
Deposed beginning of 1248/July 1832
12. Mirzā Ḥasan Neẓām ol-ᶜOlamā
Appointed beginning of 1248/July 1832
13. Moshir ol-Molk (I), second term (see No. 11)
Appointed Dhu'l-Qaᶜda 1249/March–April 1834
14. Mirzā Moḥammad Taqi Qavām ol-Molk
Appointed Rabiᶜ II 1252/July–August 1836
15. Mirzā Jaᶜfar Mostoufi Savādkuhi
Appointed after Shaᶜbān 1252/November–December 1836
16. Mirzā Fażlollāh-e ᶜAliābādi Naṣir ol-Molk (son of No. 1)
Appointed Ramażdān 1257/October–November 1841
17. Moshir ol-Molk (I), third term (see No. 13)
Appointed 1260/1844–1845
Died 1262/1846–1847
18. Mirzā Abu'l-Ḥasan Khān Moshir ol-Molk (II), son of Moshir ol-Molk (I)
Appointed 1262/1846–1847
19. Mirzā Fażlollāh Naṣir ol-Molk, second term (see No. 16)
Appointed Dhu'l-Ḥejja 1264/October–November 1848
20. Mirzā Abu'l-Qāsem-e Tafrishi
Appointed beginning of 1266/end of 1849
21. Moshir ol-Molk (II), second term (see No. 18)
Mentioned in Shaᶜbān 1269/May–June 1853
22. Mirzā Moḥammad Taqi Āshteyāni
Appointed middle of Dhu'l-Ḥejja 1269/September 1853
23. Moshir ol-Molk (II), third term (see No. 21)
Appointed 1272/1855–1856
24. Mirzā Moḥammad Ḥosein-e Hamadāni
Appointed 1275/1858–1859
25. Moshir ol-Molk (II), fourth term (see No. 23)
Appointed after Shavvāl 1276/1860
26. Moḥammad Nāṣer Khān-e Qājār Ẓahir od-Doula
Appointed after New Year 1279/March 1863
27. Mirzā Moḥammad-e Farahāni ᶜFrāqi Qavām od-Doula
Appointed after Shavvāl 1280/March–April 1864

28. Moshir ol-Molk (II), fifth term (see No. 25)
    Appointed after 19 Rabi^{c} II 1282/11 September 1865
29. Haji Moḥammad Qoli Khān-e Qājār Āṣaf od-Doula
    Appointed beginning of 1286/April 1869
30. Moḥammad Qāsem Khān Vāli
    Appointed Ṣafar 1288/April–May 1871
31. Haji Moḥammad Nāṣer Khān Ẓahir od-Doula, second term (No. 26)
    Appointed beginning of 1289/March 1872
21. Moshir ol-Molk (II), sixth term (see No. 28)
    Appointed after 17 Rabi^{c} I 1291/4 May 1874
    Deposed after middle of Sha^{c}bān 1293/5 October 1876
33. Mirzā Fatḥ ^{c}Ali Khān-e Shirāzi Ṣāḥeb Divān
    Appointed after 20 Rabi^{c} II 1298/22 March 1881.

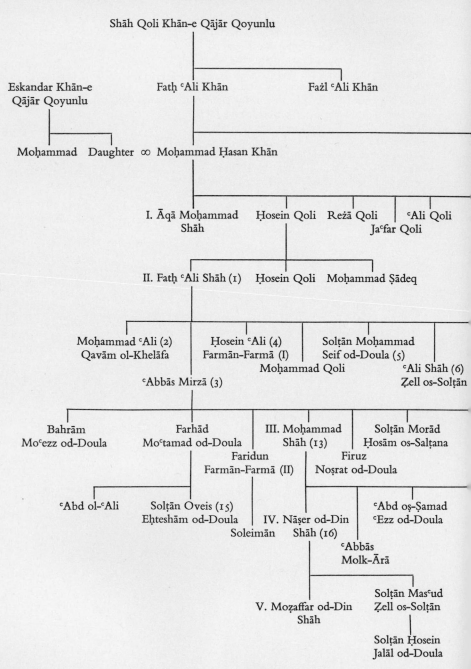

Shāh Qoli Khān-e Qājār Qoyunlu

Eskandar Khān-e
Qājār Qoyunlu

Faṭḥ ᶜAli Khān

Fażl ᶜAli Khān

Moḥammad   Daughter ∞ Moḥammad Ḥasan Khān

I. Āqā Moḥammad   Ḥosein Qoli   Reżā Qoli   ᶜAli Qoli
Shāh   Jaᶜfar Qoli

II. Faṭḥ ᶜAli Shāh (1)   Ḥosein Qoli   Moḥammad Ṣādeq

Moḥammad ᶜAli (2)   Ḥosein ᶜAli (4)   Solṭān Moḥammad
Qavām ol-Khelāfa   Farmān-Farmā (I)   Seif od-Doula (5)
                         Moḥammad Qoli   ᶜAli Shāh (6)
          ᶜAbbās Mirzā (3)   Ẕell os-Solṭān

Bahrām   Farhād   III. Moḥammad   Solṭān Morād
Moᶜezz od-Doula   Moᶜtamad od-Doula   Shāh (13)   Ḥosām os-Salṭana
                     Faridun   Firuz
                     Farmān-Farmā (II)   Noṣrat od-Doula

ᶜAbd ol-ᶜAli   Solṭān Oveis (15)   ᶜAbd oṣ-Ṣamad
                 Eḥteshām od-Doula   IV. Nāṣer od-Din   ᶜEzz od-Doula
                 Soleimān   Shāh (16)
                                      ᶜAbbās
                                      Molk-Ārā

                                 Solṭān Masᶜud
          V. Moẓaffar od-Din   Ẕell os-Solṭān
                Shāh

                                 Solṭān Ḥosein
                                 Jalāl od-Doula

Daughter

Mortażā Qoli

Moṣṭafā Qoli

Moḥammad Qoli

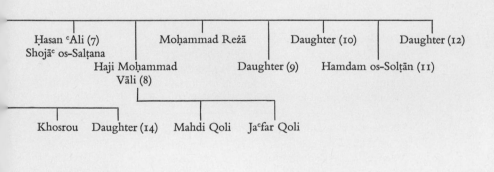

Ḥasan ᶜAli (7)
Shojāᶜ os-Salṭana

Haji Moḥammad
Vāli (8)

Moḥammad Reżā

Daughter (9)

Daughter (10)

Hamdam os-Solṭān (11)

Daughter (12)

Khosrou

Daughter (14)

Mahdi Qoli

Jaᶜfar Qoli

Moḥammad Taqi
Rokn od-Doula

Abu'l-Qāsem

NOTES TO APPENDIX II ARE ON THE FOLLOWING PAGES

APPENDIX III: ḤOSEIN ʿALI MIRZĀ FARMĀN-FARMĀ (I) AND HIS FAMILY

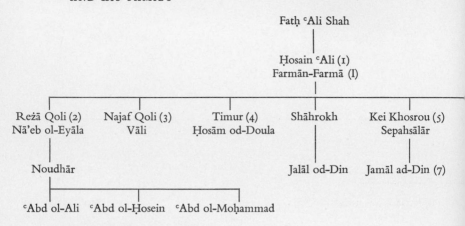

- Fatḥ ʿAli Shah
  - Ḥosain ʿAli (1) Farmān-Farmā (I)
    - Reżā Qoli (2) Nā'eb ol-Eyāla
      - Noudhār
        - ʿAbd ol-Ali
        - ʿAbd ol-Ḥosein
        - ʿAbd ol-Moḥammad
    - Najaf Qoli (3) Vāli
    - Timur (4) Ḥosām od-Doula
    - Shāhrokh
      - Jalāl od-Din
    - Kei Khosrou (5) Sepahsālār
      - Jamāl ad-Din (7)

Other sons of Farmān-Farmā

Emām Qoli Ghażanfar od-Doula
Naṣrollāh
Jahāngir Ṣāḥeb Ekhteyār
Akbar
Moḥammad Kāẓem
Kāmrān
Moḥammad
Solṭān Ebrāhim
Manuchehr

Daughters of Farmān-Farmā (I)

Daughter, married to Mirzā Abu'l-Ḥasan Khān-e Fasā'i (see Table IV)
Daughter, married to Shokrollāh Khān-e Nuri
Daughter, married to Seiyed Saʿid Khān, Imam of Masqaṭ
Daughter, married to Mirzā Abu'l-Ḥasan Khān, son of Moshir ol-Molk.

NOTES TO APPENDIX II

1. Wives: *a*) daughter of Jaʿfar Khān, the son of Qāder Khān-e ʿArab-e ʿĀmeri-ye Besṭāmi; *b*) daughter of Fatḥ ʿAli Khān-e Qājār Devehlu; *c*) Gorjiya (a Georgian woman); *d*) daughter of Moḥammad Khān-e Qājār; *e*) Tāj od-Doula (Eṣfahāniya); *f*) daughter of Ebrāhim Khalil Khān-e Janvānshir, ruler of Karabagh.

2. Son of 1*c*. Ṭahmāsp Mirzā Mo'eiyed od-Doula was a son of Moḥammad ʿAli Mirzā Qavām ol-Khelāfa. Ṭahmāsp Mirzā had four sons: a) ʿAbd ol-Bāqi Mirzā; b) Abu'l-Qāsem Khān; *c*) Loṭf ʿAli Mirzā; and *d*) Jalāl od-Din Mirzā.

3. Son of 1*b*. ʿAbbās Mirzā married (among others) a daughter of Mirzā Moḥammad Qājār Devehlu, the son of Amir Khān-e Qājār Devehlu.

4. Son of 1*a*. For his family, see Appendix III.

5. Son of 1*e*.

6. Sons: Seif od-Doula Mirza and Seif ol-Moluk Mirzā; the latter married a daughter of ʿAbbās Mirzā.

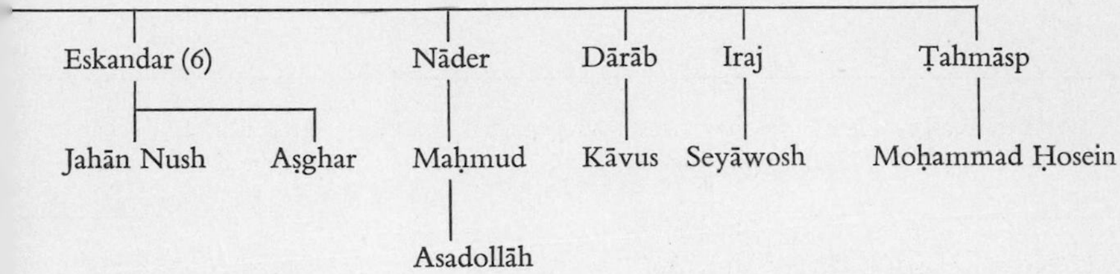

1. His wives: *a*) the "Hajiya," a daughter of Moḥammad Qoli Khān-e Afshār; and *b*) a daughter of Amir Guna Khān-e Kord Za^{c}farānlu, the ilkhāni of Khorasan.

2. Son of the "Hajiya."

3. Son of the "Hajiya"; married a daughter of Mirzā Manṣur Khān-e Behbehānī, governor of Behbehān.

4. Son of the "Hajiya"; married a daughter of Vali Khān, son of Khub Yār Khān-e Bakash Mamassani.

5. Son of 1*b*; married a daughter of Shojā^{c} os-Salṭana (see Appendix II).

6. Brother of Režā Qoli, see note 2.

7. Son of the daughter of Shojā^{c} os-Salṭana, see note 5.

---

7. He had four sons: *a*) Hulāgu Mirzā; *b*) Arghun Mirzā; *c*) Abāqā Mirzā; and *d*) Ügetai Qā'ān Mirzā. A daughter was married to Kei Khosrou Mirzā, a son of Ḥosein ^{c}Ali Mirzā Farmān-Farmā (I).

8. Son of 1*e*.

9. Married to Soleimān Khān Neẓām od-Doula, the father of Mohammad Qāsem Khan-e Qājār Qoyunlu.

10. Married to Allāh Yār Khān-e Qājār Devehlu Āṣaf od-Doula. Son: Moḥammad Qoli Khān.

11. Married to Moḥammad Zaki Khān-e Nuri.

12. Married to Ebrāhim, a son of the daughter of Haji Ebrāhim Khān E^{c}temād od-Doula (see also Appendix IV).

13. Married a daughter of Moḥammad Qāsem Khān-e Qājār Qoyunlu, see also note 9.

14. Married to Seif ol-Moluk, a son of ^{c}Ali Shāh Ẓell os-Solṭān.

15. Married a daughter of Solṭān Morād Mirzā Ḥosām os-Salṭana.

16. Son of the daughter of Moḥammad Qāsem Khān-e Qājār Qoyunlu, see note 13.

APPENDIX IV: FAMILY OF GRAND VIZIER HAJI EBRĀHIM KHĀN E[c]TEMĀD OD-DOULA

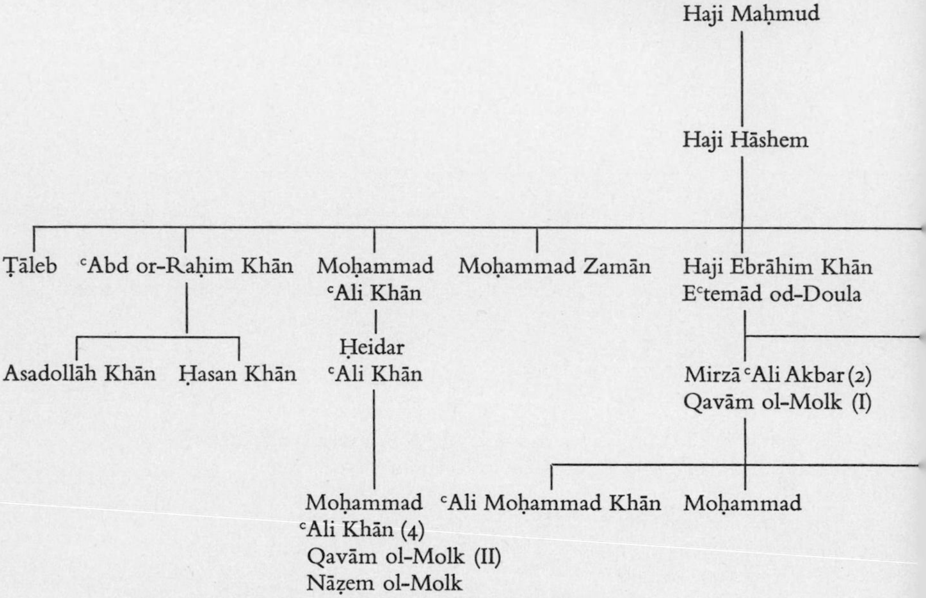

1. Married to Moḥammad ᶜAli, their son was Ambassador Mirzā Abu'l-Ḥasan Khān.
2. Married a daughter of Naṣrollāh Khān-e Nuri.
3. Married to Moḥammad Ḥosein Khān Amin od-Doula Eṣfahāni.
4. Married a daughter of Moshir ol-Molk.
5. Married a daughter of Moḥammad ᶜAli Khān Ilkhāni.
6. Married to Kheirollāh Khān-e Nuri, nephew of Naṣrollāh Khān-e Nuri.
7. Married to Moḥammad Qoli Khān, brother of Moḥammad ᶜAli Khān Ilkhāni.
8. Married a daughter of Fatḥ ᶜAlī Shāh.

Moḥammad Ḥosein Khān   Daughter (1)

Moḥammad   Asadollāh Khān   ᶜAli Reżā   Daughter (3)   Daughter

Ḥasan ᶜAli Khān Daryābegi   Fatḥ ᶜAli Khān (5)   Daughter (6)   Daughter (7)   Ebrāhim (8)

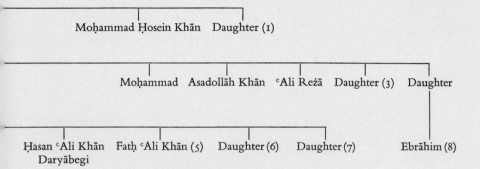

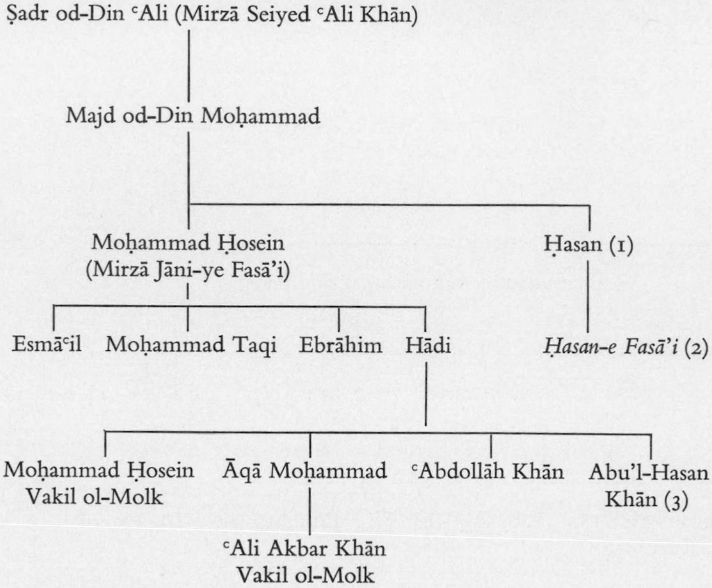

1. Married a daughter of Haji Moḥammad Taqi, merchant in Shiraz.
2. Son of the daughter of Ḥaji Moḥammad Taqi; married *a*) a daughter of Mirzā Seiyed ^{c}Ali, *b*) a daughter of Haji Mollā Āqā Bābā, merchant in Shiraz.
3. Married a daughter of Ḥosein ^{c}Ali Mirzā Farmān-Farmā (I), governor of Fārs.

BIBLIOGRAPHY

Abbott, K. E. "Notes Taken on a Journey Eastwards from Shiraz..." etc., in *Journal of the Royal Geographical Society*, Vol. XXVII (1857).

^{c}Abd or-Razzāq Maftun Dombali. [*Ma^{c}āther-e solṭāniya*]. *The Dynasty of the Kājārs. To which Is Prefixed a Succinct Account of the History of Persia Previous to That Period.* Translated from the Original Persian Manuscript of Abd Al-Razzák ibn Najaf Kulí by Sir H. J. Brydges Assisted by D. Shea. Illustrated with Plates and a Map of Western Persia by Colonel J. Sutherland. London, 1833.

Aḥmad (Qāḍi Aḥmad). *Calligraphers and Painters. Translated from the Persian by V. Minorsky.* Washington D. C., 1959 (Freer Gallery of Art Occasional Papers, Vol. III, No. 2).

Babin C., and F. Houssay. "A travers la Perse méridionale," in *Le tour du monde*, Vol. LXIV (1892), 65–128.

Badger, G. P. *History of the Imāms and Seyyids of ^{c}Omān, by Salīl-ibn-Razīk, from A.D. 661–1856.* Translated from the Original Arabic and Edited with Notes, Appendices, and an Introduction, continuing the history down to 1870. London, 1871.

Bosworth, C. E. *The Islamic Dynasties. A Chronological and Genealogical Handbook.* Edinburgh, 1967 (Islamic Surveys, No. V).

Bradford, Martin G. *German-Persian Diplomatic Relations, 1873–1912.* The Hague, 1959.

Braun, Hellmut. "Iran Under the Safavids and in the 8 Century," in *The Muslim World. A Historical Survey.* Part III: *The Last Great Muslim Empires.* Translations and Adaptations by F. R. C. Bagley. Leiden, 1969, pp. 181–218.

Brockelmann, Carl. *Geschichte der arabischen Litteratur.* Leiden, 1937–1943.

Browne, Edward G. *A Travellers Narrative, Written to Illustrate the Episode of the Bab.* Edited in the Original Persian and Translated into English, with an Introduction and Explanatory Notes. Vol. I: Persian Text. Cambridge, England, 1891.

—— *A Year Amongst the Persians.* London, 1897.

—— *Materials for the Study of the Bābī Religion.* Cambridge, England, 1918.

—— *A Literary History of Persia.* Vol. IV: *Modern Times (1500–1924).* Cambridge, England, 1924. Reprinted, 1953.

Brugsch, Heinrich. *Reise der Königlich Preussischen Gesandtschaft nach Persien 1860 und 1861.* 2 vols. Leipzig, 1862–1863.

Brydges, Sir Harford Jones. *An Account of the Transactions of His Majesty's Mission to the Court of Persia in the Years 1807–11. To which is Appended a Brief History of the Wahaby*. 2 vols. London, 1834.

Bushev, P. P. "Angliiskaye voennaya ekspediciya v Akhvaz (Epizod iz anglo-iranskoy voyny 1856–1857," in *Kratkiye Soobshcheniya Instituta Vostokovedniya*, XIX (1956), 65–71.

Costello, D. P. "Griboedov in Persia in 1820. Two Diplomatic Notes," in *Oxford Slavonic Papers* (1954), pp. 81–92.

Curzon, George Nathaniel. *Persia and the Persian Question*. 2 vols. Reprinted London, 1966.

Démorgny, D. "Les réformes administratives en Perse. Les tribus du Fars," in *Révue du monde musuman*, Vol. XXII (1913), 85–150; Vol. XXIII (1913), 3–108.

Dictionary of National Biography, The. Founded in 1882 by George Smith, and edited by Sir Leslie Stephan and Sir Sidney Lee. *From the Earliest Times to 1900*. London, 1917.

Dodwell, H. H., ed. *The Cambridge History of the British Empire*. Vol. IV: *British India, 1497–1858*. Cambridge, England, 1929.

Drouville, Gaspar. *Voyage en Perse pendant les années 1812–1814*. St. Petersburg, 1819.

Dubeux, Louis. *La Perse*. Paris, 1841.

Dutemple, Edmond. *Les Kadjars. Vie de Nasser-ed-din Chah*. Paris, 1873.

Enzyklopaedie des Islām. Leiden and Leipzig, 1913–1938. *The Encylopaedia of Islam*. 2d ed., Leiden and London, 1960 seq.

ᶜErfān, Maḥmud. "Pasarhā-ye Fatḥ ᶜAli Shāh dar London," in *Āyanda*, Vol. III, 479–83.

Farhang-e Joghrāfiyā-ye Īrān. *Az entesharāt-e dā'ere-ye joghrāfiyā'ī setād-e ātesh*. 10 vols. Tehran, 1949–1954.

Frommhold, Friedrich. *Traités etc. conclus par la Russie avec les puissances étrangères*. 14 vols. St. Petersburg, 1874–1905.

Gabriel, Alfons. *Die Erforschung Persiens. Die Entwicklung der abendländischen Kenntnis der Geographie Persiens*. Vienna, 1952.

Gardane, Comte Alfred de. *Mission du général Gardane en Perse sous le Premier Empire*. Paris, 1865.

Gardane, Paul-Ange-Louis de. *Journal d'un voyage dans la Turquie d'Asie et la Perse*. Paris, 1808.

Gasteiger, F. *General Gasteiger-Khan, ein Tiroler in Persien*. Innsbruck, 1950.

Gobineau, Joseph Arthur Cte de. *Trois ans en Asie de 1855–1858*. Paris, 1859.

—— See Hytier.

Gramlich, Richard. *Die schiitischen Derwischorden Persiens*. Part I: *Die Affiliationen*. Wiesbaden, 1965. (Abhandlungen für die Kunde des Morgenlandes, ed. Deutsche Morgenländische Gesellschaft, Vol. XXXVI, No. 1.)

Habberton, William. "Anglo-Russian Relations Concerning Afghanistan, 1837–1907," in *Illinois Studies in the Social Sciences*, Vol. XXI, No. 4 (1937).

Harkins, William E. *Dictionary of Russian Literature*. London, 1937.

Hartmann, Richard. "Die Wahhabiten," in *Zeitschrift der Deutschen Morgenländischen Gesellschaft*. Vol. LXXVIII (1924), 176–213.

Ḥasan-e Fasā'ī. *Fārsnāma-ye Nāṣeri*, 2 vols. Reprinted, Tehran, ca. 1965.

Ḥasan ibn Moḥammad ibn Ḥasan-e Qomi. *Ketāb-e Tārikh-e Qom*. Translated into Persian by Ḥasan ibn ᶜAli ibn Ḥasan ibn ᶜAbd ol-Malek-e Qomi in A. H. 804–5/A.D. 1401–1402. Edited by Seyyed Jalāl od-Din Tehrāni. Tehran, 1353.

Havell, R. *The Court of Persia in the time of Fath Ali Shah, From a Painting in the Possession of Thomas Alcock . . . Copied from the Wall of the Palace of Nugaristan*. Engraved by R. Havell. London, 1834.

Hedin, Sven. *Zu Land nach Indien durch Persien, Seïstan, Belutschistan*. 2 vols. Leipzig, 1910.

Hinz, Walther. *Islamische Masse und Gewichte umgerechnet ins metrische System*. Leiden, 1955 (Handbuch der Orientalistik, edited by Bertold Spuler, Ergänzungsband I, No. 1).

Houtum-Schindler, A. *Eastern Persian Irak*. With map. London, 1897.

Hurwitz, Jacob Coleman. *Diplomacy in the Near and Middle East. A Documentary Record: 1535–1914*. Vol. I. Princeton, New Jersey, 1956.

Hytier, Adrienne Doris. *Les dépêches diplomatiques du Comte de Gobineau en Perse. Textes inédits présentés et annotés*. Geneva and Paris, 1959.

Jahāngir Mirzā (son of ᶜAbbās Mirzā). *Tārikh-e nou. Shāmel-i ḥavādeth-e doura-ye qājāriya az sāl-e 1240 tā 1247 qamari, be sa'y va-ehtemām-e ᶜAbbās Eqbāl*. Tehran, 1327.

Jenkinson, Anthony. *Early Voyages and Travels to Russia and Persia by Anthony Jenkinson and Other Englishmen, with Some Account of the First Intercourse of the English with Russia and Central Asia by Way of the Caspian Sea*. Edited by E. Delmar Morgan and C. H. Coote. 2 vols. Reprinted, New York, 1965 (Works issued by the Hakluyt Society, First Series, No. LXXIII.)

Kaye, Sir John William. *The Life and Correspondence of Sir John Malcolm.* 2 vols. London, 1856.

Keihān, Mas^cud. *Joghrāfiyā-ye mufaṣṣal-e Irān.* 3 vols. Tehran, 1932.

Khormuji, Mirzā Moḥammad Ja^cfar Khān. *Āthār-e Ja^cfari.* Tehran, 1276: 1860.

Kinneir, J. M. *A Geographical Memoir of the Persian Empire.* London, 1813.

Kispal, P. N. "The East India Company and Persia (1800–1810)," in *Journal of the Punjab Historical Society* (1941), pp. 1–65.

Kotzebue, Moritz von. *Reis naar Perzie in den Jahre 1817.* The Hague, 1819.

Lang, David Marshall. *The Last Years of the Georgian Monarchy, 1658–1832.* New York, 1957.

Le Strange, G. *The Lands of the Eastern Caliphate: Mesopotamia, Persia and Central Asia from the Moslem Conquest to the Time of Timur.* London, 1966.

Lézine, Alexander. "Hérat, notes de voyage," in *Bulletin d'études orientales,* Vol. XVIII (1963--1964), 127–45.

Lindberg, K. *Voyage dans le sud de l'Iran: Carnet de route d'un médicin, à la poursuite du ver de Médine.* Lund, 1955.

Litten, Wilhelm. *Persien. Von der "pénétration pacifique" zum "Protektorat." Urkunden und Tatsachen zur Geschichte der europäischen "pénétration pacifique" in Persien 1860–1919.* Berlin and Leipzig, 1920.

McNeill, Sir John. *Memoir of the Right Hon. Sir John McNeill, K.C.B., and His Second Wife Elizabeth Wilson.* London, 1910.

Malcolm, Sir John. *Sketches of Persia. From the Journals of a Traveller in the East.* 2 vols. London, 1815.

—— *The History of Persia from the Most Early Period to the Present Time.* 2d ed., 2 vols. London, 1829.

—— *Persia, A Poem. With Notes.* 2d ed. London, 1814.

Midhat, Ali Haydar. *The Life of Midhat Pasha. A Record of His Services, Political Reforms, Banishment and Judicial Murder.* London, 1903.

Miles, S. B. *The Countries and Tribes of the Persian Gulf.* With a New Introduction by J. B. Kelly. Reprinted, London, 1966.

Millard, Charles W. "Mirzā Abu'l-Ḥasan Khān," in *Apollo* (February, 1967). Persian Translation by Muhammad Javād Sheikh ol-Eslāmi, in *Rāhnamā-ye Ketāb.* Vol. X (1346:1967), 339–56.

Minorsky, V. *Ḥudūd al-^cĀlam: The Regions of the World. A Persian Geography 372 A.H.: 982 A.D.* Translated and Explained, with the Preface by

V. V. Barthold; Translated from the Russian. London, 1937 (E. J. W. Gibb Memorial Series, New Series, No. XI).

Moḥammad Kalāntar, Mirzā. *Ruznāma-ye Mirzā Moḥammad Kalāntar-e Fārs. Shāmel vaqā'iᶜ-e qesmathā-ye junubi-ye Irān az sāl-e 1142 tā 1199 hejri qamari.* Edited by ᶜAbbās Eqbāl, Tehran, 1325:1947.

Moḥammad Kāẓem. *Nāma-ye ᶜālam-ārā-ye Nāderi.* Edited by N. D. Miklukho-Maklay and G. V. Shitov. 3 vols. Moscow, 1960–1966 (Pamyatniki Literatury Narodov Vostoka. Teksty, Bolshaya Seriya, Vol. XIII).

Moḥammad Ṣādeq Musavi Nāmi Eṣfahāni. *Tārikh-e giti gushā.* Edited by Saᶜid Nafisi. Tehran, 1317:1939.

Moḥiṭ Ṭabāṭabā'i, Moḥammad. "Shāhzādagān-e Qājār dar London," in *Moḥīṭ.* Vol. II, No. 12, 11–13; No. 13, 15–16.

Monteith, W. "Notes on the Routes from Bushir to Shiraz," in *Journal of the Royal Geographical Society*, Vol. XXVII (1857).

Morier, James. *A Second Journey Through Persia, Armenia, and Asia Minor to Constantinople, Between the Years 1810 and 1816, with a Journal of the Voyage by the Brazils and Bombay to the Persian Gulf.* London, 1818.

Najaf Qoli Mirzā. *Journal of a Residence in England, and of a Journey from and to Syria, of their Royal Highnesses Reeza Koolee Meerza, Najaf Koolee Meerza, and Taymour Meerza, of Persia. To which are Prefixed Some Particulars Respecting Modern Persia, and the Death of the Late Shah.* Originally written in Persian. Translated with explanatory notes by Assaad Y. Kayat. 2 vols. London, 1839.

Nāṣer od-Din Shāh Qājār. *Safarnāma-ye Nāṣer od-Din Shāh beh Orupā.* Tehran, 1308:1890. [*The Diary of H.M. the Shah of Persia during His Tour of Europe in A.D. 1873.* A verbatim translation by J. W. Redhouse.] London, 1874.

National Biography, see *The Dictionary of National Biography.*

Neumann, Karl Friedrich. *Geschichte des englischen Reiches in Asien.* 2 vols. Leipzig, 1857.

Niẓām al-Mulk. *Siyāsatnāma. Gedanken und Geschichten.* Translated into German, with an Introduction by Emil Schabinger Freiherr von Schowingen. Freiburg and Munich, 1960.

Noradounghian, Gabriel. *Recueil d'actes internationaux de l'Empire Ottoman. Traités, conventions, arrangements . . . et autres documents relatifs au droit public extérieur de la Turquie.* Vol. II, 1789–1856; Vol. III, 1856–1878. Paris, 1900, 1902.

Oberling, Pièrre. "The Turcic Tribes of Southwestern Persia," in *Ural-Altaische Jahrbücher*, Vol. XXXV, fasc. B (1963), 164–80.

Ouseley, W. *Travels in Various Countries of the East . . . etc.* 3 vols. London, 1819–1823.

Outram, James. *Lieutenant-general Sir James Outram's Persian Campaign in 1857–1858, Comprising General Orders and Despatches . . . also Selections from His Correspondence.* London, 1860.

Pelly, Lewis. "Report on the Tribes, Trade and Resources around the Shore of the Persian Gulf," in *Transactions of the Bombay Geographical Society*, Vol. XVII (1863), 32–112.

Qāḍi Aḥmad, see Aḥmad (Qāḍi Aḥmad).

Qā'em Maqāmi, Jahāngir. "Touṭṭeᶜe-ye Ḥosein ᶜAli Mirzā Farmān-Farmā dar Fārs," in *Yaghmā*, Vol. V, 35–40.

Rabino di Borgomale, H. L. "Une tentative de réformes en 1875 (Tanzīmāt-i ḥasana)," in *Révue du monde musulman*, Vol. XXVI (1914), 133–39.

—— "Une lettre familière de Fath Ali Chah," in *Révue du monde musulman*, Vol. XL–XLI (1920), 131–35.

—— *Coins, Medals and Seals of the Shahs of Iran, 1500–1941.* Hertford, England, 1945.

Reżā Qoli Khān Hedāyat. *Rouẓat oṣ-Ṣafā-ye Nāṣeri.* Tehran, 1270–1274: 1853–1856.

Röhrborn, Klaus-Michael. *Provinzen und Zentralgewalt Persiens im 16. und 17. Jahrhundert.* Berlin, 1966. (Studien zur Sprache, Geschichte und Kultur des islamischen Orients. Beihefte zur Zeitschrift "Der Islam", New Series, Vol. II).

Rypka, Jan. *Iranische Literaturgeschichte.* Leipzig, 1959.

Saᶜādat-e Nuri, Ḥosein. "Mosāfarāt-e Nāṣer od-Din Shāh ba Khorāsān va moṣāḥaba-ye u bā yek offiser englisi," in *Yaghmā*, Vol. XI, 130–31.

Sardari, Reżā. *Un chapitre de l'histoire diplomatique de l'Iran. Les traités entre l'Iran et la Russie depuis le XVIe siècle jusqu'à 1917.* Paris, 1941.

Sarkisyanz, Emanuel. *Geschichte der orientalischen Völker Rußlands bis 1917. Eine Ergänzung zur ostslawischen Geschichte Rußlands, mit einem Vorwort von Bertold Spuler.* Munich, 1961.

Schiemann, Theodor. *Geschichte Russlands unter Kaiser Nikolaus I.* 4 vols. Berlin, 1904.

Schlechta-Wssehrd, Ottokar Freiherr von. *Fetḥalī Schāh und seine Thronrivalen . . . vorzüglich nach orientalischen Quellen dargestellt.* Vienna, 1864

Sitzungsberichte der Kaiserlichen Akademie der Wissenschaften, Philosophisch-historische Classe, Vol. XLV.)

Schwarz, Paul. *Iran im Mittelalter nach arabischen Geographen.* 9 vols. Stuttgart and Berlin, 1896–1936.

Sergeant, R. B. "Naṣer od-Din Shāh Qājār wa safarhā-y-e u ba Inglistān," in *Ruzgār-e nou,* Vol. IV, No. 5, 17–23.

Sheil, Lady M. L. *Glimpses of Life and Manners in Persia.* London, 1856.

Sheil, Sir Justin. "Notes on a Journey from Tabriz . . . ," in *Journal of the Royal Geographical Society,* Vol. VIII (1838).

—— "Itinerary from Teheran to Alamut," in *Journal of the Royal Geographical Society,* Vol. VIII (1838).

Shirāzi, Abu'l-Ḥasan. "Mehmāni-ye Mirzā Abu'l-Ḥasan-e Shirāzi dar London," in *Sokhan,* Vol. VI, 711–17, 775–79.

Siassi, Ali Akbar. *La Perse au contact de l'Occident: Étude historique et sociale.* Paris, 1931.

Spies, O., and E. Pritsch. *Klassisches islamisches Recht.* Leiden, 1964 (Handbuch der Orientalistik, Part I. Edited by Bertold Spuler. Ergänzungsband No. I).

Steingass, F. *A Comprehensive Persian-English Dictionary.* London, 1947.

Storey, Charles Ambrose. *Persian Literature. A Bio-biographical Survey.* London, 1927–1953.

Sykes, P. M., Translator. *The Glory of the Shia World: The Tale of a Pilgrimage.* Translated and edited from a Persian manuscript by P. M. Sykes, assisted by Khan Bahadur Ahmad Din Khan. London, 1910.

—— *A History of Persia.* New York, 1921; 3d ed. reissue, New York, 1952.

Taqizāda, Seyyed Ḥasan. "I^{c}lān-e jang-e rusiya beh Irān," in *Yaghmā,* Vol. II, 528–32.

Ṭehrāni, Ḥosein Thoreiyā. *Dar aḥvāl-e Sīvand.* French translation by C. Huart: "Le dialecte persan de Sīwand," in *Journal asiatique,* 1893, pp. 241–65.

Thaqafi E^{c}zāz, Ḥosein. "Jang-e Irān va Inglis dar 1273 qamari," in *Yādgār,* Vol. III, No. 10, 38–53.

Thornton, H. P. "British Policy in Persia 1858–1890," in *The English Historical Review,* Vol. LXIX (1954), 554–79; LXX (1955), 55–71.

Treaties . . . Concluded Between Great Britain and Persia and Other Foreign Powers, Wholly or Partially in Force on the 1st April 1891. Edited by Sir Edward Hertslet. London, 1891.

Watson, Robert Grant. *History of Persia from the Beginning of the Nineteenth Century to the Year 1858*. London, 1866.

Winder, R. Bayly. *Saudi Arabia in the Nineteenth Century*. New York, 1965.

"Yāddāshthā-ye tārikhi (rāje^c ba jang-e Irān va Inglis dar 1272 qamari," in *Peymān*, Vol. II, 521–28, 585–92, 649–56, 721–44.

Yapp, M. E. "The Control of the Persian Mission, 1822–1836," in *University of Birmingham Historical Journal*, Vol. VII (1959), 162–79.

Zambaur, E. von. *Manuel de généalogie et de chronologie pour l'histoire de l'Islam*. Hannover, 1927.

NAMES OF PERSONS, PLACES, AND TRIBES

Abāqā Khān Mirzā, son of Ḥasan ^{c}Ali Mirzā Shojā^{c} os-Salṭana, 201

Abarj, district in Fārs, 44, 52, 55

Abarquh, near Yazd, 27, 57

Ābavān (Ābdān), in Fars, 393

^{c}Abbās I, Safavid ruler (1588–1623), 12*n*, 17*n*, 191, 354*n*, 355

^{c}Abbās II, Safavid ruler (1642–1666), 30*n*

^{c}Abbās-e Erevani, *see* Haji Mirzā Āqāsi

^{c}Abbās Khān-e Shirāzi (Hamadāni), sent with troops to Bandar ^{c}Abbās, 307; governor of Bandar ^{c}Abbās, 309; surrenders Bandar ^{c}Abbās without battle, 310

^{c}Abbās-e Māzandārāni, valet of Āqā Moḥammad Shāh, 74, 80

^{c}Abbās Mirzā, crown prince, his birth, 36; accompanies the shah on campaign to Shushā, 73; returns to Tehran, 75; appointed crown prince, 104 seq.; marries Qājār princess, 104 seq.; his campaigns in the Russian War, 107 seq., 118, 130, 134, 176 seq., 178 seq., 181; puts on Mongolian mail shirt, 108; fabricates guns, 109; appointed governor of Ādherbāyjān, 110; Russian peace offer, 133; meets shah at Solṭāniya, 150; receives Russian ambassador, 152; campaign to the Kurdish frontier, 166; meets shah and Russian ambassador at Solṭāniya, 175; opposition against him in Ādherbāyjān, 182; rumors about deposal, 184; negotiates peace treaty of Torkmānchāy, 185; takes measures after murder of Griboyedov, 189; appoints his son on mission to Russia, 190; settles affairs in Yazd and Kerman, sent to Khorasan, 200; rivalry between him and Farmān-Farmā (I), 206, 216; his son is governor of Kerman, 214; introduces military reforms, 221; his death at Mashhad, 222

^{c}Abbās Mirzā Molk Ārā, son of Moḥammad Shāh, 281

^{c}Abbās Qoli Khān Sardār-e Lārijani, 296*n*, 299

^{c}Abd ol-^{c}Ali Mirzā, son of Mo^{c}tamad od-Doula, 396

^{c}Abd ol-^{c}Aziz I, of Saudi Arabia (1765–1803), 101 seq.

^{c}Abd ol-Bāqi Mirzā, son of Ṭahmāsp Mirzā, appointed deputy governor of Fārs, 307, 345; sent to conquer Bandar ^{c}Abbās, 310 seq.; appointed governor of Lārestān and Bandar ^{c}Abbās, 312; receives gifts from Imam of Masqaṭ, 318; sent to settle affairs of Sab^{c}a and Lārestān, 337; returns to Shiraz, 359

^{c}Abd ol-Ḥosein Khān, son of Grand Vizier Haji Moḥammad Ḥosein Khān, 112

^{c}Abd ol-Ḥosein Khān, son of Khan Bābā Khān, 384

^{c}Abd ol-Ḥosein Khān Mir Panj, son of Moḥammad Ḥasan Khān Sardār-e Erevani, 310 seq.
^{c}Abd ol-Ḥosein Khān-e Shirazi, Mirzā, ambassador to Austria, 155, 159
^{c}Abdollāh-e Eṣfahāni, Haji, chief eunuch, 168 seq.
^{c}Abd ol-Maleki, tribe, 46, 178
^{c}Abd ol-Moḥammad-e Maḥallāti, Haji Mollā, 257 seq.
^{c}Abd ol-Moḥammad Malek ot-Tojjār-e Bushehri, Haji, 313 seq., 316 seq.
^{c}Abd on-Nabi Khān Tājer-e Bushehri, Haji, 397, 401
^{c}Abd or-Raḥim Khān, brother of Haji Ebrāhim Khān, in the service of the Zand, 27, 43; commander of Qājār army in Fārs, 51; governor of Esfahan and ^{c}Erāq, 97 seq.; killed after deposal of his father, 99
^{c}Abd or-Raḥim Khān, son of Taqi Khān-e Yazdi, 59
^{c}Abd or-Raḥim Mostoufi-ye Shīrāzi, Mirzā, 222
^{c}Abd or-Raḥmān, astronomer, author of "Ketāb-e Ṣowar," 273
^{c}Abd or-Raḥmān-e Qeshmi, Sheikh, 306, 308
^{c}Abd or-Rasul Khān-e Bushehri Daryābegi, lord of Bushehr, his role in policy, 201 seq.; prisoner of Imam of Masqaṭ, 203; surrenders Bushehr to local chieftains, 204; imprisons rebels on island of Khārk, 205; sent back to Bushehr, 206, 210; his murder, 211
^{c}Abd or-Razzāq Khān-e Kāshi, 25
^{c}Abd oṣ-Ṣamad-e Hamadāni, Ākhund Mollā, 241
^{c}Abd oṣ-Ṣamad Mirzā ^{c}Ezz od-Doula, son of Moḥammad Shāh, 281
^{c}Abd ol-Vahhāb, founder of the Vahhābiya, 101 seq.
^{c}Abd ol-Vahhāb-e Eṣfahāni Mo^{c}tamad od-Doula "Nashshāt," chancellor of the empire, 131; writes Arabic letters, 145; receives Russian envoys, 152; his career, 172; opponent of Holy War with Russia, 175; prime minister in office, but not in name, his death, 191
^{c}Abd ol-Vahhāb Khān-e Shirāzi Naṣir od-Doula, Mirzā: appointed deputy minister of foreign affairs, 337 seq.; receives title Naṣir od-Doula, 374; minister of commerce, 379
^{c}Abdollāh I ibn Sa^{c}ud (1814–1823), 164
^{c}Abdollāh Khān, son of Naṣir Khān-e Lāri, 28; defeated by Loṭf ^{c}Ali Khān, 28; submits to Fatḥ ^{c}Ali Khān, 64
^{c}Abdollāh Khān, commander at Shahr Babak, 212
^{c}Abdollāh Khān, Mirzā, brother of Moḥammad-e Fasā'i, 221
^{c}Abdollāh Khān, Mirzā, brother of Moḥammad Ḥosein Khān Vakil-e Fārs, governor of Fasā, 247
^{c}Abdollāh Khān, Mirzā, son of Mirzā Manṣur Khān-e Behbehāni, 207
^{c}Abdollāh Khān Amin od-Doula, son of Haji Moḥammad Ḥosein Khān Amin od-Doula, beglerbegi of Esfahan, then mostoufi ol-mamālek, 144; sent to Mashhad with gifts, 165; appointed prime minister, 168; receives Turkish ambassador in his house, 169; married to Bakhteyāri woman,

170; his son appointed governor of Esfahan, 171; deposed from office, 172; mehmāndār of theologians in Holy War, 174 seq., 180; again appointed prime minister, 186; sent to settle accounts of Fārs, 200 seq., 228 seq.; favors succession to the throne of Farmān-Farmā (I), 231
^{c}Abdollāh Khān-e Qiri, 115
^{c}Abdollāh Khān-e Qaraguzlu Ṣārem od-Doula, 308
^{c}Abdollāh Khān-e Zand, uncle of Loṭf ^{c}Ali Khān, 26, 53, 58 seq.
^{c}Abdollāh Masqaṭi, Sheikh, 314, 318
^{c}Abdollāh Mirzā, governor of Khamsa, 141, 152
^{c}Abdollāh Munshi-ye Māzandarāni, Mirzā, 284
Abu ^{c}Abdollāh ol-^{c}Āmeli, theologian of fourteenth century, 107
Abu Dolaf, Dulafid emir, 148
Abu'l-Fatḥ Khān, son of Karim Khān Vakil, 6 seq., 8 seq., 10 seq., 62, 239
Abu'l-Fatḥ Khān Ṣārem od-Doula, Amir ol-Omarā, son of Khān Bābā Khān, 367
Abu Ḥanifa, 370
Abu'l-Ḥasan Khān, Āqā, mayor of Behbehān, 380
Abu'l-Ḥasan Khān, Haji Mirzā, his career, appointed ambassador to London, 129, 134, 137; returns to Persia with Sir Gore Ouseley, 138; signs peace treaty of Golestān, 143; ambassador to Russia, 146 seq.; his mission unsuccessful, 151 seq.; sent to Turkey, France, and England, 155; returns to Tehran, 163; becomes minister of foreign affairs, 172; opponent of Holy War with Russia, 175 seq.; signs treaty of Torkmānchāy, 184 seq.; sent to Fārs, 228 seq.
Abu'l-Ḥasan Khān, Mirzā, son of Mirzā Hādi, son-in-law of Farmān-Farmā (I), 196; governor of Fasā, 207; receives Farmān-Farmā at Fasā, 210; removed from office, 216
Abu'l-Ḥasan Khān, Mirzā, mojtahed, brother of Āqā Mirzā Moḥammad, 309
Abu'l-Ḥasan Khān, Seiyed, 37*n*
Abu'l-Ḥasan Khān-e Kuhaki, Seiyed, governor of Kerman, 37 seq.
Abu'l-Ḥasan Khān Moshir ol-Molk, Mirzā, son-in-law of Farmān-Farmā (II), 220; vizier of Fārs, 276; intendant of Fārs, 294; goes to Tehran to close accounts, 305; returns to Shiraz three years later, is appointed vizier, 318; removed from vizierate and fined, 339, 343; summoned to Tehran, 347; intrigues against beglerbegi of Fārs, 351; again vizier of Fārs, 352, 380; quarrels with Qavām ol-Molk, 360 seq.; appropriates irrigation canal near Shiraz, 382 seq.; his influence in Fārs, 386; his death, 419
Abu'l-Qāsem-e Farāhāni Qā'em Maqām, Mirzā, son of Mirzā ^{c}Isā Farāhāni, succeeds his father in vizierate, 166; concludes treaty with Turkey, 169; present at Torkmānchāy, 184; introduces military reforms, 221; advises Moḥammad Shāh to take over, 232; arrested and executed, 241
Abu'l-Qāsem-e Gilāni (Qommi), Ḥojjat ol-eslām, 127
Abu'l-Qāsem-e Hamadāni Dhu'r-Reyāsatain, Mirzā, brother of Mirzā Yusof, scholar, then vizier

Abu'l-Qāsem-e Hamadāni *(Cont.)* of Kermanshah, 116; sent with Mo^{c}tamad od-Doula to Fārs, 234, 236, 239
Abu'l-Qāsem-e Tafrishi, Mirzā, vizier of Fārs, 294
Abu'l-Qāsem Khān, son of Ṭahmāsp Mirzā, 307
Abu'l-Qāsem Mirzā, son of Moḥammad Shāh, 281
Abu Sa^{c}id, Ilkhanid ruler, 1*n*
Abu Torāb, Sheikh, imam of prayers at Shiraz, 237, 342
Abu'l-Vardi, tribe, 416
^{c}Ādel Shāh, Afshār ruler, 3 seq.
Ādherbāyjān, home of Qājārs, 1; ruled by Shaqāqi Kurds, 16*n*; ravaged by plague, 80; governor appointed, 83, 89, 109, 223, 374; fugitives come to Shiraz, 263; Ādherbāyjāni soldiers (detachment), 283, 285 seq., 337, 349 seq.; vizier appointed, 374, 379; *see also* Shushā, Tabriz.
Adinabāzār, in Ādherbāyjān, 73, 75
Afghanistan, 69, 92, 95, 222, 253 seq.
Afshār, tribe, in the region of Qazvin, 11; belonged to Qizilbash order, 15*n*; disunity, 74; Afshār cavalry, 332, 334
Afzar, town in Fārs, 226, 270
Aḥmad, Haji Mirzā, mayor of Shiraz, 345
Aḥmad, Mirzā, physician from Esfahan, 50
Aḥmad-e Jāmi, Sheikh, saint and mystic, 254*n*
Aḥmad Khān, Haji, governor of Bandar ^{c}Abbās, 344; son of the vizier of Masqaṭ, 365 seq.; removed from office, 377
Aḥmad Khān, Mirzā, treasurer in Fārs, 253, 263 seq.
Aḥmad Khān-e Afghān, son of Āzād Khān-e Afghān, in the service of the Zand, 22; subdued by Qājārs, 23
Aḥmad Khān-e Bastaki, governor of Lārestān, 208, 210
Aḥmad Khān-e Masqaṭi, governor of Bandar ^{c}Abbās, 346
Aḥmad Khān-e Navā'i ^{c}Amid ol-Molk, deputy chamberlain, sent to Shiraz, 287; appointed daryābegi and governor of Bushehr, 336, 347 seq.
Aḥmad Khān-e Tabrizi, Mirzā, administrator of Fārs, 262
Aḥmad Narāqi Kāshāni, Haji Mollā, mojtahed, 127, 175
Aḥmad Shāh Dorrāni, ruler of Afghanistan, 271*n*
Aḥmad Shāh Khān, brother of Ra'is Ḥosein-e Tangestāni, 205
Aḥmad Shāh Khān-e Minābi, mayor of Mināb, 312, 318; governor of Bandar ^{c}Abbās, 377, 385
Aḥmad-e Shirāzi, Haji Mirzā, 360
Aḥmad-e Tangestāni, son of Bāqer Khān, 323
Aḥmadi, district in Fārs, 64, 276, 337*n*
Ahrom, town in Fārs, 399
Akbar, grandson of Mo'men Khān-e Saruzaki, 265
Akbar Mirzā, son of Farmān-Farmā (I), 240
Akbar Navvāb-e Shirāzi, Haji, scholar, author of "Ketāb-e Delgoshā," 167, 192*n*, 197
Āl-e Ḥaram, Arab chiefs on the Persian Gulf, 30 seq.
^{c}Alā Marvdasht, district in Fārs, 240*n*, 340, 345, 397
^{c}Alam Khān-e ^{c}Arab, 63

Alexander I, Russian czar (1801–1825), 120
Alexander II, Russian czar (1855–1881), 395*n*
^{c}Ali, Mollā, Sheikh, 304
^{c}Ali, Seiyed, *see* ^{c}Ali b. Sa^{c}id
^{c}Ali, Sheikh, envoy from Baḥrein, 144
^{c}Ali Akbar, Mollā, son of Mollā Moḥammad ^{c}Ali, 342, 343
^{c}Ali Akbar Khān-e Fasā'i, Mirzā, governor of Fasā, 363
^{c}Ali Akbar Khān-e Nafar, 208, 213, 219, 237
^{c}Ali Akbar Qavām ol-Molk, Haji Mirzā, son of Haji Ebrāhim Khān, appointed lord mayor of Shiraz, 142; accompanies Farmān-Farmā (II) to Esfahan, 172, 228; marries a daughter of Naṣrollāh Khān-e Nuri, 193; receives title Qavām ol-Molk, 196; quarrels with the ilkhāni, 206; marches with Farmān-Farmā (I) to Kerman, 210; returns from mission to the ilkhāni, 213; intrigues against Moshir ol-Molk, 219 seq.; arrested by Farmān-Farmā and fined, 224 seq.; goes on pilgrimage during civil war, 263; goes to Tehran to complain about governor of Fārs, 274; rebels against governor of Fārs, 283 seq.; willing to fight the English at Bushehr, 327; arrested and sent to Tehran, 342 seq.; summoned to Tehran, 347; appointed administrator of shrine at Mashhad, 348; dies at Mashhad, 349 seq.
^{c}Ali Aṣghar-e Hezār Jaribi Mazandārāni, chief mollā, 90, 213
^{c}Ali Aṣghar Khān, brother of Haji Zein ol-^{c}Ābedin Khān of Niriz, 292
^{c}Ali Fakhri, son of Haji Mirzā Raḥim, 192*n*
^{c}Ali Himmat Khān-e Kolyā'i, son of Naẓar ^{c}Ali Khān-e Zand, 32
^{c}Ali b. Sa^{c}id, ruler of Zanzibar (1890–1893), 318*n*
^{c}Ali Khān, from Marāgha, 349
^{c}Ali Khān, Mirzā, beglerbegi of Shiraz, 351 seq., 357 seq.
^{c}Ali Khān ^{c}Allāma Shirāzi (Madani), grandfather of Mirzā Jāni, 24, 197
^{c}Ali Khān-e Eṣfahāni, vizier of Rasht, 162
^{c}Ali Khān-e Ḥayyāt Dā'udi, Amir, 32, 45 seq.
^{c}Ali Khān-e Khamsa'i, 24 seq.
^{c}Ali Khān-e Māfi, 9
^{c}Ali Khān-e Marandi, 178
^{c}Ali Khān Noṣrat ol-Molk Sartip, son of Rostam Khān-e Qaraguzlu, 311
^{c}Ali Khān-e Qazvini, Seiyed, 46, 50
^{c}Ali Khān-e Zand, Sheikh, 6
^{c}Ali Moḥammad, Mirzā, son of Mirzā Bazzāz-e Shirāzi, 277
^{c}Ali Moḥammad Bāb, Mirzā, founder of the Bābi sect, 290
^{c}Ali Moḥammad-e Kāshāni, Haji, ascetic, 168
^{c}Ali Moḥammad Khān, Mirzā, son of ^{c}Abdollāh Khān Amin od-Doula, 171
^{c}Ali Moḥammad Khān, Mirzā, son of Na^{c}im-e Nuri, 340
^{c}Ali Moḥammad Khān-e Astarābādi, 126
^{c}Ali Moḥammad Khān-e Fili Sang-e Seyākhi, grandson of Mo'men Khān-e Saruzaki, 265
^{c}Ali Moḥammad Khān-e Nuri, Mirzā, chief registrar of the army, 313

ᶜAli Moḥammad Khān Qavām ol-Molk, Mirzā, son of ᶜAli Akbar Qavām ol-Molk, governor of Kāzerun, 325; receives title "Vakil," 335, inherits office and title from his father, 350; oppresses tribes of Fārs, 360, 362 seq.; quarrels with Abu'l-Ḥasan Khān Moshir ol-Molk, 382 seq., 419 seq.; appointed governor of several places and tribes in Fārs, 387, 419; conquers fortress of Tebr, 388*n*, 390 seq.; settles affairs of Lārestān, 394, 419; repairs irrigation canals near Shiraz, 398; deputy governor of Fārs, 416; his death, 419
ᶜAli Morād Khān-e Zand, assumes rule, captures Esfahan and Tehran, 8 seq., 13; conquers Qazvin, 11; tries to conquer Māzandārān, 17; fails to capture Astarābād, 18 seq.; dies near Esfahan, 20
ᶜAli Naqi Khān, son of Reżā Qoli Khān-e Kāzeruni, 47
ᶜAli Naqi Khān, governor of Yazd, 56
ᶜAli Naqi Khān-e Qājār Qoyunlu, 214 seq.
ᶜAli Naqi Khān-e Qaraguzlu, 337
ᶜAli Naqi Mirzā Rokn od-Doula, governor of Qazvin, 190; son of Fatḥ ᶜAli Shāh, 229
ᶜAli Naqi Mostoufi, Mirzā, nephew of Moshir ol-Molk, 220
ᶜAli Pāshā, governor of Baghdad, 118 seq.
ᶜAli Qoli Khān, brother of Aqā Moḥammad Shāh, brought from Astarābād to Qazvin, 4; left with troops at Esfahan, 29; goes to Kāshān, 30; sent to Kuh-e Giluya, 36; tries to occupy the throne after his brother's death, 75 seq.; exiled to Bārforush, 78
ᶜAli Qoli Khān, son of Jaᶜfar Khān-e Bayyāt, 89 seq.
ᶜAli Qoli Khān, nephew of the ilkhāni, 334
ᶜAli Qoli Khān-e Afshār, *see* ᶜĀdel Shāh
ᶜAli Qoli Khān-e Kāzeruni, Haji, in the service of the Zand, 24; arrested, 25 seq.; among the murderers of Jaᶜfar Khān-e Zand, 31; his life spared by Loṭf ᶜAli Khān, 33; sent to Āqā Moḥammad Shāh as an envoy, 46
ᶜAli Qoli Khān-e Shāhsevan, 109
ᶜAli Reżā, Mirzā, son of Haji Ebrāhim Khān, 99, 139
ᶜAli Reżā Behbehāni, Mirzā, governor of Behbehān, 36*n*
ᶜAli Reżā Garāshi, governor of Lārestān, 307
ᶜAli Reżā Khān-e Bakhteyāri, 298
ᶜAli Shāh (ᶜAli Shāh-e ᶜEvaż), fortress near Tehran, 75
ᶜAli Shāh Ẓell os-Solṭān, 200, 227
ᶜAli Torāb Khān, Mirzā, grandson of Mo'men Khān-e Saruzaki, 264
ᶜAli Veis Khān-e Kur, brother of Khān ᶜAli Khān, 268
Allāh Akbar, pass near Shiraz, 49
Allāh Yār Khān, lord of Sabzavār, 93
Allāh Yār Khān-e Qājār Devehlu Āṣaf od-Doula, son-in-law of Fatḥ ᶜAli Shāh, appointed prime minister, 172; besieges Shushā together with ᶜAbbās Mirzā, 177 seq.; defeated by Madatov near Ganja, 179 seq.; honorably imprisoned by the Russians in Tabriz, 182 seq.; accompanies Paskievich to Torkmānchāy, 185; renounces office, 185 seq.; Geor-

gian slaves in his palace handed over to Griboyedov, 188; takes measures after the shah's death, 231; governor of Khorasan, 251
Alp Arslan, Saljuqid ruler, 388*n*
ᶜĀmeri Arabs, 24*n*
ᶜAmid ol-Molk ("Refuge of Kingdom"), *see* Aḥmad Khān-e Navā'i
Amin od-Doula ("Trustee of the Empire"), *see* ᶜAbdollah Khān; Farrokh Khān; Moḥammad Ḥosein Khān
Amin ol-Molk ("Trustee of Kingdom"), *see* Farrokh Khān
Āmol, town in Māzandārān, 155, 335, 385
Anjira, village near Shiraz, 34
Anvah, pass near Bastak, 344
Anzān, town in Māzandārān, 18
Āqā Khān, head of Ismailis, his ancestors, 38*n*
Āqā Khān-e Nuri Eᶜtemād od-Doula, Mirzā, vizier of the army, appointed grand vizier, 301; mentioned as grand vizier, 314; removed from office, 338
Āqā Moḥammad Shāh, his birth and early life, 3; brought to Shiraz, stays with Karim Khān Vakil, 4; goes to northern Persia upon Vakil's death, 5; wins over Qājār Devehlu khāns, goes to Māzandārān, 6; defeats army of ᶜAli Morād Khān, 11; rebellion of his brothers, 12 seq.; conquests in Khorasan, 14; conquest of Gilān, Qazvin, and Zenjān, 15; besieges Tehran, 16; gives up Māzandārān, defends Astarābād, 17 seq.; returns to Māzandārān, 19; conquers Esfahan, 22; conquest of Tehran, 23; recaptures Esfahan, marches to Khamsa, 25; marches to southern Persia, 29; new campaign to Esfahan, 30; first campaign to Shiraz, 33 seq.; gives up siege of Shiraz, 35; marches to Gandomān, 36; thence to Zenjān and Qazvin, 37; campaign to Ādherbāyjān, 39 seq.; sends troops to Shiraz, 46; suffers a stroke, sends army to Shiraz, 50; marches to Shiraz, defeats Loṭf ᶜAli Khān, 52 seq.; enters Shiraz, has Karim Khān Vakil's corpse transferred to Tehran, 55; travels to Āsopās in Fārs, orders destruction of citadel of Shiraz, 56; conquers Kerman, 59; cruelty towards a scribe, 61; travels to Shiraz, 64; campaigns to Armenia and Georgia, 65; conquest of Tiflis, cruelties committed, 67; his coronation, 67 seq.; conquest of Mashhad, 69; destroys sepulcher of Nāder Shāh, extorts jewels from Shāhrokh Shāh, 70; his murder at Shushā, 73; his character depicted: pious, just, and humble, 74; provisional burial at Shushā, 80; then transferred to Najaf, 75, 372; his last will and testament, 88 seq., 104, 122, 160, 242; appoints Seiyed Saᶜid of Masqaṭ governor of Bandar ᶜAbbās, 317; rebuilds Ashraf in Māzandārān, 354*n*
Āqā Qoli, brother of Moḥammad ᶜAli Khān-e Tabrizi, governor of Jahrom, 340
Āqāsi, Haji Mirzā, *see* Haji Mirzā Āqāsi
Āqāsi Khān, 12 seq.
ᶜArabestān, *see* Khuzestān
Arabs, tribes in Fārs, Arab detachment at Shiraz, 221, 301, 305,

Arabs (*Continued*)
310, 327 seq., 331, 336 seq., 391*n*; near Bushehr, 294; in Fārs, 418; *see also* ^{c}Āmeri, Bani Damukhi, Farāmorzi, Javāshem, Lāveri, Osfur, Sharifat
Arāk, *see* Solṭānābād
Aras Khān, Russian officer, taken prisoner, embraces Islam, 109
Ardebil, 40, 68, 177
Ardekān, town in Fārs, 275
Ardestān, 27, 236
Arghun, Ilkhanid ruler, 15*n*, 139
Arghun Mirzā, son of Ḥasan ^{c}Ali Mirzā Shojā^c os-Salṭana, 201, 215
Armenia, 65 seq., 107, 123 seq., 151
Arsenjān, town in Fārs, 50, 387*n*
Āru, castle near Behbehān, 380
Asad, Haji, citizen of Shiraz, 265
Asad Khān, Qashqā'i commander, 349
Asadollāh Khān, son of Haji Ebrāhim Khān, sent as hostage to Tehran, 56; governor of Qom, 67; governor of Borujerd, Lorestān-e Fili, Shoshtar, and Dezful, 98
Asadollāh Khān, son of ^{c}Abd or-Raḥim Khān, 99
Asadollāh Khān-e Nuri, Mirzā, minister of the army, 193
Asadollāh Khān-e Qā'eni, 254
Asadollāh Mirzā, nephew of Ḥosām os-Salṭana, deputy governor of Fārs, 341; street riots at Shiraz, 342 seq.; governor of Bushehr, 352; governor of Lārestān, Sab^{c}a, and Bandar ^{c}Abbās, 364; returns to Shiraz, 365
Āṣaf od-Doula ("Counselor of the Empire"), *see* Allāh Yār Khān-e Qājār Devehlu, Moḥammad Qoli Khān-e Qājār
Ashraf (Ashraf ol-Belād), town in Māzandārān, 17*n*, 19, 155, 354, 385
Ashshāqbāsh, Qājār group, 1
Āsib, 17*n*
Asir, in Fārs, 240*n*, 340, 345, 397
^{c}Askar Khān-e Afshār Orumi, ambassador in Paris, 122
^{c}Askari, in Kuh-e Giluya, 248*n*
Aṣlān Khān, Amir, 287
Aṣlānduz, in Ādherbāyjān, 110
^{c}Asluya, *see* Bandar ^{c}Asluya
Āsopās, town in Fārs, 55 seq., 225*n*
Astarābād (Gorgān), home of Qājār dynasty, 2 seq., 6*n*, 14; called "dār ol-mo'menin," 3*n*; attacked by the Zand, 17 seq., 19; Turkomans near the town, 69; governor mentioned, 147; region called Kabud Jāma, 150
Astrakhān (Haji Tarkhān), 141, 379
Atābeg ("Guardian, Preceptor"), *see* Taqi Khān, Mirzā
Aurangzeb, Moghul ruler, 70
Austria, diplomatic mission to Austria, 155, 159
^{c}Aziz Khān-e Mokri, Ādherbāyjāni commander, envoy to Herāt, 255; put under command of Āqā Mirzā Moḥammad-e Fasā'i, later on commander in chief of Persia, 276; stays at Shiraz, 283; envoy of governor of Shiraz to rebels, 284 seq.; fights rebels in the city, 286 seq.
^{c}Azizollāh-e Tāleshi, Seiyed, mojtahed, 175

Bābā Eiyub, village near Shiraz, 117*n*
Bābā Khān, *see* Fatḥ ^{c}Ali Shāh
Bābā Khān-e Barforushi Māzandārāni, his career: tutor, commander, 196; accompanies Farmān-Farmā to Bushehr, 204; stays at Shiraz, 210; subdues

Qashqai khans, 223 seq., 225; styled "Amir-e Kabir," 367
Bābā Khān-e Bavānāti, Āqā, 287
Bābā Monir, town in Fārs, 248*n*
Bābā Tājer-e Shirāzi, Haji Mollā, father-in-law of Ḥasan-e Fasā'i, 399
Bābā Yusof, courier, 77
Bābi sect, its foundation, 277; disturbances in Fārs, 290 seq.; attempt at the shah's life, 302 seq.
Bābol, *see* Bārforush
Badakhshān, 147
Baden-Baden, visited by Nāṣer od-Din Shāh, 395
Bāgh, plain of Bāgh in Fārs, 343
Bāgh-e ᶜAliābād, in Fārs, 337
Bāgh-e Eram, *see* Bāgh-e Shāh
Bāgh-e Shāh (Bagh-e Eram), in Māzandārān, 12*n*, 16*n*, 225, 354
Baghdad, home of Bani Kaᶜb, 26*n*; governor mentioned, 80, 118, 136, 369; annexation to Persia proposed by Russia, 130; stay of Persian princes, 236; visited by Nāṣer od-Din Shāh, 370; *see also* Kāẓemein
Bahā' ad-Din Moḥammad ibn Ḥosein al-ᶜĀmili, 412*n*
Bahādorān, village in Fārs, 261
Bahārlu, Turkish tribe in Fārs, 208 seq.; Bahārlu horsemen, 219, 418; Bahārlu detachment at Shiraz, 221, 307, 336, 391*n*; winter quarters, 336*n*; subdued by governor of Fārs, 340 seq.; rebel against their governor, 360 seq., 363 seq., 388*n*; belong to the "Five Tribes," 387; in possession of Tebr, 390; *see also* Five Tribes
Bahman, near Bushehr, 322 seq.
Bahmani, castle near Forg, 337
Bahmani, district in Kuh-e Giluya, 403
Bahrām Mirzā Moᶜezz od-Doula, appointed governor of Fārs, 287; returns to Tehran, 290; settles quarrels at Behbehān, 296
Baḥrein, governed by local ruler of Bushehr, 32*n*; envoy sent to Persia, 144 seq.; captured by Bani ᶜOtub, 145*n*, 217
Bājgāh, village near Shiraz, 9, 49
Bakash Mamassani, *see* Mamassani
Bakhteyāri, tribe in Fārs, in the service of the Zand, 17; subdued by the Qājārs, 23; quarrel with the Qāshqā'i, 163; Bakhteyāri soldiers, 179, 298; robbers punished, 196, 228 seq.; governor appointed, 252; plundered by Bavir Aḥmadi, 319, *see also* Jā'iki Bakhteyāri
Baku, possession of Shaqāqi Kurds, 65 seq.; submits to Russian troops, 71, 119; Zizianov killed near Baku, 111; ceded to Russia, 144*n*
Balkh, 71
Bam, in Kerman, local ruler mentioned, 8*n*, 37*n*; supports Loṭf ᶜAli Khān, 58; Loṭf ᶜAli Khān taken prisoner near Bam, 61 seq.; occupied by Qājārs, 64; Persian tribes migrate to Bam, 213; Farmān-Farmā (I) marches to Bam, 214
Bām, in Khorasan, 156
Bampur, in Beluchistan, 271, 271*n*
Band-e Pāy, village in Māzandārān, 12 seq.
Bandar ᶜAbbās, ceded to Sultan of ᶜOmān, 134*n*; station on land route to India, 199; rent paid to Persia increased, 302; Persian governor appointed, 306; conquered by Persian troops, 307

Bandar, ᶜAbbās *(Continued)* seq.; reconquered by Sultan of ᶜOmān, 310; new treaty concluded with ᶜOmān, 314 seq.; Sultan of ᶜOmān appoints new governor, 344; Persian control re-established, 358 seq.; restituted to Sultan of ᶜOmān, 365 seq.; new governor appointed, 377, 385, 387, 417, 419; ravaged by highway robbers, 388*n*
Bandar ᶜAsluya, 30 seq., 269, 340, 393
Bandar Bushehr, *see* Bushehr
Bandar Dayyer, 393
Bandar Deilam, 25*n*, 44*n*, 398*n*
Bandar Enzeli, 110, 379
Bandar Hendeyān, 269, 275, 297*n*
Bandar Kangān, 269, 345, 392 seq., 397, 401
Bandar Khamir, 315
Bandar Kong, 327
Bandar Langa, 340
Bandar Maghu, 153, 155
Bandar Nāband, 30
Bandar Nakhl-e Taqi, 393
Bandar Ra's ol-Kheima, *see* Ra's ol-Kheima
Bandar Rig, 32*n*, 45
Bandar Ṭāheri, 223, 393, 397
Bani Kaᶜb, Arab tribe, 26
Bani Montafeq, Arab tribe, 7*n*
Bani Moᶜin, Arab tribe, 317
Bani ᶜOtub, Arab tribe, 145, 217 seq.
Bāqer, grandson of Mo'men Khān-e Saruzaki, 265
Bāqer, Shāh, *see* Bāqer Khān-e Khorāsgāni
Bāqer-e Famuri, Mirzā, governor of Kāzerun, 148
Bāqer Khān, son of Vali Khān-e Mamassani, 250
Bāqer Khān-e Galladāri, 30, 48
Bāqer Khān-e Galladāri, Āqā, governor of Galladār, 340
Bāqer Khān-e Khorāsgāni, Āqā, appointed beglerbegi of Esfahan by the Zand, 11, 20; closes gates to Zand troops, 19; assumes rule, styles himself "Bāqer Shāh," 21; arrested by Jaᶜfar Khān-e Zand, 22; appointed governor of Esfahan by Āqā Moḥammad Shāh, 23
Bāqer Khān-e Tangestāni, son of Aḥmad Shāh Khān, appointed governor of Tangestān, 205; among the murderers of ᶜAbd or-Rasul Khān, 211; protects family of Vali Khan, 248; arrested and sent to Shiraz, thence to Tehran, dies at Tabriz, 250
Bāqer Khān-e Tangestāni, rebels at Bushehr, 260; besieges Bushehr, 289; sent with troops to Bandar ᶜAbbās, 312; fights English troops at Bushehr, 322 seq., 329, 333
Bāqer-e Salmās, Haji Mollā, 127
Bāqer Solṭān, citizen of Shiraz, 265
Bardestān, on the Persian Gulf, 393
Bardi Khān, commander of the artillery of ᶜAbbās Mirzā, 216
Bārforush (Bābol), in Māzandārān, early Qājār residence, 12, 14; Qājār prince exiled to Bārforush, 78; visited by Fatḥ ᶜAli Shāh, 155, by Nāṣer od-Din Shāh, 355, 385
Bārkhudār Khān-e Zand, 37, 40, 42 seq., 44
Bāṣeri, one of the "Five Tribes" in Fārs, 387
Bāsht, town in Fārs, 198
Basra, occupied by the Zand, 7; founder of Vahhābiya studies at

Basra, 101; residence of English consul, 106; supplies English troops with victuals, 325
Bastak, town in southern Fārs, 343 seq.
Bavānāt, district in Fārs, 57, 59, 211, 214, 337*n*
Behbehān, visited by Fatḥ ᶜAli Shāh, 197 seq.; castle of Nārin, 298; tribal population settled, 349; construction of water conduit, 352 seq.; hail storm ravages town and surroundings, 356; *see also* Kuh-e Giluya
Beiżā, town near Shiraz, 34, 52
Belochestan, 271, 314
Berlin, visited by Nāṣer od-Din Shāh, 395
Besṭām, town in Khorasan, 14, 16*n*, 24*n*
Bibi Shirvān, town in Khorasan, 252
Bidel, *see* Raḥim-e Shirāzi
Bidshehr, in Fārs, 86, 223*n*, 288*n*, 318
Bigard, 248*n*
Bikhā-ye Fāl, district in southern Fārs, 153 seq.
Bishāpur, near Kāzerun, 174*n*
Bojnurd, town in Khorasan, 358
Bombay, *see* India
Borāzjān, in Dashtestān, position 32*n*, 45; visited by Farmān-Farmā (I), 205; rebels subdued by Farhād Mirzā, 269; camp of Persian army in 1856–1857, 329 seq.
Borujerd, 98, 100, 198 seq., 232, 415, 418
Bozorg, Emām Haji Mollā Āqā, 408
Bozorg, Mirzā (Mirzā ᶜIsā Qā'em Maqām), son of Mirzā Ḥosein-e Farāhāni "Vafā," appointed adjudant of ᶜAbbās Mirzā, 89; vizier to ᶜAbbās Mirzā, appointed vizier of Tehran, 108; fabricates guns at Tabriz, 109; introduces military reforms, 122; expected to guarantee peace between Persia and Russia, 124; author of treatise on Holy War, 127 seq.; appointed deputy of the prime minister, receives title "Qā'em Maqām," 131; sent to negotiate with Tormasov, 133; dies from plague, 166
Bozorg Mostoufi, Mirzā Seiyed, appointed procurator to Ṭahmāsp Mirzā, 307; vizier of Kuh-e Giluya and Behbehān, 312
Bursa, 236*n*
Bushehr, governors mentioned, 32, 45, 132, 212, 288, 294, 356, 340, 343, 345, 347, 352, 364, 384, 388, 397, 398 seq., 417, 419; port for pilgrimage to Mecca, 202, 373; besieged by khāns of Dashtestān, 204 seq.; attacked by Arabs, 217 seq.; threatened by English fleet in 1838, 260; besieged by Nāẓem ol-Molk, 288 seq.; governor of Fārs settles affairs, 304, 341 seq.; occupied by English troops in 1856, 319 seq.
Buzjān, *see* Torbat-e Sheikh Jām

Catherine II (1762–1796), 66*n*, 71 seq.
Caucasia, Russian governors, 107*n*, 120*n*, 128*n*, 151
Chaghādak, near Bushehr, 333
Chaghākhur, near Esfahan, 163
Chahār Danga, in Māzandārān, 13
Chahār Maḥāll, region near Esfahan, 21, 199 seq., 334
Chāh Kutāh, village near Bushehr, 217, 329 seq.

Chāl-e Seyākh, near Esfahan, 21, 84
Chām Mollā, castle in Kuh-e Giluya, 297 seq.
Charāgh ᶜAli Khān-e Navā'i, chief keeper of the arsenal, appointed vizier of Fārs, 92; restricted to keeping the accounts, 98; guns manufactured under his supervision, 110; removed from vizierate, 114 seq.; his learning, 116; his buildings at Shiraz, 116*n*
Chenār-e Rāhdār, village near Shiraz, 326
Chenār-e Shāhejān, village near Shiraz, 197
Chorām, town in Lorestan, 350
Christie, Captain, 234*n*

Dāghestān, 3, 65, 73, 144*n*
Dālaki, village near Kāzerun, 32, 205, 211, 329 seq.
Dāmghān, governor mentioned, 4; Qājār conquest, 14; Dāmghāni musketeers, 52; Shāhrokh Shāh dies at Dāmghān, 71; visited by Nāṣer od-Din Shāh, 358
Damukhi, Arab tribe near Bushehr, 217
Dārāb (Dārābjerd), citadel captured, 57; governors mentioned, 86, 196, 207, 243, 253, 276, 288*n*, 307, 318, 346, 361, 363 seq., 387, 399, 417, 419; visited by governor of Fārs, 210 seq., 307, 359; soldiers from Dārāb, 221; winter quarters of Inālu and Bahārlu, 336*n*, 340 seq., 361
Dārāb Khān, nephew of the ilkhāni, 334; appointed ilbegi, 389
Dārāb Mirzā, son of Farmān-Farmā (I), 240
Darband, 65, 71*n*, 110, 119
Dārenjān-e Khvāja, near Shiraz, 86*n*
Darjazzin (Dargezin), near Hamadān, 84; Dargezin detachment, 337
Darvish Nadim (Naqqāl), Haji, 226
Daryābegi ("Admiral"), *see* Hasan ᶜAli Khān; Aḥmad Khān-e Nava'i ᶜAmid ol-Molk
Dāryān, near Shiraz, 216
Dāshlu, branch of the Ashshāqbāsh, 2
Dasht-e Arjan, village near Shiraz, 197, 218
Dashti and Dashtestān, the region of Bushehr, 32, 44; khāns opponents of Zand rule, 45; governors mentioned, 132, 294, 336, 340, 343, 345, 347 seq., 352, 384, 417, 419; troops sent to ᶜOmān, 134; khāns lay siege to Bushehr, 204 seq.; names of khāns listed, 211; rebels subdued, 269; affairs settled, 304, 397 seq., 399
Dāyen, village near Kāzerun, 148
Deh Bid, town near Shiraz, 243
Deh Dasht, in Kuh-e Giluya, 269, 300
Deh Kord, near Esfahan, 200
Deh Ram, town in Fārs, 393; *see also* Nāḥahi Arbaᶜ
Deh Rud, in Fārs, *see* Navāḥi Arbaᶜ
Delgoshā, plain near Shiraz, 284
Derāz, *see* Qeshm
Derᶜiyya, capital of Vahhābi movement, 102, 135, 164
Devehlu, *see* Qājār
Dez-e Sapid, *see* Qalᶜa-ye Safid
Dezāshub, village near Tehran, 101
Dezgāh, village in southern Fārs, 393
Dhahabi, Sufi order, 161*n*
Dhu'l-Feqār Khān-e Afshār, 11
Dhu'l-Qadr, of the Qizilbash order, 15*n*
Dinkān, village near Shiraz, 34

Do Danga, district in Māzandārān, 13
Do Gombadān, town in Kuh-e Giluya, 198, 249
Dolafābād, *see* Zolfābād
Doshmanzeyāri, *see* Mamassani
Douraq, district in Khuzestān, 26*n*
Dudāgh, *see* Moḥammad Ḥosein Khān-e Qājār Qoyunlu
Dudasht (Tudashk), near Esfahan, 22, 28
Dulāb, village near Tehran, 76
Dulafids, 148
Dust Ali Khān, essayer of the empire, 374
Dust Moḥammad, Barakzay ruler of Afghanistan, 258*n*
Dutch Company, at Bandar ᶜAbbās, 311; building on island of Khārk, 400

East India Company, *see* India
Ebrāhim, Haji Mirzā, son of Jāni-ye Fasā'i, sent as hostage to Tehran, 56; mojtahed at Shiraz, gives fetvā for Holy War, 127; the shah visits his house, 197; death (1839) and works, 262; exercizes great influence, 263
Ebrāhim Khalil Khān-e Javānshir, ruler of Karabagh, 65; surrenders Shushā to Qājār army, 66; Shushā again besieged, 72 seq.; ordered to transfer corpse of the murdered shah, 80; his daughter married to Fatḥ ᶜAli Shāh, 139
Ebrāhim Khān, nephew of the governor of Baku, Ḥosein Qoli Khān, 111
Ebrāhim Khān, son of grand vizier Haji Moḥammad Ḥosein Khān, 197
Ebrāhim Khān-e Ashrafi Māzandārāni, 52
Ebrāhim Khān Eᶜtemād od-Doula, Haji Mirzā, lord mayor of Shiraz, 32; arrests Seiyed Morād Khān-e Zand, 33; appointed vizier of Shiraz, 37; dissension with Loṭf ᶜAli Khān, 40 seq.; arrests Zand emirs at Shiraz, 43 seq.; closes gates to Loṭf ᶜAli Khān, 44 seq.; appointed beglerbegi of Fārs by Āqā Moḥammad Shāh, 46; expels tribal soldiers from Shiraz, 47 seq.; refuses Zand peace offer, 49; sends to Tehran, 50; expels Māfi and Nānkoli from the city, 52; Malcolm on Ebrāhim's aims and abilities, 54; confirmed in office, 55; gives hostage to Āqā Moḥammad Shāh, 56; accompanies shah on campaign to Kerman, 59; appointed grand vizier, 64; present at coronation, 68; royal princes entrusted to him, 73; marches to Tehran after murder of the shah, 75; meets Fatḥ ᶜAli Shāh near Tehran, 78; camp of Saruq entrusted to him, 84; plots downfall of the pretender Ḥosein Qoli Khān, 85 seq.; accompanies shah to Khorasan, 89; proceeds to Nishāpur, 90; meets prime minister of Afghanistan, 92; receives Malcolm in his palace, 94; seals treaty with England, 95; his ancestors and career, 96 seq.; influence of his family, 98; victim of false accusations, his deposal, and death, 98 seq.; his son restored to office of lord mayor of Shiraz, 142; *see also* Appendix IV
Ebrāhim Khān-e Qājār Joveini Khorāsāni, sent to accept submission of Ṣādeq Khān, 80; governor of Kuh-e Giluya and Behbehān, 340

Ebrāhim Khān-e Zand, son of Karim Khān Vakil, 6
Ebrāhim Khān-e Zand, son of Esma^c^il Khān-e Zand, 31
Ebrāhim Pāshā, son of Moḥammad ^c^Ali, ruler of Egypt, 164
Ebrāhim-e Shirāzi, Mirzā, son of Mirzā Moḥammad ^c^Ali, appointed lord mayor of Shiraz, 100
Ebrāhim-e Tabrizi, Mirzā, governor of Fasā, Dārāb, 253
Echmiadzin ("Unigenitus descendit"), called Üch Kilise by the Turks, 181
Egypt, 163 seq.
Eḥteshām od-Doula ("Respect of the Empire"), *see* Solṭān Oveis Mirzā
Elisavetpol (Elizabeth Paul), *see* Ganja
Ellis, Sir Henry, 256*n*
^c^Emād od-Din, Mir, calligrapher, 146
^c^Emād ol-Molk ("Support of Kingdom"), *see* Amir Ḥasan Khān
^c^Emāda Deh, in Fārs, 346*n*
Emām Qoli Khān, 311
Emām Qoli Mirzā Ghażanfar od-Doula, son of Farmān-Farmā (I), 208, 210, 240
Emām Verdi Beg, 116
England, treaty with Persia, 94 seq., 121, 125; English ambassadors to Persia, 125 seq., 133 seq., 137 seq., 143, 184 seq., 232; Persian ambassador sent to England, 128 seq., 155, 163; English military instructors, 221, 227, 234 seq., 256 seq., 258 seq.; English intervention in the Persian Gulf, 260 seq., 319 seq.; English telegraph line installed, 338*n*; English resident in ^c^Omān, 361*n*, 365*n*; visited by Nāṣer od-Din Shāh, 379; English books translated, 413*n*
Enzeli, *see* Bandar Enzeli
Eqlid, village south of Esfahan, 195
Erakli Khān, *see* Irakli
^c^Erāq (^c^Erāq-e ^c^ajam, ^c^Erāq-e Irān), region northwest of Esfahan, 23*n*; crown prince sent to ^c^Erāq, 39; governors mentioned, 98, 130, 186, 415, 418; disciplined army of ^c^Erāq, 122
Erevan, home of Qājārs, 1, 2*n*; attacked by Qājār army, 65; besieged by Russians, 107, 109; Friday mosque outside the town, 108; occupied by Russia, 124, 181; Russians defeated, 128; crown prince stationed near Erevan, 130
Erzerum, 130, 169*n*, 236*n*
Esfahan, ^c^Ali Qapu, 21*n*; Bāgh-e Sa^c^ādatābād, 30, 228; Behesht Ā'in Palace, 21; Kākh-e Hasht Behesht, 21*n*; Lombān-quarter, 170; Ṭabaruk (citadel), 23; Ṭālār-e Ṭavila, 21
——public treasure, 9, 21; governor appointed, 11, 97, 367, 415; garrison of Lakziya army, 21; Shāh Bāqer claims rule of the whole of Persia, 21; conquered by Qājār army, 23; physicians from Esfahan at Qājār court, 50; occupied by Ḥosein Qoli Khān, 83, 100; founder of Vahhābiya studies at Esfahan, 101; released from payment of taxes, 135; fabrication of brocaded silk, 147; Kadkhodā family, 167; inhabitants molested by evildoers, 170 seq., 267
Esfahaniya, mother of Moḥammad Mirza Vāli, 35

Esfandābād, near Hamadān, 166
Esfandeyār, Persian hero, 207, 223
Esfarjān, town south of Esfahan, 30
Esḥāq Khān, governor of Torbat-e Ḥeidari, 69
Eskandar Khān-e Qājār Qoyunlu, 3
Eskandar Mirzā, son of Farmān-Farmā (I), 240
Esmāᶜil, Mirzā, son of Jāni-ye Fasā'i, 56
Esmāᶜil, Mirza, nephew of Moshir ol-Molk, 220
Esmāᶜil Beg, citizen of Shiraz, 265
Esmāᶜil Khān, governor of Hamadān, 24
Esmāᶜil Khān-e Dāmghāni, Dāmghāni commander, 125, 137
Esmāᶜil Khān-e Qarāchlu, 248, 250
Esmāᶜil Khān-e Zand, 31
Esmāᶜil Mirzā, 176
Esmāᶜil-e Shirāzi Kotvāl, Mirzā, 82
Esmāᶜil Vazir, Haji Mirzā, vizier of Fārs, governor of Bushehr, 388
Eṣṭahbānāt, town and district in Fārs, 57, 86, 216, 221, 243, 253, 261, 291, 340
Eᶜtemād od-Doula ("Confidence of the Empire"), *see* Ebrāhim Khān; Āqā Khān-e Nuri
Eᶜtemād os-Salṭana ("Confidence of the Rule"), *see* Moṣṭafā Qoli Khān-e Qaraguzlu
ᶜEzz od-Doula ("Glory of the Empire"), *see* ᶜAbd oṣ-Ṣamad Mirzā

Fahleyān, in Fārs, 25*n*, 197 seq., 244*n*, 268
Fakhr od-Doula ("Pride of the Empire"), *see* Bidel
Fakhri, *see* ᶜAli Fakhri
Fāl, *see* Galladār
Falā Rad, in Fārs, 163, 226*n*
Falāḥi, in Khuzestān, 26, 268 seq., 270, 297
Famur, near Kāzerun, 148
Fandarask, in Gorgān, 5
Farāḥ, in Afghanistan, 258
Farāhān, district in Fārs, 84, 149
Farakhābād, in Māzandārān, 355
Farāmorzi, tribe in Lārestān, 344
Farazdaq, Arab poet, 419 seq.
Farhād Mirzā Moᶜtamad od-Doula, son of ᶜAbbās Mirzā, 81; punishes the Lors, 245*n*; deputy governor of Fārs, 267; marches against Lors, 268; campaign to southern Fārs, 269 seq.; appoints new governor of Behbehān, 271; summoned to Tehran, 272; governor of Kurdistan, 367; governor of Fārs, 368; examples of his wise government, 403 seq.; his scholarship and writings, 412 seq.; returns to Tehran, 415
Faridun, Persian hero, 300
Faridun, Mirzā (Haji Khān-e Jān), brother of Reżā Qoli Khān, 12 seq.
Faridun Khān-e Tavalloli, 308
Faridun Mirzā Farmān-Farmā (II), brother of Moḥammad Shāh, governor of Fārs, 253 seq.; deposed, 266, 272
Farmān-Farmā ("Issuer of Orders"), *see* Faridun Mirzā; Ḥosein ᶜAli Mirzā
Farrāshband, town in Fārs, 328
Farrokh Khān-e Kāshāni Amin ol-Molk, sent to Fārs to collect taxes, 271; Persian ambassador to Paris, 334; styled "Amin od-Doula," 364
Fārs, governed by Loṭf ᶜAli Khān-e Zand, 28*n*; nobles rebel against Zand rule, 33; conquered by Qājārs, 36 seq.; mares of the Zand

Fārs *(Continued)*
on pasture in Fārs, 46; locust plague, 51; Saljuqid governor mentioned, 88; manufacture of cannons, 109; inspection of revenues and expenditure, 131, 201, 228, 405; kalāntar of Fārs appointed, 142; ilkhāni of Fārs appointed, 160; tribal quarrels settled, 163; military reforms introduced, 221 seq.; famine in several parts of province, 376, 409; new assessment of taxes, 389; extension of province described, 403; *see also* Kāzerun, Shiraz etc.)

Fasā, town in Fārs, governors mentioned, 83, 207, 216, 243, 247, 253, 276, 309, 346, 363 seq., 417, 419; taken away from Ḥasan-e Fasā'i's family, 83, 207; situated on highway Bandar ᶜAbbās–Shiraz, 199; visited by governor of Fārs, 210 seq., 270; soldiers from Fasā in reformed army, 221, 319; encroachments of governor of Lārestān, 261; Bābi disturbances, 290; winter quarters of Inālu and Bahārlu, 336*n*, 363

Fatḥ Ali Khān, Mir, of Talpor dynasty of India, 199*n*

Fatḥ ᶜAli Khān, son of Qavām ol-Molk, 206

Fatḥ ᶜAli Khān-e Kāshāni (Ṣabā) Malek osh-shoᶜarā, 81

Fatḥ ᶜAli Khān Kotval, protector of Mashhad, 71

Fatḥ ᶜAli Khān Mostoufi, Mirzā, 335

Fatḥ ᶜAli Khān-e Nuri, 94

Fatḥ ᶜAli Khān-e Qājār Devehlu, 16, 36

Fatḥ ᶜAli Khān-e Qājār Qoyunlu, ancestor of the Qājār dynasty, 2

Fatḥ ᶜAli Khān-e Shirāzi Ṣāḥeb Divān, Mirzā, son of ᶜAli Akbar Qavām ol-Molk, grand vizier, given title Ṣāḥeb Divān, 335; governor of Yazd, 339; of Shoshtar, Dezful, and ᶜArabestān, 350; vizier, then governor of Esfahan, 367; vizier to crown prince Moẓaffar od-Din Mirzā in Ādherbāyjān, 374; appointed grand vizier, 379; vizier of Fārs, 416; gives aldermen regular pay, 417; efficient administrator, 418; orders to pave streets of Shiraz, 419

Fatḥ ᶜAli Shāh, son of Ḥosein Qoli Khān, his birth, nicknamed Bābā Khān, 4 seq.; stays at Bārforush, 12; his marriages, 16; sent on campaign to Yazd, 28 seq.; his children, 35 seq., 230; designated crown prince, 39; transfers corpse of Karim Khān Vakil to Najaf, 55; conquers southern parts of Kerman, appointed governor of Fārs, Kerman and Yazd, 64; transfers corpse of Nādar Shāh to Najaf, 70; appointed crown prince anew, 72; accession to the throne, 77; appoints ᶜAbbās Mirzā crown prince, 88; gives instructions to historiographer, 96 seq.; celebrates thirtieth anniversary of coronation, 173; alleged attempt on his life, 198; appoints Moḥammad Mirzā crown prince, 227 seq.; dies at Esfahan, 228 seq.
——*administrative reforms:* issues farmān with regard to dress, 115; institutes board of "Four Viziers," 117; introduces military reforms, 122
——*buildings:* renovates shrine of

Qom, 87; builds Takht-e Qājār, 87; builds new courtyard at Mashhad, 158
——*receives ambassadors:* from England, 94 seq., Turkey, 136, 169; Russia, 120, 152 seq., 161, 175; Sind, 199; Yemen, Baḥrein, Najd, 144 seq.
——*campaigns:* to Khorasan, 89, 93 seq., 103 seq., 155 seq.; against Ḥosein Qoli Khān, 100 seq.; against Turkoman tribes, 105; to Ādherbāyjān, 78 seq., 107 seq., 110, 130, 133 seq., 136 seq., 143, 176 seq.
——*travels:* to Astarābād, 150; Behbehān, 198; Borujerd, 198; Esfahan, 135, 170 seq., 199, 228 seq.; Firuzkuh, 147; Hamadān, 166, 198; Kāshān, 159; Kermānshāh, 199 seq.; Khorasan, 164; Mashhad, 158; Māzandārān, 155; Nehāvand, 166; Qom, 100 seq., 150, 159, 168, 186; Shiraz, 195 seq.; Solṭānābād (Arāk), 186; Solṭāniya, 81, 107 seq., 110, 119, 125, 130, 133, 136, 142 seq., 150, 152 seq., 159, 161, 165, 175; Tabriz, 180 seq.; Ṭārom, 162
——*religious life:* renovates shrine of Qom, 87; refuses to capture Mashhad by force, 104; allows drinking of wine at wedding feast of crown prince, 105; asks ulema for fetvā for Holy War, 127; pays debts of a courtier, 145; does not allow plundering in Ramażān, 156; pilgrimage to Mashhad, 158; builds new courtyard at Mashhad, 158; honors Moḥammad ᶜAli of Egypt, 164; sends precious gift to Mashhad, 165; pilgrimage to Qom, 168; sends gift to Medina, 168; performs duty of Holy War mentally, 176; buried at Qom, 229
Fatḥ ᶜAli Shāhsevan, 140 seq.
Fatḥollāh-e Ardelāni, Mirzā, 53 seq.
Fatḥollāh Khān, son of Lord Mayor Mirzā Ebrāhim, 221
Fatḥollāh Khān-e Zand, son of Loṭf ᶜAli Khān, 60
Fattāḥ, Mir, son of mojtahed of Tabriz, 182
Fāżel Khān-e Garrusi, chief courier, 162
Fażl ᶜAli Beg-e Bahārlu, besieged in castle of Tebr, 388*n*, 390 seq.
Fażl ᶜAli Khān-e Karabaghi Amir-e Tumān, 333 seq., 328, 332
Fażl ᶜAli Khān-e Qājār Qoyunlu, ancestor of Qājārs, 2
Fażl ᶜAli Khān-e Zand, son of Naẓar ᶜAli Khān, 32
Fażlollāh-e ᶜAliābādi Naṣir ol-Molk, Mirzā, son of Grand Vizier Naṣrollāh, appointed vizier of Fārs, 267; vizier of crown prince Nāṣer od-Din Mirzā, 283; vizier of Fārs, 287, 291; sends troops against Bābis, 293
Fażlollāh-e Khāveri Shirāzi, Mirzā, author of Tārikh-e Dhu'l-Qarnein, quoted, 82, 95 seq., 105, 159, 222 seq., 230; his gazel cut into marble block and sent to Mecca, 169
Fażluya Shabānkāra, 388*n*
Firuz Mirzā Noṣrat od-Doula, brother of Moḥammad Shāh, appointed governor of Fārs, subdues Farmān-Farmā (I), 234 seq.; settles affairs of Fārs, 242 seq.; marches to Shulestān, 247, 249; appointed governor of Kerman, 253; again governor of Fārs, 290; sends troops against Bābis, 292; appoints vizier in

Firuz Mirzā Noṣrat od-Doula (*Continued*)
Fārs, 294; travels to Bushehr, 300; campaign to Lārestān, 301; increases taxes on Bandar ᶜAbbās, 302, 306; returns to Tehran, 305
Firuzābād, in Fārs, 30, 86, 113, 225, 393
Firuzkuh, in Māzandārān, visited by the shah, 147, 165, 251, 349; Firuzkuh detachment sent to Fārs, 271, 277
Five Tribes, tribal group in Fārs (Nafar, Bahārlu, Inālu, ᶜArab, Bāṣeri), 387, 399, 417, 419; *see also* the single names
Forg, in Fārs, 64*n*, 199
France, 95, 118, 120 seq., 123 seq., 155; *see also* Gardane, Napoleon
Fumestān, district in Lārestān, 402*n*

Gaikhātu Khān, Mongol ruler, 1*n*
Galladār (Fāl), in southern Fārs, occupied by Zand army, 31; Vahhābis subdued, 153 seq.; governors mentioned, 240*n*, 339, 340, 345, 393, 397, 401 seq.; affairs settled, 269, 399; Sunni creed has majority, 272; capital of Persian Gulf area, 339
Ganāva, in Fārs, 398*n*
Gandomān, in Fārs, 29, 36 seq., 40, 43
Ganja (Kirovabad), home of Qājārs, 1 seq., 2*n*; Qājār army at Ganja, 66 seq.; occupied by Russians, 71, 107, 119, 174; restitution to Persia announced, 151; attacked by Persian troops, 177; defeat of Qājār army near Ganja, 178
Gardane, Claude-Matthieu, French ambassador, 120 seq., 123 seq., 125
Gardane, Paul-Ange-Louis de, brother of Claude-Matthieu, 120*n*
Garmābād, near Qomisha, 226*n*, 278
Garmrud, in Ādherbāyjān, 80
Gāvbandi (Gāvband), in southern Fārs, 393, 397, 402
Georgia, her women appreciated for beauty, 35*n*; Qājār campaigns, 65 seq., 67; Russian intervention, 71 seq., 125; Russian governor-general, 128; ceded to Russia, 143*n*; accepts Russian sovereignty, 151; Georgian prisoners in Persia, 188
Ghafur Khān-e Ṭehrāni, 16
Ghażabān, Sheikh, governor of Falāḥi and Moḥammara, 26
Ghāzān Khān, Ilkhanid ruler (1295–1304), 1*n*, 140*n*
Ghażanfar od-Doula ("Lion of the Empire"), *see* Emām Qoli Mirzā
Gholām Ḥosein-e Bālā Kefti, citizen of Shiraz, 265
Gholām Ḥosein Khān Sepahdār, governor of Persian ᶜErāq, second corps commander, 186, 231
Gholām Reżā Aḥmadi, 307
Ghureyān, fortress near Herāt, 254
Ghurids, 254*n*
Gilān, 14 seq., 110, 162, 379
Giorgi XII (Gurgin Khān), king of Georgia, 107*n*
Gobineau, Joseph Arthur Comte de, 313
Göklen, Turkoman tribe, 251 seq.
Gojārāt, 195
Gol and Golāb, castle in Kuh-e Giluya, 248 seq., 298
Golbād, in Māzandārān, 17 seq., 19
Golbād, Ditch of, 17–19
Golpāygan, near Esfahan, 100*n*, 267, 307 seq., 415, 418
Gombad-e Qābus, 252
Gorgān, *see*, Astarābād

Gorgin Khān, governor of Tiflis, 107
Gorjiya, mother of Moḥammad ᶜAli Mirzā, 35
Goshtāsp, Persian hero, 223
Griboyedov, Alexander Sergeyevich, Russian writer and ambassador, 187 seq., 189
Gudovich, Ivan Vasilevich, 120, 123 seq., 128
Guna Khān-e Afshār-e Ṭāromi, commander of Zand army, 14
Guna Khān-e Kord Zaᶜfarānlu, Amir, governor of Khabushān, 91, 157

Ḥabibollāh Khān, governor of Kerman, 271
Ḥabibollāh Khān, grandson of ᶜAli Moḥammad Qavām ol-Molk, beglerbegi of Shiraz, 418
Hādi-ye Fasā'i, Mirzā, 86 seq.; son of Jāni-ye Fasā'i, 142; his sons listed, 196
Hādi Khān, son of Vali Khān-e Mamassani, 250
Hādi Khān-e Beiżā'i, son of Haji Mirzā Ebrāhim, appointed lord mayor of Shiraz, 274
Hādi Khān-e Borujerdi, 48
Ḥāfeẓ, the poet, 85, 96, 396, 407
Haji Ebrāhim Khān, *see* Ebrāhim Khān Eᶜtemād od-Doula
Haji Mirzā Āqāsi (ᶜAbbās-e Erevāni), his biography, appointed grand vizier, 241 seq.; protects the ilbegi of Fārs, 250 seq.; friend of Farmān-Farmā (II), 266, 272 seq.
Haji Tarkhān, *see* Astrakhan
Hamadān, Zand rule not fully established, 20; visited by the shah, 23, 198, 368; Zand defeat near Hamadān, 24; Hamadāni Qaraguzlu detachment, 212; soldiers from Hamadān, 214; "The judge of Hamadān" in Saᶜdi's Golestān, 369
Hamdam os-Solṭān ("Intimate Companion of the Sultan"), sister of Farmān-Farmā (I), 194
Ḥamza Khān-e Noukandi (Ḥamza Solṭān), 18 seq.
Hangām, *see* Navāḥi Arbaᶜ
Ḥannā, town south of Qomesha, 225*n*, 278
Harford Jones, Sir, English ambassador, 125 seq., 128 seq., 134, 137, 139
Ḥasan, Mirzā, brother of Mirzā Jāni-ye Fasā'i, 56
Ḥasan, Mirzā, astrologer, 72
Ḥasan, Sheikh, mojtahed of the ᶜOṣfur tribe, 260
Ḥasan ᶜAli Khān-e Bayyāt Zarandi, 246 seq.
Ḥasan ᶜAli Khān Daryābegi Naṣir ol-Molk, son of ᶜAli Akbar Qavām ol-Molk, appointed governor of Bushehr, 294 seq.; fights English landing, 321 seq., 323 seq.; brought to Bombay, 327; returns to Shiraz, 336; appointed governor of Lārestān, Sabᶜa etc., 339 seq., 345; granted title "Naṣir ol-Molk," 350; at Shiraz, 351; governor of Bushehr, 364, 367; again governor of Lārestān, 387; governor of Kuh-e Giluya and Bandar ᶜAbbās, 417; governor of Bushehr, 419
Ḥasan ᶜAli Khān-e Kheshti, governor of Khesht, 384
Ḥasan ᶜAli Khān-e Qājār, 60
Ḥasan ᶜAli Mirzā Shojāᶜ os-Salṭana, governor of Khorasan, on campaign against Afghans, 155;

Ḥasan ᶜAli Mirzā Shojāᶜ os–Salṭana *(Continued)*
subdues khāns of Khorasan, 165; plans revolt, returns to Tehran, 166 seq.; allegedly appointed crown prince, 184; his sons sent to Farmān-Farmā (I), 201; governor of Kerman, 227, 231; joins Farmān-Farmā (I) in revolt, 223 seq.; suffers defeat near Ābāda, 235; arrested at Shiraz, 239; his death, 240
Ḥasan-e ᶜArab Damukhi Chāh Kutāhi, Sheikh, 323
Ḥasan-e Fasā'i, author of "Fārsnāma-ye Nāṣeri," visits Kuh-e Giluya, 249*n*; his pilgrimage to Mecca and Medina, 372 seq.; accompanies Eḥteshām od-Doula to the Persian Gulf, 392 seq.; is given share of irrigation canal, 397; a son born to him, 399; visits island of Khārk, 400 seq.
Ḥasan ibn Zain ad-Dīn al-ᶜĀmili, 262*n*
Ḥasan Khān, son of ᶜAbd or-Raḥim Khān, 99
Ḥasan Khān, Amir, governor of Ṭabas, 26*n*, 56, 58
Ḥasan Khān-e Darb Shāhzāda'i, citizen of Shiraz, 265
Ḥasan Khān-e Firuzkuhi, Seiyed, commander of Firuzkuh detachment, 271, 277
Ḥasan Khān-e Galladāri, 269
Ḥasan Khān-e Qarāchadāghi Ādherbāyjāni, governor of Bushehr, 340
Ḥasan Khān-e Sāru Aṣlān, 180
Ḥasan Nāẓer-e Māzandarāni, Haji Mirzā, 240
Ḥasan Neẓām ol-ᶜOlamā, vizier of Fārs, 213, 220; introduces military reforms, 221; flees to Kerman, 227
Hāshem, Haji, father of Haji Ebrāhim Khān, 97, 129
Hāshem ᶜEvażi Lāri, Mirzā, 301 seq.
Hāshem Khān, Haji, nephew of Āqā Khān-e Nuri, chief magistrate of Fārs, 338
Hāshem Khān-e Bakhteyāri, Haji, 170 seq., 172
Ḥātem oṭ-Ṭā'i, famous for his generosity, 168, 202
Hayyāt Dā'ud, near Bushehr, 32*n*, 398*n*
Hedāyat, *see* Reżā Qoli Khān-e Māzandarāni
Hedāyatollah, Mirzā, motjahed, 165
Hedāyatollāh Khān, governor of Gilān, 14
Hedāyatollāh-e Tafashi, Mirzā, minister of the army, 118
Ḥeidar ᶜAli Khān, nephew of Haji Ebrāhim Khān, envoy to Egypt, 164
Ḥeidar Khān, son of Moḥammad Ḥasan Khān-e Borāzjāni, 392 seq.
Ḥeidar Khān-e Ṭālesh, Mir, governor of Kāzerun, 340
Ḥeidar Qoli Khān-e Qashqā'i, son of Mortażā Qoli Khān Ilbegi, 277
Ḥeidar Qoli Mirzā, 234
Herāt, famous for carpets, 147; campaign to Herāt planned, 250 seq.; second campaign in 1837–1838, 253 seq.; captured in 1856, 319; evacuated after peace treaty of Paris, 334
Herāt-e Morust, 50
Herouābād, in Ādherbāyjān, 11*n*
Ḥeshmat od-Doula ("Magnificence of the Empire"), *see* Moḥammad Ḥosein Mirzā
Hezār, near Shiraz, 34

Hezār Jarib, in Māzandārān, 13

Holāgu Mirzā, son of Ḥasan ^{c}Ali Mirzā Shojā^{c} os-Salṭana, sent to Shiraz, 201; accompanies Farmān-Farmā (I) to Bushehr, 204; appointed governor of Kerman, 216, 218

Holeila, near Bushehr, 323

Homā'ejān, in Fārs, 278

Hormoz, 317

Ḥosām os-Salṭana ("Sharp Sword of the Rule"), *see* Solṭān Morād Mirzā

Ḥosein, sheikh of Damukhi Arabs, 217

Ḥosein, Ra'is, brother of Aḥmad Shāh Khān, 205

Ḥosein ^{c}Ali Khān, master of the imperial mint, 174

Ḥosein ^{c}Ali Mirzā Farmān-Farmā (I), governor of Fārs, son of Fatḥ ^{c}Ali Shāh, his birth, 36; stays at Adinabāzār, 73; returns to Tehran, 75; marries daughter of Amir Guna Khān, 91; appointed governor of Fārs, 91 seq.; attends marriage of ^{c}Abbās Mirzā, 104; manufactures guns at Shiraz, 109; receives Sir Harford Jones, 126; finances of Fārs in state of confusion, 131; receives Sir John Malcolm, 133; sends troops against Vahhābis, 134; opens Achaemenian tombs at Persepolis, 141 seq.; takes blood revenge, 148; travels to Tehran, 167; meets shah at Esfahan, 171 seq.; expels Nuri soldiers from Shiraz, 192 seq.; the shah comes to Shiraz, 195 seq.; accompanies shah as far as Fahleyān, 198; marches to Bushehr; his wives, 201 seq.; 204 seff.; returns to Shiraz, 206 seq.; appoints his son governor of Dārāb, 207, another son governor of Sab^{c}a, 208; undertakes campaign to Kerman, 210; deposes Moshir ol-Molk, 213; marches to Bam and Narmāshir, 214; refuses to occupy Yazd, 215; appoints governor of Kerman, 216; takes measures against Moshir ol-Molk, 219; subdues the Qashqā'i khāns, 223 seq.; violates shrine at Shiraz, 224 seq.; reconciliation with Moshir ol-Molk, 226; meets shah at Esfahan, 228; refuses to go to Tehran after shah's death, 231; revolts against Moḥammad Shāh, 233 seq.; arrested, dies in Tehran, 239; list of his sons, 240; his buildings at Shiraz, 241; appoints son governor of Kuh-e Giluya, 296*n*

Ḥosein ^{c}Ali Shāh Eṣfahāni, Sufi, 161

Ḥosein ol-Bokhāri, 401

Ḥosein-e Farāhāni (Vafā), Mirzā, vizier of Karim Khān Vakil, 89

Ḥosein Khān, Sheikh, uncle of Naṣr Khān, deputy governor of Bushehr, 294 seq.

Ḥosein Khān-e Bavir Aḥmadi, 380

Ḥosein Khān-e Dashti, 333

Ḥosein Khān Neẓām od-Doula, governor of Fārs, repairs Masjed-e Vakil, 266; appointed governor of Fārs, 274; repairs irrigation canal, 275, 278 seq.; travels to Tehran, receives title "Neẓām od-Doula," 277; fights rebels at Shiraz upon Moḥammad Shāh's death, 283 seq.

Ḥosein Khān-e Qājār Qazvini, commander in chief, 78, 104 seq.
Ḥosein Khān Ṣāḥeb Ekhteyār Neẓām od-Doula, *see* Hosein Khān Nezām od-Doula.
Ḥosein Khān Sepahsālār, Haji Mirzā, appointed grand vizier, 374; announces reforms, 375; accompanies shah to Europe, 378; renounces office on return, appointed governor of Gilān, 379
Ḥosein Qoli Beg, 90
Ḥosein Qoli Dombali, governor of Khoy and Tabriz, 40
Ḥosein Qoli Khān, father of Fatḥ ᶜAli Shāh, at Karim Khān Vakil's court, governor of Dāmghān, 4; murdered by Turkomans, 5
Ḥosein Qoli Khān, nephew of Āqā Moḥammad Shāh, accompanies shah on campaign to Khorasan, 69; left with crown prince Fatḥ ᶜAli Khān at Adinabāzār, 73; goes to Tehran, 75; appointed governor of Fārs, 79; joins Fatḥ ᶜAli Shāh, 81; his character analyzed, 82; imprisons nobles of Fārs, 82 seq.; marches to Farāhān, 84; reconciled, appointed governor of Semnān, 85 seq.; alleged letters of Haji Ebrāhim Khān to him, 98; governor of Kāshān, rebels again, 100; appointed governor of Qom, then sent to a village near Tehran in exile, 101
Ḥosein Qoli Khān, governor of Baku, 111
Ḥosein Qoli Khān-e Kort Beglu Mir Panj, governor of Khesht, 384
Ḥosein Qoli Khān-e ᶜEzz od-Dinlu, 80
Ḥosein-e Tangestāni, 204 seq.
Ḥouż-e Solṭān, near Qom, 59
Hyderabad/Decan, 129

Ilbegi ("leader of the tribe"), *see* Moḥammad Qoli Khān-e Qashqā'i; Mortażā Qoli Khān
Ilkhani ("khān of the tribe"), *see* Jāni Khān-e Qashqā'i; Moḥammad ᶜAli Khān-e Qashqā'i; Solṭān Moḥammad Khān
Imāni Khān, governor of Farāhān, 98, 149
Inālu, tribe in Fārs, agreement with Qashqā'i, 209; Inālu detachment, 336; rise in rebellion, 340 seq., 363 seq.; Inālu horsemen, 418; *see also* Five Tribes
India, Ismaili sect, 38*n*; jewels from India, 70; East India Company, 91, 94 seq., 121 seq., 125, 132 seq.; Persian ambassador killed in Bombay, 106; plague from India strikes Persia, 166; threatened by Persian occupation of Herāt, 256 seq.; a merchant from Shiraz in Bombay, 306
Iraj Mirzā, son of Farmān-Farmā (I), 240
Irakli II (Erakli Khān), king of Georgia, 66 seq.
ᶜIsā-ye Farāhāni, Mirzā, *see* Bozorg Qā'em Maqām
Ishpokhdur, *see* Zizianov
Isin, near Bandar ᶜAbbās, 315
Istanbul, 164, 169
Izadkhvāst (Aulād-e ᶜAli), south of Esfahan, 9, 235, 336*n*, 360 seq.

Jabbāra Khān-e Kangani, Sheikh, 269
Jaᶜfar, Āqā Seiyed (Eṣṭahbānāti), 290, 294
Jaᶜfar Khān, son of Qāder Khān-e

^{c}Arab, his daughter married to Fatḥ ^{c}Ali Shāh, 16, 36
Ja^{c}far Khān-e Bayyāt, governor of Nishāpur, 89 seq., 93
Ja^{c}far Khān-e Dārābi, lord of Dārāb, 57
Ja^{c}far Khān-e Khormuji, Mirzā, 204 seq., 206
Ja^{c}far Khān-e Zand, half-brother of ^{c}Ali Morād Khān, brother of Ṣādeq Khān, 7; rules over southern Persia 1784–1788, 20–31; his murder, 31, 41
Ja^{c}far Mostoufi-ye Savādkuhi, Mirzā, vizier of Fārs, 253, 262, 264
Ja^{c}far-e Najafi, Sheikh, mojtahed, 119, 127
Ja^{c}far Qoli Khān, brother of Āqā Moḥammad Shāh, brought to Qazvin, 4; defeats army of ^{c}Ali Morād Khān-e Zand, 11; conquers Khamsa, 15; defeats Zand army of Rostam Khān, 19; stationed at Esfahan, 25; defeats khan of Ṭabas, pretender to the throne, 28; accompanies shah on first campaign to Shiraz, 34; his pretensions to the throne, murdered, 38 seq.
Ja^{c}far Qoli Khān, Qarāchadāghi general, 234, 246
Ja^{c}far Qoli Khān, commander of the artillery, 337
Ja^{c}far Qoli Khān-e Dombali, chief of rebels, 81
Ja^{c}far Qoli Mirzā, son of Moḥammad Vāli Mirzā, appointed governor of tribes, 340
Ja^{c}farābād, village near Shiraz, 47
Jahāngir Khān, brother of Seiyed Morād Khān-e Zand, 31
Jahāngir Khān-e Qashqā'i, son of Moḥammad ^{c}Ali Khān Ilkhāni, 221
Jahāngir Khān-e Sistāni, lord of Bam and Narmāshir, 58, 61 seq.
Jahāngir Mirzā, son of Farmān-Farmā (I), governor of Dārāb, 207, 240
Jahāngiriya, district in Fārs, 344
Jahrom, in Fārs, home of family of Mirzā ^{c}Abd ol-Vahhāb, 191, 192*n*; visited by governor of Fārs, 270, 307, 362 seq.; governors mentioned, 228*n*, 307, 318, 340, 387; encroachments by Inālu tribe, 416
Jā'iki Bakhteyāri, tribe, 26
Jājarm, in Khorasan, 155
Jalāl od-Din Mirzā, son of Kāmrān Mirzā, governor of Farāḥ, 258
Jalāl od-Doula ("Majesty of the Empire"), *see* Solṭān Ḥosein Mirzā
Jalāl od-Doula Mirzā, son of Mo'eiyed od-Doula, governor of Lārestān, 318
Jamāl Khān-e Shirāzi, vizier of Sheikh ^{c}Abd or-Rasul Khān, 206, 212
Jān, Mirzā, mostoufi of Herāt, 255
Jandaq, 24
Jān Moḥammad Khān-e Qājār, sent with army to Fārs, 50; enters Shiraz, 51; pulls down citadel of Shiraz, 56; sent to Lārestān, 79; flees to Persian ^{c}Erāq, 83
Jani, Mirzā, brother of Lord Mayor Mirzā Moḥammad, 10, 83, 197
Jāni-ye Fāsā'i, Mirzā, uncle of Ḥasan-e Fasā'i, governor of Esfahan, 24; aids Loṭf ^{c}Ali Khān, 33; sends hostages to Tehran, 56; appointed counselor of crown prince, 64; accompanies crown prince to Tehran, 77; arrested and murdered by Ḥosein Qoli Khān, 82 seq.

Jāni Khān-e Qashqā'i Ilkhāni, ilbegi, appointed ilkhāni, 160; sent to settle affairs of the Qashqā'i, 163
Jāni-ye Qiri (Sā'el), Āqā, governor of Qir va-Kārzin, 114, 116
Jarir, the poet, 420
Jāshk, near Bandar ᶜAbbās, 315
Javād Khān-e Qājār Zeyādlu, governor of Ganja, 107
Javānshir, tribe, 66
Javāshem, Arab tribe on Persian Gulf, 145, 154, 217
Jāvidi, *see* Mamassani
Jiroft, in Kerman, 64
Jochi Khān, son of Chingis Khān, 108
John IV, prince regent of Portugal, 138*n*
Jones, Captain, 320
Jouhar, Haji Āqā, chief eunuch, 240
Juyom, in Fārs, 47, 86, 223*n*, 288*n*

Kabud Jāma, *see* Astarābād
Kadkhodā, *see* Moḥammad Kāẓem Khān-e Shirāzi
Kahak, *see* Qohestān
Kāki, in southern Fārs, 393
Kakuya, near Lar in southern Fārs, 270*n*
Kām Firuz, in Fārs, 250
Kamara, district southeast of Arāk/Solṭānābād, 85
Kamārej, near Kāzerun, 45
Kamin, district in Fārs, 87, 336*n*, 387*n*
Kamiz, castle in southern Fārs, 307
Kāmrān Mirzā, son of Farmān-Farmā (I), 240
Kāmrān Mirzā, governor of Herāt, 255 seq., 258
Kanāra Gerd, near Tehran, 78, 239 seq.
Kandahār, 58, 93
Kangān, in southern Fārs, 223, 402
Karabagh, Qājār campaign to Karabagh, 65, 72, 109, 111, 177; governor appointed, 110; occupied by Russia, 124 seq., 130, 174, 183, 185; ceded to Russia, 143*n*; submits to Russia voluntarily, 151
Karaj, near Tehran, 15*n*, 148*n*, 161
Karim Khān-e Bidshehri, 223 seq.
Karim Khān Vakil, Zand ruler (1750–1779), honors Qājār princes at his court, 4; his death, 5; list of his sons, 6; sends Ṣādeq Khān to Basra, 7*n*; last will and testament, 36*n*; builds Masjed-e Vakil at Shiraz, 47*n*; his offspring of the Lak, 52*n*; his sepulcher at Shiraz, transferred to Tehran, then to Najaf, 55, 70; builds citadel at Shiraz, 56; jewels in his possession, 63; changes administrative division of Shiraz, 92*n*; builds irrigation canals, 395 seq.
Kars, in Turkey, 136
Kāshān, Zand army defeated near Kāshān, 22; governed by Qājār prince, 100, 240*n*; visited by Fatḥ ᶜAli Shāh, 135, 159
Kavār, in Fārs, 86, 387*n*, 393
Kāẓem-e Bāzār-e Morghi, citizen of Shiraz, 265
Kāẓemein, near Baghdad, murder of Akhbāri theologian, 113; visited by Nāṣer od-Ḍin Shāh, 368, 371 seq.; building erected by governor of Fārs, 412
Kāzerun, governor subdued by Zand, 25; battle between Zand and Qājār army, 47; Qanāt-e Qarācha, 88*n*; earthquake, 170; Bāgh-e Naẓar, visited by Fatḥ ᶜAli Shāh, 197; visited by governor of Fārs, 205; fief of Farmān-Farmā's spouse, 219;

plundered by Mamassani tribe, 244; governors mentioned, 340, 352; home of experienced canal builders, 354
Kazzāz, district near Arāk/Solṭānābād, 20, 186
Kedar, son of Ishmael, 140
Kei Khosrou Mirzā Sepahsālār, son of Farmān-Farmā (I), his mother mentioned, career after return to Persia, 240*n*
Kerbelā, sacked by Vahhābis, 101, 103; ulema give fetvā for Holy War, 127; burial of grand vizier, 159; residence of "Pole" of Sufi order, 161*n*; exile of disgraced officials, 220; shrine of Ḥosein and ᶜAbbās, 371; visited by Nāṣer od-Din Shāh, 371 seq.
Kerman, in Zand possession, 8, 10, 28*n*; besieged by Zand army, 37 seq.; governor mentioned, 28*n*, 38*n*, 196, 216, 218, 253, 271, 310; conquered by Loṭf ᶜAli Khān, 58 seq., by Āqā Moḥammad Shāh, 59 seq.; slaughter of inhabitants, 61; Solṭāniya Gate, 61; Zoroastrian astrologer, 62; affairs settled, 200, 222; tribes of Fārs move to Kerman, 208 seq.; citadel captured, 215; ravaged by highway robbers, 388*n*
Kermānshāh, governors mentioned, 116, 119, 130, 150, 199, 252, 415, 418; vizier mentioned, 116, 234
Keyāsar, in Māzandārān, 13*n*
Khabushān, in Khorasan, 91, 156 seq.
Khafr, in Fārs, 86, 336*n*, 416
Khafrki, *see* Mirzā Moḥammad ᶜAli Shirāzi
Khāk-e ᶜAli, near Qazvin, 19
Khāksār, Sufi order, 161*n*
Khalᶜat Pushān, near Bushehr, 322, 324
Khalfān Khān-e ᶜAslu'i, Sheikh, 269
Khalil Khān-e Koroghlu Qazvini Malek ot-Tojjār, Haji, envoy to India, 95, 105; killed by accident at Bombay, 106; married to sister of Moḥammad Nabi Khān, 132
Khalkhāl, region near Ardebil, 11, 24*n*
Khallār, in Fārs, 278
Khālu, *see* Moḥammad ᶜAli Khān-e Qājār Qoyunlu
Khamsa, conquered by Zand army, 11; Qājār conquest, 15; revolts against Qājārs, 25; shah marches to Khamsa, 37; royal court at Khamsa, 46
Khān ᶜAli Khān, mayor of the Rostam tribe, 268, 271
Khān-e Jan, Haji, *see* Mirzā Faridun
Khān-e Lor Māzandārān, Mirzā, chancellor of the empire, 191
Khān Mirzā, in Fārs, 163
Khān-e Qājār, Amir, governor of Ganja, 178
Khān-e Zenjān, village near Shiraz, 218 seq.
Khārk, island in the Persian Gulf, provisions brought from Bushehr to Khārk, 205; occupied by English troops, 260 seq.; refuge of lord of Bushehr, 289; visited and described by Ḥasan-e Fasā'i, 400 seq.
Kharqān, in Ādherbāyjān, 182 seq., 184
Kheir, in Fārs, 57, 216
Kheirābād, in Fārs, 198, 403
Kheirollāh Khān, son of Moḥammad Zaki Khān-e Nuri, 193
Khesht, village near Bushehr, 45, 205, 248*n*, 384
Khezānadārlu, ancestors of Qājārs, 2

Khir, in Fārs, 57, 216
Khodādād-e Eṣfahāni, valet of Āqā Moḥammad Shāh, 73, 79
Khodā Karam Khān-e Bavir Aḥmadi, 319, 412
Khonj, in southern Fārs, 226, 270
Khorasan, Afshār capital Mashhad, 16*n*; alleged conspiracy of khāns in favor of Ja^cfar Qoli Khān, 39; Qājār claim to Khorasan, 68; campaigns to Khorasan, 69 seq., 80 seq., 92 seq., 150, 155, 164 seq.; hostages sent to Tehran, 71; governors mentioned, 79, 131, 166 seq., 222 seq., 227, 251, 345; conquest of Khorasan, 103 seq.; stipulations regarding Khorasan in treaty with France, 121; manufacture of swords, 147; head of tribes styled "ilkhāni," 160; governor plans revolt, 166 seq.; crown prince sent to Khorasan, 200, 210*n*, 228; ravaged by plague, 251; Khorasani soldiers, 254; domicile assigned to Afghan emirs, 260 seq.; *see also* Mashhad
Khormuj, in southern Fārs, 393, 399
Khorramābād, 198
Khorramshehr, 26*n*, 236*n*
Khosh Yeilaq, near Dāmghān, 165, 254
Khosrav-e Shirin, district in Fārs, 33
Khosrou, black slave, 224
Khosrou Khān-e Zand, brother of of Lotf ᶜAli Khān, 37, 42
Khosrou Mirzā, son of ᶜAbbās Mirzā, 179, 190
Khour, village south of Qomesha, 225*n*
Khoy, 40, 81, 181
Khub Yār Khan-e Mamassani, 245
Khuzestān (ᶜArabestān-e Irān), Arab tribes, 26*n*; Saljuqid vizier mentioned, 88; named ᶜArabestān, 197*n*; governors mentioned, 252, 270, 297, 350, 415, 418
Khvāja, district in Fārs, 86
Khvāja Vand, Kurdish tribe, 178
Khvānsār, district in Fārs, 267, 415, 418
Khvārezm, 3, 63*n*, 155, 158
Kinneir, English instructor, 227
Kinneir, Sir John Macdonald, 177, 184
Kirovabad, *see* Ganja
Kohandel Khan-e Afghān, brother of Dust Moḥammad, 258
Korbāl, region near Persepolis, 216, 387*n*
Kordon, near Esfahan, 21
Koshan, near Shiraz, 35, 51
Kotal-e Dokhtar, 218*n*
Kuchek, Mirzā, governor of Mamassani, 269
Kuchek Vaṣṣāl-e Shirāzi, poet, 273
Kuh-e Giluya, Zand campaign, 25 seq.; submits to Qājār army, 36; governors mentioned, 81, 86, 98, 100, 207*n*, 221, 271, 289 seq., 196*n*, 299, 300, 312, 335, 339 seq., 345 seq., 348, 351 seq., 367, 380 seq., 383 seq., 389, 392, 394, 417, 419; occupied by local ruler, 207; eastern border described, 247; castles of Gol and Golāb, 248 seq.; inhabitants neglect payment of taxes, 268 seq.; quarrels about governorship, 296 seq.; successful administration, 348 seq.; *see also* Behbehān
Kuh-e Marra, district in Fārs, 86, 218
Kuhpāya, near Esfahan, 27
Kurdistan, occupied by the Zand, 20; visited by Nāṣer od-Din Shāh,

341; governor mentioned, 367, 415, 418
Kushk-e Bibi Chāh, near Shiraz, 49
Kushk-e Kenār, in southern Fārs, 31
Kushk-e Zard, in Fārs, 29, 59
Kuweit, 145*n*

Lak, Kurdish tribe, 4*n*, 52*n*, 178*n*
Lakz (Lakziya), people in southern Dāghestān, 21
Lār, Lārestān, governors mentioned, 27, 27*n*, 208, 210, 243, 253, 307, 312, 318, 336, 339, 343, 345, 352, 359, 364 seq., 387, 399, 417, 419; subdued by Zand army, 28; conquered by Qājār crown prince, 64; affairs settled by governor of Fārs, 79, 273, 301, 394; troops of Lārestān fight Vahhābis in ᶜOmān, 134; Vahhābis in coastal area subdued, 153; musketeers from Lārestān support governor of Fārs, 213; encroachments on district of Dārāb, 261; exempted from taxes for delivery of gun powder, 270; subdued by governor of Fārs, 336 seq.; winter quarters of Bahārlu, 336*n*; Bandar ᶜAbbās added to Lārestān, 362, 387; highway robbery, 388*n*; *see also* Sabᶜa
Lārijān, 12, 14, 17, 299
Lāvari, tribe in Lārestān, 344
Lindsay-Bethune, Sir Henry, 216, 234 seq., 234*n*
Lirāvi, region of Bandar Deilam, 25, 247, 349, 381, 398*n*
Lishtarr, in Kuh-e Giluya, 198
Lor, tribe in Fārs, in the service of the Zand, 15; Lors at Esfahan, 170; attack Qājār army, 221; punished by governor of Fārs, 245*n*, 246 seq.; defend Bushehr, 294; a group settles down at Shiraz, 343; united by governor of Behbehān, 349
Lorestān (Lorestān-e Fili), 98, 100, 197, 234, 252, 343, 418
Loṭf ᶜAli Khān, son of Jaᶜfar Khān, Zand ruler, 1789–1794, given title Jahānbāni, sent to Lārestān, 28; sent to Galladār, 30 seq.; assumes rule, 32 seq.; defeated by Qājār army, 34 seq.; undertakes campaign to Kerman, 37 seq.; change of attitude toward Haji Ebrāhim Khān, 40 seq.; marches to Esfahan, his army revolts, 42 seq.; marches to the Persian Gulf, 44 seq.; defeats Qājār army near Kāzerun, 46 seq.; puts up camp at Masjed-e Bardi, 47; occupies Zarqān, 48; fails to recapture Shiraz, 50 seq.; goes to Ṭabas, 55; conquers Kerman, 56 seq.; gives up Kerman, 60 seq.; his flight and death, 61 seq.; hands over jewels to Qājārs, 63
Loṭf ᶜAli Khān-e Firuzābādi, 47
Loṭf ᶜAli Khān-e Qashqā'i Sartip, 328
Loṭf ᶜAli Mirzā, son of Ṭahmāsp Mirzā, governor of Behbehān, 312, 335, 339
Loṭf ᶜAli Shirāzi, son of Moḥammad ᶜAli Khān Ilkhāni, 301
Loṭfollāh Mostoufi-ye Shirāzi, governor of Sabᶜa, 336

Mac Mahon, French president, 395*n*
Mac Neill, Sir John, English ambassador, 256 seq., 258
Madā'en, in ᶜErāq, 370
Madatov, V. G., Russian general, 178 seq.
Madhkur Khān-e Kangani, Sheikh, 392 seq., 397, 401 seq.
Māfi, Kurdish tribe, 9*n*, 52

Maḥallāt, region south of Qom, 257*n*
Mahān (Mahun), near Kerman, 60, 60*n*
Mahārlu, in Fārs, 5
Mahdi, Mirzā, secretary of the Zand army, 41
Mahdi, Mirzā, mojtahed at Mashhad, 69, 104 seq.
Mahdi ᶜAli Khān-e Khorāsāni, Mirzā, ambassador of the British governor general of India, 91
Mahdi Khān, Mirzā, brother of Nāẓem ol-Molk, 288 seq.
Mahdi Khān-e Nehāvandi, 321 seq.
Mahdi Qoli Mirzā, son of Moḥammad Mirzā Vāli, governor of Dārāb, 340; then governor of Lārestān, 343; marches to Bastak, 344; governor of Sabᶜa and Lārestān again, 352; sent to conquer Bandar ᶜAbbās, 359 seq., 361; appointed governor of Bandar ᶜAbbās, 364
Maḥjub ᶜAli Shāh, Sufi, 162*n*
Maḥmud, Dorrāni ruler of Afghanistan, 255*n*
Maḥmud, Haji, grandfather of Haji Ebrāhim Khān, 96
Maḥmud II, Ottoman sultan, 135, 164, 169
Maḥmud Khān, 234
Maḥmud Khān-e Afghān, son of Āzād Khān, 11
Māhur-e Milāti, district in Fārs, 247, 248 seq., 250, 275
Majnun Khān-e Pazuki, 23
Makku, in southern Fārs, 270
Malcolm, Sir John Badādur, quoted, 42, 54; ambassador to Persia, 94 seq.; travels to India, 95, 106; second mission to Persia, 125; third mission, 133 seq.
Mamassani, Lor tribe in Kuh-e Giluya, punished by the Zand, 25; Shulestān their home, 34, 275; the district and its capital, 197, 248*n*; governor appointed, 208; plunder family of Moshir ol-Molk, 221; chiefs subdued, 268 seq., 300 seq.
——*groups:* Bakash, 208, 244; Rostam, 271; Jāvidi (Jāvi), 299*n*; Doshmanzeyāri, 299*n*; plunder Bakhteyāri, 319
Manṣur Khān-e Behbehāni, Mirzā, son of Solṭān Moḥammad Khān, occupies Behbehān, 207; helps Moshir ol-Molk on flight, 221; confirmed in office, 243; welcomes Firuz Mirzā, 249; a case of blood revenge in his family, 380
Manṣur Khān-e Farāhāni, in Firuz Mirzā's army, 234; escorts Farmān-Farmā (I) to Tehran, 239; sent to collect taxes at Behbehān, 269
Manuchehr Khān-e Gorji Moᶜtamad od-Doula, chief chamberlain, 185; sent to Torkmānchāy, 185; given title "Moᶜtamad od-Doula," 191; sent to subdue Farmān-Farmā (I), 234 seq.; vizier of Fārs, 251 seq.; stays at Esfahan, 269; governor of ᶜArabestān and Shoshtar, 270
Manuchehr Mirzā, son of Farmān-Farmā (I), 240
Marāgha, in Ādherbāyjān, 24*n*, 81
Marand, near Tabriz, 24*n*, 181
Marv, 251*n*
Marvdasht, district in Fārs, 52 seq., 55, 142, 336*n*, 346*n*
Mashhad, shrine of Emām Reżā, 8*n*; Afshār capital of Khorasan, 16*n*; conquered by Qājārs, 69; shrine renovated, 71; authority

of Nāder Mirzā re-established, 89; besieged by Qājār army, 91, 104; conquered by Qājārs, 105; shrine visited by the shah, 158, 261, 358; shrine presented with gift, 165; mayor appointed by the shah, 345, 353; administrator of shrine appointed, 348; *see also* Khorasan
Mashhad-e Mādar-e Soleimān (Mashhad-e Omm on-Nabi, Mashhad-e Morghāb), 29, 352*n*
Masiḥ, Mirzā, physician from Esfahan, 50
Masjed-e Bardi, town near Shiraz, 35, 47 seq., 51, 396
Masjed-e Soleimān, in Khuzestan, 26*n*
Masqaṭ, 134 seq., 202 seq., 311, 344, 358
Maᶜṣum Khān-e Inālu, 209, 213
Maᶜṣum-e Kheżri, Āqā, 83
Māzandārān, conquered by Qājārs, 5 seq.; Zand attack fails, 16 seq.; Ditch of Golbād, 17; soldiers called "Jānbāz," 122; visited by the shah, 155, 385, 402 seq., 419; soldiers sent to southern Persia, 271
Mazinān, in Khorasan, 93
Mecca, 163 seq.
Medina, 103, 163 seq.
Mehr ᶜAli Khān, chief of the guard of ᶜAli Morād Khān, 19
Mehr ᶜAli Khān-e Nuri Shojāᶜ ol-Molk, commander of the Shirāzi horsemen, 293; fights against Bābis, 294; governor of Behbehān, 300; included into treaty with Imam of Masqaṭ, 300; receives envoys from Masqaṭ in his house at Shiraz, 318; marches against British troops at Bushehr, 321 seq., 327, 329 seq., 332; promoted to rank of Amir-e Tumān, 335; mediates for Naṣrollāh Khān-e Lāri, 338; appointed governor of Bushehr, Dashti, and Dashtestān, 345
Meḥrāb Khān, 133 seq.
Mehrebān, in Ādherbāyjān, 181
Meyān Kotal, near Kāzerun, 218*n*, 373
Meyāna, in Ādherbāyjān, 80*n*, 180
Mināb, near Bandar ᶜAbbas, 306, 312, 315, 362, 377
Mo'eiyed od-Doula ("Strengthener of the Empire"), *see* Ṭahmāsp Mirzā; Bahrām Mirzā
Moᶜezz od-Doula ("Glorifier of the Empire"), *see* Bahrām Mirzā
Mofid-e Astarābādi, Seiyed, Āqā Moḥammad Shāh born in his house, 3
Mogadishu, 310*n*
Moghān, in Ādherbāyjān, 65, 67
Moghestān-e ᶜAbbāsi, region east of Bandar ᶜAbbās, 403
Moḥammad, Āqā Seiyed, mojtahed, son of Āqā Seiyed ᶜAli, 174 seq., 180
Moḥammad, Mirzā, lord mayor of Shiraz, author of "Rūznama," quoted, 9 seq., 20 seq., 23; dies in Tehran, 97
Moḥammad, Mirzā Seiyed, son of Ḥasan-e Fasā'i, 399
Moḥammad, Seiyed, son of sultan of Masqaṭ, 317
Moḥammad ᶜAli, son of Jāni Khān-e Qashqā'i, appointed ilbegi, 160
Moḥammad ᶜAli, son of Āqā Abu'l-Ḥasan Khān, 380
Moḥammad ᶜAli, from Lārestān, 28
Moḥammad ᶜAli, Haji (Tājer-e Kabab), vizier of Masqaṭ, 314 seq.

Moḥammad ᶜAli, Haji Mirzā, chief servant at Masjed-e Vakil of Shiraz, 412
Moḥammad ᶜAli Jāberi Anṣāri Eṣfahāni, Mirzā, chief of Fasā, 345 seq.
Moḥammad ᶜAli Khān, brother of Haji Ebrāhim Khān, 43 seq., 51
Moḥammad ᶜAli Khān, son of Aḥmad Shāh Khān-e Tangestāni, 205, 217
Moḥammad ᶜAli Khān, Mirzā, brother of Fatḥ ᶜAli Khān Ṣabā, scribe of Loṭf ᶜAli Khān, 61
Moḥammad ᶜAli Khān, Mirzā, son-in-law of Moshir ol-Molk, 220
Moḥammad ᶜAli Khān-e Eṣfahāni, 172
Moḥammad ᶜAli Khān Nāẓem ol-Molk, Mirzā, 288, 307, 318
Moḥammad ᶜAli Khān-e Qājār Qoyunly (Khālu), governor of Fārs, 80; conducts corpse of Āqā Moḥammad Shāh to Najaf, 86
Moḥammad ᶜAli Khān-e Qashqā'i Ilkhāni, son-in-law of Farmān-Farmā (I), 173; arrests Bakhteyāri robbers, 196; enmity between him and Qavām ol-Molk, 206 seq., 213, 220; leads Qashqā'i tribes to Kerman, 208 seq.; orders tribes to return to Fārs, 213; arrested, his houses plundered, 224; released, 225; refuses to pay hommage to Farmān-Farmā (I), 237; his house plundered again, 238; summoned before the shah, 251; allowed to return, stays in Tehran, 252; returns to Shiraz thirteen years later, 287
Moḥammad ᶜAli Khān-e Sistāni, 61 seq., 63
Moḥammad ᶜAli Khān-e Tabrizi, governor of Jahrom etc., 340
Moḥammad ᶜAli Khān-e Zand, 37, 40, 43
Moḥammad ᶜAli Mirzā Qavām ol-Khelāfa, son of Fatḥ ᶜAli Shāh, his birth, 35; appointed governor of Fārs, 77; summoned to Tehran, 79; governor of Kermānshāh, 119; sent on campaign to Tiflis, 130; settles affairs of the Two ᶜErāqs, 137; meets shah at Solṭāniya, 150, 159
Moḥammad ᶜAli Moshir ol-Molk, Mirzā, vizier of Fārs, receives title Moshir ol-Molk, 196; accompanies Farmān-Farmā (I) to Bushehr, 204; tribes of Fārs his opponents, 209; the ilkhāni demands his deposal, 213; accused of peculation and fined, 219 seq.; goes to Esfahan, 221; reappointed vizier of Fārs, 226 seq.; given administrative duties after Farmān-Farmā's revolt, 243; appointed vizier of Fārs again after many years of retirement, 274; his death, 276
Moḥammad ᶜAli Pāshā, Ottoman governor of Egypt (1805–1848), the shah sends him a gift, 163
Moḥammad ᶜAli-ye Shirāzi (Khafrki), Mirzā, intendant of Fārs, 172, 192; ambassador of governor of Sind, 199
Moḥammad ᶜAli Solṭān-e Shirāzi, 217
Moḥammad Amin, Sheikh, sheikh ol-eslām of Fārs, 210 seq., 213
Moḥammad Amin Khān-e Shabankāra, son of Aḥmad Shāh Khān-e Tangestāni, 211
Moḥammad Bāqer, Ra'is, son of Ḥosein-e Tangestāni, 204 seq.

Moḥammad Bāqer-e Kāshāni, Āqā, vizier of Fārs, 152, 158
Moḥammad Bāqer Khān, beglerbegi of Tehran, 240
Moḥammad Bāqer Khān, alderman of the Jāvi tribe in Kuh-e Giluya, 299
Moḥammad Bāqer Khan, Haji, governor of Jahrom etc., 387; governor of Bushehr, 297, 398 seq.
Moḥammad Bāqer-e Majlesi, famous theologian of Safavid times, 221
Moḥammad Bāqer Mollā Bāshi, Mirzā, 192
Moḥammad Ebrāhim Beg, 402
Moḥammad Ebrāhim Khān Sehām ol-Molk Miri Sartip, 328
Moḥammad Esmāᶜil Khān, son of Haji Khalil Khān, lives in London and Paris, 106
Moḥammad-e Farāhāni Qavām od-Doula, Mirzā, vizier of Fārs, 348, 350 seq.
Moḥammad-e Fasā'i, Āqā Mirzā, son of Mirzā Hādi, governor of Dārābgerd, 196; brother of Moḥammad Ḥosein Vakil, 210 seq., 214; governor of Ḥumā-ye Shiraz etc., 216; arrested and sent to Tehran, released, enters service of the court, 243; accuses governor of Fārs, 251; returns to Shiraz, appointed governor of Fasā, Dārāb etc., 253, 261, 291; confirmed in office, further districts added, 276; bans Bābi missionary from Fasā, 290 seq.; flees to Tehran, returns later, 309, 318; sent on difficult mission, 319; promises to provision troops at Bushehr, 327
Moḥammad Ḥasan Āqā, alderman at Shiraz, 264 seq.
Moḥammad Ḥasan Khān, father of Āqā Moḥammad Shāh, 2 seq., 4, 66
Moḥammad Ḥasan Khān-e ᶜArab ᶜĀmeri, governor of Jandaq, 24
Moḥammad Ḥasan Khān-e Borāzjāni, mayor of Borāzjān, 324 seq., 330, 393
Moḥammad Ḥasan Khān-e Māfi, brother of Ḥosein Qoli Khān Saᶜd ol-Molk, 393
Moḥammad Ḥasan Khān Sardār-e Erevāni, governor of Kerman, 310
Moḥammad Ḥasan Khān-e Sistāni, ruler of Bam, 8, 37*n*
Moḥammad Ḥasan-e Lārijāni, Mirzā, scholar from Shiraz, 407
Moḥammad Ḥasan-e Qazvini, Haji, theologian, 127
Moḥammad Hāshem Khān, Haji, chief magistrate of the empire, 327
Moḥammad Hāshem Khān-e Kheshti, Haji, 333
Moḥammad Hāshem Khān-e Nuri Amir ol-Omarā, Haji, 404
Moḥammad Ḥosein, Mirzā, physician of the shah, 198
Moḥammad Ḥosein-e Eṣfahāni, Haji, Sufi, 161 seq.
Moḥammad Ḥosein-e Farāhāni, Mirzā, vizier of Fārs, 32 seq.
Moḥammad Ḥosein-e Hamadāni, Mirzā, vizier of Fārs, 339, 343
Moḥammad Ḥosein Kamāl Khān, Āqā, citizen of Shiraz, 264 seq.
Moḥammad Ḥosein Khān, brother of Haji Ebrāhim Khān, 43; governor of Kuh-e Giluya, 81, 98; killed after deposal of his father, 99, 296*n*

Moḥammad Ḥosein Khān Amin od-Doula Mostoufi ol-Mamālek, Haji, governor of Esfahan, 100; minister of finance, 117; seals treaty with France, 122; English ambassador put up in his house, 126, 138; inquiries into financial affairs of Fārs, 131, 144; intercedes in favor of ᶜAli Akbar Qavām ol-Molk, 142; granted title Neẓām od-Doula, 144; appointed prime minister, 159; his death, 167; his career, 167 seq.
Moḥammad Ḥosein Khān-e Garrusi, 24
Moḥammad Ḥosein Khān-e Qājār Devehlu, beglerbegi of Astarābād, 4
Moḥammad Ḥosein Khān-e Qājār Qoyunlu (Dudāgh), cousin of Āqā Moḥammad Shāh, 57, 75, 109
Moḥammad Ḥosein Khān-e Qaraguzlu, 59
Moḥammad Ḥosein Mirzā Ḥeshmat od-Doula, governor of Kermānshāh, 116, 199
Moḥammad Ḥosein Sheikh ol-Eslām, Haji Sheikh, 351
Moḥammad Ḥosein Solṭān ol-ᶜOlamā, Haji, imam of prayers at Esfahan, 127
Moḥammad Ḥosein Vakil, Mirzā, son of Hādi-ye Fasā'i, 172; granted favors by the shah, 196; deposed from governorship of Fasā and Dārāb, 207; goes to Kerman, 209; received in audience by ᶜAbbās Mirzā, 222; governor of Fasā, 243; accuses governor of Fārs, 251; in the service of the court, 252; his death, 335
Moḥammad ibn Ḥanafiya, hidden on island of Khārk, 400
Moḥammad ibn Saᶜud, ruler of Saudi Arabia (1746–1765), 102*n*
Moḥammad ibn Seif, Sheikh, 135
Moḥammad Jaᶜfar-e Astarābādi, Haji Mollā, mojtahed, 175
Moḥammad Jaᶜfar Khān, brother of Moḥammad Nabi Khān, governor of Dashtestān and Bushehr, 132
Moḥammad Jaᶜfar Khān-e Khormuji, *see* Jaᶜfar Khān-e Khormuji
Moḥammad Jaᶜfar-e Qaraguzlu Hamadāni, Haji, Sufi, 162
Moḥammad Karim Khān-e Qājār, governor of Kuh-e Giluya and Behbehān, 290, 296
Moḥammad Karim Khān Vakil, *see* Karim Khān Vakil
Moḥammad Kāẓem Mirzā, son of Farmān-Farmā (I), 240
Moḥammad Kāẓem-e Shirāzi, Haji, alderman at Shiraz, 274; appointed mayor of Mashad, 345; has knowledge of canal building, 353
Moḥammad Khān, son of Aᶜzam Khān-e Afghān, 58
Moḥammad Khān, son of Naṣir Khān-e Lāri, 27
Moḥammad Khān, Maku'i general, 234
Moḥammad Khān, Mirzā, son of Haji Ebrāhim Khān, tax collector of Fārs, 86; executed, 99
Moḥammad Khān, Mirzā, son of ᶜAli Akbar Qavām ol-Molk, fined by Farmān-Farmā (I), 225; arrested and threatened with death, 233; appointed lord mayor of Shiraz "as before," 237
Moḥammad Khān, Mirzā, son of Amir Khān-e Qājār Devehlu, maternal uncle of ᶜAbbās Mirzā, 234

Moḥammad Khān-e ᶜArab Zangu'i, Amir, governor of Ṭabas, 26 seq., 28
Moḥammad Khān-e Borāzjāni, Haji, son of Aḥmad Shāh-e Tangestāni, 211
Moḥammad Khān-e Dashti, 324, 399
Moḥammad Khān-e ᶜEzz od-Dinlu, grandfather of Fatḥ ᶜAli Shāh, 4
Moḥammad Khān-e Lārijāni, Mirzā, 55
Moḥammad Khān-e Qājār, maternal uncle of Āqā Moḥammad Shāh, 35
Moḥammad Khān-e Qājār Amir ol-Omarā, commander in chief, 327 seq., 332
Moḥammed Khān-e Qājār Devehlu, Amir Mirzā, father-in-law of ᶜAbbās Mirzā, 104, 160
Moḥammad Khān-e Qājār Devehlu, Mirzā, 5, 76, 239
Moḥammad Khān-e Qājār ᶜEzz od-Dinlu, 4, 39
Moḥammad Khān-e Qājār Qoyunlu, governor of Erevan, 107 seq.
Moḥammad Khān-e Qājār Zeyādlu Erevāni, 67
Moḥammad Khān-e Zand, brother of Jaᶜfar Khān, appointed commander of the army, 25; sacks Bani Kaᶜb, 26; sent to Qomesha, 30; guards palace at Shiraz, 42; with Loṭf ᶜAli Khān at Bushehr, 45; in battle with Qājārs, 53
Moḥammad Mirzā, son of Farmān-Farmā (I), 240
Moḥammad Mofid, Sheikh, 83
Moḥammad Mostoufiy-e Neẓām, Mirzā, governor of Bushehr, 417
Moḥammad Nabi Khān-e Shirāzi, ambassador to India, 106, 121; returns to Tehran, 122; appointed vizier of Fārs, 123; removed from office, 131
Moḥammad Nāṣer Khān-e Qājār Devehlu Ẓahir od-Doula, vizier of Fārs, 347, 377; returns to Tehran, 380
Moḥammad-e Nishāpuri, Haji Mirzā, theologian, 111 seq.
Moḥammad ᶜOmar Khān, son of Kohandel Khān-e Afghān, 258, 261
Moḥammad Qāsem Khān-e Beiżā'i 352
Moḥammad Qāsem Khān-e Qājār Qoyunlu, Amir-e Kabir, son of Soleimān Khān Neẓām od-Doula, 163; father-in-law of Moḥammad Shāh, 160, 200, 281
Moḥammad Qāsem Khān Vāli, governor of Fārs, 374, 376
Moḥammad Qāsem Pirānā Vand, 100
Moḥammad Qoli Khān, cousin of Āqā Moḥammad Shāh, 36
Moḥammad Qoli Khān-e Qashqā'i Ilbegi, marries daughter of Qavām ol-Molk, 206; appointed ilbegi, 226; flees to Tehran, 250 seq.; complains about governor of Fārs, 274; stays in Tehran, returns to Shiraz, 277 seq.; rebels against governor of Fārs, 284; meets shah at Esfahan, 300; fights the English at Bushehr, 321, 327, 329; promoted to rank of Amir Panj, 335; summoned to Tehran, 347
Moḥammad Qoli Khān-e Qājār Āṣaf od-Doula, Haji, vizier of Fārs, 367 seq.; summoned to Tehran, 374
Moḥammad Qoli Khān-e Afshār Orumi, father-in-law of Farmān-Farmā (I), 201

Moḥammad Qoli Khān-e Javānshir, 328
Moḥammad Qoli Khān-e Qājār, 34
Moḥammad Qoli Khān-e Qājār Devehlu, son of Allāh Yār Khān-e Astarābādi, 176
Moḥammad Qoli Mirzā, son of Fatḥ ᶜAli Shāh, 35, 73, 75
Moḥammad Raḥim, dyer at Shiraz, 265 seq.
Moḥammad Raḥim Khān, king of Khvārezm, 158
Moḥammad Raḥim Khān-e Shirāzi, Haji, 306
Moḥammad Raḥim Khān-e Zand, son of Moḥammad Karim Khān Vakil, 6 seq.
Moḥammad Reżā Beg-e Zeyārati, 324
Moḥammad Reżā Khān, Mirzā, 297 seq.
Moḥammad Reżā Mirzā, governor of Gilān, 162, 258
Moḥammad Reżā Mostoufi, Mirzā, 347
Moḥammad Reżā-ye Khoy'i, theologian, 174
Moḥammad Reżā-ye Shirāzi, Mirzā, 222
Moḥammad Ṣādeq Khān, 329, 349
Moḥammad Ṣādeq Khān, Haji, son of Ḥosein Qoli Khān, 216
Moḥammad Saᶜid (Āqā Jāni-ye Qiri), Āqā, son of ᶜAbdollāh Khān-e Qiri, 114n
Moḥammad Ṣāleh-e Minābi, Ra'is, 312
Moḥammad Shāh, son of ᶜAbbās Mirzā, his birth, 122; marries Qājār Qoyunlu princess, 160; takes part in Russian War, 178; appointed governor of Ādherbāyjān and Khorasan, 223; summoned to Tehran, appointed crown prince, 227 seq.; his coronation, 232; appoints crown prince, 242; campaign to Herāt, 250 seq.; travels to Esfahan, 267; his death, 280; list of his sons, 281
Moḥammad Ṭāher Khān-e Galladāri, 392
Moḥammad Ṭāher Khān-e Qazvini, 234, 236, 239, 246 seq.
Moḥammad Taqi-ye Āshteyāni, Mirzā, vizier of Fārs, 305, 307
Moḥammad Taqi Khān, son of ᶜAbdollāh Khān-e Qiri, 115
Moḥammad Taqi Khān, governor of Behbehān, 380
Moḥammad Taqi Khān-e Farāhāni, Mirzā, prime minister, 301
Moḥammad Taqi Khān-e Shirāzi, beglerbegi of Fārs, 192*n*
Moḥammad Taqi Mirzā Ḥosām os-Salṭana, son of Fatḥ ᶜAli Shāh, undertakes campaign to Khvārezm, 157; governor of Borujerd, 199; sent to Fārs to collect taxes, 228 seq.; sent to Borujerd by Farmān-Farmā (I), 232
Moḥammad Taqi Mirzā Rokn od-Doula, son of Moḥammad Shāh, 281
Moḥammad Taqi Moustoufi-ye Kāshāni (Sepehr), 148, 301
Moḥammad Taqi Qāvam od-Doula, Mirzā, vizier of Fārs, 251 seq.; 253
Moḥammad Taqi-ye Qazvini, Haji Seiyed, 175
Moḥammad Vali Khān-e Qajar Qoyunlu, 62, 71, 79
Moḥammad Vali Mirzā, son of Fatḥ ᶜAli Shāh, 35; governor of Khorasan, 104 seq., 131
Moḥammad Ẓāher Khān-e Zand, 17 seq.

Moḥammad Zaki Khān-e Nuri, Mirzā, welcomes English ambassador at Bushehr, 126, 133, 138; leader of campaign to Persian Gulf, 154; accompanies Farmān-Fārmā (I) to audience at Esfahan, 171; vizier, marries sister of Farmān-Farmā, 173; deposed, his family and followers expelled from Shiraz, 192 seq.; vizier of Kerman, 196
Moḥammad Zamān, Āqā, brother of Haji Ebrāhim Khān, lord mayor of Shiraz, 77; imprisoned during Ḥosein Qoli Khān's revolt, 82
Moḥammad Zamān Khān-e Qājār ᶜEzz od-Dinlu, governor of Astarābād, 39, 147
Moḥammara, town in Khuzestān, 268
Moḥsen, Āqā, 82
Molk Āqā, *see* ᶜAbbās Mirzā, son of Moḥammad Shāh
Mo'men-e Reżavi, Seiyed Āqā Mir, 274
Morād ᶜAli, 298 seq.
Morad ᶜAli, Mir, governor of Sind, 199
Morād-e Meidān-e Shāhi, citizen of Shiraz, 265
Morier, deputy of Sir Gore Ouseley, 147
Mortażā Qoli Khān, brother of Āqā Moḥammad Shāh, 4, 6, 12 seq., 17
Mortażā Qoli Khān, lord of Bām, 156
Mortażā Qoli Khān-e Qashqā'i Ilbegi, brother of Moḥammad ᶜAli Khān Ilkhāni, leads tribes to Kerman, 208, 213; returns to Fārs, 214; arrested, died from wounds, 224 seq.
Moscow, visited by Nāṣer od-Din Shāh, 394
Moseiyeb, village near Kerbelā, 371
Moshir ol-Molk ("Counsellor of Kingdom"), *see* Abu'l-Ḥasan Khān; Moḥammad ᶜAli
Moslem-e Erevāni, Mirzā, father of Haji Mirzā Āqāsi, 241
Moslem ibn ᶜAqil, 372
Moṣṭafā Khān-e Bastaki, 309, 342, 344
Moṣṭafā Khān-e Qājār Devehlu, 46, 49, 50, 65
Moṣṭafā Qoli Khān, brother of Āqā Moḥammad Shāh, 4
Moṣṭafā Qoli Khān-e Qaraguzlu Eᶜtemād os-Salṭana Mir Panj, on campaign against Bābis, 239 seq.; sent to Bushehr, 295; deputy governor of Lārestān, 319; at Bandar Kong, 327
Moṣṭafā Qoli Khān-e Qashqā'i, 214 seq.
Moṣṭafā Qomesha'i, theologian, 80
Moᶜtomad od-Doula ("Trust of the Empire"), *see* ᶜAbd ol-Vahhāb-e Eṣfahāni; Farhād Mirzā; Manuchehr Khān-e Gorji
Moula Verdi Khān-e Dhu'l-Qadr, governor of Qazvin, 15
Moẓaffar od-Din Mirzā (Shāh, 1896–1907), appointed crown prince, 347; governor of Ādherbāyjān, 374; deputy during shah's visit to Europe, 378
Murcha-ye Khurt, village near Esfahan, 20
Musā, Mirzā, chief astrologer, governor of Gilān, 80, 85, 110

Nabi Khān-e Qazvini, Amir-e Kabir Mirzā, vizier of Qazvin, 190; chief magistrate, sent to

Nabi Khān-e Qazvini *(Continued)* Fārs, 266 seq.; governor of Fārs, 273 seq., 383

Nāder Mirzā, son of Shāhrokh Shāh, 69, 89, 91, 104 seq.

Nāder Mirzā, son of Farmān-Farmā (I), 221, 240

Nāder Shāh (Ṭahmāsp Qoli Khān), in the service of the Safavid Ṭahmāsp II, 2*n*; famous jewels in his possession, 63; his sepulcher at Mashhad destroyed, his corpse transferred to Tehran, thence to Najaf, 70; blinds Haji Hāshem, mayor of Shiraz, 97; brings big cannon to castle of Cham Mollā, 298

Nafar, tribe in Fārs, moves to Kerman, 208 seq.; Nafar horsemen, 219; Nafar detachment, 221; united with Bahārlu, 340; belong to the "Five Tribes," 387; *see also* Five Tribes

Na^{c}im-e Nuri, Āqā Mirzā, chief registrar of the army, governor of Dārāb, Jahrom, 318; delivers provisions to the army, 327; arrests Naṣrollāh Khān-e Lāri, 338

Nā'in, town in Khorasan, 27

Najaf, burial of Karim Khān Vakil, 55, of Nāder Shāh, 70, of Āqā Moḥammad Shāh, 80, of mojtahed from Shiraz, 262; learned mojtahed of Najaf mediates between Turkish and Persian government, 119; ulema gives fetvā for Holy War, 127; shrine of Ḥosein, visited by Nāṣer od-Din Shāh, 371; Lake of Najaf, 372

Najaf Khān-e Zand, maternal uncle of Ja^{c}far Khān, 22

Najaf Qoli Khān-e Khorāsāni, citizen of Kerman, 60

Najaf Qoli Mirzā Vāli, son of Farmān-Farmā (I), governor of Behbehān, 207; 296*n*; flees from Shiraz, 236; writes journal of his exile in London, 236*n*; pays half of his jewels as transit duty to Mamassani chief, 245

Najib Efendi, Turkish ambassador, 169

Nakhchevān, in Ādherbāyjān, 181

Nanizak, village near Bushehr, 328, 330, 332 seq., 334

Napoleon I, offers treaty of friendship, 118, 121; Persia not mentioned in peace treaty of Tilsit, 123 seq.; his campaign to Russia, 143

Naqd ^{c}Ali Khān-e Zand, son of Naẓar ^{c}Ali Khān, 32

Nārin, castle near Behbehān, 297 seq.

Narmāshir, in Kerman, 58, 64, 213 seq.

Nāṣer Khān, governor of Bushehr, 32

Nāṣer od-Din Shāh, of pure Qājār Qoyunlu offspring, 160; his birth, 200; appointed crown prince, 242; appointed governor of Fārs, 267; ascends the throne, 282 seq.; Bābi attempt on his life, 302 seq.; introduces celebration of the birthday of the Twelfth Eman, 338; appoints Moẓaffar od-Din Mirzā crown prince 347; visits Russian ships in the Caspian Sea, 355; new distribution of government schedules, 362; author of "Safarnāma," quoted, 368, 371; decree issued to the army, quoted, 378; royal autograph to Mo^{c}tamad od-Doula, quoted, 378 seq.; ——*travels*: to Esfahan, 300;

Kurdistan and Solṭāniya, 341; Firuzkuh, 349; Māzandārān, 354, 377, 385, 402 seq., 419; Dāmghān, 358; Gilān, 367; Europe, 377 seq.; 394 seq.;
——*religious life*: pilgrimage to Mashhad, 358; pilgrimage to Holy Places in Mesopotamia, 368 seq.
Nashshāt, *see* ᶜAbd ol-Vahhāb-e Eṣfahāni
Naṣir od-Doula ("Defender of the Empire"), *see* ᶜAbd ol-Vahhāb Khān-e Shirazi
Naṣir Khān, beglerbegi of Lārestān, 27*n*, 271*n*
Naṣir Khān-e Lāri, beglerbegi of Lārestān, 153, 208, 210, 213; son of ᶜAbdollāh Khān-e Lāri, 243; encroaches on district of Dārāb, 261
Naṣir ol-Molk ("Defender of Kingdom") *see* Fażlollāh-e ᶜAliābādi; Ḥasan ᶜAli Khān Daryābegi
Naṣr Khān, governor of Bushehr, 32, 45, 46
Naṣr Khān, son of ᶜAbd or-Rasul Khān, takes refuge on English ship, 212; attacks Bushehr, 217 seq.; appointed governor of Bushehr, 288 seq., 290; sent to Tehran, 294
Naṣrābād, near Kāshān, 22
Naṣrollāh-e ᶜAliābādi Māzandārāni, Mirzā, minister of finance of Fārs, 64; vizier of Fārs, 77, 79; imprisoned, 82; again vizier of Fārs, 267
Naṣrollāh-e Astarābādi, Āqā Seiyed 175
Naṣrollāh Khān-e Nuri, 92, 193
Naṣrollāh Khān-e Lāri, 336 seq., 338
Naṣrollāh Khān-e Qājār Devehlu, governor of Fārs, 267
Naṣrollāh Khān-e Qaraguzlu, Amir, vizier of Fārs, 30, 114, 123
Naṣrollāh Khān Sartip, son of Mirzā Nabi Khān, 307
Naṣrollāh Khān-e Zand, uncle of Loṭf ᶜAli Khān, 57
Naṣrollāh Mirzā, son of Farmān-Farmā (I), 208, 240
Navāḥi Arbaᶜ, district in Fārs, composed of Deh Rām, Deh Rud, Hangām und Rudbāl (Rudbār?), 226*n*
Naẓar ᶜAli Khān-e Zand, 6 seq., 32
Nāẓem ol-Molk ("Arranger of Kingdom"), *see* Moḥammad ᶜAli Khān
Nehāvand, 166
Neᶜmatollāh, Sufi order, 161 seq., 265*n*
Neyāvarān-e Shemrān, near Tehran, 302, 304
Neẓām od-Doula ("Administrator of the Empire"), *see* Ḥosein Khān Ṣāḥeb Ekhteyār; Moḥammad Ḥosein Khān Amin od-Doula; Soleimān Khān-e Qājār Qoyunlu
Neẓām ol-ᶜOlamā, *see* Ḥasan Neẓām ol-ᶜOlamā
Niriz, in Fārs, 37; occupied by Loṭf ᶜAli Khān, 57; occupied by Qājārs, 64; governor mentioned, 86, 243, 253, 261; on Shiraz–Kerman highway, 209 seq., 211, 216; Bābi activities, 291 seq., 293, 318
Nishāpur, 89 seq., 93
Noṣrat od-Doula ("Assistance of the Empire"), *see* Firuz Mirzā
Noṣrat ol-Molk ("Assistance of Kingdom"), see ᶜAli Khān
Noubandagān, 34*n*, 210

Noudhār, Persian hero, 33
Noudhār Mirzā, son of Reżā Qoli Mirzā, 240*n*
Noudhār Mirzā, grandson of Farmān-Farmā (I), governor of Galladār, 340
Nouruz Khān-e Qājār ᶜEzz od-Dinlu, 86
Nur (Nur va-Kujur), in Māzandārān, 17, 92, 377, 385
Nurābād, in Fārs, 208, 244*n*, 246

Ögetei Qā'ān Mirzā, son of Ḥasan ᶜAli Mirzā Shojāᶜ os-Salṭana, 201
ᶜOmān, 134, 344, 365; *see also* Masqaṭ
Ordshonikidse, *see* Vladikavkaz
ᶜOṣfur, Arab tribe, 260
ᶜOtubi, *see* Bani ᶜOtub
Oulād-e ᶜAli, *see* Izadkhvāst
Ouseley, Sir Gore, English ambassador, 137, 139, 143, 147
Outram, Sir James, English general, 320, 324 seq., 331

Pādonā, south of Qomisha, 225*n*
Panj ᶜAli Beg, of the Abu'l-Vardi branch of Inālu, 416
Paris, peace treaty signed in, 334; visited by Nāṣer od-Din Shāh, 395
Parkān, *see* Qir va-Kārzin
Pas Kuhak, near Shiraz, 336
Pasargadae, 29*n*
Paskevich, I. V., Russian general, 178, 181 seq., 183 seq., 185, 189 seq.
Pazuki, tribe in northern Persia, 23*n*
Persepolis (Takht-e Jamshid), center of Marvdasht, 49*n*; tombs of Achaemenids, 141; named "Takht-e Jamshid," 142*n*; camp of governor of Fārs, 352
Pelly, Lewis, "Political resident on the Persian Gulf," 361*n*, 365*n*
Pir Qoli Khān, 109
Pol-e Dallāk, near Qom, 59
Pol-e Fasā, near Shiraz, 416
Pol-e Khān, in Fārs, 346*n*
Poli, castle near Behbehān, 299
Posht-e Kuh, 98*n*, 343*n*, 350

Qā'āni, the poet, 242*n*
Qabus-e Voshmgir, ruler of Gorgān (978–1012), 252*n*
Qāder Khān-e ᶜArab-e ᶜĀmeri Besṭāmi, 16, 36
Qā'em Maqām, *see* Borzorg, Mirzā
Qā'en, town in Khorasan, 58
Qahhār Qoli Mirzā, son of Shāhrokh Shāh, 69
Qahnir, region near Esfahan, 199 seq.
Qājār Nuyān, son of Sertuq Nuyān, 1
Qalᶜa-ye Bahman, near Bushehr, 322
Qalᶜa-ye Gol, *see* Gol and Golāb
Qalᶜa-ye Mirzā, near Fasā, 57
Qalᶜa-ye Poli, *see* Poli
Qalᶜa-ye Safid, in Kuh-e Giluya, 244, 246 seq., 268
Qalᶜa-ye Shahreyāri, in southern Fārs, 270
Qalᶜa-ye Shirvān, in Khorasan, 157
Qalᶜa-ye Ṭūs, in Fārs, 268
Qalāt-e Sorkh, castle in southern Fārs, 401 seq.
Qalamrav-e ᶜAli Shakār (province of Hamadān), 20
Qanāt-e Nāṣeri, *see* Behbehān
Qanāt-e Qarācha, *see* Kāzerun
Qarācha, Atabeg, Saljuqid vizier, 88
Qarācha Dāgh, region north of Tabriz, 40; Qarācha Dāghi detachment, 321, 324

Qarachlu, tribe and horsemen, 250
Qaraguzlu, tribe near Hamadān, 24; Qaraguzlu soldiers at Shahr Babak, 212, at Kerman, 214 seq., in Fārs, 293, 311, 319, 331, 334, in Lārestān, 327; trained by English instructors, 216
Qarya-ye Riz, in Fārs, 393
Qāsem Khān-e Khalaj, Mirzā, son-in-law of Moḥammad ᶜAli Khān Ilkhāni, 209 seq., 224
Qāsem Khān-e Kuh-e Marra'i, Ra'is, 47
Qashqā'i, Turkish tribe in Fārs, sacked by Āqā Moḥammad Shāh, 29; quarrels with the Bakhteyāri, 163; a case of blood revenge at Shiraz, 194; tribes move from Fārs to Kerman, 208 seq.; fight against Qaraguzlu soldiers, 215; reformed detachment at Shiraz, 221, 301, 308, 321, 327 seq., 332, 350; subdued by governor of Fārs, 223; homeland described, 225*n*; leader styled ilbegi and ilkhāni, 226, 389, 419; *see also* "ilbegi"; their winter camp, 248*n*; Lors steal their cattle, 268; quarrels among the Qashqā'i khāns, 276; Qashqā'i horsemen, 331, 334, 418
Qaṣr-e Qomisha, near Shiraz, 279, 396
Qaṭif, 217
Qaṭru, in Fārs, 292
Qavām od-Din-e Behbehāni (Mirzā Qavāmā), governor of Behbehān, 269, 296 seq., 298 seq.
Qavām od-Dine-e Shirāzi, Haji, 96
Qavām od-Doula ("Support of the Empire"), *see* Moḥammad-e Farāhāni
Qavām ol-Khelāfa ("Support of the Caliphate"), *see* Moḥammad ᶜAli Mirzā
Qavām ol-Molk ("Support of Kingdom"), *see* ᶜAli Akbar; ᶜAli Moḥammad
Qavāmā, Mirzā, *see* Qavām od-Din-e Behbehāni
Qāvi, near Bushehr, 212
Qazvin, exile of Qājār princes, 4; occupied by Zand army, 11; conquered by Qājār army, 15; temporary residence of Āqā Moḥammad Shāh, 37; and captured women, 40; and hostages from Shiraz, 56; and Shaqāqi hostages, 78; and battle of 1797–1798, 79; grand vizier deposed and exiled to Qazvin, 99; governor mentioned, 190
Qebla, near Shiraz, 35, 51
Qebla, near Tabriz, 181
Qeshm (Derāz), island near Bandar ᶜAbbās, 145, 154, 261, 306, 316 seq., 366
Qeyākhlu, branch of the Yukhāri-bāsh, 2
Qir va-Kārzin, district in Fārs, governor mentioned, 114 seq, 240*n*, 288*n*, 318, 340, 387; position described, 209*n*, 270; castle of Parkān, 223 seq.; plundered by Inālu tribe, 416
Qizil Ayāgh, *see* Zubov, V.
Qobād, mythical Persian king, 142
Qobād Khān, nephew of the ilkhāni, 334
Qohestān (Kahak), district south of Qom, 150
Qom, shrine of Fāṭema, 8*n*, 100; Qājār camp near Qom, 22, 24; governor mentioned, 67, 100 seq.; renovation of the shrine, 87; ulema give fetvā for Holy War, 127; visited by the shah,

135, 159, 168; burial of Fatḥ ᶜAli Shāh, 229; burial of Moḥammad Shāh, 280
Qomesha (Shahreżā), 21, 30, 43, 200
Quchān, in Khorasan, 91*n*, 157*n*, 358
Qunqāri, district in Fārs, 337*n*

Rabiᶜ Khān-e Kazzāzi, Haji, 98
Rabiᶜ Khān-e Marvdashti, 49
Raḥim-e Shirāzi (Bidel), Haji Mirzā, physician, chancellor of the empire, 172, 191
Ramażān Khān-e Zand (Reżā Khān-e Zand), 15
Rāmhormuz, in Khuzestān, 268 seq., 270, 297
Rāmjerd, in Fārs, 336*n*
Rashmāyjān, castle in Fārs, 52
Ra's ol-Kheima, in ᶜOmān, 145, 154, 217
Rasht, in Gilān, 14 seq., 162, 367, 379
Reiy, 16
Reżā, musketmaker at Shiraz, 265
Reżā, Mirzā, intendant of Bushehr, 325
Reżā Bazzāz-e Shirāzi, Mirzā, Bābi leader, 302
Reżā Khān-e Farāhāni, Haji, 19
Reżā Khān-e Qājār Qoyunlu, 5
Reżā Khān-e Zand, *see* Ramażān Khān-e Zand
Reżā-ye Qāri, Haji, 343, 351 seq.
Reżā Qoli Khān-e ᶜArab Fārsi Sartip, son of Āqā Khān and alderman of the Arabs, 221, 301, 310, 336 seq.
Reżā Qoli Khān-e Kāzeruni, 45, 47, 51
Reżā Qoli Khān-e Kord Zaᶜfarānlu, lord of Khabushān, 157 seq.
Reżā Qoli Khān-e Māzandarāni (Hedāyat), Amir-e Kabir, author of "Roużat oṣ-Ṣafā-ye Nāṣeri," 148; in the service of Reżā Qoli Mirzā, 204 seq. 212 seq.; quoted, 218 seq., 229, 281
Reżā Qoli Khān-e Qājār, colonel, 246
Reżā Qoli Khān-e Qājār Devehlu, 50
Reżā Qoli Khān-e Qājār Qoyunlu, brother of Āqā Moḥammad Shāh, 4, 6, 12 seq.
Reżā Qoli Khān-e Shāhsevan, 45 seq., 47
Reżā Qoli Mirzā, son of Farmān-Farmā (I), son of Hājiya, 202 seq.; accompanies Farmān-Farmā to Bushehr, 204 seq.; occupies Behbehān, 207; Shiraz entrusted to him, 210; marches to Bushehr, 211 seq., 213, 216 seq.; returns to Shiraz, intercedes for Qavām ol-Molk, 225 seq.; flees from Shiraz, 236; his house at Shiraz occupied, 239; his son returns to Tehran, 240*n*
Reżā Qoli Navā'i Solṭān, Haji Mirzā, given title "Solṭān," 46; sent from Shiraz to Tehran as envoy, 50; with the shah at Shushā, 75; friend of vizier of Fārs, 114; chancellor of the empire, 117; writes text of treaty with France, 122; appointed vizier of Khorasan, 131
Rokn od-Doula ("Pillar of the Empire"), *see* ᶜAli Naqi Mirzā; Moḥammad Taqi Mirzā
Rommān, famous for hyacinths, 164
Rostam, hero of Persian epics, 33, 207, 247
Rostam, branch of Mamassani, *see* Mamassani

Rostam Khān-e Bayyāt, 83
Rostam Khān-e Qarācha Dāghi, 321
Rostam Khān-e Zand, 19 seq.
Rostamdār, district in Māzandārān, 17
Rostāq, near Qom, 293
Rouniz, in Fārs, 57, 209 seq.
Rour va-Ravāt, region in Fārs, 29
Rudān, district in Fārs, 64, 276, 337*n*
Rudbāl (Rudbār), in Fārs, see Navāḥi Arba^c
Rudbār, in Kerman, 60, 64
Ruḥ ol-Amin (the faithful spirit, that is, the angel Gabriel), imam of the Friday prayers, 90

Ṣabā ("Zephyr"), *see* Fatḥ ^cAli Khān-e Kāshāni
Sab^ca, district in Fārs, governor mentioned, 210, 261, 276, 340; affairs settled, 301; winter quarters of Arab tribes, 337*n*; *see also* Lār, Lārestān
Sabza Meidān, near Tehran, 14
Sabzavār, in Khorasan, 93 seq., 254
Ṣādeq, Georgian servant, 73, 79
Ṣādeq Khān Āqā-ye Qājār, governor of Behbehān, 296*n*
Ṣādeq Khān-e Qājār Devehlu, 134 seq.
Ṣādeq Khān-e Shaqāqi, lord of Sarāb, 40, 74, 78, 80 seq.
Ṣādeq Khān-e Zand, Zand ruler of Shiraz (1779–81), brother of Ja^cfar Khān, returns from Basra to Shiraz, 7; goes to Kerman, 8; returns to Shiraz, 10; arrests Abu'l-Fatḥ Khān, 11; stays at Shiraz, 13; deposed, 14*n*; counted as Zand sovereign, 62
Sa^cdi, the poet, 369
Ṣadr od-Din Moḥammad-e Tabrizi, Mollā, 127
Sā'el ("Beggar"), *see* Jāni-ye Qiri
Safavids, Āqā Moḥammad Shāh visits shrine at Ardebil, 40; model for choice of honorific titles, 64; ceremonial of coronation imitated by Qājārs, 68; introduce division into Ḥeidari and Ne^cmati, 264*n*; *see also* ^cAbbās I, ^cAbbās II, Ṣafidābād
Ṣafidābād, in Māzandārān, Safavid foundation, 355
Ṣāḥeb Divān ("Chief of Divān"), *see* Fatḥ ^cAli Khān Mostoufi; Shafi^c-e Shirāzi
Ṣāḥeb Ekhteyār-e Dārāb ("Governor of Dārāb by Free Option of the Ruler"), *see* Jahāngir Mirzā
Sa^cid, Solṭān Seiyed, ruler of ^cOmān and Zanzibar (1806–1856), assisted by Persian troops against Vahhābis, 134 seq.; becomes son-in-law of Farmān-Farmā (I), 202 seq.; mediates for ^cOtubi and Javāshem Arabs, 218; quarrels with Persian government about possession of Bandar ^cAbbās, 303 seq.; offers negotiations, 313 seq.; new treaty concluded, 314 seq.; his death, 318
Sa^cid, Sheikh, nephew of Sheikh Ṣafi, 306, 308
Sa^cid ibn Aḥmad, governor of Bandar ^cAbbās, 317
Sa^cidābād, *see* Sirjān
Saint Petersburg, 151, 190, 395
Salduz, in Ādherbāyjān, 81
Sālekhān, region east of Baku, 119
Sālem, Seiyed, ruler of ^cOmān (1866–1868), 359, 365 seq.
Sālem Khān-e Borāzjāni, 204 seq.
Sāleyān, south of Baku, 71
Salim Khān-e Chagani, 234, 246
Salmān, Sheikh, of the ^cOṣfur tribe, 260

Salmān-e Fāresi (Salmān ol-Fāresi), 197, 370
Salmān-e Musavi Ḥoseini (Bidel), ancestor of ᶜAbd ol-Vahhāb Moᶜtamad od-Doula, 191
Samal and Abād, plain east of Bushehr, 205
Sāmarrā, 338*n*, 372
Sāmer Khān, Sheikh, chief of the Bani Kaᶜb and governor of Falāḥi, 269
Samirom, center of Sarḥadd-e Shesh Nāḥiya, 9*n*, 21, 43, 225*n*
Sanandaj (Senānda, Senna), 341
Sang-e Safid, near Herāt, 255
Sangbārān, northwest of Esfahan, 25
Sar-e Jahān, district in Fārs, 337*n*
Sarāb, in Ādherbāyjān, 40, 80, 130 seq., 181
Sarāb-e Bahrām, near Kāzerun, 197 seq., 319
Sarāb-e Seyākh, in Fārs, 198, 221
Sarakhs, in Khorasan, 251*n*
Ṣārem od-Doula ("Sharp Sword of the Empire"), *see* Abu'l-Fatḥ Khān; ᶜAbdollāh Khān-e Qaraguzlu
Sarḥadd-e Chahār Dānga, district in Fārs, 225
Sarḥadd-e Shesh Nāḥeya, district in Fārs, 163, 225, 278, 300
Sāri, in Māzandārān, 13, 19, 155, 354
Sāruq, near Arāk/Solṭānābād, 84
Sarvestān, district in Fārs, 57, 199, 310, 216, 221, 387*n*
Saᶜud, son of ᶜAbd ol-ᶜAziz, ruler of Arabia (1803–1814), plunders Kerbelā, 101; fights the Arabs, 103; defeated by Persian troops in ᶜOmān, 134 seq.; promises to protect Persian pilgrims, 144
Seh Chāh, in Fārs, 210
Sehām od-Doula ("Arrow of the Empire"), *see* Soleimān Khān-e Armani
Sehām ol-Molk ("Arrow of Kingdom"), *see* Moḥammad Ebrāhim Khān
Seif od-Doula ("Sword of the Empire"), *see* Solṭān Moḥammad Mirzā
Seif od-Doula Mirzā, brother of Seif ol-Muluk Mirzā, 215
Seif ibn Badr, of Masqaṭ, 302, 306
Seif ibn Mālek, Sheikh, Saᶜudi commander, 135
Seif ibn Nebhān, governor of Bandar ᶜAbbās, 302*n*
Seif ol-Moluk Mirzā, son of ᶜAli Shah Ẓell os-Solṭān, governor of Kerman, 200, 209, 212, 213
Seiyed Morād Khān-e Zand, 26, 32
Semnān, 14, 23*n*, 86
Senānda, *see* Senandaj
Senna, *see* Sanandaj
Sepahsālār, *see* Keikhosrou Mirzā; Ḥosein Khān
Sepehr, *see* Moḥammad Taqi Mostoufi-ye Kāshāni
Sertāq Nuyān, father of Qājār Nuyān, 1
Seyākh, district in Fārs, 86
Shabānkāra, region in Fārs, 147
Shafiᶜ-e Māzandārāni, Mirzā, accompanies Qājār army to Khorasan, 89 seq.; appointed grand vizier, 99; appointed counselor of ᶜAbbās Mirzā, 108; head of the board of "Four Viziers," 117; receives Russian ambassador in his house, 120; given title "Ṣadr-e aᶜẓam," 131; Ottoman ambassador put up in his house, 136; his function in audience, 152 seq.; with the army in Khorasan, 157; dies at Qazvin, 159

Shafiᶜ-e Shirāzi, Mirzā, secretary of the grand vizier, 339
Shāh Moḥammad, Mollā, 148
Shāh Morād Khān-e Zand, takes part in murder of Jaᶜfar Khān, 31; sent against Loṭf ᶜAli Khān, 32; murdered during revolt, 33
Shāh Qoli Khān-e Qājār Qoyunlu, ancestor of the Qājār dynasty, 2
Shahr Bābak, in Fārs, fief of Qājār princess, 211, 219
Shahrak, in Fārs, 52
Shahrazur, in Kurdistan, 136
Shahreyāri, castle in southern Fārs, 270
Shahreżā, *see* Qomesha
Shāhrokh Shāh, 69 seq., 71
Shāhrud, in Khorasan, 14
Shāhsevan, tribe, 46, 328, 334
Shakkāk, Kurdish tribe, 40*n*, 286
Shakki, 119, 328
Shamil, near Bandar ᶜAbbās, 306, 315, 362, 377
Shams od-Din Khān-e Afghān, commander of Herāt, 255, 261
Shams od-Din-e Noudāni Kāzeruni, Mir, 148
Shapur Dhu'l-Aktāf, Sasanid ruler, 173
Shaqāq, *see* Shahkkāk
Sharifat, Arab tribe in Khuzestān 297
Sheil, Lady M. L., wife of J. Sheil, 234*n*
Sheil, Sir Justin (Sheil Ṣāḥeb), 234, 320*n*
Shekār Masila, region near Qom, 150
Shemrān, near Tehran, 186, 355, 419
Shib Kuh, region in southern Fārs, 154 seq., 334
Shif, near Bushehr, 331
Shir Khān-e Nuri, 338
Shir Moḥammad Khān-e Afghān, lord of Ghureyān, 254
Shiraz, siege of one year by ᶜAli Morād Khān-e Zand, 14*n*; beleaguered by Qājār army, 35; tribal soldiers expelled, 44; Nuri soldiers settle down at, 92; Russian prisoners sent to, 109; ravaged by plague, 166, 336, 367; earthquakes (1824), 170, (1853) 305; fugitives from Ādherbāyjān, 263; revolt of inhabitants (1839–1840), 263 seq., (1847–1848), 285 seq., quarters enumerated, 264*n*; commercial center, 285*n*; reconstructed after earthquake, 309; famine (1866–1867), 356 seq., (1872–1873), 376, 1878, 409; decorated in 1876, 390; aldermen receive regular pay, 417; streets paved, bazaars vaulted, 419;
——Ark-e shāhi, 31, 37, 56; Bāgh-e Delgoshā, 219 seq., Bāgh-e Farhādābād, 273; Bāgh-e (Jahān-namā-ye) Vakili, 49, 55, 83, 195, 227, 237, 321; Bāgh-e Naẓar-e Vakili, 239, 241; Bāgh-e Nou, 195, 238, 241, 305, 339; Bāgh-e Shāh Gate, 236 seq., 250, 279; Bālā Keft quarter, 97, 264*n*, 398; Bāzār-e Āqā, 117*n*; Bāzār-e (Karim Khān) Vakil, 47 seq., 146, 263, 285 seq., 419; Bāzār-e Mesgerān, 419; Bāzār-e Mirzā Yusof, 146; Bāzār-e Morgh, 117*n*, 264*n*; Caravanserai of Charāgh ᶜAli Khān, 116; Caravanserai Emāmiya, 117*n*; citadel, *see* Ark-e shāhi; Darb-e Kāzerun quarter, 116*n*; Darb-e Shāhzāda quarter, 164*n*, 274, 345; Darvāza-ye Masjed quarter, 264*n*; Dashtak quarter, 44;

Shiraz *(Continued)*
Emāmzada Seiyed ᶜAlā od-Din Ḥosein, 224; Emāmzāda Seiyed Mir Moḥammad, 220; Emāmzāda Shāh Charāgh, 83, 117*n*, 262, 273, 417; Enderun-e kuchek, 7*n*, 239; Esfahan Gate, 238, 419; Esḥāq Beg quarter, 264*n*, 275; Ḥeidari Khāna quarter, 97, 264*n*, 265; house of Āqā Bashir, 239; Jewish quarter, 264*n*; Karim Khāni irrigation canal, 395 seq.; Karim Khāni prison, 393; Labb-e Āb quarter, 264*n*, 398; Madrasa-ye Emāmiya, 117*n*; Madrasa-ye Khān, 265 seq.; Madrasa-ye Qarācha, 88*n*; Masjed-e Hāshemiya, 97; Masjed-e (Jāmeᶜ) Nou, 148, 264, 342; Masjed-e Jāmeᶜ Aṭiq, 412; Masjed-e Ṭāheri, 412; Masjed-e Vakil, 47 seq., 264 seq., 266, 285 seq., 381, 412; Meidān-e Shāh quarter, 191, 264*n*, 275, 345, 356; Meidān-e Ark, 114, 158 237, 263; Meidān-e Naᶜlbandān, 286; Meidān-e Naqqāra Khāna, 264; Meidān-e Tubkhāna, 222; Murdestān quarter, 92, 193; Nahr-e Aᶜẓam, 279, 396; Neᶜmati Khāna quarter, 100, 264*n*, 265, 274; Sang-e Seyākh quarter, 117*n*, 264; Sar Dezak quarter, 264*n*; Sarbāgh quarter, 264*n*; sword-cutlers Bāzār, 48; Takht-e Qājār, 87 seq.; Takht-e Qarācha, 88; Tekke of Ḥāfeẓ, 77, 286; Teppe-ye Salām, 415; Tubkhāna, 240*n*; Vakili Palace, *see* Bāgh-e Vakili; Vakili storehouses, 286
Shirvān, region northwest of Baku, 15; invaded by Qājār army, 65, 67, 72, 177; Shirvāni detachment defeated by Russians, 71, 151, 174; ceded to Russia, 144*n*
Shojāᶜ ol-Molk ("Intrepid of the Empire"), *see* Mehr ᶜAli Khān
Shojāᶜ os-Salṭana ("Intrepid of the Rule"), *see* Ḥasan ᶜAli Mirzā
Shojāᶜ Shāh Dorrāni, 258*n*
Shokrollāh Khān-e Nuri, son of Mirzā Asadollāh, commander of Nuri soldiers, 193; marries daughter of Farmān-Farmā (I), 194; returns to Shiraz after expulsion, 201; accompanies Farmān-Farmā to Bushehr, 204; deputy governor of Bushehr, 225; intercedes for Qavām ol-Molk's eldest son, 233; appointed governor of Kuh-e Giluya and Behbehān, 271
Shoshtar, in Khuzestān, governor mentioned, 98, 129, 270, 350; visited by the shah, 198
Shul-e Jouzag, in Mamassani, 250
Shulestān (Shul), in Mamassani, home of Mamassani tribe, 34, 220; also called Mamassani, 197; governor appointed, 208; Vali Khān subdued, 246 seq., 249; castles in Shulestān, 268
Shulgestān, near Ābāda, 195, 235
Shushā, in Karabagh, besieged by Qājār army, 65 seq., 72 seq., 176 seq., 178
Silākhur, region southeast of Borujerd, 100
Ṣimekān, district in Fārs, 86, 416
Sind, ambassador sent to Persia, 199
Sirjān (Saᶜidābād), in Kerman, 37, 64, 209 seq., 216
Sivand, village in Fārs, 346*n*
Skandar Shāh, Neẓām of Hyderabad, 129*n*
Sobodār Khān, of Hyderabad, 199*n*
Sohrāb Khān, nephew of the ilkhāni, 334

Sohrāb Khān-e Shabānkāra, 333
Sojās Rud, district near Solṭāniya, 140, 143
Soleimān I, Safavid ruler, 282n
Soleimān Khān, son of Yaḥyā Khān-e Tabrizi, adherent of the Bābi sect, 302
Soleimān Khān-e Armani Sehām od-Doula, nephew of Manuchehr Khān Moʿtamad od-Doula, 297 seq.
Soleimān Khān Mir Panj-e Afshār, 334 seq.
Soleimān Kjān-e Qājār Qoyunlu, Amir-e Kabir, cousin of Āqā Moḥammad Shāh, 3; sent to Ṭālesh, 39; present when the shah suffered a stroke, 50; besieges Shushā, 65; occupies Mashhad, 69; guards princes at Adinabāzār, 73; favored by the shah, 74; mediates for Ṣādeq Khān-e Shaqāqi, 81; appointed governor of Ādherbāyjān, 83; adjudant of ʿAbbās Mirzā, 89
Soleimān Khān-e Qājār Qoyunlu Neẓām od-Doula, 200
Soleimān Mirzā, son of Faridun Mirzā Farmān-Farmā (II), 234, 343, 365
Soleimān Pāshā, governor of Baghdad, 80
Soleimān Pāshā Kahyā, 118 seq.
Solṭān ʿAli Khān-e Zand Hezāra'i, 45
Solṭān Ebrāhim Mirzā, son of Farmān-Farmā (II), 240
Solṭān Ḥeidar, ancestor of the Safavids, 265n
Solṭān Ḥosein Mirzā Jalāl od-Doula, son of Solṭān Masʿud Mirzā Ẓell os-Solṭān, governor of Fārs, 372, 415, 417
Solṭān ibn Aḥmad, Seiyed, Sultan of ʿOmān (1792–1806), 134n, 317

Solṭān Masʿud Mirzā Yamin od-Doula Ẓell os-Solṭān, appointed governor of Fārs, 347, 349; returns to Tehran, 351; again governor of Fārs, 367 seq.; returns to Tehran, 380; appointed governor of Fārs, Esfahan, Borujerd, etc., 415; goes to Esfahan, 418
Solṭān Moḥammad Khān, Mirzā, son of Mirzā ʿAli Reżā-ye Behbehāni, governor of Behbehān, 36, 100, 296n
Solṭān Moḥammad Khān Ilkhāni, governor of the Qashqā'i, 419
Solṭān Moḥammad Khān-e Ṭabāṭabā'i, Mirzā, governor of Behbehān, 289; nephew and son-in-law of Mirzā Qavāmā, 296; fights Mirzā Qavāmā, 297 seq.; arrested and sent to Shiraz, 299; again governor of Behbehān, fights the English at Bushehr, 328, 333; arrested at Behbehān, 346; appointed governor of Lārestān, 340; granted a pension, 348
Solṭān Moḥammad Mirzā Seif od-Doula, governor of Esfahan, 171
Solṭān Morād Mirzā Ḥosām os-Salṭana, uncle of Nāṣer od-Din Shāh, governor of Fārs, 339
Solṭān Oveis Mirzā Eḥteshām od-Doula, son of Farhād Mirzā Moʿtamad od-Doula, visits Qalʿa-ye Golāb, 248n; appointed governor of Kuh-e Giluya and Behbehān, 348 seq.; marches to Posht-e Kuh, 350; confirmed in office by Ḥosām os-Salṭana, 351; builds water conduit at Behbehān, 353 seq.; travels to Kurdistan, 366 seq.; governor of Hama-

Solṭān Oveis Mirzā Eḥteshām od-Doula *(Continued)*
dān, 368 seq.; again governor of Kuh-e Giluya, 381 seq., 382 seq., 389; undertakes campaign to the Persian Gulf, 392 seq.; returns to Kuh-e Giluya, 394; undertakes another campaign to that area, 397; third campaign, 398 seq.; visits island of Khārk, 400; subdues Madhkur Khān-e Kangani, 402; returns to Tehran, 403
Solṭānābād (Arāk), 148*n*, 186
Solṭāniya, Qājār conquest, 15; Mongol foundation, 15*n*; visited by the shah, 72, 81, 108, 110, 118, seq., 123, 125, 128, 133, 137, 142, 150, 152, 159, 161, 156 seq., 175, 341; Qajar army assembled and mustered, 128
Soula Deh, in Māzandārān, 355
Soveini, Seiyed, ruler of ᶜOmān (1856–1866), 306, 308 seq., 310 seq., 316 seq.

Ṭabas, in Khorasan, 27*n*, 28, 55 seq., 58, 210
Tabriz, residence of Turkish ambassador, 136; garrison of special detachment, 169; visited by the shah, 180, 341; occupied by Russian troops, 181 seq., 185; coronation of Nāṣer od-Din Shāh at Tabriz, 282; Tabrizi (the fourth) detachment, 286; *see also* Ādherbāyjān
Ṭāher Khān, Mirzā, son of Mirzā Manṣur Khān of Behbehān, 380
Ṭāheri, *see* Bandar Ṭāheri
Ṭāhmāsp Khān-e Fili, 43
Ṭahmāsp Mirzā, son of Farmān-Farmā (I), 240
Ṭahmāsp Mirzā Mo'eiyed od-Doula, son of Moḥammad ᶜAli Mirzā, appointed governor of Fārs, 305; undertakes campaign to Bandar ᶜAbbās, 307; honored by the shah, 309; sends his son to Bandar ᶜAbbās, 310; appoints another son governor of Behbehān, 312; receives French ambassador, 313; envoys from ᶜOmān received in audience, 318; settles quarrels between tribes of Fārs, 319; prepares campaign to Bushehr against the English, 321 seq.; marches to Dālaki, 324; arrests people who supply English troops, 333; has summer camp at Pas Kuhak, 336; removed from governorship of Fārs, 339; again governor of Fārs, 345; summoned to Tehran, 347
Ṭahmāsp Qoli Khān, *see* Nāder Shāh
Ṭahmāsp Qoli Khān-e Qazvini, chief of Dārāb, 346
Tāj od-Doula, spouse of Fatḥ ᶜAli Shāh, 35*n*, 171
Takht-e Jamshid, *see* Persepolis
Ṭāleb, Haji, son of Haji Hāshem
Ṭāleqān, region near Qazvin, 99
Ṭālesh, coastal area east of Ardebil, 40, 71, 144*n*, 151
Tang-e Karam, in Fārs, 57, 209
Tangestān, district in Fārs, 46, 205, 393, 399
Ṭāq-e Gerra, in Kurdistan, 119
Taqi-ye Farāhāni, Mirzā, commander of the regular army, then grand vizier 282; given title "Atabeg," 283
Taqi Khān, governor of Yazd, 26, 29
Ṭārom, region near Qazvin, 14*n*, 39, 162
Ṭārom, in Fārs, 199

Tassuj, district in Lārestān, 350
Tāzyān, near Bandar ᶜAbbās, 315
Tebr, castle in Fārs, 387, 388*n*, 390 seq.
Tehran, besieged by Qājār army, ravaged by plague, 16, 22; conquered by Qājārs, 23; residence of Qājār dynasty, 23, 25; ——Bāgh-e Negārestan, 165, 227, 233, 241, 250, 254; Doulat Gate, 377; Emāmzada Zeid, 62; ᶜErāq Gate, 139; Karim Khāni Convent, 55, 70; Qaṣr-e Jadid, 280; Takht-e Qājār, 87 seq.; Takya Doulati, 419
Tekke, Turkoman tribe, 251
Tell-e Beiżā, *see* Beiżā
Tiflis, ruled by Shaqāqi Kurds, 65; ruler called "vāli," 66; occupied by Qājār army, 67; submits to Russian army, 107; restitution to Persia promised by Napoleon, 121, 123
Tilsit, peace treaty of Tilsit, 123
Timur Gurkān (Timur Leng), 1, 245*n*
Timur Mirzā Ḥosām od-Doula, son of Farmān-Farmā (I), 240; his mother mentioned, 202; incites khāns of Dashtestān to plunder Bushehr, 204; flees from Shiraz, 236; returns to Tehran, 236*n*; marries daughter of Vali Khān-e Mamassani, 245
Timur Shāh Dorrāni (Timur Shāh Afghān), 58
Torbat-e Ḥeidari, 69, 157
Torbat-e Sheikh Jām (Buzjān), in Khorasan, 254
Torkmānchāy, peace treaty of Torkmānchāy, 185
Tormasov, A., Russian general, 128, 130, 133
Ṭorra Bāz Khān, Afghan vizier, 92 seq., 94
Tudashk, *see* Dudashk
Turkey, exile proposed by Loṭf ᶜAli Khān, 49; Kurdish rebels flee to Turkey, 81; Turkish campaign to Kurdistan fails, 118 seq.; Turkey and Russia on hostile terms, 120; Turkish ambassador in Tehran, 135 seq.; Persian ambassador sent to Turkey, 155; campaign of ᶜAbbās Mirzā in Kurdistan, 166*n*; treaty concluded between Turkey and Persia, 169; *see also* Nāṣer od-Din Shāh
Turkoman tribes, 18, 69, 105, 240*n*, 251; *see also* Göklen, Tekke, Yomut

Üch Kilise ("Three Churches," *see* Echmiadzin
Ujān, district in Ādherbāyjān, 130, 134, 143
Urmiya, 81

Vafā, *see* Ḥosein-e Farāhāni
Vafādār Khan, prime minister of Afghanistan, 92
Vagarshapat, *see* Echmiadzin
Vahhābis, sack Kerbelā, their teachings and history, 102 seq.; Persian troops fight them in ᶜOmān, 134 seq.; adherents in southern Persia, fought by governor of Fārs, 154; prisoners brought to Tehran and released, 155
Vali Khān-e Mamassani, kalāntar of Bakash Mamassani tribe, son of Khub Yār Khān, 244; revolts against governor of Fārs, 208; campaign against him planned, 229; his plunderings, 244; son-in-law of Farmān-Farmā (II),

Vali Khān-e Mamassani *(Cont.)* 245; subdued by governor of Fārs, 246 seq.; arrested and sent to Tabriz, dies there, 250
Vāli Moḥammad Khān-e Qājār, sepahsālār of Khorasan, 89
Vaṣṣāl-e Shirāzi, *see* Kuchek
Van, 136
Varāmin, 5, 173
Vardasht, south of Qomisha, 266*n*
Veis Khān-e Zand, Sheikh, son of ᶜAli Morād Khān, 17, 19 seq., 24
Veis Morād Khān-e Zand, brother of Seiyed Morād Khān, 31
Victoria, Queen, 325*n*
Vladikavkaz (Ordshonikidse), 394

Walter, John, 222

Yaḥyā, Haji Sheikh, imam of the prayers, 351, 406
Yaḥyā, Seiyed, son of Āqā Seiyed Jaᶜfar-e Eṣṭahbānāti, 291 seq., 293 seq.
Yaḥyā Khān Moᶜtamad ol-Molk, son of Nabi Khān-e Qazvini, 383
Yakh chāl, locality near Shiraz, 49
Yamin od-Doula ("Strength of the Empire"), *see* Solṭān Masᶜud Mirzā
Yār Moḥammad Khān, vizier to Kāmrān Mirzā, 255, 257 seq.
Yāri Khān, brother of Seiyed Morād Khān, 31
Yazd, governor mentioned, 26, 28*n*, 56, 59, 64, 215, 239, 415, 418; besieged by Zand army, 27; Qājār army sent to Yazd, 28 seq.; affairs settled by crown prince, 200; inhabitants send petition to Farmān-Farmā (I), 215
Yemen, 144 seq.
Yermelov, A., Russian general, 151 seq.
Yomut, Turkoman tribe, murder father of Fatḥ ᶜAli Shāh, 5; chastised by Fatḥ ᶜAli Shāh, 251; nobles submit to the shah, 252; their cattle plundered, 253
Yukhāribash, Qājār group, 1
Yusof, Mirzā, scholar, 116
Yusof-e Ashrafi Māzandarāni, Mirzā, vizier of Fārs, 132, 146
Yusof Khān-e Gorji, appointed sepahsālār of reformed army of ᶜErāq, 122; subdues rebels of Zolfābād, 149 seq.; appointed vizier of Esfahan, 171; founder of town of Solṭānābād/Arāk, 186; vizier of Shulestān and Mamassani, killed by Vali Khān-e Mamassani, 208

Ẓahir od-Doula ("Supporter of the Empire"), *see* Moḥammad Naṣir Khān
Zaki Khān-e Zand, 6 seq., 8 seq., 11
Zāl Khān, governor of Khesht, 45
Zamān Khān, Haji Mirzā, uncle of Farrokh Khān Amin od-Doula, 364
Zamān Shāh, ruler of Afghanistan (1793–1800), 92
Zande-ye Kāla, 52*n*
Zanjirān, 87*n*
Zarand, in Kerman, 246 seq.
Zarqān, near Shiraz, 48, 50 seq.
Zeidun, in Kuh-e Giluya, 248*n*, 275, 349, 381
Zein ol-ᶜĀbedin-e Kāshāni, Mirzā, vizier of Fārs, 146, 152
Zein ol-ᶜĀbedin Khān, Haji, governor of Niriz, 291 seq., 293
Zein od-Din, Sheikh (Ḥosein ᶜAli Shāh), Sufi, 161 seq.
Ẓell os-Solṭān ("Shadow of the Sultan"), *see* Solṭān Masᶜud Mirzā

Zeyādlu, branch of the Ashshāqbash, 2
Zenjān, center of "Five Districts," 11*n*; conquered by Qājārs, 15; visited by the shah, 25, 80, 97
Zizianov (Ishpokhdur), Russian general, 107 seq., 109 seq., 111 seq.
Zohāb-e Kermānshāh, 119
Zolfābād, near Solṭānābād/Arāk, 149
Zubov (Qizil Ayāgh), V., 71 seq.

GLOSSARY OF TECHNICAL TERMS

^{c}abbāsi, a coin, 376
afvāj, *see* fouj
ajudan bāshi, chief adjudant, 274
akbar shāhi, famous jewel, 63
aliq, fodder (part of pay of horsemen), 390, 405
^{c}āmel, ^{c}ommāl, administrative officer, taxation agent, 83, 299, 405
^{c}āmeli, the financial administration, 384
amir-e divān-khāna-ye ^{c}adliya, chief magistrate, 266
amir-e neẓām, commander of disciplined army, 282
amir panj, high military rank, 335
amir-e tomān, commander of a tomān, 335
amlāk-e żabṭi, confiscated estates, 99
^{c}aql, reason (in theological context), 105
aqsāt, tax installments, 390
araba-ye khompara, cannon wagon, 322
arbāb-e dafātir, accountants, 117
ariża-negar, secretary of petitions, 404
ark, citadel, 31, 37, 56
ashrafi, gold coin, 173
^{c}ashur, tithe, 325
asl-e māleyāt, the ordinary budget, 201; the principal taxes, 363

bāj va-kharāj, (general) taxes, 66, 128
bakhsh, district (modern term), 5*n*
balada, capital of province, 367
balliyuz, consul, 106
bānu, title of spouse of the shah, 139
baqāyā-ye māleyāt, tax arrears, 196
baravāt-e divani, government decrees, 362
beglerbegi, governor of province, 4, 23, 27*n*, 64, 98, 144, 167, 208, 210
boluk, bolukāt, district (within a province), 82, 248*n*
boyutāt, the royal household, 75

daftar-e ḥesāb-e divani, account book of financial administration, 404
dalil-e ḥaqqiyat, witness in court of justice, 404
dārugha, night-guard, 325
darya-ye nur, "Ocean of Light," famous jewel, 63, 68
dastur ol-^{c}amal, official instruction for collection of taxes, 195, 362
dehestān, municipality (modern term), 307*n*
dhekr, commemoration, prayer, 200
dinār, monetary unit, 173
dirā^{c}-e malek, measure of length, 138*n*
divān, ministry, office of administration, 77

divān-khāna, tax office, 170
divān-khāna-ye ᶜadliya, chief magistrates court, 362
divān-e maẓālem, court of complaints, 362

ejtehād, decision issued by mojtahed, 101 seq.
eᶜlām-nāma, (letter of) information, 351
eshik āqāsi, chamberlain, 37
eshik āqāsi bāshi, chief chamberlain, 43, 287, 360, 404

farmān, royal patent, decree, 80, 115
farr, divine grace (attributed to the king), 55*n*
farrāsh bāshi, chief warden, 196
farrāsh khāna, guardroom, 170, 196
farzand, prince of royal blood, 375
farzand maqām, prince adopted (honorific title), 196
fetvā, religious sentence pronounced by mofti or mojtahed, 105, 127, 175
fouj, afvāj (afvāj-e qāhera), detachment (military unit), 274
fouj-e jānbāz, detachment of reformed army, 150
fouj-e khāṣṣ, special detachment, 169

ghāzi, fighter in the Holy War, 127
gholām-e divāni, Divān servant, 321
gholām-e neẓām, soldier of regular army, 332
gholām-e pishkhedmat, page of the presence, 125
gholām-e pishkhedmat-e khāṣṣa, special page of the presence, 205

hadiya, present, gift, 375, 389
ḥākem, governor, 144, 315
ḥākem-e sharᶜ, judge of religious court, 404
ḥakim bāshi, title of physician in ordinary, 191
ḥāmi, protector, 361
ḥaqq-e maẓlumi, extorted money, 375, 389
ḥisab al-ᶜaqd, digital computation, 117*n*
ḥokm-e ᶜarab-shāhi, a tax, 389, 404
ḥokm-e doulati, decision issued by secular court, 407, 408*n*
ḥokm-e sharᶜ, decision issued by religious court of justice, 408*n*

jārchi bāshi, chief courier, 162
jang-e madhhabi, religious war, 291
jens, contribution in kind, 410
jeld, bag, measure used with dates, 325
jānebdār, deputy, 361
jira, tips, daily allowance, victuals, 390, 405, 418

kalām, theology, 101
kadkhodā bāshi, chief alderman, 100
kalāntar, mayor, chief of tribe, castellan, 30, 142, 298
kār-pardāz, intendant, 325
keshvar-setān, gold coin, 173
ketābchehā-ye dastur ol-ᶜamal, *see* dastur ol-ᶜamal
khādem bāshi, chief servant (of a mosque), 412
khalᶜa, khalᶜat, robe of honor, gift, 164, 322*n*
khāleṣa-ye divan-e aᶜlā, the crown property, 117*n*
khāleṣajāt-e divāni, state property, 99
khāna sālār, chief of royal household, 197

khāngāh, convent for dervishes, 140*n*
kharāj, *see* bāj
khaṭṭa, district, 243
khedmatāna, allowance, provision paid to official, 389 seq.
kolāh-e kayāni, the imperial crown, 81
kotval, commander (guard) of town or castle, 90, 392*n*

lala, tutor, 179
lala bāshi, chief tutor, 196, 205*n*
lashgar-nevis, secretary of the army, 41, 92
lashgar-e neẓām, the disciplined (reformed) army, 232

maḥall, maḥalla, district, 92, 264*n*, 276, 304
māl-e sovari, fodder money paid to horsemen, 325
malek osh-shoᶜarā, poet-laureat, 61*n*
malek ot-tojjār, alderman, chief of merchants, 95, 306
māleyāt-e mostamerra, the ordinary budget, 195
māleyāt va-vojuhāt, taxes and fees, 382
mann, a weight, 376*n*
mann-e shāhi, 410*n*
mann-e Shirāzi, 88*n*, 410*n*
mann-e Tabrizi, 88*n*
manshur, decree, 253
mashhad, sepulcher (or place of martyrdom) of a saint, 401
maṭlab, claim advanced in court of justice, 404
mavājeb, pay, emoluments, 405, 409
mavājeb-e divāni, pension, 338
mehmāndār, official in charge of visitors to the court, 94, 126, 133, 137 seq., 175, 238
mir akhur, official in charge of the stable, 416
miskāl, a weight, 63*n*, 173, 259*n*, 376, 404
miskāl-e Ṣirāfi, 88
mo'ākhadha-ye doulati, official fine, 375
moᶜāmalāt, proceedings (of taxation agents), 383, 405
mobāsher, agent, 383
moᶜeiyer ol-mamālek, essayer of the imperial mint, 174, 374
mofti, theologian issuing decisions in religious matters, 127*n*
moḥāsabāt va-ḥavālajāt, the account books, 243
mohletāna, fee to be paid for delay of taxes, 389
moḥtaseb, superintendant of markets and life in public, 411
mojtahed, theologian approximately the same as a mofti, 101 seq, 113*n*, 176 seq., 178 seq., 180
mokhber, scout (military), 311
molāzem, follower, bodyguard, 5, 223
monajjem bāshi, chief astrologer, 110
monshi, scribe, 61
monshi ol-mamālek, chancellor of the empire, 46, 75, 172
monshi-ye rasā'il, scribe in charge of the letters, 117
moqaddam, chief, 274
moqarrari-ye divāni, regular pay, 110
moqaṣṣer, a man causing detriment to the state, 351, 405
moqāṭaᶜa-ye divāni, farming out of taxes, 384
morshed, spiritual guide in Sufi order, 162
mosāmara, discussion, 290

mostaḥdath, new agricultural settlement, 186
mostamarri, pay or pension granted by the state, 65, 409
mostoufi, financial officer, 243 seq.
mostoufi ol-mamālek, minister of finance, 117, 144
motavalli, administrator of shrine or pious foundation, 116

nadim, boon companion, 226*n*
nā'eb, lieutenant, 216
nā'eb ol-ḥokuma, deputy governor, 345
nā'eb os-salṭana, crown prince, 89, 131, 228
nāhār, "supper," accommodation of official on travel, 390
nāḥeya, district, 25*n*, 247*n*
nasaqchi bāshi, chief of bodyguard, 19
nastaᶜliq, style in Persian calligraphy, 281
nāẓer, inspector, 197
neshān-e shir o khorshid, Order of the Lion and Sun, 228, 242
neshān-e timthāl-e homāyun, Order of the Effigy of the Shah, 309, 318
neẓām, the disciplined (regular) army, 122, 388*n*
nimethāl-e divānkhāna, tax collection, 71
nokhud, a weight, 63, 173, 376
noqṣān, deductions from pay, 418
noukar, servant, 148, 297
noukarhā-ye divān, divan servants, 405

ᶜolum-e ilāhiya, theological sciences, 406*n*
ᶜolum-e rasmiya, ordinary sciences, 406*n*
ᶜommāl, *see* ᶜāmel

ordubāzār, bazaar of the camp, 53

peimān, a square measure, 88
peshkash, present, gift, 36 seq., 117, 389 seq.
pir, *see* morshed, 162
pishkār, administrator, 196, 206

qalāvuz, scout (military), 28, 329
qanāt, qanawāt, irrigation canal, 83
qarār-nāma, letter of obligation, treaty, 314
qarāvol, qarāvolān, guard, 53
qasam-nāma, written oath, 408
qāżi, judge of religious court of justice, 37
qoṭb, "pole," leader of Sufi order, 161*n*
qollar āqāsi, commander of the pages, 79, 122*n*
qur yasāvol bāshi, chief keeper of the arsenal, 92

rafiq, companion (honorific title), 87
ra'is-e arbāb-dārān, chief of the landowners, 309
ra'is-e daftar-khāna, chief of the registers, 243
raqam, decree, 389
reshva, "bribery," a kind of taxes, 389 seq.
reyāl, a silver coin, 173, 376

ṣadr-e aᶜẓam, title of grand vizier, 131, 159; *see also* vazir
ṣāḥeb-e, mansab, officer, 405
ṣāḥeb qerān, a silver coin, 173
saḥiḥ ast, formula written on margin of decisions, 404
ṣaḥn-e moqaddas, courtyard of holy shrine, 371
salṭana, the rule, 375
sang-e posht, part of construction of irrigation canal, 398

sar keshik bāshi, chief of bodyguard, 267
sar khaṭṭ, assessment, 382
sar reshta-dār, intendant (of the army), 129
sarbāz, regular soldier of reformed army, 122, 212
sarbāz-e qarāvol, soldier of the vanguard, 270
sardār, commander of the army, 26, 39, 104
sarhang, military commander, 321
sartip, commander, general, 214, 277, 319
sartip-e avval, rank above commander, 312
sepāh-e neẓām, the disciplined (reformed) army, 234
sepahdār, commander of the army, 122, 171
sepahsālār, commander-in-chief, 240*n*, 374
seyāsat, "punishment," a kind of tax, 375
shāh, title of mystics and saints, 40*n*
shāhi, a coin, 404
shām, "dinner," accommodation of official on travel, 390
shamkhalchi, crossbow man, 266
shari^{c}a, the religious law, 74 seq., 168, 174, 180
shari^{c}a court, 303, 304*n*; *see also* ḥokm-e shar^{c}, qāżi
shāṭer bāshi, chief groom, 303
sheḥna, policeman, 325
sheikh ol-eslām, chief mofti, 37
shekasta, style in Persian calligraphy, 288*n*
shir-ḥāji, name of breastwork in Afghanistan, 259
ṣonduq-e ^{c}adālat, "Chest of Justice," 381
sonduqdār, treasurer, 164
sovar-e neẓām, regular cavalry, 331
soyurghāl, fief, 101
soyursāt, provisions free of charge, 186*n*, 315*n*, 388*n*
ṣurat-e ḥesābi, the accounts, 98

ta^{c}ahhod-nāma, letter of obligation, 316
ṭabib-e khāṣṣa, physician in ordinary, 172
tadbir, administration (of household or state), 418
tadhkera-dār, diplomatic representative, 315
tāj-e māh, "Crown of the Moon," famous jewel, 63, 68
takhfif, alleviation of taxes, 201, 389
taqṣirāt, peculiations (of money belonging to the state), 286
tiyul, fief, 13, 87
tofangchi, musketeer, 14*n*
toḥfa va-hadiya, gifts, 388*n*
tomān, monetary unit, 173; district supposed to furnish 10,000 fighting men, *see also* amir-e tomān
tub-khāna, arsenal, 271

vajh ol-ḥalāl, money acquired in conformity with the prescriptions of the religious law, 412*n*
vajh-e molzami, tax arrears, 219
vakil, deputy, viceregent, 244, 364
vakil or-ra^{c}āyā, deputy of the subjects, 196
vāli, governor of province, 315
vaqf, pious foundation, 396
vaẓifa, vaẓāyef, pay, pension, emoluments, 65, 87, 409
vazir-e avval va-ṣadr-e a^{c}ẓam, prime minister, 117
vazir-e a^{c}ẓam, grand vizier, prime minister, 301
vazir-e doval-e khāreja, minister of foreign affairs, 172

vazir-e lashgar, vizier of the army, 301
velāyat, district, province, 140
voyuh-e divāni, divan fees, 382
vojuhāt-e aṣnāf, taxes paid by the guilds, 382
voṣul-e māleyāt, payment of taxes, 201
voṣuli, sum, 389

yasāvol, life guardsman, 129
yāver, major (military rank in reformed army), 212

żābeṭ, żābet-e bolukāt, governor of district, 45, 279
żabṭ, governorship of district, 205
ẓālem, "oppressor," oppressive official, 375, 389
zauraq, a small vessel, 212

TITLES OF BOOKS

Āthār-e Ja^c^fari, 206
Baḥr ol-ḥaqā'eq, 262
Ḥaqā'eq ol-akhbār, 206*n*
Ḥāsheya-ye mabsuṭa bar ketāb-e Ma^c^ālem oṣul-e feqh, 262
Ḥāsheya bar ketāb-e Sharḥ-e Lom^c^a, 262
Hedāyat os-sabil va-kefāyat od-dalil, 413*n*
Jām-e Jam, 244*n*, 413 seq.
Kanz ol-ḥesāb, 412
Ketāb-e Amthela, 407
Ketāb-e Delgoshā, see *Tārihk-e Delgoshā*
Ketāb-e Qamqām, see *Qamqām-e zakhkhāt*
Ketāb-e Ṣowar, 273
Ketāb-e Taṣrif, 407
Kholāṣa-ye Ḥesāb, 412
Kholāṣat al-ḥisāb al-bahā'iya, 412*n*
Kitāb al-lum^c^a ad-Dimashqiya, 262*n*
Leila and Majnun, 401
Ma^c^ālim ad-din wa-malādh al-mujtahidin fī uṣul ad-din, 262*n*
Nāṣekh ot-Tavārikh, 112
Qamqām-e zakhkhār va-ṣamṣām-e battār, 413*n*
Resāleya jehādiya, 128
Roużat oṣ-Ṣafā-ye Nāṣeri, 148, 205*n*, 218, 281
Ruznāma, 9*n*, 20*n*
Ruznāma-ye Safar-e Madinat os-Salām va-Beit Ollāh ol-Ḥarām, 413
Safar-nāma-ye Shāhenshāhi ba-aṭabāt-e ^c^āliyāt, 370
Tadhkera-ye Mojma^c^ ol-Foṣaḥā, 229
Tārikh-e Delgoshā, 167*n*, 192*n*
Tārikh-e Dhu'l-Qarnein, 82, 95, 105, 145, 148, 159, 230
Tārikhee Nāṣekh ot-Tavārikh, 148
Tārikh-e Nozhat ol-Akhbār, 206
Tārikh-e Qājāriya, 112, 301